E18 RESOURCE BASE

KU-736-938

Aristotle

Nicomachean Ethics

TRANSLATION (WITH HISTORICAL INTRODUCTION) BY

CHRISTOPHER ROWE

PHILOSOPHICAL INTRODUCTION AND COMMENTARY BY

SARAH BROADIE

OXFORD

UNIVERSITY PRESS

OXFORD

UNIVERSITY PRESS

Great Clarendon Street, Oxford OX2 6DP

Oxford University Press is a department of the University of Oxford.
It furthers the University's objective of excellence in research, scholarship,
and education by publishing worldwide in

Oxford New York

Auckland Bangkok Buenos Aires Cape Town Chennai
Dar es Salaam Delhi Hong Kong Istanbul Karachi Kolkata
Kuala Lumpur Madrid Melbourne Mexico City Mumbai Nairobi
São Paulo Shanghai Taipei Tokyo Toronto

Oxford is a registered trade mark of Oxford University Press
in the UK and in certain other countries

Published in the United States
by Oxford University Press Inc., New York

Translation and Historical Introduction © Christopher Rowe 2002
Philosophical Introduction and Commentary © Sarah Broadie 2002

The moral rights of the author have been asserted
Database right Oxford University Press (maker)

First published 2002

All rights reserved. No part of this publication may be reproduced,
stored in a retrieval system, or transmitted, in any form or by any means,
without the prior permission in writing of Oxford University Press,
or as expressly permitted by law, or under terms agreed with the appropriate
reprographics rights organization. Enquiries concerning reproduction
outside the scope of the above should be sent to the Rights Department,
Oxford University Press, at the address above

You must not circulate this book in any other binding or cover
and you must impose this same condition on any acquirer

British Library Cataloguing in Publication Data
Data available

Library of Congress Cataloging in Publication Data
Data available

ISBN 0–19–875271–7

5 7 9 10 8 6 4

Typeset in Dante and Gill Sans
by RefineCatch Limited, Bungay, Suffolk
Printed in Great Britain by
Biddles Ltd King's Lynn
www.biddles.co.uk

8 0000893

Luton Sixth Form College
Learning Resources Centre

Luton Sixth Form College
Learning Resources Centre

WITHDRAWN E18 RESOURCE BASE

Aristotle

N

80000893

Luton Sixth Form College

To the memory of
Gwen Beese and Mildred Taylor,
teachers of ancient Greek and Latin,
S.B. dedicates her part of this work
in gratitude and affection

Acknowledgements

Christopher Rowe thanks the Leverhulme Trust, whose generous award to him of a Personal Research Professorship has enabled him to bring this project to completion (along with much else).

We both thank Carrie Swanson and Agnes Gellen for their scholarly vigilance in checking our typescript, and Heather Rowe for hers in reading the proofs.

Acknowledgements

Contents

PART I

Introduction

PART 1

Historical Introduction

Christopher Rowe

Aristotle, son of Nicomachus and Phaistis, of Stagira [in Chalcidice, in northern Greece]. Nicomachus, according to Hermippus in his *On Aristotle*, was descended from Nicomachus son of Machaon, grandson of Asclepius [the legendary founder of Greek medicine]; and he resided with Amyntas [II], king of the Macedonians, in the role of physician and friend [so medicine ran in Aristotle's family; he frequently quarries medicine for analogies and examples]. Aristotle was Plato's most genuine student; he spoke with a lisp, according to Timotheus the Athenian in his *On Lives*; he also had thin legs, they say, and small eyes, and his clothes, his rings and the cut of his hair were distinctive. According to Timaeus, he had a son—also called Nicomachus—by Herpyllis, his concubine.

(Diogenes Laertius, *Lives and Opinions of Famous Philosophers*, v. 1)

Diogenes, who wrote at least five centuries after Aristotle, goes on to report that Aristotle 'seceded' from Plato's Academy (he joined it in 367 BCE, at the age of 17) while Plato was still alive. Whether or not this story is true, Aristotle's relationship with his philosophical mentor was a complex one. His *On Ideas*, which subjects one of Plato's key 'doctrines' to detailed criticism (cf. *Nicomachean Ethics* I. 6), was written before Plato's death in 347; nevertheless Plato's influence on his thinking is everywhere apparent, and nowhere more clearly than in ethics (despite his criticisms, themselves gently expressed—at least in the *Ethics*). Aristotle certainly left Athens in 347, perhaps for political reasons (relating either to the Academy, or to his family connections with Macedonia), and did not return until 335, when he founded his own philosophical school, the Lyceum (or 'Peripatos'). In the meantime, among other things he apparently served for a short period as tutor to the future Alexander the Great, although this episode, astonishingly, has left no clear trace in the genuine parts of the Aristotelian corpus. Most of the large body of his writing that we still have probably dates from the period between 335 and 323, the year of Alexander's death; forced out, for one reason or another, from Athens, where he lived, taught and wrote as an outsider, Aristotle himself died the following year.

The corpus of Aristotle's works handed down to us by tradition includes four ethical treatises: the *Nicomachean Ethics* (named, it appears—by whom, and for what reason, we do not know—after his son); the *Eudemian Ethics* (named after a much-loved student of Aristotle's, though again we have no clear evidence about the precise origins of the title); the so-called *Magna Moralia*, or *Great Ethics* (actually much shorter than either the *Nicomachean* or the *Eudemian*); and the diminutive *On Virtues and Vices*. The last is incontrovertibly not by Aristotle, and while some have defended, and continue to defend, the authenticity of the *Magna Moralia*, its special features seem likely to be best explained by treating it as the work of a student who followed Aristotle's lectures. But the *Nicomachean* and *Eudemian Ethics* are indubitably by Aristotle. These two mostly cover the same range of subjects; and indeed they actually appear—on good but not quite certain authority—to share three books in common (*Nicomachean* v–vii, *Eudemian* iv–vi). Now recent scholarly opinion is probably on the side of treating the *Eudemian* as an earlier work, superseded, perhaps, by the *Nicomachean* (even though some powerful voices have claimed the *Eudemian* in fact to be the more philosophically subtle); and if this is right, the easiest hypothesis is that Aristotle simply decided not to rewrite the central books for the *Nicomachean*, but instead to transfer *Eudemian* iv–vi to it, despite the fact that this would leave the new work with two separate, and rather different, treatments of pleasure (vii. 11–14, x. 1–5). Alternatively, perhaps Aristotle intended to write a new version of *Eudemian* iv–vi, but failed to complete the project, and an editor (Nicomachus?) subsequently made good the gap by transplanting the three old books.

In any case, if the balance of opinion, and of the evidence, makes the *Eudemian* earlier than the *Nicomachean*, there is also something like the same balance in favour of an Eudemian origin for the 'common' books, particularly in light of some stylistic evidence. This may be important for readers of the *Nicomachean* to know (and might make them want to read the *Eudemian*—or the rest of the *Eudemian*—as well). While Aristotle may have been the person who put *Eudemian* iv–vi—if that is what they originally were—into the *Nicomachean*, and in that case will evidently not have been over-concerned about inconcinnities of content (one consequence being the double treatment of pleasure), nevertheless there *are* significant philosophical differences between the undisputed books of the *Nicomachean* and the undisputed books of the *Eudemian*, the most notable perhaps being between *Nicomachean* x. 6–8 and the end of the *Eudemian*, and between the respective treatments of 'friendship'. Thus, if *Nicomachean* v–vii were originally Eudemian, we need not expect complete harmony between the contents of these books and those of *Nicomachean* i–iv and viii–x; and indeed there is in any case some disharmony of a fairly moderate sort, i.e. between the treatments of pleasure in *Nicomachean* vii and x.

However, one should not make too much of such problems. Aristotle's treatises are usually regarded as being lecture notes, rather than as works intended for publication (whatever that would have meant in the fourth century BCE: at any rate wide circulation, as probably with a number of Plato's dialogues). The *Nicomachean Ethics* is in fact far more readable than that might suggest; and furthermore it is considerably more readable than any other extant complete work of Aristotle's (some, especially early ones, admired for their style, have been lost). Some parts, especially in the last three books, are even close to being beautifully written, a few actually moving; the ellipse and the indeterminacy, as well as most of the dryness, of works like the *Metaphysics*—I write as translator—are largely absent here. Yet despite all this, the *Nicomachean Ethics*, even (or especially) at its best, is typically a mixture of the orderly and the disorderly. (My point, then, is that any problems of disunity or discontinuity we may discover are unlikely to begin, or end, with the 'common' books.) At his most orderly when developing a specific argument, Aristotle is also capable of treating a subject or developing an idea more or less as the thought takes him, so that it is sometimes easier to trace the connection between individual sentences than to say overall, how a longer stretch goes. Aristotle's mind is quick, sharp, and above all fertile, always ready to notice another perspective or another avenue to follow. Even though he evidently likes, and wants, to tie things down, the complexity of his subject matter (human behaviour), which he openly recognizes, is perpetually mirrored in the complexity of his writing. (More mechanical explanations of the peculiarities of the text, e.g. in terms of the presence of layers of writing from different periods, then become largely redundant, despite the case of books V–VII; or if not redundant, more difficult to justify.)

All of this has the immediate practical consequence that it is extremely difficult to break up his text into smaller portions. The divisions into books do, on the whole, coincide with major changes of subject, but not all major changes of subject are marked by a book division, and a book division need not indicate such a change; in truth, whoever divided the *Nicomachean Ethics* into books was more swayed by other considerations, e.g. what would easily fit within the limits of a papyrus roll. The chapter divisions which we traditionally use, and which are reproduced in the translation in the present volume, are a modern invention, representing a particular view of the way the text might be broken up into sections smaller than 'books' . My own judgements in this matter are indicated by *indentation*. The accepted chapter divisions are used, with spacing in between chapters, as a way of dividing the text into some smaller chunks—so giving the modern reader some relief of the sort he or she will expect (we are not used, as ancient readers were, to being faced with huge, unbroken quantities of prose). But what I take to be significant pauses in Aristotle's argument or thought are indicated *only* by indentations, which often but by no means always coincide with the beginnings of the traditional chapters; and the reader will find relatively little such indentation. This represents a significant difference from the practice of some recent translators, who paragraph much more freely—thus, in my view, obscuring a major feature of Aristotle's style, at least in the *Nicomachean Ethics*: its habit, as it were, of flowing. (Nor is this likely to be just a matter of obscuring a facet of style.) But at the same time I have tried to take particular care with Aristotle's particles, and to bring out the relationship between one sentence and the next.

The text translated is essentially that of Bywater's Oxford Classical Text (first published in 1894; my copy is the reprint of 1962), and any departures from what he chose to print (apart from frequent changes to his punctuation) are indicated by footnotes to the translation. The text handed down to us by tradition, as mended by generations of textual critics, appears to be only very rarely corrupt and beyond repair. The manuscript tradition *may* sometimes, or often, have let us down, and failed to preserve, or give us enough evidence to reconstruct, what Aristotle wrote; and Bywater's reporting of the tradition may also have been inaccurate (it is certainly incomplete), and his choices—and mine—may have been bad ones. But if all this, together with other factors, means that the translation may not be, quite, of *Aristotle* (sometimes), still there is no good reason to suppose that the text translated is significantly different from what readers not long after his death would have had in front of them. My aim as translator has above all been to reproduce this text accurately and, so far as possible, readably, but always putting accuracy before readability; on the relatively few occasions when the Greek seems genuinely indeterminate, I hope to have reproduced that indeterminacy. Sarah Broadie and I have worked closely together on the translation throughout; the most likely explanation of any large errors, infelicities, or other shortcomings is obstinacy on my part.

NOTE TO THE HISTORICAL INTRODUCTION

The historical and philological issues raised in this part of the Introduction will be referred to but, in the main, not discussed in Sarah Broadie's Philosophical Introduction and Commentary—which is why it seemed appropriate to introduce them here. The commentary is determinedly philosophical, and only rarely touches on the history, language, or other non-philosophical aspects of the *Nicomachean Ethics*. The literature relating to the issues in question is large but easily accessible; a good place to start is the bibliography to Jonathan Barnes (ed.), *The Cambridge Companion to Aristotle* (Cambridge: Cambridge University Press, 1995).

Line numbers in the translation keep pace in principle with the standard line-numbering of the original Greek text. However, mainly because of differences between Greek and English syntax, correspondence is sometimes not quite exact. Since the commentary numbers its lemmata in accordance with the Greek, there is sometimes a slight mismatch between a lemma's line-number and that of the words as they appear in the translation. But it seems best to accept this inconvenience so as to retain throughout this book the numbering system used by all modern editors, translators, and interpreters of Aristotle.

Philosophical Introduction[1]

Sarah Broadie

I: **The chief human good**[2]

SUMMARY:

'The chief good' not a quantitative notion; the chief good as what makes other goods worth while; the meaning of 'political' concern; method of examining existing views; qualifications of the audience; practical purpose of the *Ethics*; identification of the chief good as happiness (*eudaimonia*), and meaning of the term; Aristotle's definition in terms of excellence; the definition's practical indubitability for his audience; reasons for identifying the chief good with happiness; preparing the way for X. 7–8, where it will be argued that the highest form of human happiness has something godlike about it; the chief good not the reference point for deciding which actions are right.

Aristotle's *Nicomachean Ethics* is about what is good for human beings. It asks and proposes an answer to the question 'What is the chief or primary good for man?', and it looks at the implications of its answer.

Let us begin by considering what is meant here by 'chief' or 'primary' (also 'highest', 'best') human good. Does it mean the greatest good available to, or suitable for, human beings? Not if we understand 'greatest' in a straight-forwardly quantitative way. Aristotle's chief good is not simply more of something that non-chief goods exemplify in lesser degrees. There are two reasons why this is so. First, the 'something' that it might be thought the greatest good presents or exemplifies more or most of, the other goods less, cannot be mere good or goodness. Aristotle will argue (against the Platonists) that there is no such property of good or goodness that all goods, or even all intrinsic goods, share in common,[3] whether or not to different degrees. Secondly, Aristotle's chief good is not ahead of the others by being the largest amount or the widest distribution of something independently desirable. This conception is exemplified by the supreme objective of classical utilitarianism: the greatest pleasure (or happiness) of the greatest number. If this is the chief good, then presumably at least some of the inferior goods will be lesser amounts of pleasure, or pleasure for lesser numbers of people. But Aristotle's chief good is not like this. Just as pleasure according to the classical utilitarians is something valuable in itself, before the question of its quantity ever arises, so Aristotle's chief good is valuable in itself. It, too, can occur in wider or narrower distributions, i.e. in the lives of more or fewer individuals. So its status as 'chief' is not based on its consisting, itself, in the maximal occurrence, by comparison with occurrences sparser or less plentiful, of something that is valuable regardless of quantity or extent of spread. On the contrary, the other goods over which the chief good predominates differ from it (and from each other) by being of different kinds, not amounts; and the chief good is related to them as the principle and cause of their being worth while:[4] i.e. worth pursuing, worth conserving, worth regretting the lack of.

The other goods, most obviously, are familiar desirables like health, wealth, pleasure, honour and respect, beauty, love and friendship: objects which most people spend most of their active time pursuing or tending for themselves and others. But according to the idea of the chief good as that which makes the others worth while, there is nothing to be gained by success in any of these directions if it is achieved at the expense of the chief good. This has the rather severe implication that if we miss the chief good, then, whatever else we manage to achieve, we achieve nothing worth while any more than if we had not done anything at all or had failed in all our undertakings. Though probably without our knowing it, our efforts are completely pointless. By contrast, if instead the chief good were pre-eminent by being the largest or most widely distributed amount of something independently desirable, then if we fail (even if the entire human race fails) to bring about the chief good, nevertheless it will still have been possible for us to bring about smaller amounts or distributions of the independently desirable thing, and succeeding in that would have certainly have been more worth while than completely failing or not doing anything at all. One could say: if the point of being practical, which is something human beings are by their very essence, is to make a difference for the better, then, according to the conception being examined here, our practicality as such, not merely this or that project, is 'empty and vain' if the chief good is missing from it.

It follows from the general value-dependence of the other goods on the chief one that practical concern for the latter should be in control of practical concerns for any of the former.[5] Aristotle calls this magisterial concern 'political',[6] and he says that his inquiry into the nature of its object is 'political in a way'.[7] This characterization tells us less about the chief good than it does about Aristotle's conception of what political theory should be. For him, the theory of political institutions should start from a reasoned account of the chief human good; consequently, political inquiry, rightly conceived, should contain as part of itself the inquiry into the chief good. Aristotle, moreover, inherits from Plato the assumption, which he never questions, that the primary purpose of political power is to help realize the chief good in the lives of the citizens.[8] But for Aristotle this in no way implies that the chief good is simply a collective as distinct from an individual phenomenon. Achieving it requires a political and social context—of course, since man is essentially political and social; but the chief good is achieved only in individual lives and through the active engagement of individuals themselves. Thus that organizing of the other goods that helps secure the chief one is not, and should not be, the special preserve of community leaders and their advisers. It is the proper concern of anyone free to shape his or her own life,[9] and of anyone responsible for helping to shape the lives of others. When such shaping is conducted thoughtfully, the thinking involved is 'political' in Aristotle's sense, whether it is done solely for one's own benefit, or for members of one's family or community.

In working out a systematic account of the chief good, which is the object of political thinking and the end or goal of any political activity, Aristotle proceeds by examining existing views.[10] He attends to the opinions of ordinary people, of the 'better class of people', and of intellectuals. He taps the common culture, the works of the poets in particular, for ethical materials. He invokes customs and practices, and appeals to 'what we say' (and sometimes to etymology). He believes that most views that are widely held, or have been handed down, or have been carefully arrived at, contain some truth, although the truth often leads to error unless it is corrected and qualified. Aristotle finds a position of his own to be corroborated if its being true would explain why others, reaching less effectively for the same truth, have arrived at their own positions. Particularly satisfactory forms of corroboration occur when his own position on a subject explains, and so in a way justifies, each of a set of conflicting existent views,[11] or when it solves recognized puzzles or problems (*aporiai*).[12]

In addition to the already existent views and questions, which are like materials for a philosophical account, Aristotle begins his ethical inquiry with certain expectations of the kind of mentality his audience will bring to the subject. These expectations divide into two kinds, both educational. On the one hand (as Aristotle constantly shows, rather than says), the audience will be familiar with, and will accept, a range of technical logical and metaphysical distinctions and turns of argument that are the stock-in-trade of Aristotelian philosophy. On the other hand (as he finds it necessary to declare), he expects the audience to be 'well brought up'.[13] This is because the study of ethics is practical philosophy, not merely in the sense of being about human practice, but above all in the sense of being intended to make a practical difference for the better.[14] Aristotle evidently hopes to make a difference via his audience; but if they have not learned to live disciplined lives, then whatever they learn from his discourse will fail to be translated into consistent patterns of practical thought and action. And if members of the audience have grown up disciplined, but with wrong values and bad priorities, or, as an uninvolved observer would say, with values and priorities that seriously diverge from those endorsed by Aristotle himself in his *Ethics*, then again the discourse will leave them unmoved on the practical level. This will be true even if they are intellectually impressed by Aristotle's arguments. For values and priorities develop through our practising the kinds of actions that express such values and priorities; discourse alone cannot form or reform us on this level.[15]

Let us now turn to the first positive proposal of the *Nicomachean Ethics*, which is that the chief human good is happiness—that is to say, *eudaimonia*, which like many interpreters we have decided to translate by 'happiness'. The difficulty with this translation is that 'happiness' in ordinary usage often means a good feeling or a feeling good; in fact, a sort of pleasure or being pleased. But an ancient Greek, knowing that someone is in such a state, either in general or about something in particular, would not on that account attribute *eudaimonia* to the person. For one thing, the person might, as we could put it using English words in the ordinary way, be simultaneously happy about this and unhappy about that; but one cannot be said to be *eudaimōn* (the adjective) about one thing, and the opposite (*dusdaimōn*) about something else. This is because being *eudaimōn* is not *about* something: it is not a feeling or an attitude that has an object. For another reason, too, regarding someone as '*eudaimōn*' is not attributing a feeling or a subjective attitude to him or her. Regarding someone as *eudaimōn* is more like ascribing a status, or applauding. It is to imply that the person is admirable, even enviable, an exemplar of life at its best.[16] But one can sincerely describe a person as 'happy' in our ordinary English sense because of the way they are feeling, even if one also considers them to be hateful or pathetic (for example, deluded about the very thing that makes them feel happy), or feeble-minded, or hopelessly unfulfilled, or repulsive, or in general pitiable or contemptible. Hogarthian gluttons smacking greasy lips are happy but not *eudaimones*. By contrast, to ascribe *eudaimonia* is to honour the recipient. It would be misleading to ascribe it to someone of whom one had any of the above opinions, just as it would be misleading in such a case to praise the person; in fact, according to Aristotle the *eudaimōn* is beyond praise.[17]

So if 'happiness' means ancient Greek *eudaimonia*, it is not too difficult to identify the chief human good with happiness.[18] Aristotle says, in fact, that this is a common identification, and he accepts it himself. But, he says, people disagree on what happiness is.[19] One might well complain then that the identity tells us nothing about the nature of the chief good, and wonder what he achieves by giving that good the label 'happiness'. In anticipation of this complaint,[20] Aristotle proceeds to lay out an argument that culminates in the second positive proposal of the *Nicomachean Ethics*, namely the famous definition of the chief good as activity of reason in accordance with excellence, in a complete life.[21] This definition sets the agenda for the rest of the work, which unfolds into a study of human excellence and closely related topics.

The human excellences are the qualities that make for a good human being, and then as now a good human being was normally understood as one who is courageous, moderate, wise, and above all just, in the global sense of fair and decent in dealing with others, and properly respectful of them. Certainly this is how Aristotle understands 'good human being'. However, the proposition that the chief human good principally consists in having and actively exercising these qualities is certainly open to question. This is not a proposition such that to reject it is to show that one has failed to understand it. It was a familiar subject for debate whether the chief good is a matter of excellence, or pleasure, or material goods, or some sort of intellectual enlightenment.[22] There were also questions about the interpretation of 'human excellence'. Not everyone took the common-sense excellences for granted. Justice, in particular, had come under attack. Through the characters of Thrasymachus and Callicles,[23] Plato had presented memorable arguments to show that whoever believes in justice as a human excellence has been indoctrinated with propaganda invented by the naturally weak as self-protection against the naturally strong.

Aristotle accepts the challenge of some of these rival views, and counters them. Some of his replies may be considered conceptually compelling. For example: wealth is essentially a means, not an ultimate end; the chief good is obviously an ultimate end; therefore, the chief good is not wealth.[24] But the view that the chief good is indiscriminate pleasure is not so easily dispatched. Aristotle's first short argument against it—that a life devoted to such pleasure is the life not of human beings but of grazing cattle[25]—will seem like empty rhetoric to someone who not only wants to live like that, but is convinced that pleasure—any pleasure—is the chief good. And the careful discussions of pleasure that come later[26] presuppose, rather than prove, the superiority of excellence to some kinds of pleasure (with 'excellence' being interpreted in the common-sense way).

A critic who accepts Aristotle's assumption that the chief human good must express something distinctive in human nature might argue that the despotic ideal of Callicles and Thrasymachus satisfies this assumption: it is, after all, distinctively human to want unlimited power and to revel in trampling on the rights of others and in letting them know their nothingness by comparison with oneself. Thus one might have expected Aristotle to attempt to cover this sort of gap in his argument by proposing, or at least gesturing towards, a theory of human nature, or the human function, from which it would follow that a good example of human nature, one that carries out the human function well, is a person who possesses the traditionally acclaimed excellences including justice. On the other hand, a critic who seriously suggests that justice is not an excellence will probably not be convinced by any theory that yields the opposite result. In any case, whether because this seems a fruitless dialectic or for some other reason, Aristotle makes no effort to strengthen his starting point in this way.

The foundation of his system of ethics and politics is not, then, absolutely secure: it lacks the indubitability of what cannot be rationally denied. Even so, Aristotle can point out that if he has the appropriate audience, the system is as firmly based as it needs to be, and in just the way it needs to be, if it is to fulfil its practical purpose. His well brought up listeners, already because of their upbringing, are committed above all to the cultivation and practice of excellence as ordinarily understood. Their past development has formed them to reject lives shaped round the pursuit of wealth for its own sake, or indiscriminate pleasure. They are incapable, then, of receiving to practical effect any account of the chief good that does not place excellence at the centre, along with anything entailing or entailed by excellence. One can imagine that some of them entered Aristotle's course on ethics without any expectation of being made aware that their own lives already incorporated, or were well on the way to incorporating, the main ingredient of *eudaimonia* or happiness. But if they allow that this legendary status can apply to persons like themselves, they are bound to realize that the chief good, or its nucleus, consists in that which they themselves have been reared to care about most. To this realization Aristotle's philosophy brings some essential and somewhat technical clarifications: one that ties the excellence of a thing to its function (*ergon*), and ties function to the thing's distinctive nature or type;[27] one that views human beings anthropologically in comparison with the rest of animate nature, and locates the distinctively human function at the level of reason rather than sense-perception or nutrition;[28] and one that identifies the chief good with activity rather than quiescence.[29]

Let us turn back to a question touched on earlier: What does Aristotle achieve by equating the chief human good with happiness? Well, first it enables him to engage directly with existing views in which 'happiness' and 'happy' are the operative terms, for example Solon's adage 'Call no man happy until he is dead', which Aristotle makes the basis of an extraordinarily rich and complex discussion.[30] Secondly, the equation helps prepare for a position which remains unannounced until the penultimate chapters of the *Nicomachean Ethics*, where Aristotle will argue that the very best human life is that of the theoretical thinker, and that excellent intellectual activity engaged in just for its own sake is the most complete form of happiness.[31] This is quite a surprising conclusion to a work almost entirely devoted to the topic of practical excellence and its ramifications. However, Book I contains sundry pointers in this direction, one of them being the equation of the chief human good with happiness, another the argument by which Aristotle supports it.

To explain: for Aristotle, the main difficulty in showing that the theoretical thinker's life is a splendid human possibility lies in the fact that one of his strongest considerations in favour of this position would have seemed to many in his culture a reason against it. The consideration is that excellent intellectual activity engaged in for its own sake is godlike: the most godlike phenomenon that human life can show. But deeply entrenched in ancient

Greek tradition, and backed by a large stock of horrific legends, was the belief that the gods are jealous—not, as the deity of the Bible, jealous so much of our straying to other gods (for this did not necessarily entail straying away from *them*), but jealous of sharing their attributes with us. From this perspective, if the human good is, or contains, something godlike, then that good is not practicable by us, because to aim at it would be religiously unsafe. Although for an Aristotelian it verges on self-contradiction to hold that the good of a certain species is in principle better not aspired to, let alone attained, by members of the species, a doctrine of this generality would not have carried much weight against the traditional pessimism, according to which, whatever may be true of other species, human beings must be careful not to aim too high[32] (even though the fact that this warning is constantly needed proves that those who do aim too high are seeking something that draws them naturally, as if the fullness of their own nature were somehow already up there). Alternatively, the same perspective will allow that the human good is practicable by us, but denies that it is or contains anything godlike. Aristotle, then, is faced with an existing attitude according to which it is irrational, as well as impious, to stress the godlikeness of unfettered intellectual activity as a reason for placing it on the highest echelon of a *practicable, human,* good.[33]

It is interesting that he does not attempt to sidestep this problem by staging a purely humanistic defence of the importance in human life of the theoretical employment of reason.[34] Nor, in the *Ethics*, does he engage in theological analysis and argue, as Plato had done before him,[35] that god is essentially good, and therefore incapable of jealousy.[36] Instead, Aristotle relies on what people and tradition say about happiness. One of the most important things traditionally said is that the gods are happy and blessed; another is that heroes whose labours have won special divine favour go after death to the Islands of the Happy Ones (the Isles of the Blessed). Moreover, people find it conceptually inappropriate (as we would say) to apply the term 'happy' ('*eudaimōn*') to any species of animal apart from the human.[37] And, finally, they *do* apply it, at least in principle, to humans, since all sides agree in calling the chief human good 'happiness'. By accepting this appellation himself and getting us used to it as the natural label for his main topic, Aristotle marshals resources of existing opinion against that traditional injunction to keep our heads down and not emulate the gods, thereby clearing the way for his own view that a godlike activity constitutes the pinnacle of human life, and is a proper objective for human beings.

Aristotle does not rely only on common agreement to secure the equation of the chief human good with happiness. He also gives this argument: the chief human good, whatever it may be, (*a*) is the most complete of human ends, being chosen only for its own sake and never for anything else, and (*b*) confers self-sufficiency; but of the various goods which have been mentioned in the discourse so far, such as wealth, honour, pleasure, intelligence, excellence, and happiness itself, only happiness conforms to the above conditions. Therefore happiness is the chief human good.[38] Since we do not yet know what happiness is, except that it is the same as the chief good, the declaration that only happiness conforms to those conditions does not convey fresh information about something already identified as happiness; instead, it says in effect that nothing will count as happiness that fails to conform (whereas obviously something that fails to conform to *those* conditions may still count as honour or wealth or pleasure or excellence etc. by meeting the standard criteria for those things). Now the attributes of completeness and self-sufficiency undoubtedly make a contribution to the ensuing arguments of Book I,[39] but given Aristotle's rather elaborate introduction of them they seem in the end to do less work here than might have been expected. Much later, however—in Book X—it will appear that completeness and self-sufficiency were deployed at that early stage partly so that it will have been true that they were on the scene and accepted from almost the very beginning. Because of the elaborate introduction we remember them as old acquaintances when Aristotle calls them back into active service in x. 7. In this second appearance they explicitly function as criteria (among others) on what is to count as happiness. This time they are invoked to show that while human happiness takes different forms, one practical, the other theoretical, the theoretical version is the one most truly called 'happiness', because it meets the criteria more fully than the other.[40]

In concluding this introductory section on the chief human good, we should point to a remarkable difference between Aristotle's ethics and modern ethics or moral philosophy. It is that, for Aristotle, articulating the chief good and its relation to other goods is not merely one task of fundamental ethics: it is *the* task. We see this from the following. At the end of the *Nicomachean Ethics*, when he has finished discussing happiness and other major goods such as the excellences, friendship, and pleasure, he turns to the question of *implementation*, the next stage in the 'political' inquiry.[41] He argues that the laws of a society should play a major role in the training for excellence without which happiness is impossible. So we must now begin a new work, which will be an inquiry about legislation and political institutions in general, 'so that as far as possible that part of philosophy that deals with things human may be brought to completion'.[42] In other words, now that the project of outlining the chief good is complete,[43] what remains to be considered under the heading of human affairs is the political and social reality in which this good may be realized. The implication is that ethics or moral philosophy, as distinct from political theory, jurisprudence, sociology, and economics, consists solely in the study of the good.

We have already seen that Aristotle does not consider it necessary to produce a philosophical defence of the standardly recognized excellences, especially justice. In other words, that major topic of modern ethics, 'the justification of morality', is no part of his basic ethical agenda.[44] Another problem on which he turns his back, one that is central to modern ethics, is that of uncovering principles, or the principle, of right action. Talk of the chief good reminds modern readers of the *summum bonum* of utilitarianism, whose principal function in the theory is to provide the standard for right action or a rule for deciding what to do.[45] Thus they easily assume that Aristotle's chief good is meant to be that by reference to which we should reach and justify every decision. It is true that he regards it as the standard for decision in 'political' planning, just as the health of the patient is the standard for medical decisions, but he certainly does not think that every decision in our lives is or ought to be political, i.e. an express decision to arrange things so as to promote the chief good or excellent activity in a complete life.[46] Most of the time the good Aristotelian agent is *engaged in* the excellent activity in question, and is taking decisions with all sorts of ends in view.[47] If Aristotle thought that 'Always act so as best to promote excellent activity in a complete life' is the rule that ought to guide every decision, he would not have said, as he emphatically does, that philosophy cannot lay down guidelines for conduct in general[48]—that it is for the wise and excellent agent to see for himself what to do in the particular situation.[49]

2: **Excellence of character: general**[50]

SUMMARY:

The two kinds of human excellence; they cannot occur apart; excellence of character (*ēthikē aretē*) a disposition acquired through practice; how it differs from skill or expertise; has to do with pleasures and pains; intermediacy of excellent dispositions and the responses expressing them; implications of the theory; its pluralism by contrast with other views; the practical significance of this.

For the purposes of ethics, Aristotle focuses on two aspects or 'parts' of the human soul, one of which he identifies with reason strictly speaking, the other with the capacity to 'listen to reason'. Human excellences fall into two corresponding kinds, of intellect and of character (*ēthos*).[51] Now, this division is misleading if it gives the impression that the two kinds can occur apart—an impression unfortunately aggravated by the fact that Aristotle deals with them in separate parts of the *Ethics*. For according to his complete doctrine, excellences of character are impossible without the intellectual excellence which he calls '*phronēsis*', often translated as 'practical wisdom' and in this work simply as 'wisdom'.[52] For an excellence is a condition whereby its possessor or subject operates well,[53] and for the human subject to operate well it is not enough that his or her listening part of the soul be in the right condition, since the listening part must also (following the metaphor) be given the right orders. But, again, the subject cannot yet be said to operate well as a human individual as long as the orders have to come from outside, any more than one can be said to have mastered an expertise if one can only practise it under another's guidance.[54] (This is so even though obeying and imitating wise external authorities is certainly, in Aristotle's view, the way to begin to develop excellence of character.) Thus the good condition of the listening part of the soul does not strictly speaking constitute finished excellence unless the rational, prescriptive, part of the same soul is in the right condition for prescribing well. And when this is so, the individual has the excellence called 'wisdom'. However, in his discussion of excellence of character, Aristotle for the most part treats it in abstraction from its essential connection with wisdom. This is partly because it is usual with him to give separate consideration to the different parts of a topic, but also because in the present case he is particularly concerned with the question of how the listening part *acquires* the good state proper to it, and this process of acquisition is mainly pre-rational even though what is acquired does not come into its own until put to the service of reason. Consequently, much of the time when Aristotle is discussing excellence of character, he is in fact talking about a good state of the listening part that strictly counts as excellence of character if and only if it occurs in the context of autonomous wisdom; and this commentary will mostly follow his practice in this respect.

We acquire excellence of character, or excellences, rather, since they are plural, by practising and becoming used to behaving in ways typical of the excellences. We become just by doing just actions, and also by being encouraged to feel as a just person feels.[55] In a well brought up person this process of character-shaping through practice will have started at an early age under the care of parents or guardians. But Aristotle also assigns responsibility to developing individuals themselves for becoming the sorts of person they become, since as we grow up we are more and more left to ourselves to choose what to do and to monitor our responses to situations.[56]

What we acquire through this process is the disposition (*hexis*)[57] to act and feel in certain ways. The activities that build the disposition are the same in kind as those that manifest it once it has developed.[58] And the same is true of the contrary dispositions, the character faults and defects. In this, qualities of character are like skills: these, too, are dispositions, and we acquire them by practising doing what the expert already does with more assurance and at a higher level of difficulty. Another similarity is that excellences of character, like skilful expertises (*technai*), make their possessors good at getting things right—not going too far, not falling short—in the relevant sphere.[59]

In what way, then, does excellence of character differ from skill or expertise? The question points back to the well-known discussions in which Socrates compared human excellence to expertise, and even sought to identify it with expertise of some special kind. The word 'excellence' cannot explain the difference, since an expertise in its given sphere *is* excellence. In medicine, the medical expert counts as the 'excellent' person. And the difference is not that skilful expertises are necessarily restricted to specialists, for some skills everyone is expected to have, such as the ability to speak a language, numeracy, and literacy, just as everyone in principle is expected to live up to standards of human excellence. What distinguishes human excellence from expertise is that the former is an *unconditional preparedness* to act, feel, and in general respond in the ways typical of the humanly excellent person, whereas the latter is only an *ability* to act and respond (and perhaps, in some cases, to feel) in the ways typical of the sort of expert in question.

This has two closely connected consequences. First: let it be typical of a certain kind of expert that he or she does act A in situation S, and suppose I am in S. Then if I prefer not to do A, or to do something contrary to A, perhaps because I don't feel like doing A or feel like doing the contrary thing, it does not follow that I am not the kind of expert in question. I can be thoroughly possessed of an ability yet prefer not to exercise it; I can also prefer, for some reason, to exercise it badly rather than well. But if it is typical of a humanly excellent person that he or she does A in S, then if I am in S and fail to do A or prefer to do the opposite, it follows that I am not humanly excellent.[60] *Mutatis mutandis*, the same holds for the various forms of human badness: each of them is a practical preparedness rather than an ability. Thus from the point of view of ethics these dispositions of character, and (at a less developed stage) our tendencies towards developing them, constitute the self, for one cannot both have one of these dispositions *and* hold it at arm's length so to speak, to use or not use in accordance with some extraneous purpose or inclination. (This feature of the ethical dispositions is marked in Aristotle's Greek by the word '*prohairetikos*', from his technical term '*prohairesis*', translated 'decision' in this work.[61]) Secondly, one can possess an expertise and then let it go, even deliberately decide to let it go, by ceasing to practise it. By contrast, being prepared *unconditionally* to act in certain ways entails being prepared, now, to act in those ways whenever the situation should arise in the future.[62] Because of these two features, an ethical disposition is maximally self-reinforcing and self-perpetuating. For to the extent that such a disposition exists, it always, whenever the occasion offers, practises the behaviour that strengthens it and ensures its continuation. Hence when marking differences between character-excellence and expertise, Aristotle speaks of the former as a 'firm and unchanging disposition'.[63]

Aristotle says of character-excellence that it 'has to do with pleasures and pains'.[64] On the one hand, excellence and its opposites show up in our liking or disliking right or appropriate forms of conduct, and disliking or liking the opposite forms. These are the pleasures and discomforts of ethical approval and disapproval.[65] They will be different in persons of different ethical dispositions. Propensities for them are acquired as we acquire the dispositions; in fact, to feel these ethical likes and dislikes is already to exercise one's ethical disposition. Such likes and dislikes may be aroused by the conduct of others as well as oneself. On the other hand, the ethical dispositions also show themselves in the ways we deal with basic and ethically neutral pleasures and pains common to all human beings: the various physical ones, and those experienced in experiencing universal affections such as anger, fear, joy, longing, love, and others.[66] In the undisciplined soul, attraction to what is pleasant on this level, and revulsion from what is unpleasant, assume the role that ought to be occupied by excellence: the role of determining[67] how we actually act and feel in a given situation.

Some pleasures and pains, then, are allies of excellence, while others threaten its possibility by competing for the ground that has to be given over to good ethical training if excellence is ever to develop. The allies are ethical pleasures and pains directed to the right objects, since feeling these and acting according to them obviously strengthens good dispositions. (Similar pleasures and pains directed towards the wrong objects equally reinforce bad ones.) The eventual effect of this strengthening is not, however, a power that puts a brake on the basic pleasure/pain impulses, blocking them in mid-trajectory as they try to push beyond the limit of what is appropriate. The effect, instead, is an easy compliance on their part, a reformation of their trajectories so that the completed shapes fit gracefully with the excellent response. Otherwise, the excellent agent will always be fighting with himself. That is not necessarily an incredible notion of human excellence. Regularly to emerge victorious from anguished self-struggle is surely a kind of heroism. But it is alien to the Aristotelian conception, according to which excellence lies at the core of happiness, and human happiness is godlike. For Aristotle cannot conceive of god or the gods except as engaged in activity that is utterly effortless and unconstrained.[68]

Let us turn to Aristotle's proposal that the excellences of character are intermediate dispositions: the famous 'doctrine of the intermediate'. The idea that excellence, accomplishment or expertise in any sphere issues in acts that are just right in that they *neither go too far nor fall short* was, of course, familiar and intuitively obvious to everyone, but Aristotle gives it clarity[69] and a degree of rigour, and makes it the framework for his entire approach to the excellences of character. In his hands it turns out to have quite interesting practical implications.

The excellence mildness, for example, operates in the 'continuum'[70] of temper. It is 'intermediate' for several reasons: first, because the responses it issues on particular occasions 'hit the intermediate between too much and too little'.[71] Aristotle lets this quantitative notion do duty for the whole gamut of dimensions in which a response might go wrong.[72] The apt responses of mildness are 'intermediate' by comparison with various imaginable inferior responses, which (he assumes) fall into two groups: excessive (irascible) and deficient (spiritless). Mildness, the disposition, logically inherits the 'intermediacy' of its responses. Secondly, for every excellence of character, there is (in theory) a corresponding pair of faulty dispositions, one issuing 'excessive' particular responses, the other 'deficient' ones in the same 'continuum'. Thus, for mildness, there are irascibility and spiritlessness. As above, these bad dispositions are called after the quality of their respective responses, i.e. 'excessive' and 'deficient' respectively, with the result that mildness can now be viewed as intermediate in direct comparison with the associated bad dispositions. Thirdly, Aristotle holds that the faulty ones develop because the young person is allowed to rush forward indiscriminately in every instance of some type of situation, e.g. danger, or else to recoil indiscriminately from every instance, whereas excellence is developed by applying a 'mixed' and therefore intermediate diet of challenges.[73]

Aristotle applies the conception of excellence as intermediate to a large variety of contexts, such as facing danger; physical pleasures; laying out wealth and receiving income; receiving honours; different aspects of social intercourse. These each constitute or suggest a continuum of human feeling or action. One of the main messages of the account is that explaining a response by simple reference to some standard human feeling, motive, or interest fails to justify it, and also fails to convey the information needed to know whether it was justified, or whether the agent acted well. Because we are all more or less familiar from within with the standard feelings, motives, and interests, it can seem justificatory to cite one of them in everyday discussions of conduct, our own or somebody else's. Asked why one did or is going to do so and so, one tends to say: 'I am going to be giving my friends a treat, aren't I?' or 'It tasted so good' or 'I was angry with him', on the assumption that the interlocutor, having had more or less the same kinds of human experience, will not only understand, but will also accept, one's behaviour. And this often works. But it ought not to work, and we ought to be more critical. We should consider whether what is felt or done is the right amount, to the right people, on the right occasion, and so forth, and refrain from judging the quality of the behaviour until we know these circumstances.

The account also explains, or at any rate neatly presents, the fact that members of the identical human species display such enormous ethical differences. We all participate in the same 'continua': these constitute the universal and in itself neutral human condition; but we are differently positioned along a given range, and our position determines the quality of our responses to situations. The model also explains misjudgements about others: we all tend to assume that our own perspective is undistorted, in other words that we see things as an excellent person sees them; but if in fact we are at or near an extreme of excess or deficiency in some continuum, our view is foreshortened and we fail to see the radical difference between the other two positions, i.e. the intermediate and the opposite extreme. In reality these are opposed to each other just as each is opposed to the extreme we are at, but foreshortening makes cowards see the courageous as rash, and rash persons see them as cowardly.[74] Hence the model can even be used as a means of self-correction if one is already theoretically convinced of it; for whenever, in a given area, we find ourselves tending to view everyone else on the range as 'opposite to us' without discrimination, or (what comes to the same thing) tending to act and feel as if there were just two positions, our own which is good, and an opposite one which is bad, then we have strong evidence that we ourselves are tending towards an extreme of excess or deficiency—possibly a nameless one. For, far from following existing categorizations, Aristotle uses the triadic framework to identify a number of nameless dispositions of character.[75] Some are unnamed because they hardly exist (for example, in his view, the trait of being insufficiently interested in physical pleasures, which shares a triad with moderation, the excellence, and self-indulgence, the fault of excess).[76] But other nameless ones exist, only for some reason they have never before been properly identified[77] or they have gone unnoticed or never become topics of discussion.

The account is schematic and pluralistic by comparison with the substantial and reductive approaches of Socrates and Plato (before the *Republic*). Those earlier philosophers had tended to answer the question 'What is excellence?' by singling out one of the commonly recognized admirable qualities, e.g. wisdom (knowledge) or moderation, and arguing either that the supposedly other excellences were identical with it, or that it was the fundamental one of which the others were different forms.[78] Aristotle privileges none of the character-excellences in quite this way, and his theory of triads each with its own continuum seems designed to emphasize the multiplicity of the areas of human life, every one of which offers a distinct kind of opportunity for the cultivation and exercise of the excellence proper to it, as well as distinct opportunities for ethical failure.[79]

Aristotle prefaces his examination of the specific dispositions by saying: 'Now let us . . . discuss each of the excellences individually, saying what they are, what things they relate to, and how; and it will be clear, too, at the same time, how many they are.'[80] 'How many' could mean that we shall be shown what the total number of ethical triads is. But nothing in what follows suggests a reason why he considers just the number of them that he does, or that this is necessarily a complete set.[81] Thus 'it will be clear how many they are' may well mean simply that we shall see what a lot there are, as distinct from just one (Socrates), or four (the *Republic*). The triadic schema brings out this plurality, precisely because it is so clearly schematic. What, according to it, the good dispositions share, i.e. their intermediacy, is obviously not an attribute to which they could all be *reduced* in the way in which Socrates believed all the other excellences were reducible to wisdom.[82] And the schema helps alert us not only to nameless dispositions on already recognized continua, but also to the possibility of continua which Aristotle does not discuss that would define additional triads.

This respect for the plurality of character-excellence shows practical concern for the needs of the would-be good and the requirements of ethical training. An ideally developed character may view all circumstances as simply posing the identical question, 'What is called for in this situation?', but anyone in charge of a developing person is surely helped by a lively sense of the specificities of different kinds of situation, and the different kinds of human weakness that have to be overcome for decent responses to be possible in each. The challenges to courage are painful, those to moderation pleasant. As a natural scientist, Aristotle would take seriously the psycho-physiological differences between the way it feels to be in mortal danger and the way it feels to be sexually tempted, for example.[83] And it is common sense that plenty of practice in coping with mortal danger does not substitute for the plenty of different sorts of practice needed to inculcate justice, mildness, moderation, and friendliness.

3: The specific excellences of character[84]

At II. 7 Aristotle lists the ethical triads to be treated, and after discussing voluntary agency he begins the detailed studies of them. He does not explain the order of treatment. Still, it makes sense to start as he does, with courage and moderation and their opposites,[85] since in both cases the challenges arise from our physical nature. At stake here is one category of non-psychic good, the goods of the body.[86] Then come two pairs of triads concerned with external goods,[87] namely: open-handedness and munificence, and their opposites (to do with wealth); and greatness of soul and ambition, and their opposites (to do with honour). Aristotle probably meant to end with justice,[88] which requires an extended treatment to itself; if so, he reasonably places the three social triads of friendliness, truthfulness, wittiness, and their opposites, next to justice. Perhaps mildness and its opposites come just before them because these too are social qualities in a way.

The portraits Aristotle gives us of the specific excellences each correspond to an aspect of the perfect character. Aristotle tends to personify them, speaking of 'the courageous person', 'the great-souled person', and so on. The courageous person, in this logical sense, cannot be the moderate or great-souled or mild person, any more than any of these qualities can be any of the others. But the ideal, which Aristotle hopes he can help his 'political' audience to advance, is the fostering of concrete individuals who are excellent in all the areas of life in which they might participate.

Courage (*andreia*; literally, 'manliness')[89]

Nothing in Aristotle's general account of character-excellence prepares us for the complexity of courage, which turns out to be intermediate in respect of two continua, one of fear, the other of boldness and defiance.[90] Excess of fearfulness coincides with deficiency of boldness to produce the character of the coward, but in the reverse directions the continua part company. The person deficient in fear is too insensitive to danger (hence takes foolish risks), whereas the over-bold are apt to swagger beforehand, only to lose their nerve in the event.[91] The dimension of boldness has to do with anticipating an ordeal, that of fear with response to the situation itself. Aristotle assumes a natural connection between correct attitude beforehand and in the event itself; thus the quality of courage combines the two mid-positions in a natural unity.[92] (Cowardice is likewise a natural combination of demoralization beforehand and timorousness in the action.) If, however, one considers possible the case of a person who is too bold or not bold enough beforehand, but just right in the event itself, and also that of a person who is appropriately bold in advance but then, say, panics,[93] one can ask which of these hybrids more closely approximates courage. Obviously it is the former. Whether by this or some other route, Aristotle sees that the fear-dimension is more central. For the courageous person is one who, above all, stands firm and keeps his head in the midst of danger.[94]

But not everything fearsome offers an occasion for courage. Some situations are so terrifying that any normal human being will panic. And there are outcomes which it would be wrong not to fear. The courageous person is not fearless of these. And some prospects which one ought to face fearlessly (such as becoming poor through no fault of one's own) are not on that account occasions for courage. Courage, in Aristotle's account, is for facing death and wounds: the worst that can happen to the individual human organism.[95]

The audience will have recognized here a repudiation of Socrates' statement in Plato's *Laches*, according to which courage is simply general strength of character.

I wanted to include not only those who are courageous in warfare, but also those who are brave in dangers at sea, and the ones who show courage in illness and poverty and affairs of state; and then again I wanted to include not only those who are brave in the face of pain and fear but also those who are clever at fighting desire and pleasure . . . (191d–e).

Not even one who calmly faces an unpleasant death at sea or in illness exemplifies Aristotelian courage. For that, there has to be the possibility of running away from the danger,[96] and also of warding off evil (from others if not oneself) by standing firm.[97] The link with appropriate boldness beforehand shows that courage is not the excellence for facing a hopeless situation. It comes in when there is opportunity for gallant action. It is readiness, not to undergo a difficult death with dignity, but to *give* one's life in a noble cause. But only if necessary. The courageous person holds his own life dear, the more so the better he is, because he knows the value of what he is prepared to give up.[98] (Aristotle leaves us to spell out the performative dynamic whereby the brave man's act of risking his life renders that life all the more precious, hence all the more worth his cherishing, and so a more painful and admirable sacrifice.)

The *Nicomachean Ethics* essay on courage particularly emphasizes the fineness or beauty (*kallos*) of this excellence and its activity, and draws attention to the motive 'for the sake of the fine' (*tou kalou heneka*) that distinguishes courageous action from various lookalikes.[99] The essay signs off with the observation that courageous men as here defined may be less useful for military purposes than mercenaries whose lives are not worth much to them, so that they are willing to risk death for low wages.[100] To some readers, this separation of the true value of courage from its undoubted usefulness in real life, especially for certain groups or certain stages of social development, seems to beckon towards a cult of pointless heroism. But we must consider the position in the context of the *Ethics* as a whole. Many facts suggest to the thoughtful person that the value of courage lies primarily in its usefulness. This would explain why courage is not called into play in hopeless situations. One is then naturally led to suspect that people glorify the beauty of courage because of the need to inculcate it. Now if the value of courage and courageous activity is simply their usefulness, the same is surely true for other major excellences such as moderation, justice, and wisdom. And so, it will seem, for excellence in general. But then what will the chief good be, for the sake of which these excellences are to be valued? It cannot consist mainly in the activity of excellence, since by definition the chief good cannot be something that is useful for a further good. So, on this theory about courage and the other excellences, it must mainly consist in physical or external goods (the possession and use of which would now have to be regarded as an end in itself[101]), or in pleasures associated with having and using such goods. In short, Aristotle's emphasis on the beauty of courage is not meant to prompt us to manufacture opportunities to display it,[102] but to stave off a general coarsening of our values.

Moderation (*sōphrosunē*)[103]

'*Sōphrosunē*' (literally, 'soundness of mind') originally connoted self-restraint in general, like the English 'moderation', but later came to be restricted to restraint in the pleasures of the flesh. Aristotle uses the term in this narrower sense.[104]

Whereas the *Laches* theory (see p. 24) implied that moderation in the narrow sense is a subdivision of courage, moderation and courage for Aristotle are not merely coordinate but are opposed in a way that renders it impossible to see how the concept of either could be extended to include the other. The potential pain, to one's body, of situations calling for courage creates a contrary challenge to that of the pleasure, to one's body, of things that call for moderation. This contrast reflects a more general one between appetite (*epithumia*), the impulse towards something attractive, and temper (*thumos*), the impulse to fight back against harm, danger, and interference. The former is typified by its object, which is the pleasant; the latter by its occasion, which is threatening and hence unpleasant. Moderation is about the governance of certain pleasures, courage about the correct channelling of temper in response to certain kinds of repugnant situation.

All pleasures occur 'in' the soul,[105] and all, including intellectual pleasures, depend (in human beings) on physiological conditions.[106] But the pleasures of eating, drinking, and sex are the terrain of moderation, and these are peculiarly 'bodily', since what is enjoyed is sensations occurring in the organs as they operate in these functions. Contrast this with seeing and hearing, where we are equally dependent on bodily organs, but where the associated pleasures feature beautiful external objects, not one's own eyes and ears.

Whatever forms and meanings they receive under social conditioning, the functions of eating, drinking, and sex are naturally designed to further the biological system. But biological continuation in higher animals has as its natural purpose a richer life of perception and movement, and, in the case of man, a life of reason, emotion, and action. Yet the pleasures of eating, drinking, and sex represent the sensations of parts of the organism as ends in themselves rather than as nature's means, which from a biological point of view they really are.[107] Aristotle calls those sensations 'necessary',[108] which says both that the pleasures they provide are compulsive in nature and that we should have no more truck with them than necessary. These are not the kinds of pleasure we should revel in or make a fuss about.

Aristotle associates them solely with the sense of touch, the one sense common to all animals because necessary for existence.[109] One can see the theoretical attraction of connecting the pleasures of the biological functions with animality as such, and of locating them in the one sense-modality shared by all animals. This restriction to the sense of touch would make it possible for Aristotle to integrate two aspects of the processes of feeding and copulation. There are, on the one hand, the sensations by which the organism is aware of those processes, and, on the other, the internal physiological changes that result. Like all chemical effects in Aristotle's universe, these physiological changes are produced by heat, cold, dryness, moisture, and the common sensibles such as movement and size. Now, these chemically effective qualities are all tangibilia, and tastes, smells, sounds, and colours are not among them.

Suppose, then, that the qualities that explain the physiological changes by which eating, drinking, and copulation contribute to the life of the species also explain the associated pleasures that drive the organism: it follows that the associated pleasures can only be pleasures of touch.[110]

This view implies that when we enjoy the tastes and smells of the food and drink we consume, our pleasure in these is not part of our pleasure in the basic activities of consumption. Rather, it is like the pleasure of wine connoisseurs, who taste and smell without a view to consumption.[111] What Aristotle finds objectionable about self-indulgence (*akolasia*), the excessive member of the pleasures-in-consumption triad, is not simply that the self-indulgent consume too much, but that they take excessive pleasure in the purely tactile aspect of the activity, to the extent that they hardly care about tastes and smells except as external signs or reminders of a meal. They are interested in the tastes and smells only in the way the lion is interested in the mooing of his prey, i.e. as a sign of the meat he will devour.[112]

We need some degree of moderation, or some approximation towards it, as we need courage, to safeguard bodily and external goods, and to maintain or protect our social institutions.[113] But whereas courage involves risking something so precious that a loss or gain of great magnitude must be at stake, the pleasures which the moderate person forgoes, as well as the ones he legitimately enjoys, are of little value in themselves. The courageous very much want not to die, but when the moderate refrain from some physical pleasure, they do not mind it.[114] As with courage, the usefulness of moderation is real but is not the point. By rejecting our sheer animality, Aristotelian moderation affirms our humanity instead. It is distinctively human to think in terms of means to ends at all, and to desire the kinds of thing—long-term health and security, participation in society—that moderate practices do so much to promote. The person who is genuinely moderate practises moderation not for the sake of those results, nor perhaps sheerly for its own sake, but to assert and reinforce the human nature, unique among mortal living beings, by which we value rational ends and approach them in a rational way.

Open-handedness (*eleutheriotēs*)[115]

Literally, this is the excellence to be expected in those who enjoy civic freedom (*eleutheria*), and more generally in all with property or funds at their disposal. It has to do with the continua of giving and taking financial assets.[116] The contrary defects are wastefulness (*asōtia*) and avariciousness (*aneleutheria*), but they are not necessarily contrary to each other (even though open-handedness is said to be 'intermediate'), since one form of avariciousness tends to go with wastefulness.[117]

Giving and taking are considered together, because outlay requires income, but open-handedness is immediately expressed in appropriate giving, not taking.[118] The giving side is essential, and is done for the sake of the fine, whereas

27

the taking is done only because it is necessary for the sake of giving.[119] And one can still count as open-handed even if one's giving out is somewhat excessive,[120] but not if one's taking is so, i.e. if one takes too much or in wrong or sordid ways or from inappropriate sources. In sum, the giving out that typifies open-handed people implies appropriate possession of the wealth they use, and that in turn implies appropriate acquisition.[121]

As before, 'too much, too little, the right amount' stand for a multiplicity of dimensions in which one can get things right or wrong. Thus wastefulness is typified not by just any 'excessive' spending, for a self-indulgent person spends 'more than he should' in spending on excessive physical pleasures, but if he does it intelligently, and—by his own standards, at least—gets something worth while in return, he is not wasteful. The wasteful type fritters wealth away, thereby destroying his means of living.[122] It is perhaps logically to be expected that someone who does not 'know the value of money' will be deficient about taking as well as excessive about giving, and theoretically perhaps the wasteful person combines these characteristics. However, the necessity of getting what one spends makes this an unstable situation: this sort of wastefulness runs out of resources, and the enforced curtailment of spending provides the chance of a 'cure'. (By contrast, avariciousness contains no such principle of self-correction, and is a much uglier characteristic.)[123] However, most wasteful people are not cured, and therefore they lapse into taking 'too much' in order to support their inordinate spending.[124]

Taking too much is the mark of an avaricious person, so this sort of wastefulness actually coincides with avariciousness. But the latter quality comes in different kinds. The one that is compatible with wastefulness consists in not being particular about how one acquires one's wealth. The other kind, which excludes wastefulness, and which Aristotle might therefore have denominated its true opposite, is miserliness, which values having wealth above any kind of spending it.[125]

Munificence (*megaloprepeia*)[126]

Wealthy Athenians were required to take responsibility for certain public goods and services: for example, fitting out and maintaining a ship of war for one year; entertaining official foreign visitors; leading delegations to sacred centres such as Delphi and Delos; hosting public banquets; staging a tragedy or comedy at one of the festivals. Evidently there was a great deal of latitude in the execution of these duties, providing a sphere for *megaloprepeia*, the excellence that discharges them with suitable (*prepon*) grandness (*to mega*).[127] The good and successful leader whose happy life is surpassed only by that of the thinker (x. 7–8) will certainly need this quality.

Munificence presupposes open-handedness, which it resembles in being 'about money'. It differs in being entirely to do with spending rather than getting, and in its scale. But munificent spending is not simply open-handed spending multiplied. Open-handedness avoids the mistakes of failing to spend when one should, and of being forward in spending when one should not, by choosing the right occasions and recipients. Munificence, by contrast, has its occasions and recipients already set by civic and religious custom. It does not spend more often than open-handedness (its occasions are comparatively rare), nor does it simply spend more. It spends more in response to the eminence of the occasion, and does what it does 'for the sake of the fine'— which covers not only the spirit of munificent action, but the beauty and grandeur of the public event in which it is expressed. For Aristotle's munificent type is not merely suitably generous in financing such events, but is personally involved in deciding how to stage them. So good taste, and a sense of how the city should present itself, are essential aspects of Aristotelian munificence. Shabbiness (*mikroprepeia*), one of the opposite states, economizes at the expense of rising to the occasion; vulgarity (*banausia*), the other, treats the communal occasion as an opportunity for personal display of wealth.

Greatness of soul (*megalopsuchia*)[128]

Right attitudes to expendable possessions, to physical pleasure, to personal safety, have been crucial to the excellences considered so far. Greatness of soul[129] has to do with a person's right attitude to his own worth—but not any person's. Just as munificence was coupled with a more ordinary excellence also concerned with spending, so for greatness of soul too we go by the name[130] and locate it as the grand member of a similar pair. It is the excellence of one who esteems himself worthy of receiving great things, and rightly so.[131] Its opposites are conceitedness (*chaunotēs*) and littleness of soul (*mikropsuchia*).

Aristotle's next step connects greatness of soul with honour and respect from others. Since worth can only be estimated by reference to external goods,[132] and the greatest external good is honour, greatness of soul is to do with honours and the lack of them.[133]

The idea of one who considers himself worthy of great things, in particular honour, was of course a familiar notion to Aristotle's audience. They would have thought of Homeric heroes such as Achilles and Ajax,[134] for whom it was dishonour to tolerate an insult or accept second place. They would have thought of Odysseus' harangue to the Achaeans by their ships at Troy, when he argued the disgrace of going home in despair after nine fruitless years instead of holding out for the great destiny once foretold them.[135] And Aristotle's audience would have found nothing new in this reasoning: 'if the great-souled person is in fact worthy of the greatest things, he will be best (*aristos*); for it is always the better person who is worthy of what is greater, and the best of what is greatest'.[136] 'Best' here is schematic, meaning 'the true élite by whatever standard'. Achilles and Ajax were *aristoi* by the standard of their society.

Now, however, Aristotle moves forward. If we recognize such an excellence as greatness of soul (and this is never in doubt), and spell it out as the excellence of the best, we must accept that the great-souled man is *good* (*agathos*), since the best is at least good. But when we say that the great-souled as such are good, i.e. good without qualification, we must mean 'by *our* standards'. Aristotle's audience[137] must mean 'good, i.e. patriotically courageous, moderate, just, and the rest', interpreting these in the usual way. The 'greatness', then, of true greatness of soul implies possession of *these* qualities to superlative degree.[138]

Greatness of soul not only presupposes the familiar excellences: it enhances them like an adornment (*kosmos*).[139] We soon see how greatness of soul has this effect. The great-souled person, it is implied, not only is not mistaken in regarding himself as worthy of highest honour, but he understands the ground of this desert. He therefore honours excellence, in general and in himself, more highly than anything else.[140] So he is detached about wealth, power, noble birth, and so forth,[141] since excellence as we understand it is none of these. He need not therefore regard these things as valueless, but since he knows that excellence alone deserves honour, and that even honour cannot measure up to it since the value of honour is less,[142] he knows (*a*) that he is not to be honoured for wealth and power etc. if he has them, and (*b*) that it is an insult to excellence to suppose that any of these things, including even honour itself, is or should be its compensation. This reflective commitment to excellence roots it more firmly in him than if he were less clear about the place of excellence in the scale of things. For those who are deeply impressed by wealth or power or social position, or deeply disappointed at not having them (whether for themselves or for those they care about), are already on the way to regarding a life of excellence as not worth while[143] just on its own terms: an attitude that paves the way towards reluctance to pursue what is best when doing so undermines or fails to augment those other goods. In misfortune, in particular, greatness of soul stands between us and the temptation to give up doing our best as if it were true that 'it makes no difference'.[144]

The defects of excess and deficiency each exhibit a mismatch between self-estimated and actual desert. These mismatches could occur in two ways. The subject may share the great-souled person's understanding of 'worth' and 'excellence', but simply over- or underestimate himself in these terms. Alternatively, the subjects may understand 'worth' and 'excellence' differently, for example equating them with the possession of wealth. In that case, the conceited think too much of themselves because they are rich, the little-souled too little of *them*selves because they are not.[145] In any event, Aristotle says that conceitedness and littleness of soul are foolish but harmless.[146] This statement is true only on a certain assumption, however. No doubt the little-souled type is ineffectual in any context; but if the conceited one has, and prides himself on, significant wealth or power, he is potentially dangerous: arrogant and wantonly offensive towards his supposed inferiors. In fact, such a one is not merely conceited; for measured in terms of wealth and power his worth *is* great, just as he believes it to be. This is a simulacrum of true greatness of soul. Often, it begins because others honour the wealthy and powerful for their wealth and power, and they accept the evaluation.[147]

Aristotle says that it is hard not to be spoilt by external good fortune unless one has excellence.[148] Clearly, the acquisition of wealth etc. might catalyse behaviour the agent might not have manifested before, when there was less chance of getting away with it. But if that was *because* he would not get away with it, then he was not excellent. What, though, if someone begins as a person of simple excellence unadorned by greatness of soul?[149] He stands up for his rights and concedes to others on particular occasions, but has not developed an attitude to his own worth in general. Again, on particular occasions he does what is right or fine because it so is, but himself has hardly reflected on values in general, or the place of excellence compared with other goods. Will he remain ethically unchanged if he enters the lifestyle of the rich and famous? It seems impossible if we assume that certain others now honour him for these attributes, or act as if they do, and he takes himself to be honoured on these grounds. For then either he accepts this evaluation—he is a better human being than others because richer or more powerful—and simple excellence is eroded; or the new status and attention jolt him into genuine greatness of soul. To find himself unmoved by their honourings is to have made the step to great-souled love of excellence. Greatness of soul, then, keeps simple excellence intact in times of great good fortune as well as bad.[150]

Aristotle might have defined greatness of soul as the excellence called into play when ordinary excellence is challenged by major turns of fortune. Or he might straightforwardly have identified it as the disposition to prize excellence above all else. But while these are effects of Aristotelian greatness of soul, its essence remains linked to respect from others.[151] The implication is that in principle there can be external respect that it would be right to care about within reason. We should therefore expect the great-souled person to go to some trouble, rather than none at all, to explain himself where necessary to those whose respect he deserves, i.e. those who respect excellence. Presumably his knowing that he cannot explain himself to the others, and his refusal to dissemble—his authenticity, as we would call it—lie at the root of the famous disdain[152] that makes him unattractive to some of us today. If the great-souled person is notorious for this disdain, presumably it is because there is (Aristotle assumes) a preponderance of people who give honour, or expect to get it, for the wrong reasons.

In living up to his own standard, the great-souled person, like the ancient hero, holds himself ready for opportunities to do great things. Thus he is uncluttered by affairs, and not in a hurry to respond to lesser calls on his time and attention.[153] This description, we must remember, is intended to portray not a concrete type, but one aspect of the all-round excellent person. By definition the great-souled person is just and open-handed etc., a good father, friend, and citizen, and as such he attends to all sorts of predictable duties and commitments that he has in common with everyone. Thus he cannot literally loiter like Achilles in his tent until the moment arrives to unsheath his greatness. The point must be that, just as his centre remains unswayed by the approval and disapproval of the vulgar, so in the midst of humdrum necessities he keeps a part of himself in reserve for the chance to do something out of the ordinary. Such chances go unnoticed if one is wholly immersed in familiar things. So in so far as a person is great-souled, he or she is not bustling or shrill, as people are who throw themselves completely into whatever they happen to be doing.[154]

This link between greatness of soul and extraordinary initiative explains why Aristotle regards conceitedness as a lesser failing than littleness of soul.[155] At first sight this is surprising, since littleness is said to be clearest in one who is actually worthy of great things,[156] hence one who possesses admirable qualities. But the point is that littleness of soul is worse in this particular dimension. The vain person, whose excellence is lightweight, is presumably worse all round, but his pretension to special honours shows a sort of idealism; whereas to have developed admirable qualities, yet hang back from chancing one's arm at some achievement that would bring them out, is a betrayal of one's excellence.

A nameless excellence to do with honour[157]

Aristotle says that this quality stands to greatness of soul more or less as open-handedness to munificence.[158] But his treatment is perfunctory. It is not clear whether he means that the nameless quality involves a true self-estimate of small-scale excellence,[159] or that it has to do with honour on a smaller scale. In fact, the difference may not be exactly quantitative, any more than the difference between munificence and open-handedness. For it may be that greatness of soul has to do with respect for what is most important about a human being, whereas the nameless excellence is about institutional honours, such as titles, privileges, and prizes, that are awarded for particular contributions or achievements. It also seems that the difference between the nameless excellence and the corresponding defects is not that of true versus false estimates of one's own (minor) worth, but that of caring the right amount (in the right way, etc.), versus caring too much or too little, about going in for such honours. Whereas there is no reason why the munificent person should not be open-handed, since these two excellences operate in different contexts, the great-souled type cannot have the nameless excellence if it necessarily involves minor worth, and in any case is likely to lack it by being too unambitious for the honours in question.

Mildness (*praotēs*)[160]

This is excellence in the sphere of anger. Although the term 'mildness' actually suggests deficiency in respect of anger, Aristotle lacks a better word for the intermediate state. So he emphasizes that, if 'mild' is to connote an excellence, the mild person *does* get angry when it is appropriate.[161] The study is interesting for its distinctions between the different excessive types: the person who is too quick off the mark; the one who seethes ready to be angry about anything; the one who nurses his anger in secret, and is stuck with it for a long time, and is vengeful.[162] Since anger is in a way susceptible to reason (anyway by comparison with appetite for physical pleasure[163]), the open excessive forms are easier to deal with, giving others an opportunity to persuade one out of it.[164]

Three social excellences[165]

Before turning to justice, the most fundamental of the social excellences, Aristotle considers some less obvious ones: those that pertain to interactions where no great thing is at stake, where there is nothing to trigger the potentials for fear or lust or anger or material greed, where honour and law and binding duty are not at issue.[166] We could call these the three conversational excellences.

The first, which is nameless, has to do with pleasing and displeasing others.[167] One extreme seeks always to please and never give offence; the other is contentious and confrontational. The former comes in two forms: the obsequious (*areskos*) person who wants to be liked and not spoil the other's pleasure, and the ingratiating (*kolax*) person who aims at material profit. (One might distinguish corresponding forms of the other extreme: the person who likes opposing others or making them feel uncomfortable, and the person who does it to show that he is not the ingratiating type. One might also contrast timidity about confrontation with the indiscriminate desire to be liked, since they need not go together.)

The next conversational excellence, also nameless, has to do with self-presentation.[168] Its opposites are imposture (*alazoneia*) and self-deprecation (*eironeia*). Aristotle faults these qualities not primarily because of their effect on others (even if we are not misled, the lack of straightforwardness is unpleasant), but because they show disregard for truth.[169]

While the first two conversational excellences contribute to any social situation, the context of the third[170] is relaxation. Relaxation and play are a necessary part of human existence,[171] and—Aristotle assumes—we relax in each other's company. The relevant excellence is wittiness (*eutrapelia*), the intermediate between buffoonery (*bōmolochia*) and humourless boorishness (*agroikia*, literally 'rusticity', the opposite of urbanity[172]). Aristotle may be mainly thinking of raillery, where one person ridicules another to his face.[173] The witty person not only has a fine sense of humour, but also chooses similar companions with whom to laugh and joke.[174]

This discussion of wittiness gives two impressions that will be corrected later: (*a*) that active life is divided between *practical doings* and *relaxation*, and (*b*) that this division coincides with the contrast *serious* and *not-serious*. In Book X Aristotle will continue to equate relaxation with the non-serious,[175] but he will go on to argue that the best life includes an activity that is neither practical nor a relaxation.

4: Justice[176]

SUMMARY:

General justice and particular justice; the attempt to characterize particular justice by reference to (*a*) the motive 'graspingness', and (*b*) fair apportionments of gain and loss; fair apportionment divides into 'distributive' and 'rectificatory'; justice and commercial exchange; a series of important questions about general justice.

In a broad sense we act justly when practising the other excellences of character, since in each area what counts as appropriate ('intermediate') conduct is to some extent determined by what we owe others or what they have a right to expect from us. And the laws of a society, written and unwritten, lay down constraints in many different areas, so if we call an act 'unjust' because it is against the law or shows disrespect for lawfulness, we are not placing it in a special category coordinate with categories such as 'self-indulgent', 'cowardly', 'wasteful'; and similarly with acts that are said to be 'just' in this broad sense.

But although the field of general justice is more or less coextensive with all the departments of life considered under the excellences examined so far, this notion of justice is not the same as that of character-excellence in general ('the whole of excellence', as Aristotle calls it[177]). For the notion of excellence is, by comparison, simple, whereas that of general justice includes the qualification: *directed towards another*.[178] One might wonder what exactly this adds, since some of the specific excellences are, in various ways, essentially other-oriented, e.g. open-handedness, the qualities that have to do with honour, and the 'conversational' excellences. The point, however, is that in calling an action just in the general sense we attend to the fact that it fits in with what is owed to all concerned, whereas in calling it, for example, open-handed we attend to the fact that the agent logically might have been, but is not, put off by the motives associated with avarice or wastefulness; and so on.

A person who is just in the general sense will be one who acts out of respect for all concerned and with respect for the law. One can therefore have and exercise the specific excellences studied so far without having and exercising general justice, for one might be in the habit of doing what is courageous or open-handed simply by seeing that the actions in question are appropriate without spelling this out by reference to the rights of others. But to exercise general justice in any of the special areas one needs the relevant special excellence. However, general justice across the board does not merely subsume the other excellences; it also perfects each one by extending its operation beyond our personal circle.[179] General justice, then, is a sort of meta-excellence: one that has its own sort of motive and gives rise to some actions of its own, but is not expressed in any area that is special or exclusive to itself.

However, there are kinds of procedure and arrangement, e.g. distributions of goods or burdens, that we judge to be 'just' or 'unjust' in the special sense of 'fair', 'equitable', or the opposite. Impartiality, or treating equals as equals, is the essence of just conduct in this narrow sense, whereas broadly just actions are not, as such, impartial (or, of course, partial). (A person who, in the spirit of general justice, refuses to consider an adulterous relationship because it would infringe on someone's marriage is not being *impartial* towards that person.) Aristotle not only marks off certain sorts of *arrangement* and *action* as just (or the opposite) in this special sense, but he also strains to prove the existence of a corresponding special *quality of character*, which, like excellences already considered, is a 'part' of general excellence.[180]

He homes in on this postulated quality along two lines which do not quite neatly converge. Book V as we have it is an amalgam of different treatments: this is clear from a number of repetitions and abrupt turns in the sequence of presentation. It is reasonable to infer that the two approaches to narrow or particular justice were devised independently and were not entirely integrated. According to one, this excellence comes to light as the opposite of a disposition called 'particular injustice', which Aristotle characterizes by the notorious motive of graspingness (*pleonexia*).[181] According to the other, we begin from a special area of life, that of apportioning gains and losses, on the assumption that particular justice is the character-trait that values and produces fair apportionments.[182] But on this approach, the contrary quality is not graspingness. For graspingness has one's own gain as object, whereas the contrary of fairness in apportionment is bias or partiality, which may favour a third party at the expense of someone else. In distributing goods, one can treat someone unfairly not for the sake of gain to oneself , but because one dislikes one of the participants or his type. Even if it is said that in such a case one obtains the unfair gain of seeing the disliked person lose, it is still true that what was unjust about the original action was that it treated the person unfairly by comparison with the other participants in the distribution, regardless of the consequences for the distributing agent.

It is also rather unclear what graspingness is. The word 'pleonexia' literally means 'tendency to get more for oneself'. Aristotle explains this by saying that the goods aimed at by graspingness are the ones that are subject to fortune;[183] when discussing friendship, he calls them, more illuminatingly, the goods that are 'fought over'.[184] These are goods that can in principle be shared even when they belong to someone (unlike someone's health or courage or good deeds, no part of which can belong to anyone else), and are such that if one person has more, another has less. However, Aristotle leaves us guessing how to understand the 'more' that graspingness aims for. Is it for more than others have or will get, or for more and more, i.e. more than one has already? And does the grasping person actually want more than his share as such, so that part of his satisfaction is that others get less than they deserve, or does he simply want what in fact is more than his share without considering others? However this may be, we can allow that graspingness (given certain obvious conditions) tends to result in apportionments that unfairly favour oneself, even though one who apportions unfairly does not necessarily thereby act in a way that is grasping.

No doubt Aristotle would like to represent particular justice as an inter-mediate *disposition* like the other excellences of character. But he can only state that its characteristic *acts* achieve intermediacy between too much and too little for the parties concerned. He cannot place the disposition to perform such acts in a triad whose other members are a defect of excess and a defect of deficiency, for particular justice has but a single opposite, injustice, which by one and the same act favours the agent and deprives someone else.[185] No doubt some people exhibit the opposite tendency, that of taking less than their share of good things or more than their share of burdens, but this is not a new kind of injustice. For if they seem to act unjustly, it is only against themselves, and Aristotle insists that it is impossible to do injustice to oneself.[186]

Particular justice, according to the second approach, which seeks to dis-tinguish it by what it does rather than through contrast with the injustice of graspingness, is manifested in two kinds of operation: *distribution* of goods or burdens, and *rectification* of injuries.[187] The common factor is apportionment of *gain* and *loss*, which he interprets very schematically. The hallmark of a just apportionment is *equality*. In distribution, this consists in maintaining the same ratio of quantified goods or burdens to quantified merit for all recipi-ents. In rectification, it consists in restoring the parties to the relative position (schematized as 'equality') they were in before one harmed the other. Ideally this is done by 'taking from' the perpetrator the 'gain' (or an equivalent) which he 'took from' the victim, and 'returning' it. At one place Aristotle seems close to admitting the artificiality of applying this schema to injuries in general.[188] Yet he does not discuss the problem presented by wrongs such as murder, where the victim cannot be compensated.[189]

Under *rectification* Aristotle does not distinguish *forced reparation* and *punishment.*[190] This is bound up with the fact that he applies 'rectification' (in the same sense) to what later came to be contrasted as civil and criminal cases.[191] In the former, a satisfactory outcome consists in the wrongdoer's compensating the victim, whereas in the latter it includes punishment of the wrongdoer by the state. Athenian law recognized the difference between these outcomes, and in some cases it exacted both. Possibly Aristotle understands punishment as just one variety of compensation (paid to the state) and hence as not needing special discussion. At any rate he offers none. Nor does he dwell on the aspect of punitive fairness that comes under distributive justice, i.e. similar punishments for similar offences.[192]

His analysis of different kinds of just assignment includes a discussion of *commercial exchange.* This arises out of a consideration of the Pythagorean view that the just should be defined in terms of reciprocity (the *lex talionis*).[193] Although Aristotle rejects this view, he sees reciprocity, and in particular the reciprocity of commercial exchange, as important for understanding justice. Reciprocity in general is what holds the city together. Commercial exchange is the necessary condition for the kind of association that results in a city-state. Not only does it fulfil economic needs, but it sets its participants on the footing of equality that must exist between fellow citizens. This is not equality of merit, since merit can vary among fellow citizens, but equality of (as we would put it) the right to a fair deal and to being treated according to one's merit, and equality in respect of the corresponding responsibilities. Without this equality, there is no such thing as life under the rule of law, and the basic context is lacking in which arrangements and actions can properly be judged either 'just' or 'unjust'.[194]

The examination of particular justice is followed by short studies on a number of fundamental questions concerning justice in the broad sense: the scope of justice;[195] the relation of natural justice to law;[196] the difference between an action that is forbidden by the rules of justice and an unjust act;[197] ways in which voluntariness is involved in committing and suffering unjust acts and in being just and unjust;[198] the need to exercise humane reasonableness (*epieikeia*) as a corrective to the inadequacies of law;[199] and whether one can commit injustice against oneself.[200]

5: **Voluntary agency**[201]

SUMMARY:

The voluntary and the counter-voluntary; correct distinctions in this area are needed if one is to respond to people's actions with praise, blame, or pity, as appropriate; external force is one ground for denying voluntariness, factual ignorance is the other; 'what depends on us'—an important concept, but its implications remain unclear; Aristotle and determinism; character, bad as well as good, is not genetically determined, and is the individual's voluntary acquisition to some extent.

Voluntary agency is an important topic for several reasons. Ethical dispositions are expressed in voluntary action, and they are built up by repeated voluntary action. It is only on account of voluntary actions that agents are said to be, or to be becoming, good or bad, and only on account of voluntary actions do they deserve praise or censure, reward or punishment.[202] And there are also voluntary actions that prima facie call for such responses, but turn out in fact to be grounds for being sorry for the agent.

'Voluntary' translates 'hekousion' (adjective for a thing done or suffered) and 'hekōn' (adjective for a subject or agent). For the contrary terms, 'akousion' and 'akōn', we have chosen the translation 'counter-voluntary', an unfamiliar rendition of two perfectly familiar ancient Greek words. The reason is that the only (and commonly used) alternative, 'involuntary', is less satisfactory. 'Akousion' and 'akōn' express pain and rejection on the part of the subject or agent, 'involuntary' does not.

The most obvious sort of voluntary action is that in which the agent acts gladly or without reluctance: as we say, 'willingly' as opposed to 'unwillingly' or 'reluctantly'. In fact, Aristotle's contemporaries would have felt most comfortable using the words 'hekousion' and 'hekōn' of non-reluctant agency, and of things happening that are welcome, just as they naturally used the contrary terms to imply pain on the part of the agent or subject. Now, when someone is made to do something after being overpowered by an external force, this is an obvious example of the counter-voluntary since that kind of episode normally involves pain for the subject and a struggle to resist. Similarly, the episode is obviously *not* voluntary or *hekousion*. But what exactly is it about it that makes it not voluntary? Is it the person's pain and reluctance, or is it the fact that he or she is overpowered by external force? Aristotle's first major step in his Book III treatment is to drive a wedge between the way the person feels about the episode as it takes place, and the question whether it is voluntary. In the example it is the external force that makes the episode not voluntary. So where there is no external force (and the agent knows what he is doing), something can be done reluctantly yet still is a voluntary action. It can be the kind of action that, considered in the abstract, we think we never would do unless literally forced to do it, but under certain circumstances we may find ourselves choosing to do it.

In ordinary parlance, 'voluntary' and 'counter-voluntary' were contrary terms, and Aristotle wants to preserve this contrariety in his own account.[203] Thus he refuses to apply 'counter-voluntary' to all cases of pain and reluctance, and reserves it for cases of pain and reluctance in which the episode has been found to be not voluntary on some other ground. We might be inclined to think that the important difference is the one between what is voluntary and what is not, and that the presence or absence of pain and reluctance is a side issue. Perhaps this is true in a context where the only purpose is to establish whether someone is legally responsible for something. But how a person feels about something that was not his fault usually says something about his ethical disposition, and it therefore helps in determining our attitude towards the person. For instance, we are sorry for one who is externally forced into a shameful situation if he hates it, but perhaps not so much otherwise.

Thus, as Aristotle notes, there is an important similarity between counter-voluntary episodes and one class of voluntary cases involving pain and reluctance, namely that it is appropriate to be sorry for the person concerned. If the circumstances are such that the agent must choose an evil, and he chooses the lesser evil and reluctantly carries it out, we may well be sorry for him in much the same way as if he had been externally forced to do that thing. His doing that bad thing is voluntary but not his fault. On the other hand, we might even admire the person for choosing and carrying out the lesser evil, if doing so required particular intelligence or courage, whereas it would not make sense to admire someone for a counter-voluntary episode, even if the result were better than some alternative. Moreover, when it is a case of someone's choosing between evils, if we disagree with his judgement of what *is* the lesser evil, in that what he does seems to us the inferior course, we shall not admire, but find fault; nor should we be sorry for him for the action, however reluctantly it was taken.[204]

The modern analyst might extend the concept of being compelled by irresistible force so that it covers cases of duress by threat and other kinds of severe psychological pressure. These would therefore fall outside the class of the voluntary. Aristotle recognizes such cases, but in Book III he assimilates them to choices between evils, making them voluntary.[205] Normally they deserve pity, and we no more find fault than if they were counter-voluntary; but he holds open the possibility that even in such a case there might be reason to fault the agent, if what he did under extraordinary pressure was sufficiently horrendous.[206]

External force is one of the criteria for judging an episode not to be voluntary action. The other is factual ignorance on the part of the agent. Here Aristotle might have made good use of a distinction which he employs frequently throughout his philosophy, between sameness in *actuality* and sameness *in account*. Oedipus' killing the obstreperous old man at the crossroads was the same actuality as Oedipus' killing his father, but the 'accounts' differ, which is why Oedipus knew he was doing one of those things but not the other, and did only the first one voluntarily. What is not voluntary because of factual ignorance is placed in the class of the counter-voluntary if the agent is pained on discovering what he has done. As above, the presence or absence of retrospective pain makes no difference to legal responsibility, but gives valuable ethical information about the agent.

It is easy to be misled about what is voluntary and what is not, not only because the same attitude of pity is appropriate for counter-voluntary acts or episodes and for some that are voluntary, but also because the language of force and compulsion is very naturally applied to motives such as pleasure or appetite or anger. Aristotle insists that nothing is voluntary if actions done from these are not.[207] And the fact that actions done just from these motives are not rational is not for him a reason for regarding them as not voluntary.[208] Drunkenness and anger cause a kind of ignorance, but actions done in this condition still count as voluntary.[209] And although at times Aristotle, like Socrates and Plato, speaks of ethical failings as 'ignorance', he does not follow them in holding that conduct that flows from such ignorance—the ignorance of good and bad, right and wrong—is on that account not voluntary. In much of his discussion he is clearly guided by the principle that if a decent person disapproves of such and such behaviour, the behaviour is voluntary.[210]

He also makes considerable use of the concept of 'what depends on us', but its implications are not always clear. He says that when doing something depends on us, not doing it likewise depends on us, and vice versa.[211] Apparently, one is a voluntary agent only with respect to the actions that depend on one.[212] Presumably Aristotle means that as a voluntary agent I can refrain from doing what in fact I do, and vice versa. But two things are unclear about the sense in which he thinks that both the 'no' and the 'yes'[213] are open to me. First, it is one thing to claim that while I am still considering whether or not to do A, both courses are open to me (unless I am misinformed), and another to claim that once I become definite that it would be better, for example to do A, *then* it is still open to me to refrain. Secondly, he does not explain whether he thinks that both courses are open to me in the sense that, given everything about the situation I am actually in, each course represents a physically possible future stretching forward from my present; or whether he merely thinks that I might have been (though I am not) in a situation from which a future would have stretched forward that was different from my actual future. The fact that Aristotle does not explain where he stands on these questions suggests that he is not preoccupied with the problems of determinism, in particular the problem of showing that there is a sense in which 'The agent could have done otherwise' can still be true even if the universe is deterministic, or deterministic on the level at which human agency occurs.

Two aspects of modern determinism seem to threaten our notion of ourselves as responsible individuals. One follows from the implication that whatever happens happens of necessity, given the circumstances; the other from the doctrine that whatever happens is to be explained by, or at least falls under, laws that apply to the entire natural universe.[214] Aristotle's account of voluntary agency in the *Nicomachean Ethics* is compatible with the former implication, although there is little reason to think that he framed it with that in view.[215] As for the latter doctrine, his position in the *Ethics* and elsewhere is incompatible with it, for he speaks of man and nature as distinct kinds of principle or cause.[216]

In the cases considered so far, it is taken for granted that the agent who operates from an undesirable situation, e.g. one in which he is externally forced, or is factually ignorant, or is stuck with a choice between evils, is not responsible for being in that situation. However, Aristotle does recognize that if I voluntarily act in a way that foreseeably leads to a certain result, then I am the voluntary producer of that result. The most important application of this principle is to character-development. Aristotle argues that although genetic endowment may play a part in determining our ethical characteristics, and although early upbringing certainly plays a major part, nevertheless to some extent it depends on the developing individual himself whether or not he comes to be one or another sort of person, ethically speaking.[217] And since the sort of person he is determines how he interprets the Good in particular situations, the individual is to some extent responsible for his own ethical values and intuitions. In arguing this out, Aristotle is mainly concerned to emphasize two things. First, good character and bad character are on the same footing: it is not the case that we can take credit for good character and good actions, while blaming something outside ourselves for the bad; and, secondly, ethical character is not set by the individual's biological infrastructure, but is due to distinctively human or personal influences.

It is enough for his purpose that biological nature does not completely dictate our actions; he can allow that it may make a very important contribution. He does not need to refute theorists who hold that biological nature determines what end appears good to us. (In any case, there is *some* truth in that theory, since many human ends, such as to live unharmed, to bring up a family, to be part of a society, are biologically implanted in us. And if one considers happiness or the chief human good, certainly in most people's view it contains elements, such as those just mentioned, that answer to our biological nature.) Even if those theorists were right, it does not follow that our actions, and the ethical dispositions that develop from them, are or flow from our genetic endowment. For different individuals may have the same end genetically, but approach it in different ways. These different approaches are what they embrace in their decisions, and are what they voluntarily implement; and these differences in action and decision develop, and reflect, their different ethical dispositions.[218]

6: **Decision** *(prohairesis)*[219]

SUMMARY:
'Practical immediacy' the hallmark of the technical concept of 'decision'; what is decided-for is a subclass of what is voluntary; why excellences and defects of character are defined as 'issuing in decisions'; decision and deliberation; decision as shaped by the particularities of a situation.

Aristotle put an existing word, *'prohairesis'*, to a new and somewhat technical use as the term for a concept which presumably in some sense existed, but which he himself was the first philosopher to bring out into discussion. In this respect, our principal translation, 'decision',[220] is similar, since its ordinary sense is not yet loaded with the implications it must come to bear as the English equivalent of Aristotle's technical *'prohairesis'*. *'Prohairesis'* as we find it in the non-philosophical writings of some of his contemporaries is usually translated by 'undertaking' or 'policy'.[221] The general meaning, which Aristotle carries forward and elaborates for his own purposes, is: 'something practical to which one is committed'. This general meaning underlies the two main directions in which he develops the concept; what is common to the two directions is the idea of *practical immediacy*.

1. Aristotelian *decision* (as from now on we call it) is a sort of prescription. It is an all-things-considered judgement of what to do. This means that it is immediately practical by contrast with prescriptions (decision-analogues) based on considerations belonging to a limited field, like that of a special expertise such as medicine. A prescription reached from a purely medical point of view (the medical analogue of a decision in the proper sense) has only conditional practicality; even if, in the actual case, there is no question that the patient's health is indeed desired, medical science as such cannot determine whether taking the best medical steps is in fact best: i.e. best in view of the family's entire situation, which involves other individuals, limited resources, other goals and commitments. Thus even if the medically best advice is finally followed, the decision to implement it is not a medical verdict.[222]

2. Aristotelian decision has practical immediacy by comparison with a 'wish' *(boulēsis)*, i.e. the desire for an object which, if attainable, can only be attained through intermediate steps not yet identified. The process by which a wish becomes a determinate practical project is 'deliberation' *(bouleusis)*. If deliberation is brought to a satisfactory conclusion, i.e. to a point where one need not deliberate further to find out how to achieve the wish, the conclusion is a decision, and the next step should be action.[223]

Because an Aristotelian decision is reached 'all things considered', and most obviously through deliberation, it differs from various other springs of voluntary action. Actions that have been *decided-for*, or *objects of decision* (*ta prohaireta*)—are a subclass of the voluntary.[224] Voluntary actions done from appetite (*epithumia*) or temper (*thumos*) are not decided-for, because they are impulsive. Actions against one's better judgement (un-self-controlled actions) are voluntary but not decided-for; in fact Aristotle often describes such agents as 'not sticking to their decision'.[225] The same is true of actions which, though fuelled by an appetite or by temper, are not completely impulsive but based on calculation of how best to satisfy the desire in question. Since this sort of calculation is answerable only to the limited objective of obtaining one particular satisfaction, action based upon it is not decided-for, and may be contrary to a decision which the agent has made.[226]

Unlike the verdicts of expertise, the decision-analogues sometimes yielded up by calculation in the service of appetite or temper are of immediate practical import, since they are automatically enacted unless something interferes. So too, of course, for the uncalculated impulses of appetite and temper. The type of interference that is ethically most significant comes from decisions with which these other springs of action conflict. We need to consider how this can happen. For although Aristotle thinks of decision as an essentially practical attitude, and is careful to show that it is not any kind of belief,[227] his model of practical reason as issuing decisions to a potentially obedient and in itself non-rational part of the soul suggests that decision as such does not carry an inherent psychological power or forceful tendency to suppress or push past recalcitrant elements within the soul. According to the model, decision becomes enacted through the obedience, which may be more or less complete, of the non-rational part. It is clear that reason, which constructs the decision (most obviously, through deliberation) has an *interest* in its being enacted (presumably first a general rational concern for acting rationally, and then, in a given case, determinate concern embodied in a particular decision); but the *will* to enact it is a matter of character, built up by habituation. In this respect, a decision is more like a judgement than it is like a desire, if by 'desire' is meant something analogous to a physical force. If, then, a decision confronts a recalcitrant element in the soul in such a way that the agent is actually torn between conflicting practical tendencies,[228] this can only be because the non-rational part already to some extent sides with reason. Now since decisions are all-things-considered practical judgements, they ought to be enacted: both because there is no authority overriding them, and because they constitute fully determinate practical projects, so that there is, as it were, no logical direction in which they can go except forward into action. They therefore should not have to face conflicting tendencies within the soul. The soul of a rational agent should be in a settled condition in which it is ready to carry out its own decisions without fuss. Good and bad dispositions of character are this kind of settled condition, which is why Aristotle defines them as 'issuing in decisions'.[229] For they make it possible for a decision to *be* as it should be, i.e. unconditionally practical.

However, the association of character-qualities with the potentially obedient part of the soul is misleading if it suggests that they are simply concerned with the execution of decisions. In fact, Aristotle makes it amply clear in Book II that these dispositions play a major role in shaping the decisions themselves. In so far as they are dispositions for liking and disliking the ethically right, or wrong, things, they encapsulate a variety of values and priorities. Respect for reason and its prescriptions (i.e. decisions[230]) is one aspect of excellence across the board, but every specific excellence also involves its own kind of sensitivity and concern for what is fine and disgraceful in its sphere. And the defects of excess and deficiency partly consist in the corresponding insensitivities, and partly make their own kinds of evaluative claim about what is fine and good for a human being to do and feel. In so far as these claims, concerns, sensitivities, and insensitivities are dispositional, they are or correspond to evaluative generalizations, which are expressed as particular responses to particular situations. Thus they affect the content of decisions, and for this reason too the dispositions of character are said to 'issue in decisions'.

Naturally, all-things-considered deliberation concludes in decision; but Aristotle goes further: he explains decision as the conclusion of deliberation.[231] This too is reasonable up to a point. Aristotle generally explains mental attitudes and capacities by specifying the kind of object they are 'of'; thus he wants to demarcate the object of decision, and he makes progress on this by looking at the kind of question to which a decision is answer. The question is the kind that it makes sense to settle through deliberation; thus what we decide-for emerges from the field of things concerning which it makes sense to deliberate. So it is not an object of theoretical science, since the objects of science are eternal or regular features of the universe, and we do not deliberate about these. It is something that depends on us, since it makes no sense to deliberate about things that do not depend on us.[232] But Aristotle also says in Book III that we only deliberate when it is difficult to see what to do, when it is unclear what the outcome will be of this or that course of action;[233] and although this is true about deliberation, there is no warrant for restricting expressions of the ethical dispositions to situations where it is difficult to see what to do, so that deliberation is needed to decide. It is not just that one can act from an ethical disposition without having to deliberate to know what to do, for one might already know because one had deliberated about this sort of thing in the past. But it is also the case that responses expressing the excellences can be formed spontaneously in the sense that, although they are backed by experience, they are not guided by decisions reached through any deliberation present or past.[234]

Perhaps what Aristotle has in mind is that even such spontaneous and immediately creative responses have a complicated rational structure, as appears from the fact that the agent, when questioned why exactly he did this in this way, to these people, at this moment, to this degree, aiming at such and such an effect, etc., sees that these questions are appropriate and is generally able to answer them. This shows that the response, unlike a mere voluntary impulse, is full of thought, even if it did not become so through a process of deliberation.

However, this interpretation does not fit very well with one of the cornerstones of the Book III account of deliberation, namely the statement that whereas wish is for the end, deliberation is about the means to it and has the sole task of bringing us to a decisive grasp of the first step of action.[235] For it is not at all clear that the structure of thought that informs a spontaneous ethical response is most typically means–end reasoning. In the above spelling-out, the 'effect aimed for' is just one of many factors that seem equally important. No doubt when the witty person decides to entertain with a certain joke, or the great-souled one to refuse an invitation, they take account of the effects of their actions, but it is extremely artificial to insist that in these and all other cases means are employed to realize an end.

There is, however, something important in common between decisions considered as the conclusions of deliberation, and decisions considered as expressions of ethical dispositions. Both are responses to the particularities of a situation, and in both cases the objectives or values that we bring to the situation are relatively abstract by comparison. But facing these with the particularities under which they will be instantiated (if at all) on this occasion makes the commitments determinate, brings out qualifications and priorities that could not have been thought of when the disposition remained only a disposition, the end only an object of wish. Presumably Aristotle thinks that character is shown above all when abstract or general objectives and values are exposed to the constraints of our particular circumstances under pressure of the necessity to evince a particular response. And the thought-process he calls 'deliberation' is for him paradigmatic of the kind of practical thought that brings about that exposure and follows it through in detail.[236]

In the light of this parallel between decision as expression of ethical disposition and decision as conclusion of deliberation, let us look at the Book III statement that we deliberate only about means, not ends. He cannot mean by this that we rational animals do or should endorse our ends in life without thoughtful consideration, since thoughtful consideration is exactly what he asks for in encouraging his audience to follow an inquiry about the highest end of all. Instead, the point may be that this philosophical sort of thinking (as well as lower-level but nonetheless entirely general thinking about politics, economics, and legislation), though ultimately practical, is not 'deliberation', because it is remote from, and therefore unconstrained by, the thinkers' particular personal circumstances. Consequently, its conclusions are not 'decisions', since they cannot immediately govern particular actions. And for the same reason he might say that this sort of practical thinking is not the kind that brings out or builds or exercises good character (even if being of bad character means that one cannot empathize with the ideal being sketched in the *Ethics*), because this kind of thinking cannot put us in the practical tight spots to which character responds by 'issuing decisions'.

7: **Wisdom** (phronēsis)[237]

SUMMARY:

The account of wisdom, which completes that of character-excellence, is developed by contrasting wisdom with intellectual accomplishment, on the one hand, and technical expertise, on the other; the importance for the *Ethics* as a whole of explaining wisdom as a genuinely intellectual quality; its relation to truth; how wisdom depends on character-excellence; how character-excellence ensures that the goal is correct, while the intellectual factor in wisdom takes care of the means to the goal; why the Aristotelian contrasts of desire versus thought, and the character- versus the intellectual aspects of wisdom, cast no light on the modern question 'Do moral judgements come from reason or from the feelings?'

It is time to consider the intellectual excellences, of which Aristotle distinguishes two main forms: a theoretical[238] one to which he gives the name '*sophia*', here translated 'intellectual accomplishment', and a practical one, which he calls '*phronēsis*', here translated 'wisdom'. Wisdom in particular needs to be examined so that the account of character-excellence will be complete. For wisdom provides the right prescription that is referred to in the definition of character-excellence.[239]

Aristotle expounds the nature of wisdom by developing accounts of other valuable intellectual qualities, which he compares with wisdom. Summarily, the others are: intellectual accomplishment (*sophia*)—which for Aristotle is excellence in purely theoretical studies—and technical expertise (*technē*). In approaching his discussion we must bear in mind that he is drawing distinctions that had not been made systematically before in Western philosophy. It would not have been obvious to his audience at the outset that technical expertise is not the right paradigm for understanding practical wisdom. Socrates, after all, had constantly argued as if it were.[240] And Plato in the *Republic* had confused matters still further. Not only did he take it for granted that wisdom is identical with the art of government, which he represented as an expertise requiring specialist training. He also insisted that the training include mastery of pure mathematics and astronomy, as well as 'dialectic', a science which, according to the *Republic*, excels mathematics in clarity and intelligibility no less than mathematics excels experiential judgements about the everyday world.[241] The implication is that a mind trained in the most abstract and exact theoretical disciplines is essential for practical wisdom.

Aristotle seems to have been the first to teach that abstract theoretical understanding does not confer practical wisdom, is not a precondition of that sort of wisdom, and is to be prized entirely for its own sake; and the first to see clearly that these are two quite different kinds of excellence.[242] Whereas Plato used the terms '*phronēsis*' and '*sophia*' without distinction, Aristotle makes them names of different qualities,[243] and brings out the differences to the point of being able to say that wisdom is 'antithetical to [theoretical] intelligence'.[244]

This is a crucial point for Aristotle's *Ethics*. If, like Plato in the *Republic*, we believe that practical reasoning, to be genuinely excellent, must be backed by, or even express, an exact science of abstract relations, then we cannot look upon ordinary good judgement as the product of excellent practical reasoning. So either we must dismiss ordinary good judgement as an unreliable guide for action, or we must treat it as reliable even though subrational.[245] But in the latter case it becomes doubtful whether reason has a genuinely practical function at all, or is in any way connected with practical excellences such as courage, justice, or good practical judgement itself. No one in Aristotle's audience can suppose that these are not central and essentially human excellences. But perhaps they are kinds of sensibilities rather than dispositions for rational response. We have already seen how excellence can operate without deliberate thinking. In this respect it is like a sensory faculty, and Aristotle, like Plato, tends to contrast sense-perception with reason. There is, then, a real question whether *rational* animals are what we most essentially are.[246] If we are not, Aristotle will lack a basis from which to argue that theoretical accomplishment—an indubitably rational asset—belongs among the *human* excellences, its exercise being, in his view, the crowning perfection of animals such as ourselves.[247] He could not supply his audience with an answer to anyone who claimed that while thinking purely for thinking's sake may be a privilege of the immortals, thinking, for us, is not a good way of spending time except when it serves a practical goal.[248]

Accordingly, Aristotle insists on these two features of wisdom: (1) its objects are contingent particulars, non-abstract, imprecise, never completely articulable, by contrast with the objects of intellectual accomplishment, which are necessary, universal, abstract, capable of being made completely precise.[249] Yet, in case these contrasts seem to cast doubt on wisdom's claim to intellectuality, (2) it is an intellectual excellence coordinate with intellectual mastery. Each of the two is the excellence of a distinct kind of reason—a distinct 'part' of the strictly rational part of the soul—and each enables its own kind of reason to achieve its own kind of truth.[250] Wisdom shows itself in good deliberation, and deliberation is plainly a kind of reasoning.[251] Finally, critics are wrong who question the value of wisdom, on the ground that it adds nothing to conduct that is not already well taken care of by excellence of character (understood simply as a condition of the non-rational part of the soul).[252] If this charge were correct, wisdom would be intellectual, but it would not be an excellence, since it adds nothing. Aristotle responds by arguing that wisdom and character-excellence each make a necessary contribution to good conduct, and that character-excellence strictly speaking is essentially linked to wisdom, and therefore to reason.[253]

What, then, *is* wisdom, granted that it is an intellectual excellence? What is the disposition by which we find the right prescription or, what comes to the same thing, the apt decision? Aristotle defines it as a 'true disposition accompanied by rational prescription, relating to action (*praktikē*) in the sphere of what is good and bad for human beings'.[254] 'What is good and bad for human beings' means 'what it is good that the agent do or avoid considered simply as a human individual, not as a type defined by some limited concern'.[255] This is one of the differences between wisdom and technical expertise, making the former 'practical', the latter 'productive' (*poiētikē*).[256] Another difference is that what is achieved when someone operates as a technical expert is 'other' than his act of producing it, whereas what is achieved when one operates well in a practical way (and therefore when one operates from wisdom) is sheer doing well, or good-in-the-action-itself (*eupraxia*).[257]

Wisdom resembles technical (productive) expertise in that both have to do with contingent things.[258] It resembles intellectual accomplishment in being a human excellence (a quality whereby someone is praiseworthy as a human being). It differs from both in being inseparable from excellence of character. For since it is the disposition that generates prescriptions that are apt all things considered, and since a prescription cannot be apt in this way unless it measures up to the ethical requirements of one's situation, wisdom must include openness and sensitivity to these. Aristotle speaks of wisdom as 'true'; i.e. its responses reliably reflect the ethical reality of the state of affairs in which one is placed. The wise person is alive to the ethically significant details, and takes them in as significant in the way that they are. Deliberation (which in III. 3 Aristotle compared to analysis[259]) may be necessary before the facts and factual possibilities group and regroup themselves under the wise person's eye so as to elicit the right response; but the process can also be compared to looking and seeing. It is excellence of character that ensures that the eye will be looking in the right direction, for the kinds of things that ought to be taken into account. This is because the kind of answer that the wise person seeks to form (by contrast with answering a purely theoretical or technical question) is the kind that one can be twisted astray from finding, if one is a person who likes or dislikes the wrong things.[260]

Wisdom, however, is also an intellectual excellence, which is to say that it succeeds in cases that pose intellectual difficulties, for instance where many things have to be held in mind together, or where the causal relationships are complicated, or where individually familiar aspects are juxtaposed in an unfamiliar way. For wisdom's eye actually to see as it should rather than look myopically in generalized right directions, it needs more than the qualities that make for character-excellence; it also needs cleverness (*deinotēs*), penetration, thoughtfulness, and the experience necessary for shrewd reflection.[261] In a word, wisdom requires practical intelligence (*nous*). This is because it deals with particulars,[262] by which Aristotle means not merely that its objects are not logical universals, but that the standard groupings of them, reflected in the general terms of our language, cannot be expected always to capture what is significant from the practical point of view. The truly practical agent looks upon his situation not simply as a *PQR* situation, even where that description is true and relevant, but as *this P, this Q, this R*, scanning for particularities that could upset rules and forecasts founded on something's being *P, Q*, or *R*, or any combination, in the abstract.

But although Aristotle must be right in holding that complete practical excellence combines qualities of intellect and of character, he makes a puzzling statement about their respective contributions. He says: 'excellence [sc. of character] makes the goal (*skopos*) correct, while wisdom makes what leads to it correct'.[263] ('Wisdom' here means the intellectual factor in wisdom.) At first sight this appears to mean that the character-element is solely responsible for setting up the goal or end, and cleverness is solely responsible for selecting means. But this is very problematic. Presumably, the wise person's formal goal is to *do what is good (or best) in this situation, all things considered*. But this formal goal is common to all purposeful agents, including those with corrupted ethical vision. Presumably, again, the wise person is aiming for some specific wished-for objective. But very many objects of wish are the same for almost everyone, good people and bad. We all wish for pleasure, honour, material resources, health, friends; and wisdom is exercised in pursuing these common goals in appropriate ways. One would have thought, too, that this is where good character comes in—not in simply desiring those goals or finding them desirable.[264] It is absurd to suggest that character plays, or should play, no part in selecting means to our ends, and equally absurd to suggest that the intellectual side of wisdom plays no part in assessing whether something is a worthwhile goal.

An acceptable interpretation would be as follows. Let us understand 'the goal' to be some specific, empirical, object of wish *O* framed by the formal requirement that one do what is best or good in this situation, all things considered. The only limitation on the content of *O* is that it not be something that a decent person would reject outright on any terms. As one begins to deliberate about means to *O*, one assumes, for lack of reason to the contrary, that pursuing it would (from the human point of view) be a good thing given the situation *S*. Now, in deliberating how we might go about obtaining *O*, we are testing the hypothesis that it would be a good thing to try to obtain it, placed as we are. One could say that the role of character-excellence is to determine whether the hypothesis is true and ought to be acted upon. But no definite answer is possible until we make the question more determinate by deliberating on the detail of what must be done, and the wider effects, if O is pursued in S. Practical cleverness makes an analysis that converts the original question into one to which character-based likes and dislikes may constitute an answer. 'Would it be good to pursue O in S, given that this would require me to do T or U, with consequences V or W?' A negative answer might be apparent at an early stage. But the non-appearance of 'no' is not an immediate licence for 'yes'. The likes and dislikes due to character may be inconclusive because it is still not clear exactly what the courses of action would involve. Then cleverness must analyse further until either a negative answer is returned, or the hypothesis remains unrefuted up to the point where analysis can find no more distinctions that have practical significance. Now, it is true that in this process qualities of character select and reject means to O, but the role of character throughout is to decide, in the light of more and more factual discriminations, on the merits of pursuing O, given that one is in S. This is the single constant theme. Thus throughout the deliberation, character is particularly associated with the one goal of pursuing O, provided that this is good all things considered, given that one is in S. The goal survives the analysis only because character allows it to do so. Consequently, if the character is good, the goal that survives has proved itself good.[265] If we think of the goal as simply O, then excellence of character ensures that the goal is correct, i.e. one that will be pursued correctly, by eliminating inappropriate ways of going after it. If instead we think of the goal as *pursuing O, provided that it is good to do so all things considered*, then—again—excellence of character, by the elimination-process, ensures that this correctly describes what the agent will achieve. Cleverness works out possible means, i.e. determinate forms which the O-project might take, but it is character that turns them into a test of the project's acceptability. And it is typical of a good character not merely to react one way rather than another at any given stage of testing, but to insist on testing until the O-project is either eliminated or reduced to a form such that, if there is more than one way of realizing it, it makes no ethical difference which is chosen. For it is typical of many kinds of character-defect to stop testing too soon, i.e. to accept and act upon a causal pathway traced out by cleverness simply because it is an effective pathway to the desired O.

Wisdom, then, turns out to be impossible without excellence of character, just as excellence of character is impossible without wisdom.[266] When Aristotle 'puts them together' in his exposition, what in fact he puts together is an unfinished infrastructure of character-excellence with an abstract or ethically footloose capacity called 'cleverness'. Neither is an excellence (since neither can reliably generate or issue in good decisions) in the absence of the other.[267]

When each becomes the excellence it is supposed to be, they are what Aristotle would call the same in actuality though different in account.[268] In the case of anyone who fully achieves both, the ground for distinguishing them is visible only in retrospect: it is that they grew up from different origins. Now, Aristotle has said a great deal about the way in which character-excellence is generated; by comparison, he says hardly anything about ways or necessary conditions of gaining practical wisdom. Yet this is not because he thinks that it automatically develops through the practices by which we acquire excellences of character, even if in concrete reality wisdom often grows up alongside. For the different excellences of character are acquired by practising the right responses in situations where it is easy to know what to do perhaps because we are told by others or because the situation falls neatly under a simple rule of conduct (although not so easy for the non-excellent to get themselves to do it). Even though, in such a situation, the excellent person's response is informed by the rational structure of a decision, this is not the type of situation that requires one to be excellent in finding out what to do, or that forces one to take the mental exercise that improves one in that respect. Aristotle surely thinks that persons of good character develop wisdom by learning to recognize situations that require deliberation, and by deliberating in them, as well as by following the deliberations of others.[269] And perhaps he also thinks that for some people he can make wisdom more accessible by clearing away false models of it.

Aristotle's distinctions between desire and thought as factors in decision, between character-excellence and wisdom, and between unintellectualized ethical decency and ethically unconditioned cleverness, have led many twentieth-century scholars and philosophers to mine the *Ethics* for insights on a dynasty of problems that has tyrannized moral philosophy in the last 250 years. The dynasty's founding question was 'Are moral judgements expressions of reason or sentiment?' Among the offspring: 'Are moral qualities and relations properties of persons and actions in the mind-independent fashion of properties like *weighing 140 pounds* or *taking effect at such-and-such a time or place*? 'Can moral judgements be validly inferred from empirical facts?' And, if 'no' to either of the above, then: 'How can moral judgements be true or false? And how can they be justified?' Aristotle seems to emphasize just the distinctions that underlie these questions, but he shows no obvious interest in taking up definite positions in reply. This is one reason why his discussions of wisdom and decision can often seem maddeningly obscure. For if we expect Aristotle to have a line that would give him a position on the above questions, then, if we cannot see clearly what it is, we assume that he is very cryptic in the way he expresses his line. And interpretative efforts to bring his texts one way or another into the modern debate have been singularly unrewarding.

In fact, there is only superficial resemblance between the modern polarity of reason and sentiment and the Aristotelian distinctions mentioned above.

The modern questions are about the philosophical justification of moral judgements in general. Rationalist answers line moral judgements up with logical or mathematical truths, the justification of which is assumed to be well understood. The sentimentalist answer rejects this model of justification, and splits over whether to reject the idea of justification in ethics altogether, or whether to offer a different model for it. Aristotle, however, for better or worse, and whatever the historical explanation, is undisturbed by the ethical scepticism that fuels the demand for wholesale justification of moral judgements. If he thought about the matter at all, he may have thought that how we meet that demand would or should make no difference to practice, in which case it is not the business of practical philosophy.[270] In practice we know that some people have better ethical judgement than others, and the practical problem is to develop this ability to make good judgements in those for whom we are responsible. The fact that developing it requires two manifestly different kinds of training is the sole basis for Aristotle's distinction between rational and non-rational elements in ethical judgement. From his perspective, as we have seen, the distinction is notional as applied to the actually wise. By contrast, the questions about justification, and the associated polarity of reason and sentiment, apply to moral or ethical judgements as such, or in virtue of their distinctive ethical content. From the point of view of the problematic about justification, the judgements are treated as propositions; it is irrelevant who asserts them—whether those whom in practice we consider wise, or those whom in practice we consider stunted in one way or another. Finally, part of the modern debate turns on the correctness or not of assimilating moral judgements to observations of empirical fact, or to theories of natural science, or to logical or mathematical intuitions, all of which, it is taken for granted, are epistemologically more respectable. But, according to the interpretation suggested in this commentary, Aristotle's stress on the common rationality of theoretical and practical knowledge has a very different motive. Partly, at least, he hopes to win more *social* respect for the theoretical employment of reason, by declaring that practical wisdom, whose value nobody doubts, is akin to it because practical wisdom is rational.

8: Intellectual accomplishment *(sophia)*[271]

SUMMARY:

The precision of Aristotelian intellectual accomplishment; the sublimity of its objects; human affairs not among them; the Platonic and Aristotelian conception of intellectual culture versus that of Isocrates.

The adjective 'sophos' was ordinarily used in connection with a particular expertise or subject, to ascribe virtuosity in that area.[272] It was predicated on the basis of the *precision* (*akribeia*)[273] of someone's work: its finished perfection, rigour, exactness, exquisite attention to detail. Opposite qualities: sketchiness, clutter, irrelevance, crudeness. 'Precision' in a work of art or a performance manifests a penetrating sensitivity to the medium and subject matter. However, in Book VI Aristotle restricts accomplishment in the strict, primary, and unqualified sense to refinement, mastery, and creativity in theoretical science and theoretical philosophy. Even his own work in ethics and political science would be too 'rough' to qualify as a product of intellectual accomplishment in this restricted sense.[274] In *Metaphysics* I. 1–2 he is yet more restrictive, elaborating further criteria satisfied only by the 'science of causes' (i.e. metaphysics and theology). But elsewhere in the *Metaphysics* he recognizes the natural scientist, too, as 'a kind of intellectually accomplished person', and allows natural science and mathematics to count as 'parts of intellectual accomplishment'.[275]

As well as being characterized by precision, intellectual accomplishment deals with sublime objects. What these objects are depends on what should count as sublime. Aristotle is definite that human affairs do not meet this criterion: 'there are other things that have a far diviner nature than a human being'.[276] The objects of intellectual accomplishment are necessary and universal,[277] but perhaps not everything necessary and universal is a domain for intellectual accomplishment, since in one place he implies that mathematical expertise is not intellectual accomplishment in the strict sense.[278] The objects of the latter are 'divine', which for Aristotle includes not only immaterial divinities, but eternal physical substances such as he took the heavenly bodies to be. It may also include eternally ongoing natural cycles.[279] Sublimity of subject matter and precision are not independent features of intellectual accomplishment, since the more trivial a subject is, the less it deserves to be treated with precision. Intellectual accomplishment is a human excellence, hence *misplaced* exactness is not intellectual accomplishment.

The presentation of intellectual accomplishment in Book VI achieves two goals. One, which is obvious, is to bring out the contrast between theoretical attainments and wisdom, in order to get rid of a false model for wisdom. The other can easily escape the modern reader. It is to declare that, according to Aristotle's understanding of human life, the pinnacle of culture and education is not practical, but *theoretical* or *purely reflective*, accomplishment. This declaration must be seen in its historical context. Aristotle makes a substantial claim when he identifies intellectual accomplishment (*sophia*) with theoretical mastery. For 'sophia' did not *mean* this to his audience. The word and its associate 'philosophia' (literally, 'love of sophia'[280]) meant: *the pinnacle of culture and education, whatever it might be*. It was Plato, followed by Aristotle, who gave this status to rigorous theoretical studies, and tied 'philosophy' down to something like its modern meaning.

It was a contested status. The opposition was one of the most powerful intellectuals on the fourth-century Athenian scene: Isocrates (436–338), a contemporary of Plato as well as Aristotle. He was a consummate rhetorician, an imaginative political thinker, an influential teacher, and an educational idealist tirelessly dedicated to propagating his own conception of high culture. Like Plato (*Republic*), Isocrates fervently believes that rulers should be 'philosophers'. Like Aristotle, he holds that culture at its best is noble and lofty, detached from narrow concerns and from the workaday detail of practical life, deserving of honour for its own sake. But *philosophia* to Isocrates is essentially an instrument of statecraft and a celebration of great events. Its highest expression is found in the grand political rhetoric he himself practised brilliantly. To him, human history-in-the-making (specifically, the history of Athens and Greece) is the proper subject for the truly cultivated person's keenest intellectual interest, and he says of the Academic curriculum that while it helps to sharpen the mind for more serious things, he would not call it 'philosophy'. As for the theories of such thinkers as Parmenides and Empedocles (who, in Aristotle's phrase, studied the 'constituent parts of the universe'[281]), Isocrates writes: 'I think such curiosities of thought are on a par with jugglers' tricks which, though they do not profit anyone, yet attract great crowds of the empty-minded.'[282] Today, we might take it for granted that only a completely uneducated person, or a complete philistine, could hold such views. (Aristotle would probably find it unnecessary to take a stand against people like that, as if their opinions in this matter carried any weight.) But in fact these were the views of the cultured, and in his own way splendidly artistic, Isocrates. It is in this context that Aristotle presents his own interpretation of intellectual accomplishment.

9: **Self-control** (*enkrateia*) **and the lack of it** (*akrasia*)[283]

SUMMARY:
Dispositions that must be distinguished from the excellences and defects: (*a*) brutishness and godlike excellence, (*b*) self-control and the lack of it; the nature of un-self-controlled behaviour must be explained so that it is clear, *pace* Socrates, that it can occur; unqualified versus qualified forms of appetitive un-self-control; un-control of appetite versus un-control of temper.

After surveying the excellences and defects, Aristotle turns to other sets of characteristics which it is important to distinguish from them. The commonest are self-control and the lack of it, i.e. the tendency to let some appetite or emotion override one's decision or better judgement. These dispositions are the concern of anyone concerned about training character, for they are fostered by such training or the neglect of it. This differentiates them from another pair which Aristotle considers alongside them, namely brutishness (*thēriotēs*) and 'divine' (*theios*) excellence.[284] Brutishness results from an impaired or diseased nature; educators cannot hope to cure it any more than they can reasonably aim to foster superhuman excellence in general. In any case, such an aim would be superfluous, because while it is true that human happiness has something godlike about it, and that we should try to surpass ourselves,[285] superhuman excellence like that of a legendary hero such as Heracles is not a necessary condition for human happiness.

Nor is the exercise of self-control under otherwise propitious circumstances sufficient for happiness (from which it should be clear that self-control is not excellence or a kind of excellence). For the self-controlled person has to force himself not to indulge an appetite, and being conflicted in this way is not a happy way of being. However, Plato sometimes spoke as if excellence just is self-control.[286] But confusing these qualities can lead to mistakes with practical implications: for instance, the belief that genuine human excellence need not involve a harmony of practical judgement and desire, and the belief that self-control is good enough for humans as if anything more would be a superhuman ambition. By talking about excellence in ways that set its standard too high or too low, we diminish it in practice. Similarly, if we confuse lack of self-control with a genuinely bad disposition, we shall either be too forgiving towards genuinely bad people, who are shameless and irremediable, or too unforgiving towards those deficient in self-control, who repent of their behaviour and can be cured.[287]

These distinctions are in danger of being shaken by the argument of Socrates, a man of legendary (perhaps superhuman?) excellence or self-control. According to him, there can be no such thing as un-self-controlled behaviour, for such behaviour would consist in voluntarily doing what one knows is bad, and according to Socrates this is not possible: bad conduct necessarily proves the agent ignorant that what he does is bad.[288] If one assumes that every type of disposition has just one contrary,[289] it follows from Socrates's view that excellence and self-control are identical, since otherwise there will be two kinds of good disposition contrary to the bad kind. It is important, therefore, for Aristotle to come to terms with Socrates on this, and to explain what un-self-controlled behaviour is in a way that makes clear that it can and does happen.[290]

Another major question for Aristotle is whether there is a logically central type of lack of self-control (and presumably, therefore, of self-control) which should be called, simply, 'lack of self-control'; or whether 'lack of self-control' said without qualification is just a generic term covering different species each called 'lack of self-control with respect to appetite or emotion X' for variable X. Aristotle holds that the unqualified title should go to the kind of lack of self-control that has to do with the field of moderation, in other words with certain physical pleasures.[291] Where the lack of self-control has to do with other sorts of pleasures, such as pleasure in getting wealth, or being honoured, or winning a victory, or in having splendid children, we have in each case a distinct type that is called 'lack of self-control' only by analogy with the former.[292]

This very deliberate restriction of the unqualified term adds to the distinctions Aristotle can draw between self-control and excellence, lack of self-control and badness, in that 'excellence' and 'badness', said without qualification, are clearly generic terms. But the more obvious reason for his restriction is that, unqualified, 'un-self-controlled' carries a note of strong condemnation which in Aristotle's view is the right attitude towards un-control about pleasures of the flesh, but not towards forms involving those other kinds of pleasures. This difference follows from his doctrine that the activities that give rise to pleasures of the flesh are merely 'necessary',[293] whereas the objects of those other pleasures are 'desirable in themselves'.[294] Given some of the examples, this cannot mean that they are desirable as ends in themselves;[295] it must mean that their desirability is not a mere matter of biological necessity, but engages our distinctively human nature.

In a different classification, Aristotle compares lack of self-control in respect of appetite with lack of self-control in respect of temper.[296] One difference is that appetite is for the pleasant (and away from the painful), whereas an outburst of temper attacks something distressing: specifically, a present danger or threat.[297] Another is that temper, as Aristotle considers it here, is more rational. Other animals, too, are driven by temper to lash out against danger to themselves,[298] but the distinctively human temper-reaction is directed against a threat to one's *dignity*. Aristotle says that when reason or sensory appearance indicates that one has been the object of an insult or humiliation, temper gets angry at once as though it has reasoned that one ought to fight back against the word or deed in question. When it bursts out even against one's better judgement, this is lack of self-control of temper. But the uncontrolled reaction is fuelled by something rational and reflective, since the evaluation it embodies can be unpacked as the thought that one's worth is to be preserved by asserting itself against anything that denies it. This general evaluation functions as a premiss from which the particular response follows as conclusion. Appetite, by contrast, is a simple tendency to move, with no sense that the move is fitting, towards or away from an object as soon as it is realized that the object is pleasant or painful.[299] However misguided its behaviour sometimes is from the standpoint of a detached rational decision, human temper moves in 'the space of reasons', whereas behaviour powered by appetite is mechanical by comparison. Hence, not surprisingly, Aristotle considers lack of self-control in respect of appetite to be more shameful than its temper-related counterpart.

It is not entirely clear whether he means this comparison to apply to all forms of appetitive lack of self-control, beginning with the unqualified kind and going on to those where the pleasant object is wealth, victory, honour, etc.; or whether he means it to apply only to the unqualified kind that has to do with pleasures of the flesh. On the latter interpretation, the unqualified type is inferior to the qualified appetitive types and to the type that relates to temper, and these are not ranked *vis-à-vis* each other. On the former, the type that relates to temper is less shameful than every kind of appetitive un-control, even those whose objects rational beings alone can appreciate. This is the more interesting position. It implies that there are two reasons, which come apart in the two contrasts (qualified versus unqualified, appetitive versus temper-driven), why the one he calls 'unqualified lack of self-control' is the most shameful type of all: it is partly because of the biological nature of its pleasures and partly because it involves the defeat of better judgement by the completely non-rational force of pleasure as such.

10: **Love and friendship** *(philia)*[300]

SUMMARY:
The three main kinds of friendship, corresponding to the three kinds of value; general conditions for friendship; the best kind of friendship, combining the three kinds of value; the friend as 'another self'; the self and reason; since happiness is supposed to combine the three kinds of value, the presence in it of the best kind of friendship would help to explain how this can be so; reasons why the best kind of friendship is necessary for happiness.

The conventional translation of '*philia*' is 'friendship', but this one Greek word covers every type of attachment from kinship relations to membership of the same political community. However, Aristotle's main division in the *Ethics* is not, as such variety might lead us to expect, sociological; instead it is in terms of the three 'lovables' (*philēta*), i.e. qualities for which someone is cherished. These are usefulness, pleasantness, and goodness or excellence.[301] The perspective that makes this partition the natural starting point is the assumption that friendship is not merely a universal human phenomenon, but a human *good* (in turn a natural assumption for a discussion undertaken in the context of ethics). For the three lovable qualities correspond to the three standard categories of value: the beneficial (or useful), the pleasant, and the fine (which includes deeds, characters, and persons that are excellent).[302]

A relation between two people[303] counts as friendship only if (*a*) it is reciprocal; (b) each wishes the other well for his or her own sake; (c) there is mutual awareness of this reciprocal good will; and (d) the good will on both sides is founded on one of the three lovable qualities.[304] Since the three types of value are irreducibly different, one must recognize analogous differences between the corresponding types of friendship.[305] Still, the fact that the structure is the same in all three might lead one to expect that they all count equally as *friendships*, even though each has its own kind of ethical significance. However, Aristotle takes a different line. He focuses on certain general attributes of friendship, such as *stability* and loving the other *for himself*, and he argues that these belong most of all to the type founded on excellence, precisely because it is so founded. He argues further that excellence-friendship entails the mutual usefulness and pleasantness of the parties, whereas the other two types are not correspondingly inclusive. He concludes that excellence-friendship is the complete and perfect kind, that it is *philia* in the primary and central sense, and that the other forms count as friendships only because of their resemblance to it.[306] So if it is granted that friendship based on excellence is the best kind, ethically speaking (which is hardly controversial), there is a necessary coincidence between the type of friendship that best exemplifies *friendship*, and the type that it is ethically best to prefer.

One difficulty in understanding Aristotle on friendship is that he seems to affirm and also deny that in relationships based on usefulness or pleasure, each party cares about the other for his own sake. He sets this down as a feature of all three basic types,[307] but he also says that friends drawn together by utility or pleasure do not care about each other 'for themselves'.[308] There is no contradiction, however. Aristotle recognizes two levels of personal involvement. At the first, we take a positive interest in the other as an independent self rather than as a tool or object for our use or enjoyment. This is common to all types of friendship. At the second, we take the above sort of interest in the other just because he is who he is and not because of some relation of usefulness or pleasantness in which he happens to stand to us. Thus suppose that M and N are friends because they are members of a car-pool or play squash together. 'Because they are in the same car-pool' cannot mean or entail that M treats N merely as part of the system by which he, M, gets to work and vice versa, for such a relation would not be any sort of *friendship*. The 'because'-clause must allow for such genuinely friendly phenomena as inquiries about each other's health regardless of effects on the squash games or the car-pool; interest in each other's news; a certain amount of laughing together and commiserating with one another. But the mutual interest is not strong enough to survive the demise of the utility- or the pleasure-relationship. Since relations of utility and pleasure depend on the individuals' changeable circumstances, friendships based on them are unstable by comparison with those in which the togetherness, for either side, arises out of who the other is—his personality. But they are still friendships.

Aristotle regards personality-based friendship (loving the other for 'who he is') as the deepest, most stable, most satisfying kind, and the one that makes most difference to individual development. More controversially, he equates friendship based on personality with friendship based on excellence, as his triple division requires. We can agree that each party in the deepest kind of friendship admires and appreciates the other's character, and therefore regards him as excellent. Thus excellence, anyway in each other's eyes, is necessarily part of the picture. But, we want to object, to say that they love each other 'because of excellence' is absurd as an explanation, since it completely fails to capture the individuality of what each side means to the other. However, 'because of excellence' is not intended to capture this but to draw a broad contrast with the two other types of friendship, which are also very broadly or abstractly conceived. It is true that Aristotle does not dwell in modern fashion on the uniqueness and irreplaceability of our near and dear. But there is no reason, apart from his silence, to think that he is unaware or dismissive of this dimension of the experience of friendship. Book VI on wisdom shows his awareness that much practical and personal knowledge cannot and need not be put into words.[309]

Some of Aristotle's most telling passages on friendship develop from the aphorism that the friend or loved one is 'another self' (*allos autos* or *heteros autos*). He brings in this notion in order to characterize a broad range of attitudes that are typical of love and friendship.[310] What they have in common, according to Aristotle, is that they all 'seem to derive from'[311] attitudes the human individual has to him- or herself: I want the friend, as I want myself, to live and be happy, I grieve with his grief, rejoice with his joy, and so forth. It is clear from a passage in the *Eudemian Ethics* that 'the friend is another self' is not a novel notion, but is based on the proverbial phrase 'another Heracles', which was presumably said by the hero himself in some story.[312] Aristotle seeks to improve on the existing commonplace by not taking it for granted that each individual necessarily does have friendly attitudes towards himself. There are those who hate themselves, would like to be dead or to destroy themselves. If the commonplace is to function in the way it is meant to, i.e. as a handy formula covering the characteristic feelings, actions, and attitudes of love and friendship, then the 'self' which it invokes must be that of an inwardly harmonious person, who loves his own existence and 'wishes to spend time in his own company'.[313] But Aristotle goes further still, insisting that the self invoked must be that of a good person, one who is right to like himself and to value his own existence. Perhaps this further requirement can be justified if we consider that loving normally carries with it a kind of approval of the person (at least for the side that one finds lovable), and an assumption that one is right in approving. The analogy between attitudes to the self and attitudes to the friend then yields the conclusion that the self is one that at least takes itself to be good. At any rate, if one has a friend, and is proud of or revels in the relationship, and hence wants the aphorism to be true of one's friend in relation to oneself,[314] there are two ways in which it can be true. (1) One's attitude to the other is like that which an inwardly harmonious, self-valuing person *would* have towards himself. Presumably one can have such an attitude to another, and even have it consistently, without *being* (or being consistently) a harmonious, self-valuing, person. However, it might seem rather unreasonable to be glad to have such an attitude towards another, and at the same time be contented with failing to have it towards oneself. (2) One's attitude to the other (agreeing with, valuing the existence of, wishing to spend time with, etc.) is like one's actual attitude to oneself. For this to be true, one must *be* a harmonious, self-valuing, person. For someone who is 'well brought up',[315] i.e. brought up in the right values and confident about them in general, the project of becoming more harmonious and self-valuing, so more like a self whose self-reflexive attitudes are the model for how we should be to friends, is inseparable from the project of becoming actually better.[316] In this way, perhaps, we can justify Aristotle's position.

But now if I can be at enmity or at peace with myself, then I am not a simple being; so which of the elements within me is me most of all? This is really an ethical question: which side of me should my friend who loves me support? And when reason in me is at war with inclination, which side should I take—I, the agent who has to act in the world? Only reason can ask such a question. So the I who asks it is reason, and the answer, of course, is that I, reason, should take reason's part.[317]

If each of us is our reason most of all, and we are aware of this (even if only in a practical way), then in loving my friend for who he is (the mark of excellence-friendship), I love him as the reflective, controlling, discriminating, centre of his considered attitudes, thoughts, and decisions, since this is the self he is, or the part of himself that he 'sides with'. In fact it is appropriate not only for his friends but for him to love that self of his; for when 'self' is rightly understood as 'reason', 'self-love', contrary to vulgar opinion, is seen to be admirable and wise.[318] (It would surely be a mistake to interpret this as the chilly doctrine that what should be loved in friends and self is Reason, i.e. what is common to all rational beings. Aristotle cannot afford to lose touch with common sense to that extent. One should, on the contrary, think here of a person's reason as individualized through and through by his or her experiences.)

As we have seen, 'the friend is another self' naturally suggests a model of the healthy self as one whose different elements are on 'friendly' terms with each other. However, Aristotle brings in the aphorism mainly to characterize the attitudes of friendship by reference to those one has to or about oneself, not to explain healthy selfhood as friendship between parts of the soul. But in so far as he needs to refer to self-reflexive attitudes in order to make his point, it is difficult for him, as it would be for anyone, to do so without employing language that is primarily used about attitudes towards separate individuals. Our understanding of the idea that the good person shares grief with (*sunalgein*) himself and shares pleasure with (*sunhēdesthai*) himself[319] derives from our prior understanding of someone's entering into the grief etc. of another: which in turn rests on our understanding of what it is for someone simply to feel pleasure (*hēdesthai*) or grief (*algein*). Aristotle wants to answer the question 'How should we characterize the attitude of regarding someone as a friend?' by saying 'See how a person is about himself: it's like that, but towards someone else'. But in the detail of his answer he ends up closer to explaining the way a good sort of person is about himself as a likeness of friendship between separate individuals.[320]

One can, however, spell out 'the friend is another self' in a way that shows what is distinctive about attitudes towards friends (by comparison with attitudes towards non-friends) without implying that the self in question is experienced as, or even that it is, a unity of actually distinct parts. It is enough to say that M enters into his friend N's joys and disappointments as if they were his own. This simply bypasses the possibility that M is the kind of being that can be divided against, and therefore needs to be elaborately united with, itself. One can spell the point out further by saying that concern for a friend approximates self-concern *in respect of immediacy*. 'I am in danger' explains without more ado my taking steps to protect myself,[321] and '*He* is in danger' is similarly related to my taking steps to protect him, given that he is my friend.[322] I am no more 'going out of my way' to take care of him than when I act on my own[323] behalf. This way of looking at it fits in better with Aristotle's intended order of logical or explanatory priority. For immediate concern for oneself is prior to immediate concern for another, since the first is necessarily with us, being partly constitutive of selfhood, whereas the second depends on the contingency of having a friend.

The examination of friendship contains results that are of particular importance for Aristotle's theory of the chief good, in the following way. In Book I, after equating the chief human good with happiness, and defining it as activity of excellence in a complete life,[324] Aristotle sought corroboration for his account by checking its implications against numerous existing views.[325] All those he cited supported it, with one notable exception: the famous Delian inscription, according to which, in practice, the fine, the beneficial, and the pleasant necessarily tend to diverge. If this piece of lore is true, it follows that happiness, in which the three values would presumably hang together in stable unity, is a will o' the wisp for mortals, or at best a fluke. Naturally Aristotle rejected the inscription, asserting that excellent actions are pleasant and good (i.e. beneficial) as well as fine.[326] That they are 'fine' is uncontroversial, but he did not so much as sketch an argument for 'beneficial' (sc. to the agent), and his easy argument for 'pleasant' came under strain later when he looked at concrete examples drawn from the case of courage.[327] But as

Aristotle takes stock of excellent activity within the reciprocating context of excellence-friendship, it emerges that this sort of friendship necessarily combines excellence with pleasure and benefit. And since friendship is a human good and excellence-friendship is the kind that is ethically best, this sort of friendship will obviously be part of the best life available to human beings. So now there is a credible basis for rejecting the Delian pessimism, and for proposing happiness as a genuine human ideal.

In ix. 9 Aristotle gives detailed consideration to the question whether the happy person needs friends. It can seem that the answer is 'no' if one parses the question perversely so that it asks, concerning a person already assumed happy, who is consequently assumed self-sufficient,[328] whether he or she needs friends. Likewise if 'The friend is another self' is understood as meaning that the role of the friend is to procure or protect material goods on one's behalf; for in that case one needs friends only when one lacks or might lack material good fortune. Thus one would need friends not as a positive element of happiness, but only because happiness without them is hard to attain and fragile.[329] And if, as Aristotle claimed at the beginning, happiness is mainly the activity of excellence, and this activity is pleasant of itself, the happy person hardly needs friends in order to inject extraneous pleasure and amusement into his life.[330] In fact, Aristotle's development of the 'other self' notion may make it seem as if the excellent person is such good company for himself that external friends are superfluous.[331] It is, of course, common sense that friends and loved ones are part of a happy life, but Aristotle cannot allow himself the luxury of this piece of common sense unless he explains more precisely what friendship contributes to happiness.

On the question of friends and material goods, he points out that it is better, and more friend-like, to do good than to receive it; hence especially when we are flush we need friends as objects of beneficence.[332] On the question of friends and pleasure, his response is a complex exegesis of the dictum that the excellent person takes pleasure in his excellent activity. Although it had always been clear that the pleasure is not incidental to the activity, but intrinsic, it now begins to emerge that what is pleasant is activity as such. This is the basic tenet of the account of pleasure that is to be developed in Book X. Now, the presence of friends makes us more active. It is not just that they create occasions and directions for specific activities that would not have been possible otherwise. It is that by ourselves we droop; we have less zest for life; we are less interested in everything. Aristotle is saying that in human beings aloneness naturally breeds depression.[333] Moreover, the active presence of his excellent friend enables the excellent person to enjoy *his own* (*oikeios*) activity of excellence in a way that is impossible for a person who lives among strangers.

This is because human activity focuses on objects other than itself,[334] and on the circumstances, and these are what the agent as such remembers. Once an activity is over it is gone; it is not a piece of property which is still there when one is not using it. Yet a person's activities are the most interesting, the most distinctive, and if he is excellent the best, things about him. And an activity that is his own ought particularly to please the excellent person *because* it is good and his own, since in general this combination of attributes makes whatever has them a source of exceptional pleasure to the person concerned. (Perhaps Aristotle is particularly thinking of an artist's pleasure in an excellent work of art he has made; the pleasure is unique because the artist not only brings to the contemplation his agent's remembrance of what he was trying to do and the feel of the medium and the way it yielded here and had to be persuaded with special ingenuity there, etc., but he can also now see it as a whole as perhaps not before, and begin to discern non-accidental felicities that came into being as part of what he created, but which he could not grasp, or which passed unnoticed, while he was making it.) At any rate, there is no moment when the excellent person, taken on his own, *can* grasp, enjoy, and appreciate what is most precious about him, and in itself most suited to delight him. Evidently, the company of a friend holds the answer or anyway an alleviation for this otherwise tragic paradox of the human condition, which if untreated would, in the extreme, leave us in this respect as impoverished as other animals: fascinating, in fact wondrous, creatures aware of their particular surroundings and objects, but for ever cut off from being able to love and marvel at the ingenuity and richness and, in a sense, significance of what they themselves do and are—matters that can only be appreciated by the human observer.

One might expect Aristotle at this point to speak about how we come to see and learn of ourselves 'through the eyes of' those who love us or take a friendly interest: i.e. about the feedback about ourselves that others give us, which need not always be admonition or praise, since it is also natural for human beings to offer each other (when they are close enough really to follow each other's activities) appreciation and comprehension. Perhaps Aristotle takes this for granted; in any case, instead of explicitly pursuing this line, he declares that the unique pleasure that arises from something that is both good and one's own comes to the excellent person via the spectacle[335] of his friend's excellent activity.[336] It is not clear what this means, however. The thought may be that because the friends are both excellent they behave or would behave in the same ways in the same situations, so that one sees conduct which he recognizes to be like his own unfolding from the other. This relies rather heavily on the assumption that friends who are alike in excellence tend to be alike in other significant ways, which seems to rule out many interesting human possibilities. Alternatively, the thought may be that the friend's activity counts in a way as one's own for the logical reason that the friend is one's own, i.e. one of one's own people, so that what is immediately his is indirectly one's own; so in this way his good activity gives us the special pleasure we take in things that are good and our own. This allows for the friend's activity to be interestingly different from what one's immediately own activity would be in a similar situation, as long as it were not so different that one could not, as we say, empathize with it. Aristotle may not even distinguish these alternatives.

Finally, he elaborates on the two commonplaces: 'man is a civic (*politikon*) being, one whose nature is to live with others (*suzēn*)'[337] and 'Being alive (*zēn*) is something that is good and pleasant in itself'.[338] The argument shows that the happy individual needs a certain kind of friend because the living together that is distinctive of human beings is not simply living in proximity to others of their kind (like herd animals grazing side by side), or in a mutual arrangement designed for physical protection and economic advantage. It is living together as rational beings, sharing talk and exchanging thoughts. In fact, for Aristotle the activity of thought *is* a mode of living or vital functioning in creatures capable of it, in exactly the same sense as that in which the physiological activity evinced by respiration, pulse, metabolic changes, and the like is a mode of living or vital functioning. And between these two levels, the biological and the intellectual, there is also the sense-perceptual mode of being alive: this includes the activities of memory and imagination, as well as desires, emotions, and motor activity. Now, the good person recognizes as good, and takes pleasure in, the things that are naturally good and pleasant. Consequently, he values and enjoys his own vital activity.[339] Moreover, in seeing or hearing or walking we are automatically aware of what we are doing; our awareness of the activity is a dimension of the activity itself. So also for intellectual activity. In the very act, then, of perceiving or thinking, we are aware (*aisthanesthai*) that we are alive—that we exist. This awareness is naturally pleasant, since it is naturally pleasant to be aware of something as good and as belonging to oneself; this is especially the case when what one is aware of in this way is not simply one's existence, but the especially desirable existence of a good person. So especially the good person finds his own existence desirable. But since 'the friend is another self' he will find his friend's existence desirable in much the same way. However, the desirability to him of his own existence is, we saw, due to his awareness-in-activity of himself as good. The friend's existence can only be desirable to him in the same sort of way if he concurrently perceives (*sunaisthanesthai*) his friend's good activity in the same sort of way as he is aware of his own. Linguistically, the point may be either that *M*'s awareness of his own activity includes or is bound up with (*sun*) a simultaneous awareness of *N*'s activity as if from *N*'s point of view; or that *M* shares (*sun*) *N*'s awareness-in-activity of himself (i.e. *N*) as good. This happens in and only in the course of their actively living together in the way that is distinctively human, i.e. by sharing talk (*logoi*) and exchanging thoughts. And the more this is done on both sides for its own sake, not for any independent utility or entertainment, the closer it comes to being complete and perfect friendship.

Thus the desirability to a good person of his good friend's existence, and his pleasure in being aware of it through activity, are almost as great as the desirability and pleasure to him of his own. So since his own is desirable and pleasant to a very high degree, his lack, if he lacked good friends, would be very serious. This explains why he needs such friends if he is to be happy.[340]

11: Pleasure *(hēdonē)*[341]

SUMMARY:

The discussion in Book VII mainly devoted to correcting negative views about pleasure; pleasure discredited by the widespread false view of the coarsest pleasures as paradigmatic; in general, pleasures are good and desirable; explanation for prevalence of the false paradigm; the discussion in Book X mainly directed to correcting the hedonist theory of Eudoxus; pleasure in something the signal that it is good—a signal true for the well-conditioned subject; pleasure and completeness; pleasure and cognitive activity; the variety of pleasures; how to allow that some pleasures are better than others while keeping the general hedonist inference from 'pleasant' to 'good'; healthy versus perverted pleasures at the same level of functioning; higher (purer) versus lower pleasures corresponding to different levels of functioning; the higher not only better but pleasanter.

The *Nicomachean Ethics* contains two accounts of pleasure. One is in the common book *NE* VII = *EE* VI, following the discussion of self-control and the lack of it—a natural position given the fact that these character-traits are defined by reference to pleasure. The other is between *NE* VIII–IX on friendship and the final discussion of happiness in x. 7–8. This too is natural, since Aristotle cannot leave the question of happiness or the chief human good without settling accounts with a serious rival to his own definition of it, namely the theory that the chief good is pleasure.

These different contexts bring different concerns. Pleasure in the context of self-control and the lack of it figures, of course, as the adversary. Moreover, there is a temptation to think that, just as lack of self-control about pleasures of the flesh is the strict and unqualified type (and similarly with self-control),[342] so too these pleasures themselves are the paradigms of pleasure. Thus all pleasure comes to be identified with or assimilated to the grossest kind. Some people conclude that no pleasure is good, considering that excellence (moderation) sets little stock on the gross pleasures, and that they hinder the activity of thought, and that caring about pleasure is childish or brutish. Some, following the same paradigm, have added the more philosophical consideration that pleasures are physical processes in which the body returns from a defective condition to a better one, and have argued that since a process of coming to be (*genesis*) is necessarily for the sake of the state in which it terminates, pleasure is not any sort of intrinsic good, since it is only for the sake of something else which is not itself a coming to be. It follows that the chief good cannot be a pleasure or anything pleasant, since it cannot be for the sake of anything beyond itself, and that the best condition is the neutral one devoid of both pleasure and pain.[343] In Book VII Aristotle corrects these negative views. He points to pleasures that involve no transition from a defective condition, and argues that pleasure is not a coming to be, but an 'activity' (*energeia*) whose end or completion is within it. This is true even of the physical pleasures.[344] He contends that activities of thought and moderate conduct have their own pleasures, and that pleasure is no impediment in general to these activities, since the pleasures that do impede them are alien ones.[345] It follows that there is no reason why the chief good might not be a pleasure or something pleasant, which fits in with the common-sense intuition that pleasure is bound up with happiness.[346] As his opponents agree, all animals, including man, tend towards pleasure; but Aristotle sees this as indicating not that human pleasure is brutish, but that the chief good for every species is something pleasant to the members of the species.[347] More generally, he emphasizes that pleasures are good and desirable. For even if some are not good and desirable without qualification (i.e. good and desirable for those who are in a healthy, natural, or good condition), even these are nonetheless good and desirable *for* those who want them, because these people are in some special, less than ideal, condition.[348] This implies that if one takes pleasure in a certain kind of thing, but considers that pleasure to be bad or wrong, either one should draw the conclusion that one's condition is not as it should be, and try to improve it if possible, or one should take a different view about the pleasure and not reject it. For if one's condition *is* good, the pleasant thing is good, and to resist taking it because it is pleasant is to deprive oneself of a good, one that might not make itself known in any other way. So if, as a result of continual resistance, we end by not finding the thing pleasant any more, we have broken through to a kind of calm, but it is not the self-harmony of excellence (as opposed to the conflicted state of self-control), but death of some aspect of our sensibility. Furthermore, if we completely reject the idea that what is good might actually, for that reason (i.e. because it suits our condition, and our condition is good), present itself to us as something pleasant, then we ought to be equally monolithic in refusing to believe that painful things are bad. But then we ought to cease to avoid pain just as much as we should cease to pursue pleasure; yet no one can live like that, and even the opponents of pleasure do not encourage it.[349]

Summarily, then, the position of Book VII is that pleasures are good, though in certain cases this judgement must be qualified in a way that fits in with the standard view that certain pleasures do not attract the good person. We ought not to trust our pleasure-instincts outright, but we certainly ought not to be suspicious of them through and through and in principle. This applies even to the pleasures of the flesh, which have their limited place in life.[350] But now there is something he has to explain. Very many people, according to Aristotle, regard those pleasures as immensely desirable, but this is a mistake. Yet if it is a mistake that just happens for no particular reason, but because human beings are prone to error, then the same could be, and presumably was, said by Aristotle's opponents about all pleasure, namely that it is just a human error to consider it desirable at all—especially if the opponents accept the view of many ordinary (and pleasure-loving) people that pleasures of the flesh constitute the paradigm of pleasure. So Aristotle has to provide a definite explanation, that does not apply to all human beings, for why so many people are deluded about the value of the physical pleasures. His explanation is that physical existence is full of pain and distress, even in the normal course of events, and these pleasures, especially when most intense and compulsive, are an escape from pain[351] (whereas, he implies, we normally have to be out of physical pain before we can attend to more refined pleasures); and consequently these are the only pleasures that many people are aware of or are able to enjoy, given their condition. (This explanation assumes that the people in question think (a) that it is very desirable to be out of physical pain, and (b) that pleasure is very desirable, views which Aristotle shares though with qualification.)

The last point, that the majority are unacquainted with other kinds of pleasure, also explains why they identify pleasures of the flesh with pleasure as such, giving it a bad name with various moralists and philosophers, who hold that pleasure belongs to the brutish side of human nature, so that it becomes improper to attribute pleasure to god. Aristotle ends by replying that we fall short of god not in having pleasure, but in being able to have it only intermittently and from different objects at different times; and that, far from its being the case that god is in a state of neither pleasure nor pain, as those other thinkers imply,[352] god's activity is supremely pleasant;[353] the neutral condition, by contrast, is a thoroughly mortal phenomenon: it occurs because our constitution, unlike the simple divine nature, is a mixture of contrary elements whose effects sometimes cancel each other out, bringing us into neutral.[354]

The Book X discussion of pleasure covers some of the same ground as the Book VII one, but the main perspective is different. It is set by the need to define his own position in contradistinction to that of the hedonist philosopher Eudoxus.[355] (Aristotle says that Eudoxus' arguments carried conviction less because of their intrinsic quality than because of their author's extraordinary moderation, which made people think that such an unbiased advocate of pleasure must be speaking the truth.[356])

Eudoxus held that all beings seek pleasure, and that this shows that pleasure is *the* good, i.e. the chief good.[357] Aristotle agrees that all creatures seek pleasure,[358] and he regards this as certain proof that pleasure is good. Eudoxus argued for this weaker conclusion, too; and he should have stopped short at it, because one of his arguments suggests a point which Plato then turned against him to show that pleasure is not the chief good. Eudoxus argued that if X is good, and adding Y to X makes X better, this can only be because Y is good; hence pleasure must be good, since if pleasure is added to just or temperate action, the action is better, and so on with other examples. But Plato latched on to the implication that if X is good and adding Y, another good, makes X better, then X alone is not the chief good, since X can be surpassed; and he argued that pleasure is not the chief good since adding wisdom to it makes something better.[359]

Now Aristotle cannot be satisfied to let the question rest here, i.e. at the conclusion that, while pleasure is *a* good (a position for which he and Eudoxus can muster numerous arguments, and to which he will wish to add certain refinements and qualifications[360]), even so it is not *the* good (the chief good). For in the first place, Aristotle launched the *Nicomachean Ethics* from the very principle which Eudoxus used: 'the good is that which all things seek',[361] and Aristotle then went on to give his own account of what this chief good is. And he agrees with Eudoxus that 'all things' (i.e. animals now, not sorts of expertise, inquiries, actions, and undertakings[362]) seek pleasure. But if it is now a mistake to conclude from this premiss that pleasure is the chief good, how was it all right earlier to argue, as he did, that what 'all things' seek is the goal of political expertise, and that this goal, therefore, is the chief good?[363] If all that Eudoxus can show by his 'All things seek' argument is that pleasure is *a* good, one among others, then all that Aristotle can show by *his* is that the political goal is *a* good too. Secondly, it has been becoming clear from the Book IX discussion of friendship[364] that the pleasantness of excellent activity is not merely not adventitious, but intimately essential to it; so that if excellent activity lies at the centre of the chief good, or happiness, pleasure lies there too—a state of affairs that calls for further investigation.

From Aristotle's report, we know that Eudoxus did not pass immediately to 'pleasure is the chief good' from 'all creatures seek pleasure', but justified the inference with the dictum 'each creature [or kind of creature] finds what is good for itself, just as it finds its own food'.[365] It seems that Eudoxus simply identified the pleasure that a creature naturally seeks (and finds) with the chief good that that kind of creature naturally finds (upon seeking). But Aristotle draws from the same two premisses the more sophisticated conclusion that a well-constituted creature, *in* seeking what it finds pleasant, is seeking its own distinctive kind of good, and, *in* finding that good, it finds pleasure as well. Again, whereas Eudoxus had argued that pleasure is what is most desirable on the ground that 'by general agreement' pleasure is something 'we do not choose because of something else, or for the sake of something else',[366] Aristotle's more developed theory locates pleasure in activity, and assigns to pleasure the role of a sort of signal—one that tells the agent: 'this is your proper activity, your good and your end, and your engaging in it brings out your excellence'. The signal works by making the activity appear to us *as* an end in itself, to absorb us so that we do not look beyond it, as we tend to do when an activity is not going well, or when we are engaged in something as a means or as part of a wider project. In short, the signal's information comes to us in a form that makes us act as it would be good to act if the information were true, since it makes us embrace the activity all the more strongly.

Aristotle begins his positive account by expounding the telic nature of pleasure, i.e. its end (*telos*)-likeness or completeness (*teleiotēs*). Pleasure is not, as some have claimed, a process, for a process is directed towards completion in a state or product beyond itself, and therefore is incomplete (*atelēs*) throughout the time during which it goes on. This is by contrast with, for example, seeing, the form of which is complete (*teleios*) at every moment. By this Aristotle means that if an act of seeing is incomplete, or, as we more naturally say, 'imperfect', if it does not fully measure up to what an act of seeing should be, this is *not because it has not gone on long enough*. (It will be, rather, because the eyes are in poor condition or tired, or because they are obstructed, or because the object does not lend itself to being properly seen, say because it is moving too fast, or is too far away, or is dazzling.) But an act of building such as building a temple depends for its perfection not only on the quality of the builder and the materials, but also on its being carried on right to the moment when its end, the temple, is completed. If this act is to be complete or perfect of its kind, then, for any given moment *M* of its duration, it must go on beyond *M*, because if it is stopped at *M* it falls short of its goal. Since the process is necessarily tending towards completion, and since it is over once completed, it is a sort of rush to get itself out of existence and into the past. Thus our taking pleasure in something is of a contrary nature to our being subject to some sort of process, for when we take pleasure in something we want the pleasure, and what we take pleasure in, not to be over, not to be getting closer and closer to the point where they are gone from us. Now the basic activities in which we take pleasure are the vital functions of perception and thought,[367] which are not processes but are complete in form at each moment.[368] And pleasure too is complete in this way. At first Aristotle asserts this result about pleasure as if it is immediately clear that pleasure resembles seeing (the example he first uses) in this respect. Later, however, it seems as if his thought is this: perceiving (or thinking) is so closely related to pleasure in perceiving (or thinking) that the cognitive activity could not possess the stability of something that is complete in form at each moment if the pleasure in it had the opposite metaphysical structure of a process that is racing to be over.

Since pleasure is not a process, the question naturally arises whether it comes into the contrasting metaphysical category of 'activity', where Aristotle placed it in the discussion in Book VII.[369] Since perceiving and thinking are activities in that sense, it is now clear that pleasure, or taking pleasure, is not another activity alongside perceiving or thinking;[370] if it were, there would be a question whether one takes pleasure in it too, and a possible infinite regress. According to the present doctrine, pleasure completes (*teleioun*) the activity, as 'a sort of supervenient end' (or 'completion') (*epigignomenon ti telos*).[371] This implies two connected points: that the pleasure is not an end to which the activity is a means, and that pleasantness is not the criterion by which the quality of the activity, good or bad, should be judged. The activity is to be assessed by standards appropriate to that sort of activity, which are different in each kind of case. Pleasantness is not the, or a, feature of the activity that makes it good of its kind; instead, pleasure arises *because* the activity is good of its kind; it is how the excellence of the activity makes itself known to the agent.[372] (This does not contradict the common-sense view, which Aristotle thoroughly endorses,[373] that the fact that an activity is pleasant is sometimes a good reason for engaging in it. Consider a particular action of tennis-playing: the player's pleasure in his activity (*energeia*) is a feature of the action (*praxis*), one which, under certain circumstances, makes it a good action to choose to do or to carry on doing. However, in order get the pleasure specific to tennis-playing, the player must not be watching for this pleasure (even if his playing on this occasion will turn out to have been pointless if he does not get pleasure from it), but must concentrate on doing what it takes to play well.

The activity is good of its kind, so that there is pleasure in it, when the subject and the object (he continues to think of the activities as basically cognitive[374]) are each in the best condition to be subject and object of that kind of activity, and when nothing impedes.[375] The nature of the pleasure reflects the nature of the activity, and there are as many different kinds of pleasure as kinds of activity.[376] Yet there is a single reason why all animals desire pleasure; it is that in tasting it we experience activity, and thereby taste what it is to be alive, and everything wants to be alive.[377] It might seem from this unity that runs through all the kinds of activity and kinds of pleasure that Aristotle believes in a single fundamental energy or primal life force that takes different forms, rather as a plastic material takes on many shapes. Now, in the course of explaining why friends are necessary for happiness, he says that life is *determinate*.[378] This may be taken to mean that the single life-force is never found except in one or another determinate form, or it may mean that the many determinate kinds of life and activity are metaphysically primary, with the in itself indeterminate universal activity being merely an abstraction derived by considering the many forms together. Aristotle does not make clear which of these possibilities he intends, but they suggest different models for a phenomenon that interests him greatly: the fact that pleasures of different kinds can, in the same individual, impede one another. The pleasure that belongs to an activity makes it more intense and more refined and more in command of detail; but the activity, and therefore its pleasure, tend to be weakened and dulled by the pleasure of a simultaneous different sort of activity. We could think of this as due to the channelling of a single fund of energy from one direction to another, or as more like a clash between distinct living beings, where one overpowers another. The kind of compromise in which both hold back, or each makes do on a fraction of the energy, is not a satisfactory solution, since it means the deadening of both parties.

So far[379] not a word of this theory would particularly lead one to expect that some pleasures are bad and to be avoided; in fact, the general emphasis on completeness and perfection might seem to pave the way towards a conclusion that, even if it differs academically from the strict hedonism that identifies the chief good with pleasure, would carry the same practical consequences, since it would consist in the teaching that the chief good is activity of whatever kind, and that we should accept the guidance of every form of pleasure that appeals to us, since, whatever its kind, it will be riding on the back of an activity. On the other hand, the theory so far gives ample grounds for concluding that *if* some activities are good and others not, we should be extremely careful to practise good ones, because the associated pleasure strengthens an activity and extinguishes any of opposite nature, thereby making us unfit to engage well in the latter[380] and unable to derive pleasure from them.

Although Aristotle seems to be committed to the view that life and activity are generally speaking good, he does not, of course, follow this line to the point where it coincides with out-and-out hedonism. For he holds not only that we are prone to be misled by pleasure because we easily interpret the attractiveness of a pleasure as an injunction or licence to engage with it there and then, regardless of other considerations. This can happen with activities and pleasures that are good in themselves and even fine. But Aristotle also holds that some kinds of activity, and therefore some kinds of pleasure, and so, by implication, some ways of being actively alive, are in themselves low-grade and undesirable from the point of view of life as a whole.

Broadly speaking, there are two ways in which a philosopher might develop such a view. He or she might say that the judgement that activity *A* is undesirable in the above unqualified way is an assessment in terms of a kind of value, ethical or moral, that is fundamentally different in nature from the hedonic value which has been the topic so far. Alternatively, the philosopher might say that the judgement that *A* is undesirable is an assessment in terms of the realization of truly human potential—a value that limits what pleasures are valuable, but nonetheless subsumes or explains the value of those that are. For example, one might say that the activity of malicious gossip, and pleasure in it, are bad because (aside from the damage to others) they spring from a perverted use of such basically good human things as intelligence and interest in other people, whereas the pleasure of what non-malicious people regard as good conversation about worth while or innocently amusing subjects is due to a healthy use of the same faculty and sensibility. This is Aristotle's line.

Now according to one way of developing this line, we can hold that the pleasure of malicious gossip, to those who are cut out for it, is just as much a pleasure as that of conversation at no one else's expense to those who are cut out for *it*, although the first is due to a misuse, the second to a healthy use, of the same human faculties. We might say this on the basis of observation of the persons concerned: the pleasure in each case plays the same sort of role in motivating the person to seek out opportunities and materials of conversation; it shows itself in the same way, by sparkling eyes, animated gestures, and so forth. In that case, we can express the ethical inferiority of malicious gossip in the following way: although it is just as true to say that malicious gossip is pleasant as to say that innocent conversation is pleasant—for each is pleasant *for* those who like it, and (in the present discussion) saying that X is pleasant is simply shorthand for saying that it is pleasant for someone or other—still, one kind of conversation is good or at least acceptable while the other kind is bad. According to this way of looking at the matter, something's being pleasant is not a sufficient condition for its being good, and hedonism is shown up as clearly mistaken.

However, Aristotle in Book X and elsewhere[381] maintains that we should not always say only that something is pleasant *for* the individual who is constituted so as to find it pleasant; for we should allow that some things are pleasant without qualification, namely those that are pleasant *for* the person of excellence. In and only in the case of excellent Y,[382] there is a valid inference from 'Z is pleasant for Y', to 'Z is pleasant' said without qualification. Moreover, it is clear that Aristotle thinks that, where the inference is valid, the unqualified statement is preferable to the ' . . . for Y' statement from which it is inferred. Now, this is not the absurd view that the excellent person has the ability to detect pleasures that exist in objects out there independently of any relation in which they stand to him as subject.[383] Rather, the point is that the unqualified 'Z is pleasant', between human beings, is a recommendation of Z, and only the good person can be relied on to recommend rightly. The recommendation is lost if one returns to or stays with 'Z is pleasant for Y', the longer but, from a practical point of view, the more impoverished form. By contrast, when 'W is pleasant' issues from a person V whom we regard as unwise or of poor character or (if W is a taste, colour, etc.) as perceptually handicapped in the relevant way, we reject the recommendation, but retain the psychological information about V, by modifying what we have heard into 'W is pleasant for V (or: for someone like V)'. The upshot is that for anyone who despises malicious gossip, but not innocent conversation, it is not just as true to say that malicious gossip is pleasant as that innocent conversation is, for if 'is pleasant' is qualified by 'for (or: to) someone or other', it applies to the first but not to the second, whereas if it is said without qualification, it applies to the second but not to the first. Moreover, because Aristotle is willing to say that malicious gossip is pleasant to or for a certain sort of person, he is also willing to say that it is good, too, but not without qualification: it is good *for* that sort of person.[384] Thus 'good' follows from 'pleasant', the unqualified use entailing the unqualified, the qualified the qualified, and hedonism remains in a way unrefuted. But it is a way that preserves the values that Aristotle endorses, and that Eudoxus also endorsed by the way he lived.

In the discussion above, the examples given of a good activity and a degraded one both stood at more or less the same level of psychic functioning. Conversation, to be good, need not be dramatically more intellectual in content than malicious gossip, and in many quite typical cases both activities muster the same powers of memory, imagination, experience, and feeling. But there is another form of degradation from that in which a faculty or sensibility is put to bad use; in this other form the activity itself is good, but too much importance is attached to it. It is degrading to the person who loves and gets pleasure from it, not because of what it is, but because it occupies space in his or her life that ought to be available for better and finer activities and pleasures. Pursuit of the degrading activity in ways that cause harm to the agent or violate the rights of others is evidence that he or she attaches too much importance to it. But, from Aristotle's point of view, what is wrong here is not merely that the attachment raises the probability of harmful conduct. This alone is not why the attachment is 'excessive'; it is excessive also because human beings ought not to make this type of activity and pleasure so central to their lives: a judgement that still applies even if they are circumstanced, as indeed wealthy and powerful people are,[385] in ways that enable them to indulge these pleasures without robbing anyone, without using resources that should be saved against a rainy day or for their children's education, and even perhaps, since they can afford the care of the best doctors and the best gymnastic trainers, without irreversibly compromising their own health.

Evidently this sort of judgement presupposes a ranking of natural and healthy activities and pleasures into lower and higher. For Aristotle, the ranking is in degree of what he calls 'purity' (*kathareiotēs*).[386] By linking pleasure so closely as he does to *cognitive* activity, he is able to rank the purity of pleasures by reference to the logically antecedent purity of various cognitive activities. He states that in respect of purity, sight and hearing are superior to touch and taste, intellectual to sensory activities,[387] one kind of thinking (purely reflective) to another (practical). Clearly, purity consists in independence from physical involvement, or at any rate experienced physical involvement, with the object of cognition; such independence is assumed to permit greater cognitive steadiness and refinement: the reception of information at cost of less 'noise' or degradation in our modern technical sense. The kinds of pleasure that complete the purer activities are the kinds proper to man, Aristotle says. This tells us a good deal about what he considers it is to be human: it is to be a being whose fulfilment depends on living *beyond* the biological infrastructure in which it is essentially embodied.

In comparing the pleasures in respect of purity, Aristotle is probably not just introducing an important attribute which pleasures have to a greater and lesser degree, in the way in which some horses run faster than others although all are equally horses. For the Book X discussion was surely intended not only to respond to Eudoxus, but also to take up some of Plato's arguments in the *Philebus*; and Plato had argued that the purer a pleasure is, the more it is a *pleasure*.[388] Aristotle can reach the same conclusion. By binding pleasure so closely to cognitive activity, he is able to suggest that the more fully an activity lives up to the title of 'cognitive', the more fully its pleasure deserves to be called 'pleasure'. Thus the activity of intellectual accomplishment turns out to be 'pleasantest'.[389] This is a conceptual, not just (if at all) an experiential, statement. It carries the practical implication that anyone who thinks that pleasure as such has an important place in human life should be receptive to the claim, which Aristotle is about to defend with his all but final arguments,[390] that this place should be filled as far as possible by the pleasure of purely reflective activity.

12: **Three ideals**[391]

SUMMARY:
The three ideal lives in I. 5 and X. 6–8; making the case for the reflective (theoretic) ideal; why a competition between it and the political one? Of two extraordinary forms of happiness, one is logically primary; the place of theoretical reflection in the happiest life; the relation of intellectual accomplishment to the practical excellences; ordinary happiness recognized in X. 9; the narrowly theoretical reflective ideal can be expanded; if the chief human good is godlike, its nature depends on one's conception of god.

In *NE* I. 5, in the course of getting his discussion of happiness off the ground, Aristotle briefly considers three 'kinds of lives that stand out' as ideals in the eyes of certain people. There is what he calls the life of the consumer, which is focused on pleasure interpreted according to the vulgar paradigm. This is the dream of 'the utterly slavish sort of people'. 'People of quality' (which is certainly how they see themselves) prefer the political life, which is focused on honour. Aristotle says that what they really want, in wanting honour, is the credible assurance that they are excellent; excellence, then, is the real point, anyway by comparison with honour. Thirdly, there is the reflective life (*bios theōrētikos*), concerning which he says only that it will be discussed later. At this stage we are given no explicit impression of what sort of person they are who make this their ideal. Still, it is obvious that they are not the slavish sort. What is not obvious is how the better sort, whose initial stance about honour was un-self-analytic and even confused, might see themselves in relation to those who choose the reflective life. Would it be clear to them on consideration that they are superior measured by *this* yardstick, as distinct from the one which the 'slavish' type constitutes? And if it is not, because they hardly know what the other term of the comparison amounts to,[392] should they be left to forget about the reflective life as a possibly respectable ideal, so that in practice they will go on taking it for granted that when decent and reasonable people aspire to distinction, these aspirations are, of course, practical and political in nature? Or should they be educated a bit, so that they come to understand something about the reflective ideal, enough at least to see that it deserves respect and that those who try to pursue it should be given an honourable place in society?[393]

After concluding the Book X discussion of pleasure, Aristotle returns to the topic of happiness. It is clear now that happiness is a pleasant activity; but it is not a gross, trivial, or childish pleasant activity, like the ones in which people dissipate themselves at the courts of tyrants and kings. The fact that lovers of these activities are serious about them, sometimes even to the point of sacrificing health and fortune in the cause of indulgence, does not mean that the activities are of serious value; it only shows that these individuals have rotten judgement, as one might expect, since being in and around the seats of power is not what breeds wisdom and personal excellence.[394]

Now why is Aristotle saying this at this point? If the discussion of pleasure and friendship has not convinced his audience that happiness does not consist in mindless pleasures, these new remarks cannot, and if it has, they add nothing. And in any case his well brought up audience has always known it all along.[395] However, this labouring the obvious is not in order to establish it as a conclusion, but to set it up as a machine of persuasion about something else. He is in fact reverting to the three lives of I. 5, and starting an argument that begins: 'The reason why decent people, people of some refinement, scorn this elevation of mindless pleasures, namely, that they are unworthy of a serious (*spoudaios*[396]) person's time—so *they* cannot be what the rest of life, the toil and sweat, is "all about" (for that is what we mean by 'happiness')—this is just the reason why those same decent people should hail the devotees of the reflective ideal as cousins, even if not (quite yet) as brothers: for so far as it is a question of doing something fine and serious with one's life, their values are the same.'

Now this sort of statement, too, can hardly be intended to persuade Aristotle's audience. Whether or not they all share his sense, which he will articulate in the next stage of the argument, that the reflective ideal is actually *higher* than the political one, they do not need to be convinced of the value of reflection. He speaks to them as to persons versed in, at home with, able to appreciate, rigorous reasoning, the careful crafting of arguments, the pleasures of intellectual illumination.[397] Surely what he is about to give them are elements, materials, for presenting a case on behalf of theoretical studies to decent citizens *outside* the academy. Here we should bear in mind that there was no established attitude of respect, in the wider society, for theoretical science and philosophy—in fact, precious little understanding, even at arm's length, of what these activities were. It is true there was quite a tradition of philosophers and intellectuals coming under the patronage of rulers and rich men, but these relationships were personal, and were vulnerable to the vicissitudes of politics;[398] in this period there was no such thing as regularized, institutionalized, state endorsement of purely theoretical studies.[399] The laws of a state, according to Aristotle, can and should be a powerful instrument for communicating and reinforcing the standard ethical values.[400] Presumably he also hoped that places where theoretical studies went on would one day become objects of public concern and pride, with legal charter; but for that, the support of ordinary decent citizens would be required.

To return to the final discussion of happiness: in Book I and again at the end of the Book X discussion of pleasure, Aristotle left markers indicating that the chief human good, once its general nature is thoroughly understood, may turn out to take distinct forms, each counting as happiness, and each, therefore, representing an ideal which it is the political mission[401] to uphold; and he has also left markers indicating that if there are distinct forms, one of them will be best and most 'complete', and is therefore most entitled to be called 'happiness'.[402] In x. 7–8 these intimations are borne out: once the ideal of vulgar pleasure has been dismissed, the other two ideals of I. 5, the political life and the reflective life, remain in place; both are said to be happy, and by many criteria the reflective life is shown to be superior.

Now it is remarkable the extent to which the question 'Which is superior?' dominates this final discussion.[403] Aristotle sets up the comparison as a contest which the reflective candidate wins hands down. Why should this be so? This format is surely not necessary for his purpose of supplying ammunition for promoting theoretical studies in the wider society. Aristotle could certainly have made the case for honouring and respecting the reflective life by pointing out its superiority in terms of the very criteria he actually uses. But to do this is not the same as, and does not entail, designing the discussion *so that its governing purpose is to show which ideal is better*. It is possible to argue that both are good and that one (his personal choice) is, as a matter of fact, better, without presenting them as *competitors*. Why are they presented so? And what is being competed for?

One possible answer is that he chooses to work within a traditional genre: Choice of Lives or Contest of Ideals. Other examples are: the just versus the unjust life in the *Republic*; wisdom versus pleasure in the *Philebus*; the Choice of Heracles (excellence versus pleasure);[404] the Judgement of Paris (wisdom, power, and pleasure versus each other); the brothers Zethus and Amphion (practical versus theoretical lives).[405] And apart from traditional genres,

Aristotle is quite likely responding to contemporary hyperbole like the following, which comes from Isocrates' address to Philip of Macedon. Isocrates is urging the king to unite the Greek city-states in a war against the Persians:

> if some god were to give you the choice of the interests and the occupations in which you would wish to spend your life, you could not, at least if you took my advice, choose any in preference to this; for you will not only be envied by others, but you will count yourself blessed. For what happiness (*eudaimonia*) could then surpass your own? Men of the highest renown will come as ambassadors from the greatest states to your court; you will advise with them about the general welfare, for which no other man will have been found to have shown a like concern; you will see all Greece on tiptoe with interest in whatever you happen to propose; and no one will be indifferent to the measures which are being decided in your councils . . . And what man that is even moderately endowed with reason would not exhort you to fix your choice above all upon that course of action which is capable of bearing at the same time the twofold fruits, if I may so speak, of surpassing pleasures (*hēdonai*) and imperishable honours?[406]

In face of this kind of sentiment, expressed, of course, for consumption by a general public which the author evidently expects to throb to his drumbeat, a philosopher whose own reflections have convinced him that when intellectual activity unfetters itself from practical affairs, *then* one is most alive, enjoys what is most truly pleasant, identifies most completely with the most authoritative element in oneself, engages in projects whose success depends least on external chance and on winning the cooperation of uncongenial people—this philosopher naturally responds with impassioned, though reasoned, support for his own candidate.

There is, however, a further explanation, compatible with the above, for the competitive format. In stating that there are two forms of happiness, Aristotle is committed on general logical grounds to the assumption that one and only one of them constitutes the primary sense of the word, while the other constitutes a derivative sense dependent on some relation to the first. Otherwise, 'happiness' used of both is simply an equivocation, and there will be no unitary chief good and goal of political expertise.[407] The same goes for the phrase 'chief good' (and equivalents) as used of both of them. Now, Aristotle would find it logically natural to say that these terms apply 'most of all' to whichever form is identified as primary, and indeed to say (in a manner apparently closer to the material mode) that the primary one most of all is happiness or *the* human good. And in general when he says that A_1 and A_2 are both kinds of A, he easily passes to saying that the primary one is 'more A' or 'A-er' than the other. For example, he says that demonstrative premisses are 'better known' than the conclusion, because knowledge of them is logically primary in that it 'causes' knowledge of the conclusion.[408] But there is no implication that we are more certain of them, either psychologically or in the sense of being more justified in asserting them. Consequently, when he considers the two forms of the chief good, the question 'Which is logically primary?' naturally presents itself as the question 'Which is better?', and he will seek to answer the first by settling the second. The comparison with the case of 'better known' suggests that, just as being better known in this logical sense does not imply epistemic superiority, so the fact that one form of the chief good is 'better' in this sense does not imply that it has a stronger *practical* claim than the other, i.e. should always or normally be put first, whether in policy-making or in everyday decisions. In fact the two are so different that it is tempting to say that, from a practical point of view, neither is even slightly better than the other in the way in which each is vastly better than something that Aristotle regards as *not* happiness, e.g. a degrading pleasure.[409]

Resemblance is the key to the fact that both are forms of happiness. The question then is 'Does fine theoretical reflection count as happiness because it resembles outstanding political activity, or is it the other way round?' If we take the first alternative,[410] we shall fasten on whatever seems most distinctive about outstanding political activity, and look upon the fine theoretical kind as in some way analogous. We might say that getting intellectual control over a subject matter, marshalling arguments, building a theory, is a substitute or sublimation for controlling events in society, marshalling human beings in war or peace, building institutions, monuments, and utilities that outlast their founder. If, with Aristotle, we take the second, we shall say that what gives dignity to the life of a political leader is that he operates by means of the intellect and by discourse, and minimally by physical strength, in which respect he is surpassed by his purely reflective prototype, whose legacy consists in viaducts for men's minds rather than their bodies. In fact, according to Aristotle's clinching argument, the respect in which we should be comparing the political and theoretical ideals is the degree to which they approximate the life of gods, the paradigms of happiness.[411] If we apply traditional ideas of the gods (as deploying or as somehow present in elemental physical forces, 'rulers over land and sea',[412] and also as great interferers in human affairs), then one result follows; but if these notions are set aside in favour of a more rational conception of the divine life as wholly independent of physical and social environment, then purely reflective activity plainly emerges as closer in nature to the divine activity than any other human phenomenon.[413] The political form of the human chief good is thus secondary to the reflective, since both resemble the perfect divine paradigm[414] (and therefore each other) enough to count as happiness, but the former lags behind the latter in this respect.[415]

One important implication of this construction is that while it upholds the traditional view that fine political activity is happiness, it enforces a novel intuition as to *what about* the activity makes this true. And for devotees of either ideal, the intuition carries the message that they should respect each other for what they have in common.

So far, I have not attempted to characterize these ideal lives except in terms of their distinctive activities, and Aristotle gives us little clue about how he thinks the distinctive activity relates to the rest of the life in each case. Some interpreters think Aristotle implies that the superlative quality of theoretical activity requires its devotee to sacrifice everything else to it, or at least put it first in every conflict. Thus either he must live as a hermit, or he is sure to fail at times in what is expected of him as citizen, family member, and human being. Aristotle, however, sees him as involved to some extent in a life shared with others, and as practising the practical excellences to that extent.[416] Clearly this means having commitments besides the commitment to theoretical work; and justice, love, and friendship will sometimes entail giving that work second place. But the reflective thinker's special kind of life still differs from contrasting lives by such facts as: this sort of work is what occupies him when he is free from other commitments; he plans so as to be as free of other commitments as human nature and practical excellence allow; he finds in this work his greatest pleasure and personal fulfilment. It is true that Aristotle refers to him as 'intellectually accomplished',[417] and gives us no reason why we should think, contrary to experience and common sense, that intellectual accomplishment is open only to persons of true practical excellence. Some scholars conclude that, whether Aristotle realized it or not, nothing in the profile of his reflective paragon prevents it from fitting an unscrupulous, warped, or morally slovenly person, provided the person is intellectually talented and puts the talent to good theoretical use. Yet to proclaim that the life of such a person is an example of the acme of human happiness is completely at odds with Aristotle's initial definition of happiness as activity of excellence, 'excellence' having been interpreted in a way that made it natural to pass on to examine the standard excellences of character together with practical wisdom.

This difficulty disappears once we see that the division of happiness into two ideal forms is a bifurcation in the life characterized by activity of excellence as this was understood at the start, i.e. as involving the practical excellences. Such a life, given the elements necessary to make it 'complete', is happy. But the happy life, we now see, is generic, and can take two extraordinary forms, whose distinguishing features in both cases can also be found elsewhere than in a happy life. For it is equally true that the conjunction of talents and circumstances that make someone a brilliant politician (let us suppose entirely in the service of good causes) can coexist with serious faults of character. But the purely reflective excellence that makes one kind of life superlatively happy can only have this effect if the life is anyway happy in accordance with the definition as interpreted earlier. And similarly with the political distinction that renders a life splendidly happy even though inferior in the way we have seen to the former. In x. 7–8, where kinds of happiness are under discussion, individuals who by reason of their ethical defects have no chance of happiness, even though they may be intellectual geniuses or brilliant politicians, are beyond the universe of discourse. This is why Aristotle simply calls the supremely happy individual 'intellectually accomplished'; it is not the meaning of this designation that implies possession of practical excellence, but the context in which it is imposed.

As well as the two extraordinary forms of happy life, Aristotle must also recognize more common forms that resemble these more and less. For otherwise the 'political' goal becomes a mission to foster only the elevated forms, which would be absurd. The elevated ones hold the limelight in the two penultimate chapters of the *Nicomachean Ethics*, and then in the final chapter Aristotle implicitly reincludes the common forms. For he ends by considering the role of social institutions in the training of character, which is the necessary basis for all human happiness, ordinary or not. No doubt he hopes to add a new dimension to this basic training by forging an argument in favour of a new kind of cultural hero, so that it will come about in the normal course of things, and in the wider society, that traditional zeal for personal excellence and its exploits will broaden to include admiration and respect for adventures of purely reflective reason, and a taste for sampling their results, and the desire to participate in such adventures oneself on a modest scale or a larger one. This argument proceeds by showing that activity in accordance with the practical excellence that everyone traditionally respects is at the core of human happiness; that activity in accordance with all forms of the latter is an operation of human *reason*; that such activity makes for happiness precisely in virtue of its complex rationality; hence if there is another kind of activity (and we know there is) that is much more obviously rational or less beholden to what is non-rational, this kind expresses an excellence as fundamental as the traditionally respected sort (even if at present it is hardly recognized), and constitutes (therefore) a unique enhancement of human happiness.

In assessing this argument and its practical implications, the modern reader must bear in mind that from Aristotle's standpoint the reflective and political ideals are the only serious competitors. We can expand this sparse gallery of cultural icons by including under 'reflective' all kinds of creative and artistic activities that call forth the utmost of human imagination and perfectionism, both in themselves and in their products. But this expansion leaves out a major contender of an entirely different kind, one that is very clearly recognized by us.[418] This is the ideal of beneficence to the poor, sick, oppressed, or in whatever way deprived, who lie outside what would ordinarily be considered one's sphere of responsibility. Such an ideal seems to have little to do with happiness, because those who try to live according to it set little store by their own happiness, and in so far as they work to improve the social and material conditions of the needy, their avowed objective may not be those people's happiness, which easily seems a distant and even irrelevant luxury, but preliminary goods such as health, security, freedom from slavery, basic education, jobs. Still, this is clearly an ideal. It is interesting to consider the disparity between the biblical tradition that gave us this central ideal,[419] and Aristotelian *eudaimonia*. God in the Bible enters into human history: he suffers with his people, is not satisfied until they are saved, and in Christianity even becomes a human being himself for that purpose. Even if he is in some sense complete and self-sufficient, he cannot rest in completeness and self-sufficiency as long as there is a world in trouble. Nor is he self-sufficient in coming to its aid, since he depends on human cooperation to heal the world and ourselves. Such a being lacks essential aspects of Aristotelian *eudaimonia*—ones, moreover, that are critical for deciding which is its highest form. A humanitarian or charitable ethic based on the biblical model of divinity may resemble Aristotle's approach in declaring godlike (or godly) whoever lives up to its ideal; but it cannot conceive of that ideal as *eudaimonia* in Aristotle's sense.

POSTSCRIPT

Early on in writing the Commentary, I decided not to discuss or even refer to works of other commentators and interpreters. This was in the interest of sustaining as far as possible a purely conceptual focus, and of making Aristotle its object throughout. Scholarship on Aristotle's *Ethics* is a vast and thriving industry, so that citing even a fair sample of the valuable contributions at any given turn would have resulted in a work of entirely different character from what was intended, and one, moreover, that must have been authored by somebody else. But in preparing this actual Commentary and Introduction, I have been helped beyond measure by what others have done. In this connection, I wish to mention the following in particular:

A. Grant, *The Ethics of Aristotle*, 3rd edn. (London: Longman, 1874).

J. A. Stewart, *Notes on the* Nicomachean Ethics *of Aristotle* (Oxford: Oxford University Press, 1892).

J. Burnet, *The Ethics of Aristotle, Edited with an Introduction and Notes* (London: Methuen, 1900).

F. Dirlmeier, *Aristoteles*, Nikomachische Ethik. *Übersetzung und Erlaüterungen* (Berlin: Akademie-Verlag, 1960).

R. A. Gauthier and J. Y. Jolif, *L'Éthique à Nicomaque: Introduction, Traduction et Commentaire*, 2nd edn. (Louvain: Publications Universitaires, 1970).

T. H. Irwin, *Aristotle*: Nicomachean Ethics (Indianapolis: Hackett, 1985).

C. Natali, *Aristotele*: Etica Nicomachea (Rome: Editori Laterza, 1999).

NOTES TO THE PHILOSOPHICAL INTRODUCTION

1. The Philosophical Introduction is not meant to give a comprehensive account of all the subjects with which it deals, but to focus on matters that seem to be of particular interest or difficulty.

2. *NE* I. 1–12 (1094a1–1102a4), x. 6–8 (1176a30–1179a32).

3. *NE* I. 6 (1096a11–1097a14).

4. *NE* I. 12, 1102a2–4, and see comment on 4, 1095a26–28.

5. The nature of the dependence is different in different cases, and the question is complicated by the fact that what does the 'good-making' turns out not to be so much

the chief human good (i.e. human happiness, according to Ar.), but the principal element of this, namely excellent rational activity (see comment on I. 12, 1102a3–4). However, this complication does not undermine the contrast between the Aristotelian *summum bonum* and the utilitarian one.

6. *NE* I. 2, 1094a26–7.
7. Ibid. 1094b11.
8. See e.g. *NE* I. 9,1099b29–32, and x. 9 (1179a33–1181b23) on legislation.
9. *EE* I. 2, 1214b6–7.
10. Phrases such as 'it seems' (*dokei*; sometimes translated as 'it is thought') are ubiquitous in the *Ethics*. Their function is not to indicate doubt or uncertainty on Ar.'s part, but to invoke the way things ordinarily present themselves to us as grounds for taking them indeed to be that way.
11. e.g. *NE* I 10, 1100a32 ff., 'Happiness is excellence/is good luck'; VII. 2, 1145b25–31, 'The uncontrolled knows/does not know that what he is doing is wrong.'
12. See *NE* VII. 2 (1145b21–1146b8) for a series of problems deliberately set out to test his theory; and *Metaph.* II. 1, 993a30 ff, and III. 1, 995a24–b4, for methodological reflections.
13. *NE* I. 4, 1095b4–6.
14. *NE* I. 2, 1094a22–4; 3, 1095a2–11; II. 2, 1103b26–9; x. 9, 1179a35–b4.
15. *NE* II. 4, 1105b12–18; x. 9, 1179a35–b31.
16. This hits it off: 'In fine, we thought that he was everything | To make us wish that we were in his place', from 'Richard Cory' by Edward Arlington Robinson.
17. *NE* I. 12, 1101b25–7.
18. Etymologically the *eudaimōn* is one who has a good *daimōn* ('guardian spirit'). Ar. rejects the implication that whether or not one is *eudaimōn* is due to an external supernatural dispensation, or is a matter of cosmic luck (*NE* I. 9, 1099b14–25). Similarly when we translate this as 'happy', we reject the English etymological implication that it is just happenstance whether or not one is happy.
19. *NE* I. 4, 1095a17–26.
20. *NE* I. 7, 1097b22–4.
21. Ibid. 1098a7–18.
22. *NE* I. 4 (1095a14–b9).
23. In *Republic* I and *Gorgias* respectively.
24. *NE* I. 5, 1096a5–7. However, one type of miser might simply not accept the first premiss (as distinct from accepting it and acknowledging the irrationality of his predilection).

25. Ibid. 1095b19–20.
26. *NE* VII. 11–14 (1152b1–1154b34); x. 1–5 (1172a19–1176a29).
27. *NE* I. 7, 1097b24 –33.
28. Ibid. 1097b33–1098a3.
29. Ibid. 1098a5–7; cf. I. 5, 1095b31–3.
30. *NE* I. 10–11 (1100a10–1101b9).
31. *NE* x. 7–8 (1177a12–1179a32).
32. Cf. *Metaph.* I. 2, 982b29–32.
33. Cf. *NE* x. 7, 1177b31–3.
34. Such a defence could be developed from 'All men by nature reach out for understanding', the first sentence of the *Metaphysics*.
35. *Timaeus* 29e.
36. On divine goodness, see *NE* I. 6, 1096a23–5; on god not being jealous, *Metaph.* I. 2, 982b32–983a3.
37. *NE* I. 9, 1099b32–1100a1; x. 8, 1178b24–5.
38. *NE* I. 7, 1097a15–b21.
39. See *NE* I. 8, 1098b31–1099a2, for self-sufficiency (though the word is not used), and 11, 1101a18–19, for completeness.
40. *NE* x. 7, 1177a27–b26.
41. *NE* x. 9 (1179a33–1181b23).
42. Ibid. 1181b14–15.
43. Cf. ibid. 1179a33–4. However, *details* may be filled in later and by others; cf. I. 7, 1098a20–3.
44. See also pp. 51–2 below for his silence on a group of meta-ethical problems that preoccupy us today.
45. See the first page of J. S. Mill's *Utilitarianism*.
46. Similarly, a religion can pervade a person's life without its being the case that every decision that he or she makes is aimed at promoting, or strengthening the conditions of, the religion.
47. Cf. comment on VI. 1, 1138b18–34.
48. *NE* II. 2, 1103b26–1104a10. And where Ar. does give rules, i.e. in the field of particular justice, they do not refer to the chief good. It is true that the excellent agent is determined in every situation to *respond appropriately*, but phrased as an injunction this gives no guidance. How he or she actually responds is a matter of character and judgement, but character-cum-judgement is not a rule telling its possessor what to do.
49. Moreover, the good 'which all things seek' of *NE* I. 1, 1094a3 turns out, on the next page, to be the political objective, where 'political expertise' is explained as authoritative over production and use of the other *goods* (2, 1094a26–b11), not as laying down right *action* for everyone concerned. We can

agree with Ar. that every action and under-taking etc. seeks some good, and even agree, further, that in so doing every action and undertaking seeks the chief good (that is: presupposes or ought to presuppose concern for the chief good, whatever it is—it has not yet been defined—since apart from it any lesser goal is worthless), with-out thereby being committed to the view that this latter seeking is the sole determin-ant of right action. Suppose, for example, I hold that pleasure is the chief good which 'all things seek'. That some project of mine would be pointless if carrying it out suc-cessfully entailed eliminating pleasure from much of my life or the life of whomever I mean to benefit, certainly need not be the only consideration that weighs with me when I decide not to undertake the project or to seek its goal in another way. I may also be swayed by independent considerations of morality (cf. Eudoxus as described at *NE* x. 2, 1172b9–18). (Modern philosophers are familiar with the idea that the determin-ation of what is right does not (or not in general) depend on reference to some good which the action will produce, but possibly not so familiar with the idea of an ethical theory in which the chief good has a role, only not the role of being reference-point for right action. If so, this is because they overlook the ancient role of 'source of the value of every other good'.) Suppose, for example, I am a Eudoxan hedonist, and seek to promote pleasure in ways that respect ordinary morality (which perhaps never strikes me as requiring to be 'justi-fied', nor therefore as requiring to be justi-fied by conduciveness to pleasure): if I then come to accept Ar.'s definition of the chief good, what counts as right action for me may well remain largely unchanged; the main changes will be (*a*) I now see myself (even while only laying the groundwork for the pleasures I had in view) as having *already* (granted the elements that 'com-plete' a life) been enacting the chief good; (*b*) pleasure loses its ethical glamour; (*c*) now, when operating in the 'political' mode, I work for the Aristotelian ideal. (Note that when operating in the political mode, whether for the hedonic or the Aris-totelian ideal, the person imagined above will do so in a way that respects ordinary morality.) With the i. 1 passage, cf. i. 7, 1097a18–24 and i. 12, 1102a2–3, in each of which, as the context shows, the topic is the chief good in relation to other goods; or,

more precisely, the chief good in relation to actions considered not in respect of their rightness but in respect of their aiming at one or another of the lesser goods.

50. *NE* ii.

51. *NE* i. 13, 1102b13–ii. 1, 1103a18.

52. In *NE* vi, where he deals with wisdom, he will also argue that wisdom is impossible without excellence of character (vi. 12, 1144a29 ff.).

53. *NE* ii. 6, 1106a15–24.

54. *NE* ii. 4, 1105a22–6.

55. *NE* ii. 1–2 (1103a14–1104b3).

56. *NE* iii. 5, 1113b3–1114b25.

57. *NE* ii. 5 (1105b19–1106a13).

58. *NE* ii. 2, 1104a27–b3.

59. *NE* ii. 4, 1105a17–26; 6, 1106b5–14.

60. *NE* vi. 5, 1140b22–4.

61. See *NE* ii. 4, 1105a31–2, with note (*b*) ad loc., and pp. 42–6 below on decision.

62. It does not entail that at any given future time one will be prepared to act in those ways, since one might become incapaci-tated, but it does entail that if in the future one is not thus prepared, this will not be because one has preferred to give up the disposition, or preferred not to act (when one could) in the ways that maintain it.

63. *NE* ii. 4, 1105a33; cf. i. 10, 1100b12–17.

64. *NE* ii. 3 (1104b3–1105a16); cf. 9, 1109b1–12.

65. *NE* ii. 3, 1104b3–13.

66. *NE* ii. 5, 1105b21–3. See *Rhetoric* ii. 1–11 for discussions of many of these.

67. 'Determining' here does not mean 'abso-lutely necessitating'. Probably there is usu-ally a margin of contingency between a given pleasure/pain impulse and the behaviour motivated by it.

68. See e.g. *On the Heavens* ii. 1, where he argues that the movement of the divine celestial system cannot be due to an external agency, since then the movement would be effortful, and the life of the external agency (if it were a soul) could not be painless and blessed—all of which is inconsistent with 'our premonitions concerning god' (284b3–4).

69. The most important clarification is that the ethical intermediate is not arithmetically calculable from pre-established extremes, but is 'relative to us'; see *NE* ii. 6, 1106a29–b7.

70. *NE* ii. 6, 1106a26.

71. Ibid. 1106b5–35.

72. Ibid. 1106b21–3.

73. *NE* ii. 2, 1104a11–27.

74. *NE* II. 8, 1108b19–26.

75. *NE* II. 7, 1107b2, 7, 30; 1108a5, 17–19; cf. III.
7, 1115b25–6; IV. 4, 1125b17; 5, 1125b28–9;
6, 1126b19 and 1127a12–14.

76. *NE* II. 7, 1107b6–7. At II. 2, 1104a22–5 Ar.
writes as if the fault of 'running away from
every pleasure' does occur (in 'boors'), but
he seems to consider it only notional in his
study of moderation, since he does not discuss it. The studies of each of the other
character-excellences (except for justice, on
which see below, p. 36) all include some
discussion of both defects.

77. Cf. *NE* II. 7, 1107b27–1108a1 on proper
ambition and its opposites.

78. Plato, *Phaedo* 69a–c; *Protagoras* 329d ff.,
349a–360e; Xenophon, *Memorabilia* III. ix.
4–5; *NE* VI. 13, 1144b17–19, 28–30.

79. By contrast, practical wisdom, an intellectual excellence, is supposedly the same
in all areas of life; cf. *NE* VI. 13, 1144b6–21.
For the various continua, see the table at
p. 307.

80. NE III. 6, 1115a4–5.

81. However, it is certainly not an arbitrarily
chosen set. The *Eudemian Ethics* and *Magna
Moralia* recognize the same character-triads,
except that they add one for an excellence
called 'dignity' (*semnotēs*).

82. Cf. Ar.'s approach in *Physics* I and II to the
question of the fundamental principles and
causes of nature. Whereas his predecessors
had tried to reduce the natural world to a
handful of empirical factors such as the Hot
and the Cold, or four elements and two
forces of attraction and repulsion, Ar. gives
us metaphysical analyses of change and
causal relations as such: schemata which are
instantiated by indefinitely many physically
distinct types of change or entity.

83. Cf. *NE* III. 12, 1119a21–5, and IV. 9,
1128b13–14.

84. *NE* III. 5, 1115a4–IV.

85. The *EE* and *MM* begin with these too; then
the order becomes different in each.

86. Cf. I. 8, 1098b12–14.

87. Ibid.

88. We cannot be certain, as the ordering of the
books of the *NE* may be due to an early
editor.

89. *NE* III. 6, 1115a6 – 9, 1117b22.

90. *NE* III. 6, 1115a6–7.

91. *NE* III. 7, 1115b29–33.

92. Ibid. 1116a8–9.

93. It may be objected that the second combination is impossible since appropriate boldness beforehand would be partly based on a
reasonable estimate of one's nerve.

94. *NE* III. 6, 1115a24–6; 7, 1115b11.

95. *NE* III. 6, 1115a10–27; 9, 1117b7–8.

96. Cf. *NE* III. 8, 1116a30–b2.

97. *NE* III. 6, 1115b4.

98. *NE* III. 9, 1117b9–15.

99. '*kalos*' can also be rendered by 'admirable'
and 'noble'. '*kalos*' occurs in connection
with courage at NE III. 6, 1115a30–3; 7,
1115b11–24, 1116a12, 15, 28, 1116b2–3, 19,
31, 1117a16–18. The theme is repeated in
the studies of several other excellences:
open-handedness, IV. 1120a23–31 and
1121b4–5; munificence, IV. 2, 1122b6–7
and 1123a24–5; friendliness, IV. 6,
1126b29–33.

100. *NE* III. 9, 1117b17–20; cf. 8, 1116b13–15.

101. Since this view more or less requires that
something has to be treated as an end in
itself that in fact is not, it seems preferable
to subject excellent activity to this
treatment.

102. Cf. *NE* X. 7, 177b6–12.

103. *NE* III. 10, 1117b23 – III. 11, 1119b18.

104. For the wider one, see *NE* IV. 3, 1123b5; 4,
1125b12–13.

105. Cf. *NE* I. 8, 1099a7–8.

106. This is implied at *NE* VII. 14,
1154b20–6.

107. See *NE* X. 4, 1174a13–b14, on the
'completeness' of pleasure, i.e. its
desirability for itself; cf. I. 7, 1097a30–4.

108. *NE* VII. 4, 1147b23–31.

109. *On the Soul* III 12.

110. Ar. is a direct realist about sensible
properties, including the tangibles which
have the power of affecting non-sentient
beings in various ways. Thus the very
same heat that I feel is what melts the wax
(*On Generation and Corruption* II. 2–3).

111. *NE* III. 10, 1118a23–9.

112. Ibid. 1118a18–23.

113. Cf. *NE* IV 1, 1119b31–2, on the
wastefulness of self-indulgence; v. 1,
1129b19–22, on courage and moderation
in relation to general justice.

114. *NE* III. 11, 1119b14.

115. *NE* IV. 1, 1119b22 – 1122a17.

116. Ibid. 1119b22–7.

117. Ibid. 1121a30 ff.

118. Ibid. 1119b25–6, 1120a9–23.

119. Ibid. 1120a34–b2.

120. Ibid. 1120b5–6.

121. Ibid. 1120b31–1121a1.

122. Ibid. 1119b34–1120a4.

123. Ibid. 1121a16–29.

124. Ibid. 1121a30–b12.

125. Ibid. 1121b17–1122a13.

126. *NE* IV. 2, 1122a18–1123a33.

127. The word is sometimes translated 'magnificence'.
128. *NE* IV. 3, 1123a34–1125a35.
129. 'Magnanimity' in some translations.
130. *NE* IV. 3, 1123a34–5.
131. Ibid. 1123b2.
132. Because 'worth' implies the possibility of something like exchange, with giving and receiving, and only external goods can be given and received.
133. Ibid. 1123b17–22.
134. Ar. gives them as examples at *Posterior Analytics* II. 13, 97b17–18.
135. *Iliad* II. 297 ff.
136. *NE* IV. 3, 1123b26–8.
137. See above, pp. 11–12 and 14.
138. *NE* IV. 3, 1123b29 ff.
139. Ibid. 1124a1–3.
140. Ar. overlooks the distinction he made in I. 12 (1101b10–1102a4), by which honour is for activity of excellence, praise for the disposition.
141. *NE* IV. 3, 1123b32, 1124a12–20.
142. Ibid. 1124a6–7, 16–17.
143. Worth while even if less than happy.
144. Cf. I. 10, 1100b22–1101a6, especially 1100b32–3.
145. Cf. *NE* IV. 3, 1125a27–32 on the vain.
146. *NE* IV. 3, 1125a18–19.
147. Ibid. 1124a20–b5.
148. Ibid. 1124a30–b2.
149. This 'simple excellence' is set forth for the purpose of analysis. It may be that no such actuality is possible for human beings, although this depends on how much or little one means by 'reflection'.
150. Comparable possibilities of a shift to either servility or greatness of soul arise if one imagines the person of simple excellence suddenly precipitated into proximity with the rich and famous, without becoming one of them. He sees others honouring them, is expected to himself, etc.
151. It is this that gives it a specific sphere. Otherwise, it would be simply coextensive with all the specific excellences, like general justice and wisdom.
152. *NE* IV. 3, 1124b5–6, 26 – 1125a1.
153. Ibid. 1124b6–9, 24–6. No doubt the range of possible exploits is not confined to practical deeds. Certainly, as some have suggested, exploring theoretical philosophy and science would befit a great-souled person who had the talent. Aristotle may be hinting at this in portraying him as supine, since this was a

standard charge against intellectuals. See note (*b*) on I. 7, 1097b33–1098a4.
154. *NE* IV. 3, 1125a12–16.
155. Ibid. 1125a32–4.
156. Ibid. 1123b12.
157. *NE* IV. 4, 1125b1–25.
158. Ibid. 1125b2–8.
159. *NE* IV. 3, 1123b5–6; cf. 'moderate' at 4, 1125b12–14.
160. *NE* IV. 5, 1125b26–1126b10.
161. Ibid. 1125b26–1126a1.
162. Ibid. 1126a8–28.
163. Cf. *NE* VII. 6, 1149a24–b3.
164. *NE* IV. 5, 1126a23–4.
165. *NE* IV. 6, 1126b11– 8, 1128b9.
166. Cf. *NE* IV. 7, 1127a33–b3.
167. *NE* IV. 6, 1126b11–1127a12.
168. *NE* IV. 7, 1127a13–b32.
169. Cf. ibid. 1127a33–b7.
170. *NE* IV. 8, 1127b33–1128b9.
171. Ibid. 1127b33–4; 1128b3–4; cf x. 6, 1176b34–5.
172. The *agroikos* or country bumpkin was a standard character in comedy.
173. He calls wittiness 'civilized insult' at *Rhetoric* II. 12, 1389b11.
174. *NE* IV. 8, 1128a2.
175. *NE* X. 6, 1176b27–1177a5.
176. *NE* V.
177. *NE* V. 1, 1130a8–10.
178. Ibid. 1130a10–13.
179. Ibid. 1129b33–1130a1.
180. *NE* V. 2, 1130a14–15.
181. Ibid. 1130a14–b5.
182. Ibid. 1130b30 ff., with 1, 1129a6–9.
183. *NE* V. 1, 1129b1–4.
184. *NE* IX 8, 1168b19, 1169a21.
185. *NE* V. 9, 1133b32–1134a11.
186. *NE* V. 11, 1138a4–28.
187. *NE* V. 2, 1130b30–1131a1.
188. *NE* V. 4, 1132b11–16.
189. Applying the gain/loss model to all types of injury and rectification generates a taxonomical problem for Ar.: the opposite of a just distribution is an unfair one, but what is the opposite of just rectification? Apparently it has two opposites, an unjust arrangement by the rectifier, and the original wrong requiring rectification. In so far as the latter is modelled in terms of gain, loss, and imbalance, it comes under particular (in)justice; but in so far as *any* sort of wrong is supposed to fit this model, it comes under general (in)justice.
190. Even under this conflation, rectification in Book V is not punishment as Socrates interprets it, i.e. reformation of the wrongdoer's soul or conduct (Plato,

Gorgias 477a–481b, and cf. Ar. himself, *EE* I. 3, 1214b32; II. 1, 1220a35–6; *NE* II. 3, 1104b16–18). For the good produced by such a reversal (were it possible) would be a degree of excellence, whereas particular justice is concerned with equalizing the goods of fortune.

191. This distinction resembles but does not exactly coincide with Ar.'s division of interactions requiring rectification into 'voluntary' and 'counter-voluntary' (*NE* v. 2, 1131a1–9).

192. In *NE* x. 9, 1180a4 ff. he speaks of judicial punishment as an aspect of law enforcement, whether by way of deterring potential law-breakers or teaching a lesson to actual ones. From this point of view, the topic of punishment belongs with that of law-abidingness in general, as distinct from particular justice.

193. *NE* v. 5, 1132b21–31.

194. Ibid. 1132b31–1133a5, 1133b14–20; 6, 1134a23–b1.

195. *NE* v. 6, 1134a23–b18.

196. *NE* v. 7, 1134b18–1135a5.

197. *NE* v. 6, 1134a17–23; 7–8, 1135a8–20.

198. *NE* v. 8–9, 1135a19–1136a34.

199. *NE* v. 10 (1137a31–1138a3).

200. *NE* v. 11 (1138a4–b13).

201. *NE* III. 1–5 (1109b30–1115a3); v. 8–9 (1135a15–1137a30).

202. Most of Ar.'s examples are cases where, prima facie, it is a question of judging the act or the agent to be bad.

203. But at v. 8, 1135b4–8 agents who act from fear or under duress are said to be counter-voluntary although by principles stated at 1135a23–5 and 31–3 such actions are voluntary. Perhaps here Ar. means only that they act 'unwillingly', for which he has no separate word.

204. *NE* III. 1, 1110a19–b1.

205. However, at *EE* II. 8, 1225a2–36 he classes some such cases as counter-voluntary, and possibly also at *NE* v. 8, 1135b4–8, on which see note 203.

206. *NE* III. 1, 1110a26–9.

207. Ibid. 1110b9–11.

208. Ibid. 1111a24–b3; but cf. IX. 8, 1168b35–1169a1.

209. But at v. 8, 1136a6–9 he recognizes a distinct class of actions done because the agent is demented by an affection (passion) that is 'neither natural nor human', and says they are counter-voluntary.

210. Cf. *NE* III. 4, 1113a29–33.

211. *NE* III. 5, 1113b7–11.

212. *NE* III. 1, 1110a17–18.

213. *NE* III. 5, 1113b8.

214. This can also be given an indeterministic interpretation.

215. Cf. the argument at *EE* II. 6 that man is a kind of cause that is able to go either way; but again it is not obvious what this amounts to.

216. e.g. at *NE* III. 3, 1112a31–3; and cf. VI. 2, 1139b5.

217. *NE* III. 5 (1113b3–1115a3).

218. Ibid. 1113b3–5, 1114b17 –19.

219. *NE* III. 2–3 (1111b4–1113a14); VI. 2 (1139a17–b13).

220. Other translators and commentators have used 'choice', 'rational choice', 'purpose', for Aristotelian *prohairesis*.

221. The present translation has 'undertaking' for *prohairesis* at I. 1, 1094a2 and 4, 1095a14–15; and 'programme' at x. 9, 1179a35.

222. Cf. *NE* VI. 2, 1139a35–b3.

223. *NE* III. 3, 1112b15–1113a7; VI. 2, 1139a31. The action is the next step logically speaking. Ar. is not committed to holding that (in the suitably conditioned soul, on which see below) action is triggered as soon as a decision is reached. Action begins when an occasion arises, and recognizing the occasion is not a matter of further deliberation, but of something like perception; cf. III. 3, 1112b34–1113a2.

224. *NE* III. 2, 1111b6 ff.; v. 8, 1135b8–11.

225. *NE* VII. 8, 1150b30; 9, 1151a29–35; cf. I. 13, 1102b18–21.

226. Cf. *NE* VII. 6, 1149b13–18, where lack of control with respect to physical appetites is said to be 'a plotter'. The quotation from Homer suggests that appetite's cleverness is not only in working out external means to its end, but also in temporarily winning the agent over by specious reasons (i.e. self-deception).

227. *NE* III. 2, 1111b 30–1112a13.

228. Self-controlled and un-self-controlled action give examples of this; cf. the 'contrary impulses' at *NE* I. 13, 1102b21 (un-self-controlled agents are mentioned here, the self-controlled are included just above; 1102b14–21). However, there are also cases of un-self-controlled action where it simply goes contrary to the decision, without struggle.

229. *NE* II. 5, 1106a2–4 and 6, 1106b36, where the connection with decision is explicit for excellence, but applies to the bad dispositions too.

230. The terminology of 'right prescription'

(*orthos logos*) and the metaphor of obedience were commonplace (cf. *NE* II. 2, 1103b31–2), whereas the technical concept of decision is Ar.'s own contribution.

231. *NE* III. 2, 1112a15–16; 3, 1113a2–12. See also VI. 2, 1139a23.

232. *NE* III. 1112a18–34; VI. 1, 1139a5–14; 2, 1139b5–11.

233. *NE* III. 3, 1112b3–9.

234. At III. 8, 1117a17–22 Ar. recognizes decisions reached 'without calculation and reasoning'.

235. *NE* III. 3, 1112b11–19; 5, 1113b3–4; cf. VI. 12, 1144a7–9 and 20–1.

236. The *NE* VI. discussion emphasizes particularity; the *NE* III. one does not. See especially VI. 11, 1143a25–b5 with commentary. The link between this passage and decision, discussed in VI. 2, is provided by the concept of wisdom (1143a6–26, defined as 'practical' at 5, 1140b5; cf. 2, 1139a21 b1).

237. *NE* VI.

238. The translation uses 'reflective' for *theōrētikos*, 'reflection' for *theōria*. See also n. 335 below.

239. *NE* II. 6, 1107a1; cf. 4, 1105a31–2; 5, 1106a3–4.

240. e.g. Plato, *Republic* I, 332c–334c, 349a–350c.

241. *Republic* VI, 510d–511e; VII, 522a–534d.

242. *NE* VI. 5, 1141b3–9, 21–2. He had not always seen this. In his early work, *Exhortation to Philosophy* [*Protrepticus*], of which portions survive, Ar. emphasizes both the theoretical character of philosophical wisdom, and its practical benefits (*Protrepticus*, B46–51, Düring).

243. This new stipulation builds on a distinction of meaning already present: '*phronein*' ordinarily means 'to have one's wits about one', 'to be switched on to what concerns one', while the *sophos* is one who has mastered a body of knowledge or a method. The contrary of *phronēsis* is *anoia*, foolishness, while the contrary of *sophia* is *amathia*, lack of learning.

244. *NE* VI. 8, 1142a25. Since the reasons for the contrast become apparent only in the course of Ar.'s argument, it is a mistake to translate '*phronēsis*' and '*sophia*' in a way that makes it obvious in advance, e.g. as 'practical wisdom' and 'theoretical wisdom'. This trivializes Ar.'s conclusion at *NE* VI. 5, 1140b5, that *phronēsis* is a practical disposition.

245. Cf. the last suggestion of Plato's *Meno*

(96d–100a) that wisdom is not knowledge but true opinion.

246. This is not settled by self-reflection on the indubitable fact that in asking it we are doing something that only rational beings could do. In the ethical context we are essentially rational only if *the excellences central to happiness* are rational in nature or essentially dependent on rational excellence. This would not be the case if rational excellence were only instrumentally valuable or if it showed itself only in areas peripheral to whatever the main thing in life is assumed to be.

247. *NE* x. 7–8 (1177a12–1179a32).

248. Cf. ibid. 1177b30–4.

249. *NE* VI. 1, 1139a6–8; 7, 1141a16–17, 1141b14–22; 11, 1143b11–14.

250. *NE* VI. 1, 1138b35–2, 1139b13.

251. *NE* VI. 1, 1139a11–12; 5, 1140a24–31; 9 (1142a31–b33).

252. *NE* VI. 12, 1144a11–31; b18–33.

253. *NE* VI. 12–13 (1143b18–1145a6).

254. *NE* VI. 5, 1140b4–6, 20–1.

255. Ibid. 1140a27–8. Thus the judgements of the wise are all-things-considered judgements.

256. Ar. thinks of the limited objective of a technical expertise as a 'product'.

257. *NE* VI. 5, 1140b6–7; see note ad loc.

258. *NE* VI. 4, 1140a1–2.

259. And perhaps also at VI. 8, 1142a28–9.

260. *NE* VI. 5, 1140b13–20.

261. *NE* VI. 12, 1144a20–9.

262. *NE* VI. 11, 1143a25–b5.

263. *NE* VI. 12, 1144a7–9. Cf. 12, 1144a22–7; 13, 1145a4–6.

264. Cf. *NE* III. 5, 1113b6, where he says that the activities of the excellences are particularly to do with what forwards the end, as distinct from the end itself.

265. This follows on the principle that the good person's judgement in such matters is true: *NE* III. 4, 1113a29–33.

266. See above, p. 17–18.

267. *NE* VI. 12–13, 1144a11–1145a6.

268. Cf. *NE* III. 12, 1119b16, where (speaking about moderation) he says that appetite and reason alike aim at the fine.

269. Cf. *NE* VI. 11, 1143b11–14; 10, 1143a8–15; III. 3, 1112b10–11.

270. Cf. *Physics* I. 2, 184b27 ff., where he says that it is not the business of the natural scientist to argue against those who deny the existence of motion. His reason is, in effect, that refuting them or not makes no difference to the content of natural science.

271. *NE* VI. 7, 1141a9–b8; 12, 1143b18–20 with 13, 1145a6–11; X. 7–8 (1177a12–1179a32).
272. The application to ditch-diggers in the *Margites* fragment at 1141a15–16 may be ironic.
273. Cf. *NE* VI. 7, 1141a9–12.
274. Cf. I. 3, 1094b11–27; 7, 1098a26–b1.
275. *Metaph.* IV. 3, 1005b1; XI. 4, 1061b33; cf. the juxtaposition at *NE* VI. 8, 1142a17–18.
276. *NE* VI. 7, 1141a34–b3.
277. This follows from the fact that it in a sense contains 'systematic knowledge' (*epistēmē*), which strictly speaking is Aristotelian science (*NE* VI. 7, 1141a17–20; cf. 3, 1139b18–35).
278. *NE* VI. 8, 1142a16–18.
279. The objects of mathematics are not substances, but abstractions; knowing this perhaps means that we cannot have towards them the awe implied by calling something 'divine'. Yet Ar. does speak of their beauty at *Metaph.* XIII. 3, 1078a31–b6.
280. Cf. *NE* X. 7, 1177a24–7.
281. *NE* VI. 7, 1141b1–2; cf. the reference at lines 3–4 to Anaxagoras and Thales, philosopher-scientists like Parmenides and Empedocles.
282. Isocrates, *Antidosis* 264–9, trans. Norlin. Isocrates is not merely attacking, but competing with, philosophers like Plato and Aristotle. The *Antidosis* shows him staking a claim to be the true successor of Socrates; see comment on X. 8, 1179a22–32.
283. *NE* VII. 1–10 (1145a15–1152a36).
284. Ibid. 1145a16–30.
285. *NE* X. 7, 1177b31–4.
286. e.g. *Rep.* IV. 430e, 431d; *Laws* I. 626e.
287. *NE* VII. 8, 1150b29–32.
288. *Protagoras*, 352b ff.; cf. Xenophon, *Memorabilia* III. ix. 4.
289. Socrates assumes this in the *Protagoras*; see 332d. Ar. seems to assume it in his contrasts excellence/vice, godlike excellence/brutishness, self-control/un-control.
290. *NE* VII. 3 (1146b8–1147b19). Contemporary philosophers generally treat this chapter as containing all that is of interest that Ar. has to say about un-control.
291. *NE* VII. 4 (1147b20–1148a14). Plato too takes these pleasures as paradigmatic of what the self-controlled (i.e., for him, excellent) person has under control, but then he writes as if self-control in this area is automatically the key to self-control in

292. any other, and in fact hardly distinguishes them (e.g. *Gorgias* 507a–c).
292. *NE* VII. 4, 1148b10.
293. See above, p. 26.
294. *NE* VII. 4, 1147b29–31.
295. On wealth, see I. 5, 1096a5–7; on victory, cf. X. 7, 1177b5–6.
296. *NE* VII. 6, 1149a24–b25.
297. Cf. *NE* III. 8, 1117a6.
298. Ibid. 1116b31–4.
299. *NE* VII. 6, 1149a32–b3.
300. *NE* VIII and IX.
301. *NE* VIII. 2, 1155b17–19.
302. *NE* II. 3, 1104b30–2.
303. This is the simplest case, and the one Ar. mostly considers.
304. *NE* VIII. 2, 1155b27–1156a5.
305. i.e. in which the lovable quality is the same on both sides. These are the three basic types. Here it is assumed that the parties are equal or have equal stake in the friend-ship. Later he introduces variations involving inequalities and different lovable qualities on either side.
306. *NE* VIII. 4 (1156b33–1157a36).
307. *NE* VIII. 2, 1155b27–9.
308. *kath' hautous*, VIII. 3, 1156a11; cf. 1156b9–11.
309. *NE* VI. 11, 1143b4–5, 11–14; cf. II. 9, 1109b21–3; IV. 5, 1126b3–4.
310. *NE* IX. 4 (1166a1–b29).
311. Ibid. 1166a1–2.
312. See *EE* VII. 12, 1245a30. Apparently Ar. coined the phrases translated 'another self'.
313. *NE* IX. 4, 1166a23–4.
314. Recalling legendary friendships; cf. n 312 above.
315. See above, pp. 11–14.
316. The considerations obviously become logically more complicated if one adds in (*a*) the possibility that the friend is a self divided against itself, and then (*b*) the fact that in Aristotelian friendship the friendly attitude is reciprocated.
317. *NE* IX. 4, 1166a16–17; 8, 1169a2; cf. X. 7, 1178a2–6.
318. *NE* IX. 8 (1168a28–1168b2).
319. *NE* IX. 4, 1166a27.
320. But he does not take it for granted that one can have friendship with oneself: see *NE* IX. 4, 1166a33–b1, and *EE* VII. 6, 1240a7–21, where he says that it is friendship only by analogy.
321. It is a defeasible connection in both cases.
322. Neither this, nor 'the friend is another self', requires reciprocity; thus 'friend' here means 'loved one'. Cf. 4, 1166a5, with VIII.

8, 1159a28–33, on mothers. It is assumed that infants are hardly capable of friendship.
323. In Homeric usage, 'philos' meant 'one's own'.
324. *NE* I. 7, 1098a7–18.
325. *NE* I. 8–9 (1098b9–1100a9).
326. *NE* I. 8, 1099a21–30.
327. *NE* III. 9, 1117a33–b8.
328. Cf. I. 7, 1097b6–16.
329. *NE* IX. 9, 1169b3–8.
330. Ibid. 1169b25–7.
331. This is how god is conceived. *EE* VII. 12, 1244b7–11 objects that the happiest human being should need friends least, because god (the paradigm of happiness) is completely self-sufficient. Ar. replies *inter alia* that the comparison with god is misconceived: ibid. 1245b13–19. This dialectic is unsuitable at a point in the *NE* where the arguments of Book X are already in view, i.e. those of X. 7–8 elevating the thinker's life as godlike.
332. *NE* IX. 9, 1169b8–16; 11 (1171a21–b28).
333. *NE* IX. 9, 1170a5–13.
334. Unlike divine activity; cf. *EE* VII. 1245b16–19.
335. Cf. 'observe' (*theōrein*) at *NE* IX. 9, 1169b33. The word should not be taken necessarily to imply dispassionate or humanly disengaged contemplation, or the purely theoretical stance in the modern sense, because for Aristotle's audience one of its most familiar uses was in application to spectators of athletic events, dramatic performances, and religious pageants, where the natural point of being thus 'theoretically' involved is not to 'obtain knowledge' or 'scientific understanding' of what is going on, but a kind of cognition that might be described as 'being part of the fun but without participating physically', or 'entering into something imaginatively'. This original connection places 'theōria' a good distance away, on the spectrum of cognitive or quasi-cognitive attitudes, from mystical contemplation, at least in the Christian tradition; but translators of Aristotle often render it by 'contemplation', and some interpreters have understood this in a mystical sense.
336. *NE* IX. 9, 1169b28–1170a4.
337. Ibid. 1169b18–19.
338. Ibid. 1170a19–20.
339. Aristotle restricts this to lives not marred by pain of various kinds (1170a22–4).
340. *NE* IX. 9, 1170a13–b19.

341. *NE* VII. 11–14 (1152b1–1154b34); x. 1–5 (1172a19–1176a29).
342. See above, pp. 55–6.
343. *NE* VII. 11, 1152b12–15; cf. Plato, *Philebus* 53c–54e.
344. *NE* VII. 12, 1152b33–1153a14.
345. Ibid. 1153a17–23.
346. *NE* VII. 13, 1153b14–15.
347. Ibid. 1153b25–31; cf. 11, 1152b19–20.
348. *NE* VII. 12, 1152b26–31. On the relativization 'for so-and-so', see also pp. 72–3 below.
349. *NE* VII. 13, 1153b1–7, 1154a1–5.
350. *NE* VII. 14, 1154a8–21.
351. This includes but is not confined to the pain of the associated lack. Thus eating removes the pain of hunger and blocks or distracts from other pains.
352. *Philebus* 22a–c, 33a–b.
353. Cf. *Metaph.* XII. 7, 1072b14–16.
354. *NE* VII. 14, 1154b20–31; cf. IX. 9, 1170a20–1: 'the determinate is of the nature of the good'.
355. See comment (*b*) on I. 1, 1094a2–3.
356. *NE* x. 2, 1172b15–18.
357. Ibid. 1172b9–15.
358. *NE* x. 4, 1175a 10 ff. 2; 1172b35–1173a5; VII. 13, 1153b25–8.
359. *NE* x. 2, 1172b23–34; cf. *Philebus* 20e–22b. Plato also reversed the terms so as to argue that wisdom is not the chief good either.
360. Principally, that in some cases it is correct to say that *X* is pleasant *for* the subject, and therefore only good *for* them as distinct from *good*.
361. *NE* I. 1, 1094a2–3.
362. Ibid. 1094a1–2.
363. *NE* I. 2, 1094a18–b2. The numerous thematic connections between Books I and X make it unreasonable to suppose that he would not notice this inconsistency. Cf. x. 2, 1172b14–15, with I. 1, 1094a2–3; x. 2, 1172b20–3, with I. 7, 1097a30–b6; x. 2, 1172b32–4, with I. 7, 1097b16–20; see also the reference to Eudoxus at I. 12, 1101b27–31; cf. the three lives in I. 5 (1095b14–1096a10) and x. 6–8 (1176a30–1179a32); and I. 7, 1097a28 and b7–8, with x. 7, 1177b25–6, and a27–8.
364. Especially at IX. 9, 1170a13 ff.
365. *NE* x. 2, 1172b13–14.
366. Ibid. 1172b20–3. It is not clear that Aristotle agrees, since he points out that we choose or should choose certain activities (commonly called pleasures) for the sake of recreation; *NE* x. 6, 1176b33–1177a1.

367. Cf. IX. 9, 1170a16 ff.
368. *NE* x. 4, 1174a14–16; cf. b12. It is not clear how Ar. would apply 'complete at each moment' to such apparent processes as trying to solve a pre-set problem.
369. See above, p. 66.
370. This was not the theory in *NE* VII, of course. Rather, Ar. there identified the pleasure of thinking or eating with the latter activity itself, when it is unimpeded. It has been suggested that the topic in Book VII is *what we take pleasure in*, whereas in Book X it is, rather, *the pleasure we take*. This seems largely correct as an external description, but there is no sign that Ar. himself distinguishes the two discussions by reference to this distinction.
371. *NE* x. 4, 1174b31–3.
372. Cf. *NE* IX. 9, 1170b1–3.
373. *NE* x. 4, 1175a16–17.
374. Ibid. 1175a32–b20 he mentions pleasures (and pains) of doing geometry, music, building, playing pipes and listening to them being played, watching a play, drawing, calculating. At *NE* IX. 12, 1172a3–5 he gives as examples of pleasant activities shared with friends: drinking, playing dice, gymnastic exercising, hunting, philosophizing.
375. *NE* x. 4, 1174b14–1175a1. Impediments include distracting pleasures; 5, 1175b1–24; cf. VII. 12, 1153a15; 13, 1153b9–19.
376. *NE* x. 5 (1175a21–1176a29).
377. *NE* x. 4, 1175a10–17.
378. *NE* IX. 9, 1170a19–21.
379. i.e. in the exposition from *NE* x. 4, 1174a13 to 5, 1175b24.
380. On the principle that exercise is needed to maintain a capacity in good condition.
381. *NE* x. 5, 1176a10–22; III. 4, 1113a25–33, on which see comment.
382. Proviso: when (1) the statements and inference are made by one human being communicating with another, and (2) *Y* is a human being; or, more generally, when the communicators and *Y* belong to the same kind. All this because donkeys can be excellent in their own way; cf. *NE* x. 5, 1176a3–8.
383. Ar. cannot think this, as he locates pleasure in cognitive activity.
384. Cf. *NE* VII. 12, 1152b26–31. The prepositions in 'pleasant to . . .' and 'good for . . .' are both rendered by the dative in Greek.
385. Cf. *NE* x. 6, 1176b12–19; cf. I. 5, 1095b21–2.

386. *NE* x. 5, 1176a1; 7, 1177a26; cf. 6, 1176b20 ('refined', *eilikrinēs*); cf. *Philebus* 51b–53c.
387. *NE* x. 5, 1175b36–1176a3; 7, 1177a25–6.
388. *Philebus* 53a–c.
389. *NE* x. 7, 1177a23; cf. 'the truly pleasant' at 9, 1179b15.
390. The final arguments of the *NE* have to do with the role of law in ethical training, and the qualifications for legislators (x. 9, 1179a33–1181b23).
391. *NE* x. 6–8 (1176a30–1179a32).
392. Cf. the anecdote in which the philosopher Anaxagoras, on being asked 'Who is the happy man?' said: 'a strange sort', and went on to describe someone like himself; *NE* x. 8, 1179a13–15, with comment. In the 5th and 4th centuries intellectuals were standardly accused of being 'idle'; cf. Ar.'s response in *Politics* VII. 3.
393. For Isocrates, on whom see above, p. 54, this was clearly no part of his task as higher educator.
394. *NE* x. 6, 1176b12–19; cf. I. 5, 1095b21–2.
395. See above, pp. 11–14.
396. The word also means 'good'. See comments (*d*) on I. 7, 1098a7–17 and (*b*) on x. 7, 1177619–20
397. For example: recent argumentation in IX. 9, 1170a13 ff. ('if we examine the matter more from the point of view of natural philosophy') is quite technical; so is x. 4 (1174a13–1175a21); and x. 1–3 (1172a19–1174a12) assumes intimate knowledge of the Academic debate on pleasure.
398. Thus Socrates suffered by his association with the politically controversial Alcibiades; if Plato had dreams of setting up a branch of his school in Syracuse, they were dashed by court politics; earlier Anaxagoras, a foreigner in Athens but a member of Pericles' set, was target of a formal charge of impiety because of that association.
399. Cf. Plato's complaint, *Republic*. VII. 528b–c, that there has been little progress in the study of solid geometry (Eudoxus' speciality, incidentally) 'because no city values it', unlike the potentially useful sciences of arithmetic, plane geometry, and astronomy.
400. *NE* x. 9, 1179b31–1180b3.
401. See above, pp. 10–11.
402. See *NE* I. 7, 1097a22–4 and x. 5, 1176a26–9 for multiplicity of the chief good; I. 7, 1098a16–18 and 8, 1099a29–31 for superiority of one form over any other(s).
403. See e.g. how the superlatives 'best' and 'happiest' occur (respectively) at *NE* x. 7,

1177a13 and 8, 1179a31— the first and last sentences of the entire comparison.

404. Xenophon, *Memorabilia* II. 1.

405. In Euripides' lost play *Antiope*.

406. *Address to Philip* 68–71. This extract reproduces, with a few changes, the translation of La Rue Van Hook, Isocrates v. 1, Loeb Classical Library. It is meant to illustrate a general point, for Aristotle may not have known this particular work, which was written in 346 BCE. All we know for certain about the date of composition of the last stretch of the *NE* is that it was later than 354–353.

407. To take Ar.'s own illustration: the healthy is a unitary field, the concern of the single expertise of medicine, despite the fact that 'the healthy' means different things: (1) health without qualification, i.e. a suitable balance of physiological factors; (2) what is healthy as in healthy complexion, i.e. a sign of (1); (3) what is healthy as in healthful diet , i.e. the cause of (1). The relations to (1) unify the field; *Metaph.* IV. 2, 1003a31–b4.

408. *Posterior Analytics*, I. 2, 70b29–30.

409. See, however, *Politics* VII. 13, 1332a8–25, which may ground the superiority of theoretical activity on the fact that it, unlike typical political and practical activity, is what is proper to engage in when circumstances are all good, whereas the former are responses to evils and lacks. Obviously superiority for this reason does not entail a prior practical claim; on the contrary: in general where there are

practical problems, they must be dealt with first. (The references at *Pol.* 1332a9 and 22 are to the *EE*.)

410. There is no need to take either alternative if one is not committed to the view that a unitary concept of happiness requires that one form be primary, the other dependent.

411. This paradigmatic function of the gods in the argument does not presuppose the actual existence of anything godlike apart from the human intellect itself. However, for Aristotle and his audience it is a given that there are superhuman divinities.

412. *NE* X. 8, 1179a4, where the phrase applies to human rulers.

413. Ibid. 1178b7–28.

414. Cf. *NE* I. 2, 1094b9–10, where it is 'finer and more godlike' to bring about the chief good 'for a nation or for cities' than for one individual.

415. Once it is clear that this is the nature of the priority, there is no temptation to suppose (what is unwarranted by the text) that the political life is posterior because its one goal is purely reflective activity.

416. *NE* X. 8, 1178b5–7. The life of a hermit is also ruled out by I. 7, 1097b8–11, and by the arguments of IX. 9 (1169b3–1170b19).

417. *NE* X. 7, 1177a32; 8, 1179a32–3.

418. For the ancient Greeks it was adumbrated in the myths about Heracles and Prometheus.

419. And articulated the virtue of universal compassion, a quality undreamed of by Aristotle.

PART II

Translation

BOOK I

(I. 1) Every sort of expert knowledge and every inquiry, and similarly every action and undertaking, seems to seek some good. Because of that, people are right to affirm that the good is 'that which all things seek'. But there appears to be a certain difference among ends: some are activities, while others are products of some kind, over and above the activities themselves. Where there are ends over and above the activities, in these cases the products are by their nature better than the activities. Since there are many sorts of action, and of expertise and knowledge, their ends turn out to be many too: thus health is the end of medicine, a ship of shipbuilding, victory of generalship, wealth of household management. But in every case where such activities fall under some single capacity, just as bridle-making falls under horsemanship, along with all the others that produce the equipment for horsemanship, and horsemanship along with every action that has to do with expertise in warfare falls under generalship—so in the same way others fall under a separate one; and in all activities the ends of the controlling ones are more desirable than the ends under them, because it is for the sake of the former that the latter too are pursued. It makes no difference—as in the case of the sorts of knowledge mentioned—whether the ends of the actions are the activities themselves, or some other thing over and above these.

(I. 2) If then there is some end in our practical projects that we wish for because of itself, while wishing for the other things we wish for because of it, and we do not choose everything because of something else (for if *that* is the case, the sequence will go on to infinity, making our desire empty and vain), it is clear that this will be the good, i.e. the chief good. So in relation to life, too, will knowing it have great weight, and like archers with a target would we be more successful in hitting the point we need to hit if we had this knowledge? If so, then one must try to grasp it at least in outline, that is, what it might be, and to which sort of expertise or productive capacity it belongs. It would seem to belong to the most sovereign, i.e. the most 'architectonic'. Political expertise appears to be like this, for it is this expertise that sets out which of the expertises there needs to be in cities, and what sorts of expertise each group of people should learn, and up to what point; and we see even the most prestigious of the productive capacities falling under it, for example

1094a1

1094a5

1094a10

1094a15

1094a20

1094a25

1094b1

1094b5 generalship, household management, rhetoric; and since it makes use of the practical[1] expertises that remain, and furthermore legislates about what one must do and what things one must abstain from doing, the end of this expert-ise will contain those of the rest; so that this end will be the human good. For even if the good is the same for a single person and for a city, the good of the city is a greater and more complete thing both to achieve and to preserve; for

1094b10 while to do so for one person on his own is satisfactory enough, to do it for a nation or for cities is finer and more godlike. So our inquiry seeks these things, being a political inquiry in a way.

(I. 3) But our account would be adequate, if we achieved a degree of precision appropriate to the underlying material; for precision must not be sought to the same degree in all accounts of things, any more than it is by

1094b15 craftsmen in the things they are producing. Fine things and just things, which are what political expertise inquires about, involve great variation and irregularity, so that they come to seem fine and just by convention alone, and not by nature. Something like this lack of regularity is found also in good things, because of the fact that they turn out to be a source of damage to many people: some in fact have perished because of wealth, others because of

1094b20 courage. We must be content, then, when talking about things of this sort and starting from them, to show what is true about them roughly and in outline, and when talking about things that are for the most part, and starting from these, to reach conclusions too of the same sort. It is in this same way, then, that one must also receive each sort of account; for it is a mark of an educated

1094b25 person to look for precision in each kind of inquiry just to the extent that the nature of the subject allows it; it looks like the same kind of mistake to accept a merely persuasive account from a mathematician and to demand demon-strations from an expert in oratory. Each person judges well what he knows,

1095a1 and is a good judge of these things (so the person who is educated in a given thing is a good judge of that, and the person who is educated in everything is a good judge without qualification). This is why the young are not an appropri-ate audience for the political expert; for they are inexperienced in the actions that constitute life, and what is said will start from these and will be about these. What is more, because they have a tendency to be led by the emotions,

1095a5 it will be without point or use for them to listen, since the end is not knowing things but doing them. Nor does it make any difference whether a person is young in years or immature in character, for the deficiency is not a matter of time, but the result of living by emotion and going after things in that way. For having knowledge turns out to be without benefit to such people, as it is

1095a10 to those who lack self-control; whereas for those who arrange their desires, and act, in accordance with reason, it will be of great use to know about these

---

[1] Retaining πρακτικαῖς (1094b4).

things. Let this stand as our preamble: about audience, about how the present inquiry is to be received, and about what we are proposing.

(I. 4) Let us then resume the argument: since every sort of knowledge, and every undertaking, seeks after some good, let us say what it is that we say political expertise seeks, and what the topmost of all achievable goods is. Pretty well most people are agreed about what to call it: both ordinary people and people of quality say 'happiness', and suppose that living well and doing well are the same thing as being happy. But they are in dispute about what happiness actually is, and ordinary people do not give the same answer as intellectuals. The first group identifies it with one of the obvious things that anyone would recognize, like pleasure or wealth or honour, while some pick some other thing and others another (often, too, the same person picks a different thing: when he falls ill, it's health, and if he is poor, it's wealth); but out of consciousness of their own ignorance they are in awe of those who say something impressive and over their heads. Some people used to think that besides these many goods there is another one, existing by itself, which is cause for all of these too of their being good. Now it is presumably rather otiose to examine all these opinions, and enough to examine those that are most widely held, or seem to have some justification. However we must keep in mind that there is a difference between arguments that begin from first principles and arguments that work to first principles. Plato too used to raise difficulties here, and rightly: he would inquire whether the movement of the discussion was from first principles or to them, just as in the stadium the runners might be moving away from the race stewards towards the turn or in the reverse direction. For one must begin from what is knowable, but there are two senses of 'knowable': there is what is knowable *in relation to us*, and what is knowable *without qualification*. Presumably, then, in our case, we must start from what is knowable to us. Consequently, in order to listen appropriately to discussion about what is fine and just, i.e. about the objects of political expertise in general, one must have been well brought up. For the starting point is *that* it is so, and if this were sufficiently clear to us—well, in that case there will be no need to know in addition *why*. But such a person either has the relevant first principles, or might easily grasp them. As for anyone who has neither of the things in question, he should listen to what Hesiod says:

1095a15

1095a20

1095a25

1095a30

1095b1

1095b5

> Best out of everyone he who himself sees all that concerns him;
> Excellent too is that man who listens to others' good counsel.
> But the one who neither sees for himself, nor, hearing another,
> Takes the words to his heart—now that is a useless man.

1095b10

(I. 5) But let us return to the point from which we digressed. On the good and happiness: to judge from their lives, most people, i.e. the most vulgar, seem—not unreasonably—to suppose it to be pleasure; that is just why they

1095b15

favour the life of consumption. The kinds of lives that stand out here are
especially three: the one just mentioned; the political life; and the life of
1095b20   reflection. Now most of the utterly slavish sort of people obviously decide in
favour of a life that belongs to grazing cattle, and not without reason, given
that many of those in high places behave like Sardanapallus. People of quality,
for their part, those who tend towards a life of action, go for honour; for
pretty much this is the end of the political life. But it appears more superficial
1095b25   than what we are looking for, as it seems to be located in those doing the
honouring rather than in the person receiving it, and our hunch is that the
good is something that belongs to a person and is difficult to take away from
him. Again, people seem to pursue honour in order to be convinced that they
themselves are good: at any rate they seek to be honoured by people of
discernment, and among those who know them, and to be honoured for
1095b30   excellence. So it is clear, at any rate according to them, that excellence is of
greater value. In fact, perhaps one might suppose that this is even more the
end of the political life than honour is. But excellence too appears somewhat
incomplete: for it seems to be possible actually to be asleep while having one's
1096a1   excellence, or to spend one's life in inactivity, and furthermore to suffer, and to
meet with the greatest misfortunes; and no one would call the person who
lived this kind of life happy, unless to defend a debating position. That will
suffice on these questions, since they have also been adequately discussed in
the books that have circulated. Third of the three lives in question, then, is the
life of reflection, about which we shall make our investigation in what follows.
1096a5   The life of the money maker is of a sort that is chosen under compulsion of
need, and wealth is clearly not the good we are looking for, since it is useful,
and for the sake of something else. Hence one might be more inclined to take
as ends the things mentioned before, because they are valued for themselves.
But it appears that they are not what we are looking for either; and yet there
1096a10   are many established arguments that focus on them.

Let these things, then, be set aside;

(I. 6) but perhaps we had better discuss the universal good, and raise difficulties about how 'good' is predicated—although such an investigation goes
against the grain because it was friends of ours who introduced the forms. But
it would seem perhaps better, even imperative, certainly when it is a matter of
1096a15   saving the truth, to destroy even what is one's own, especially if one is a
philosopher; for while both friends and the truth are dear, the right thing is to
honour the truth first. Well then, those who introduced this view used not to
set up forms for things to which they applied the notions of prior and posterior, which is why they also did not construct a form of numbers; but 'good'
1096a20   is said in the categories of 'what it is', quality, and relative to something: and
what is in its own right, i.e. substance, is by nature prior to what is relative to
something (for the latter resembles an offshoot or accident of what is); it

follows that there will not be some common form over these. Again, since
'good' is said in as many ways as 'being' (since it is said in the category of
'what', e.g. god and intelligence, in that of quality, e.g. the excellences, in that
of quantity, e.g. the moderate amount, in that of relative to something, e.g.
the useful, in that of time, e.g. the right moment, in that of place, e.g. habitat,
and other things like this), it is clear that there will not be some common and
unitary universal in this case; for otherwise good would not be said in all the
categories, but only in one. Again, since in relation to the things corresponding to a single form there is also a single kind of knowledge, there would also
be some single knowledge of all goods; but as it is there are many even of
goods falling under a single category, as for example there are many kinds of
knowledge of the right moment, since in war there is generalship, and medicine in the case of disease, while for the moderate amount there is medicine in
diet and athletic training in physical exertion. One might raise difficulties, too,
about what it might be that they *mean* by talking about the (whatever it may
be in each case) 'itself', if in fact there is one and the same definition both in
the case of 'man-itself' and in that of man, namely the definition of man. For
in so far as both are man, they will not differ at all; and if that is so, neither will
there be a difference in the other case, in so far as both 'good-itself' and good
are good. Nor will 'good-itself' be more good by virtue of being eternal,
unless it is also true that what is white and long-lasting is whiter than what is
white and short-lived. The Pythagoreans seem to have something more persuasive to say about the matter, when they place the One in the column of
goods; and apparently Speusippus followed their lead. But let us leave these
people for another occasion. As for those others we referred to, we may detect
something of a dilemma arising for them, from their not having said the same
things about every good: rather, those that are pursued and valued for themselves are called good by reference to a single form, while those that tend to
bring these about or somehow preserve them or prevent their opposites are
called good because of them, and in another way. It is clear, then, that goods
will be called good in two ways, i.e. some will be good in themselves, while
the other sort will be good because of them. Well then, let us separate off
those good in themselves from those that are useful, and consider whether
they are called good by reference to a single form. These goods in
themselves—what sort of goods would one suppose these to be? Or are they
those that are pursued even on their own, like understanding, or seeing, or
certain pleasures or honours? For even if we do pursue these because of
something else, still one might suppose them to belong among things good in
themselves. Or is there nothing that is good in itself at all apart from the form?
In which case, the form will have no point. If on the other hand the things
mentioned also belong among things good in themselves, the same definition
of the good will need to show up in all of them, just as the definition of
whiteness shows up in snow and white lead. But in fact the definitions of

1096a25

1096a30

1096a35
1096b1

1096b5

1096b10

1096b15

1096b20

1096b25 honour, understanding, and pleasure are distinct and different according to the way in which they are goods. In that case the good is not something in common and relating to a single form. But then on what principle *is* it predicated? For it does not look like a case of mere chance homonymy. Or is it on the principle that other goods derive from a single one, or that they all converge on it; or is it rather a matter of analogy: as sight is in the case of body,

1096b30 intelligence is in the case of soul, and so on with other goods, other contexts? But perhaps for now we should leave these questions aside; for to get precision on them would belong to a different sort of inquiry. Similarly in relation to the form; for even if the good that is predicated in common of things is some one thing, something separate 'itself by itself', it is clear that it will not be anything doable or capable of being acquired by a human being, whereas, as things

1096b35 stand, it is something like this that we are looking for. But perhaps someone
1097a1 might think it better to get to know it with a view to getting those goods that *are* capable of being acquired and doable; they might think that by having this as a kind of model we shall also be better able to identify those things that are good for us, and in that case to attain them. Well, the idea has a certain plausibility, but seems not to be in accord with what we find with the various

1097a5 sorts of expert knowledge; for all of them seek some particular good, and though they look for whatever is lacking, they leave out knowledge of the form of the good. And yet it is hardly likely that all the experts should be unaware of so great a resource, and should fail even to go looking for it. But it is also difficult to see how a weaver or a carpenter will be helped in relation to

1097a10 his craft by knowing this good 'itself'; or how someone who has seen the form itself will be a better doctor or a better general. For the doctor appears not even to look into health in this way; what he looks into is human health, or perhaps rather the health of this individual, for he deals with his patients one by one.

So much for these subjects:

1097a15 (I. 7) let us go back to the good we are looking for—what might it be? For it appears to be one thing in one activity or sphere of expertise, another in another: it is different in medicine and in generalship, and likewise in the rest. What then is the good that belongs to each? Or is it that for which everything

1097a20 else is done? In medicine this is health, in generalship victory, in housebuilding a house, in some other sphere some other thing, but in every activity and undertaking it is the end; for it is for the sake of this that they all do the rest. The consequence is that if there is some one end of all practical undertakings, this will be the practicable good, and if there are more than one, it will be these. Thus as the argument turns in its course, it has arrived at the same point;

1097a25 but we must try even more to achieve precision in this matter. Since, then,[2]

---

[2] Reading ἐπεὶ δὴ (1097a25).

the ends are evidently more than one, and of these we choose some because of something else, as we do wealth, flutes, and instruments in general, it is clear that not all are complete; and the best is evidently something complete. So that if there is some one thing alone that is complete, this will be what we are looking for, and if there are more such things than one, the most complete 1097a30 of these. Now we say that what is worth pursuing for itself is more complete than what is worth pursuing because of something else, and what is never desirable because of something else is more complete than those things that are desirable both for themselves and because of it; while what is complete *without qualification* is what is always desirable in itself and never because of something else. Happiness seems most of all to be like this; for this we do 1097b1 always choose because of itself and never because of something else, while as for honour, and pleasure, and intelligence, and every excellence, we do choose them because of themselves (since if nothing resulted from them, we would still choose each of them), but we also choose them for the sake of happiness, supposing that we shall be happy through them. But happiness no one 1097b5 chooses for the sake of these things, nor in general because of something else. The same appears also to follow from considerations of self-sufficiency; for the complete good seems to be self-sufficient. By 'self-sufficient', we do not mean sufficient for oneself alone, for the person living a life of isolation, but also for one's parents, children, wife, and generally those one loves, and one's 1097b10 fellow citizens, since man is by nature a civic being. But there must be some limit found here: if the point is extended to ancestors and descendants and loved ones' loved ones, an infinite series will result. But this we must look at on another occasion: the 'self-sufficient' we posit as being what in isolation makes life desirable and lacking in nothing, and we think happiness is like 1097b15 this—and moreover most desirable of all things, it not being counted with other goods: clearly, if it *were* so counted in with the least of other goods, we would think it more desirable, for what is added becomes an extra quantity of goods, and the larger total amount of goods is always more desirable. So 1097b20 happiness is clearly something complete and self-sufficient, being the end of our practical undertakings.

But perhaps it appears somewhat uncontroversial to say that *happiness* is the chief good, and a more distinct statement of what it is is still required. Well, perhaps this would come about if one established the *function* of human 1097b25 beings. For just as for a flute-player, or a sculptor, or any expert, and generally for all those who have some characteristic function or activity, the good—their doing well—seems to reside in their function, so too it would seem to be for the human being, if indeed there is some function that belongs to him. So does a carpenter or a shoemaker have certain functions and activities, while a human being has none, and is by nature a do-nothing? Or just as an eye, a 1097b30 hand, a foot, and generally each and every part of the body appears as having some function, in the same way would one posit a characteristic function for a human being too, alongside all of these? What, then, should we suppose this to be? For being alive is obviously shared by plants too, and we are looking for what is peculiar to human beings. In that case we must divide off the kind of life that consists in taking in nutriment and growing.[3] Next to consider would be some sort of life of perception, but this too is evidently shared, by horses, oxen, and every other animal. There remains a practical sort of life of what possesses reason; and of this, one element 'possesses reason' in so far as it is obedient to reason, while the other possesses it in so far as it actually has it, and itself thinks. Since this life, too, is spoken of in two ways, we must posit the *active* life; for this seems to be called a practical life in the more proper sense. If the function of a human being is activity of soul in accordance with reason, or not apart from reason, and the function, we say, of a given sort of practitioner and a good practitioner of that sort is generically the same, as for example in the case of a cithara-player and a good cithara-player, and this is so without qualification in all cases, when a difference in respect of excellence is added to the function (for what belongs to the citharist is to play the cithara, to the good citharist to play it well)—if all this is so, and[4] a human being's function we posit as being a kind of life, and this life as being activity of soul and actions accompanied by reason, and it belongs to a good man to perform these well and finely, and each thing is completed well when it possesses its proper excellence: if all this is so, the human good turns out to be activity of soul in accordance with excellence (and if there are more excellences than one, in accordance with the best and the most complete). But furthermore it will be this in a complete life. For a single swallow does not make spring, nor does a single day; in the same way, neither does a single day, or a short time, make a man blessed and happy.

Let the good, then, be sketched in this way; for perhaps we need to give an outline first, and fill in the detail later. To develop and articulate those elements in the sketch that are as they should be would seem to be something anyone can do, and time seems to be good at discovering such things, or helping us to discover them; this is also the source of advances in the productive skills—it is for anyone to add what is lacking. But one must also bear in mind what was said before, and not look for precision in the same way in everything, but in accordance with the underlying material in each sphere, and to the extent that is appropriate to the inquiry. For a carpenter and a geometer look for the right angle in different ways: the one looks for it to the extent to which it is useful towards his product, while the other looks for what it is, or what sort of thing it is; for his gaze is on the truth. We should proceed in just the same way in other areas too, so that the side issues do not overwhelm the main ones. One should not demand to know the reason *why*,

1098a1
1098a5
1098a10
1098a15
1098a20
1098a25
1098a30
1098b1

---

[3] Reading τὴν θρεπτικὴν καὶ αὐξητικὴν ζωὴν (1098a1).
[4] Retaining 1098a12 ἀνθρώπου δέ . . . 16 εἰ δ᾽ οὕτω.

either, in the same way in all matters: in some cases, it will suffice if *that* something is so has been well shown, as indeed is true of starting points; and that something is so is primary and a starting point. Of starting points, some are grasped by induction, some by perception, some by a sort of habituation, and others in other ways: one must try to get hold of each sort in the   1098b5 appropriate way, and take care that they are well marked out, since they have great importance in relation to what comes later. For the start of something seems to be more than half of the whole, and through it many of the things being looked for seem to become evident.

(I. 8) But we must inquire into it not only on the basis of our conclusion and   1098b10 the premisses of our argument, but also on the basis of the things people say about it: for a true view will have all the available evidence in harmony with it, while a false one quickly finds itself in discord with what is true. Well then, given the division of goods into three, with some said to be external, and others said to relate to soul and body respectively, we commonly say that those relating to soul are goods in the most proper sense and good to the   1098b15 highest degree, and we count actions, and soul-related activities, as 'relating to soul'. So what we have said will be right at any rate according to this view, which is an old one, and has the agreement of those who reflect philosophically. Our account will be right too in so far as certain actions and activities are being identified as the end; for in this way the end turns out to belong among goods of the soul and not among external goods. In harmony with our   1098b20 account, too, is the idea that the happy man both lives well and does well; for happiness has virtually been defined as a sort of living well and doing well. Also all the things that are looked for in relation to happiness appear to belong to what we have said it is. For some people think it is excellence, others that it is wisdom, others a kind of intellectual accomplishment; others think that it is   1098b25 these, or one of these, together with pleasure or not without pleasure, while others include external prosperity as well. Some of these views have been held by many people from ancient times, while some belong to a few people of high reputation; and it is not reasonable to suppose that either set of people are wholly wrong, but rather that they are getting it right at least in some one respect, or else in most respects. Well, our account is in harmony with those   1098b30 who say that happiness is excellence, or some form of excellence; for 'activity in accordance with excellence' belongs to excellence. But perhaps it makes no little difference whether we suppose the chief good to be located in the possession of excellence, or in its use, i.e. in a disposition or in a form of activity. For it is possible for the disposition to be present and yet to produce   1099a1 nothing good, as for example in the case of the person who is asleep, or in some other way rendered inactive, but the same will not hold of the activity: the person will necessarily be doing something, and will do (it) well. Just as at the Olympic Games it is not the finest and the strongest that are crowned but

1099a5 those who compete (for the winners come from among these), so too in life it is the doers that become achievers of fine and good things—and rightly so. Their life, too, is in itself pleasant. For enjoying pleasure is something that belongs to the soul, and to each person that thing is pleasant in relation to which he is called 'lover of' that sort of thing, as for example a horse is to the

1099a10 horse-lover, a spectacle to the theatre-lover; and in the same way what is just is also pleasant to the lover of justice, and generally the things in accordance with excellence to the lover of excellence. Now for most people the things that are pleasant are in conflict, because they are not such by nature, whereas to lovers of the fine what is pleasant is what is pleasant by nature; and actions in accordance with excellence are like this, so that they are pleasant both to

1099a15 these people and in themselves. So their life has no need of pleasure in addition, like a piece of jewellery fastened on, but contains pleasure within itself. For to add to what we have said, the sort of person who does not delight in fine actions does not even qualify as a person of excellence: no one would call a person just if he failed to delight in acting justly, nor open-handed if he

1099a20 failed to delight in open-handed actions; and similarly in other cases. If that is so, actions in accordance with excellence will be pleasant in themselves. But they will be *good*, too, and fine, and will be each of these to the highest degree, if the person of excellence is a good judge here—which he is, and he judges in

1099a25 the way we have said. So happiness is what is best, and finest, and pleasantest, and these qualities are not divided as the inscription at Delos says:

> What's finest—perfect justice; what's best—not that, but health.
> What's most pleasant—none of those, but getting the thing one adores.

1099a30 All these accolades in fact belong to the best kinds of activity; and it is these, or the one of them that is best, that we say happiness is. Nevertheless it clearly also requires external goods in addition, as we have said; for it is impossible, or not easy, to perform fine actions if one is without resources. For in the first

1099b1 place many things are done by means of friends, or wealth, or political power, as if by means of tools; and then again, there are some things the lack of which is like a stain on happiness, things like good birth, being blessed in one's children, beauty: for the person who is extremely ugly, or of low birth, or on his own without children is someone we would be not altogether inclined to

1099b5 call happy, and even less inclined, presumably, if someone had totally depraved children or friends, or ones who were good but dead. As we have said, then, one seems to need this sort of well-being too; and this is the reason why some people identify good fortune with happiness, others excellence.

(I. 9) This is the reason too why people debate whether happiness is some-
1099b10 thing learned, or the product of habituation, or the product of training in some other way, or whether it comes by some sort of divine dispensation, or even through chance. Well, if anything is a gift of the gods to mankind, it is

reasonable to suppose that *happiness* is god-given—more than any other human possession, by the same degree that it is best. But, while this subject will perhaps belong more to a different investigation, it appears nevertheless that, even if happiness is not sent by gods but comes through excellence and 1099b15 some process of learning or training, it is one of the most godlike things; for the prize and fulfilment of excellence appears to be to the highest degree good, and to be something godlike and blessed. It will also be something available to many; for it will be possible for it to belong, through some kind of learning or practice, to anyone not handicapped in relation to excellence. And 1099b20 if it is better like this than that we should be happy through chance, it is reasonable to suppose that it is like this, if in fact things in the natural world are as fine as it is possible for them to be, and similarly things in the realm of artifice, or causation generally, and most of all in relation to the best cause.[5] To hand over the greatest and finest of things to chance would be too much out 1099b25 of tune. But the answer we are looking for is evident from our account too: for we have said that happiness is a certain sort of activity in accordance with excellence; and of the remaining goods, some are necessary to happiness, while others contribute to it by being useful tools. This will agree, too, with our opening remarks; for we were there positing that the end of political 1099b30 expertise is best, and this expertise is dedicated above all to making the citizens be of a certain quality, i.e. good, and doers of fine things. So it makes sense that we do not call either an ox, or a horse, or any other animal 'happy', because none of them is capable of sharing in this sort of activity. For this 1100a1 reason a child is not 'happy', either; for he is not yet a doer of the sorts of things in question, because of his age; those children that *are* said to be happy are being called blessed because of their prospects. This is because, as we have said, happiness requires both complete excellence and a complete life. For 1100a5 many changes occur in life, and all sorts of things happen: it is possible for a person who flourishes to the highest degree to encounter great disasters in old age, as happened to Priam in the story of events at Troy; and no one who has had a fate like that, and died miserably, is counted happy by anyone.

(I. 10) Is it the case, then, that we should not count anyone else happy, either, 1100a10 so long as he is alive? Must we agree with Solon, and look to a man's end? And if we *should* posit that view, is it then that one is really happy—when one is dead? Or is that a completely strange notion, especially in our case, when we are saying that happiness is a kind of activity? But if we do not call the dead happy, and if this is not what Solon means, either—only that that is the time 1100a15 when it will be safe to call a human being blessed, on the grounds that he is now beyond the reach of evils and misfortunes: even this one might dispute, for someone who is dead seems in a way to be affected by both good and bad,

---

[5] Reading μάλιστα κατὰ τὴν ἀρίστην (1099b23).

1100a20   as much as someone who is alive but not perceiving what is happening to him; so for example the dead seem to be affected when their children are honoured or disgraced, and generally by whether their descendants do well or encounter misfortune. But this too raises a difficulty. Take someone who has lived a blessed life up until old age, and died in a manner that accords with that: the way his descendants turn out is something that will be liable to great

1100a25   variation, and some of them may be good and enjoy the life they deserve, while for others the opposite happens; and it is clearly possible for them to be separated by all sorts of different intervals from their dead ancestors. It would then be a strange result if the dead person were to change along with his descendants, and were to be happy at one time and miserable at another; and

1100a30   it would be odd too if the fortunes of descendants did not touch their ancestors to any degree, or over any period of time. But we should go back to the first problem, for perhaps from that we shall also be able to observe the answer to the question we are now considering. If, then, one must look to a man's end, and call a man blessed at that point, not on the grounds that he is then blessed, but because he was so before, is it not plainly strange if, when he

1100a35
1100b1   is happy, what actually belongs to him will not be truly predicated of him, as a result of our not wanting to call the living happy because of the changes that can occur, and because of our assumption that happiness is something firm-rooted and not in any way easily subject to change, while often the same people find their fortunes circling back on themselves? For clearly if we were

1100b5   to track a person's fortunes, we shall find ourselves often calling the same person happy, and then miserable, thus revealing the happy man as a kind of 'chameleon, and infirmly based'. Or is it completely wrong to track a person's fortunes like this? For *they* are not where living well or badly is located, but

1100b10   rather human life needs them in addition, as we have said, and it is activities in accordance with excellence that are responsible for our happiness, and the opposite sort of activities for the opposite state. The present difficulty itself bears witness to our account. For in no aspect of what human beings do is there such stability as there is in activities in accordance with excellence: they seem to be more firm-rooted even than the various kinds of knowledge we

1100b15   possess; and of these very kinds of knowledge the most honourable are more firm-rooted because of the fact that those who are blessed spend their lives in them more than in anything, and most continuously, for this is likely to be why forgetfulness does not occur in relation to them. What we are looking for, then, will belong to the happy man, and throughout life he will be such as

1100b20   we say; for he will always, or most of all people, do and reflect on what is in accordance with excellence, and as for what fortune brings, 'the man who is truly good and four-square beyond reproach' will bear it in the finest way, without any note of discord of any kind. Given that many things happen by chance, things that differ in magnitude and smallness, small instances of good

1100b25   fortune, and similarly of the opposite, clearly do not alter the balance of a

man's life, whereas turns of fortune that are great and repeated will if good
make one's life more blessed (since they are themselves such as to add lustre
to life, and the use of them is fine and worth while), and if they turn out in the
opposite way, they crush and maim one's blessedness; for they bring on pains,
and obstruct many sorts of activities. Nevertheless, even in these circum-   1100b30
stances the quality of fineness shines through, when someone bears repeated
and great misfortunes calmly, not because he is insensitive to them but
because he is a person of nobility and greatness of soul. If one's activities
are what determines the quality of one's life, as we have said, no one who is
blessed will become miserable; for he will never do what is hateful and vile.   1100b35
For we consider that the truly good and sensible person bears what fortune   1101a1
brings him with good grace, and acts on each occasion in the finest way
possible given the resources at the time, just as we think that a good general
uses the army he has to the best strategic advantage, and a shoemaker makes
a shoe as finely as it can be made out of the hides he has been given; and   1101a5
similarly with all the other sorts of craftsmen. If so, then the happy man will
never become miserable, though neither will he be blessed if he meets with
fortunes like Priam's. Nor indeed will he take on many colours, or be subject
to easy change; for on the one hand he will not be readily dislodged from his
happy state, and not by any misfortune that happens along, but only by great   1101a10
and repeated ones, and on the other hand he will not recover his happiness
from such misfortunes in a short time, but if at all in some extended and
complete passage of life in which he achieves great and fine things. What then
stops us from calling happy the one who is active in accordance with complete
excellence, sufficiently equipped with external goods, not for some random   1101a15
period of time but over a complete life? Or must we add that he will also
continue to live like that, and die accordingly, since his future is not apparent
to us, and we posit happiness as an end, and complete in every way and every
respect? If so, we shall call blessed those living people who have and will have 1101a20
the things we have mentioned, but blessed as human beings.

On these issues, let us draw the line at this point:

(I. 11) as for the question we left behind, the idea that the fortunes of one's
descendants and all one's loved ones should make not the slightest contribution to one's state seems too devoid of fellow feeling, and contrary to what
people think; however since the things that come about are many and exhibit
all sorts of variety, and some penetrate to us more and some less, to make   1101a25
distinctions in each and every case appears a long, even endless task, and it will
perhaps be enough if we deal with the matter in general terms and in outline.
If, then, there is a similarity between the misfortunes that affect oneself and
those affecting all one's loved ones, with some possessing weight and influ-   1101a30
encing the quality of life, and others looking like lighter occurrences, and if,
for any given incident, whether it involves the living or the dead makes much

more difference than whether in tragedies lawless, terrible deeds have happened beforehand or are presently being enacted, we must then take this difference too into account in our argument, or rather perhaps we must bring in the difficulty, in relation to the dead, whether they share in any good or in the things opposite to that. For it seems likely from these considerations that even if anything at all does penetrate through to them, whether good or the opposite, it is something feeble and small, either small generally or small to them, or if not, at any rate of such a size and such a sort as not to make happy those who are not already, nor to take blessedness away from those who are. Thus the dead do seem to be somehow affected when their loved ones do well, and similarly when they do badly, but in such a way and to such an extent as neither to render the happy unhappy nor do anything else of the sort.

(I. 12) With this clarified, let us consider whether happiness comes under the heading of what is to be praised or rather of what is to be honoured; for obviously it is not found among the potentialities. Everything praised appears to be praised for being of a certain quality and being disposed in a certain way towards something; for we praise the just man, the courageous man, and in general the good man, and excellence, because of his actions, i.e. what he does, and we praise the strong man, too, and the one who is good at running, and so on in other cases, because they are of a certain quality and disposed in a certain way towards something good and worth doing. This is also clear if we consider praises offered to the gods; for they appear laughable if they are offered by reference to our case, and this actually occurs, because of the fact that we have mentioned, that praise is always with reference to something. But if praise is of things like this, it is clear that it is not praise that is appropriate to things that are good to the highest possible degree, but something greater and better, as in fact accords with our practice, for we call both gods and the most godlike men 'blessed' and 'happy'. Similarly in the case of good things: for no one praises happiness as one does justice, but ranks it blessed, as being something more godlike and superior. It seems, in fact, that Eudoxus put well the claims of pleasure to first place in the competition of goods: he thought that the fact that it is not praised, even though it is a good, indicated that it was superior to the things that *are* praised, as he thought god and *the* good are superior, because it is to these that the other things are referred. For praise is appropriate to excellence, since excellence is what makes people disposed to fine actions; whereas encomia belong to things done, whether in the sphere of the body or in that of the soul. However to achieve precision in these things perhaps belongs more to those who have worked on the subject of encomia; for our purposes it is clear, from what we have said, that happiness is one of the things that are honourable and complete. This also seems to be so because of the fact that it is a principle; for it is for the sake of happiness that we all do everything else we do, and we lay it down that the principle and cause of goods is something honourable and godlike.

(I. 13) Since happiness is some activity of soul in accordance with complete excellence, we should discuss the subject of excellence; for perhaps in this way we shall get a better view of happiness too. In fact it seems that the true political expert will have worked at excellence more than anything; for what he wants is to make the members of the citizen-body good, and obedient to the laws. A model in this case is provided by the lawgivers of the Cretans and the Spartans, and any others there have been like them. If the present inquiry belongs to the sphere of political expertise, the investigation into excellence will be in accordance with our original purpose. But clearly it is human excellence we should inquire about, because it was the human good that we were looking for, and human happiness. By 'human excellence' we mean excellence of soul, not of body; happiness, too, we say, is activity of soul. If all this is so, clearly the political expert should know, in a way, about soul, just as the person who is going to treat people's eyes should know about the entire body, too; and more so, by the same degree that political expertise is more honourable than and superior to the doctor's; and the better sort of doctor is in fact much occupied with knowing about the body. It is for the political expert too, then, to reflect about the soul, but he should do so for the sake of the things in question, and to the extent that will suffice in relation to what is being looked for; to go into greater detail is perhaps a task too laborious for our present enterprise. There are some things said on the subject of soul in our published works too that are quite adequate, and we should make use of them: for example, that one aspect of soul is non-rational, while another possesses reason. It makes no difference for present purposes whether these are delimited like the parts of the body, and like everything that is divisible into parts, or whether they are two things by definition but by nature insepar-able, like the convex and the concave in the case of a curved surface. Of the non-rational, one grade looks likely to be shared, and to have to do with growth—by which I mean what is responsible for the taking in of food and for increase in size; for this sort of capacity of soul one would posit as being in all things that take in food, and in embryos, and this same one too as being in them when they are full-grown, for it is more reasonable to suppose the presence of this one than of any other. Excellence in the exercise of this capacity, then, appears to be something shared and not distinctively human: this part, and this capacity, seem to be most active when things are asleep, and it is most difficult to tell the good and the bad man apart when they are asleep (which is why people say that there is no difference at all between the happy and the miserable for half of their lives—but this is a perfectly reasonable consequence, because sleep is inactivity of soul in that respect in which it is said to be excellent or worthless), unless to some small degree some

1102a5

1102a10

1102a15

1102a20

1102a25

1102a30

1102b1

1102b5

1102b10 movements really do penetrate us in sleep, and in this way the dream-appearances of reasonable people are better than what appears to any random person. But on these subjects that will suffice, and we should leave the nutritive aspect of soul to one side, since it appears by nature devoid of any share in human excellence. But another kind of soul also seems to be non-rational, although participating in a way in reason. Take those with and without self-
1102b15 control: we praise their reason, and the aspect of their soul that possesses reason; it gives the right encouragement, in the direction of what is best, but there appears to be something else besides reason that is naturally in them, which fights against reason and resists it. For exactly as with paralysed limbs,
1102b20 which when their owners decide to move them to the right take off in the wrong direction, moving to the left, so it is in the case of the soul: the impulses of the person lacking self-control are contrary to each other. The difference is that in the case of the body we actually see the part that is moving wrongly, which we do not in the case of the soul. But perhaps we should not be any less inclined to think that in the soul too there is something
1102b25 besides reason, opposing and going against it. How it is different is of no importance. But this part too seems to participate in reason, as we have said: at any rate, in the self-controlled person it is obedient to reason—and in the moderate and courageous person it is presumably still readier to listen; for in him it always chimes with reason. The non-rational, then, too, appears to be
1102b30 double in nature. For the plant-like aspect of soul does not share in reason in any way, while the appetitive and generally desiring part does participate in it in a way, i.e. in so far as it is capable of listening to it and obeying it: it is the way one is reasonable when one *takes* account of advice from one's father or loved ones, not when one *has* an account of things, as for example in mathematics. That the non-rational is in a way persuaded by reason is indicated by our practice of admonishing people, and all the different forms in
1103a1 which we reprimand and encourage them. If one should call this too 'possessing reason', then the aspect of soul that possesses reason will also be double in nature: one element of it will have it in the proper sense and in itself, another as something capable of listening as if to one's father. Excellence too is
1103a5 divided according to this difference; for we call some of them intellectual excellences, others excellences of character—intellectual accomplishment, good sense, wisdom on the one hand counting on the side of the intellectual excellences, open-handedness and moderation counting among those of character. For when we talk about character, we do not say that someone is accomplished in a subject, or has a good sense of things, but rather that he is mild or moderate; but we do also praise someone accomplished in something for his disposition, and the dispositions we praise are the ones we
1103a10 call 'excellences'.

BOOK II

(II. 1) Excellence being of two sorts, then, the one intellectual and the other   1103a15
of character, the intellectual sort mostly both comes into existence and
increases as a result of teaching (which is why it requires experience and time),
whereas excellence of character results from habituation—which is in fact the
source of the name it has acquired [*ēthikē*], the word for 'character-trait' [*ēthos*]
being a slight variation of that for 'habituation' [*ĕthos*]. This makes it quite
clear that none of the excellences of character comes about in us by nature;
for no natural way of being is changed through habituation, as for example   1103a20
the stone which by nature moves downwards will not be habituated into
moving upwards, even if someone tries to make it so by throwing it upwards
ten thousand times, nor will fire move downwards, nor will anything else that
is by nature one way be habituated into behaving in another. In that case the
excellences develop in us neither by nature nor contrary to nature, but
because we are naturally able to receive them and are brought to completion   1103a25
by means of habituation. Again, in the case of those things that accrue to us
by nature, we possess the capacities for them first, and display them in actuality later (something that is evident in the case of the senses: we did not acquire
our senses as a result of repeated acts of seeing, or repeated acts of hearing,
but rather the other way round—we used them because we had them, rather   1103a30
than acquired them because we used them); whereas we acquire the excellences through having first engaged in the activities, as is also the case with the
various sorts of expert knowledge—for the way we learn the things we should
do, knowing how to do them, is by doing them. For example people become
builders by building, and cithara-players by playing the cithara; so too, then,
we become just by doing just things, moderate by doing moderate things, and   1103b1
courageous by doing courageous things. What happens in cities testifies to
this: lawgivers make the citizens good through habituation, and this is what
every lawgiver *aims* at, but those who do it badly miss their mark; and this is   1103b5
what makes one constitution different from another, a good one from a bad
one. Again, it is from the same things and through the same things that every
excellence is both produced and destroyed, and similarly every expertise; for it
is from playing the cithara that both the good and the bad cithara-players
come about. So too both with builders and the rest: good building will result   1103b10
in good builders, bad building in bad ones. If it were not like this, there would
be no need at all of anyone to teach them, and instead everyone would just
become a good builder or a bad one. This, then, is how it is with the excellences too; for it is through acting as we do in our dealings with human beings   1103b15
that some of us become just and others unjust, and through acting as we do in
frightening situations, and through becoming habituated to fearing or being

confident, that some of us become courageous and some of us cowardly. A similar thing holds, too, with situations relating to the appetites, and with those relating to temper: some people become moderate and mild-tempered, others self-indulgent and irascible, the one group as a result of behaving one way in such circumstances, the other as a result of behaving another way. We may sum up by saying just that dispositions come about from activities of a similar sort. This is why it is necessary to ensure that the activities be of a certain quality; for the varieties of these are reflected in the dispositions'. So it does not make a small difference whether people are habituated to behave in one way or in another way from childhood on, but a very great one; or rather, it makes all the difference in the world.

1103b20

1103b25

(II. 2) Since, then, the present undertaking is not for the sake of theory, as our others are (for we are not inquiring into what excellence is for the sake of knowing it, but for the sake of becoming good, since otherwise there would be no benefit in it at all), we need to inquire into the subjects relating to actions, i.e. to how one should act; for as we have said, our actions are also responsible for our coming to have dispositions of a certain sort. Now, that one should act in accordance with the correct prescription is a shared view— let it stand as a basic assumption; there will be a discussion about it later, both about what 'the correct prescription' is, and about how it is related to the other kinds of excellence. But before that let it be agreed that everything one says about practical undertakings has to be said, not with precision, but in rough outline, just as we also said at the beginning that the sorts of account we demand must be determined by the subject matter: things in the sphere of action and things that bring advantage have nothing stable about them, any more than things that bring health. But if what one says universally is like this, what one says about particulars is even more lacking in precision; for it does not fall either under any expertise or under any set of rules—the agents themselves have to consider the circumstances relating to the occasion, just as happens in the case of medicine, too, and of navigation.

1103b30

1104a1

1104a5

1104a10

But even though the present discussion is like this, we must try to give some help. First of all, then, one must keep in view that the sorts of things we are talking about are naturally such as to be destroyed by deficiency and excess, just as we observe—since we have to use what is obvious to testify on behalf of what is not so—in the case of strength and health; for both excessive training and too little training will destroy our strength, and similarly if we drink or eat too much, that will destroy our health, whereas drinking and eating proportionate amounts creates, increases, and preserves it. So too it is, then, with moderation, courage, and the other excellences. For someone who runs away from everything, out of fear, and withstands nothing, becomes cowardly, and correspondingly someone who is frightened of nothing at all and advances in the face of just anything becomes rash; and similarly, too,

1104a15

1104a20

someone who takes advantage of every pleasure offered and holds back from none becomes self-indulgent, while someone who runs away from every pleasure, as boors do, is insensate, as it were. Moderation, then, and courage are destroyed by excess and deficiency, and preserved by what is intermediate between them. But not only are the excellences brought about, increased, and destroyed as a result of the same things, and by the same things, but it is in the same things that we shall find them activated too. This in fact holds in the other, more obvious cases, as for example with bodily strength; for strength comes about from taking plenty of nourishment and withstanding repeated exertion, and the strong person would be most capable of doing these things. So it is with the excellences as well: from holding back from pleasures we become moderate, and also when we have become moderate we are most capable of holding back from them; and similarly, too, with courage—from being habituated to scorn frightening things and withstand them we become courageous people, and having become courageous we shall be best able to withstand frightening things.

(II. 3) The pleasure or pain that supervenes on what people do should be treated as a sign of their dispositions; for someone who holds back from bodily pleasure and does so cheerfully is a moderate person, while someone who is upset at doing so is self-indulgent, and someone who withstands frightening things and does so cheerfully, or anyway without distress, is a courageous person, while someone who is distressed at them is cowardly. For excellence of character has to do with pleasures and pains: it is because of pleasure that we do bad things, and because of pain that we hold back from doing fine things. This is why we must have been brought up in a certain way from childhood onwards, as Plato says, so as to delight in and be distressed by the things we should; this is what the correct education is. Again, if the excellences have to do with actions and affections, and every affection and every action is accompanied by pleasure and pain, this will be another reason for thinking that excellence has to do with pleasures and pains. A further proof is afforded by the practice of forcible correction, which takes place through pleasures and pains; for it is a kind of medical treatment, and it is in the nature of medical treatments to be effected through opposites. Further, as in fact we said just now, every disposition of the soul by nature relates to and has to do with the sorts of things that make the soul worse and better; and it is through pleasures and pains that people become bad, i.e. by pursuing them and running away from them, either the ones they shouldn't, or when they shouldn't, or in a way they shouldn't, or however many other distinctions are made in one's prescriptions. This is also why people define the excellences as kinds of impassivity and immobility; but they go wrong because they say what they say without specifying—they don't add 'as one should', 'as one shouldn't', 'when one should', and all the other specifications. It is, then, a

1104a25

1104a30

1104a35
1104b1

1104b5

1104b10

1104b15

1104b20

1104b25

basic assumption that this kind of excellence is a disposition to act in the best ways in relation to pleasures and pains, while badness is the opposite. That excellence and badness have to do with the same things will also become clear to us from the following considerations. The things pertinent to choice being three, and those pertinent to avoidance also three, i.e. what is fine, what is advantageous, and what is pleasant, and their opposites, the excellent person tends to get things right in relation to all of them, while the bad person tends to get things wrong, and especially in relation to pleasure; for pleasure both is something shared with the animals, and accompanies all the things falling under the heading of choice (since in fact what is fine and advantageous seems pleasant). Again, pleasure is something we have all grown up with since infancy; the result is that it is hard to rub us clean of this impulse, dyed as it is into our lives. And we measure our actions too, some of us more, some less, by pleasure and pain. Because of this, then, our whole concern is necessarily with these; for it makes no small difference with regard to action whether someone feels pleasure and pain in a good way or a bad way. Again, it is harder to fight against pleasure than to 'fight temper' (as Heraclitus says), and it is always in relation to what is harder that we find both technical expertise and excellence; for it is also a better thing to do something well if it is difficult. So that for this reason too the whole concern both for excellence and for political expertise is with pleasures and pains; for someone who behaves well in relation to pleasure and pain will be a person of excellence, while someone who behaves badly in relation to them will be bad. So much, then, for these subjects—that excellence has to do with pleasures and pains, that the things from which it comes about are also the ones by which it is both increased and—if they come about in a different way—destroyed, and that the things from which it has come about are also the things in relation to which it is activated.

(II. 4) But someone may raise a problem about how we can say that, to become just, people need to do what is just, and to do what is moderate in order to become moderate; for if they are doing what is just and moderate, they are already just and moderate, in the same way in which, if people are behaving literately and musically, they are already expert at reading and writing and in music. Or does this fail to hold, in fact, even for skills? One can do something literate both by chance and at someone else's prompting. One will only count as literate, then, if one both does something literate and does it in the way a literate person does it; and this is a matter of doing it in accordance with one's own expert knowledge of letters. Again, neither do the case of the skills and that of the excellences resemble each other: the things that come about through the agency of skills contain in themselves the mark of their being done well, so that it is enough if they turn out in a certain way, whereas the things that come about in accordance with the excellences count as done

1104b30

1104b35
1105a1

1105a5

1105a10

1105a15

1105a20

1105a25

justly or moderately not merely because they themselves are of a certain kind,   1105a30
but also because of facts about the agent doing them—first, if he does them
knowingly, secondly if he decides to do them, and decides to do them for
themselves, and thirdly if he does them from a firm and unchanging disposition. When it is a matter of having skills, these conditions are not rele-   1105b1
vant, except for knowledge itself; but when it comes to having the excellences,
knowledge makes no difference, or a small one, whereas the force of the other
conditions is not small but counts for everything, and it is these that result   1105b5
from the repeated performance of just and moderate actions. So things done
are called just and moderate whenever they are such that the just person or
the moderate person would do them; whereas a person is not just and moderate because he does these things, but also because[6] he does them in the way in
which just and moderate people do them. So it is appropriate to say that the
just person comes about from doing what is just, and the moderate person   1105b10
from doing what is moderate; whereas from not doing these things no one
will have excellence in the future either. But most people fail to do these
things, and by taking refuge in talk they think that they are philosophizing,
and that they will become excellent this way, so behaving rather like sick   1105b15
people, when they listen carefully to their doctors but then fail to do anything
of what is prescribed for them. Well, just as the latter, for their part, won't be
in good bodily condition if they look after themselves like that, neither will
the former have their souls in good condition if they philosophize like that.

(II. 5) After these questions, we must consider what excellence is. Now since
the things that occur in the soul fall into three kinds, i.e. affections, capacities,   1105b20
and dispositions, excellence will be one of these. By affections I mean appetite, anger, fear, boldness, grudging ill will, joy, friendly feeling, hatred,
longing, envy, pity—generally, feelings attended by pleasure or pain; while
capacities are what people are referring to when they say we are susceptible to
the affections, as for example with those capacities in terms of which we are
said to be capable of becoming angry, or distressed, or of feeling pity; as for   1105b25
dispositions, it is in terms of these that we are well or badly disposed in
relation to the affections, as for example in relation to becoming angry, if we
are violently or sluggishly disposed, we are badly disposed, and if in an intermediate way, we are well disposed—and similarly too in relation to the other
things in question. Well then, neither the excellences nor the corresponding
bad states are affections, because we are not called excellent or bad people on   1105b30
account of affections, whereas we are so called on account of excellences and
bad states; and because we are neither praised nor censured on account of
affections (for the frightened person isn't praised, nor is the angry person, nor
is the person who is simply angry censured, but the person who is angry in a   1106a1

---

[6] Retaining ὁ (1105b8).

certain way), whereas we are praised or censured on account of excellences and bad states. Again, we are angry and afraid without decision, whereas the excellences are kinds of decision, or anyway involve decision. In addition to these considerations, when it comes to the affections we are said to be moved, whereas with the excellences and the bad states we are said, not to be moved, but to be in a certain condition. For these reasons they are not capacities either; for neither are we called excellent by virtue of being capable of being affected, simply, nor are we called bad, nor are we praised, nor censured. Again, we are by nature capable of being affected, whereas we do not become excellent or bad by nature—but we talked about this earlier. If, then, the excellences are neither affections nor capacities, the only thing left for them to be is dispositions. We have said, then, what the genus of excellence is.

(II. 6) But we must not restrict ourselves to saying that it is a disposition; we must also say what sort of disposition it is. Well, one should say that every excellence, whatever it is an excellence of, both gives that thing the finish of a good condition and makes it perform its function well, as for example the eye's excellence makes both it and its functioning excellent; for it is through the excellence of the eye that we see well. Similarly the excellence of a horse both makes it an excellent horse and good at running, carrying its rider and facing the enemy. If, then, this is so in all cases, the excellence of a human being too will be the disposition whereby he becomes a good human being and from which he will perform his own function well. In what way this will be, we have already said, but it will also be clear in this way, too, i.e. if we consider what sort of nature excellence has. Now with everything continuous and divisible it is possible to take a greater and a lesser and an equal amount, and these either with reference to the object itself or relative to us. The 'equal' is a kind of intermediate between what exceeds and what falls short; by intermediate 'with reference to the object' I mean what is equidistant from each of its two extremes, which is one and the same for all, whereas by intermediate 'relative to us' I mean the sort of thing that neither goes to excess nor is deficient—and this is not one thing, nor is it the same for all. So for example if ten count as many and two as few, six is what people take as intermediate, with reference to the object, since it exceeds and is exceeded by the same amount; and this is intermediate in terms of arithmetical proportion. But the intermediate relative to us should not be taken in this way; for if ten minae in weight is a large amount for a particular person to eat and two a small amount, the trainer will not prescribe six minae, because perhaps this too is large for the person who will be taking it, or small—small for Milo, large for the person just beginning his training. Similarly with running and wrestling. It is in this way, then, that every expert tries to avoid excess and deficiency, and looks instead for the intermediate, and chooses this; the intermediate, that is, not in the object, but relative to us. If, then, it is in this way

that every kind of expert knowledge completes its function well, by looking
to the intermediate and guiding what it produces by reference to this (which is
why people are used to saying about products of good quality that nothing   1106b10
can either be taken away from them or added to them, because they suppose
that excess and deficiency destroy good quality, while intermediacy preserves
it—and skilled experts, as we say, work by looking to this), and if excellence is
more precise and better than any expertise, just as nature is, it will be effective   1106b15
at hitting upon what is intermediate. I mean excellence of character; for this
has to do with affections and actions, and it is in these that there is excess and
deficiency, and the intermediate. So for example it is possible on occasion to
be affected by fear, boldness, appetite, anger, pity, and pleasure and distress   1106b20
in general both too much and too little, and neither is good; but to be affected
when one should, at the things one should, in relation to the people one
should, for the reasons one should, and in the way one should, is both intermediate and best, which is what belongs to excellence. In the same way with
actions, too, there is excess, deficiency, and the intermediate. Excellence has to
do with affections and actions, things in which excess and deficiency go   1106b25
astray, while what is intermediate is praised and gets it right—features, both,
of excellence. Excellence, then, is a kind of intermediacy, in so far as it is
effective at hitting upon what is intermediate. Again, there are many ways of
going astray (for the bad belongs to what is unlimited—as the Pythagoreans   1106b30
used to say by analogy—the good to what is limited), whereas there is only
one way of getting it right (which is exactly why the one is easy and the other
difficult—missing the mark is easy, but hitting it is difficult); for these reasons
too, then, excess and deficiency belong to badness, whereas intermediacy
belongs to excellence—

   for single and straight is the road of the good; the bad go bad every which way.   1106b35

Excellence, then, is a disposition issuing in decisions, depending on intermediacy of the kind relative to us, this being determined by rational prescrip-   1107a1
tion and in the way in which[7] the wise person would determine it. And it is
intermediacy between two bad states, one involving excess, the other involving deficiency; and also because one set of bad states is deficient, the other
excessive in relation to what is required both in affections and in actions,   1107a5
whereas excellence both finds and chooses the intermediate. Hence excellence, in terms of its essence, and the definition that states what it is for
excellence to be, is intermediacy, but in terms of what is best, and good
practice, it is extremity. But not every action admits of intermediacy, nor
does every affection; for in some cases they have been named in such a way
that they are combined with badness from the start, as e.g. with malice,   1107a10
shamelessness, grudging ill will, and in the case of actions, fornication, theft,

---

   [7] Reading καὶ ὡς ἂν (1107a1).

murder; for all these, and others like them, owe their names to the fact that they themselves—not excessive versions of them, or deficient ones—are bad. It is not possible, then, ever to get it right with affections and actions like 1107a15 these, but only to go astray; nor does good practice or the lack of it in relation to such things consist in (e.g.) fornicating with the woman one should, when one should, and how—rather, simply doing any one of these things is going astray. So it is like expecting there to be intermediacy and excess and deficiency also in relation to unjust, cowardly, and self-indulgent behaviour; 1107a20 for that way there will be intermediate excess and deficiency, excessive excess, and deficient deficiency. But just as in moderation and courage there is no excess and deficiency, because the intermediate is in a way an extreme, so neither can there be intermediacy in those other cases, or excess and 1107a25 deficiency—one goes astray however one does them; for, in short, neither is there intermediacy in excess and deficiency, nor excess and deficiency in intermediacy.

(II. 7) But we should not simply state this in general terms; we should also show how it fits the particular cases. For with discussions that relate to 1107a30 actions, those of a general sort have a wider application, but those that deal with the subject bit by bit are closer to the truth; for actions have to do with particulars, and the requirement is that we should be in accord on these. So we should take these cases, from the chart. Thus with regard to feelings of 1107b1 fear and boldness, courage is the intermediate state; while of those people who go to excess, the one who is excessively fearless has no name (many cases are nameless), the one who is excessively bold is rash, and the one who is excessively fearful and deficiently bold is cowardly. With regard to pleas- 1107b5 ures and pains—not all of them, and still less with regard to all pains—the intermediate state is moderation, the excessive state self-indulgence. As for people deficient with regard to pleasures, they hardly occur; which is why people like this, too, have even failed to acquire a name. But let us put them down as 'insensate'. With regard to the giving and receiving of money the 1107b10 intermediate state is open-handedness, while the excessive and deficient states are wastefulness and avariciousness. But in these states excess and deficiency work in opposite ways: the wasteful person is excessive in handing money out and deficient in taking it, while the avaricious person is excessive in taking it and deficient when it comes to giving it out. (For the moment we are talking 1107b15 in outline, and giving the main points, contenting ourselves with just that; later we shall give more precise descriptions.) With regard to money there are also other states: an intermediate state, munificence (for the munificent person differs from the open-handed one: the former deals in large amounts, the latter with small), while the excessive disposition is tastelessness and vulgarity, 1107b20 the deficient one shabbiness; these differ from the excessive and deficient states relating to open-handedness, but what the differences are we shall say later. With regard to honour and dishonour the intermediate state is greatness of soul, while the excessive state is called a kind of conceitedness, the deficient one littleness of soul. And just as we said open-handedness was related to munificence, differing from it in having to do with small amounts, so there is a state with the same kind of relationship to greatness of soul, that being concerned with honour on the large scale while this other is concerned with it on a small scale; for it is possible to desire honour both more than one should and less than one should. The person who is excessive in his desires in this case is said to be honour-loving, while the one who is correspondingly deficient is said to be indifferent to honour; and the intermediate person lacks a name. (The states themselves, too, are nameless, except that the name given to that of the honour-lover is love of honour.) Consequently those at the extremes lay claim to the ground between them; and even we ourselves sometimes call the intermediate person 'honour-loving', sometimes 'indifferent to honour', sometimes using the first as a term of praise, sometimes the second. We shall talk about the reason for our doing this in what follows; for now, let us talk about the remaining states, on the pattern we have adopted with the previous ones. With regard to anger, too, there are excessive, deficient, and intermediate states, but since they are practically nameless, let us—since we say that the intermediate person is mild-tempered—call the intermediate state 'mildness'; and of those at the extremes, let the one who goes to excess be 'irascible', and the corresponding state 'irascibility', with the deficient one being in a way 'spiritless', and the deficiency 'spiritlessness'. There are also three other intermediate states, ones which have a certain similarity to one other, but which at the same time differ from one another; for while all have to do with the sharing by people in conversation and in actions, they differ in so far as one of them has to do with truth in these contexts, whereas the others have to do with what is pleasant; and of this, part is found in play, part in all aspects of life. So we must talk about these states too, in order to gain a broader perspective on the fact that in everything intermediacy is an object for praise, whereas the extremes are neither to be praised, nor correct, but to be censured. Well, more of these too lack a name than have one, but we must try—just as we did in the other cases—to create names for them ourselves, to make things clear and easy to follow. With regard to truth in social contexts, let the intermediate individual be said to be in a sense 'truthful', and the intermediate state 'truthfulness', while the sort of pretending about oneself that tends to overstatement will be 'imposture', the person having the state being an 'impostor', and the sort that tends to understatement will be 'self-deprecation', the corresponding person being 'self-deprecating'. With regard to the part of the pleasant that lies in play, let the intermediate person be 'witty' and the state 'wittiness'; the excessive state, for its part, will be 'buffoonery' and the person having it a 'buffoon', the deficient person perhaps a 'boor' and the disposition 'boorishness'. With regard to the remaining part of the pleasant, i.e. the part

1107b25

1107b30

1108a1

1108a5

1108a10

1108a15

1108a20

1108a25

to be found in any part of life, if someone is pleasant in the way one should be, let us call him 'friendly', and the intermediate state correspondingly; if without ulterior motive, someone with the excessive state will be 'obsequious', but if it is for his own benefit, he will be 'ingratiating'; while someone

1108a30 with the deficient state, someone who is always unpleasant, will be a 'contentious' and 'morose' sort of person. There are also intermediates in the affective feelings and in relation to things that happen to people; for (e.g.) a sense of shame is not an excellence, but people are praised for having a sense of shame too. For in fact in these contexts one person is said to be intermediate, while another is said to be excessive, as with the nervous sort who feels shame at

1108a35 everything; the person who is deficient in shame or does not feel it at all is called shameless, and the intermediate person is said to have a sense of shame.

1108b1 Righteous indignation is intermediate between grudging ill will and malice, all of these having to do with pain and pleasure at things that happen to one's neighbours: the person who tends towards righteous indignation is distressed at those who do well undeservedly, while the grudging person exceeds him,

1108b5 being distressed at anyone's doing well, and the malicious person is so deficient when it comes to being distressed that he is even pleased. But there will be an opportunity to discuss these questions later; and as for justice, since the term is not used merely in one sense, we shall (after these other subjects) make a division and talk about how justice in each of the two senses is an

1108b10 intermediate. And likewise with the excellences of reason too.

(II. 8) There being, then, three kinds of dispositions, two of them bad states, i.e. the one relating to excess and the one relating to deficiency, and one excellence, the intermediate state, all three are in one way or another opposed to all; for the states at the extremes are contrary both to the intermediate state

1108b15 and to each other, and the intermediate to the ones at the extremes; for just as what is equal is larger when compared with the smaller and smaller when compared with the larger, so the intermediate dispositions are excessive when compared with the deficient ones and deficient when compared with the excessive ones, in the spheres both of affections and of actions. For the

1108b20 courageous appear rash in comparison with cowards, but cowardly in comparison with the rash; similarly the moderate, too, appear self-indulgent in comparison with the 'insensate', but 'insensate' in comparison with the self-indulgent, and the open-handed appear wasteful in comparison with the avaricious, but avaricious in comparison with the wasteful. This is why those at either extreme try to distance themselves from the one between

1108b25 them, associating him with the other extreme: the courageous person is called rash by the coward, cowardly by the rash person, and analogously in the other cases. This being the way these things are opposed to each other, there is most contrariety between those at the extremes—more than between them and the intermediate; for they stand further away from each other than they do from the intermediate, just as the large stands further away from the small and the small from the large than either of them from the equal. Again, in some cases what is at the extremes has a certain similarity to the intermediate, as rashness has to courage and wastefulness to open-handedness; whereas there is most dissimilarity between the extremes in relation to each other, and things that are furthest away from each other are defined as contraries, so that things that are further apart will also be more contrary to each other. What is more opposed to the intermediate is in some cases the deficient state, in others the excessive, as in the case of courage it is not rashness, an excessive state, but a deficient one, cowardliness, whereas with moderation it is not 'insensateness', a state involving lack, but self-indulgence, an excessive state. This comes about for two reasons, the first being the one deriving from the thing itself; for by virtue of the fact that one of the extremes is closer to and more like the intermediate, we do not oppose that to the mean so much as its opposite. So for example because rashness seems to be something more like and closer to courage, and cowardliness more unlike it, it is the latter that we oppose more to courage—because things that are further removed from the intermediate seem to be more contrary to it. This, then, is one reason, deriving from the thing itself; but the second derives from our own selves, namely that the things towards which we ourselves have a certain natural inclination appear more contrary to the intermediate—as for example we are ourselves naturally more inclined towards pleasures, which is why we are more easily drawn in the direction of self-indulgence than of orderliness. So it is these things, the things to which we are more prone, that we call more contrary; and for this reason it is self-indulgence, the excessive state, that is more opposed to moderation.

(II. 9) This, then, will suffice on the themes we have been treating: that excellence of character is an intermediate state; in what way it is intermediate; that it is intermediate between two bad states, one relating to excess and the other to deficiency; and that it is such because it is effective at hitting upon the intermediate in affections and in actions. This is why being excellent is also something difficult to achieve. For in any context getting hold of the intermediate is difficult—as for example finding the centre of a circle is not a task for anyone, but for the skilled person; so too, whereas getting angry, or giving money away, or spending it are things anyone can do, and easy, doing them to the person one should, to the extent one should, when one should, for the reason one should, and in the manner one should—this is no longer for anyone, nor is it something easy, which explains why getting things right is a rare thing, a proper object of praise, and something fine. Hence the person who is aiming at the intermediate should first move away from the more opposed extreme, following Calypso's advice:

That spray and surging breaker there—keep your ship well clear of that.

1108b30

1108b35

1109a1

1109a5

1109a10

1109a15

1109a20

1109a25

1109a30

For to arrive at one of the two extremes is more erroneous, to arrive at the other less; so, since it is hard to hit upon the intermediate with extreme accuracy, one should take to the oars and sail that way, as they say, grasping what is least bad of what is available, and this will be most easily done in the way we say. And we should consider the things that we ourselves, too, are more readily drawn towards, for different people have different natural inclinations; and this is something we shall be able to recognize from the pleasure and the pain that things bring about in us. We should drag ourselves away in the contrary direction; for by pulling far away from error we shall arrive at the intermediate point, in the way people do when they are straightening out warped pieces of wood. In everything we must guard most against the pleasant, and pleasure itself, because we are not impartial judges in its case. We ourselves should feel towards pleasure as the elders of the people felt towards Helen, and repeat on every occasion what they uttered; by proposing to send pleasure packing like this we shall get things less wrong. In short, by doing these things we shall be best able to hit upon the intermediate. But to do this is difficult, perhaps, and most of all in particular cases; for it is not easy to determine not only how, but with whom, in what sorts of circumstances, and for how long one should be angry, since we ourselves sometimes praise those deficient in anger and call them 'mild', while at other times we praise those who get angry and call them 'manly'. But it is not the person who deviates a little from the right path who is censured, whether he does so in the direction of excess or of deficiency; rather it is the person who deviates significantly, for there is no missing *him*. But as to how far and to what extent one has to deviate to be worthy of censure, it is not easy to fix it in words, any more than anything else that belongs to the sphere of perception; for such things depend on the particular circumstances, and the judgement of them lies in our perception. This much, then, shows that the intermediate disposition is to be praised in all circumstances, but that one should sometimes incline towards excess, sometimes towards deficiency; for in this way we shall most easily hit upon what is intermediate, and good practice.

BOOK III

1109b30   (III. 1) Since, then, excellence has to do with affections and actions, and in response to what people do that is voluntary we praise and censure them, whereas in response to what is counter-voluntary we feel sympathy for them, and sometimes even pity, those inquiring into the subject of excellence must presumably determine the boundaries of the voluntary and the counter-voluntary; and to do so is also useful for those framing laws, when it comes to fixing honours and methods of forcible correction. The counter-voluntary, then, seems to be what comes about by force or because of ignorance; and what comes about by force seems to be that of which the origin is external, i.e. such that the person acting, or the person having something done to him, contributes nothing, as for example if a wind were to carry him somewhere, or human agents who had him in their power. As for what is done because of fear of greater evils, or because something fine is at stake (suppose, for example, that a tyrant gave one orders to do something shameful, when he had one's parents and children in his power, and they would be kept alive if one did as ordered, but put to death if not)—such cases make one doubt whether they are voluntary or counter-voluntary. Something of this sort also arises when it comes to throwing things overboard in a storm: no one throws goods away voluntarily, if it is just a matter of throwing it away, whereas if it is a condition of saving oneself and the rest of what is on board, any sensible person would do it. Such actions, then, are mixed, but they look as if they belong more to the class of the voluntary, for the actions in question are desired at the time of acting, and the end for which actions are done varies with the occasion; so we must assign both 'voluntary' and 'counter-voluntary', too, with reference to the time when one acts. And a person acts voluntarily in the cases in question; for in fact in actions of this sort the origin of his moving the instrumental parts is in himself, and if the origin of something is in himself, it depends on himself whether he does that thing or not. Doing such things, then, is voluntary, but just in themselves they are presumably counter-voluntary; for no one would choose anything of this sort for itself. And for actions of this sort, people are sometimes even praised, i.e. whenever they put up with something shameful or painful in exchange for great and fine consequences, while if they do it in exchange for what is neither great nor fine, we censure them; for putting up with the most shameful things as a condition of getting something not at all fine, or something only moderately so, is a vile person's behaviour. In some cases it is not praise we accord someone, but sympathy—cases where a person does the sorts of things one shouldn't do because of what is such as to over-extend the natural capacity of human beings—what no one could withstand. But perhaps in some cases there is no such thing as 'being constrained', but one should rather accept the most agonizing death: the things that 'constrained' Euripides' Alcmaeon to commit matricide are plainly ludicrous. But it is sometimes hard to make out what sort of thing to choose in exchange for what, and what to put up with in exchange for what—and harder still to abide by what one has determined, for mostly what we are expecting in such cases is something painful, and what we are being constrained to do is shameful, which is why there is praising and

1110a1

1110a5

1110a10

1110a15

1110a20

1110a25

1110a30

1110b1   censuring in the case of those who have or have not been constrained. What
kinds of things, then, should we say are forced? Or is it that things are
unqualifiedly forced if their cause lies in the externals, and the agent contributes nothing, whereas ones which, considered in themselves, are counter-
voluntary but desirable on this occasion and in exchange for these particular

1110b5   results, given that the origin is in the agent—these are counter-voluntary
considered in themselves, but on this occasion and in exchange for these
particular results, they are voluntary? And they look more like things that are
voluntary; for actions are located among particulars, and these are voluntary.
But as to what sorts of things one should choose in return for what, it is not
easy to supply an answer, for there are many differences among particular

1110b10   situations. If someone were to say that pleasant things and fine things force us,
on the grounds that they constrain us, and are external, he will get the result
that everything is forced; for these two things motivate everything everyone
does. And those who are forced, and act counter-voluntarily, are distressed at
what they do, whereas those who act because of what is pleasant and fine do
so with pleasure. It is ludicrous too to put the responsibility on external
objects, rather than on oneself for falling an easy victim to such things, and to

1110b15   put it on oneself for fine things, but on the objects that please for shameful
ones.
       What comes about by force, then, appears to be that of which the origin is
external, with the person forced contributing nothing. What comes about
because of ignorance, for its part, is all non-voluntary, whereas being counter-
voluntary belongs to what causes the agent pain and involves regret; for the

1110b20   person who has done whatever it is because of ignorance, if he feels nothing
by way of discomfort at his action, has not acted voluntarily, in so far as it was
something he didn't know he was doing, but he has not acted counter-
voluntarily either, in so far as he is not distressed at it. What comes about
because of ignorance, then, seems to fall into two types: someone who feels
regret seems to have acted counter-voluntarily, while the one who does not
feel regret—well, since he is distinct from the other person, let him be 'non-
voluntary'; for since he is different, it is better that he should have a name to

1110b25   himself. Acting *because of* ignorance also appears to be distinct from acting *in*
ignorance; for the person who acts while drunk or angry does not seem to act
because of ignorance but because of one of the things just mentioned,
though not knowing what he is doing, but in ignorance of it. Now it is true
that every worthless person is ignorant of what one should do and what one
should abstain from, and it is because of this sort of mistake that there come

1110b30   to be unjust people, and bad people in general; but 'counter-voluntary' is not
meant to cover the case where someone is ignorant of what is to his
advantage—for ignorance in decision-making is not a cause of something's
being counter-voluntary; rather, it is a cause of worthlessness, nor is ignorance at the level of the universal a cause of the counter-voluntary (people are

censured for *that* sort of ignorance), but rather ignorance at the level of particular things, which are where action is located and what action is about. For both pity and sympathy depend on particulars; it is the person who is in ignorance of one of these that acts counter-voluntarily. Perhaps, then, it is no bad thing to determine what these particular factors are, and how many they are. So: there is the matter of who is acting, what he is doing, in relation to what or affecting what, sometimes also with what (as for example with a tool), what the action is for (e.g. saving someone), and how it is done (e.g. gently or vigorously). Now no one, unless he were mad, could be ignorant of all of these things, and neither, clearly, could anyone be ignorant of the person acting; for how could that be, given that it is himself? But someone might be ignorant of what he is doing, as when people say 'it just came out', in conversation, or 'I didn't know the subject was prohibited', as Aeschylus said about the Mysteries, or 'I let it off when I meant to demonstrate it', as the man said who let off the catapult. And someone might also think her son to be one of the enemy, as Merope did, and that the spear had a button on the end of it when it did not, or that the stone was a pumice stone; and one might give someone a drink to save him but end up killing him, and mean to give someone a touch, as in sparring, but land a blow on him instead. Given, then, that ignorance is possible in relation to all these factors, in which action is located, it seems that the person who was ignorant of any one of these things has acted counter-voluntarily, and most of all if the ignorance is related to the things that most determine the nature of the action; and these are what things are affected and what the action is for. In the case, then, of what is said to be counter-voluntary on the basis of this sort of ignorance, the action must in addition cause distress to the agent and involve regret.

So, given that 'counter-voluntary' applies to what comes about by force and what comes about because of ignorance, the voluntary would seem to be that of which the origin is in oneself, when one knows the particular factors that constitute the location of action. For presumably it is not right to say that things done because of temper or appetite are counter-voluntary. For in the first place none of the other animals will act voluntarily, nor will children; and secondly, is nothing we do because of appetite and temper done voluntarily, or are the fine things done voluntarily and the shameful ones counter-voluntarily? Or is that ridiculous, given that one and the same thing is the cause in all cases? One would think it strange to assert that things we should desire are counter-voluntary; and one *should* be angry at certain things and have an appetite for certain things, like health and learning. The counter-voluntary also seems to be distressful, whereas what falls under appetite seems to be pleasant. Again, what difference is there, in respect of counter-voluntariness, between things we get wrong through acting in accordance with rational calculation, and those we get wrong through temper? For both are to be avoided, but the non-rational affections seem to be no less typical of

1111a1

1111a5

1111a10

1111a15

1111a20

1111a25

1111a30

1111b1

human nature, so that actions deriving from temper and appetite will belong to human beings too. Strange, then, to count these things as counter-voluntary.

(III. 2) Now that the voluntary and the counter-voluntary have been defined, the next task is to discuss decision; for decision seems to be something highly germane to excellence, and to indicate the differences between people's characters more than actions do. Decision, then, is clearly something voluntary, but is not the same thing as the voluntary, for the voluntary is a wider type: the voluntary is shared in by both children and the other animals, whereas decision is not, and things done on the spur of the moment we say are voluntary, but not done from decision. Those who say that it is appetite, temper, or wish, or a sort of judgement seem not to be correct. For decision is not something shared by non-rational creatures, whereas appetite and temper are. And the person without self-control acts from appetite, but not from decision; conversely the self-controlled person acts from decision, but not from appetite. Next, appetite goes contrary to decision, whereas appetite does not go contrary to appetite. Again, we have appetite for what is pleasant and what brings pain, whereas decision is neither for what is painful nor for what is pleasant. Still less is decision temper; for things we do because of temper seem least to be from decision. And yet neither, for that matter, is it wish, although it appears quite closely related to it; for there is no decision for impossible things, and if someone were to *say* he was deciding on one of these, he would be taken for an idiot—whereas there is wish for the impossible[8] as e.g. for immortality. And there is wish also in relation to the sorts of things that could in no way be brought about by one's own agency, as for example that a particular actor or athlete should win; whereas no one decides on things of this sort, only on those one thinks *could* come about by one's own agency. Further, wish is more for the end, whereas decision is about what forwards the end, as e.g. we wish to be healthy, whereas we decide on the things through which we shall be healthy, and we wish to be happy, and say that we wish it, whereas it is out of keeping to say 'we decide to be happy'; for generally decision appears to be about things that depend on us. It will not, then, be judgement either; for judgement seems to be about anything, and no less about the eternal and the impossible than about the things that depend on us; and we divide judgements into false and true, not into bad and good, whereas decisions we divide more in the latter way. So perhaps no one even claims that decision is the same thing as judgement in general. But neither should it be identified with a certain kind of judgement; for what makes us people of a certain quality is deciding for, not making judgements about, good things or bad ones. And we form a decision to take or avoid some such thing, whereas we make a judgement about what it is, or to whom it is of

——————————

[8] Reading ἐστὶ τῶν ἀδυνάτων (1111b22).

advantage, or how; we certainly do not 'make a judgement' to take or avoid something. Again, decision is praised more by reference to its being for what it should be, or to its being correctly made, whereas judgement is praised by reference to how true it is. Again, decision is for what we most know to be good, whereas we make judgements about what we do not know at all to be good; and it seems that those who make the best decisions and those who make the best judgements are not the same people—but rather that some people make better judgements, but because they are bad choose things other than those they should. If there is judgement preceding the decision, or following it, this makes no difference; for we are not considering that point, but rather whether decision is the same thing as a certain kind of judgement. What then, or what sort of thing, is it, since it is none of the things we have mentioned? Well, it is clearly something voluntary, but the voluntary is not all a matter of decision. So is it, at any rate, what has been reached by prior deliberation? In favour of this view is that decision is accompanied by reasoning and thought—and even the name indicates that what we decide to do is chosen before other things.

(III. 3) Do people deliberate about everything, and is everything an object of deliberation, or are there some things about which there is no deliberation? Presumably one should say 'object of deliberation' with reference not to what an idiot or a madman might deliberate about, but to what a sane person would. Well, no one deliberates about eternal things, as for example about the universe or about the fact that the diameter and side of a square are incommensurable. But for that matter neither does anyone deliberate about things which involve change, but which always occur in the same pattern, whether from necessity, or indeed by nature, or through some other cause (e.g. turnings and risings of celestial bodies); nor about things that happen sometimes one way, sometimes another, like droughts and rainstorms; nor about things that happen from chance, like discovering a cache of treasure. But there is no deliberation, either, about all human affairs, as for example no Spartan deliberates about how Scythians might best manage themselves politically—for none of these things will come about through our agency. What we do deliberate about are the things that depend on us and are doable; and these are in fact what is left once we have been through the rest. For the causes of things seem to be nature, and necessity, and chance, and then, in addition to these, intelligence and everything that occurs through human agency; and among human beings, each group deliberates about what is doable through their own agency. And in relation to those forms of knowledge that are precise and self-contained, there is no deliberation, as e.g. with writing (for we are not in two minds about how to write); but those things that come about through us, but not in the same way on every occasion—*these* are the things we deliberate about, as e.g. we do about things falling within the spheres of

1112a5

1112a10

1112a15

1112a20

1112a25

1112a30

1112b1

1112b5 medicine and business, and in relation to navigational expertise more than to that of athletic training, to the degree that the former has been less precisely worked out, and again deliberation is involved similarly in the remaining cases, but more, too, in relation to productive than to other forms of knowledge, for we are more in two minds about the productive forms. Deliberation, then, occurs where things happen in a certain way for the most part, but where it is unclear how they will in fact fall out; and where the outcome is

1112b10 indeterminate. For large projects, we get people to provide us with advice, because we do not believe we have the capacity ourselves to see our way through. But we deliberate, not about ends, but about what forwards those ends. For a doctor does not deliberate about whether he'll make his patients healthy, nor a public speaker about whether he'll persuade his audience, nor a political expert about whether he'll bring about good government—and nei-

1112b15 ther do any of the others deliberate about the end, but rather they take the end for granted and examine how and by what means it will come about; and if it appears as coming about by more than one means, they look to see through which of them it will happen most easily and best, whereas if it is brought to completion by one means only, they look to see how it will come about through this, and through what means *that* will come about, until they

1112b20 arrive at the first cause, which comes last in the process of discovery. For the person who deliberates seems to investigate and to analyse in the way we have said, as if with a diagram (and while not all investigation appears to be deliberation, as e.g. mathematical investigations are not, all deliberation is investigation); and what is last in the analysis seems to be first in the process of

1112b25 things' coming about. And if people encounter an impossibility, they desist, as e.g. if money is needed, and there is no possibility of providing it; while if it appears possible, they set about acting. Things are possible that might come about through our agency; for what comes about through our friends in a way comes about through us, since the origin of it is in us. What is sought is sometimes the tools for what is to be done, sometimes how they are to be

1112b30 used; and similarly in the other cases too, what is sought is sometimes the thing to do the job with, sometimes how it is to be done or by what means. It seems, then, as has been said, that a human being is the origin of his actions; and that his deliberation is about those things that are doable by him, while his actions are for the sake of other things—for it will not be the end that is deliberated about but the things that forward ends. So there will not be

1113a1 deliberation about particulars either, as e.g. about whether this is a loaf, or whether it has been cooked as it should; for these belong to the sphere of perception. And if a person deliberates at every point, he will go on for ever. What we deliberate about and what we decide on are the same, except that what is decided on is, as such, something definite; for it is what has been

1113a5 selected as a result of deliberation that is 'decided on'. For each person ceases to investigate how he will act, at whatever moment he brings the origin of the

128

action back to himself, and to the leading part of himself; for this is the part that decides. This is clear also from those ancient forms of government that Homer used to represent in his poems: the kings would announce to the people what they had decided. Given that what is decided on is an object of 1113a10 deliberation and desire among the things that depend on us, decision too will be deliberational desire for things that depend on us; for it is through having selected on the basis of having deliberated that we desire in accordance with our deliberation. Let this, then, stand as our outline treatment of decision— both of what sorts of things it has to do with, and of the fact that what we decide about are the things that forward our ends.

(III. 4) That wish is for the end, we have already said; but to some it seems to 1113a15 be for the good, whereas to others it seems to be for the *apparent* good. The consequence, for those who say that the object of[9] wish is the good, is that what the person making an incorrect choice wishes for is not wished for (for if it is wished for, it will also be good; but in fact it may have been bad); while for 1113a20 those who say that the apparent good is wished for, the consequence is that there is nothing naturally wished for, only what seems an object of wish to each particular person; and different things appear so to different people, perhaps even contrary ones. But if, then, we are not content with these views, should we say that the good is without qualification and in truth the object of wish, whereas what appears good to a given person is the object of wish for that person? We shall then be saying that for the person of excellence the 1113a25 object of wish is the one that is truly so, whereas for the bad person it is as chance will have it, just as on the physical level too the things that are truly healthful are healthful for people in good condition, whereas a different set of things is healthful for those that are diseased; and similarly too with bitter, sweet, hot, heavy, and every other sort of thing; for the good person dis- 1113a30 criminates correctly in every set of circumstances, and in every set of circum- stances what is true is apparent to him. For each disposition has its own corresponding range of fine things and pleasant things, and presumably what most distinguishes the good person is his ability to see what is true in every set of circumstances, being like a carpenter's rule or measure for them. But most people are deceived, and the deception seems to come about because of pleasure; for it appears a good thing when it is not. So they choose what is 1113b1 pleasant as something good, and they avoid pain as something bad.

(III. 5) Given, then, that what is wished for is the end, while what we deliber- ate about and decide on are the things that forward the end, the actions relating to the latter will be based on decision and voluntary. But the activities 1113b5 that constitute the excellences are concerned with these. Excellence too, then,

---

[9] Retaining τὸ (1113a17).

depends on us, and similarly badness as well. For when acting depends on us, not acting does so too, and when saying no does so, saying yes does too; so that if acting, when it is a fine thing to act, depends on us, not acting also

1113b10 depends on us when it is shameful not to act, and if not acting, when it is a fine thing not to act, depends on us, acting when it is a shameful thing to act also depends on us. But if it depends on us to do fine things and shameful things, and similarly not to do them too, and this, it is agreed, is what it is to be, respectively, a good person and a bad one, then being decent people, and

1113b15 being worthless ones, will depend on us.[10] To say that no one is vicious voluntarily, or counter-voluntarily blessed with happiness, looks false in one way, true in another; for no one is blessed counter-voluntarily, but badness is something voluntary. Or should one dispute what has just been said—should one say that a human being is *not* an origin, or begetter, of his actions as he is of

1113b20 children? But if he obviously is, and we are unable to trace actions back to origins beyond their origins in us, then, in so far as they are things that have their origins in us, they themselves, too, depend on us and are voluntary. Testimony to this effect seems to be provided by the practice both of different sorts of private groups and of lawgivers themselves; for they forcibly correct and impose penalties on wrongdoers, provided they did not act under force,

1113b25 or because of ignorance for which they are not themselves responsible, while they honour those who perform fine actions, in order to encourage the latter and put a stop to the former. By contrast no one encourages us to do the things that neither depend on us nor are voluntary, on the assumption that nothing is gained by getting someone *persuaded* not to become hot, or feel

1113b30 pain, or hunger, or anything of this sort; we shall be affected just the same. In fact ignorance itself constitutes grounds for penal correction, if the agent seems to be responsible for his ignorance—as when penalties are doubled for people acting while drunk; for the origin is in the agent; it was in his power not to get drunk, which was cause of his ignorance. And they correct people who are ignorant of something laid down in the laws—one of the things one

1114a1 *should* know, which are not difficult either; and similarly too in the other cases where people seem to be ignorant through carelessness, on the grounds that it depended on them not to be ignorant; for it was in their power to take the appropriate care. But perhaps the agent is the kind of person not to take care?

1114a5 But we are ourselves responsible for having become this sort of person, by living slackly, and for being unjust or self-indulgent, in the first case by treating people badly, in the second by passing our time in drinking and that sort of thing; for it is the sort of activity we display in each kind of thing that gives us the corresponding character. This is clear from those who practise for any sort of competition or performance: they go on and on actually *doing* whatever it is. So only a thoroughly stupid person could fail to know that the dispositions

---

[10] Reading ἐφ' ἡμῖν ἔσται τὸ . . . (1113b13–14).

come about as a result of the sort of activity we display in relation to each   1114a10
kind of thing. But again it runs counter to reason to suppose that the person
engaged in unjust action does not wish to be unjust, or that the person
engaged in self-indulgent action does not wish to be self-indulgent. But if
someone does, not in ignorance, the things that will result in his being unjust,
he will be unjust voluntarily—and yet he will not stop being unjust, and be
just, merely if he wishes it. For no more will the sick person be healthy merely   1114a15
for wishing it; and it may be that he is ill voluntarily, by living a life in weak-
willed disobedience to his doctors. Previously, then, he had the option not to
be ill, but once he has let himself go, he no longer has it, any more than it is
possible for him to retrieve a stone after it has left his hand; but all the same it
depended on him that it was thrown, for the origin of it was in him. So too at
the beginning the unjust person and the self-indulgent one had the option not   1114a20
to become like that, and hence they are voluntarily unjust and self-indulgent;
but once they have become like that, it is no longer possible for them not to
be. Not only are bad states of the soul voluntary, but with some people those
of the body are so too, and these people too we blame; for while no one
blames those who are naturally ugly, we *do* blame those who are ugly through
lack of training and through neglect. Similarly with physical weakness, and   1114a25
disability; for no one would find fault with someone born blind, or blind as a
result of disease or a blow—one would rather pity him; whereas everyone
would blame someone whose blindness resulted from drunkenness or some
other form of self-indulgence. As for bad physical states, then, for those that
depend on us people find fault with us, whereas for those that do not depend
on us they do not. But if this is so, in the other cases too the bad states that   1114a30
people get blamed for will be ones that depend on us. Suppose someone said
that while every one of us aims at what appears to us good, we are not in
control of the appearance, but rather the sort of person each of us is, what-   1114b1
ever that may be, determines how the end, too, appears to him. Well, if each
of us is himself somehow responsible for causing his disposition in himself, he
will also be somehow responsible for the appearance in question. If he is *not*
somehow responsible for his disposition, no one is responsible for its being the
case that he himself does bad things; he does these things because of ignorance of the end, thinking that by means of them he will get what is best. In   1114b5
this case aiming at the end will not be self-chosen, but one must be born with
the capacity for a kind of sight by which to discriminate well and choose what
is truly good, and the person who has this capacity by nature will be the one
who counts as 'naturally well endowed'; for it is the greatest and finest of
things, and something it will not be possible to get from anyone else, or to   1114b10
learn from anyone—rather, one will have it in just the form in which it was
born in one, and to have been born well and beautifully endowed in this
respect will be to be naturally well endowed in the full and true sense. If, then,
all this is true, how will excellence be any more voluntary than badness? For

whether the end appears to us by nature, or however its appearance is to be explained, it appears and is fixed in the same way for both, i.e. the good person and the bad one, and since they act by referring everything else to the end, the same explanation—whatever it is—will apply to their action. Whether, then, it is not by nature that the end appears to each person in whatever form it does, but this is also to an extent under his control, or whether the end is natural, but because the good person acts voluntarily in all other respects, his excellence is voluntary—in either case badness too will be no less voluntary; for 'through him' applies to the bad person too, in respect of his actions even if not of his end. If, then, as people say, the excellences are voluntary (for we ourselves are partly responsible, in a way, for our dispositions, and it is by virtue of being people of a certain sort that we suppose the end to be of a certain sort), bad states too will be voluntary; for they come about in a similar way.

So now we have discussed the excellences in a general way, giving an outline of their genus, i.e. that they are intermediates, and that they are dispositions; saying that the kinds of things by which they come about are the kinds they dispose us to do, i.e. in accordance with themselves; that they depend on us and are voluntary; and that they relate to actions that are such as the correct prescription lays down. (But actions and dispositions are not voluntary in the same sort of way; for we are in control of our actions from beginning to end, because we know the particulars involved, whereas we only control the beginning of our dispositions, and the process of incrementation is not something we are aware of in its particulars, any more than we are when we are becoming ill; but because it depended on us either to react to things in such-and-such a way, or not in that way—this makes them voluntary.) Now let us pick up our subject again and discuss each of the excellences individually, saying what they are, what things they relate to, and how; and it will be clear, too, at the same time, how many they are.

First, let us discuss courage.

(III. 6) Well, that it is an intermediate state relating to fearing and being bold has already become apparent; and clearly, what we fear are fearsome things, and these are, broadly speaking, bad things—which is why people define fear itself as expectation of what is bad. Now we fear all bad things, e.g. loss of reputation, poverty, disease, friendlessness, death; but courage seems not to be to do with all of them, since there are some things which we actually should fear, and fearing them is a fine thing, while not fearing them is shameful, e.g. loss of reputation, for someone who fears this is a decent person and has a sense of shame, whereas the one who does not fear it is shameless. But some do call the latter person courageous, in a transferred sense; for he has a certain resemblance to the courageous person, in so far as the courageous person too is in a sense fearless. On the other hand there is presumably no requirement

1114b15

1114b20

1114b25

1114b30

1115a1

1115a5

1115a10

1115a15

on one to fear poverty, or disease, or in general the sorts of things not due to
badness, or to one's own agency. But neither is the person who is fearless
about these things courageous, although we do call him, too, courageous,
picking out a resemblance; for some people who are cowardly in face of the
dangers of war are open-handed, and so altogether bold when it comes to
losing money. Nor, then, is a person cowardly if he fears assault on his children and wife, or fears grudging ill will, or anything like that; nor is he
courageous if he is bold when facing a whipping. So what sorts of fearsome
things is the courageous person courageous about? Or is it the greatest of
them? No one, after all, is better at withstanding what is frightening. And the
most fearsome thing is death; for it is an end, and there seems to be nothing
any longer for the dead person that is either good or bad. But neither would
courage seem to have to do with death under any set of circumstances: e.g.
death at sea, or from illness of some sort. Death under what circumstances,
then? Or is it under the finest? Such deaths are deaths in war; for then
the danger is greatest and finest. In agreement with these conclusions are the
honours accorded in cities, and where there are monarchs in power. In the
primary sense, then, the courageous person will be said to be the one who is
fearless about a fine death, or about sudden situations that threaten death; and
those that occur in war are mostly of this sort. Of course the courageous
person *is* fearless on the sea too, and when affected by disease, but not in the
way people familiar with the sea are: whereas others have given up hope of
survival and find this sort of death hard to stomach, these are optimistic
because of their experience. Again, the situations in which people really show
courage are those in which one can put up a fight, or, if that fails, the death is
a fine one; and neither feature obtains when one perishes in situations like the
ones just described.

(III. 7) What is fearsome is not the same for everyone; but there is a sort of
thing we say it is actually beyond human capacity to endure. This, then, *is*
fearsome to everyone—everyone, that is, who has any intelligence; but the
things that are within the capacity of human beings differ in magnitude, i.e. in
being more fearsome or less, and similarly too with the things that make for
boldness. But the courageous person is as unshakeable as a human being can
be. So he will be afraid of those sorts of things too, but he will withstand
them in the way one should, and following the correct prescription, for the
sake of achieving what is fine; for this is what excellence aims at. But one can
fear these things more and one can fear them less, and in addition one can fear
the sorts of things that are not fearsome as if they were. Of the ways people
go wrong in these cases, one occurs because they fear what one shouldn't,
another because they don't fear in the way one should, another because they
don't fear when one should, or something else of this sort; and similarly, too,
with the things that make for boldness. So the person who withstands and

fears the things one should and for the end one should, and in the way and when one should, and is bold in a similar way, is courageous; for the courage-
1115b20 ous person feels and acts as the occasion merits, and following the correct prescription, however it may direct him. But in every case, an activity's end is the one that accords with the corresponding disposition. This, then, holds for the courageous person too. Now, courage is something fine.[11] So the end, too, is such, since each thing is distinguished by its end. So it is for the sake of achieving the fine that the courageous person stands firm and acts in those ways that accord with courage. Of those who go to excess, the person who
1115b25 exceeds in fearlessness is nameless (we have said in our earlier discussions that many qualities are nameless), but he would be some sort of madman, or someone immune to pain, if he feared nothing, not even an earthquake or stormwaters—like Celts, as people say; whereas the person who goes to excess in being bold about what is fearsome is rash. The rash person seems
1115b30 also to be an impostor, and to be the sort of person who pretends to courage; at any rate he wishes to appear to be as the courageous person actually is in relation to the fearsome, and so mimics him in those situations in which he can. Hence most rash people in fact combine rashness with cowardice, for while they brazen it out in circumstances that allow it, they do not withstand what is actually fearsome. The person who goes to excess in fearing, on the
1115b35 other hand, is cowardly; for he fears the sorts of things one shouldn't and in a way one shouldn't, and every other feature of this sort goes along with his
1116a1 disposition. He is deficient, as well, in boldness, but the excess in the distress he experiences is the more obvious. The coward, then, is a kind of person who lacks hope, because he is afraid about everything. The brave man is in the contrary condition; for someone who keeps up hope has a bold attitude. So
1116a5 the cowardly person, the rash one, and the courageous one all have to do with the same things, but relate to them in different ways; for the first two display excess and deficiency, whereas the third is in an intermediate condition, and is as one should be. Again, rash people are impetuous, and for all their willing-ness in advance of the dangers they pull back when the dangers arrive; cour-ageous people by contrast are energetic when it comes to doing things but are
1116a10 quiet beforehand. As has been said, then, courage is an intermediate state relating to things that make for boldness and things that make for fear, in the circumstances we have stated, and it makes its choice and stands firm because doing so is fine, or because not doing so is shameful. Dying to escape from poverty, or sexual passion, or something painful, is not a feature of courage but rather of cowardice; for it is softness to run away from things because they
1116a15 are burdensome, and the person in this case accepts death not because it is a fine thing to do, but because he is running away from something bad.

    What courage is, then, is something like this;

---

[11] Reading καὶ τῷ ἀνδρείῳ δή. ἡ δ' ἀνδρεία καλόν (1115b21).

(III. 8) but there are also other 'courages', so called, which take five forms. First there is the 'civic' kind—for this has the greatest resemblance to real courage. For citizens seem to withstand the dangers facing them because of the penalties inflicted by the laws' and people's reproaches, and because of the honours; and it is because of this that the most courageous peoples seem to be those among whom cowards are dishonoured and the courageous honoured. Individuals of this sort one finds portrayed by Homer too, e.g. Diomedes and Hector—as in

1116a20

> Polydamas will be first to lay up disgrace against me,

and

1116a25

> For one day Hector will speak out among the Trojans, and say
> 'By me was the son of Tydeus . . . .'.

This 'courage' has the greatest resemblance to the one described before because it comes about through excellence; for it comes about through shame and through desire for what is fine (because for honour), and in order to escape reproach, because that is something shameful. One might also put in the same category those acting under constraint from their commanders; but these are inferior, to the extent that they do it not through shame but through fear, and in order to escape not what is shameful, but what is painful—for the ones applying the constraint have control over them, just like Hector:

1116a30

> But any man I find cowering, away from the battle,
> Make no mistake—he will be meat for the dogs.

1116a35

And those who issue orders and beat anyone who retreats are doing the same thing, as are those who draw up their men in front of ditches or things of that sort; for they are all using constraint. But one should not be courageous because of constraint; one should be courageous because it is fine to be so. People also think of experience in each particular sphere as courage; this is also why Socrates thought courage to be expert knowledge. There are different people like this in different spheres, but in the sphere of warfare it is the soldiers; for there are many situations in war that contain nothing to be afraid of, and soldiers have the best perspective on these; so they appear courageous, because everyone else lacks the knowledge of what sorts of situations these are. Again, their experience gives them the greatest ability to inflict damage and avoid it themselves, since it gives them the ability to use weapons and provides them with the kinds of weaponry that will have the greatest power, both for inflicting damage and for avoiding it; so when they fight it is as if armed men are fighting with unarmed ones, and trained athletes against non-athletes, for in contests of this sort too it is not the most courageous people that are the most effective fighters but those with the greatest strength and in the best physical condition. But soldiers turn cowardly when the danger is

1116b1

1116b5

1116b10

1116b15

extreme and they are at a disadvantage in terms of numbers and equipment; for they are the first to run away, while the citizen elements stand and die (which is what actually happened at the temple of Hermes). For to the latter, running away is something shameful, and death is more desirable than saving oneself in that sort of way; whereas the soldiers from the very beginning were ready to face the dangers because they believed they had the advantage, and once having seen they do not, they run away, because they fear death more than the shameful. But the courageous person is not someone of this sort. People also count temper as courage; for the courageous are thought also to include people who act through temper, like wild animals that rush at the people who have wounded them, because courageous people too are strong-tempered; for temper especially strains to go out and meet dangers, which is what explains Homer's 'he infused their temper with strength', 'aroused their force and temper', 'and in his nostrils, bitter force', and 'his blood boiled'—all such expressions seem to indicate the arousal and impulse of temper. Well then, courageous people act because of the fine, and temper cooperates with them; by contrast, the wild animals in question act because they are distressed—after all, it is because they have been hit by a weapon, or because they are frightened (since they do not approach if they have the cover of a wood). That they are driven out by distress and temper and so impelled towards the danger, without seeing in advance any of the frightening aspects of the situation—that, then, does not make them courageous, since at that rate even donkeys would be brave when they are hungry; after all beating them doesn't stop them from feeding. Adulterers too go through with many daring things because of their appetite. But the 'courage' that comes about through temper does seem to be the most natural form, and to *be* courage once the factors of decision and the end for the sake of which have been added. Human beings too, then, are distressed when angry, and take pleasure in retaliating; but people who fight from these motives are effective in fighting, not courageous, since they do not fight because of the fine, or as the correct prescription directs, but because of affection. But they do have something that resembles courage. Nor, then, are people who act because they are optimistic courageous, for they are bold in dangerous situations because they have defeated many people and on many occasions; and while they are comparable with the courageous, because both sorts of people are bold, courageous people are bold because of the factors mentioned before, whereas optimistic people are so because they think that they are strongest and that no harm will come to them. (When people are getting drunk they behave in the same sort of way—they become optimistic.) And whenever they find things not turning out as they expect, they run away; but as we said, it is characteristic of the courageous person to withstand those things that are and appear frightening to human beings, because doing so is fine and not doing so is shameful. This is why a person also seems more courageous if he is fearless and undisturbed in

the face of sudden fears than of ones that are foreseen; for it was more the   1117a20
result of a disposition, in so far as it was less the result of preparation. For in
the case of what is clearly foreseen, one can decide also as a result of calculation and reasoning about it; with what comes suddenly one decides according
to one's disposition. Another set of people who appear courageous are those
who act in ignorance, and they are not far removed from the optimistic sort,
but they are inferior to the extent that they have no expectations of themselves, whereas the others do. This is why the others stand firm for a time;   1117a25
whereas if those who are deceived about the situation recognize that it is not
what they guessed it to be, they run away (which is what happened to the
Argives when they fell in with the Spartans, thinking they were Sicyonians).
This, then, is our account of what sort of people the courageous are, and
those who seem courageous.

   (III. 9) Now while courage has to do both with being bold and with fearing,
it does not have to do with the two things equally, but more with what is   1117a30
fearsome; for the person who is undisturbed in face of fearsome things and is
in the condition one should be in relation to these is courageous, more than
the person who is so in relation to the things that make for boldness. It is by
virtue of their withstanding what is painful, then, as has been said, that people
are called courageous. Hence courage is also something that brings pain with
it, and is justly an object of praise; for it is harder to withstand what is painful   1117a35
than to hold back from what is pleasant. All the same, the end that accords   1117b1
with courage would seem to be pleasant, but to be obscured by the circumstances, as also happens e.g. in athletic competitions; for to the boxers the
end—what they do it for, i.e. the wreath and the honours—is pleasant,
whereas being punched hurts them, given that they are made of flesh, and is   1117b5
painful—and so is all the slogging; and because the painful aspects are many,
its small size appears to leave the end for which it is all done without anything
pleasant about it. If, then, it is like this with courage too, then while death and
wounds will be painful to the courageous person, and counter-voluntary, he
will withstand them because doing so is fine or because not doing so is
shameful. And the greater the extent to which he possesses excellence in its   1117b10
entirety, and the happier he is, the more he will be pained at the prospect of
death; for to such a person, most of all, is living worth while, and *this* person
will knowingly be depriving himself of goods of the greatest kind, which is
something to be pained at. But he is no less courageous because of that, and
perhaps even more courageous, because he chooses what is fine in war in   1117b15
place of those other goods. So not all the excellences give rise to pleasant
activity, except to the extent that pleasant activity touches on the end itself.
But presumably it is perfectly possible that the most effective soldiers will not
be people of this sort, but rather the sort who while being less courageous
possess nothing else of value; for these people are ready to face dangers, and

1117b20   put up their lives for sale for small profits. Let this much stand, then, as our account of courage; and from what has been said, it is not difficult to grasp what it is, at least in outline.

      (III. 10) After this excellence, let us discuss moderation; for these seem to be
1117b25   the excellences of the non-rational parts. Well then, we have said that it is an intermediate state relating to pleasures (for it relates less, and not in the same way, to pains); and self-indulgence too appears in the same context. So let us now determine what *sorts* of pleasures it relates to. Let there be a distinction, then, between pleasures of the soul, like love of honour and love of learning,
1117b30   and those of the body—since each of these two, the lover of honour and the lover of learning, delights in what he is a lover of without his body being affected at all, but rather his mind. People concerned with pleasures of this sort are not called either moderate or self-indulgent. Nor, similarly, are those who are concerned with the other non-bodily pleasures: if people love stories,
1117b35   are always telling how something happened, and spend their days on matters
1118a1   of no consequence, we call them chatterers, not self-indulgent; nor do we call someone self-indulgent if he is distressed about money or friends. It will be to the pleasures of the body that moderation relates—but not all of these, either; for those who enjoy what comes to us through sight, e.g. colours, shapes, or
1118a5   painting, are not said to be either moderate or self-indulgent; yet it would seem possible in these cases too to take pleasure as one should, or excessively or deficiently. Similarly too in the field of hearing: no one calls self-indulgent those who find inordinate enjoyment in singing or drama, or moderate those who enjoy them in the way one should. Nor are these terms applied when it
1118a10   comes to smells, except incidentally; for we do not call people self-indulgent who enjoy smells of apples, roses, or incense, but rather ones who enjoy smells of perfumes or tasty dishes; for the self-indulgent do enjoy these, because through them they are reminded of the objects of their appetites.
1118a15   One will see other people too, when they are hungry, enjoying the smells of food, but to enjoy such things is characteristic of the self-indulgent person; for in his case these are objects of appetite. Pleasure does not occur from these senses among other animals either except incidentally. For again, it is not the scent of the hares that the hunting-dogs enjoy, but consuming them—the
1118a20   scent just told the dogs the hares were there; nor is it the ox's lowing that the lion enjoys, but rather eating it up, and he merely sensed through the lowing that the ox was nearby, so appearing to enjoy the sound itself; similarly, what pleases him is not the sight of 'a stag or a goat running wild', but that he is to get a meal. Moderation and self-indulgence relate to the sorts of pleasures
1118a25   that are shared in by all the other animals too, which is why they appear slavish and bestial; and these are touch and taste. But the extent to which they involve taste, too, is little or nothing; for it is the function of taste to tell one flavour from another, as people do when approving wines or preparing tasty

dishes; but what people, or at least the self-indulgent sort, really get pleasure   1118a30
from is not this but rather the consumption involved, which comes about
wholly by means of touch, whether it is a matter of eating or of drinking or
so-called 'venery'. This is why a certain individual, a gourmandizer, actually
prayed for a throat longer than a crane's—so showing that it was the sense of
touch that he enjoyed. The sense, then, that is the most widely shared is the   1118b1
one connected with self-indulgence, which would justly seem a matter for
reproach because it belongs to us not in so far as we are human beings but in
so far as we are animals. To take enjoyment in such things, then, and to be
attached to them more than anything, is bestial. For the touch-related pleas-   1118b5
ures most appropriate to free men lie outside the sphere of self-indulgence,
e.g. the ones in gymnasia produced through rubbing and warming; for the
touching that is characteristic of the self-indulgent person has to do not with
the whole of the body but only with certain parts of it.

   (III. 11) Of the appetites, some seem to be shared, others peculiar and
acquired; so e.g. the appetite for nourishment is natural to us, since everyone   1118b10
has an appetite for nourishment when they lack it, dry or liquid, or sometimes
both; and for 'bed', in Homer's phrase, when one is young and in one's
physical prime; but as for the appetite for this or that sort of food, not
everyone has *that*—or an appetite for the same people. Hence it appears to be
peculiar to us. All the same, it *does* have an element of the natural about it,
since different things are pleasant for different individuals, and everyone gets
more pleasure from certain things than from just anything. With the natural   1118b15
appetites, then, few people get things wrong, and only in one direction, that
of excess; for eating or drinking whatever is to hand until one is overfull is to
exceed the natural limit in quantity, since the object of natural desire is
replenishment of the lack. (That is why these people are said to have 'belly-
lust'—because they fill their belly more than is necessary. Those who are   1118b20
excessively slavish become people of this sort.) With the kinds of pleasures
peculiar to us, on the other hand, many people get things wrong, and there
are many ways of doing so. For given that people are called lovers of such-
and-such either because they enjoy the sorts of things one shouldn't, or
because they enjoy things more than most people do, or because they don't
enjoy them in the way one should—well, the self-indulgent go to excess in all
respects; for they too enjoy some things one shouldn't (being ones they should   1118b25
hate), and if there are some things of the sort in question that one *should*
enjoy, they enjoy them more than one should and more than most people do.
Excess in relation to pleasures, then, is clearly self-indulgence and a matter for
censure; as for pains, the moderate person does not get his name for with-   1118b30
standing them, as the courageous person does, nor the self-indulgent person
for not withstanding them—rather, the self-indulgent person is so called for
being more distressed than one should be at not getting what is pleasant (the

pain, too, is caused for him by the pleasure), and the moderate person for *not*
being distressed at its absence and for holding back from the pleasant. So the
self-indulgent person, for his part, has an appetite for any pleasant things, or
for the most pleasant, and he is driven by his appetite so as to choose these
instead of anything else; this is why he is distressed both when he fails to get
them and when he has the appetite for them—since the appetite is accompanied by pain, though it seems a strange thing to be pained because of
pleasure. People who are defective in relation to pleasures and enjoy them less
than one should hardly occur; for to be insensate like this is not human—all
the other animals too, after all, make distinctions between foods, and enjoy
some but not others. If there is someone to whom nothing is pleasant, and
nothing is preferable to anything else, he would be a long way from being
human; and there is no name for him, because of the fact that he hardly
occurs. As for the moderate person, he is in an intermediate state in these
respects; for neither does he take pleasure in the things the self-indulgent
person most enjoys, which actually disgust him, nor in general does he enjoy
the things one shouldn't, or get intense enjoyment from anything of this sort,
nor is he distressed at their absence—and neither does he have an appetite for
them, or only a sober one, and not more than one should, or on the sort of
occasion when one shouldn't, or generally anything of that sort. But such
things as conduce to health or fitness and are pleasant he will desire moderately and in the way one should, as he will any other pleasures if they do not
impede these, or are not contrary to what is fine, or not beyond his means. For
someone disregarding these conditions is fonder of such pleasures than they
deserve; and the moderate person is not of this sort, but as the correct
prescription lays down.

(III. 12) Self-indulgence looks more like a voluntary thing than cowardice
does. For self-indulgence comes about because of pleasure, cowardice because
of pain, and of these the one is something one chooses, the other something
avoided; and while pain puts things out of joint and even destroys the natural
state of the person who has it, pleasure does nothing of the sort. So self-
indulgence is a more voluntary thing. Hence it is also more a matter for
reproach; for it is also easier to acquire the habit of resisting pleasures, since
there are many such things in one's life, and the occasions for habituation are
without danger, whereas with fearsome things it is the reverse. But the disposition of cowardice would seem to be voluntary in a way in which particular acts of cowardice are not; for it is in itself painless, whereas they put things
out of joint, through pain, even to the extent of causing the throwing down of
weapons and the other sorts of disgraceful behaviour—which is why they also
seem to be forced. For the self-indulgent person it is the reverse: the particular
acts seem voluntary, because they accord with his appetite and desire,
while the thing as a whole appears less so, for no one has an appetite to be

self-indulgent. The term 'indulgence' is one we also apply to the ways children
go wrong, for these have a certain resemblance to self-indulgence. Which is   1119b1
called after which makes no difference for present purposes, but clearly the
later is called after the earlier. Nor does the transfer of usage seem inappropriate; for *least* to be indulged is the part of us that not only desires shameful
things but can become big, and this characteristic belongs to appetite, and to   1119b5
the child, above all—since children too live according to appetite, and the
desire for the pleasant is strongest in them. If, then, whatever desires shameful
things is not ready to obey and under the control of the ruling element, it will
grow and grow, for the desire for the pleasant is insatiable and indiscriminate,
in a mindless person, and the activity of his appetite augments his congenital
tendency; and if his appetites are strong and vigorous, they knock out his   1119b10
capacity for rational calculation as well. This is why they should be moderate
and few, and offer no opposition to rational prescription (which is the sort of
thing we mean by 'ready to obey' and 'not indulged'); for[12] just as a child should
conduct himself in accordance with what the slave in charge of him tells him
to do, so too the appetitive in us should conduct itself in accordance with
what reason prescribes. Hence in the moderate person the appetitive should   1119b15
be in harmony with reason; for the fine is goal for both, and the moderate
person has appetite for the things one should, in the way one should, and
when—which is what the rational prescription also lays down. Let this, then,
be our account of moderation.

BOOK IV

(IV. 1) Let us next discuss open-handedness. Well, it seems to be the intermediate state relating to money; for the open-handed person is not praised in
the context of war, or in the same one as the moderate person, or again in
legal judgements, but in relation to the giving and taking of money—but more   1119b25
in relation to giving. (By 'money', we mean anything whose value is measured
by currency.) Both wastefulness and avariciousness consist in behaving excessively and deficiently in relation to money; and we ascribe avariciousness
always to those who are more concerned with money than one should be,   1119b30
whereas in imputing wastefulness to people we sometimes combine different
states, since we give the name 'wasteful' to those who lack self-control and

---

[12] Reading ὥσπερ γὰρ τὸν παῖδα (1119b13).

spend lavishly on self-indulgence. This is why these people also seem the worst—because they have several forms of badness at the same time. The name 'wasteful', then, is not properly theirs; for by 'wasteful' is meant the person who has one failing, that of destroying his substance; for the person who is being ruined through his own agency is wasteful, and the destruction of one's substance seems to be another sort of ruining of oneself, the thought being that life depends on these things. This, then, is how we are taking wastefulness.

1120a1

Things that have a use can be used both well and badly; wealth is something that has a use; and each thing is used best by the person possessing the excellence relating to that thing: wealth, then, too, will be used best by the person possessing the excellence relating to money, and this is the open-handed person. Using money seems to be a matter of spending and giving; taking it and keeping it seem more to do with possessing it. This is why giving to the people one should is more the mark of the open-handed person than taking from sources one should take from, and than not taking from sources one shouldn't. For bestowing benefits is more the mark of excellence than receiving them, and doing fine things than not doing shameful ones; and it is not hard to see that bestowing benefits and doing fine things go with giving, receiving benefits, and not acting shamefully with taking. Then too the gratitude goes to the giver, not to the person who doesn't take; and the giver also gets more of the praise. Again, not taking is easier to do than giving; for people are less often found parting with what belongs to them than not taking what belongs to others. What is more, it is those who give that are called open-handed; those who don't take are praised not for being open-handed but, if anything, for being just, while those who do take are not even praised at all. And of those who are loved for their excellence, the open-handed are loved perhaps most of all; for they are useful, and their usefulness lies in their giving. Actions in accordance with excellence are fine and for the sake of the fine. So this will apply to the open-handed person too: he will give for the sake of the fine, and in the correct way. He will give to the people one should, as much as one should, when one should, and so on with all the other features that belong with correct giving; and he will do all this with pleasure, or without pain, since what is in accord with excellence is pleasant or painless—least of all is it painful. The person who gives to the sorts of people one shouldn't, or not for the sake of the fine but for some other motive, will be called not open-handed but something else. Nor will someone be called open-handed if it pains him to give; for he would choose money over acting finely, and that is not a characteristic of the open-handed person. But neither will the open-handed person take from the sorts of sources he shouldn't; that kind of taking is not a characteristic of someone who does not set a high value on money. Nor will he be the kind of person to ask for things; for neither is it characteristic of the benefactor to be an easy recipient of benefaction. But he

1120a5

1120a10

1120a15

1120a20

1120a25

1120a30

will take from the sources one should, e.g. from his private possessions,   1120b1
regarding taking not as something fine but as something necessary, in order
that he should have something to give. Nor will he neglect his possessions,
given that there are people he will want to use these to assist. Nor will he give
to people at random, since otherwise he will have nothing to give the people
one should give to, when one should, and in the circumstances where giving is
something fine. But it is emphatically the mark of the open-handed person   1120b5
even to go to excess in giving, so as to leave too little for himself; for it is
characteristic of the open-handed person not to look to his own interests.
Attributions of open-handedness do, however, take account of a person's
resources; for the essence of open-handedness does not lie in the quantity of
what is given, but in the disposition of the giver, and this ensures giving that
takes account of his resources. So it is perfectly possible for the person who   1120b10
gives less to be more open-handed, if he has less from which to give. Open-
handedness seems to belong more to the sort who have not acquired their
resources by their own efforts, but who have inherited it; this is both because
they have no experience of lacking resources, and because everyone is more
attached to what they have themselves made, like parents and poets. It is not
easy for an open-handed person to be wealthy, given that he is not the sort of   1120b15
person either to take things or to keep what he has, but rather to part with it,
and that he does not value money for itself, but for the purpose of giving. This
in fact is why people complain against fortune that the most deserving are the
least wealthy. But it is not unreasonable that it should turn out like this, since
it is not possible to have money without concerning oneself about how to get
it—as with everything else. All the same, the open-handed person will not give   1120b20
to the people one shouldn't, or on the sort of occasion one shouldn't, and so
on; for in that case he would not be acting in accordance with open-
handedness, and having spent on these things he would have nothing to spend
on the things he should. For as we have said, a person is open-handed if he
spends in accordance with his resources, and on the things one should; and the
person who overspends is wasteful. This is why we do not call tyrants waste-   1120b25
ful; for it does not seem easy for them to exceed the quantity of their possessions in their giving and spending. Since, then, open-handedness is an intermediate state relating to the giving and taking of money, the open-handed
person will give and spend on what one should and as much as one should, in
small matters and great ones alike, and he will do it with pleasure; he will also   1120b30
take from the sources one should and as much as one should. For since the
excellence is an intermediacy relating to both things, he will do both in the
way one should; for with acceptable taking goes the same sort of giving, while
the sort that is not like this is contrary to it. So the giving and taking that go
with each other will be found at the same time in the same person, whereas
those that are contrary to each other clearly will not. If it turns out that he   1121a1
does not spend as one should, or in accordance with what is fine, he will be

distressed, but moderately, as one should be; for it is the mark of excellence that one be both pleased and pained at the things one should be and in the way one should be. Again, the open-handed person is easy to deal with as a

1121a5 partner in financial matters; for he can be treated unjustly, given that he does not set a high value on money, and that it upsets him more if he has not spent when he should than it distresses him if he has spent when he should not have done—so failing to conform to Simonides' example. The wasteful person, by contrast, goes wrong in these respects too, for he is neither pleased at the things one should be, or as one should be, nor distressed; but this will be more evident as we proceed.

1121a10   We have said, then, that wastefulness and avariciousness consist in behaving excessively and deficiently, and in two things, i.e. in giving and taking (for spending too we count under giving). So: wastefulness goes to excess in giving and not taking, and is deficient in taking, whereas stinginess is deficient in

1121a15 giving but excessive in taking—but only on a small scale. The features of wastefulness, then, are hardly found in combination; for it is not easy to give to everybody while taking from nowhere, since if private individuals are giving, their resources quickly run out (and 'wasteful', in fact, seems to apply to private individuals)—and yet this sort of person would seem to be more

1121a20 than a little better than the avaricious sort, since he is easily cured both by adulthood and by poverty, and he is capable of arriving at the intermediate. For he possesses the features of the open-handed person, since he both gives and does not take, though he does neither as one should, and neither of them well. If, then, he were to change in this respect, through habituation or in some other way, he would be open-handed; for then he will give to the people

1121a25 one should, and he will not take from the sources from which one should not. Hence he actually seems not to be a bad character; for it is not the mark of a worthless person, or of an ignoble one, to go to excess in giving and not taking, but rather of a fool. The person who is wasteful in this way seems to be a much better sort than the avaricious person both for the reasons stated,

1121a30 and because he benefits lots of people, while the other benefits no one, not even himself. However, as we have said, most wasteful people also take from the sorts of sources one should not take from, and to this extent they are actually avaricious. But they acquire a tendency to take because, while they want to spend, they cannot do so readily, because what is available to them

1121b1 runs out; so they are compelled to find other sources. At the same time because they have no concern at all for the fine they also take from any source, not caring what it is; for they have an appetite for giving, and how or from what source they give makes no difference to them. For this very reason neither do their acts of giving count as open-handed; for they are not fine, nor

1121b5 done for the sake of the fine, nor done as they should be done. Instead, sometimes these people enrich those who should be poor, and would give nothing to people of decent character, whereas they would give plenty to those who flatter them or provide some other kind of pleasure. Hence most of them are self-indulgent as well: since they spend readily, they also spend lavishly on acts of self-indulgence, and because they do not live with a view to the fine they incline towards what brings them pleasure. So if the wasteful person finds no one to guide him, he changes in this direction, but with the right attention he could reach the intermediate, where one should be. But avariciousness, as well as being incurable (for old age and any sort of incapacity seems to make people avaricious), is a condition more congenital to human beings than wastefulness; for most people are inclined to love money more than they are inclined to give. It also covers a wide range of things, taking many forms; for there seem to be many ways of being avaricious. For involving two factors as it does, deficiency in giving and excess in taking, it does not occur in its full-blown form in all cases: sometimes it divides itself, with some people going to excess in taking, and others being deficient in giving. For while the people who come under such descriptions as 'miserly', 'niggardly', or 'skinflint' are all deficient in giving, they do not go after what belongs to other people, or want to take it, some because of a certain decency, and wariness of doing the shameful (for there are those who seem to keep what they have, or at any rate say they do, in order to prevent their ever being compelled to do something shameful; to this sort belong the cheese-parer, and everyone of that sort—the name comes from his excessive reluctance to give anything away); some, again, hold back from other people's property through fear, on the basis that it is not easy to take other people's oneself while not having others taking one's own, with the result that they are content to do without either taking or giving. The other sort, by contrast, go to excess in taking, in that they take anything and from any source, as do e.g. those who work in occupations not fit for free men—pimps and everyone of that sort, and moneylenders who make small loans for a high return. For all these take from sources one shouldn't take from, and in amounts one shouldn't. A feature they share seems to be their readiness to scavenge for profit; for all of them put up with getting a bad name for the sake of profit, and a small one at that. For those who take on a large scale, and not from the sources one should, nor what one should, e.g. tyrants when they sack cities and plunder sanctuaries—we don't call these avaricious, but rather vicious, impious, and unjust. The avaricious do, however, include the dicer, the petty thief, and the brigand; for they are scavengers for profit—both sorts ply their trades, and put up with being called names, for what they can get in the way of profit, the one sort putting up with the greatest dangers for the sake of the takings, the other making a profit out of their friends, to whom they should be giving. Both sorts, then, are scavengers in that they are prepared to make a profit from sources one shouldn't profit from; all such ways of taking, then, are a matter of avariciousness as well. And it is reasonable that avariciousness should be said to be contrary to open-handedness; for it is a greater evil than

1121b10

1121b15

1121b20

1121b25

1121b30

1122a1

1122a5

1122a10

1122a15 wastefulness, and people get things wrong more in this direction than in that of what we have described under the heading of wastefulness. Let so much, then, stand as an account of open-handedness and of the bad states opposed to it.

1122a20 (IV. 2) It would seem appropriate next to talk about munificence too. For it seems itself, too, to be a sort of excellence relating to money; but it does not, like open-handedness, extend to all actions to do with money, but only to those involving expenditure, and in these it exceeds open-handedness in scale. For as its very name [*megaloprepeia*] tends to indicate, it consists in expenditure that is suitable [*prepousa*] in scale [*en megethei*]. But the scale involved is relative: the 1122a25 costs are not the same for someone fitting out a trireme and for someone leading an official delegation. What is suitable, then, is relative to the person concerned, and to the context and what the expenditure relates to. The person who spends as the situation merits in small or moderate things—as in

many times to a vagabond would I give

—is not called munificent, but rather the one who does so in big things. For the munificent person is open-handed, but for all that the open-handed person 1122a30 is not a munificent one. The deficiency corresponding to this sort of disposition is called shabbiness, while the excess is vulgarity, tastelessness, and anything else of that sort, which involves not spending excessively on what one should but rather spending ostentatiously in contexts one shouldn't and in ways one shouldn't; but we shall discuss these subjects later. The munifi-1122a35 cent person resembles a technical expert; for he is able to observe what is 1122b1 suitable and spend large amounts with good taste: as we said at the outset, a disposition is distinguished by its activities, and by its objects. So the expenditures of the munificent person, then, are on a large scale, and suitable. Its effects, then, are of this sort too; for in this way there will be a large expend-1122b5 iture and one suiting the effect. Thus the effect should be worthy of the expense, and the expense worthy of the effect, or even exceed it. And the munificent person will incur such expenditure for the sake of the fine, since this is a shared feature of the excellences. Moreover he will enjoy spending, and do it readily; it is shabby to budget precisely. Again, he will be more concerned how to spend in the finest and most suitable way than with how 1122b10 much it will cost, and how to do it most cheaply. So the munificent person will necessarily also be open-handed, for the open-handed person too will spend the amount one should and in the way one should; but it is in these aspects, the ones open-handedness has to do with, that the large scale ['the *mega*'] of munificence [*megaloprepeia*]—as it were its greatness—lies, so that with the same expenditure it can create a greater and more suitable effect. For the 1122b15 excellence of a possession and of an effect achieved are not the same: a possession is valued most if it is worth most, e.g. gold, whereas the most valued effect is a great and a fine one (for the spectacle of such a thing is admirable, and munificence is something that arouses admiration); and munificence is excellence of effect, lying in its greatness. Of expenditures, some are of the sort we call prestigious, e.g. those relating to gods—votive offerings, ritual paraphernalia, and sacrifices—and similarly for any being that is worshipped, and all the kinds of public benefaction for which it is good to compete, e.g., perhaps, if people think a play should be staged brilliantly, or a trireme fitted out, or a feast provided for the city. But in all cases, as has been said, expenditure must also take the agent into account—who he is and what he has available to him; for the expenditure must be worthy of both, and be suitable not only to the effect to be achieved but to the person creating it. This is why a poor person could not be munificent, since he does not have the resources from which to spend large amounts in a suitable way; and anyone who attempts it is a fool, because it is beyond what the circumstances merit or require—and acting in accordance with excellence is getting things right. But it *is* suitable for those who have such resources stored up through their own efforts or those of their ancestors or connections, or those of noble birth, or high reputation, or anything else of that sort; for all these things bring great expectations with them. Most of all, then, the munificent person is like this, and munificence is located in expenditure of these sorts, as has been said, because such expenditure is on the greatest scale and carries the most prestige; but it also belongs to the types of private expenditure that arise only once, like weddings and things of that sort, or if there is some event that holds the interest of the whole city or of its eminent figures, or again to do with receiving or sending off foreign visitors, whether initiating the gift-giving or responding to it—for the munificent person does not spend lavishly on himself but on what is in the public domain, and his gifts have some resemblance to votive offerings. It is also the mark of a munificent person to furnish himself with a household in a way suitable to his wealth (for a household too is a kind of adornment), and to prefer to spend on things whose effects will be long-lasting (for these are the finest)—in each sort of case spending what is suitable; for the same things are not fitting for gods and human beings, nor in the case of a temple and that of a tomb. Again, since the greatness of any expenditure varies with the type of its object, and while what is most munificent[13] is great expenditure on a great object, what is munificent in this particular case is what is great in these circumstances, and greatness in the effect is different from greatness in the expenditure (for the most beautiful ball or oil-flask is munificent as a children's gift, even if in monetary value the gift is small and cheap), this means that whatever the type of context in which he finds himself, the munificent person will act munificently (for that is a sort of thing not easily outdone), and produce an effect worthy of his expenditure.

Such, then, is the munificent type; the one who goes to excess, the vulgar

1122b20

1122b25

1122b30

1122b35

1123a1

1123a5

1123a10

1123a15

---

[13] Reading μεγαλοπρεπέστατον μὲν τὸ . . . (1123a12).

1123a20   person, goes to excess in that he spends beyond what is required, as has been said. For on occasions for small expenditure he spends large amounts and behaves with tasteless ostentation, e.g. by contributing to a communal dinner on the scale on which one would spend for a wedding-feast, or introducing purple for the entrance of the chorus, as the Megarians do, when staging a

1123a25   comedy. And he will do everything like this not for the sake of the fine, but by way of showing off his wealth, in the belief that he is admired because of his behaviour, and spending little where the situation calls for a lot, but a lot when it calls for a little. The shabby spender, for his part, will be deficient in every respect, and even after spending the largest amounts he will spoil the fine

1123a30   effect over a small detail, by hesitating over whatever he is doing and trying to see how to spend the least amount, and complaining about that, and thinking he is doing everything on a larger scale than required. So these dispositions are forms of badness—though they do not actually give people a bad name, because they are neither harmful to one's neighbour nor excessively discreditable.

1123a35   (IV. 3) Even from its name, greatness of soul seems to have to do with great things; but let us first see what sort of great things these are. It makes no

1123b1   difference whether we examine the disposition or the person corresponding to the disposition. Well then, greatness of soul seems to belong to the sort of person that thinks himself, and is, worthy of great things; for the sort of person who does so not in accordance with his real worth is a fool, and none of those corresponding to any excellence is a fool, or mindless. So the great-

1123b5   souled type is the one described. For the person who is worthy of small things and thinks himself worthy of them is moderate, but not great-souled; for greatness of soul depends on scale, just as a beautiful body must possess a certain scale, and small people are neat and well-proportioned, but not beautiful. Someone actually unworthy who thinks himself worthy of great things is conceited, though not everyone who thinks himself worthy of more than he is counts as conceited. As for the person who thinks himself worthy of less

1123b10   than he is, he is little-souled, whether he is worthy of great things or moderate ones, or whether, when he actually is worthy of small things, he thinks himself worthy of even smaller ones. The most little-souled would seem to be the one worthy of great things; for what would he do if he were not worthy of so much? The great-souled person, then, is at the extreme in terms of scale, but in terms of being as one should he is intermediate; for he values himself at his actual worth, whereas the other types are excessive and deficient.

1123b15   Now if the great-souled person thinks himself worthy, and is worthy, of great things, and especially of the greatest, then his concern will be with one thing especially. Worth is stated in terms of external goods, and greatest of these we would suppose to be the one we mete out to the gods, the one the eminent

1123b20   seek most, and the one given as the prize for the finest achievements; but such

is honour, for this *is* in fact greatest of the external goods. So the great-souled type has to do with honours and dishonours, in the way one should. But that greatness of soul has to do with honour is evident even without argument; for it is of honour, especially, that the great[14] think themselves worthy, and worthy they are. The little-souled person, for his part, is deficient by comparison both with himself and with the great-souled person's self-estimate; while the conceited person goes to excess in relation to himself, though not by comparison with the great-souled one. But if the great-souled person is in fact worthy of the greatest things, he will be best; for it is always the better person who is worthy of greater, and the best of what is greatest. It follows, then, that the truly great-souled man must be good. And in fact greatness in respect of each of the excellences would seem to belong to the great-souled person— it would not be at all consistent for the great-souled person to retreat with his arms pumping, or to treat people unjustly; for what will motivate him to do shameful things, when nothing impresses him? And if one considers particular cases, the great-souled type would appear quite laughable if he were not good. But he would not be worthy of honour either, if he were bad; for honour is a prize of excellence, and it is meted out to the good. Greatness of soul, then, seems to be a sort of adornment, as it were, of the excellences; for it augments them, and does not occur without them. For this reason it is hard to be truly great-souled; for it is not possible without refinement of excellence. It is, then, honours and dishonours that the great-souled person most has to do with; and in the case of great honours, accorded him by people of excellence, he will be moderately pleased, on the grounds that he is getting what belongs to him, or actually less than that—for there could be no honour worthy of complete excellence. All the same, he will accept it in so far as they have nothing greater to mete out to him. As for honour from just anyone, and given for small things, he will wholly despise it, because *that* is not what he is worthy of—and he will treat dishonour in the same way, for it will not justly attach to him. Most of all, then, as has been said, the great-souled person has to do with honours; nevertheless he will also be moderately disposed in relation to wealth, political power, and any kind of good or bad fortune, whichever it turns out to be, and he will neither be over-pleased at good fortune nor over-distressed at bad (since his attitude even to honour is not that it is the greatest of things). Power and wealth are desirable because of the honour they bring, or at any rate people who have them wish to be the recipients of honour through them; and the person to whom even honour is of small consequence will treat the other things like that too. This is why great-souled people seem to be arrogant. But people think having good fortune also contributes towards greatness of soul; for those of noble birth are thought worthy of honour, as are people with political power or wealth; for

1123b25

1123b30

1123b35
1124a1

1124a5

1124a10

1124a15

1124a20

---

[14] Retaining οἱ μεγάλοι (1123b23).

this puts them above others, and everything that is superior in respect of a good is held in more honour. Hence even things like this make people more

1124a25 great-souled, in so far as they are honoured by some; but in truth only the good person is to be honoured, even though someone who has the other things as well is thought more worthy of honour. Those who possess goods of this sort without excellence are neither justified in thinking themselves worthy of great things nor correctly called great-souled; for neither is possible without complete excellence. And even those possessing goods of this sort

1124a30 become arrogant and wantonly offensive, since without excellence it is not easy to bear in a fitting way what good fortune brings; and because they are

1124b1 not able to bear it, and think themselves superior to everyone else, they look down on them even though there is nothing distinguished about their own conduct. For they mimic the great-souled person without actually being like him, and do it where they can; so they don't do what accords with excellence,

1124b5 but they do look down on everybody else. For the great-souled person is justified in looking down on people (since his judgements are true), whereas ordinary people do it without discrimination. He does not risk himself for small things, or often, because there are few things he values, but for great things he does, and when he does he is unsparing of his life, as one to whom there are some conditions under which it is not worth living. He is the sort of

1124b10 person to bestow benefits, but is ashamed at receiving them; for the former is the mark of a superior, the latter of an inferior. When returning benefits he tends to give more than he received; for in this way the person who started the process will owe him a debt in addition, and will be the one benefited. People of this sort also seem to remember any benefit they bestowed, but not those they have received (because the receiver of benefit is at a disadvantage, and

1124b15 being great-souled means being superior); and to be pleased at being reminded of the one but not of the other—which is actually why Thetis doesn't mention to Zeus the things she did for him; similarly the Spartans to the Athenians, but they did mention what the Athenians had done for them. It is also a mark of the great-souled person not to ask anyone for anything, or only reluctantly, but to offer his services readily, and to be grand towards the

1124b20 eminent and wealthy, but an ordinary human being towards those in the middle; for it is a hard and lofty thing to surpass the former, but easy to surpass the latter, and whereas with the former to behave loftily is not ignoble, with people of no distinction it is as vulgar as using one's strength against the weak. Another mark of the great-souled person is not to enter public competition, or where others come first; and to be slow to act, holding back except

1124b25 where there is great honour to be had or a great deed to be done; and to be a doer of few things, but great ones, and ones that will be renowned. But necessarily, he is also open about his hating and his loving (for concealment implies fear, and shows less care for the truth than for one's reputation), and he talks and acts openly (for he is the sort to speak his mind, since he tends to

look down on people, and tell the truth, except when being self-deprecating   1124b30
with ordinary people); necessarily, too, he cannot live by reference to someone
else, unless that person is a friend, since that is what a slave does (which is why   1125a1
all flatterers are like day-labourers and all people without self-respect are
flatterers). He is not the sort to feel admiration either; for nothing impresses
him. Nor does he remember past wrongs; for great-souled people do not store
things up, especially a memory of wrongs done them, but rather overlook   1125a5
them. Nor does he talk about personal things—he will not talk either about
himself or about someone else, since he is not anxious either to be praised
himself or to see others censured; nor again does he tend to praise others,
which is why he does not speak ill of them either, even his enemies, unless to
insult them to their face. Again, where it is a question of unavoidable or small
things, he is least inclined to complain or ask help; to behave like that about   1125a10
them implies that one takes them seriously. As for possessions, his tend to be
the fine and unprofitable kind rather than the profitable and useful, since that
is more a mark of self-sufficiency. Again, slow movement seems to be characteristic of the great-souled person, and a deep voice, and steady speech; for
the person who takes few things seriously is not the sort to hurry, nor is   1125a15
someone who is impressed by nothing the sort to be tense—and these are the
causes of a high-pitched voice and hasty movement.

Such, then, is the great-souled person; the deficient one is little-souled, while
the one who goes to excess is conceited. Now these people too are thought of
not as bad (for they do no harm to anyone) but as having got things wrong.
For the little-souled person, who is worthy of good things, deprives himself of   1125a20
the very things he is worthy of, and gives the impression of having some fault
in him, in so far as he does not think himself worthy of these good things, and
of not knowing himself; if he did, he would want the things he was worthy of,
given that they are worth having. All the same, such people are not thought of
as foolish, but rather as diffident. But this sort of view of themselves seems
actually to make them worse; for every sort of person seeks what accords   1125a25
with their worth, and these stand back even from fine actions and pursuits, on
the basis that they are unworthy of them, and similarly from external goods
too. The conceited sort, on the other hand, *are* foolish, and ignorant of
themselves, and patently so; for they try their hands at public competition
when they are not worthy of it, and are consequently found out. They also   1125a30
deck themselves with fine clothes, a fine manner, and things like that, and
when things have gone well for them they want that to be visible, too, to
everyone else, talking about their good fortune as if that will bring them
honour. But littleness of soul is more opposed to greatness of soul than
conceitedness is; for it both occurs more often and is worse.

Greatness of soul, then, has to do with great honour, as has been said;   1125a35

(IV. 4) but in relation to honour too there appears to be a kind of   1125b1 excellence, as was said in our first discussions, that would seem to be related to greatness of soul in the same sort of way as open-handedness is to munificence. For both of these excellences are unconnected with greatness of scale,

1125b5   instead making one disposed as one should be in relation to moderate and small things; and just as there is an intermediate state, and an excessive one and a deficient one, in taking and giving money, so too with desire for honour— there is desiring it more than one should and less, and desiring it from the sources one should and in the way that one should. For we censure both the

1125b10   honour-loving person for seeking honour more than one should and from sources one shouldn't, and the person indifferent to honour for preferring not to be honoured even for fine things. But sometimes we praise the honour-loving one as manly and loving what is fine, and the one indifferent to honour as decent and moderate, just as we said in our first discussions. Clearly, there are more ways than one in which we call people 'lovers of' such-and-such, and

1125b15   we do not always apply the term 'honour-loving' to the same feature: if we are using it to praise someone it means loving honour more than ordinary people do, whereas if we are censuring someone it means loving it more than one should. Because the intermediate state is without a name, the ones at the extremes dispute for its territory, so to speak, as if it were vacant. But where there is excess and deficiency, there is also intermediacy; and people do desire

1125b20   honour both more than one should and less; so there is also *as* one should; so this disposition is praised, being an intermediate state to do with honour, with no name. Compared to love of honour it appears as indifference to honour, compared to indifference to honour as love of honour; compared to both it appears in a way as both. This seems to be the case with the other excellences

1125b25   too. But here the people at the extremes appear to be opposed to each other because the intermediate person has no name.

(IV. 5) 'Mildness' is an intermediate state to do with being angry. Because the intermediate lacks a name (as do the extremes, almost), we apply the term 'mildness' to it, despite its leaning towards the deficiency, itself nameless. But

1125b30   the excessive state might be called a kind of 'irascibility'; for the affection involved is anger, though the things that bring it about in people are many and various. Now a person is praised if he gets angry in the circumstances one should and at the people one should, and again in the way one should, and when, and for the length of time one should; this sort of person, then, will be 'mild', if indeed mildness is praised. For being mild means being unperturbed,

1125b35   and not being carried away by one's feelings but being angry in the way, in the
1126a1   circumstances, and for the sort of length of time the correct prescription lays down; but he seems to err more towards deficiency, since the mild person tends not to look for revenge but rather to be sympathetic. But the deficiency, whether it is a kind of spiritlessness or whatever it is, is censured: the sort of

1126a5   people who do not get angry in the circumstances one should are thought to be foolish, as are the sort that do not get angry as they should, or when, or with the people one should; such a person seems to be insensate, and not to feel pain, and—if he does not get angry—not the sort to defend himself, whereas putting up with being a target of abuse, and not intervening when those close to one are treated that way, is slavish. Excess occurs in all the relevant respects (with people one shouldn't, in circumstances one shouldn't, more than one should, more quickly, for a longer time); on the other hand not all of them are there in the same person. That would not be possible in any case; for the bad destroys even itself, and if ever it is full-blown, it ceases to be bearable. 'Irascible' people, then, get angry quickly, and with people one shouldn't, in circumstances one shouldn't, and more than one should; but they stop quickly, which is their best feature. This comes about in their case because they do not hold in their anger but retaliate, in that their sharpness of temper makes them open about it—and then they are done with it. Hyper-choleric people are excessively quick-tempered, ready to get angry over anything and in any situation; hence their name. The bitter are hard to make up with, and stay angry for a long time; they hold back their temper. Relief comes when they retaliate; for paying people back makes them stop being angry, and brings them pleasure in place of the pain. But if this does not happen their anger continues to weigh on them; for because it is under the surface no one tries to help persuade them out of it either, and it takes time to work through one's anger by oneself. People of this sort cause the greatest disturbance to themselves and those closest to them. We call 'difficult' those who get angry in the sorts of circumstances one shouldn't, more than one should, and for a longer time; these are people who do not settle their differences with anyone without getting revenge, or forcible correction for the other party. It is the excessive state that we tend more to regard as opposed to mildness, since it actually occurs more; after all, to want revenge is the more human reaction, and difficult people are worse to live with.

But what we said in our previous discussions is also clear from the present one: it is not easy to determine how, with whom, in what sorts of circumstances, and for how long one should be angry, and what the dividing line is between acting correctly and going wrong. For it is not the person who deviates a little who is censured, whether he does so in the direction of excess or of deficiency; since sometimes we praise those deficient in anger and call them mild, and we call those who get angry manly, on the basis that they are capable of taking charge. So as to how far and in what way a person must deviate to be worthy of censure, it is not easy to define it in words; for the judgement of such things lies in our perception of the particular circumstances.[15] But this much at least is clear, that the intermediate disposition, in accordance with which we are angry with the people we should, in the

1126a10

1126a15

1126a20

1126a25

1126a30

1126a35

1126b1

1126b5

---

[15] Reading καὶ τῇ αἰσθήσει (1126b4).

circumstances we should, in the way we should, and so on, is to be praised, while the excessive and deficient states are to be censured—lightly, if the deviation is small, more if it is more, but severely if it is on a large scale. It is clear, then, that it is the intermediate disposition we should hold on to. So let

1126b10 this stand as our account of the dispositions concerned with anger.

(IV. 6) When it comes to mixing with others—living in their company, sharing with them in conversations and the business of life—one sort of people are thought to be obsequious: people who praise everything in order to please and offer no resistance in anything, thinking they must be no trouble

1126b15 to anyone they meet. Others, contrary to these, offer resistance in everything, and have not the slightest concern about causing distress to people; this sort are called morose and contentious. It is quite clear, then, that the said dispositions are to be censured, and that the disposition intermediate between these is to be praised—the disposition in accordance with which one will accept what one should and as one should, and take exception similarly. No special

1126b20 name is assigned to it, but it most resembles friendship. For the person corresponding to the intermediate disposition is the sort we mean by 'the good friend'—except that there special affection is an additional feature. The disposition differs from friendship in that there is no feeling of special affection for the people at whom it is directed; for it is not because of loving or hating that the type in question accepts each kind of thing in the way one should, but

1126b25 because he is a person of that sort. For no matter whether the people involved are unknown or known to him, acquaintances or not, he will do it in a similar way—except that he will do it as is fitting in each sort of case; for it is not equally appropriate to be concerned about acquaintances and strangers, or again to cause distress in the two cases. We have said, then, in general terms that he will mix with people as one should; what he will do is to aim at either

1126b30 not causing distress or contributing pleasantness with reference to what is fine and what is advantageous. For this type seems to have to do with the pleasures and pains that come about when people mix with each other; and on occasions when it is not fine, or is harmful, to be pleasant, he will object, and will decide in favour of causing distress—so that if someone is doing something that actually brings disgrace, and no slight disgrace at that, or brings harm,

1126b35
1127a1 and opposing it will cause little distress, the 'friendly' person will not accept it but will object. He will deal differently with eminent and ordinary people, and with people he knows better and those he knows less well, and so on for other relevant differences: he will mete out what is suitable to each set of people, preferring in itself the option of being pleasant to them, and taking care not to cause distress, but being guided by the consequences where these tip the

1127a5 balance the other way—and by 'consequences', I mean the fine and the advantageous. But he will also cause distress on a minor scale for the sake of great future pleasure. Such, then, is the intermediate person, though he has no name; as for the complaisant type, the sort that aim at being pleasant without any other motive are obsequious, while the sort that do it to get some benefit for themselves in terms of money and what money brings are ingratiating. As for the person who objects to everything, we have said he is morose and contentious. These extremes appear to be opposed to each other because of the fact that the intermediate has no name. | 1127a10

(IV. 7) The intermediate state between imposture and self-deprecation also has to do more or less with the same things; and this state too is nameless. But it is no bad thing to go over the nameless sorts of states as well; for in that way | 1127a15 we shall get to know the subject of character better, having gone through things one by one, and we shall be more convinced that the excellences are intermediate states once our survey has shown this to hold in all cases. In the matter of social living, then, we have discussed the types that mix with others with a view to the giving of pleasure and pain; now let us discuss those that are truthful and untruthful, whether in word or in action, in what they claim | 1127a20 about themselves. The impostor, then, seems to be a type that claims possession of things that bring repute, whether things he doesn't have at all or ones greater than he does have; while conversely the self-deprecating person seems to deny that he has what he does have, or to make less of them than they are. As for the intermediate person, he is precisely himself, which makes him characteristically truthful both in the way he lives and in the way he talks, acknowledging it to be true that he has what he has, and neither | 1127a25 more nor less. (It is possible to do each of these sorts of things either for some further end or for no further end; but each type, if he is not acting for some further end, speaks and acts in the way corresponding to his nature, and lives his life in that way.) In itself falsehood is a bad thing, and to be censured, while truth is fine and something to be praised; and so the truthful | 1127a30 person, the one in the intermediate state, is also to be praised, while the untruthful sorts are both to be censured, but the impostor more. Before we discuss each of these two, let us discuss the truthful sort. We are not here talking about the person who tells the truth in the context of agreements, or anything of that sort, which has more to do with injustice, or justice (that, after all, will belong to the sphere of a different excellence), but about contexts | 1127b1 in which, with nothing of that sort to make any difference, a person is truthful both in the way he talks and in the way he lives, by virtue of being such by disposition. Someone like this would seem to be a decent person. For the lover of truth, since he also tells the truth where it makes no difference, will tell the truth even more where it does make a difference; for there he will be guard- | 1127b5 ing against falsehood as something shameful, when he was already guarding against it in itself. Such a person is to be praised. But he leans more towards telling less than the truth about himself; it appears more fitting because of the offensiveness of going too far. The sort who claims things for himself on a

1127b10   greater scale than he has them for no further end looks like a worthless person (for otherwise he would not take pleasure in falsehood), but is evidently more ineffectual than bad; the one who does do it for a further end is to be censured (but not too much) as an impostor[16] if it is for the sake of reputation or honour, whereas if it is for the sake of money, or the sorts of things that generate money, he is a more disgraceful figure (but it is decision, not capacity,

1127b15   that makes the impostor what he is; he is an impostor by disposition, and by virtue of being that sort of person). Liars too fall into two similar types: they either enjoy the lie itself, or they do it from a desire for reputation or profit. Impostors who do it for the sake of reputation, then, claim the sorts of things that bring praise or cause people to call one happy; whereas those who do it for profit claim the sorts of things which are also of use to one's neighbours

1127b20   and which one can successfully escape detection for lacking, like the skills of a seer, a wise person, or a doctor. It is for this reason that most people lay claim to such things, when they do so falsely; for the things in question have the features described. The way self-deprecating people understate themselves makes their character appear more attractive, since they seem to do it from a

1127b25   desire to avoid pompousness, and not for the sake of profit; most of all it is things that bring repute that these people too disclaim, as indeed Socrates used to do. Those who disclaim small and obvious things are said to be silly and affected, and are easier to despise; and sometimes it is patently imposture, as when people wear Spartan dress, since imposture is a matter of both excess

1127b30   and excessive deficiency. But those who employ self-deprecation in reasonable measure, and in relation to things that are not too obvious and visible, are patently attractive. The impostor, since he is worse, appears to be more opposed to the truthful person.

    (IV. 8) Life also includes relaxation, and relaxation includes amusement of a playful sort: here too there is thought to be a way of interacting with others

1128a1   that is fitting—and sorts of things one should say, and ways one should say them, with similar limits on what one listens to. It will also make a difference to be talking, or—as the case may be—listening, to other people who are like this. Clearly, here too it is possible to go to excess and to be deficient by comparison to the intermediate. Those who go to excess in trying to raise a

1128a5   laugh are thought of as buffoons, and as vulgar, striving for comic effect by any means, and aiming more at causing laughter than at saying things that are becoming and not causing distress to the butt of their joke; while those who would not say anything funny themselves, *and* take exception to those who do,

1128a10   are thought to be boorish and stiff. Those who are playful in a fitting way are called witty [*eutrapeloi*]—'supple-witted' [*eutropoi*], as it were; for supple moves like these are thought to be ones that belong to character, and just as we judge

---

[16] Reading ὡς ἀλαζών (1127b12–13).

bodies by their movements, so too we do people's characters. But since
humour is prevalent in society, and most people enjoy play and making jokes
more than one should, buffoons too are called witty because people find them   1128a15
attractive; but that there is a difference, and no small one, is clear from what we
have said. In the same family as the intermediate disposition is also ingenious-
ness: it is a mark of the ingenious person to say and to listen to the sorts of
things that are fitting for decent and civilized people, for there are certain
things that are appropriate for people of this sort to say by way of amusement,   1128a20
and to listen to, and the civilized person's amusement differs from that of the
slavish type, the educated person's from that of the uneducated. One can see
this too by comparing old- and new-style comedies: the former treated foul
language as funny, whereas for the latter innuendo is more so, and there is no
small difference between these in terms of decorum. So should one define one   1128a25
who uses humour to good effect as someone who says things not unsuitable
for a civilized person, or as one who does not cause distress to the listener or
even gives him pleasure? Or is this sort of thing itself undefined? Different
things, after all, are hateful or pleasant for different people. The intermediate
person will also listen to the same sorts of things; for what he tolerates listening to seems also to be what he will put together himself. So there will be limits
to that, for jokes are a kind of verbal abuse, and some forms of abuse are   1128a30
forbidden by the lawgivers; presumably some forms of joking should have
been forbidden too. The person of taste and cultivation, then, will be disposed
to behave like this, being as it were his own law. Such, then, is the intermediate
person, whether we call him ingenious or witty. The buffoon cannot resist making a joke of things, sparing neither himself nor anyone else if he can raise a   1128a35
laugh, and saying the kind of things the person of taste would never say, and   1128b1
some of which he would not even listen to. The boorish person is useless for
social interaction of this sort; for he contributes nothing and takes exception to
everything. But it seems that relaxation and play are a necessity in life.

So then the intermediate states we have talked about in the sphere of ordinary   1128b5
life are three, and all of them have to do with sharing in certain sorts of
conversation and action. But they differ in that one of them has to do with
truth, while the others have to do with pleasure; and of those to do with
pleasure, one is in the sphere of playful amusement, the other in other forms
of social interaction.

(IV. 9) A sense of shame is not appropriately talked about as a kind of excel-   1128b10
lence; it resembles an affection rather than a disposition. At any rate it is
defined as a kind of fear of disrepute, and has an effect comparable to that of
fear in the ordinary sense: being ashamed of themselves makes people blush,
and fear of death makes them pale. So both appear in a way to be associated   1128b15
with the body, a feature which seems to belong to an affection rather than to a
disposition. But the affection in this case is not fitting for every time of life,

only for youth; for we think that young people should have a sense of shame because they live by emotion and so get many things wrong, but are held back by a sense of shame; and we praise those of the young who have it, whereas 1128b20 no one would praise an older person for being prone to feeling shame, since we think he shouldn't do anything that incurs shame in the first place. For shame is not something that belongs to the decent person at all, given that it is occasioned by bad actions: one shouldn't do them (if some are truly shameful, some only held to be so, it makes no difference—one shouldn't do either sort), 1128b25 and so one shouldn't feel shame. Even being the *kind* of person to do anything shameful is a sign of worthlessness. To be such as to feel shame if one did any such thing, and then think oneself a decent sort of person because of that, is strange; for a sense of shame applies to voluntary actions, and the decent person will never voluntarily do what is bad. A sense of shame will indeed be 1128b30 hypothetically something decent—*if* one did such-and-such, one would be ashamed; but this is not a feature of the excellences. If shamelessness is something bad, and so is not being ashamed at doing shameful things, that doesn't make it decent to do such things and be ashamed. Self-control is not an excellence either, but a sort of excellence that's mixed with something else. 1128b35 But what it is will be shown in our later discussions. Now let us talk about justice.

BOOK V

(V. 1) We must inquire into justice and injustice—what sorts of actions they 1129a5 relate to, what sort of intermediate state justice is, and what it is that the just is intermediate between. Let our inquiry follow the same approach as the preceding discussions. Well then, we see everyone using 'justice' to mean the sort of disposition that makes people such as to do just things, i.e. which 1129a10 makes them act justly and wish for what is just; and similarly with injustice too—it is what makes people act unjustly and wish for what is unjust. So for us too let this be laid down, as a rough starting point. For in fact there is a difference between types of expert knowledge and capacities on the one hand, and dispositions on the other: with a capacity or expertise, the same one seems to relate to both members of a pair of contraries, whereas a disposition, in so far as it is one of a pair of contraries, does not relate to 1129a15 contraries in this way; so e.g. health does not lead to our doing both healthy and unhealthy things, but only healthy ones, since we say that someone is walking healthily when he walks in the way a healthy man does, whatever that is. So a contrary disposition is often revealed by its contrary, and often too the dispositions are revealed by the subjects possessing them; for if it is evident what good physical condition is, it becomes evident what bad physical condition is too, and what contributes to good condition reveals what good condition is, and vice versa. For if good condition is firmness of flesh, necessarily bad condition must also be flabbiness, and what contributes to good condition must be what contributes to making flesh firm. And as a general rule, if one of a pair of contraries is said in more than one way, it follows that the other is too; so that e.g. if the just is, so is the unjust. Justice and injustice, in fact, *do* seem to be said in more than one way, but we fail to notice the homonymy in their case because the things referred to are close together, whereas with things that are further apart it is more obvious (for here things actually *look* quite different), e.g. that the key that locks a door and the one below the neck of an animal are called 'key' homonymously. Let us then find out in how many ways a person is said to be unjust. People[17] regard as 'unjust' both the person who breaks the law and the grasping, i.e. unequal-minded, one; hence, clearly, both the law-abiding person and the equal-minded one are just. In that case, the just is what is lawful and what is equal, while the unjust is what is unlawful and what is unequal. Because the unjust person is grasping, his sphere of operation will be goods—not all of them, but those to which good and bad fortune relate, ones which are generally good, but not always for this or that particular person. (Human beings pray for these, and go after them; but they should rather pray that what are goods generally speaking be good for them too, while choosing the things that are good for them.) The unjust person does not always choose the greater share, actually choosing less in the case of things that are generally bad; but since the lesser evil too is regarded as good in a way, and what the grasping person wants more of is what is good, this makes people think of him as grasping. In fact he is unequal-minded; this covers both cases and is a common feature of both. But because, as we said, the lawbreaker is unjust and the law-abiding person just, it is clear that everything in accordance with law is in a way just; for the things marked off by the lawgiver's art are in accordance with law, and we do call each of these just. When the laws pronounce about anything they aim either at what is of common advantage to all, or at what is of advantage to the best people, or of those in power, or on some other basis of this sort; so that in one way we call just the things that create and preserve happiness and its parts for the citizen community. But the law also enjoins us to do what the courageous person does (e.g. not leaving one's post, or running away, or throwing down one's weapons), and what the moderate person does (e.g. not committing adultery, or rape), and what the mild person does (e.g. not throwing punches, or

1129a20

1129a25

1129a30

1129b1

1129b5

1129b10

1129b15

1129b20

---

[17] Reading δοκεῖ δὲ ὅ τε ... (1129a32).

resorting to verbal abuse)—and similarly in accordance with the other excellences and the corresponding forms of badness, ordering us to do some things

1129b25 and forbidding others; correctly, if the law has been laid down correctly, but less well if it has been merely improvised. This justice, then, is complete excellence, only not without qualification but in relation to another person. It is because of this that justice is often thought to be mightiest of the excellences, so that 'neither Evening Star nor Morning equals its wonder', and the

1129b30 proverb goes 'But justice gathers in excellence entire'. And it is complete excellence to the highest degree because it is the *activation* of complete excellence; complete, too, because the person who possesses it has the capacity to put his excellence to use in relation to another person as well, and not just by himself; for many people are able to display their excellence in relation to what belongs to them, but incapable of doing so when it comes to dealing

1130a1 with another person. This is the reason why Bias' saying—'ruling will reveal the man'—seems good; for holding office already implies a relationship with, and an association with, another. It is also for this same reason, i.e. that it relates to another person, that justice alone of the excellences is thought to be

1130a5 someone else's good—because the just person does what is of advantage to someone else, whether someone in power or an associate. The worst sort of person, then, is the one whose badness extends even to his treatment of himself and of those close to him, but the best sort is not the one whose excellence extends to his treatment of himself, but to his treatment of another; for it is this that is a difficult task. This justice, then, is not a part

1130a10 of excellence but excellence as a whole, and the injustice that is its contrary is not a part of badness but badness as a whole. What we have said makes clear how excellence and justice of this sort differ from each other: while it is the same disposition, what it is to be the first is not the same as what it is to be the second; rather, in so far as the state relates to another person, it is justice, while in so far as it is this sort of disposition without such a qualification, it is excellence.

(V. 2) However, what we are looking for is the justice that is a part of

1130a15 excellence—for as we are saying, there *is* one; similarly too with the injustice that is part of badness. What indicates that there is such a form of justice is that the person who is actualizing any of the other forms of badness behaves unjustly but does not grasp after more than his share at all, e.g. someone who has thrown away his shield because of cowardice, or resorted to verbal abuse because he is a 'difficult' sort of person, or not helped someone out with

1130a20 money because of avariciousness; whereas when someone does grasp after more than his share, often the action does not correspond to any states of this sort, still less to all of them together, and yet it does correspond to *some* form of viciousness (since we censure it), i.e. injustice. There is, then, another kind of injustice relating to the first as part to whole, and another way for something to be unjust, as part of the whole that is the unjust in the sense of contrary to law. Again, if one person commits adultery for the sake of profit, taking something over and above the adultery, while another person spends money to do it and so penalizes himself through appetite, the latter sort would seem to be self-indulgent rather than grasping, and the former unjust but not self-indulgent; clearly, then, because he is doing it for the sake of making a profit. Further, in the case of all the other sorts of unjust actions, the action is referred to some particular form of badness—e.g. to self-indulgence if someone has committed adultery, to cowardice if he has deserted his comrade in battle, to anger if he has struck someone; but if the action was one of making a profit, it is not referred to any form of badness except injustice. So it is evident that there is a certain other sort of injustice besides injustice as a whole, and a part of it, sharing the same name because its definition is in the same genus; for the force of both lies in their other-regarding aspect, the difference being that the one has to do with honour, or money, or security (or whatever single term might be available to cover all these things), and because of the pleasure that comes from profit, while the other has to do with all the things that concern the person of excellence.

So then it is clear that there are more forms of justice than one, and that there is also a certain, separate, form of it over and above excellence as a whole; what it is, and what sort of thing it is, we must now establish. Well then, we have defined the unjust as what is unlawful and what is unequal, and the just as what is lawful and what is equal. The injustice talked about in the previous section will correspond, then, to the unjust in the sense of the unlawful; and since the unequal and the unlawful are not the same thing, but differ as part from whole (for everything unequal is unlawful, but not everything unlawful is unequal), so too this sort of unjust and injustice are not the same as but different from the other sort, the one sort being parts and the other wholes; for this injustice is a part of injustice as a whole, and similarly too the justice corresponding to it is a part of justice as a whole. Hence we must also talk about the justice that is a part, and the injustice that is a part, and so too about what is just and unjust in this sense. So as for the justice that is coextensive with excellence as a whole, and that sort of injustice too, the one being an activation of excellence as a whole in relation to another person, the other similarly of badness as a whole, these can now be set on one side. It is evident, too, how one should define the just and the unjust that correspond to this sort of justice and injustice, since broadly speaking most of the things enjoined by law are those that are prescribed from the point of view of excellence as a whole; for the law prescribes that one should live in accordance with each excellence and forbids living in accordance with each corresponding bad state. Again, the things that tend to produce excellence as a whole are those legal provisions that have been enacted in relation to education with a view to the common interest. (On the subject of the education of the

Marginal references: 1130a25, 1130a30, 1130b1, 1130b5, 1130b10, 1130b15, 1130b20, 1130b25

individual that makes him unconditionally a good man, it must be determined later whether this is a matter for political or for some other sort of expertise; for presumably it is not the case that being a good man and being a good citizen are the same, for every type of citizen.) Of the justice that is a part, and of what is just in this sense, one sort is the one found in distributions of honour, or money, or the other things to be divided up among those who are members of the political association (for in the case of these things it is possible for one person to have either an unequal or an equal share in relation to another); while another is rectificatory, operating in interactions between one person and another. Of the latter, there are two parts, since some interactions are voluntary, some counter-voluntary: voluntary, things such as selling, buying, lending with interest, making guarantees, giving free use of something, depositing, or hiring out (called 'voluntary' because the interactions are voluntary at the beginning); counter-voluntary, either clandestine, e.g. theft, adultery, poisoning, procuring, enticement of slaves, killing by stealth, testifying falsely against someone; or violent, e.g. assault, imprisonment, murder, kidnapping, maiming, slander, verbal abuse.

(V. 3) Given that the unjust person is unequal-minded and the unjust is unequal, clearly there is something intermediate too, between the inequality on the two sides. This is what is equal; for whatever action admits of 'too large' and 'too small' also admits of 'equal amount'. So if what is unjust is unequal, what is just is equal; which is what everyone thinks even without any argument. And since what is equal is intermediate, the just will be a sort of intermediate. But the equal involves at least two terms. So what is just is necessarily both intermediate and equal, and relative, i.e. relating to certain individuals; and in so far as it is intermediate, it will be between certain things (i.e. too large and too small), in so far as it is equal, it will involve two things, and in so far as it is just it will relate to certain individuals. Necessarily, then, the just involves at least four terms: the persons with an interest are two, and the things in which they deal are two. And there will be the same sort of equality between the people and between the things involved, in so far as the second pair, the things, stand to each other in the same relationship as the first; for if the persons are not equal to each other, they will not have equal shares—and it is here that the battles and the accusations start, when either equals get shares that are not equal or people that are not equal have and are assigned shares that are. The matter of distribution 'according to merit' also makes this clear, since everybody agrees that what is just in distributions must accord with some kind of merit, but everybody is not talking about the same kind of merit: for democrats merit lies in being born a free person, for oligarchs in wealth or, for some of them, in noble descent, for aristocrats in excellence. The just, then, represents a kind of proportion. For the proportionate is not just a property of numbers that consist of abstract units, but of number in general; proportion is equality of ratios, and it involves at least four terms. (That discrete proportion does so is clear; but so too does continuous proportion, because it treats one term as two, mentioning it twice: e.g. as line A is to line B, so line B is to line C. Line B, then, has been mentioned twice; hence, if line B is put in twice, the terms of the proportion are four.) The just, too, involves at least four terms, and the ratio is the same: the people and the things are divided similarly. In that case, as A is to B, so C is to D, and so, *alternando*, as A is to C, so B is to D. Thus one whole (A + C), too, stands to the other whole (B + D) in the same way—which is the pairing the distribution creates, and if things are put together in this way, the pairing is done justly. Thus the combination of A with C and that of B with D is what is just in distribution, and the just in this sense is intermediate, while the unjust is what contravenes the proportionate; for the proportionate is intermediate, and the just is proportionate. (Mathematicians call this sort of proportion 'geometrical'; for it is in geometrical proportion that one whole also stands to the other whole as each term stands to the other in a given pair.) But this proportion is not continuous: there is not numerically one term, representing person and thing. What is just, then, is this—what is proportional; and what is unjust is what contravenes the proportional. One share, then, gets too large and the other too small, which is what actually happens in practice; for the person who behaves unjustly has too much of what is good, the person treated unjustly too little. With what is bad it is the reverse, since the lesser evil is reckoned as a good in comparison with the greater evil; for the lesser evil is more desirable than the greater, and what is desirable is a good, and what is more so is a greater one. This, then, is one of the two forms the just takes.

(V. 4) The remaining form is the rectificatory, which is found in interactions between people, both voluntary and counter-voluntary. What is just in this sense differs in form from the just in the previous sense. For the just in the distribution of things belonging to the community always follows the proportion we have described (for in fact if the distribution is from public funds, it will follow the same ratio that the individual contributions have to one another); and the unjust which is opposed to the just in this sense is what contravenes the proportional. What is just in personal interactions, on the other hand, is in a way equal, and what is unjust is in a way unequal, but in accordance not with that other sort of proportion but with arithmetical proportion. For it makes no difference whether a decent person has defrauded a worthless one or a worthless person a decent one, or whether the adultery was committed by someone decent or someone worthless; the law pays attention solely to the difference created by the damage done, and where one person is committing an injustice, another suffering it, or one person inflicted damage and another has been damaged, it treats them as equal. So what is

1131b1

1131b5

1131b10

1131b15

1131b20

1131b25

1131b30

1132a1

1132a5

unjust in this sense the judge tries to equalize, because it is a matter of inequality; for in fact when one person is struck and another does the striking, or if one person actually kills and the other is killed, the effect of the action and the doing of it constitute unequal parts of a division—and the aim of

1132a10 imposing a loss on the doer is to equalize things, taking away from the gain realized. For by and large we talk in such cases, even if perhaps inappropriately in some, about the 'gain' accruing e.g. to the assailant, and the 'loss' suffered by the victim; but when the effect is measured the one is called a 'loss' and the other a 'gain'. So then the equal is intermediate between too

1132a15 much and too little, while the gain and the loss in these cases represent too much and too little in contrary ways, the gain too much good and too little bad, the loss the other way round; intermediate between which, we say, is the equal, which is what we are saying is just, so that what is just in terms of rectification will be intermediate between loss and gain. This is why, when

1132a20 people are in dispute, they resort to the judge, and when they make their way to the judge they are making their way to what is just, for being a judge means being as it were the just in living form; and they seek out the judge as something intermediate—sometimes judges are actually called 'mediators', the thought being that if one succeeds in getting what is intermediate, one will get what is just. The just, then, is something intermediate, if in fact the

1132a25 judge is. What the judge does is to equal things up; it is as if he were dealing with a line divided into unequal segments, taking away from the larger segment the amount by which it exceeds half of the line and adding it to the smaller segment. Whenever a whole is divided into two, people say they have what belongs to them when they receive what is equal; the equal being what is

1132a30 intermediate between the larger and the smaller according to arithmetical proportion. It is because of this, in fact, that it has the name *dikaion* ['just'], i.e. because it is a matter of cutting *dicha* ['into two'], as if one might say '*dichaion*', and as if the *dikastēs* ['judge'] were a '*dichastēs*'. For when something is taken away from one of two equal things and added to the other, one of the two exceeds the other by twice that amount—given that if it had been

1132b1 taken away from the one but not added to the other, the latter would exceed the former only by one such amount. So it exceeds the intermediate by one, and the intermediate exceeds what had something taken away from it by one. That then will enable us to see both what should be taken away from the one that has too much and what should be added to the one that has too little:

1132b5 there should be added to the latter the amount by which the intermediate exceeds it, while the amount by which the intermediate is exceeded should be taken away from the largest thing. Let there be three lines AA, BB, CC, which are equal to one another. Let segment AE be taken away from AA, and let CD be added to CC, so that DCC as a whole exceeds EA by CD and CF; it will

(1132b10) then exceed BB by CD. These terms, 'gain' and 'loss', are derived from voluntary exchange, for to have more than what belonged to one is called

making a gain, while having less than one had at the beginning is called
making a loss, as e.g. in buying and selling, and in other spheres where the law   1132b15
imposes no sanction on such outcomes; in contrast where neither more nor
less results for the two parties, but the transaction leaves the balance of
resources as it was,[18] people say they have what belongs to them, and that they
are neither making a loss nor making a gain. So then the just is intermediate
between a kind of gain and a kind of loss that are counter to what is voluntary, and it is a matter of having an equal amount both before and after the   1132b20
action.

(V. 5) Some people think that it is in fact the reciprocal that is unqualifiedly
just—as the Pythagoreans asserted; for they used, without qualification, to
define the just as what stands in a reciprocal relation to something else.
However the reciprocal does not fit the case either of the just in the distributive sense or of that in the rectificatory (even though people give this inter-   1132b25
pretation to Rhadamanthys' notion of the just too:

if what one did one suffered too, then straight would justice be),

for in many ways it fails to accord with them: so e.g. if an office-holder
struck someone, he should not be struck in return, and if an office-holder
was the person struck, the one who struck him should not only be struck but   1132b30
receive forcible correction as well. Again, there is a great difference between
what was done voluntarily and what was done counter-voluntarily. In commercial associations, however, the parties are bound together by a form of
the just that is like this, i.e. what is reciprocal in proportional terms, not in
terms of numerical equality. For it is reciprocal action governed by proportion that keeps the city together. Either people seek to return evil for evil,
and if they don't, it seems like slavery; or they seek to return good for good,   1133a1
and if they don't, there is no giving in exchange, and it is exchange that
keeps them together. This is in fact why the temple of the Graces [Charites] is
located in a prominent public place, to ensure that there is reciprocal giving;
for this is a peculiar function of gratitude [charis], which is the Graces'
sphere—the recipient should perform a service in return to the one who did   1133a5
him the favour [ho charisamenos], and on another occasion take the initiative
in doing a favour himself. What brings about proportional reciprocity is the
coupling of diametrical opposites. Let A be a builder, B a shoemaker, C a
house, D a shoe: the requirement then is that the builder receive from the
shoemaker what the shoemaker has produced, and that he himself give the   1133a10
shoemaker a share in his own product. If, then, there is first of all equality in
proportional terms, and reciprocal exchange occurs after that, the stated
requirement will be fulfilled, but if not, there is no equality, and there is
nothing to keep the parties together; for the product of the one may well be

---

[18] Reading ἀλλὰ ⟨τὰ⟩ αὐτὰ δι' αὐτῶν γένηται (1132b16–17).

superior to that of the other, so these need to be equalized. This feature is found in the various forms of productive expertise too; for they would be
1133a15   wiped out, if the effect caused by whatever it is that is causing it were not matched by what happens to the thing affected, and matched in size and kind too. For it is not two doctors that become partners to an exchange, but rather a doctor and a farmer, and in general people who are of different sorts and not in a relation of equality to each other; they therefore have to be equalized. Hence everything that is exchanged must be somehow compar-
1133a20   able. This is a role that is fulfilled by currency, so that it becomes, in a way, an intermediate; for since it measures everything, it also measures excess and deficiency—so measuring just how many shoes it does take to equal a house, or food. Then as builder is to shoemaker, so must such-and-such a number of shoes be to a house or food. For without this equalization, there will be
1133a25   no exchange and no association for exchange; and there will be equalization only if the things in question are somehow equal. Everything, in that case, must be measured by some one thing, as was said before. In truth this one thing is need, which holds everything together; for if people did not need things, or if they do not need them to the same extent, then either there will be no exchange, or the exchange will be a different one. But as a kind of
1133a30   substitute for need, convention has brought currency into existence—and it is called currency [nomisma] because of this, i.e. because it exists not by nature but by custom [nomos], and because it is in our power to change it and render it useless. There will, then, be reciprocity when equalization takes place, so that as farmer is to shoemaker, so the product of the shoemaker is
1133b1   to that of the farmer. But one should not introduce them as terms in a figure of proportion when they are already making the exchange (since otherwise one of the two terms at the extremes will have both of the excess amounts), but when they are still in possession of their own products. In this way they will be equals and partners, i.e. because this equality is capable of being
1133b5   produced in their case. Let A be a farmer, B food, C a shoemaker, D his product as equalized: if reciprocity could not be achieved in this way, there would be no sharing in activity between the parties. That it is need that holds them together, being as it were a single thing, is shown by the fact that when the parties involved do not have a need for each other—either each for the other, or one of the two—they make no exchange, just as when someone needs what one has oneself, e.g. wine, but they want to give a corn export
1133b10   licence in return. Equalization, then, is needed here; and in the interest of future exchange, if one has no need for anything now, currency acts as a kind of guarantor for us that, when there is a need, exchange will be possible; for the person bringing it is necessarily in a position to take something away. True, this same thing also happens with currency, in that it does not always have the same purchasing power; nevertheless it has a greater ten-
1133b15   dency to be stable than to vary. Everything, therefore, needs to have a value

set on it; for in this way there will always be exchange, and if exchange, association. Currency, then, acts like a measure, making things commensurable and so equalizing them; for there would be no association without exchange, no exchange without equality, and no equality without commensurability. Strictly speaking, of course, it is impossible that things so different in kind should become commensurable, but in relation to people's needs a sufficient degree of commensurability can be achieved. There must then be some single element involved in all cases, and this must be something laid down by agreement—which is why it is called 'currency' [*nomisma*], since it is this that makes everything commensurable, in so far as everything is measured in currency. Let A be a house, B ten units of currency, C a bed: A is half of B, if the house is worth five units, or is equal to that amount, and the bed, C, is a tenth part of B. It is clear, then, how many beds equal the house, i.e. five. Clearly, that is how exchange took place before currency existed; for it makes no difference whether five beds are exchanged for a house, or currency to the value of five beds. 1133b20

1133b25

So then we have said what it is for something to be unjust, and what it is for something to be just. With these defined, it is clear that just action is an intermediate between doing what is unjust and being subjected to what is unjust; for the one is to have too much, the other to have too little. Justice is an intermediate disposition, only not in the same way as the other excellences, but because it achieves something intermediate, while injustice achieves the corresponding extremes. And justice is the disposition in accordance with which the just person is said to be the sort to do what is just, as a result of decision, and to distribute things to himself in relation to another and between two others not in such a way as to give himself too much of what is desirable and his neighbour too little, and the reverse with what is harmful, but so as to give what is proportionately equal to both, and similarly where the distribution is between two others. Injustice, conversely, is a matter of doing, as a result of decision, what is unjust; and this is excess and deficiency in what is beneficial or harmful, contrary to what is proportional. Hence injustice is excess and deficiency because its effect is excess and deficiency: in the case of the agent's distributing to himself, this will be excess of what is generally beneficial and deficiency of what is harmful, while where the distribution is between others, the case is as a whole similar, but there can be disproportion either way. Of unjust action, the 'too small' is a matter of being subjected to what is unjust, the 'too large' of doing what is unjust. So as for justice and injustice, and what the nature of each of them is, let our account stand like this, and similarly in relation to what is just and what is unjust, in general terms. 1133b30

1134a1

1134a5

1134a10

1134a15

(V. 6) Given that it is possible for someone to do what is unjust without yet *being* unjust, what sorts of unjust actions make a person e.g. a thief, or an adulterer, or a brigand, i.e. unjust in terms of each of the specific forms of injustice? Or will this turn out not to be the way they differ? For in fact someone might sleep with a woman knowing who she is, only not as a result of starting from a decision, but through passion. He is behaving unjustly, then, but he is not unjust: as for example one is not a thief, though one *did* steal, and one is not an adulterer, though one *did* commit adultery; and similarly in other cases.

Well then: how the reciprocal is related to the just has been said earlier; but one should not fail to observe that what we are looking for is both what is just without qualification and what is just in the context of the political community. This is found where people share their lives together with a view to self-sufficiency: people who are free, and equal either proportionately or arithmetically. Hence for those who do not meet these conditions there is no such thing as what is just in this 'political' sense in relation to each other, only what is just in a way and in virtue of a certain resemblance. For there is justice between people who also have law governing interactions between them; and people have law if there can be injustice between them, since legal judgments distinguish between what is just and what is unjust. But where there is injustice between people, there is also unjust action (even though where there is unjust action there is not always injustice), and this is a matter of assigning to oneself too much of what is generally good and too little of things generally bad. This is why we do not allow a human being to rule, but rather rational principle, on the grounds that a human being does it for himself and becomes a tyrant; but the ruler is guardian of what is just, and if of the just, of the equal too. And since no greater share seems to accrue to him as ruler, if in fact he is just (for he does not assign more of what is generally good to himself, unless it is proportional to his own case; hence his labours are for another's benefit, and it is for this reason that people say that justice is someone else's good, as we stated before, too): given that this is so, some form of return must be provided for him, and this is honour and prestige—and it is those for whom such things are insufficient that become tyrants. What is 'just' for a master of slaves or for a father is not the same as these forms of it, but only like them. For there is no injustice in an unqualified sense in relation to what is one's own, and a chattel, or a child until it is of a certain age and becomes independent, is like a part of oneself, and oneself—no one decides to harm *that*; hence there will be no injustice in relation to oneself; nor, therefore, will there be what is unjust in the political sense, or what is just, since that, as we agreed, is what is in accordance with law, and exists among those whose interactions are by nature such as to be governed by law; and these were people sharing equally in ruling and being ruled. Hence 'the just' exists more in relation to one's wife than in relation to one's children and chattels; for this is the just as it applies to a household. But this too is different from the just in the political sense.

(V. 7) What is politically just divides into the natural and the legal: the
natural being what has the same force everywhere, and does not depend on a
decision whether to accept it or not, the legal what in the beginning makes no
difference whether enacted or not, but when enacted *does* make a difference,
e.g that the ransom for a prisoner of war be set at a particular amount, or that
the sacrifice should be of a goat, not two sheep, or again the laws laid down to
meet particular cases, e.g. that sacrifice be made to Brasidas, and enactments
in the form of decrees. Some people think that all legal enactments are of this
sort, on the grounds that what is by nature is unchangeable and has the same
force everywhere (just as fire burns both here and in Persia), whereas they see
things that are just in process of change. But in fact it is not like this, except in
a way. Granted, among gods there is presumably no change at all, but among
human beings, while there *is* such a thing as what is by nature, still everything
is capable of being changed—and yet, despite this, there is room to apply a
distinction between what is by nature and what is not by nature. It is clear
enough what sort of arrangement, among those that can also be otherwise
than they are, is by nature, and what sort is, rather, legal and the result of
agreement, given that both sorts alike are changeable. And the same distinction will fit in the case of other things; for the right hand is superior by nature,
and yet it is possible that everyone should become ambidextrous. Those just
arrangements based on agreement and what is advantageous are like units of
measure: measures of wine and corn are not everywhere of equal size, but
larger where people buy, smaller where they sell. Similarly, just arrangements
established not by nature but by human beings are not the same everywhere,
since even political constitutions are not the same everywhere, although only
one is everywhere the best by nature. Each of the things that are just in the
legal sense is related as a universal to the particulars falling under it, since the
things that are done are many, but each part of the legally just is one in
number, because it is a universal. An unjust act and what is unjust are not the
same thing, nor are a just act and what is just; for what is unjust is so by nature
or by prescription, while this same thing, when done, is an unjust act, which it
is not before it has been done, then being only something that is unjust.
Similarly with a just act too, a *dikaiōma*, though the common category is more
usually called a *dikaiopragēma*, the term *dikaiōma* being used for the rectification of an unjust act. We must consider later each particular sort of just and
unjust act, to see what sorts these are, how many they are, and what the
things are to which they relate.

(V. 8) Given that the things that are just and unjust are as we have said, a
person acts unjustly and justly when he does these voluntarily; whereas when
he does them counter-voluntarily, he neither acts unjustly nor acts justly,
except in an incidental sense; for people in fact do things that are incidentally
just or unjust. An unjust *act*, or a just one, is marked off by the distinction

1134b20

1134b25

1134b30

1134b35
1135a1

1135a5

1135a10

1135a15

1135a20

between voluntary and counter-voluntary; for when something unjust is done voluntarily, it is an object of censure, and at the same time it is, then, an unjust act. So it will be possible for something to be unjust but not yet an unjust act, if the element of voluntariness is not present as well. By voluntary, I mean—as has also been said before—whatever, from among the things that depend on him, a person does knowingly, i.e. not in ignorance of any of the relevant

1135a25 factors (the person affected, the instrument, or the effect of the action, e.g. whom one is striking, with what, and to what effect, i.e. where each of those things comes into the action non-incidentally), and not under force—as, for example, if someone's hand were seized by someone else and used to strike a third person, the first would not be a voluntary agent, since the action did not depend on him; and it could be that the person being struck was his father, but

1135a30 he knew only that he was a person, or one of those present, not that he was his father; and the same distinctions can be made in the case of the effect of the action, and with relation to the action as a whole. What is done in ignorance, then, or not in ignorance but without its depending on oneself, or rather, under force, is counter-voluntary. For there are also many of the things

1135b1 belonging to our nature that we both do and experience knowingly, none of which is either voluntary or counter-voluntary, such as ageing or dying. In the case of unjust and just actions alike there is also the element of the incidental; for someone might give back the deposit counter-voluntarily, and because of

1135b5 fear, and such a person should not be said either to be doing what is just or acting justly, except incidentally, and similarly one should say that the person who fails to give the deposit back because he is under constraint, and counter-voluntarily, is acting unjustly and doing what is unjust only incidentally. But of

1135b10 voluntary actions, some we do having decided to do them, others not; in the first case we shall have deliberated beforehand, in the second not. There being three kinds of harm, then, in interactions, the cases where ignorance is a factor are mistakes, i.e. when the person affected, or the action itself, or the instrument, or the effect is not what the agent supposed, because he did not think he was hitting the other person, or not with *this*, or not *this* person, or

1135b15 not with *this* effect, but it turned out not to be the effect he thought (e.g. he had it in mind not to wound, but only to nudge), or not the person he thought, or the instrument. Now when the harm occurs contrary to reasonable expectation, it is a misfortune; when it could reasonably have been expected, but is inflicted without bad intent, it is a mistake (since it is a mistake when the origin of what causes the effect lies in the agent, but a

1135b20 misfortune when it is outside him); when a person inflicts harm knowingly but without prior deliberation, it is an unjust act, e.g. things done through temper and other affections that are inevitable or natural for human beings, since those who inflict harm and go wrong in this way are doing what is unjust, and theirs are unjust acts, yet this does not in itself mean that they themselves are unjust, or bad characters, because the harm did not come

about because of badness; and when the harm *is* inflicted as a result of   1135b25
decision, then the doer is unjust and a bad character. Hence what is done from
temper is rightly judged as being not from premeditation, because the person
who starts it isn't the one who acts through temper but the one who made
him angry in the first place. Again, the dispute is not even about whether the
event occurred, but about what is just, since anger is occasioned by the
appearance of injustice. For in this sort of case people do not dispute about
whether the event occurred or not, as in business transactions, where one of   1135b30
the two parties must be a bad character, unless the parties are in dispute
because they have forgotten what happened; rather there is agreement that it
did happen, and the dispute is about whether it was just (whereas anyone who
has plotted to harm someone else knows perfectly well); so that one party
thinks he is being treated unjustly, while the other denies it. But if a person   1136a1
causes harm as a result of a decision to do so, he is acting unjustly; and the
doing of *this* sort of unjust act *does* mean that the agent is unjust, whenever
the action runs contrary to what is proportionate or contrary to equality of
distribution. Similarly a person will be just, too, when he acts justly as a result
of decision; but someone acts justly if he merely does the action voluntarily.   1136a5
Of things done counter-voluntarily some are such as to call for sympathy,
others not. Where a person goes wrong not only in ignorance but also
because of ignorance, his actions call for sympathy; on the other hand when
he acts not because of ignorance but in ignorance, because of a state of
feeling that is neither natural nor human, sympathy is not called for.

(V. 9) One might raise a number of problems, if we have made adequate   1136a10
distinctions in relation to being treated unjustly and acting unjustly: first of all,
whether things are as the paradoxical lines of Euripides represent them—

> 'I killed—my own mother: brief the tale.'
> 'Willing you and willing she, or unwilling both?'

Is it possible, in truth, to receive unjust treatment voluntarily; or is it impos-   1136a15
sible, and is being unjustly treated always involuntary, just as, in its turn, all
just action is voluntary? And *is* it all one thing or the other, or is it sometimes
voluntary and sometimes counter-voluntary? Similarly with being treated
justly too, since acting justly is always voluntary; the result is that it is reasonable that there should be a similar opposition in either case, and that being   1136a20
treated unjustly and treated justly be, each of them, either something voluntary or something counter-voluntary. But it would appear strange even in the
case of being treated justly, if it were all voluntary; for some people are
treated justly non-voluntarily. A second problem one might raise is whether
every person who has had something unjust done to him is being treated
unjustly, or whether it is the same in the case of having something unjust done
to one as it is in the case of doing something unjust, since it is possible to share   1136a25

in what is just incidentally, whether as agent or as patient, and it is clear that there is a similar possibility in the case of what is unjust. For doing what is unjust is not the same as acting unjustly, and neither is having unjust things done to one the same as being unjustly treated; and similarly too with doing

1136a30 what is just and being treated justly, for it is impossible to be treated unjustly without someone's acting unjustly, or to be treated justly without someone's acting justly. But if acting unjustly is harming someone voluntarily, without further specification; if the person doing it voluntarily is the one doing it knowing to whom he is doing it, with what, and how; and if the person who lacks self-control voluntarily harms himself: then this person would be voluntarily in receipt of unjust treatment, and it would be possible for one to treat

1136b1 oneself unjustly. This too is one of the problems that are raised—whether it is possible to treat oneself unjustly. Again, one might, through lack of self-control, voluntarily be harmed by someone else; in which case it will be possible to receive unjust treatment voluntarily. Or is our definition incorrect? Should we add to 'harming someone, knowing whom, with what, and how'

1136b5 the further specification 'against the subject's wish'? There is, then, such a thing as being harmed voluntarily, and having unjust things done to one voluntarily, but no one is voluntarily treated unjustly—for no one wishes it, not even the person lacking in self-control, who acts, rather, contrary to his wish; for no one wishes for the sort of thing he does not think he should go for, and the person without self-control doesn't do what he thinks he should.

1136b10 The person who gives away what belongs to him in the way Homer says Glaucus did to Diomedes,

> Gold for bronze, a hundred oxen's worth for nine,

is not being treated unjustly; for giving depends on oneself, whereas being unjustly treated does not depend on oneself—it cannot occur without the person who is acting unjustly. As for being treated unjustly, then, it is clear that it is not voluntary.

1136b15 There are still two of the problems we decided to discuss: whether we should suppose the person acting unjustly to be the one who assigned the larger share contrary to desert, or the one who has it; and whether it is possible to treat oneself unjustly. For if there exists the possibility we raised before, and it is the person assigning and not the person having the larger share that is acting unjustly, then if someone knowingly and voluntarily assigns to someone else a share larger than the one he assigns himself, this

1136b20 person treats himself unjustly (which is what reasonable, decent people are thought to do; for the decent person is the sort who takes the lesser share). Or is this, too, a more complex matter? The decent person, after all, may well be getting a larger share of a different good, e.g. reputation, or what is unconditionally fine. Again, the problem is resolved by reference to our definition of acting unjustly; for the person in question has nothing happening to him contrary to his own wish, so that by this criterion, at any rate, he is not being treated unjustly, and if indeed he is being harmed at all, it is only harm he suffers. It is evident that the person distributing does act unjustly, but that the person having too large a share does not always do so; for it is not the person to whom what is unjust belongs that acts unjustly, but the person to whom it belongs to do what is unjust voluntarily, and this is located in the source from which the action has its origin, which is in the person distributing and not in the one receiving. Again, given that there are many different ways in which we talk of the 'doing' of things, and that there is a way in which inanimate objects, or one's hand, or a slave at his master's orders, are what 'do' the killing, the person receiving does not act unjustly but merely 'does' what is unjust. Again, if someone gave an unjust judgement in ignorance, he is not acting unjustly in terms of the legally just, nor is his judgement unjust, although it is unjust in a way (since what is just in a legal sense is different from what is just in the primary sense); but if he knowingly made an unjust judgement, he himself, too, is getting too large a share of either favour or revenge. So it is as if one shared out the unjust action: the person who has given an unjust decision for these motives also has a larger share, for in fact having made the decision about the land on that condition, it is as if he took, not land, but money.

People think that acting unjustly depends on them; hence they also think that being just is easy. In fact it is not: to have slept with their neighbours' wives, or punched someone standing near them, or put money in someone's hand, is easy, and depends on them, but doing these things through being in a certain state is neither easy nor something that depends on them. Similarly they think that to have recognized what is just and what is unjust involves no special accomplishment, on the grounds that it is not hard to understand the matters on which the laws utter (although it is not these that constitute what is just, except in an incidental sense); but how things are to be done, and how distributed, to be just—knowing *this* is more of a task than knowing what makes for health, since even in that case it's easy to know that it's a matter of honey and wine and hellebore and cautery and surgery, but knowing how to administer them with a view to producing health, and to whom and when, is no less a task than being a doctor. And precisely because of this people actually think that acting unjustly is as much a mark of the just person as acting justly, on the basis that the just person would be no less or even more able to perform each kind of unjust act than just ones: after all, he could in fact sleep with a woman or punch someone, and the courageous person could abandon his shield, and turn and run no matter in which direction, left or right. But being a coward and acting unjustly do not consist in doing these things, except incidentally, but rather in doing them through being in a certain state; just as being a doctor and making people healthy does not consist in performing or not performing surgery or giving or not giving him drugs, but

1136b25

1136b30

1137a1

1137a5

1137a10

1137a15

1137a20

1137a25

in doing these things in a certain way. The sphere of the just is persons who share in things generally good, and who have too much or too little of these; since for some beings, as perhaps for gods, there is no such thing as having too much of them, while for others—the incurably bad—no amount of them at

1137a30 all is beneficial, but all are harmful, and for others again they are beneficial up to a point. It is, for this reason, something that applies only to human beings.

(V. 10) The next thing to discuss is reasonableness and the reasonable: how reasonableness relates to justice, and the reasonable to the just. If one looks into the question, they give the appearance neither of being unqualifiedly the

1137a35 same nor of being different in kind; and sometimes we praise the reasonable
1137b1 and the corresponding man, in such a way that we transfer the term to other features we are praising, too, in place of 'good'—so showing that what is more reasonable is better; while at other times it appears odd, if one follows out the argument, that the reasonable should be something praiseworthy when it is something that runs counter to what is just: for either what is just is

1137b5 not a good thing, or if it is, what is reasonable is not just, if it is different from the just; or if both are good, they are the same. These, then, are the considerations that make reasonableness problematic; yet in a way they are all correct, and there is no inconsistency between them, for the reasonable is better than what is just in one sense of 'just', but is nevertheless just, and is not better

1137b10 than the just as constituting a different kind. The same thing, in that case, is just and reasonable, and while both are good the reasonable is superior. What creates the problem is that while the reasonable is just, it is not the just according to law, but rather a rectification of the legally just. The cause of this is that all law is universal, and yet there are some things about which it is not

1137b15 possible to make correct universal pronouncements. So in the sorts of cases in which it necessarily pronounces universally, but cannot do so and achieve correctness, law chooses what holds for the most part, in full knowledge of the error it is making. Nor is it for that reason any less correct; for the error is not in the law, or in the lawgiver, but in the nature of the case; for the sphere

1137b20 of action consists of this sort of material from the start. So whenever the law makes a universal pronouncement, but things turn out in a particular case contrary to the 'universal' rule, on these occasions it is correct, where there is an omission by the lawgiver, and he has gone wrong by having made an unqualified pronouncement, to rectify the deficiency by reference to what the lawgiver himself would have said if he had been there and, if he had known about the case, would have laid down in law. Hence the reasonable is just, and

1137b25 better than just in one sense, but not better than what is without qualification just, only than the error that arises through absence of qualification. And this is the nature of the reasonable: a rectification of law, in so far as law is deficient because of its universal aspect. For this is why in fact not everything is regulated by law, namely because there are some things about which laws

cannot be established, so that decrees are needed instead. For the rule for
what is indefinite is itself indefinite, like the leaden rule used in building   1137b30
Lesbian-style: the rule adapts itself to the configuration of the stone, instead
of staying the same shape, and the decree adapts itself to actual events. It is
clear, then, what the reasonable is; and that it is just, and better than just in
one sense. From this it is also evident who the reasonable person is: the sort   1137b35
who decides on and does things of this kind, and who is not a stickler for   1138a1
justice in the bad sense but rather tends to take a less strict view of things,
even though he has the law to back him up—this is the reasonable person, and
the disposition to act in this way is reasonableness, being a kind of justice, not
some distinct sort of disposition.

(V. 11) The answer to the question whether it is possible to treat oneself
unjustly or not is evident from what has been said. For part of what is just is   1138a5
what is prescribed by the law in accordance with excellence as a whole: for
instance, in cases where the law does not enjoin[19] killing oneself (and it forbids
this action except where it enjoins it); again, whenever, contrary to the law, a
person voluntarily harms someone, not in return for harm suffered, he acts
unjustly, and the person who does it voluntarily is the one who does it knowing both the person affected and the instrument; but someone who through
anger cuts his own throat does this voluntarily, contrary to what reason   1138a10
prescribes—and does something that the law forbids: in that case he is acting
unjustly. But unjustly to whom? Or is it to the city—not himself? For he is a
voluntary recipient of the action, and no one is voluntarily treated unjustly.
This is why in fact the city imposes a penalty, and a certain dishonour is
attached to the person who has done away with himself, on the grounds that
he is acting unjustly towards the city. Again, where the unjust agent is unjust,
merely, and not wholly bad, it is not possible for him to treat himself unjustly   1138a15
(for this is a distinct case from the other one: the unjust person, in one sense
of 'unjust', is bad in the way that the coward is, i.e. not as possessing badness
as a whole—so that, when he acts unjustly, his action will not be in accordance
with that kind of badness); for in that case it would be possible for the same
thing to have been taken away from and be being added to the same person at
the same time, and this is impossible—necessarily, for something to be just or   1138a20
to be unjust there must always be more than one person involved. And again,
acting unjustly is something which is both voluntary and based on decision,
and involves doing something to someone first (since the person who acts
because of something done to him, and does the same thing back, is not
thought to be acting unjustly); but if he does it to himself, he is having done to
him and doing the same things at the same time. Again, it will be possible
to receive unjust treatment voluntarily. In addition to these considerations,

---

[19] Reading οἷον ⟨οὐ⟩ οὐ κελεύει (1138a6) [S.B.].

1138a25 acting unjustly cannot occur independently of the specific forms of unjust act, and no one commits adultery with his own wife, or breaks and enters through his own wall, or steals his own property. And in general the problem about treating oneself unjustly is also resolved by reference to the definition introduced in connection with one's being the voluntary recipient of injustice. (It is evident, too, that both are bad things, i.e. both being the recipient of injustice 1138a30 and doing it, since the one is to have less, the other more than what is intermediate—as with what makes for health in the sphere of medicine, and what makes for fitness in that of athletic training; but all the same doing injustice is worse, for doing it implies badness, and is an object of reproach, and the badness is either complete and possessed without qualification, or nearly so (for not every voluntary unjust act goes with an unjust disposition), 1138a35 whereas being the recipient implies neither badness nor injustice. In itself, 1138b1 then, being the recipient of unjust treatment is less bad, and yet there is no reason why it should not incidentally be a greater evil. But this sort of thing is of no concern to science, which declares pleurisy a worse thing to suffer from than a stumble; nevertheless on occasion the latter might incidentally turn out 1138b5 to be worse—if someone stumbled, and because of his fall happened to be captured or killed by the enemy.) In an extended sense, based on similarity, there can be a relationship of justice, not between oneself and oneself but towards certain aspects of oneself; but not justice of any variety, only the sorts appropriate to a master of slaves or to the head of a household. For it is in these sorts of relationships of disparity that the part of the soul possessing 1138b10 reason stands to the non-rational part; with these in view, people then actually think one can treat oneself unjustly, on the basis that, with the parts standing in this relationship, it will be possible for them to have things done to them contrary to their own particular desires—and so they think there is a relationship of justice between them like the one between ruler and ruled. Let that then stand as our way of marking off justice and the rest, i.e. the excellences of character.

BOOK VI

(VI. 1) Since we have said earlier that one must choose what is intermediate, 1138b20 not excess, and not deficiency, and that what is intermediate is 'as the correct prescription prescribes', let us delimit this. For with all the dispositions we have discussed, just as with everything else, there is a target, as it were, that the person with the prescription has in view as he tenses and relaxes, and a kind of mark that determines the intermediate states, which we declare to be in between excess and deficiency, being as they are 'according to the correct prescription'. But while talk like this says what is true, it is not at all illuminating; for in all other spheres of concern, ones involving specialized knowledge, while it is true to say that one shouldn't apply oneself, or slacken one's effort, either too much or too little, but just to an intermediate degree and as the correct prescription lays down, if this were the only thing a person knew he would be no further on—e.g. he would not know what sorts of remedies should be applied to the body, if someone just said 'those that medical science dictates, and in the way the medical expert would do it'. Hence in relation to the dispositions of the soul too what we need is not merely to have said this and said something true; we need also to have determined what 'the correct prescription' is, and what the determining mark of this is.

1138b25

1138b30

Now when we divided up the excellences of the soul, we said that some of them were excellences of character, others intellectual excellences. The character-excellences we have discussed; let us now discuss the others as follows, after we have first talked about soul. Previously we said that there were two parts of the soul, the one that possesses reason, and the other non-rational; now with the part that possesses reason we must in the same way make a division. Let us assume the parts possessing reason to be two, one by virtue of which we reflect upon the sorts of things whose principles cannot be otherwise, one by virtue of which we reflect upon things that can be otherwise; for with things that are generically distinct, the part of the soul that stands in a natural relationship to each genus will itself be generically distinct, given that they have cognition in accordance with a certain likeness and affinity to their objects. Of these, let the first be called 'scientific', the second 'calculative'; for deliberation and calculation are the same thing, and no one deliberates about things that cannot be otherwise. So the calculative is one distinct part of the part possessing reason. We must, then, grasp what the best disposition of each of these two parts is; for this will be the excellence of each, and its excellence will relate to its own peculiar function.

1138b35
1139a1

1139a5

1139a10

1139a15

(VI. 2) In the soul, the things determining action and truth are three: perception, intelligence, and desire. But of these, perception is not an originator of any sort of action; and this is clear from the fact that brute animals have perception but do not share in action. What affirmation and denial are in the case of thought, pursuit and avoidance are with desire; so that, since excellence of character is a disposition issuing in decisions, and decision is a desire informed by deliberation, in consequence both what issues from reason must be true and the desire must be correct for the decision to be a good one, and reason must assert and desire pursue the same things. This, then, is thought, and truth, of a practical sort; in the case of thought that is theoretical, and not

1139a20

1139a25

practical nor productive, 'well' and 'badly' consist in the true and the false
(this is, after all, the function of any faculty of thought), but that of a faculty
1139a30   of *practical* thought is truth in agreement with the correct desire. Now the
origin of action—in terms of the source of the movement, not its end—is
decision, while that of decision is desire and rational reference to an end.
Hence intelligence and thought, on the one hand, and character-disposition
1139a35   on the other are necessary for decision; for doing well and its contrary, in the
context of action, are conditional on thought and character. Thought by itself
sets nothing in motion; thought that sets in motion is for the sake of some-
1139b1   thing and practical. For this also controls productive thought, since everyone
who produces something produces it for the sake of something, and what is
an end without qualification is not the end of production (being relative to
something else, and the end of a given expertise), but the end of action; for
doing well is an end, and desire is for the end. Hence decision is either
1139b5   intelligence qualified by desire or desire qualified by thought, and human
beings are originators of this sort. (Nothing that happened in the past is
subject to decision—e.g. no one decides to have sacked Troy, for no one
deliberates about the past, either, but rather about what is to come, and what
is possible, whereas it is not possible for what has happened not to have
happened—so Agathon was right:

1139b10   For even from god this power is kept, this power alone:
                        To make it true that what's been done had never been.

It holds, then, of both intelligent parts that their function is truth; so the
excellences of both will be the dispositions in accordance with which each of
them will grasp truth to the highest degree.

1139b15   (VI. 3) Let us then discuss these parts from a more general standpoint. Let
the states by which the soul has truth through affirmation and denial be five in
number: technical expertise, systematic knowledge, wisdom, intellectual
accomplishment, and intelligence; for one can be deceived by belief and
judgement. Now what systematic knowledge is will be evident from the
following—if one is to be precise about the matter, and not be misled by
1139b20   resemblances. We all believe that it is not even possible for what we know in
this sense to be otherwise; whereas with things that can be otherwise, we
cannot tell whether they hold or not when they are outside our view. What is
known systematically therefore is by necessity. Therefore it is eternal, since
everything that is by necessity, without qualification, is eternal, and what is
eternal is subject neither to coming into being nor to passing out of being.
1139b25   Again, all systematic knowledge is thought to be teachable, and its subject
matter capable of being learned. But all teaching proceeds from things already
known, as we also say in the *Analytics*, since some of it takes place through
induction, some by means of deduction. Now induction is a starting point for

coming to grasp the universal too, while deduction proceeds from universals. There are, therefore, starting points from which deduction proceeds that are not themselves products of argument; therefore it is induction that must provide them. Systematic knowledge, then, is a disposition that is active in demonstration, and so on (we list the further defining features in the *Analytics*); for a person knows in this sense when he has conviction of a certain sort and the starting points are known to him—since if they are not clearer than the conclusion, he will have the knowledge only in an incidental sense. Let systematic knowledge, then, be marked off in this way.

1139b30

1139b35

(VI. 4) Within the sphere of what can be otherwise, there are both things that belong within the realm of production and things that belong within that of action; but production is a different thing from action (and on this subject we can rely on our published discussions too), so that rational disposition in the sphere of action will also be different from rational productive disposition. By the same token, nor is either of them a species of the other: it is not the case either that action is production, or that production is action. But since building is one sort of technical expertise, and is what constitutes a particular productive disposition accompanied by rational prescription, and since there is neither any technical expertise that is not a productive disposition accompanied by rational prescription, nor any such disposition that is not a technical expertise, technical expertise will be the same as productive disposition accompanied by true rational prescription. Every technical expertise is concerned with coming into being, that is, with the practice and theory of how to bring into being some one of the things that are capable either of being or of not being, and the origin of whose coming into being lies in the producer and not in the thing being produced; for technical expertise is not concerned with things that either are or come to be by necessity, nor with things that are or come to be by nature, since these have their origin in themselves. And because production is a different thing from action, necessarily technical expertise has to do with production, not with action. (And in a certain way, chance and technical expertise occupy the same field, just as Agathon says:

1140a1

1140a5

1140a10

1140a15

> Skill does chance embrace, and chance her love returns.)

1140a20

Technical expertise, then, as has been said, is a productive disposition accompanied by true rational prescription, while conversely inexpert technique is a productive disposition accompanied by false rational prescription; both in relation to what can be otherwise.

(VI. 5) On the subject of wisdom, we may get what we need once we have considered who it is that we call 'wise'. Well, it is thought characteristic of a wise person to be able to deliberate well about the things that are good and advantageous to himself, not in specific contexts, e.g. what sorts of things

1140a25

179

conduce to health, or to physical strength, but what sorts of things conduce to the good life in general. An indication of this is that we also call those in a

1140a30 specific field wise if they succeed in calculating well towards some specific worthy end on matters where no exact technique applies. So in fact the description 'wise' belongs in general to the person who is good at deliberation. Now nobody deliberates about things that cannot be otherwise, or about things he has no possibility of doing. So if in fact systematic knowledge involves demonstration, and there is no possibility of demonstrating the sorts

1140a35 of things whose starting points can be otherwise, since all these things can in
1140b1 fact be otherwise, nor is it possible to deliberate about things that are by necessity, wisdom will not be systematic knowledge, and neither will it be technical expertise: not systematic knowledge, because what is in the sphere of action can be otherwise, and not technical expertise, because action and

1140b5 production belong to different kinds. It remains therefore for it to be a true disposition accompanied by rational prescription, relating to action in the sphere of what is good and bad for human beings. For the end of production is something distinct from the productive process, whereas that of action will not be; here, doing well itself serves as end. It is for this reason that we think Pericles and people of that sort wise—because they are capable of forming a clear view of what is good for themselves and what is good for human beings

1140b10 in general; we think that this description applies to those who are good at managing property and at politics. That is why we give *sōphrosunē* ['moderation'] its name, as something that *sōzei tēn phronēsin* ['preserves wisdom']. And it does preserve the sort of belief in question. What is pleasant and painful does not corrupt, or distort, every sort of belief, e.g. that the internal

1140b15 angles of a triangle do or do not add up to two right angles, only beliefs in the sphere of action. For the starting points of practical projects are constituted by what those projects are for; and once someone is corrupted through pleasure or pain, he fails to see the starting point, and to see that one should choose everything, and act, for the sake of *this*, and because of *this*—for badness is

1140b20 corruptive of the starting point. The necessary conclusion is that wisdom is a disposition accompanied by rational prescription, true, in the sphere of human goods, relating to action. Further considerations: there is such a thing as excellence in technical expertise, not in wisdom; and with technical expertise it is more desirable if someone voluntarily gets something wrong, whereas with wisdom, as with the excellences, it is less so. So it is clear that wisdom is a

1140b25 kind of excellence and not a technical expertise. Given that there are two parts of the soul possessing reason, it will constitute excellence of one of the two, i.e. the part with which we form opinion; for opining things to be so or so relates to what can be otherwise, and so does wisdom. But neither is wisdom a disposition accompanied by rational prescription, merely, as is indicated by the fact that this sort of disposition can be forgotten, whereas wisdom

1140b30 cannot.

180

(VI. 6) Since systematic knowledge is a matter of holding things to be true about universals and what is by necessity, and there are starting points of what can be demonstrated and of all systematic knowledge (for systematic knowledge involves reasoning), the starting point of what is systematically known will be an object neither of systematic knowledge, nor of technical expertise, nor of wisdom; for what is systematically known is demonstrable, and the other two have to do with what can be otherwise. Neither, then, are the starting points objects of intellectual accomplishment, as it is part of such accomplishment to be able to demonstrate certain things. If, then, the states by which we have truth and which exclude our being deceived about what cannot, or even what can, be otherwise are systematic knowledge, wisdom, intellectual accomplishment, and intelligence, and if three of these cannot have starting points as their objects (the three being wisdom, systematic knowledge, and intellectual accomplishment), the only possibility remaining is that the starting points are objects of intelligence.

(VI. 7) As for accomplishment, this we ascribe, in the case of the various kinds of technical expertise, to those experts in them who are most precise, e.g. Pheidias is an accomplished worker in stone, Polycleitus in bronze, here at any rate meaning no more by 'accomplishment' than excellence in technical expertise; but we think that there are people who are accomplished in a general, not in a specific, sense, and not accomplished *in* something else, as Homer says in the *Margites*:

> Him did the gods make neither a delver, nor plougher of furrows,
> Nor accomplished in anything else.

So it is clear that intellectual accomplishment will be the most precise of the kinds of knowledge. The person possessing it, then, must not only know what follows from the starting points, but have a true grasp of the starting points themselves. So intellectual accomplishment will be a combination of intelligence and systematic knowledge—systematic knowledge, as it were with its head now in place, of the highest objects. For it is a strange thing to think—if anyone does—that political expertise, or wisdom, is what is to be taken most seriously; unless, that is, man is the best thing there is in the universe. (Now if healthy and good are different for human beings and for fish, while white and straight are always the same, everyone will agree that what is intellectually accomplished too, is always the same thing, whereas what is wise differs; for each kind of creature asserts that what is wise is what successfully considers the things relating to itself,[20] and will hand over decisions to that. Hence the fact that people say some kinds of animal are wise, i.e. those that clearly have a capacity for forethought about their own lives. It is also evident that

1140b35
1141a1

1141a5

1141a10

1141a15

1141a20

1141a25

---

[20] Reading τὸ γὰρ περὶ αὐτὸ ἕκαστον τὸ εὖ θεωροῦν (1141a25).

intellectual accomplishment and political expertise will not be the same, for if
people say expertise about what is beneficial to themselves is accomplishment,
there will be many kinds of accomplishment; there will not be one, dealing
with the good of all kinds of creatures, but a different one for each—unless
there is also a single form of medical expertise appropriate to every kind of
being.) Even if man is the best thing possible out of all animals, it makes no
difference; for in fact there are other things that have a far diviner nature than
a human being, e.g., quite the most evidently, the constituent parts of the
universe. From what has been said, then, it is clear that intellectual
accomplishment is a combination of systematic knowledge and intelligence,
with the things that are highest by nature as its objects. This is why people call
Anaxagoras and Thales and people of that sort 'accomplished', but not 'wise',
when they see them lacking a grasp of what is to their own advantage; and
they say that people like that know things that are exceptional, wonderful,
difficult, even superhuman—but useless, because what they inquire into are
not the goods that are *human*. It is wisdom that has to do with things human,
and with things one can deliberate about; for this is what we say is most of all
the function of the wise person, to deliberate well, and no one deliberates
about things that are incapable of being otherwise, or about the sorts of
things that do not lead to some end, where this is a practicable good. And the
person who is without qualification the good deliberator is the one whose
calculations make him good at hitting upon what is best for a human being
among practicable goods. Nor is wisdom only concerned with universals: to
be wise, one must also be familiar with the particular, since wisdom has to do
with action, and the sphere of action is constituted by particulars. That is why
sometimes people who lack universal knowledge are more effective in action
than others who have it—something that holds especially of experienced
people. Suppose someone knew that light meats are easily digestible and so
healthy, but not what sorts of meat are light: he won't make anyone healthy,
and the person who knows that meat from birds is light and[21] healthy will do so
more. But wisdom has to do with action; so we need to have both sorts of
excellence—no, we need wisdom more. And here too there will be a kind that
is architectonic.

(VI. 8) Political expertise and wisdom are the same disposition, but their
being is not the same. Of the disposition as it relates to the city, the architectonic form of wisdom is legislative expertise, while the form of wisdom at
the level of particulars is given the generic name 'political expertise', and this is
concerned with action and deliberation, since a decree is something to be
acted upon, as what comes last in the process. This is why only people at this
level are said to take part in politics, because only they *do* things, like the

1141a30

1141b1

1141b5

1141b10

1141b15

1141b20

1141b25

---

[21]Retaining κοῦφα καὶ (1141b20).

various kinds of manual workers. With wisdom too, what is thought to be   1141b30
wisdom most of all is the sort that relates to oneself as an individual, and it is
this that is given the generic name, i.e. 'wisdom' (of those other forms of it, one
is household management, another is legislation, another is political expertise,
the last being split into deliberative and judicial). Now knowing things for one's
own benefit will certainly be a kind of knowing. But there is room for much
disagreement here: the person who knows about what concerns him, and   1142a1
occupies himself with that, is thought wise, while those occupying themselves
with politics are thought to be busybodies—hence Euripides' lines

> I wise? How so, when free from care I could have lived
> Among the rank and file, my share of what went on
> No greater than my neighbour's? . . .   1142a5
> For those whose doing exceeds these bounds, the prominent ones . . .

For people look for what is good for themselves, and think this is what they
should do. It is this view, then, that has given rise to the idea that this sort of
person is wise, and yet presumably one's own well being is inseparable from
managing a household, and from political organization. Again, *how* one   1142a10
should govern one's affairs is unclear, and something that needs investigation.
An indication of what we have said is also that geometricians and mathematicians, and those accomplished at such things, develop when young, while this
is not thought to be the case with a wise person; and the reason is that the
objects of wisdom also include particulars, which come to be known through   1142a15
experience, and a young person is not an experienced one; for it is quantity of
time that provides experience. (After all, one might also raise the question
why it is that one can become a mathematician while a boy, but not acquire
general intellectual accomplishment, or an understanding of natural science.
Or is it because the one set of subjects are given by abstraction, while the
starting points of the others derive from experience—and in the one case the
young only talk, rather than having anything they believe, while in the other   1142a20
there is no difficulty in grasping the definitions?) Again, mistakes occur in
relation either to the universal in deliberation or to the particular; e.g. either
in supposing that all heavy liquids are bad, or that this particular liquid is
heavy. But it is evident that wisdom is not systematic knowledge, since it has
for its object what comes last in the process of deliberation, as has been said;
for what is acted on is of this sort. So wisdom is antithetical to intelligence, for   1142a25
intelligence has as its objects the definitions for which there is no account,
whereas wisdom has as its object what comes last, and this is not an object of
systematic knowledge, but of perception—not perception of the sensibles
special to each sense, but like that by which we grasp that the last element in
mathematical analysis is the triangle; for things will come to a halt in that case
too. (However, this is more a case of perception than of wisdom, but a   1142a30
different kind of perception from the one of the special sensibles.)

(VI. 9) Inquiry and deliberation are different: deliberation is a certain sort of inquiry. And we must also grasp what excellence in deliberation is—whether it is a kind of knowledge, or a kind of judgement, or a capacity for guesswork, or some other kind of thing. Now it is not knowledge, for people do not

1142b1 inquire about things they know; and excellence in deliberation is a kind of deliberation, and someone who is deliberating is inquiring, in so far as he is calculating. But again, neither is it a mere capacity to guess correctly; for this involves no reasoning and is something quick, whereas one deliberates for a· long time, and people say one should act quickly on the results of deliber-

1142b5 ation, but deliberate slowly. Again, quick-mindedness is different from deliberative excellence; but quick-mindedness is a kind of capacity to hit on things correctly. Nor in fact is deliberative excellence any sort of judgement. Since the person who deliberates badly makes a mistake, and the one who deliberates well does so correctly, deliberative excellence is clearly a kind of correct-

1142b10 ness, but neither of knowledge nor of judgement; for there is no such thing as correctness of knowledge (since neither is there mistakenness of it), and correctness of judgement is truth—and at the same time everything that is the subject of a judgement is also already determinate. But neither is deliberative excellence something non-rational. It remains, then, for it to be correctness of thinking, for thinking does not imply assertion: a judgement is not a matter of inquiring, but already a kind of assertion, whereas the person who is delib-

1142b15 erating, whether he does it well or badly, is inquiring about something, and calculating. But deliberative excellence is a kind of correctness of deliber-ation; so it is deliberation—what it is, and what its object is—that needs to be inquired into first. Since correctness is of more than one kind, clearly delib-erative excellence is not any and every kind of correctness; for by calculation the person without self-control, or the one with a bad character, will achieve

1142b20 what his project requires,[22] thereby having 'deliberated correctly', although he will have got himself a great evil. But to have deliberated well is thought to be a good thing; for it is this sort of correctness of deliberation that is delibera-tive excellence, i.e. the sort that enables one to achieve what is good. But it is also possible to achieve this by means of false reasoning, and to achieve what one should have done, but not by the means by which one should, the inter-

1142b25 mediate premiss being false; so neither is this enough to constitute delibera-tive excellence—i.e. the sort of deliberation by which one achieves what one should, yet not by the means by which one should. Again, one person can achieve it by deliberating for a long time, while another manages it quickly. The former case, then, still won't count as deliberative excellence; rather, deliberative excellence is correctness as to what one should achieve, and the way in which, and when, all in accordance with what is beneficial. Again, it is possible to have deliberated well either without qualification or in relation to

---

[22] Reading ὃ προτίθεται δεῖν ἐκ τοῦ . . . (1142b18–19).

some specific end: deliberative excellence without qualification, then, will be   1142b30
deliberation that is successful in relation to the end without qualification,
while the specific kind will be deliberation that is successful in relation to
some specific end. So if it is characteristic of the wise to deliberate well,[23]
deliberative excellence will be that sort of correctness that corresponds to
what conduces to the end, of which wisdom is the true grasp.

(VI. 10) Comprehension [*sunesis*] and excellence in comprehension   1142b35
[*eusunesia*]—the states we refer to when we say people are 'comprehending'   1143a1
[*sunetoi*] and 'good at comprehending' [*eusunetoi*]—are neither completely the
same thing as knowledge or judgement (if they were, everyone would be
'comprehending'), nor are they any one of the particular branches of knowledge, e.g. medicine, dealing with what conduces to health, or geometry,
dealing with extended magnitudes; for neither is comprehension of what   1143a5
exists for ever and is unchangeable, nor is it of just anything that comes to be,
but rather of the things one might puzzle and deliberate about. Hence it is
concerned with the same things as wisdom, but comprehension and wisdom
are not the same thing. For wisdom is prescriptive: what one should do or not
do—this is its end, whereas comprehension is merely discriminative. (For   1143a10
comprehension and excellence in comprehension are the same thing; for in
fact people who are 'comprehending' are also 'good at comprehending'.[24])
Comprehension is neither having wisdom nor acquiring it; but just as seeing
the point is called 'comprehending' when one is exercising systematic knowledge, so too one 'comprehends' when exercising judgement in order to discriminate about the things wisdom deals with, when someone else is   1143a15
speaking—and exercising it in order to discriminate rightly (for 'excellently' is
the same as 'rightly'). And this is where the name 'comprehension', in the
sense of what makes people 'good at comprehending', comes from, i.e. from
the comprehension involved in seeing a point; for we often call seeing a point
'comprehending'.

(VI. 11) The quality called 'sense' [*gnōmē*], which we refer to when we talk of
people as 'having a shared sense', i.e. 'sympathetic' [*sungnōmones*], and say that   1143a20
they 'have sense' [*echein gnōmēn*], is making correct discrimination of what is
reasonable. And there is an indication of this: it is the reasonable person that
we most of all say is inclined towards sympathy, and to be sympathetic in
some cases is a mark of reasonableness. Sympathy is a correct discriminative
sense of what is reasonable; and a correct sense of this sort is the one that
arrives at what is true.
But all these dispositions are reasonably thought of as tending towards the   1143a25

---

[23] Reading τὸ εὖ βουλεύεσθαι (1142b31).
[24] Reading καὶ γὰρ οἱ συνετοὶ καὶ εὐσύνετοι (1143a10–11).

same point—as we do think of them, since we attribute sense, comprehension, wisdom, and intelligence to the same people, and say that now they have sense and intelligence, and are wise and able to comprehend. For all these capacities have as their objects what comes last, and particulars; and it is on

1143a30 being able to discriminate in the field in which wisdom operates that being a comprehending person, and one of good sense, or sympathy, depends, for reasonable responses are common to all good qualities in their other-regarding aspect. And everything that is done belongs to the particular, and to what comes last; for not only must the wise person be familiar with these

1143a35 latter things, but comprehension and sense are concerned with what is to be done, and this is last. And intelligence has as its objects what is last in both directions; for both the primary definitions and what is last in practical reason-

1143b1 ing are to be grasped by intelligence, not with an account, the objects of the sort of intelligence that operates in demonstrations being definitions that are unchanging and first, while the object of the sort that operates with practical dispositions is what is last and contingent, and belongs to the second premiss. For these are the starting points of that for the sake of which, since things that

1143b5 are universal consist of particulars. So one must have perception of these, and this is intelligence. This is why the things in question are thought to be natural growths: while no one is thought to be a natural possessor of intellectual accomplishment, sense and comprehension and intelligence *are* thought to be natural things. An indication of this is that we also think that they depend on age, and that 'this particular age has intelligence and sense', implying that nature is the cause. [Because of this, intelligence is both starting point and

1143b10 end. For demonstrations are based on these and about these.] So one should pay attention to the undemonstrated assertions and judgements of experienced and older people, or wise ones, no less than to demonstrations; because they have an eye, formed from experience, they see correctly. So then we have

1143b15 said what wisdom and general intellectual accomplishment are, and what the field of each of the two is; and that each belongs to a different part of the soul.

(VI. 12) But one might raise a problem about them: what *use* are they? Intellectual accomplishment will not reflect on any of the things that make a

1143b20 human being happy (for it is not concerned in any way with bringing things into being), while wisdom may have this feature, but what do we need it for, if in fact wisdom has to do with[25] the things that are just and fine and good for human beings, and these are the ones that the good man characteristically does—and knowledge of them does not make us any more doers of them,

1143b25 given that the excellences are dispositions; just as with things relating to health, or things relating to physical fitness (i.e. the ones to which the terms apply not because they produce but because they flow from the disposition), for we are

---

[25] Reading ἐστι περὶ (1143b22).

no more doers of those things by virtue of possessing expertise in medicine and athletic training. And if we are to say that being wise is useful not for this, but with a view to our *becoming* doers of good things, then it will not be of any use to those who already are good; and further, wisdom won't even be useful 1143b30 for those who don't have it, since it will make no difference whether they have it themselves or listen to others who do—and that will suffice for us, just as it does in the case of health: even though we wish to be healthy we don't learn how to be doctors. In addition to these problems, it would be strange if wisdom turned out to be inferior to intellectual accomplishment, yet be more authoritative—as it apparently will be, for the one that brings the other about 1143b35 will be in control, and prescribe on everything. We need, then, to discuss these subjects; for so far we have only stated the problems they raise. First, let us 1144a1 state that wisdom and intellectual accomplishment must necessarily be desirable in themselves, if excellences they are, each of one of the two soul-parts in question, even if neither of them produces anything at all. The next point is that they are in fact productive: not in the way medical expertise produces health, but in the way health does—this is how intellectual accomplishment 1144a5 'produces' happiness; for since it is a part of excellence as a whole, it is the possession of it, and its exercise, that make a person happy. Again, the 'product' is brought to completion by virtue of a person's having wisdom and excellence of character; for excellence makes the goal correct, while wisdom makes what leads to it correct. (Of the fourth part of the soul, the nutritive, there is no excellence of a relevant sort; for there is nothing the doing or not 1144a10 doing of which depends on it.) As for wisdom's not making us any more doers of what is fine and just, we must begin at a slightly more general level, taking the following starting point. Just as we say that in some cases people do what is just without being just themselves, e.g. those who are doing things that have 1144a15 been prescribed by the laws, but either counter-voluntarily, or because of ignorance, or because of some different consideration, not because of what the things themselves are (even though they are doing what one should, and everything consistent with being a person of excellence), so, it seems, it is possible to do the various sorts of things from a certain disposition, so as actually to be a good person: I mean e.g. doing them because of decision, and for the sake of the things being done themselves. The decision, then, is made 1144a20 correct by excellence, but the doing of whatever by the nature of things has to be done to realize that decision is not the business of excellence but of another ability. But we must fix our minds on these and discuss them in a more illuminating way. There is an ability that people call 'cleverness'; and this is of a sort such that, when it comes to the things that conduce to a proposed goal, it 1144a25 is able to carry these out and do so successfully.[26] Now if the aim is a fine one, this ability is to be praised, but if the aim is a bad one, then it is

---

[26] Reading τυγχάνειν αὐτῶν (1144a25–6).

unscrupulousness; which is why we say that both the wise and the unscrupulous[27] are clever. Wisdom is not identical with this ability, but is

1144a30 conditional upon it. This eye of the soul does not come to be in its proper condition without excellence, as has been said and as is clear in any case; for chains of practical reasoning have a starting point—'since the end, i.e. what is best, is such-and-such' (whatever it may be: for the sake of argument let it be anything one happens to choose), and this is not evident except to the person

1144a35 who possesses excellence, since badness distorts a person and causes him to be deceived about the starting points of action. So it is evident that it is impos-

1144b1 sible to be wise without possessing excellence.

　　(VI. 13) We must, then, reconsider excellence as well, for excellence too is in a similar case: as wisdom stands to cleverness (not the same thing, but similar), so 'natural' excellence too stands to excellence in the primary sense. For

1144b5 everyone thinks each of the various sorts of character-traits belongs to us in some sense by nature—because we are just, moderate in our appetites, courageous, and the rest from the moment we are born; but all the same we look for excellence in the primary sense as being something other than this, and for such qualities to belong to us in a different way. For natural dispositions belong to children and animals as well; but without intelligence to accompany

1144b10 them they are evidently harmful. Still, this much appears to be a matter of observation, that just as a powerful body when moving without sight to guide it will fall with powerful impact because of its sightlessness, so in this case too; but if a person acquires intelligence, it makes a difference to his actions, and the disposition, which was merely similar to excellence in the primary sense, will then be that excellence. So, just as in the case of that part of the soul that

1144b15 forms opinions there are two kinds of thing, cleverness and wisdom, so with the character-bearing part there are also two, one being natural excellence and the other excellence in the primary sense—and of these, the latter does not come about unless accompanied by wisdom. This is why some say that all the excellences are kinds of wisdom—and why Socrates was in a way on the right

1144b20 track and in a way not: for he was wrong in so far as he thought that all the excellences are kinds of wisdom, but in so far as they are always accompanied by wisdom, what he said was fine enough. And there is an indication of this: for now, in fact, everybody when defining excellence describes the disposition and what it relates to, and then adds 'according to the correct prescription'; and the correct one is the one in accordance with wisdom. Apparently, then,

1144b25 everyone seems somehow to divine the truth that this sort of disposition is excellence, i.e. the one in accordance with wisdom. But one must go a little further on than this: it is not just the disposition according to the correct prescription, but the disposition *accompanied by* the correct prescription, that

[27] Reading καὶ ⟨τοὺς⟩ πανούργους (1144a28).

constitutes excellence; and it is wisdom that 'correctly prescribes' in contexts of this sort. Socrates, then, thought the excellences were prescriptions (since he thought they were all kinds of knowledge), whereas we think they are accompanied by a prescription. It is clear, then, from what has been said that it is not possible to possess excellence in the primary sense without wisdom, nor to be wise without excellence of character. But this conclusion also offers a means of resolving the argument one can employ, in a dialectical context, to show that the excellences can be possessed independently of one another—i.e. that the same person is not best adapted by nature to all of them, so that at a given moment he will have acquired one, but not another; for this is possible in relation to the 'natural' excellences, but in relation to those that make a person excellent without qualification, it is not possible, since if wisdom, which is one, is present, they will all be present along with it. And it is clear, even if it did not lead to action, that there would be a need for it because of its being an excellence of its soul-part, and because a decision will not be correct in the absence of wisdom, or in the absence of excellence; for the one causes us to act in relation to the end, the other in relation to what forwards the end. But neither is wisdom sovereign over intellectual accomplishment, or over the better of the two rational parts, any more than medical expertise is sovereign over health; for it does not employ it, but rather sees to it that it comes into existence, so that it prescribes on its behalf, not to it. It is as if one said that political expertise rules over the gods, because it issues prescriptions about everything in the city.

1144b30

1144b35

1145a1

1145a5

1145a10

BOOK VII

(VII. 1) After these subjects we must start on a fresh one, by saying that the undesirable states in relation to character are of three kinds: badness, lack of self-control, and brutishness. The contraries of two of these are clear enough: one we call excellence, the second self-control; as for the contrary to brutishness, it will be most appropriate to point to superhuman excellence, i.e. one of a heroic or even divine sort (as in Homer's verses where Priam says Hector was an exceedingly good man—

1145a15

1145a20

> Not the son of a mortal man, but sired by a god—so seemed he).

So if, as they say, men become gods because of an excess of excellence, clearly the disposition opposed to brutishness will be one of this sort; for just as

1145a25

animals cannot possess badness, or excellence, so neither can a god, his state being something more to be honoured than excellence, while that of an animal is different in kind from badness. And given that it is a rare thing for a man to be godlike ('a godlike man' is what, in their dialect, the Spartans like to call someone they particularly admire), so too the brutish type of human being is rare; it occurs most among non-Greeks, though some cases develop through disease or disablement too—and we do also use the word for those who exceed other human beings in badness, as a term of opprobrium. But we shall have to make some mention of this disposition later, and we have discussed badness earlier; it is lack of self-control, and softness or weakness for comfort, that must be our subjects now, along with self-control and endurance; for we should not regard either of these two things as having to do with the same dispositions as excellence and badness, or as being a different kind.

As in other cases, we must set out what appears true about our subjects, and, having first raised the problems, thus display, if we can, all the views people hold about these ways of being affected, and if not, the larger part of them, and the most authoritative; for if one can both resolve the difficult issues about a subject and leave people's views on it undisturbed, it will have been clarified well enough. Well then: both self-control and endurance are thought to be good things, and objects of praise,[28] lack of self-control and softness bad, and objects of censure; and self-control is thought to go with sticking to one's rational calculations, lack of self-control with departing from them. Again, the un-self-controlled person acts because of his affective state, knowing that what he is doing is a bad thing, while the self-controlled one knows that his appetites are bad but does not follow them because of what reason tells him. Again, people call the moderate type self-controlled and resistant, while some call anyone of this sort moderate, some do not; and some call the self-indulgent type un-self-controlled and the un-self-controlled self-indulgent, mixing the things together, whereas others say they are different. And sometimes people say it is impossible for the wise person to be un-self-controlled, while sometimes they say some people behave uncontrolledly even though they are wise and clever. Then too one can be said to be un-self-controlled in regard to temper, honour, and profit as well. These, then, are the views people express.

(VII. 2) But one might raise the problem: in what sense does a person have a correct grasp when he behaves uncontrolledly? Well, some deny that it is possible to do so if one has *knowledge*: it would be an astonishing thing if, when knowledge is in us—this was Socrates' thought—something else overpowers it and drags it about like a slave. For Socrates used completely to resist the idea, on the grounds that there was no such thing as behaving

---

[28] Retaining τῶν (1145b9).

uncontrolledly; no one, he would say, acts contrary to what is best while grasping that he is doing so, but only because of ignorance. Now to say this is to say something at odds with what patently appears to be the case (and in addition we need to ask about the agent's affective state: if it is because of ignorance, what mode of ignorance turns out to be involved). For it is evident that the person acting uncontrolledly doesn't think of doing it, before he gets into the affective state in question. But there are some who go along with Socrates' view in some respects but not in others: they agree that nothing is superior to knowledge, but they do not agree that no one acts contrary to what has seemed to him better, and because of this they say that the un-self-controlled person is overcome by pleasures not when he has knowledge of something but when it has merely seemed to him to be so. And yet if it is a matter of mere seeming and not knowledge, and the belief that is resisting is not a strong but only a light one, as with people in two minds about something, there is sympathy for any failure to stand firm in such beliefs in the face of strong appetites, but there is no sympathy for badness, nor for any other object of censure. What, then, if it is wisdom that is resisting? After all, this is something very strong. But that will be a strange state of affairs: the same person will be at the same time wise and un-self-controlled, and no one at all would assert that it is characteristic of a wise person to do the worst things voluntarily. In addition to these considerations, we have shown before that the wise person is of a sort to *act* (being of a sort concerned with 'what comes last'), and is someone who possesses the other excellences. Further, if one cannot be self-controlled unless one's appetites are strong and bad, the moderate type will not be self-controlled nor the self-controlled type moderate, since it is not characteristic of the moderate person either to have excessive appetites or to have bad ones. Yet the appetites in this case must be both, since if they are respectable, the disposition that prevents their being followed will be bad, so that self-control will not always be a good thing, while if they are weak, and are not bad, there is nothing impressive about it, and if they are bad and weak, it is no great achievement. What is more, if self-control makes one tend to stick to any and every judgement, it is bad, e.g. if it makes one stick even to the one that is false, and if lack of self-control tends to make one depart from any and every judgement, lack of self-control will have a good form, as e.g. in the case of Sophocles' Neoptolemus, in *Philoctetes*; for he is to be praised for *not* sticking to what Odysseus persuaded him to do, because of his distress at deceiving someone. Then too the argument the sophists offer provides a puzzling problem. For because they want to refute people in paradoxical ways, in order to be able to be clever (if they can get their way), the argument they construct turns into a puzzle; for one's thinking is tied down, when on the one hand it does not want to stay where it is because of dislike for the conclusion, while on the other it is unable to move forward because of inability to resolve the argument. Thus there is a kind of argument from

1145b30

1145b35

1146a1

1146a5

1146a10

1146a15

1146a20

1146a25

which it follows that mindlessness combined with lack of self-control is excellence; for the agent's lack of self-control will make him do the contrary of what he supposes he should, and since what he supposes is that good things

1146a30 are bad and not to be done, the result will be that he does the good things and not the bad. Again, someone who pursued what is pleasant out of persuasion and by decision would seem better than one who did it not through calculation but through lack of self-control; after all, he would be easier to cure—one would simply have to persuade him to change his mind. And the saying we

1146a35 use applies to the un-self-controlled person: 'when water is choking you, what
1146b1 will wash it down?' For if he had been persuaded of what he is doing, he would have stopped doing it when persuaded differently; as it is, he is already persuaded that he shouldn't do it, and does it nonetheless.[29] Then again: if one can lack self-control, and have it, in regard to anything, which is the un-self-controlled type without qualification? For no one has all kinds of lack of

1146b5 self-control, but we do say that some people are un-self-controlled without adding any qualification.

The problems, then, turn out to be of these kinds, and we must now do away with some of the assumptions involved while leaving others undisturbed; for to resolve a problem is to find things out.

(VII. 3) First, then, we must investigate whether or not it is knowledge a person possesses when he acts uncontrolledly, and if so in what sense he

1146b10 possesses it; next, in relation to what sorts of things we should locate the un-self-controlled and the self-controlled—I mean, whether to any kind of pleasure and pain or to some specified kinds; whether the self-controlled type is the same as the resistant, or different; and similarly with the other questions germane to what we are presently considering. Our investigation starts with

1146b15 the question whether what distinguishes the self-controlled person and the un-self-controlled is type of object or manner, I mean whether lack of self-control is marked off just by having to do with a particular type of things, or rather just by manner, or whether it is a combination of both; then, whether or not lack of self-control, and self-control, have every type of object. For it is not in relation to every type of object that 'un-self-controlled' applies without

1146b20 qualification, but in relation to the same ones as 'self-indulgent', nor does it apply by being, without qualification, related to them, for then lack of self-control would *be* self-indulgence, but by being related to them in a certain way. For the self-indulgent type is drawn even as he decides to go in that direction, because he thinks one should always pursue what offers pleasure now; whereas the un-self-controlled type doesn't think one should, but pursues it all the same.

Now as for the suggestion about its being true judgement and not

[29] Reading νῦν δὲ πεπεισμένος οὐδὲν ἧττον ἄλλα ποιεῖ (1146b1–2).

knowledge that the un-self-controlled person acts against, this makes no differ-   1146b25
ence to the argument; for some people when making mere judgements are not
in two minds about them, but think they possess precise knowledge. If, then, it
is because of the lightness of their conviction that those merely making
judgements will be more liable than those with knowledge to act contrary to
what they suppose they should do, knowing will be no different from judging,
since some people have no less conviction about what they judge to be the case   1146b30
than others have about what they know—as the example of Heraclitus shows.
But since there are two ways in which we say someone knows—for both the
person who has knowledge but is not using it and the one using it are said to
know—there will be a difference between doing what one shouldn't when
knowing one shouldn't but not having regard to the knowledge, and doing it
when actually having regard to it; for this is what is thought astonishing, not if   1146b35
one does what one shouldn't when *not* having regard to the knowledge. Further, since there are two types of premiss, there is nothing to prevent someone   1147a1
from acting 'contrary to his knowledge' when he has both premisses but is
using only the universal one, not the particular one; for it is particulars that are
acted on. The universal too has to be differentiated, in so far as there is one
term for the agent and one for the object of the action, e.g. that all human   1147a5
beings are benefited by dry foods, and that one is oneself a human being, or
that such-and-such is dry; but whether *this* is such-and-such—this is what the
agent either does not 'have', or does not activate; and which of *these* ways we
mean will make an immense difference, with the result that his knowing
seems, in one way, not at all strange, and in the other way amazing. Further: 1147a10
there is a way other than those just mentioned in which we humans can 'have
knowledge'; for under 'having but not using' we observe a distinction in 'having', such that a person both has knowledge in a way and does not have it, as
with someone asleep, raving, or drunk. But this is the state of those who are in
the various affective states: occurrences of temper, appetite for sex, and some   1147a15
things like this manifestly alter one's bodily state too, and in some people they
even cause kinds of madness. Clearly, then, we should say that the state of the
un-self-controlled is like these people's. That they say the things that flow from
knowledge indicates nothing, since those in the affective states mentioned, too,   1147a20
can recite demonstrative proofs and Empedoclean verses, and if those who
have learned something for the first time can string the words together, they
don't yet *know* what they have learned—because they have to assimilate it, and
that requires time. So we must suppose that those who act uncontrolledly, too,
are talking like actors on the stage.

Furthermore, one can also, in the following way, look scientifically at the   1147a25
cause. One of the premisses is a universal judgement, while the second has to
do with particulars, over which it is perception that holds sway; and when a
single proposition is formed from them, the soul necessarily assents, in one
type of case, to what has been concluded, or else, when the premisses are

1147a30   about making something happen, it acts immediately—thus if everything sweet should be tasted, and *this* (some particular item) is sweet, one will necessarily at the same time also *do* this, provided that one *can* do it, and is not prevented. So when one universal premiss is in the agent preventing tasting, and so is one saying that everything sweet is pleasant—and *this* is sweet (and the latter premiss is active), and there happens to be appetite in the agent, then

1147a35   the first one says 'avoid this', but the appetite drives him to it; for it can move

1147b1   each of the parts. So it turns out that uncontrolled behaviour is due to reason, in a way, and to judgement, but one that is not in itself, but only incidentally, contrary—for what is contrary is the appetite, not the judgement—to the correct prescription (so this is another reason why animals are not un-self-

1147b5   controlled, i.e. because they do not have a universal grasp, only the capacity to receive appearances from, and to remember, particulars). As for how the un-self-controlled type's ignorance is resolved, and his behaviour becomes once again knowledge-based, the same account applies as in the case of the drunken person and the sleeping one, and is not peculiar to the affective state we are discussing; this account one needs to get from the natural scientists. But since

1147b10   the final premiss is both a judgement about something perceived, and what determines actions, either he does not have this because he is affected as he is, or he 'has' it in the sense in which we said 'having' was not a matter of knowing but only of talking, like the drunk with the verses of Empedocles. And because the last premiss is not universal and does not seem to express systematic knowledge in the way the universal premiss does, one also seems

1147b15   to get what Socrates was looking for; for it is not what seems to be knowledge in the primary sense that the affective state in question overcomes[30] (nor is it this kind of knowledge that is 'dragged about' because of the state), but the perceptual kind. Let this much, then, stand as our treatment of the 'knowing and not knowing' aspect of the subject, and of the sense in which it is possible for someone to know and yet act uncontrolledly.

1147b20   (VII. 4) We must next discuss whether there is any type that is un-self-controlled without qualification, or whether everyone is un-self-controlled in some specified way; and if there is, what sorts of things make up the objects of this unqualified lack of self-control. Now it is evident that both being self-controlled and resistant and being un-self-controlled and soft have to do with pleasures and pains. But given that some of the things that produce pleasure

1147b25   are necessary, while others are desirable in themselves, though they can be taken to excess, it is the bodily sort that are necessary (I mean things like this: what relates to food and the need for sex, and in general the sorts of bodily concerns we stated to be the sphere of self-indulgence and moderation), while

1147b30   the other sort are not necessary but are desirable in themselves (I mean e.g.

---

[30] Reading δοκούσης περιγίνεται (1147b16).

winning, honour, wealth, and other such things that are good and pleasant):
people, then, who go to excess in relation to these things, contravening the
correct prescription that is in them, we do not call unqualifiedly un-self-
controlled, but un-self-controlled with the addition of 'with regard to money',
'with regard to profit', 'with regard to honour', 'with regard to temper'—we
do not give them the name without qualification, on the basis that they are
different, and called un-self-controlled by virtue of resemblance; as with the   1147b35
man who used to win Olympic victories, called Man, where the general   1148a1
definition hardly differed from the particular, but nevertheless was different.
An indication of what we are saying is that lack of self-control is censured not
only as a fault but also as, in a way, badness, either without qualification or in
terms of some particular sort of badness, whereas none of the types just
mentioned is censured in this way. But of those types having to do with bodily   1148a5
enjoyments that we say are the sphere of moderation and self-indulgence, the
one who pursues excess in what is pleasant without its being a matter of
decision, and avoids excess of what is painful, hunger, thirst, heat, cold, and
generally all painful things to do with touch and taste, but contrary to decision and what he thinks, is called un-self-controlled, not with an addition   1148a10
indicating 'with regard to such-and-such', e.g. anger, but just without qualification. An indication is that people are also called soft in relation to these sorts
of pains, but not in relation to any of the others. And it is for this reason that
we put the un-self-controlled and the self-controlled types, but not any of the   1148a15
others, into the same category as the self-indulgent and the moderate, because
it is to the same pleasures, in a way, that they relate. But while these types do
relate to the same things as the self-indulgent and the moderate, they do not
relate to them in the same way; the difference lies in whether the agent acts
from decision or not. Hence the term 'self-indulgent' will belong to the person who pursues excessive pleasures without, or with mild, prompting from
appetite, avoiding moderate pains, more than to the one who does it because
of intense appetite; for what would the former type do if in addition he had   1148a20
an energetic appetite and felt a powerful distress at not having the necessary
pleasures? But given that some appetites and pleasures have objects that are
generically fine and good (since some pleasant things are by nature desirable)
while the objects of others are the contrary, with those of others in between   1148a25
(the distinction we made before), e.g. money, profit, winning, honour—and
given that in relation to both all the fine and good objects and all the in-
between ones people are not censured for being affected by them in the first
place, i.e. for desiring and 'loving' them, but for being affected in a certain way,
i.e. excessively (which is why censure attaches to those who either are overcome by or pursue something naturally fine and good contrary to what   1148a30
reason prescribes, e.g. those who are more concerned than one should be
with honour, or with children or parents; for these too are good things, and
people who are concerned with them are praised, but all the same it is

possible to go to excess even in these cases, as for example if someone were even, like Niobe, to get into a fight with the gods, or behaved towards his father like Satyrus, nicknamed Fatherlover—for he was thought to be taking stupidity too far): given this, there is no badness of character involved in relation to these objects, for the reason that we have stated, namely that each of them is in itself something naturally desirable, but excess with regard to them *is* a bad thing and something to be avoided. Similarly, neither can one lack self-control in these cases, since lack of self-control is not only to be avoided but something to be censured too. But because of a resemblance to the way the un-self-controlled person is affected we do use the term in relation to each of the things in question, only putting in a qualification too, as we do when we talk about a bad *doctor* or a bad *actor*, referring to people we wouldn't call bad without qualification. So just as the state of being a bad doctor, and so on, is not just bad, because no such state is *badness*, but only resembles it, by being analogous, so in the other case too: clearly, we must take un-self-controlledness and self-control to be exclusively those having to do with the same things as moderation and self-indulgence. In relation to temper, we use the terms by virtue of resemblance; this is why we use them there with the addition '(un-self-controlled) with regard to temper', as we say 'with regard to honour' and 'with regard to profit'.

1148b1

1148b5

1148b10

1148b15   (VII. 5) Given that while some things are pleasant by nature (some of these without qualification, others with reference to particular types both of animals and of human beings), other things are not, but come to be pleasant whether because of disablement or through habituation, or again because of a natural lack of quality, in relation to each of these kinds of thing too one can observe dispositions of a corresponding sort. I mean the brutish ones, as in the case of the human female who they say used to slit open pregnant women and eat their babies, or the pleasures said to be enjoyed by some of those who live wild in the Black Sea area, some of them enjoying raw meat, some human meat, others being said to hand over their children for the communal feast on condition of a similar return; or again there is what they report about Phalaris. These dispositions are brutish, but some result from diseases (and in some cases from madness, as with the man who sacrificed and ate his mother, or the one who ate his fellow slave's liver), while others are morbid dispositions resulting from habituation,[31] e.g. pulling out one's hair or chewing on one's nails, or again on charcoal or earth, or, to add another example, the disposition to sexual activity with other males; for in some cases the dispositions in question occur naturally, while in others they result from habituation, as with those who are abused from childhood on. Where nature is responsible, then, no one would call these types un-self-controlled, any more than

1148b20

1148b25

1148b30

[31] Reading νοσηματώδεις ἐξ ἔθους (1148b27).

one would call women un-self-controlled because they have the passive rather than the active role in copulation; and similarly with those who are in a morbid condition as a result of habituation. So on the one hand *having* each of these sorts of dispositions is something outside the limits of badness of character, just as brutishness in general is; on the other, having them and exercising control, or failing to exercise control, is not the unqualified lack of self-control but the one by resemblance, just as the person who is like this when it comes to keeping or losing his temper is to be called un-self-controlled with regard to his affective state, not merely un-self-controlled. For all excessive mindlessness, cowardliness, self-indulgence, or bad temper is either brutish or morbid: someone who is naturally the sort to fear anything—even a mouse rustling—is cowardly with a brutish cowardice, while the individual who was afraid of his house-weasel was so as the result of an illness; and of mindless people, those who naturally lack reasoning capacity, so living by sensation alone, are brutish (like some distant non-Greek tribes), while those who are mindless because of disease (e.g. those involving seizures) or madness are morbid. But of these traits there are some that it is possible, sometimes, to have without being overcome by them—I mean, if Phalaris had restrained himself when he felt an appetite for a child to eat, or for some outlandish sexual pleasure; but it is also possible to be overcome by them and not just have them. So just as in the case of badness the sort on a human scale is called badness without qualification, and the other sort subject to an addition, i.e. 'brutish' or 'morbid', not without qualification, clearly in the same way lack of self-control is, some of it, brutish, and some morbid, but only the kind corresponding to human self-indulgence is lack of self-control without qualification.

It is clear, then, that un-self-controlledness and self-control are concerned only with the things that concern self-indulgence and moderation, and that in relation to the other things in question there is another form of lack of self-control, one so-called in a transferred and not in an unqualified sense.

(VII. 6) Let us then observe the fact that lack of self-control with regard to temper is also less shameful than the form relating to the appetites. For one's temper in such cases seems to hear what reason says, but to mishear it, like hasty servants who run out of the room before they have heard everything being said to them and then fail to carry out the instruction, and as dogs bark just at a sound, before discovering if it's a friend who's there; just so a hot and quick nature means that temper hears—but does not hear the order, before rushing to vengeance. For reason, or sensory appearances, indicate 'unprovoked aggression' or 'insult', and temper, as if having reasoned it out that this sort of thing is cause for going to war, moves into angry mode at once; whereas appetite only needs reason or perception to say 'pleasant' for it

1149a1

1149a5

1149a10

1149a15

1149a20

1149a25

1149a30

1149a35

1149b1 to rush off to enjoy it. So temper follows reason in a way, but appetite does not. In that case not being able to control it is the more shameful, in so far as the person behaving uncontrolledly with regard to temper is in a way giving in to reason, whereas the other sort is giving in to appetite and not to reason.

1149b5 Again, there is more sympathy for people who follow the natural desires, since there is, too, in the case of the sorts of appetites that are common to everyone, and to the extent that they are so; and temper or irascibility is more natural than appetites for excess and appetites for unnecessary things—as the man said when defending himself for the beatings he gave his father, 'Well, he

1149b10 used to beat his father, and *he* used to beat his, and what's more'—pointing to his little son—'he'll beat me when he becomes a man—it's something we're born with in our family'; or there's the man who when his son used to try to drag him out of the house would tell him to stop at the outside doors, because that's as far as he'd dragged *his* father. Again, the more plotting people do, the more unjust they are. Now the person who tends to lose his temper does not

1149b15 plot, and neither does temper, but is open; whereas appetite is a plotter, just as they say Aphrodite is—

> For of the weaver of guile, Cyprus-born . . .

and Homer's description of her 'embroidered girdle'—

> Bemusement, stealing thought from wisest minds.

So, if it is true that this kind of lack of self-control is more unjust and shameful than the kind relating to temper, it will also be lack of self-control

1149b20 without qualification and, in a sense, badness. Again, no one feels distress at committing acts of unprovoked aggression, whereas everyone who acts out of anger is distressed; the aggressor gets pleasure from what he does. If, then, the things that most justify anger are the more unjust, so too is the lack of self-control that comes about because of appetite; for temper is not an unprovoked aggressor. So it is clear that lack of self-control relating to appe-

1149b25 tite is more shameful than the sort relating to temper, and that self-control, and the lack of it, have to do with bodily desires and pleasures; but there are differences among these desires and pleasures, which we need to grasp. As we said at the beginning of this discussion, some of them are natural to human beings in terms both of kind and of quantity, some brutish, some due

1149b30 to disablement and disease. Of these, moderation and self-indulgence have to do only with the first sort, which is why in the case of brute animals, too, we do not use either term, 'moderate' or 'self-indulgent', except in a transferred sense, and unless in some respect one whole species of animals differs from another—in aggressiveness, or wanton destructiveness, or in voraciousness;

1149b35 for they do not have decision, or reasoning, but are a falling away from nature,

1150a1 like madmen among human beings. But brutishness is a lesser thing than badness, though it is the more terrifying; for the better part has not been corrupted, as it has been in the human case, but is simply not present. So it is like comparing the inanimate with the animate, and asking which is worse; for the bad qualities of what does not have an internal source of movement are always less destructive, and intelligence is such a source. The comparison is similar, then, to that between injustice and an unjust human being, in so far as there is a sense in which each is the worse thing—for a bad human being will do bad things on a vastly wider scale than a brute animal.

(VII. 7) As for pleasures and pains through touch and taste, and appetite and avoidance in relation to these (all of which we have marked off before as the sphere of self-indulgence and moderation), one can be in a condition such as to give in even to those that most people are able to overcome; and one can also overcome even those that most people are too weak not to give in to. Of these types, the ones relating to pleasures are un-self-controlled and self-controlled respectively, while those relating to pains are soft and resistant; the disposition belonging to the most people is in between these, even if most people do incline towards the worse ones. Given that some pleasures are necessary and some not, and that the necessary ones are so up to a point, but excess is not necessary, and neither is deficiency, and similarly with desires, and pains, the type of person that pursues excess in terms of what is pleasant, or pursues what is pleasant to excess, and because of decision,[32] pursuing the pleasures he does for their own sake and not because of anything else that happens to accrue from them—this type is truly *akolastos* ['self-indulgent'], since he necessarily has no regrets, and so is incurable; for the sort who has no regrets is incurable. (The deficient type is the one that is the opposite of this one, the intermediate type the moderate.) Similarly with the type of person who avoids bodily pains not because of being overcome but because of decision. Of the non-deciding types, the one is led on because of the pleasure, the other because that way he will avoid the pain arising from the appetite, so that they are different from each other; [But everyone would think a person worse for doing something shameful without or with only gentle prompting from appetite than for doing it from intense appetite, and for punching someone when not angry than for doing it in anger; for what would he do if he *were* in one of these affective states? Hence the self-indulgent type is worse than the un-self-controlled one.] of the types in question, then, one is more softness— of a sort, whereas the other is self-indulgence. And the opposite of being un-self-controlled is being self-controlled, that of being soft being resistant; for resisting is a matter of withstanding, whereas self-control is a matter of over-coming, and withstanding is different from overcoming, as not being defeated is different from winning—which is why self-control is also a more desirable thing than resistance. The type that is deficient in relation to what most

1150a5

1150a10

1150a15

1150a20

1150a25

1150a30

1150a35

1150b1

³² Reading ἢ καθ᾿ ὑπερβολήν, καὶ διὰ προαίρεσιν (1150a19–20).

people struggle against, and successfully, is the one who is soft and a slave to comfort, since weakness for comfort is a kind of softness—as with the person who lets his cloak trail on the ground so as not to be troubled by the pain of lifting it, and who even as he imitates a sick person does not consider himself a miserable specimen, like though he is to one. The case of self-control and un-self-controlledness is like this too. For it is not surprising if someone gives in to strong or excessive pleasures or pains, but rather something one tends to feel sympathy for, if he is overcome despite struggling against them, like Theodectes' Philoctetes, stricken by snake-bite, or Cercyon in Carcinus' *Alopē*, or like people trying to hold back their laughter but letting it all out in a splutter, as happened to Xenophantus; but it *is* surprising if someone is overcome by pleasures or pains that most people can withstand, and is unable to struggle against *these*—unless it is because of some natural, congenital factor (or because of disease), as for example in the case of the Scythian kings their softness is a matter of heredity, or in the way in which the female is distinguished from the male. The devotee of amusement is also thought to be self-indulgent, but in fact he is soft. For amusement is a slackening, given that it is a kind of resting; and the devotee of amusement is one of those that go to excess in this respect. As for lack of self-control, part of it is impulsiveness, part weakness. For some people deliberate and then fail to stick to the results of the deliberation because of their affective condition, while others are led by the affection because they have failed to deliberate; for just as one can't be tickled if one has tickled the other person first, so some people, if they have had advance warning and seen it coming, wake themselves and their calculative faculty up beforehand and so are not overcome by the affection, either if the object in question is pleasant or if it is painful. For the most part it is the quick-tempered and the bilious sorts of people that have lack of self-control in its impulsive variety: hastiness in the one case, intensity in the other, prevent them from waiting for reason, because their disposition is to follow perceptual appearances.

(VII. 8) The self-indulgent type, as has been said, is not the sort to have regrets, since he sticks to his decision; the un-self-controlled type, on the other hand, always has regrets. Hence it is not as we suggested when we listed the problems: it is the former that is incurable, and the latter that is curable; for badness of character resembles diseases like dropsy or consumption, while lack of self-control resembles the sort involving seizures; for the one is a continuous, the other a non-continuous way of being as one shouldn't be. And lack of self-control and badness are in fact wholly different in kind; for badness goes undetected by its possessor, while lack of self-control does not. (Of the un-self-controlled themselves, the sort inclined to depart from reason are better than those who are in possession of the prescription but do not stick to it; for the latter are overcome by a lesser state of affection, and they

do not act without prior deliberation as the other sort do.) In fact the
un-self-controlled type resembles those who become drunk quickly, after little
wine, and after less than most people. It is evident, then, that lack of self-   1151a5
control is not badness (though perhaps *in a sense* it is), because the one is
contrary to decision, the other in accordance with it; yet on the other hand it
does resemble badness when it comes to the actions resulting from it: in line
with Demodocus' comment on the Milesians—

> Stupid Milesians are not, but they do what the stupid do,   1151a10

un-self-controlled people are not unjust, either, but they will do what the
unjust do. And since the un-self-controlled type is the sort to pursue bodily
pleasures that are excessive and contrary to the correct prescription but not
because he is persuaded he should, while the other type is so persuaded,
because of his being the sort to pursue them, the former is easy to persuade
that he should change his behaviour, the latter not. For excellence and badness   1151a15
respectively keep healthy, and corrupt, the fundamental starting point, and in
action this is that for the sake of which, just as in mathematical arguments the
initial posits are starting points. Neither in that case, then, does reasoning
teach us the starting points, nor does it in the present one; instead, it is
excellence, innate or resulting from habit-training, that gives us correct
judgement about the starting point. Such a person, then, is moderate, and his   1151a20
contrary is self-indulgent. But there is a type that is inclined to depart from
reason, contrary to the correct prescription, because of his affective state, who
is overcome by that state to the extent of failing to act in accordance with the
correct prescription, but not to the extent of being the sort of person to be
persuaded that one should straightforwardly pursue such pleasures: this is the
un-self-controlled type, one who is better than the self-indulgent type, and not   1151a25
bad without qualification, since the best in him, the fundamental starting
point, remains healthy. Another type is contrary to this one—the one who
sticks to instead of departing from reason, at any rate not because of any
affective state. It is evident, then, from these considerations that one of these
dispositions is good, the other bad.

(VII. 9) Well then: does self-control consist in sticking to any reasoning,
whatever it may be, and any decision whatever, or sticking to the correct one;   1151a30
and does lack of self-control consist in not sticking to any decision, whatever it
may be, and any reasoning whatever, or in not sticking to reasoning which is
not false, and the decision that is correct (the problem we raised before)? Or is
it only an incidental case when one type sticks to, or the other departs from,
any decision whatever; but in themselves self-control and the lack of it mean
sticking to and departing from the true reasoning and the correct decision? (If   1151a35
someone chooses or pursues this because of that, he pursues and chooses the   1151b1
latter in itself, the former incidentally.) But when talking without qualification

we mean what is in itself. So there is a sense in which it is any judgement whatever that the one sticks to and the other departs from, but without

1151b5   qualification it is the true one. There are some people that tend to 'stick to their judgement' who are called stubborn, the ones who are hard to persuade, i.e. not easily persuaded to change their minds: these have a degree of resemblance to the self-controlled type, just as the wasteful do to the open-handed, and the rash to the confident, but they are different in many respects. For in the one case it is the affective state of appetite that fails to effect a change

1151b10   (since the self-controlled type will be easily persuaded in other contexts), whereas with the stubborn sort it is reason, since in fact they do acquire appetites, and many of them are led on by pleasures. It is the opinionated, the uneducated, and the boorish who are stubborn—the opinionated being motivated by pleasure and pain, in so far as they take pleasure in winning if

1151b15   someone fails to persuade them, and are pained if their own judgements are invalidated, like decrees; so they are more like the un-self-controlled type than they are like the self-controlled. There are also some who fail to stick to what has seemed right to them not because of lack of self-control, e.g. Neoptolemus in Sophocles' *Philoctetes*: true, it was because of pleasure that

1151b20   he departed from his judgement, but the pleasure was a fine one—telling the truth was, to him, a fine thing, but he had been persuaded by Odysseus to lie. Not everyone who does something because of pleasure is self-indulgent, or bad, or un-self-controlled; only the one who does it because of a shameful pleasure.

     Given that there is also a type that enjoys bodily things less than one

1151b25   should, and fails to stick to the prescription, the self-controlled person will be the intermediate between this type and the un-self-controlled; for the un-self-controlled fails to stick to the prescription because of too much in some respect, this one because of too little, whereas the self-controlled sticks to it and does not change because of either. And given that self-control is a good thing, both the contrary dispositions must be bad, as in

1151b30   fact they clearly are; but because one of these two is in evidence only rarely, in a few people, just as moderation is thought to be the only contrary to self-indulgence, so is self-control, too, to un-self-controlledness. Given that many things get their names by virtue of resemblance, the 'self-control' of the moderate person is itself the consequence of a resem-

1151b35   blance: both the self-controlled type and the moderate type do nothing
1152a1   contrary to the prescription because of bodily pleasures—only the one does it while having bad appetites, the other while not having, and the one is such as not to feel pleasure contrary to the prescription, while the other is such as to feel it but not be led by it. The un-self-controlled and self-

1152a5   indulgent types are similar too: while being different, both pursue what is pleasant in a bodily sense, only the one does it while thinking he should, the other not thinking so.

(VII. 10) Nor is it possible for the same person at the same time to be wise and un-self-controlled; for one has been shown to be excellent in character at the same time as one is wise. Again, one is not wise merely by virtue of having knowledge, but also by being the sort of person to act on one's knowledge; and the un-self-controlled is not that sort. (But there is nothing to stop the clever person from being un-self-controlled—and this is why some people are sometimes thought to be wise yet un-self-controlled, because cleverness differs from wisdom in the way we described in our original discussion, and while being close to it in terms of reasoning, differs from it in terms of the decisions made.) Neither, then, does the un-self-controlled person behave like someone knowing something and having regard to his knowledge, but like someone asleep or drunk. And he acts voluntarily (since he acts knowing in a way both what he is doing and what he is doing it for), but is not a bad person, since what he *decides* on is decent; so he is half-bad. He is not unjust either, since he is not a plotter: one of the un-self-controlled types does not stick to the things he has deliberated about doing, while the bilious type doesn't even deliberate at all. In fact the un-self-controlled person resembles a city which passes all the decrees it should, and has good laws, but makes no attempt to put them into effect, as in Anaxandrides' joke— 1152a10 1152a15 1152a20

> The city willed it—she that disregards her laws;

whereas the bad person resembles a city that puts its laws into effect, but bad ones. Uncontrolledness and self-control are a matter of going beyond the dispositions of the majority of people; for the one type has more capacity than most people for sticking to things, the other less. The type of uncontrolledness displayed by the bilious sort is more easily curable than the one belonging to people who deliberate but do not stick to it, as are those who are un-self-controlled through habituation than those naturally so; for habit is easier to change than nature. In fact this is why habit itself is hard to change—because it resembles nature; as Evenus puts it, too: 1152a25 1152a30

> It comes, my friend, by practice year on year—and see:
> At last this thing we practise our own nature is.

We have said, then, what self-control is, what un-self-controlledness is, what resistance is, and what softness is, and how these dispositions stand in relation to each other. 1152a35

(VII. 11) But pleasure and pain is a subject for consideration by the person inquiring philosophically in the sphere of political expertise; for he is the 'architectonic' craftsman of the end, to which we refer when calling each sort of thing without qualification good or bad. But further, it is actually a necessary requirement that we inquire into pleasure and pain, in so far as we laid down that excellence and badness of character had to do with pains and 1152b1 1152b5 pleasures, and most people say that happiness involves pleasure—which is why the 'blessed' [*makarioi*] are so called, after 'bliss' [*chairein*]. Now some think that no pleasure is a good, either in itself or incidentally, their reason

1152b10 being that the good and pleasure are not the same thing; while others think some pleasures are good, but most are bad. Further, there is a third one of these positions: even if all count as a good, nevertheless it is not possible for the chief good to be pleasure. A general argument, then, for saying that it is not a good is that all pleasure is a perceived process of coming to be in the natural state, but no process of coming to be belongs to the same kind as the end to which it leads, as e.g. no process of housebuilding belongs to the same

1152b15 kind as a house. There are also these arguments—that the moderate person avoids pleasures; that the wise person pursues what is painless, not what is pleasant; that pleasures are an impediment to thought, and the more so the more one enjoys them (as with the pleasure of sex: no one could have any thoughts when enjoying *that*); that pleasure is not the object of any expertise, and yet everything good is the product of some expertise; and that small

1152b20 children, and animals, pursue pleasures. For their not all being good, it is argued that there are also shameful pleasures, ones that are grounds for reproach, and that there are harmful ones; for some things that give pleasure bring disease. For saying that pleasure is not the chief good, the argument is that it is not an end but a process. These, then, are the views expressed, more or less.

1152b25 (VII. 12) But that it does not follow from these arguments that pleasure is not a good, or that it is not the chief good, is clear from the following. First, given that what is good is so in two ways, i.e. either good without qualification, or good for someone, the same will then also apply to good natures and dispositions, and therefore also to good movements and comings to be; and the ones that are thought to be bad will include those that are without qualification

1152b30 bad, but not for some particular person, instead being desirable for this person—and also some that are not even desirable for this person, but only in a specific context and for a short time, not without qualification. Others again are not even pleasures, but only appear so, i.e. those that are accompanied by pain and are for the sake of healing, such as the ones sick people undergo. Further, given that the good is part activity and part disposition, it is only

1152b35 incidentally that the processes restoring one to the natural state are pleasant; the activity in the case of the appetites belongs to one's residual natural

1153a1 disposition, since there are also pleasures unaccompanied by pain and appetite, like the activities of reflection,[33] where there is no depletion of the natural state. An indication is that people do not take pleasure in the same thing while their nature is being restored to completion and when it has been re-

---

[33] Retaining ἐνέργειαι (1153a1).

established: when it has been re-established they enjoy things that are pleasant without qualification, but while it is being restored they enjoy even things that are the contrary of these—even enjoying sharp and bitter tastes, none of which is either naturally pleasant or pleasant without qualification. In that case the same applies to the pleasures too; for as things that are pleasant are distinguished one from another, so too are the pleasures deriving from them. Further, it is not necessary that there be something else better than pleasure, in the way people say the end is better than the coming to be. For not all pleasures are comings to be, or accompanied by a coming to be, but rather they are activities, and an end, nor do they occur because a coming to be is in train but because capacities are being put to use; and not all pleasures have something else as end, but only those involved in the bringing to completion of one's nature. Hence it is not right to say that pleasure is a perceived process of coming to be; rather one should say that it is an activity of a natural disposition, and replace 'perceived' with 'unimpeded'. Some people think it is a coming to be on the basis that it is good in the primary sense; for they suppose that activity is coming to be, whereas it is something different. To argue that pleasures are bad because some pleasant things bring disease is the same as arguing that some healthy things are bad because they are bad for moneymaking. Both sets of things, then, *are* bad in this one respect, but that is not enough to make them bad, since philosophical reflection too is sometimes damaging to health. Neither wisdom nor any disposition at all is impeded by the specific pleasure deriving from it, but only by alien ones, since those from reflecting and coming to understand will make one do more reflecting and coming to understand. That no pleasure is the product of expertise is what one would reasonably expect; for expertise does not relate in this way to any other activity either, only to a *capacity*—though of course people think of the expertise of the perfumer or the cook as producing pleasure. That the moderate person avoids pleasures, and that the wise man pursues the painless life, and that small children and animals pursue pleasure—these points are all resolved by the same means. For given that we have said in what way pleasures are good without qualification, and in what way not all of them are good, it is the latter sort that both animals and small children pursue, and the painlessness of a life without these that the wise person pursues, i.e. the pleasures accompanied by appetite and pain—bodily pleasures (since these are of the relevant sort) and excess of these, which are the specific objects of self-indulgence. Hence these are the pleasures the moderate person avoids, since there are pleasures that are characteristic of moderation too.

(VII. 13) And yet it is agreed that pain, too, is a bad thing, and something to be avoided; for one sort of pain is without qualification something bad, while another is bad by virtue of being an impediment in some way. But the contrary of what is to be avoided, in so far as it is something to be avoided and

1153a5
1153a10
1153a15
1153a20
1153a25
1153a30
1153b35
1153b1

1153b5 bad, is good. Necessarily, then, pleasure is a good. For Speusippus' attempted rebuttal of this argument does not succeed, i.e. that it is like the larger's being contrary to the smaller and to the equal; for he would not say that pleasure was essentially something bad. And that some pleasures are bad is not a reason why the chief good is not a certain kind of pleasure, any more than the fact that some kinds of knowledge are bad is a reason for its not being a

1153b10 certain kind of knowledge. Given that there are unimpeded activities of each disposition, then whether happiness is the activity of all of them or of one of them, it is perhaps even a necessary conclusion that this activity, provided it is unimpeded, be most desirable; but this is pleasure. In that case the chief good will be a kind of pleasure, even if most pleasures turned out to be bad, even without qualification. And it is because of this that everyone thinks that the

1153b15 happy life is a pleasant one, and incorporates pleasure in happiness—with good reason; for no activity is complete if it is impeded, and happiness is something complete. This is why, in order for a person to be happy, he also needs the goods relating to the body, and external goods, and those fortune brings, i.e. in order for him not to be impeded in these respects. (Those who

1153b20 claim that the man being broken on the wheel and engulfed by great misfortunes is happy, provided he is a good character, are talking nonsense whether they mean to or not. And because the happy person also needs the goods of fortune, some people think being fortunate is the same thing as being happy, when it is not, for even good fortune is an impediment when it is excessive—and perhaps then one should no longer call it good fortune, since

1153b25 its limit is determined by reference to happiness.) And that all animals, and indeed human beings, pursue pleasure indicates that it is in a way the chief good:

> No message voiced abroad by a multitude of the nations
> Utterly dies . . .

But since neither the best nature nor the best disposition either is or is thought

1153b30 to be the same for all, neither do all pursue the same pleasure, though all do pursue pleasure. But perhaps they also pursue, not the one they suppose, or the one they would say they were pursuing, but the same one; for everything by nature contains something godlike. It is the bodily pleasures, however, that have taken over the title to the name 'pleasure', because these are the ones we

1153b35 most often encounter, and because everyone shares in them; so because they
1154a1 are the only ones they recognize, people think they are the only ones there are. It is also evident that, if pleasure,[34] and the activity that is pleasure, is not a good, it will not be the case that the happy person lives pleasantly—for what would he need pleasure for, if indeed it is not a good?—and indeed he may

1154a5 even live a life of pain, since pain is neither a bad thing nor a good one, if in

---

[34] Reading εἰ μὴ ἡ ἡδονὴ (1154a1).

206

fact pleasure is neither too—so what reason would he have for avoiding it? Neither, then, is the life of excellence more pleasant, unless the activities that belong to it are so too.

(VII. 14) Now as for the bodily pleasures, there is a question to be considered by those who say that some pleasures are indeed intensely desirable, e.g. the fine ones, but not the bodily ones, those the self-indulgent person is concerned with: why, then, are the contrary pains bad? After all, good is contrary to bad. Or are the necessary pleasures good in this way, that what is not bad, too, is good? Or are they good up to a point? For with those dispositions and movements for which 'exceeding the better amount' is not possible, there cannot be excess of pleasure either; while with those that can, there can be excess of pleasure too. But the bodily goods can be excessive, and what makes a person bad is pursuing the excess, not the necessary pleasures; for everyone enjoys the pleasures of the table, wine, and sex in some way or other, but not everyone enjoys them as one should. But it is the contrary with pain: one does not avoid excessive pain, but pain in general, for pain is not contrary to excess except for the person pursuing excess. But given that one must not only state the true view but explain the false one, for then one is more likely to be convinced, since when what makes the latter appear true when it is not is itself shown to be reasonable, that gives greater conviction to the true view— we must, in that case, say why the bodily pleasures appear more desirable. Well, the first reason must be that bodily pleasure displaces pain; and because of excesses of pain, as if there were a remedy for them, people pursue excessive pleasure, and bodily pleasure in general. The remedies get their intensity, which is why people pursue them, from the fact that they appear in contrast to their contrary. And indeed pleasure is thought not to be a good thing because of these two things, as has been said: that some pleasures are actions stemming from a bad nature (bad either from being born so, as with a brute animal, or because of habituation, as e.g. with the pleasures of bad human beings), while others are remedies for a nature that is lacking, and having is better than coming to be; but these occur in the process of restoration to completion, so that they are incidentally good. Again, bodily pleasures are pursued because of their intensity by those not able to enjoy other sorts of pleasures; at any rate, certain sorts of thirst they contrive for themselves. Now when they contrive harmless ones, no blame attaches to them for it, but when harmful ones, it is a bad thing; for not only do they not have other things to give them enjoyment, but to many what is neither pleasant nor painful is painful, because of their nature. For a living creature is perpetually at work, as the natural scientists also testify, claiming that seeing and hearing[35] are painful—we have just come to find them second nature, so they say. Similarly

[35] Reading τὸ ὁρᾶν καὶ τὸ ἀκούειν (1154b8).

1154a10
1154a15
1154a20
1154a25
1154a30
1154b1
1154b5

1154b10   during their youth people are in a state resembling drunkenness because they are growing, and youth is a pleasant thing; while bilious people are naturally in permanent need of a remedy, since their bodies too, because of the mixture in them, are constantly stinging, and they are always in a state of intense desire—and pain is driven out both by the contrary pleasure and by *any*

1154b15   pleasure, if it is a strong one. It is for these reasons, in fact, that people become self-indulgent and bad. But the pleasures that are not accompanied by pains cannot be taken to excess; and these are the pleasures relating to things that are pleasant by nature and not incidentally. What I call incidentally pleasant are the remedial sort; for what makes a thing seem pleasant in this case is that one happens to be cured, thanks to the activity of the part that remains

1154b20   healthy; pleasant by nature I call the things that bring about activity of a nature adapted to that activity. But in no case is one and the same thing always pleasant, because our nature is not simple, but also has in it an element of a different sort, in so far as we are mortal, with the consequence that if one of the two is active, this is contrary to nature for the other, but when they are in

1154b25   equal balance, what we are doing seems neither painful nor pleasant—since if any being's nature were simple, it will follow that it would be always the same activity that is most pleasant to him. This is why god always enjoys a single, simple pleasure; for there is activity not only of movement but also of immobility, and pleasure depends more on rest than on movement.

Of all things change is sweet,

1154b30   as the poet says, because of a kind of badness; for just as a bad human being is a changeable one, so is a nature that needs change a bad nature; for it is not simple, nor is it unflawed.

We have, then, discussed self-control and uncontrolledness, and pleasure and pain, and what each sort is, and how some of them are good and some bad; as for what remains, we shall also be discussing friendship.

BOOK VIII

(VIII. 1) After these subjects, it will be appropriate to discuss friendship, since friendship is a kind of excellence, or goes along with excellence, and further-

1155a5   more is very necessary for living. For no one would choose to live without friends, even if he had all the other good things; for even the wealthy or those who rule over or dominate others are thought to need friends more than anything—since what use would such prosperity be if they were deprived of the possibility of beneficence, which occurs most, and is most to be praised, in relation to friends? Or how could it be watched over and safeguarded without friends? For the greater it is, the more at risk. And in poverty and all other kinds of misfortune people think of their friends as their only refuge. Friends, too, can help young people in avoiding mistakes, older ones by caring for them and making up what they cannot do because of weakness, and those in their prime towards fine action—'When two go forth together', and so on, because two are able both to 'notice' and to act better than one. And friendship seems to be naturally present in parent for offspring and in offspring for parent, not only among human beings but among birds, too, and most animals; and in members of each species towards each other, particularly in the case of the human species, which is why we praise those who love mankind. One can see even with people on their travels how to a human being every human being is a kindred thing and an object of friendship. Friendship also seems to keep cities together, and lawgivers seem to pay more attention to it than to justice. For like-mindedness seems to be similar, in a way, to friendship, and it is this that they aim most at achieving, while they aim most to eliminate faction, faction being enmity; and there is no need for rules of justice between people who are friends, whereas if they are just they still need friendship—and of what is just, the most just is thought to be what belongs to friendship. Not only is it necessary, it is also a fine thing. For we praise those who cherish their friends, and having many friends is thought to be one of the things that are fine. And furthermore, it is held that it is the same men that are good and are friends.

But there are not a few disputes about the subject. Some people suppose that it is a kind of likeness, and that those that are alike are friends, which is the source of sayings such as 'Like tends to like', and 'Jackdaw to jackdaw', and so on; whereas others take the contrary position and say that like to like is always a matter of the proverbial potters. And in relation to these same things they pursue the question further, taking it to a more general and scientific level—Euripides claiming that

> Ever lusts the earth for rain

when it has become dry,

> Lusts too the mighty heaven, filling full with rain,
> To fall on earth,

Heraclitus talking of hostility bringing together, the divergent making finest harmony, and of all things coming to be through strife; but taking a view contrary to these there is Empedocles, for one, who says that like seeks like. Now those problems that come from natural science we may set to one side, since they are not germane to the present inquiry; let us look further into

1155a10

1155a15

1155a20

1155a25

1155a30

1155a35
1155b1

1155b5

1155b10 those that belong to the human sphere and relate to characters and affective states, e.g. whether friendship comes about among all types, or whether it is impossible for those who are bad characters to be friends, and whether there is one kind of friendship or more than one. For those who think that there is one kind on the ground that friendship admits of more and less have based 1155b15 themselves on an insufficient indication, since things different in kind too can be compared as more or less. But we have talked about these issues earlier.

(VIII. 2) But perhaps the issues will become clear once we have reached an understanding of what is loved. For it seems that not everything is loved, only what is lovable, and that the lovable is good, or pleasant, or useful; but that 1155b20 would seem to be useful through which some good or pleasure comes about, so that it will be the good and the pleasant that are lovable as ends. Is it, then, the good that people love, or what is good for themselves? For sometimes the one is at odds with the other—and there is a similar difference in the case of the pleasant too. It seems to be the case that each person loves what is good for himself, and that it is the good that is lovable without qualification, while 1155b25 what is good for each is what is lovable to each; but each loves not what is good for him but what seems to him to be so. But that will make no difference; for it will be what appears lovable. There being three things that cause people to love, the word 'friendship' does not apply to the loving of inanimate objects; for there is no reciprocal loving, nor wishing for the other's good 1155b30 (presumably wishing good things for one's wine is absurd, or rather, if it does happen, one wishes for it to keep, so as to have it oneself); and people say friendship demands that one wish a friend good things for his sake. Those who wish good things for someone else like this are said to have good will towards him, if the same is not forthcoming from the other party as well; friendship, people say, is good will between reciprocating parties. Or should one add, 1155b35 good will that one is aware of? For many people have good will towards those 1156a1 whom they have not met, but suppose to be decent, or useful; and one of these might in fact be in the same position in relation to *them*. Good will, then, is what these people evidently feel towards each other; but how could one call them friends, if they are not aware of their mutual feelings? If there is to be friendship, the parties must have good will towards each other, i.e. wish good things for each other, and be aware of the other's doing so, the feeling being 1156a5 brought about by one of the three things mentioned.

(VIII. 3) But these things differ in kind; so, then, does the loving, and so do the friendships. There are, then, three kinds of friendship, equal in number to the objects of love; for there corresponds to each of these objects a reciprocal loving of which both parties are aware, and those who love each other wish 1156a10 good things for each other in the way in which they love. So those who love each other because of the useful do not love them for themselves, but in so far

210

as some good accrues to each of them from the other. Similarly, too, with those who love each other because of pleasure: people do not feel affection for the witty for their being of a certain character, but for the pleasure they themselves get from them. And indeed those who love because of the useful feel fondness because of what is good for themselves, and those loving   1156a15 because of pleasure because of what is pleasant to themselves; they do not love by reference to the way the person loved *is*, but to his being useful or pleasant. And in fact these friendships are friendships incidentally; for the one loved is not loved by reference to the person he is but to the fact that in the one case he provides some good and in the other some pleasure. Such friend-ships, then, are easily dissolved, if the parties become different; for if they are   1156a20 no longer pleasant or useful, they cease loving each other. And the useful is not something that lasts, but varies with the moment; so, when what made them be friends has been removed, the friendship is dissolved as well, in so far as it existed in relation to what brought it about. This sort of friendship seems especially to occur among the old (since it is not the pleasant that people of   1156a25 that age pursue, but the beneficial), and in the case of those in their prime, or young, among those who pursue advantage. This sort don't really even live together with each other, for sometimes they are not even pleasant people; and so neither do they feel an additional need for that kind of company, unless the people concerned are of some use, since they are pleasant just to the   1156a30 extent that they have hopes of some good accruing to them. (People put guest-friendships too with friendships of this sort.) Friendship between young people seems to be because of pleasure, since the young live by emotion, and more than anything pursue what is pleasant for them and what is there in front of them; but as their age changes, the things they find pleasant also become different. This is why they are quick to become friends and to stop   1156a35 being friends; for the friendship changes along with what is pleasant for them, and the shift in that sort of pleasure is quick. The young are also erotically   1156b1 inclined, for erotic friendship is for the larger part a matter of emotion, and because of pleasure; hence they love and quickly stop loving, often changing in the course of the same day. But the young do wish to spend their days   1156b5 together, and to live together, since that is how they gain the object that accords with their kind of friendship. However, it is the friendship between good people, those resembling each other in excellence, that is complete; for each alike of these wishes good things for the other in so far as he is good, and he is good in himself. And those who wish good things for their friends, for   1156b10 their friends' sake, are friends most of all; for they do so because of the friends themselves, and not incidentally. So friendship between these lasts so long as they are good, and excellence is something lasting. Again, each party is good without qualification, and is good for his friend; for the good are both good without qualification and of benefit to one another. They are similarly pleas-ant, too, for the good are both pleasant without qualification and pleasant for   1156b15

one other; for each type of person finds pleasure in his own actions and those like them, and the actions of the good are the same or similar. That this sort of friendship should be lasting is reasonable, since it brings together all the attributes that friends should have. For every kind of friendship is because of
1156b20 some good or because of pleasure, either without qualification or for the person loving, and in virtue of some sort of resemblance between the parties; and to *this* kind of friendship belong all the attributes mentioned, in virtue of what the friends are in themselves, since in this respect they are similar, and in the others, and the good without qualification is also pleasant without qualification—and these most of all are objects of love. So loving, too, and friendship—and friendship of the best kind—exist between these people most
1156b25 of all. But it is to be expected that such friendships should be rare, since there are few such people. Further, such friendship also requires time for the parties to grow acquainted with each other's character; for as the proverb has it, people cannot have got to know each other before they have savoured all that salt together, nor indeed can they have accepted each other or be friends before each party is seen to be lovable, and is trusted, by the other. Those who
1156b30 are quick to behave like friends towards each other wish to be friends, but are not friends unless they are also lovable, and the other party knows it; for what is quick to arise is wish for friendship, not friendship.

(VIII. 4) This kind of friendship, then, is complete both in respect of time and in the other respects, and in all respects each party gets the same or similar
1156b35 things from the other, which is an attribute friendship should have. The kind
1157a1 of friendship that exists because of the pleasant has a resemblance to this kind, since the good too are pleasant to each other; similarly the kind that exists because of the useful, since the good are like this too to each other. In these cases too friendships are most lasting when the parties get the same thing
1157a5 from each other, e.g. pleasure, and not only that but from the same source, as e.g. with the witty, and not as in the case of lover and beloved; for these do not take pleasure in the same things, but one of them takes pleasure in seeing the other, while *he* takes pleasure in being looked after by the lover; and sometimes as his season of youthful beauty comes to an end, so too does the
1157a10 friendship (for to the lover the sight of the beloved is not pleasant, and the beloved does not get looked after). But then again many do continue as friends, if from mutual experience of each other's character they come to love it, being similar characters themselves. But those who do not make the pleasant but the useful the basis of exchange in erotic relationships are friends, and continue as friends, to a lesser degree. Those who are friends because of what
1157a15 is useful dissolve their friendship as soon as it ceases to be of advantage to them; for it was not each other they loved, but what profited them. So pleasure or usefulness can make even bad people be friends with each other, decent people with bad ones, and ones who are neither decent nor bad with any sort

at all, but it is clear that the only ones who are friends because of themselves are the good; for the bad get no gratification from each other, unless they might get some benefit. The friendship of the good is also the only kind that is immune to slanders; for it is not easy to give credence to anyone about a person one has scrutinized oneself over a long period; also trust exists between them, and the thought that 'he would never have treated me unjustly', and all the other features that one expects of a friendship that is truly friendship. But in the other kinds, there is nothing to prevent things like slander having their effect. For since people also universally call 'friends' those who are together because of the useful, as with cities (for alliances seem to come about between cities for the sake of advantage), and those who are fond of each other because of pleasure, as children are, presumably we too should call such people 'friends', but say that there are more kinds of friendship than one, that between the good, in so far as they are good, being friendship in the primary and strict sense, the others by virtue of resemblance—for they are friends in so far as the relationship brings something good, and so has some resemblance to the first one (since the pleasant too is good to those who love it). But these two kinds of friendship don't go together very well, nor do the same people tend to become friends because of what is useful and because of what is pleasant; for things that are merely incidental have no tendency to be coupled together. Given that friendship has been assigned to these kinds, the bad will be friends because of pleasure or usefulness, since this is where the resemblance between them lies, whereas the good will be friends because of themselves; for they will be friends in so far as they are good. The latter, then, are friends without qualification, while the former are so incidentally, and by virtue of having been compared to the latter.

(VIII. 5) But just as with the excellences predicating 'good' of people sometimes refers to disposition, sometimes to activity, so it is with 'friendship' too; for some are friends in so far as they delight in living together and provide the relevant good things for each other, while others, because asleep or separated by geographical distance, are not actively friends but are disposed so as to be active in that way—it is not friendship, unqualified, that location dissolves, only its activity. But if the absence becomes long, it seems to cause even friendship to become forgotten; as someone put it

> Cut off the talk, and many a time you cut off the friendship.

Neither old people nor the sour-tempered appear to be the sort to make friends, for the element of pleasure in them is short-lived, and no one can spend his days with what is painful, or with what is not pleasant; for more than anything nature seems to avoid the painful, and seek the pleasant. But accepting each other without living together is more like good will than friendship. For nothing is so characteristic of friends as living together (for whereas the needy

1157a20

1157a25

1157a30

1157a35

1157b1

1157b5

1157b10

1157b15

1157b20

want help, even the blessedly happy want to spend their days with others; for these are the last ones to live in solitude); but it is not possible for people to spend their time with each other if they are not pleasant, and if they do not enjoy the same things, which seems to be characteristic of comradely friendship.

1157b25   It is, then, the friendship of the good that is friendship most of all, as has been said many times; for being lovable and desirable seems to belong to what is good or pleasant without qualification, while for each person, being lovable and desirable for *him* seems to belong to what is good or pleasant for him— and good people are lovable and desirable for each other in both these ways. And loving resembles an affection of the soul, whereas friendship resembles a

1157b30   disposition; for one can feel love no less towards inanimate than towards animate objects, but reciprocal loving involves decision, and decisions flow from dispositions, and when people wish good things for those they love for these others' sake, this is not a matter of affective state but of disposition. Again, in loving their friend they love what is good for themselves; for the good person, in becoming a friend, becomes a good for the person to whom

1157b35   he becomes a friend. So each of the two parties both loves what is good for himself, and reciprocates in equal measure in terms of wishing and of what is

1158a1   pleasant; for friendship is said to be equality. But these features belong most of all to the friendship of the good.

(VIII. 6) Friendship by contrast occurs less in the sour-tempered and elderly people in so far as they are harder to get on with and get less enjoyment from interactions with other people; for these more than anything are thought to

1158a5   be characteristic of, and productive of, friendship. This is why the young become friends quickly, while the old do not—since people do not become friends with anyone whose company they do not enjoy; and neither do the sour-tempered become friends quickly. Such people do have good will towards each other, since they wish each other good things, and give help when it is needed, but they are not really friends, because of the fact that they

1158a10   do not spend their days with each other, or enjoy each other's company, the very things that most seem to be characteristic of friendship. It is not possible to be a friend to many in the case of the complete kind of friendship, just as it is not possible to feel erotic desire for many people at once (for erotic desire is like an excess of something, and a thing of that sort will naturally tend to be directed towards a single individual); and that many people at once should be intensely pleasing to the same person is not easy, nor, presumably, that many at once should be good. This type of friendship also requires that the parties

1158a15   have acquired experience of each other, and a close acquaintance with one another's character, which is very difficult to achieve. But by means of what is useful and what is pleasant it *is* possible to give satisfaction to many, for there are many of the sort that are satisfied this way, and the services involved take little time to supply. Of these kinds the one that is the more like friendship is the one that comes about because of pleasure, i.e. where both parties get the same things from the relationship, and they delight in each other or in the same things, as with the friendships of the young; for open-handedness is more a feature of these. The kind that comes about because of the useful, on the other hand, is characteristic of business types; and while the blessedly happy have no need of useful friends,[36] they do need pleasant ones; for on the one hand they wish to have people with whom to share their lives, and on the other the painful is something that people tolerate for a short time, but no one would put up with it on a continuing basis—no one would put up even with the good itself, if it were painful to him. So the friends they look for will be pleasant. But if they have this quality, presumably they should also be good, and what is more, good *for them*; in this way they will have all the attributes that should belong to friends. People in powerful positions, by contrast, appear to keep their friends distinct: some are useful, some are pleasing, and generally the same persons are not both; for powerful people do not look for those who combine being pleasant with excellence, or those useful for the achievement of fine things, but when it is pleasure they seek they look for witty friends, and on the other side they look for people clever at carrying out what they have been instructed to do, and these qualities tend not to be found together. But simultaneously pleasant and useful is what the good person has been said to be; however this sort does not become friends with someone his superior in power, unless he is exceeded by him in excellence too; otherwise he is exceeded, but cannot effect a proportional equalization. But powerful people do not tend to turn out like this.

Now the two kinds of friendship in question are based on equality; for both parties get the same and wish the same for each other, or else they exchange one kind of thing for another, e.g. pleasure for practical help—though as we have said, these are at the same time friendships to a lesser degree, and less long-lasting. (They also[37] seem both to be and not to be friendships, by virtue of similarity and dissimilarity to the same thing: in so far as they resemble friendship in accordance with excellence, they look like friendships (for one of the two has the attribute of the pleasant, the other that of the useful, and the friendship of excellence also has these), but in so far as that friendship is immune to slander, and lasting, while these kinds change quickly, and differ from the other in many other respects, they do not look like friendships, because of dissimilarity to the other kind.)

(VIII. 7) But a different kind of friendship is the one involving superiority, e.g. that of father for son, and in general of older for younger, or husband for wife, and of anyone in public office for those subject to his rule. But these also differ

1158a20

1158a25

1158a30

1158a35

1158b1

1158b5

1158b10

---

[36] Reading καὶ οἱ μακάριοι χρησίμων μὲν . . . (1158a22).
[37] Retaining καὶ (1158b5).

1158b15   from each other; for the friendships of parents for children and of rulers for
ruled are not the same. But neither are those of father for son and son for father,
nor those of husband for wife and wife for husband. For there is a different
excellence of each of these, and their function is different, as is also what causes
1158b20   them to love; so too, then, are the kinds of loving and the friendships. So, while
each of the two parties neither gets nor should seek the same things from the
other, still when children render to parents what should be rendered to those
who gave one birth, and parents render what should be rendered to children,
such parties' friendships are lasting and good of their kind. In all friendships
1158b25   involving superiority the loving should itself be proportionately distributed, so
that e.g. the better person should be more loved than loving, and the more
useful one, and similarly in each of the other types of case; for when the loving is
distributed according to merit, that produces equality of a sort, and that is
something that is thought to be characteristic of friendship.

But what is equal does not seem to take the same form in just interactions
1158b30   and in friendship; for in just interactions it is what is equal as measured by
merit that is equal in the primary sense, and the equal in terms of quantity is so
in a secondary sense, whereas in friendship the one in terms of quantity is
primary and the one in terms of merit secondary. And this is clear when there
comes to be a great disparity in excellence, or badness, or resources, or what-
1158b35   ever it may be; for then people are no longer friends, and do not even expect to
be. This is most evident in the case of the gods; for the gods are to the highest
1159a1   degree superior to us in all good things. But it is clear in the case of kings too;
for those who are much needier do not even expect to be friends with them,
and neither do those without any merit expect to be friends with the best or
most intellectually accomplished. Now there is no precise way of determining
in such cases up to what point people can be friends, for many things can be
1159a5   taken away, and friendship still remains; but if the separation between the
parties is wide, as between man and god, that is no longer possible. Hence
the problem people raise, as to whether friends might sometimes not wish
the greatest goods for their friends, e.g. being a god; for they will no longer be
friends to them, and so not good things either, since friends are good things. If,
1159a10   then, it was right to say that a friend wishes good things for his friend for the
other's sake, the other should remain whatever sort he is; his friend, then, will
wish the greatest goods for him as a human being. But presumably not all of
them; for each person wishes good things for himself most of all.

(VIII. 8) Most people are thought to wish more to be loved than to love,
because of love of honour, which is why most people love flattery; for the
1159a15   flatterer is a friend who is inferior, or pretends to be such[38], and to love more
than to be loved, and being loved is thought to be something close to being

---

[38] Reading τοιοῦτος ⟨εἶναι⟩ (1159a15).

honoured, which is something most people seek. But it seems not to be for its own sake, but only incidentally, that they choose honour. For most people delight in being honoured by those in positions of power because of the hopes it raises—they think that, if they need something, they will get it from them, and so delight in the honour they receive as an indication of good things to come; while those who long for honour from decent people, who know them, are seeking to confirm their own opinion of themselves. So they delight in it, believing that they are good people because they trust in the judgement of those who say they are. But people take delight in being loved in itself; and hence it would seem that being loved is something superior to being honoured, and that friendship is desirable in itself. But it seems to lie in loving more than in being loved. This is indicated by the delight mothers take in loving: sometimes they give their own children to be brought up by others, and they love them, knowing who they are, without seeking to be loved in return, if they cannot have both things; it seems enough to them to see them doing well, and they themselves love their children even if the children give back none of the things a mother ought to expect, because they do not know who their mothers are. But given that friendship lies more in loving, and that we praise those who love their friends, the excellence that belongs to friends seems to consist in loving; so that it will be those between whom this occurs according to worth that will be lasting friends, and whose friendship will last. This is the way, most of all, that even unequal parties will be friends; for in this way they will be brought into equality with each other. 'Equality and similarity make amity', and most of all the similarity of those similar in excellence; for since their own attributes are lasting, so is their relationship to each other, and they neither need things of negative value nor provide services of such a kind themselves—even, so to speak, preventing such things from happening, since it is characteristic of good people neither to go wrong themselves nor to allow their friends to do so. The bad, by contrast, do not have stability, since they do not remain similar even to themselves; instead they become friends for a short period, each enjoying the other's bad qualities. Useful and pleasant friends are more lasting; for they last so long as they afford each other pleasure or practical help. But the friendship that exists because of what is useful seems most of all to come about from contrary attributes, e.g. a poor man with a wealthy one, or an ignorant person with someone possessing knowledge: here someone seeks what he is lacking himself and gives something else in return. Here one might drag in the case of lover and beloved, too, and the beautiful and the ugly. This is why lovers sometimes make themselves patently laughable, by expecting to be loved in the way they love: they should expect it, then, if they are similarly lovable, but if they have no such lovable qualities it is laughable. And presumably contrary does not seek contrary as such, but only incidentally; rather the desire is for the intermediate, since this is something good—e.g. for the dry the object is not to become wet but to arrive at the

1159a20
1159a25
1159a30
1159a35
1159b1
1159b5
1159b10
1159b15
1159b20

intermediate, and likewise for the hot and the rest. Well, let us put these things to one side; for they are also hardly germane.

1159b25   (VIII. 9) It does seem, as we said at the beginning, that friendship and justice have to do with the same things, and involve the same persons. For in every kind of sharing community there seems to be a specific kind of justice, and also friendship; at any rate people address as 'friends' those sailing with them or on campaign with them, and similarly too with their partners in other
1159b30   kinds of sharing community. And to the extent that they share in it, they are friends; for that is the limit of the justice between them too. Again, the proverb says 'What belongs to friends is shared in common', and correctly so; for friendship depends upon sharing. Between brothers and between comrades everything is shared, but in other kinds of friendships only certain specified things are so, more in some and fewer in others, since among friend-
1159b35   ships too, some are friendships more, some less. And what counts as just
1160a1   differs too; it is not the same for parents in relation to their children and for brothers in relation to each other, or for comrades or citizens, and similarly with the other kinds of friendship. The unjust, then, too, is different in each of these kinds of relationship, and it increases with the degree of friendship
1160a5   involved: so e.g. it is a more terrible thing to cheat a comrade out of money than a fellow citizen, or to fail to help out a brother than a stranger, and to strike one's father than anyone else at all. And the requirements of justice also increase naturally along with the degree of friendship, both things involving the same persons and having an equal reach. But all kinds of community are
1160a10   like parts of the political one. For people make their way together on the basis that they will get some advantage from it, and so as to provide themselves with some necessity of life; and the political community too seems both to have come together in the beginning and to remain in place for the sake of advantage, since this is what is aimed at by lawgivers too, and people say that what is for the common advantage is just. The other kinds of community,
1160a15   then, seek specific kinds of advantage, e.g. seafarers for the kind to be got from sea-journeys for the sake of making money, or something like that, fellow soldiers for the one to be had by going to war, whether their object is money, or victory, or taking a city, and similarly with fellow members of a tribe or a deme; but some communities seem to come about because of
1160a20   pleasure—those of people who form cult groups or dining clubs, for these associations come about for the purpose of making sacrifice and getting together. But all of these seem to be subordinate to the political community; for the political community does not seek the advantage of the moment, but takes regard to the whole of life ** making sacrifices and gatherings in relation
1160a25   to these, giving due honours[39] to the gods and providing forms of relaxation,

---

[39] Reading τιμὰς ἀπονέμοντες (1160a24).

along with pleasure, for themselves. (For in ancient times sacrifices and gatherings appear to have taken place after the collecting in of the harvest, as a kind of first-fruits offering; it was at these moments that people were most at leisure.) All the different kinds of community, then, are evidently parts of the political one; and along with community of each sort will go friendship of the same sort.

1160a30

(VIII. 10) There are three kinds of political constitution, and an equal number of deviations from, as it were ruined versions of, these. The kinds of political constitution are kingship and aristocracy, and thirdly one based on property assessments, the proper name for which appears to be 'timocracy', though most people are in the habit of calling it 'constitutional government'. Of these, kingship is best, timocracy worst. As for the deviations, tyranny is a deviation from kingship; for both are kinds of monarchy, but there is the greatest difference between them, since the tyrant considers what is of advantage to himself, while the king considers what is of advantage to those he rules. For a king is not a king unless he is self-sufficient, and superior in all good things; but someone like that does not need anything else, and so he will not consider what would help himself, but what would help those he rules (for any king not like this will be some kind of king by lot). Tyranny is the contrary of this kind of constitution, since the tyrant pursues what is good for himself. And it is more evident, in the case of tyranny, that it is worst; and worst is contrary to the best. From kingship things change to tyranny; for tyranny is monarchy in its bad form, and the king with a bad character turns into a tyrant. From aristocracy the change is to oligarchy, through the malfeasance of those in power, who distribute what belongs to the city contrary to merit, giving all or most good things to themselves, and public offices always to the same people, putting the highest priority on being wealthy; those who hold power, then, are few and corrupt instead of the most decent people. From timocracy the change is to democracy, for these kinds of constitution are coterminous: 'timocracy' too means a mass-constitution, and all those who meet the property assessment are equal. Least bad is democracy, for the kind of political arrangement involved here is only a small deviation from the other one. These, then, are for the most part the changes constitutions undergo; in each case this is the smallest change, and the one that happens most easily. Parallels to them, and models for them, can also be found in households. The community formed by father in relation to sons has the form of kingship, in so far as a father looks after the interests of his children; and this is the reason why Homer, too, calls Zeus 'father'—because being a king means ruling like a father. But among the Persians fathers rule like tyrants; they treat their sons as if they were slaves. Tyrant-like, too, is a slave-master's rule in relation to slaves, since it is the master's advantage that is achieved by it; this type of rule, then, is clearly correct, and the Persian one

1160a35

1160b1

1160b5

1160b10

1160b15

1160b20

1160b25

1160b30

mistaken; for where the people involved are of different types, the types of rule should be different too. The community formed by man and wife is clearly of an aristocratic kind; for the man rules on the basis of worth, and in the spheres where a man should rule; those where it is fitting for a woman to

1160b35   rule he gives over to her. If the man lords it over everything, his rule changes into oligarchy; for the distribution in that case takes no account of worth, or

1161a1   of where his superiority lies. Sometimes women rule a household, because they have inherited property; their rule, then, is not based on excellence, but comes about because of wealth and power, as in oligarchies. The community formed by brothers resembles a timocracy, since brothers are equals, except to

1161a5   the extent that their ages differ; so it is that if there is a great difference in their ages, the friendship between them is no longer a brotherly one. As for democracy, that is most to be found in household arrangements where there is no master (since there everyone is on a footing of equality), or where the ruling figure is weak, and each part of the household has licence to do what he or she wants.

1161a10   (VIII. 11) Corresponding to each kind of constitution there is evidently a friendship, to the extent that there is also justice. There is, first, that of a king for his subjects, based on the excess of benefits bestowed; for he benefits his subjects, if indeed, as a person of excellence, he takes care that they do well, as

1161a15   a shepherd takes care of his sheep—hence the way Homer called Agamemnon 'shepherd of the people'. Fatherly friendship is also like this, but the scale of the benefits conferred is different; after all, a father is responsible for his son's existence, than which there seems no greater benefit, and for bringing him up and educating him. These benefits are also attributed to ancestors; and the relationships between father and son, ancestors and offspring, and king

1161a20   and subjects are all naturally those of ruler and ruled. These friendships are based on superiority—which is why parents are honoured as well as loved. And so what is just, too, in these cases is not the same thing for both parties, but according to worth; for so it is with the friendship as well. Next, the friendship of husband for wife is the same as that in an aristocracy; for it is based on excellence, assigning more of what is good to the better, and what is

1161a25   fitting to each; and this way what is just is achieved too. The friendship of brothers, for its part, resembles that between comrades, since they are equals, and of an age, and people like that are for the most part in sympathy with one another, and have a similar character; and the friendship involved in timocracy, too, resembles this one, for being citizens in a timocracy means being equals, and decent in character, so that they rule in turn, and on a basis of

1161a30   equality; so too, then, is the friendship between them. As for the deviations, just as there is little in the way of justice in them, so there is little friendship, and least in the worst deviation; for in a tyranny there is no, or little, friendship. For where there is nothing in common between ruler and ruled, there is

220

no friendship either (after all, neither is there justice)—e.g. of craftsman towards tool, or of soul towards body, or of master towards slave; for these are all benefited by their users, but there is no friendship towards inanimate things, nor justice either, and no more is there towards a horse or an ox, or towards a slave in so far as he is a slave. For there is nothing in common between the parties: a slave is an animate tool, and a tool an inanimate slave. In so far as he is a slave, then, one cannot be friends with him, but only in so far as he is a human being; for there seems to be a kind of justice that obtains for any human being in relation to anyone capable of sharing in law and taking part in agreements, and so there can be friendship too, to the extent that the other is a human being. There is little, then, by way of friendships or of justice in tyrannies either, but more in democracies; for with those who are equals the things in common are many. 1161a35
1161b1
1161b5
1161b10

(VIII. 12) Every kind of friendship, then, as has been said, involves community. But one might single out the friendship between members of the same family, and the one between comrades; by contrast those between citizens, fellow members of tribes, people sailing together—all such friendships are more like ones that exist for the sake of a common interest, since they appear to be based on a sort of agreement. One might put guest-friendships too with these kinds. Family friendship itself seems to be of many kinds, but all derived from the friendship of father for children; for parents feel affection for children as something of themselves, children for parents as being something that has come from them. And parents know better what has sprung from them than their offspring know they sprang from *them*; also the source of a thing has a closer relation of belonging to what is sprung from it than the thing produced has to what produced it, for what comes from something belongs to that something, as e.g. a tooth, a hair, or anything else belongs to its owner, whereas what it came from does not belong to *it* at all, or does so to a lesser degree. Again, there is a difference in the quantity of time involved: parents feel affection for children as soon as they are born, whereas children feel it for parents only after time has passed, when they have acquired comprehension, or the capacity to perceive. And these points also make it clear why it is that maternal love is greater. Parents, then, love children as being themselves (for those sprung from them are as it were other selves of theirs, resulting from the separation), children parents as being what they have grown from, and brothers each other by virtue of their having grown from the same sources; for the self-sameness of their relation to *those* produces the same with each other (hence the way people say 'same blood', 'same root', and things like that). They are, then, the same entity in a way, even though in discrete subjects. Both being brought up together and being of the same age contribute greatly to friendship; for 'those of an age cleave together', and those who live together are natural comrades, which is why friendship 1161b15
1161b20
1161b25
1161b30
1161b35

1162a1 between brothers is in fact compared with that between comrades. The belonging to each other of cousins and other relatives derives from these, since it exists by virtue of their being from the same origins; but some of them belong more closely while others are more distant, depending on whether the ancestral common source is near or further off. Now children's

1162a5 friendship for parents, and human beings' for gods, is as for something good and superior, since it is they who have bestowed the greatest benefits on them, being responsible for their existence and their upbringing, and their education once they have come into existence; though such friendship also has more of the pleasant and the useful about it than friendship between those not related by family, in so far as they have more of a shared life. But friendship between

1162a10 brothers has the features found in that between comrades (and more so where they are decent characters, and generally where they are similar to one another), to the extent that they belong more to each other and have been there to feel affection for each other from birth, and to the extent that there is more similarity in character between those who come from the same source, have been brought up together, and have received a similar education; what is

1162a15 more, their scrutiny of each other over time will have been longest and most secure. The features of friendship in other family relationships too will be analogous to these. As for the friendship between husband and wife, this seems to be something that is there by nature; for man is naturally a coupler more than he is naturally a civic being, to the extent that a household is something prior to and more necessary than a city, and to the extent that producing offspring is something more widely shared among animals. With

1162a20 the other animals, the sharing only goes this far, whereas human beings cohabit not only for the sake of producing offspring but also for the sake of the necessities of life; for from the beginning their functions are differentiated, so that the man's are different from the woman's, and so they complement each other, making what belongs to each available to both in common. These

1162a25 points suggest that both the element of the useful and that of the pleasant are present in this kind of friendship; but it might also be because of excellence, if husband and wife were to be decent characters, since there is an excellence that belongs to each, and it could be that each took delight in someone with that proper excellence. Children seem to bind them together; hence the fact that childless couples break up more quickly, for children are a good shared by

1162a30 both, and what is shared binds together. As for how husband should live in relation to wife, and generally friend in relation to friend, there appears no difference between asking this and asking how he will do so *justly*; for what is just for friend in relation to friend and in relation to stranger, and to comrade and to schoolfellow, does not appear to be the same.

(VIII. 13) Given that there are three kinds of friendship, as was said at the

1162a35 beginning, and that in each of them some people are friends on a basis of equality while others are so where one party is superior to the other (for just as much as good people become friends with each other, so too a better person does with a worse one, and again just as much as pleasant people become friends, so too people become friends because of what is useful, equalizing things by the help they give, even while differing from each other), equals will need to keep things equal, and strictly so, in terms of loving and everything else, while unequals will need to render what is proportionate to the superiority of one of the parties in each case. Accusations and complaints occur either exclusively in the friendship that exists because of the useful, or in that kind most of all; and for good reason. For those who are friends because of excellence are eager to do each other good (for doing good is characteristic of excellence and of friendship), and between people competing with each other in *this* regard there are no accusations, and no battles; for no one objects to someone's loving and doing him good, but if he is a person of taste, he defends himself by doing good to the other. Again, since the superior party in a friendship based on superiority is getting what he seeks, he will have no accusations to make against his friend; for each and every person desires what is good. But neither do accusations arise very much between those whose friendship is because of pleasure; for what both desire they both get simultaneously, if they enjoy each other's company; and someone who went as far as making accusations against people who didn't amuse him—when he could just not spend time with them—would obviously be ridiculous. The friendship that exists because of the useful, by contrast, is prone to accusations; for since their having to do with each other is conditional on its bringing them benefit, they always want the larger share, think they have less than they ought, and complain that they are not getting as much as they want even though they deserve it; meanwhile those conferring the benefits are not able to supply the demands of those receiving them. Now it seems that, just as what is just is twofold, part of it being unwritten and part what accords with written law, so too friendship in terms of the useful falls into a type based on character and a type based on legal requirements. Accusations occur most of all, then, when the terms on which a friendship is dissolved are not the ones on which it was formed. The legal type is the one that operates on stated terms, the wholly commercial sort from hand to hand, the more cultivated sort over time, but still by agreement, something in exchange for something. With this type what is due is clear and not for dispute, but if it is based on friendship it will allow for postponement; hence the fact that in some places lawsuits to recover such debts are not allowed, the thought being that those who have made an exchange on the basis of trust should be content with that. The type based on character does not operate on stated terms, but presents are given, or whatever else it may be, as to a friend; yet the giver expects to come away with an equal amount, or more, on the basis that it was not a gift he made but a loan, and if when the friendship is being dissolved he is not in

1162b1

1162b5

1162b10

1162b15

1162b20

1162b25

1162b30

the same position as he was when it was formed, accusations will follow. This occurs because everyone, or most people, wish for what is fine, but choose what is beneficial; and it is a fine thing to do good to someone without meaning to be repaid, but it is to one's benefit to have good done to one. A person should, then, if he can, pay back the value of what he has received, and voluntarily,[40] for he should not make the other party a friend when that will be counter-voluntary for *him*; he should pay it back, then, on the basis that he made a mistake at the beginning, and received benefits from someone he shouldn't have had them from—because they weren't from a friend, or from someone doing it because of just that—and so he should dissolve the friendship as if the benefits had been bestowed on stated terms. Someone in this position will also agree that he *will* pay it back when he can; for not even the giver will expect repayment from someone who can't repay. So that if possible one should make repayment. But one should ask at the beginning from whom one is receiving benefits, and on what terms, so that the friendship may continue or not on that basis. There is room for dispute whether one should measure in terms of benefit to the recipient, and the repayment be made with regard to this, or in terms of the beneficence of the giver; for the recipients say they have received the sorts of things from their benefactors that were small to *them*, and that could have been got from someone else, belittling the matter; conversely the givers say they were the greatest things they had to give, and things that could not have been got from anyone else, and given at a time of danger or in some similar sort of emergency. Is it, then, the benefit to the receiver that is the measure when the friendship exists because of what is useful? For he is the one asking for it, and the giver supplies it on the understanding that he will come away with equal value; the quantity of the assistance given, then, is the quantity of benefit received, and what the recipient must give back to the other is therefore the amount of the benefit he enjoyed, or else more than that, since this will be a finer thing to do. However, in friendships based on excellence there are no accusations, and the measure looks as if it is the decision of the doer; for the determinant of excellence and character lies in decision.

(VIII. 14) People quarrel in friendships based on superiority too; for each of the two parties thinks he should have more, and when this happens, the friendship is dissolved. For if one of the parties is a better character, he thinks it appropriate for him to have more because it is appropriate for good people to be assigned more; and similarly if one of the parties is in a position to bestow the greater benefits, for they say that if someone is useless he shouldn't have an equal share, because it turns into a kind of service to the community instead of friendship, if what results from the friendship is not

---

[40] Retaining καὶ ἑκόντι (1163a2).

going to accord with the value of what the parties have done. They think that it should be the same in a friendship as in a financial partnership, where those who contribute more get more. But the person in need, or the inferior character, takes the converse position: that assisting the needy is the mark of a good friend, since what use is it, they ask, to be friends with a good or a powerful person if one is not going to get anything out of it? Well, it seems that the expectations of each of the two sides are correct, and that each should be assigned more out of the friendship, only not of the same thing: the superior person should get more honour, the needy one more in the way of profit, for excellence, and beneficence, have honour as their privilege, while profit is assistance for the needy. It seems to be like this in political contexts too: no honour is given the person who contributes nothing good to the community, since what belongs to the community is given to the person who benefits the community, and honour is something that belongs to the community. For one cannot at the same time receive money from communal sources and be accorded honour; no one puts up with getting the smaller share in all respects. So they allot honour to the person who comes off worse in terms of money, and money to the one prepared to accept gifts; for what is in accordance with merit is what equals things up and preserves friendship, as has been said. This, then, is the way a person should associate with unequals too, and if he is being helped in terms of money or towards excellence he should give honour in return, paying back what he can. For friendship looks also for what is possible, not what accords with merit, for such a thing is not even possible in all cases, e.g. where it is a matter of honouring the gods or one's parents; for no one could ever render them the honour they deserve, and the person who serves them to the best of his ability is thought to be behaving decently. This is why it might well not be thought permissible for son to disavow father, while father may disavow son; for the son must repay the debt he owes, and since there is nothing he can do that is worthy of the benefits he has already received, he is always a debtor. On the other hand, a creditor can remit a debt; so too, then, can a father. At the same time presumably no one would dissociate himself from a son unless he was an exceedingly bad character; for apart from the natural friendship of father for son, it is human not to reject a source of assistance. But if the son is a bad character, then for him assisting his father is something to be avoided, or something not to take trouble about; for most people wish to receive benefits, but conferring them they avoid, as unprofitable. Let this, then, be our account of these subjects.

1163a35
1163b1

1163b5

1163b10

1163b15

1163b20

1163b25

BOOK IX

(IX. 1) In all friendships based on dissimilarity, what is proportionate equalizes and preserves the friendship, as has been said, just as in political friendship too the return the shoemaker gets for his shoes is measured by their worth, and similarly with the weaver and all the rest. Here, then, currency is available as a common measure, and it is to this that everything is referred, and by this that everything is measured; but in erotic friendships sometimes the lover charges that for all his love he is not loved in return, when it may be that there is nothing for him to be loved for, and often the beloved charges that the lover used to promise everything, but now delivers nothing. Such things happen when the lover's love for the beloved is because of pleasure, while the beloved's for the lover is because of the useful, and it is not the case that both sides get what they want. For when these form the basis of the friendship, it is dissolved when the things for the sake of which the friends were friends fail to come about; for it was not the friends they loved, but the friends' attributes, which were not lasting ones; hence the friendships are not lasting either. (By contrast, friendships based on character—being for their own sake—do last, as has been said.) People fall out when what they get from the friendship begins to be different from what they desire from it, since when one does not get what one was aiming for, it is like getting nothing; as in the case of the cithara-player who kept being promised payment, and the more the better he played, and then when dawn came and he asked for delivery of the promises, was told that he had already been paid back in pleasure received for pleasure given. Now if this were what both parties wished, it would be enough; but if one of them wanted amusement and the other a profit, and the first has what he wanted but the other hasn't, things will not be well with their relationship; for a person fixes his attention on what he actually wants, and it is for the sake of *this* that he will give what he gives. But which of them is to fix the value of what is given—the one giving first, or the one who has taken first? For the one giving first seems to leave the decision to the other. This is what they say Protagoras in fact used to do; for whenever he taught whatever it might be, he used to tell the person who had learned from him to assess how much it was worth to know what he had learned, and took that as his fee. But in such cases some recommend the principle 'to each man his fee'. If on the other hand people take money in advance, and then do none of the things they said they would because of the excessive nature of their promises, they are naturally exposed to charges being made against them, since they are not delivering what they agreed. (Sophists are presumably forced to do this because otherwise no one would have given them any money—for the things they know about.) These people, then, if they do not do what they took payment for, are naturally exposed to charges against them; but where there is no agreement about services to be rendered, those who take the initiative in giving for their friends' own sake, as has been said, make no accusations, since friendship according to excellence involves this sort of giving, and the return for it should be by reference to the giver's decision to give, since this is a mark both of his being a friend and of his excellence—and this too, it seems, is how a person should make return to those who have imparted philosophy to him, since its worth is not measured in relation to money, and honour will not balance it in the scales, though presumably what is possible will suffice, as in relation to gods and to parents. Where, on the other hand, the giving was not like this but was conditional in some way, presumably the best thing will be the paying back of what seems to both parties a worthy return, but if this turned out not to happen, it would seem to be not merely necessary but also just that the one who has received first should fix its value; for when the other party has received in return the amount of the benefit this one received, or the amount he would have chosen to pay for the pleasure, he will have got what he deserved from him. For this is obviously what happens in the case of buying and selling, and in some places there are laws prohibiting lawsuits for voluntary contracts, on the basis that a transaction with a partner one trusted should be ended in the same manner in which one entered into it; the thought is that it is more just for the person to whom the decision was turned over to make the assessment than for the person who turned it over to him. For more often than not those who have a thing and those who want to get it don't put equal value on it, since to each party what's *theirs*, so what they give, appears worth a lot; but all the same the return occurs in relation to whatever amount is fixed by the receiver. But presumably the value he puts on the thing in question should not be what he thinks it worth now he has it, but what he thought it was worth before he had it.

(IX. 2) But cases like the following also give rise to problems: e.g. should one make over everything to one's father and obey him in everything, or should one trust a doctor when sick, and elect an expert in warfare to a generalship; and similarly, should one give priority to serving a friend over serving a good person, and to returning a favour to a benefactor over taking the initiative in giving to a dear comrade, if both are not possible? Well, perhaps determining all such things precisely is not easy. For they involve many and all kinds of differences, whether in terms of importance or the lack of it, or in terms of what is fine or necessary. But that one should not make over everything to the same person is clear enough; and one should for the most part sooner pay someone back for benefits received than give to a comrade, just as one should also sooner repay a loan to a creditor than give favours to comrades. But perhaps even this is not a universal rule: for example, should the person ransomed from brigands ransom in return the one who freed him, even if he

1164a35

1164b1

1164b5

1164b10

1164b15

1164b20

1164b25

1164b30

1164b35

227

1165a1   is just anybody, or should he pay him back if he has not been captured but is just asking to be paid, or should he rather ransom his father? For it would seem that one should ransom one's father even before oneself. As has been said, then, in general one should repay what is owed, but if giving is *outstandingly* fine or

1165a5   necessary, then one should incline towards that. For sometimes returning a service previously received is not even an equal exchange, namely whenever someone benefits another person he knows to be good, while the latter would be repaying it to someone he thinks is a bad character. For even to the person who has made one a loan one sometimes shouldn't make a loan in return; for the first one made it thinking he would get it back, since it was made to

1165a10 someone decent, while the second does not expect to get it back from somebody worthless. If this really is the situation, then, the first cannot expect equal treatment; or if it is not like that, but they think it is, their behaviour won't seem strange. (Thus as has often been said, discussions about affections and actions have the same degree of determinacy as the things they are about.) So,

1165a15 that one should not assign the same priority to everyone, nor everything to one's father, just as Zeus does not get all the sacrifices, is clear enough; and since different things are owed to parents, brothers, comrades, and benefactors, one should assign to each what belongs to them and what is fitting in their case. And that is in fact how people seem to behave: if it is a matter of a wedding,

1165a20 they invite relatives, since the family, and so doings affecting the family, are things belonging to them as well, and funerals, too, people think should be attended by relatives more than anyone else, for the same reason. But it would seem that one should give priority to parents when it comes to giving support, on the basis that a debt is owed to them, and that it is a finer thing to give support in this way to those who caused one's existence than to oneself; and it would also seem that one should give honour to parents, just as one should to

1165a25 gods—but not every sort of honour, since one should not even give the same honour to father as to mother, nor again should one give a father the honour that belongs to someone intellectually accomplished, or a general, but rather the sort that belongs to a father, and similarly in the case of a mother. One should give honour to every older person, too, in accordance with their age, by getting up as they approach, giving up one's couch at table, and so on; with comrades and brothers, on the other hand, what one should give is frankness

1165a30 and a share in everything one has. And to relatives, fellow members of one's tribe, fellow citizens, and all the rest one should always attempt to assign what belongs to them, and to compare the standing of each in terms of closeness to us, and excellence, or usefulness. Now where the people concerned are in the same category, the judgement[41] is quite easy; where they are in different

1165a35 categories, it is more of a task. But that is not a reason for giving up; one must make whatever sorts of discriminations are possible.

---

[41] Reading ἡ κρίσις (1165a34).

Luton Sixth Form College
Learning Resources Centre

(IX. 3) There is also a problem about whether friendships should or should not be dissolved when friends fail to stay the same as they were. Or is there no strangeness about their being dissolved when those concerned are friends because of what is useful or what is pleasant, and they no longer have these attributes? For it was the useful and the pleasant that were the objects of the love, and when these have failed, it is reasonable enough that the loving should cease. But a person might have grounds for accusation, if someone who actually liked him because he was useful or pleasant kept pretending to like him because of his character; for as we said at the beginning, quarrels between friends occur more than anything when there is a difference between what they think the basis of the friendship is and what it actually is. Now if ever someone mistakenly supposes that he is loved because of his character, when his friend does nothing that belongs to that kind of friendship, he will blame himself; but when he is deceived by the other's pretending, he will be justified in accusing his deceiver—more justified, even, than if he were facing counterfeiters of the coinage, by the degree to which what is affected by the crime is the more precious. But now if one receives someone as a friend on the basis that he is good, but then he becomes, and seems, a bad character, should one go on loving him? Or is this not possible, given that not everything is lovable, but only what is good, and what is worthless is neither lovable, nor something one should love (for one should not be a lover of what is worthless, nor become like it, and it has been said that like is friend to like)? So should one break off the friendship at once; or not in all cases, only where the badness is incurable? Where their badness can be corrected, helping them with their character should have a greater priority than helping them with their property, by the degree to which such help is a greater good and more appropriate to friendship. On the other hand, if someone breaks it off in these circumstances it won't seem a strange thing to do, since it wasn't that sort of person he was friends with; so, not being able to restore the other person to what he was before he changed, he gives up on him. But if one party stayed the same, while the other became a more decent character than the first, and changed greatly in degree of excellence, should the first treat the second as a friend? Or is that impossible? The point becomes especially clear in cases where the distance that separates people is large, as for example with children's friendships: if one side continued to think as a child while the other became a man of the most powerful sort, how could they be friends, when they are not satisfied by the same things, and when they don't share pleasures and pains? For they won't do this even in relation to each other, and without that it is impossible, as we said, for them to be friends, since it is not possible for them to live with one another. But we have discussed these things. Should one then be no differently disposed towards someone in these circumstances than if he had never become one's friend at all? Or should one retain a memory of one's past intimacy with them, and in keeping with the way we

1165b1

1165b5

1165b10

1165b15

1165b20

1165b25

1165b30

1165b35 think favours should be granted to friends rather than strangers, should one in the same way grant something to past friends too, because of that previous friendship, so long as the dissolution of the friendship does not occur because of excessive badness?

1166a1 (IX. 4) The features typical of friendship for others, and those by which the kinds of friendship are defined, seem to derive from aspects of our relationship towards ourselves. People take a friend to be someone who wishes for and does what is good, or appears good, for the sake of the other, or someone 1166a5 who wishes the friend to exist and to live, for the friend's own sake; so it is with mothers towards their children, and with friends who are angry with each other. Others take a friend to be someone who spends time with the other and makes the same choices, or who feels grief and pleasure with his friend; this too happens most of all with mothers. And people define friend-1166a10 ship too by one or other of these attributes. But each of them belongs to the decent person in relation to himself (and to other types too, in so far as they take themselves to be decent; it seems, as has been said, that excellence and the person of excellence is a measure for every sort of case). For this sort makes the same judgements as himself, and desires the same things in respect 1166a15 of his whole soul; and he certainly wishes for what is good for himself, and what appears good, and he does it (for it is a mark of a good person to work hard at what is good), and for his own sake (for he does it for the sake of the thinking element of himself, which is what each of us is thought to be). He also wishes himself to live and to be kept safe, and most of all that with which he understands, since to the good person existing is something good, and each 1166a20 of us wishes for good things for himself—nor does anyone choose, on condition of becoming other than himself, that what has come into being in his place[42] should have everything (since even as things are god has the good), but one chooses to have it while being whatever it is one is; and that which thinks would seem to be what each of us is, or that most of all. And the sort of person in question wishes to spend time in his own company; for he does so 1166a25 pleasantly, since he has both delightful memories of things he has done and good hopes for things he will do in the future, and hopes of that sort are pleasant. He also has a good supply of material for thoughtful reflection. And he most of all shares his grief and pleasure with himself; for every time it is the same thing that he finds painful or pleasant, not sometimes this and sometimes that, since practically speaking he is a person with nothing to 1166a30 regret. So because these attitudes each belong to the decent character in relation to himself, and because he is to his friend as he is to himself (for his friend is another self), friendship is actually thought to be one or other of the attitudes in question, and friends those who have them. Let us set aside for the

---

[42] Retaining ἐκεῖνο τὸ γενόμενον (1166a21).

present whether there is or is not friendship for oneself; but it would seem to be friendship just in so far as a person is countable as two or more, from what has been said, and because friendship in its superior form resembles one's love for oneself. But the attitudes mentioned appear to occur in the majority too, despite their being inferior. Is it then in so far as they are satisfied with themselves, and suppose themselves to be decent, that they share in them? Certainly no one who is really bad and does unspeakable things has these attitudes, or even appears to have them. And this is more or less true of inferior people too; for they are at odds with themselves, and they have appetites for one set of things, while wishing for another, like the un-self-controlled; for instead of the things they themselves think good they choose those that are pleasant and in fact harmful, as do those lacking in self-control, and again others shrink from doing what they think to be best for themselves because of cowardice or laziness. Those who have done many terrible things and are hated because of their depravity even take flight from life and do away with themselves. And the depraved seek others with whom to spend their days, but are in flight from themselves; for when on their own they are reminded of many odious things in the past and look forward to more of the same in the future, but in company with others they can forget. And since they have no lovable qualities there is nothing friendly about their attitude to themselves. Nor, then, do such people rejoice with themselves, or grieve with themselves; for their soul is in a state of faction, and one side, because of depravity, grieves at holding back from certain things, while the other is pleased, the one pulling in this direction and the other in that, as if tearing the soul apart. And if it is not possible to feel pain and pleasure at the same time, at any rate after a little it pains them that they had the pleasure, and they would have wished that they hadn't got pleasure from those things; for bad people are full of regret. The bad person, then, does not appear to be disposed in a friendly fashion even towards himself, because he has nothing lovable about him. So if being like this is too miserable a condition, one must strenuously shun badness, and try for decency; for in this way one will both have a friendly disposition towards oneself and become friends with another person.

(IX. 5) Good will looks as if it is a feature of friendship, but nevertheless is not friendship; for good will occurs even in relation to people one does not know, and without their being aware of it, whereas friendship does not (this is something we have said before, too). But good will is not loving, either, since there is no intensity about it, or desire, and these go along with loving; and loving involves familiarity, whereas good will can arise all of a sudden too, as happens e.g. in relation to competitors at the games; for people start to feel good will towards them, and want what they want, but they would not join in their action at all, since as we said, people develop good will all of a sudden,

1166a35
1166b1

1166b5

1166b10

1166b15

1166b20

1166b25

1166b30

1166b35
1167a1

231

and their warmth is superficial. Good will seems, then, to be the starting point of friendship, just as the pleasure gained through sight is of being in love: no one is in love without first having felt pleasure at the way the other looks, but delighting in someone's looks does not mean that one is in love, which is rather a matter of longing for him when he is not there and wanting him to be there; just so, then, while it is not possible for people to be friends if they have not felt good will towards each other, feeling good will towards each other does not make them friends, since if a person feels good will he only wishes for good things for the other, and he would not join in his actions at all, or go to any trouble on his behalf. So one might say that this is friendship in a transferred sense, i.e. one that is inactive, but which in time, and if it gets as far as involving intimacy, does become friendship—though not the kind that exists because of the useful, or the one that exists because of the pleasant, since neither does good will arise on the basis of these. For a person who has been benefited metes out good will in return for what he has received, and justly so; but one who wishes someone else to do well in the hope of doing well through him does not seem to feel good will so much towards the other person as towards himself, just as he won't be a friend, either, if the attention he pays the other is because of some use he wants to get out of it. And generally good will occurs because of excellence, or a kind of decency, where one person appears to another a fine character, or courageous, or something like that, as we said happens when we support contestants.

(IX. 6) Like-mindedness too is evidently a feature of friendship. Hence it is not a matter of having similar beliefs, since beliefs can be shared even by those who do not know each other. Nor is it those who share a judgement on any subject whatever that are said to be like-minded, e.g. about things in the heavens (for like-mindedness about these is not an attribute of friendship); rather, a city is said to be like-minded when its citizens share judgements about what is advantageous, reach the same decisions, and do what has seemed to them jointly to be best. Their 'like-mindedness', then, is about projects for action, and of these, ones that have a certain magnitude, and can be engaged in by both parties, or by everyone, e.g. when it seems a good thing to a whole city that offices should be elective, or that an alliance be made with the Spartans, or that Pittacus should rule (during the period when he was willing to do so). When each of two parties wishes power for himself, as in *Phoenician Women*, then there are contending factions; for being like-minded is not a matter of each side's being of the same mind about whatever it may be but of being of the same mind in the same particular set of circumstances, e.g. when both the masses and decent people think the best should rule; for in that way everyone gets what they are aiming for. Like-mindedness, then, appears to be a friendship between citizens, as indeed it is said to be; for it has to do with what is advantageous, and what affects people's lives. But this sort

of like-mindedness is found among decent people, for these are like-minded 1167b5
both with themselves and with each other, since generally speaking they have
the same objectives (for what such people wish for stays the same, and does
not surge to and fro like the Euripus), and they wish for what is just and what
is advantageous, and also make these their common aim; for the bad, however, like-mindedness is impossible except to a small extent, just as there is 1167b10
only a small possibility of their being friends, since they aim at the larger share
when it's a matter of what is beneficial, but are deficient in coming forward
when it's a matter of hard work and public service. While wishing for these
advantages for himself, each carefully examines his neighbour and holds him
back, on the basis that unless they keep an eye out the common good is
ruined. The result is that they form into factions, putting pressure on each 1167b15
other to do the just thing while not wishing to do it themselves.

(IX. 7) Benefactors seem to love beneficiaries more than receivers love
bestowers of benefits; and this is made a problem for investigation, as if it
were an unreasonable thing to happen. Now to most people it appears that 1167b20
one party are debtors, the other creditors; as in the case of a loan, then, where
debtors wish creditors not to exist, while those who made the loan even take
care to ensure the safety of their debtors, so the view is that benefactors too
wish the recipients to exist so that they can recoup the favours they have
bestowed, while recipients do not give the same care to repaying them. Now 1167b25
Epicharmus might perhaps claim that those who say this say it because they
are 'observing from the bad side', but it seems human enough; for most
people are forgetful, and aim more at receiving benefits than at bestowing
them. But it would seem that the explanation lies, rather, in natural philosophy, and that the case of the lender does not even resemble this one; for 1167b30
with the lender there is no loving involved, only wishing for the other's
preservation for the sake of what is to be got from him; by contrast those who
have bestowed benefits love and feel affection for the recipients even if the
latter are of no use and will not become useful in the future. This seems to be
a feature of craftsmanship too; for every craftsman feels a greater affection for 1167b35/1168a1
his own works than his works would feel for him if they acquired a soul; and
this perhaps happens with poets most of all, since they feel an excessive
affection for their own poetic creations, loving them as if their own children.
This, then, is the sort of case which that of the benefactor resembles, in so far
as the recipient of benefit is his 'work'; his affection for it, then, is greater than
the affection the work feels for its creator. The explanation of this is that 1168a5
existence is an object of desire and love for everyone; that we exist by being in
actuality (since we do so by living and acting); and that in a way, the work *is*
the maker in actuality; so he loves his work, because he loves his existence too.
And this is a fact of nature; for what he is in potentiality, the work shows in
actuality. At the same time what is done in the action is also a fine thing for the 1168a10

233

benefactor, so that he delights in the one in whom it occurs, whereas for the recipient there is nothing fine in the one who gave the benefit, but at most something advantageous, and this is less pleasant and less lovable. What is pleasant is activity in the present, expectation of it in the future, memory of it when done; but most pleasant, and likewise most lovable, is what is *done in the activity*. So for the maker the work endures (for the fine survives the passage of time), while for the subject of his work its usefulness is gone into the past. Again, the memory of fine things is pleasant, while that of things found useful is not at all pleasant, or less so; expectation seems to be the other way round. Moreover, loving is like doing something to something, whereas being loved is like having something done to one; and it is to those who exceed in respect of being an agent that 'loves' and the features of friendship apply. Further, everyone feels greater fondness for things that have cost them effort, as e.g. those who have made their money feel more fondness for it than those who have inherited theirs; and receiving benefits seems effortless, while bestowing them seems like hard work. It is because of this that mothers also love their children more than fathers, since their role in procreation involves more effort, and they have a better knowledge that their children are their own. This would seem to be characteristic of benefactors too.

(IX. 8) The problem is also raised whether one should love oneself most or someone else. For people reproach those who love themselves most, calling them 'self-lovers', and meaning this as something to be ashamed of; and the bad person is thought to do everything for his own sake, and the more so the worse he is (so they accuse him e.g. of doing nothing that lies beyond himself), whereas the decent person is thought to act because of what is fine, and the better he is, the more so, and for the sake of a friend, while setting his own interests to one side. But people's behaviour is out of tune with these statements, and not without reason. For they say that a person should love most the one who is most a friend, and the one who is most a friend is the friend who wishes good things for the one for whom he wishes them, for that other's sake, even if no one will know; and these features belong most to oneself in relation to oneself, as in fact do all the others by which a friend is defined. For, as has been said, all the features of friendship start from oneself, and are extended to others. The same view is expressed in popular sayings, too, e.g. 'Friends are one soul', 'What is friends' is shared in common', 'Equality is amity', and 'Knee is closer than shin', for all these things will belong most of all to oneself in relation to oneself, since one is most a friend to oneself; and so one should also love oneself most. It is, then, a reasonable problem to raise, which of these two sets of statements one should follow, since both are credible. Now presumably one should draw distinctions among such statements and determine to what extent, and in what way, either set expresses the truth. So perhaps if we were to grasp what each side means by 'self-love', we might clarify matters. Now those that make self-love grounds for reproach call 'self-lovers' those who assign themselves the larger share where money, or honours, or bodily pleasures are concerned; for these are the things that most people desire, and the things they are devoted to as the highest goods, and so they also become fought over. So people who are grasping about these things indulge their appetites, and in general the affective elements and the non-rational part of the soul; and the majority are like this, which is why that way of talking about people has come about, i.e. from what belongs to the major-ity element, and is bad. Self-lovers, then, in this sense are justly objects of reproach. And that it is the type assigning things of this sort to himself that most people are used to calling 'self-lovers' is clear enough; for if anyone were always eager that *he* most of all should do what is just, or what is moderate, or whatever else it might be in accordance with the excellences, and generally always kept what was fine for himself, no one will call this person a 'self-lover', or censure him. But this sort of person would seem to *be* more of a self-lover; at any rate he assigns the finest things, the ones that are most good, to himself, and indulges the most authoritative element of himself, obeying it in every-thing; and just as a city, too, or any other composite whole, seems to *be* its most authoritative element, so with man. Thus 'self-lover' applies most to the one who cherishes this, and indulges this. Again, people are called self-controlled or un-self-controlled by reference to whether intelligence is in con-trol or not, which suggests that this is what each of us is; and it is actions accompanied by reason that people most think they have done themselves, and voluntarily. That, then, this is what each of us is, or this most of all, is quite clear, and also that this is what the decent sort of person cherishes most. Hence he will count as 'self-lover' the most—not the same kind people speak of censoriously, but different by as much as living by reason differs from living by emotion, and desiring the fine, on the one hand, from desiring what appears to bring advantage on the other. Those, then, who are exceptionally eager for fine actions are welcomed and praised by everyone; and if everyone vied for what is fine, and strained to do the finest things, not only would everything be as it should on the communal level but as individuals too each person would be possessed of the greatest goods, given that excellence is such a thing. Thus the good person should be a self-lover, since by doing what is fine he will both be better off himself and benefit others, but the bad one should not; for he will harm both himself and those round him through following worthless attractions. For the bad person, then, there is discord between what he should do and what he does, whereas with the decent one, what he should do is what he does, since every intelligence chooses what is best for itself, and the decent person obeys the commands of intelligence. But it will also be true of the person of excellence that he does many things for the sake of friends and fatherland, even dying for it if need be; for he will freely give up both money and honours, and generally all the goods people fight

1168b15

1168b20

1168b25

1168b30

1168b35

1169a1

1169a5

1169a10

1169a15

1169a20

235

over, while keeping the fine for himself, since he will choose intense pleasure for a short duration over mild pleasure for a long one, and a year's life lived in a fine way rather than many years lived indifferently, and one fine action on a grand scale over many small ones. And this, presumably, is what happens with those who die for others; they are, then, choosing a fine thing for themselves, on a grand scale. Good people will also freely forgo money when this means that their friend will get more; for while the friend gains money, the good person gains what is fine, and so he assigns greater good to himself. He will behave in the same way in relation to honours and public offices, in that he will freely forgo these in favour of his friend; for this is a fine thing for him, and praiseworthy. It is reasonable, then, that he be judged excellent, choosing as he does the fine in place of everything else. It may be that he will even forgo opportunities for action in favour of his friend, and that to have been the cause of his friend's acting is finer than his acting himself. With every praiseworthy thing, then, the person of excellence patently assigns himself more of what is fine. In this way, then, one should be a self-lover, as has been said; but in the way that the majority are, one should not.

(IX. 9) There is also a dispute about the happy person: will he need friends or not? For people say that those who are blessedly self-sufficient have no need of friends, since the things that are good they already have, and so, since they are self-sufficient, they need nothing further, the friend being another self, there to provide what one cannot provide through one's own efforts. Hence the line

To those the gods make happy, what need is there of friends?

But it seems strange to assign all good things to the happy person and not give him friends, something that seems greatest of the external goods. And if it is more characteristic of a friend to do good than to receive it, and characteristic of the good person, and of excellence, to bestow benefits on others, and if it is finer to do good to friends than to strangers, the person of excellence will need people to receive benefits from him. Hence the question that is also raised, about whether one needs friends more in good fortune or in bad, since (they say) on the one hand the unfortunate will need people who will benefit them, and on the other the fortunate will need people to benefit. It is presumably strange, too, to represent the blessedly happy person as living in isolation, since no one would choose to have the sum of all goods by himself; man is a civic being, one whose nature is to live with others. This, then, is an attribute of the happy person, too, since he possesses the natural goods, and clearly it is better to spend one's time with friends and decent people than with strangers, or just anyone. So the happy person needs friends. What, then, do the first set of people have in mind, and in what way are they expressing a truth? Or is it that most people think friends are those useful to us? Now the blessedly happy will have no need of friends of this kind, since the things that are good are

1169a25

1169a30

1169a35
1169b1

1169b5

1169b10

1169b15

1169b20

1169b25

already theirs; nor, then, will they need the friends people have because of pleasure, or only to a small extent (since their life is pleasant and has no need of adventitious pleasure)—and since they do not need friends of *these* sorts, they seem not to need friends. But perhaps that isn't true. For it was said at the beginning that happiness is a kind of activity, and clearly an activity is something that comes about, not something that is there like a piece of property. 1169b30 But if being happy lies in living and being active; and the activity that belongs to the good man is excellent and pleasant in itself, as was said at the beginning; and being one's own is one way in which things can be pleasant; and we are better able to observe our neighbours than ourselves and their actions than our own; and the actions of the good, if they are friends, are pleasant for those 1169b35/1170a1 who are good themselves (for those actions have both of the attributes that are naturally pleasant): then the blessed person will need friends of this sort, given that he decides to observe decent actions that bear the stamp of his own, and that the actions of the good person who is a friend are like this. And people think that the happy must live pleasantly: well, for an isolated person 1170a5 life is difficult, for being continuously active is not easy by oneself, but is easier in the company of people different from oneself, and in relation to others. Consequently his activity will be more continuous, being pleasant in itself, which is a necessary condition of blessedness; for the good man, in so far as he is good, delights in actions in accordance with excellence, and is disgusted by those flowing from badness, just as a musical expert takes pleasure in fine 1170a10 melodies and is distressed at worthless ones. Living in the company of good people may also provide a training in excellence, as Theognis says. And if we examine the matter more from the point of view of natural philosophy, it seems that the good friend is naturally desirable for the good person. For it has been said that what is naturally good is in itself good and pleasant to the good 1170a15 person. Now people define being alive in the case of animals by capacity for perceiving, and in the case of human beings by capacity for perceiving or thinking; but the capacity carries a reference to the activity, and the primary level is that of the activity; being alive, then, in the primary sense seems to be perceiving or thinking. But being alive is something that is good and pleasant 1170a20 in itself, since it is determinate, and the determinate is of the nature of the good, and what is naturally good is also good for the decent person—and hence it appears to be pleasant to all; but one should not take as example a life that is bad and corrupted, or lived in pain, since such a life is indeterminate, as are the attributes that belong to it (the subject of pain, however, will be given 1170a25 clearer treatment in the sequel). But if being alive is itself good and pleasant (and it seems to be, also from the fact that everyone desires it, and decent and blessed people most of all, since for them life is most desirable, and their vital activity is most blessed), and if the one who sees perceives that he sees, the one who hears perceives that he hears, the one who walks perceives that he 1170a30 walks, and similarly in the other cases there is something that perceives that we are in activity, so that if we perceive, it perceives that we perceive, and if we think, it perceives that we think; and if perceiving that we perceive or think

1170b1 is perceiving that we exist (for as we said, existing is perceiving or thinking); and if perceiving that one is alive is pleasant in itself (for being alive is something naturally good, and perceiving what is good as being there in oneself is pleasant); and if being alive is desirable, and especially so for the good,

1170b5 because for them existing is good, and pleasant (for concurrent perception of what is in itself good, in themselves, gives them pleasure); and if, as the good person is to himself, so he is to his friend (since the friend is another self): then just as for each his own existence is desirable, so his friend's is too, or to a similar degree. But as we saw, the good man's existence *is* desirable because of

1170b10 his perceiving himself, that self being good; and such perceiving is pleasant in itself. In that case, he needs to be concurrently perceiving the friend—that he exists, too—and this will come about in their living together, conversing, and sharing their talk and thoughts; for this is what would seem to be meant by 'living together' where human beings are concerned, not feeding in the same location as with grazing animals. For the blessed person, then, if, then, his

1170b15 existence is desirable in itself (being naturally good and pleasant) and so, to a similar extent, is the friend's, the friend too will be something desirable. But what for him is desirable he must have, or else he will be lacking in this respect. So: the person who is to be happy will need friends possessed of excellence.

1170b20   (IX. 10) Should one, then, make as many friends as possible, or as with guest-friendship it has been said, appositely,

Host not many, but host not none,

so too with friendship will it be appropriate neither to be friendless nor, conversely, to have excessively many friends? With friends valued for usefulness, the saying would indeed seem entirely appropriate, since to make return

1170b25 to many for services received takes time and trouble, and life is not long enough to finish the task. So those in excess of the number sufficient for the needs of one's own life are superfluous and an obstacle to living as one who is fine; there is no need, then, for them. As for friends valued for pleasure, a few of them too are enough, as a little seasoning suffices for food. But what of the

1170b30 good—should one's friends of this kind be extremely numerous, or is there a measure for quantity of friends, as there is for the population of a city? Ten people will not make a city, and ten times ten thousand no longer make one—there is presumably no single answer to the question 'how many'; it will be

1171a1 anywhere between certain specified limits. With friends too, then, there will be a limit, and presumably this is the largest number with whom a person could share his life (since this seems, as we said, to be what is most characteristic of friendship); quite clearly, it is impossible to share one's life with, and

238

distribute oneself among, a large number of people. Again, they too must be
friends with each other, if everyone is going to spend time in each other's   1171a5
company; and where there are many people involved this is a hard task to
achieve. It also becomes difficult to join intimately with many people in their
joy and grief; for it is not unlikely that one would find oneself simultaneously
sharing one friend's pleasure and another's sorrow. Presumably, then, it is a
good thing not to seek to be as many-friended as possible, but to have just as
many as suffice for living a shared life; for it would not seem even possible to   1171a10
form intense friendships with many people. This is why one cannot be in love
with more than one person, either; for being in love is a kind of extreme form
of friendship; and it is in relation to a single person; intense friendship, then,
will be felt for a few. This is how it seems to be in real life too; there are not
numerous parties to the comradely type of friendship, and the legendary ones   1171a15
are said to involve just two. Those who have many friends, and greet everyone
in an intimate fashion, are thought to be friends to nobody, except in the way
that fellow citizens are friends; in fact people call them obsequious. Merely as
a citizen, then, one can be a friend to many even while not being obsequious
but a truly decent person; but being friends because of excellence, and
because of what the parties are in themselves, is not a relation one can have
towards many, and one should be content to find even a few like that.   1171a20

(IX. 11) Are friends needed more in times of good fortune or of bad? For they
are sought after in both: the unfortunate need assistance, the fortunate need
people to share life with and to be recipients of their good deeds; for they wish
to do such deeds. Friendship is, then, more necessary in misfortune—hence the   1171a25
need here for useful friends; but it is a finer thing in good fortune—hence
the fact that in this case people also look for friends of a decent sort, since
these are the ones it is more desirable to benefit, and with whom it's more
desirable to spend time. For even the presence of friends, by itself, is pleasant,
in good fortune and in bad—since pain is made lighter when friends are there   1171a30
to feel it too. So one might raise the problem whether it's as if they are sharing
a heavy load; or whether it's rather that the pleasure of having them there,
and the consciousness that they are suffering too, lessens the pain. Well,
whether the alleviation occurs for these or for some other reasons is a question we can set aside; at any rate what we have described appears to happen.
But the presence of friends seems to have somewhat mixed features. For   1171a35
simply seeing one's friends is pleasant, especially for someone in misfortune,   1171b1
and it comes as some sort of reinforcement against the pain (for a friend is a
comfort, both for being seen to be there, and for what he says, if he is an
ingenious sort; for he will know the character of the person affected, and the
things that give him pleasure and pain); on the other hand it's painful, on top   1171b5
of one's own misfortunes, to perceive a friend in pain; for everyone tries to
avoid being a cause of pain to his friends. This is why someone of a manly

nature will be careful about having friends share his pain, and if he doesn't make excessive efforts to avoid distressing them, he won't abide the pain being caused them, and simply will not permit them to come and lament with him,

1171b10 not being the lamenting sort himself; whereas the weaker sex, and the effeminate sort of man, welcome those who join in their groans, and love them as friends and fellow mourners. Clearly, however, the better example should be followed in everything. The presence of friends in the midst of our good fortune fills our time with the pleasant consciousness that they are

1171b15 taking pleasure in the good things that are ours. Hence it would seem that we should be eager to invite our friends to share our *good* fortune (for being ready to benefit others is a fine thing), but hesitant about inviting them to share it when bad; for one should share evils as little as possible, which is the origin of the saying 'One's suffering is enough'. And we should call on our friends for help most of all when they are in a position to do us great service at the cost

1171b20 of little disturbance to themselves. Conversely it is presumably fitting to go to those in misfortune without being asked, and to be eager to do so (for a friend is one who bestows benefits, and especially on those who are in need, and didn't think they should ask; for this is finer and more pleasant for both parties), but to those enjoying good fortune we should go eagerly if it is a matter of working together (for friends are needed for this too), but in a

1171b25 leisurely fashion if it is a matter of receiving benefits, since it is not a fine thing to be eager about being helped. But presumably one should guard against seeming disagreeable in rejecting friendly approaches; for that does sometimes happen. The presence of friends, then, appears desirable in every set of circumstances.

(IX. 12) Is it then the case that, just as seeing gives the greatest satisfaction to

1171b30 lovers, and they prefer this sense to all the rest, as being the one most of all on which their passion depends for its existence and origin, so for friends what's most desirable is sharing lives? For friendship is community, and as a person is disposed towards himself, so he is towards his friend too; but his perception of

1171b35 himself as existing is desirable; hence his perception that his friend exists is so
1172a1 too. But the activity of this perception depends on shared living, so that reasonably enough friends make this their aim. And whatever it is that for each sort of person constitutes existence, or whatever it is for the sake of which they choose to live, it's this they wish to spend time doing in company with their friends: hence some drink together, some play dice together, others

1172a5 train, or hunt, or philosophize together, each kind spending their days together in doing whichever of the things in life most satisfies them; for wishing as they do to live a shared life with their friends, they follow and jointly engage in the occupations in which they think they are sharing life with others. The friendship of inferior people, then, has bad effects, since they take part in inferior occupations, not being possessed of stable character, and

become bad into the bargain, by making themselves resemble one another;   1172a10
whereas the friendship of decent people is decent, and grows in proportion to
their interaction; and they even seem to become better by being active and
correcting each other, for they take each other's imprint in those respects in
which they please one another—hence the saying 'For from good men good
things come'.

Let this, then, be our treatment of friendship; the next thing will be to   1172a15
discuss pleasure.

BOOK X

(X. 1) After these subjects, presumably the next thing to discuss is pleasure.
For pleasure, more than anything, seems an ineradicable aspect of our   1172a20
humanity. This is why those who educate the young try to steer them by
means of pleasure and pain; and it also seems that taking pleasure in the
things one should, and hating the things one should, are most important in
relation to excellence of character: their effect extends through every part of
life, constituting a powerful influence in regard to excellence and the happy
life, for it is pleasant things that people choose, and painful ones they avoid.   1172a25
Discussion of such things would seem to be least dispensable, especially since
they are the subject of much dispute: some people say that pleasure is the
good, while others on the contrary say that it is just plain bad, some presumably because they are actually convinced that this is so, others because they
think it better in relation to our lives to represent pleasure as a bad thing, even   1172a30
if it isn't, since (so they say) most people incline towards it, and are slaves to
pleasures, so that one has to draw them in the contrary direction, that way
they will arrive at the intermediate. But this may perhaps not be a good thing
to say. For what people say about matters in the sphere of affections and   1172a35
actions carries less conviction than what they actually do, so that whenever
their pronouncements disagree with what one can see before one's eyes, they
earn contempt and put paid to what is true into the bargain; for if ever the   1172b1
person who censures pleasure is observed seeking it, his falling away is taken
to indicate that all of it is worth having, since making distinctions is not a
characteristic of most people. It seems, then, that true statements are the
most useful ones in relation not only to knowledge but to life; for since they   1172b5
are in agreement with what is seen to happen, they carry conviction, and so
encourage those who comprehend them to live accordingly. Enough, then, of

matters of this sort; let us go on to the things that have been said about pleasure.

(X. 2) Now Eudoxus used to think that pleasure was the good because he saw
every sort of creature seeking it, whether rational or non-rational; and since
he thought that what was desirable in all cases was what was good, and that
what was most so exercised the greatest attraction, he concluded that every
creature's being drawn towards the same thing showed this as being best for
all of them (since each finds what is good for itself, just as it finds its own
food), and that what was good for every creature, and what every creature
sought, was the good. Eudoxus' pronouncements carried conviction more
because of the excellence of his character than in themselves; for he was
thought to be a person of exceptional moderation, and so it was not thought
that he made them as a lover of pleasure, but that things were truly as he said.
He held that it was no less evident from the contrary, since pain is in itself, for
all creatures, something to be avoided, so that the contrary must similarly be
desirable for all; and that what is most desirable is what we do not choose
because of something else, or for the sake of something else—but that pleasure is by general agreement a thing of this sort, since nobody asks a person
'What are you enjoying yourself for?', which implies that pleasure is desirable
in itself. Again, he argued that when added to any good whatever, e.g. just
actions, or moderate behaviour, pleasure makes it more desirable, and that the
good is increased by itself. This argument, then, at any rate, appears to show it
to be *a* good, and no more so than any other; for every good is more desirable
when combined with another one than it is in isolation. Why, it is by this sort
of argument that Plato in fact tries to do away with the view that pleasure is
the good; for he says that the pleasant life is more desirable in combination
with than apart from wisdom, and if the result of the combination is better,
then pleasure is not the good, since there is nothing which when added to the
good makes *it* more desirable. And clearly nothing else will be the good,
either, if it becomes more desirable when combined with something else
good in itself. What, then, is there of this nature, which we have a share in
too? For it is something of that nature that we are trying to discover. Those,
on the other hand, who contend that what all creatures seek is not good may
well be talking nonsense. For what seems to all to be the case, that we assert
to be the case; and the person who does away with this conviction will hardly
have anything more convincing to say. For if it is unintelligent creatures that
desire the things in question, the claim would make sense; but if it is intelligent ones too, how could it make sense? And perhaps even in inferior creatures there is some natural element of goodness that transcends what they are
in themselves, and has as its object their own proper good. But the point about
the contrary does not seem to be well made either. For they deny that, if pain
is something bad, it follows that pleasure must be a good, since bad is opposed

1172b10

1172b15

1172b20

1172b25

1172b30

1172b35

1173a1

1173a5

to bad, too, and both bad and good to what is neither; and in saying this, so far
as it goes, they are not wrong, but at the same time they are missing the truth
in the case of the things under discussion. For if both were bad,[43] both would   1173a10
also have had to be things to be avoided too, and something that is neither
good nor bad is neither to be avoided nor to be sought, or both equally; but as
things are people patently avoid pain as something bad and choose pleasure as
something good; this, then, is the way they are opposed.

(X. 3) But neither does it follow, if pleasure is not a quality, that it is not a
good either; for neither are the activities of excellence qualities, nor is happi-   1173a15
ness. Again, they say that the good is determinate, whereas pleasure is
indeterminate, because it admits of more and less. Now if they reach this
judgement by considering being pleased, the same will hold of justice and the
other excellences—qualities of which these thinkers openly say that the persons qualified by them are more so or less so, and act more in accordance with   1173a20
the excellences, or less: people can be just to a greater degree, or courageous,
and they can also perform just acts or behave moderately to a greater or lesser
degree. But if the judgement in question refers to the pleasures, they are
perhaps failing to give the explanation; that is, if some pleasures are unmixed
while others are mixed. And why should pleasure not be in the same case as
health, which while being determinate nevertheless admits of more and less?   1173a25
For the same kind of balance does not exist in everyone, nor is there always
some single balance in the same person, but even while it is giving way it
continues to be present up to a certain point, so differing in terms of more and
less. The case of pleasure too, then, may be of this sort. Again, they suppose
the good to be something complete, movements and comings to be
incomplete, and try to show pleasure to be movement and coming to be. But   1173a30
they do not seem to be right even in saying that it is a movement; for it seems
to be characteristic of every movement to be quick or slow, and if not in itself,
as e.g. the movement of the cosmos, then in relation to something else; but
pleasure is neither quick nor slow. For it is possible to become pleased quickly,
as it is to become angered quickly, but not to *be* pleased quickly, even in   1173b1
relation to something else, in the way that one can walk quickly, or grow, and
all that sort of thing. It is possible, then, to change quickly or slowly to being
pleased, but it is not possible actually to *be* in that condition quickly—I mean
the condition of being pleased. Again, how could it be a coming to be? For it   1173b5
seems that not just anything comes to be from just anything, but that a thing
is dissolved into that from which it comes to be; and pain is a destruction of
that of which pleasure is a coming to be. But they also say that pain is lack of
what is in accordance with nature, and pleasure replenishment of it. And
these affections are bodily. If, then, pleasure is a replenishment of what is in   1173b10

---

[43] Reading ἀμφοῖν γὰρ ὄντων κακῶν (1173a10).

accordance with nature, it would follow that the subject of the replenishment
is what is being pleased; so it is the body; but it seems not to be; nor, then, is
the replenishment pleasure, but rather someone will undergo pleasure while
replenishment is in process, and pain during emptying.[44] This view of pleasure
seems to have its origins in the pains and pleasures connected with nourishment: the claim is that lack comes first, and so pain, then the pleasure of
replenishment. But this does not happen with all pleasures; for there are no
pains involved with the pleasures of coming to understand, or, if it is a matter
of sensory pleasures, those that arise through the sense of smell; and sounds
and sights, too, are often painless, as is remembering and looking to the
future. So of what will they be comings to be? For there has occurred no lack
of anything for there to be a replenishment of. To those who cite the pleasures
that bring reproach, one can reply that these things are not pleasant: that they
are pleasant for those in a bad condition does not mean that we should think
them to *be* pleasant, except for this sort of person, any more than we should
think things healthy or sweet or bitter that are so to people who are ill, or
again think things to be white that appear so to those suffering from eye-
disease; or else one can reply that pleasures really are desirable, only not
pleasures deriving from these sources, just as it is desirable to have wealth, but
not to have it as a result of betraying one's country, and to be healthy, but not
at the cost of eating anything whatever; or that pleasures differ in kind, for
those deriving from fine things are distinct from those deriving from shameful
ones, and one cannot come to feel the pleasure of the just person without
being just, or that of the musical expert without being musical, and similarly
in other cases. The distinction between friend and flatterer also seems to be
evidence either that pleasure is not a good thing, or that pleasures are different
in kind, since the one seems to offer his company with the good in view, the
other with a view to pleasure, and whereas the latter is an object of reproach,
the former receives praise, on the basis that he offers his company for quite
different purposes. Again, no one would choose to live the whole of life with
the thoughts of a small child, enjoying to the utmost the pleasures of small
children; or to delight in doing something of the most shameful sort, even
without the prospect of ever having to suffer pain for it. Again, there are many
things we would regard as important to us even if they brought no pleasure,
e.g. seeing, remembering, knowing, possessing the excellences; and if these
things are necessarily accompanied by pleasures, it makes no difference, since
we would choose them even if no pleasure did come from them. It seems
clear, then, both that pleasure is not the good, and that not all pleasure is
desirable; also that some pleasures are desirable in themselves, differing from
others either in kind or in terms of their sources.

[44] Reading κενούμενος or ⟨ἐνδεὴς⟩ γινόμενος in place of τεμνόμενος (1173b12).

244

So we have said enough about the things people say on the subject of pleasure and pain;

(X. 4) as for what pleasure is, or what kind of thing, this will become plainer if we start again from the beginning. The activity of seeing seems to be complete over any given span of time: it is not lacking in anything which by coming to be at a later time will complete its specific form; and pleasure too seems to be like this. For it is a kind of whole, and there is no length of time such that if a pleasure someone takes during it goes on for a time that's longer, the form of the pleasure will be completed. Hence it is not a movement either. For every movement involves time, and relates to some goal, as does e.g. the movement that is building, and it is complete when it finally does what it aims at. So that will be either in the whole time, or in this. But if it is divided up into temporal parts, the resulting movements are all incomplete, and distinct in form both from the whole and from each other; for the putting together of the stone blocks is distinct from the fluting of the column, and both of these from the making of the temple—and the making of the temple is a complete movement, since it is not lacking anything required for the task in hand, whereas that of the base, and of the triglyph, is incomplete, since each of these is a making of a part. So they are different in form, and it is not possible in any of the portions of the time to find a movement that is complete in terms of its form; if such a movement *is* to be found, it is to be found in the whole time. And similarly with walking, and the other cases. For if locomotion is movement from one place to another, there are different forms of this too, i.e. flying, walking, leaping, and so on; but there are not only these divisions, but divisions in walking itself, since the where from/where to is not the same thing for a race-track and for a part of it, or for one part and for another; nor is crossing this line the same as crossing that one; for one is not only traversing a line, but a line that also has a location, and this line has a different location from that one. Well, a precise account of movement has been given elsewhere; however, it seems that movement is not complete in every portion of time, but rather that most movements are incomplete and differ in form, given that the where from/where to determines the form. But the form of pleasure is complete in any and every portion of time. So it is clear that pleasure and movement will be distinct from one another, and that pleasure is something whole and complete. And this would also seem to follow from the fact that it is not possible to move, while it is possible to be pleased, without taking time; for what occurs in the now is a whole of some kind. From these points it is also clear that it is not correct to say, as people do, that there is a movement or coming to be *of* pleasure.[45] For one does not talk of a movement or coming to be of everything, but of things that are divisible

1174a15

1174a20

1174a25

1174a30

1174b1

1174b5

1174b10

---

[45] Reading . . . εἶναι τῆς ἡδονῆς (1174b10).

into parts, and are not wholes; for there is no coming to be of seeing either, or of a point, or of a mathematical unit, nor is there movement of these things at all, or coming to be; nor, then, is there movement or coming to be of pleasure either, because it is a kind of whole.

1174b15 But since every sense is active in relation to the sense-object, and completely active when the sense is in good condition and its object is the finest in the domain of that sense (for something like this, more than anything else, is what complete activity of a sense seems to be; let it be a matter of indifference whether we say the sense itself, or what it is in, is active)—this being so, well, in the case of each of the senses the activity that is best is the one whose subject is in the best condition in relation to the object that is most worth

1174b20 while in the domain of that sense. But this activity will be most complete and most pleasant. For all the kinds of sensory activity give rise to pleasure, and so too do thought and reflection; but the most complete is the most pleasant, and most complete is that whose subject is in good condition, in relation to the most worth while of the objects in the domain of the sense; and pleasure is what completes the activity. But pleasure does not complete it in the same

1174b25 way that the sense-object and the sense do so, when they are good of their kind, any more than health and a doctor are causes in the same way of being healthy. That pleasure does arise with each sense is clear (for we say that sights and sounds are pleasant), and it is clear too that it arises most when the sense is at its best and is active in relation to an object of which the same is true; and

1174b30 when both sense-object and what is doing the sensing are like this, there will always be pleasure, at any rate so long as there is something to produce the sense-perception and something to receive it. Pleasure completes the activity not in the way the disposition present in the subject completes it, but as a sort of supervenient end, like the bloom of manhood on those in their prime. For so long, then, as the object of thought or sense-perception is as it should be,

1175a1 and so is what discriminates or reflects, there will be pleasure in the activity; for when receptor and producer are similar, and in the same relation to each other, the same result naturally occurs. How then is it that no one enjoys pleasure continuously? Or is it because one gets tired? Continuous activity,

1175a5 after all, is impossible for any human capacity. So pleasure does not occur continuously either, since it accompanies the activity in each case. That some things delight when new but later on not so much has the same explanation; for at first thought is called forth, and is intensely engaged with them, like someone focussing on something in the case of sight, but afterwards the activ-

1175a10 ity is no longer like this but rather is allowed to lapse, so that the pleasure too is dimmed. That everyone desires pleasure one might put down to the fact that everyone also seeks to be alive, and living is a sort of activity, each person being active in relation to those objects, and with those faculties, to which he also feels the greatest attachment: the musical person, e.g., with hearing in relation to melodies, the lover of understanding with thought in relation to

the objects of reflection, and so on in the case of every other type too; and   1175a15
pleasure completes the activities, and so the life, that they desire. It makes
sense, then, that they seek pleasure; for it adds completeness to living, which is
something desirable, for each. As for whether we choose living because we
want pleasure or pleasure because we want to be alive, this is something
that may be set aside for the present; for the two things appear to be   1175a20
yoked together, and not to allow themselves to be separated: without activity
pleasure does not occur, and every activity is completed by pleasure.

(X. 5) This is also, it seems, why pleasures differ in kind. For we think that
where things differ in kind, what completes them is different (this is evidently
the case with both natural and artificial objects: animals and trees, a picture, a
statue, a house, a piece of furniture); and similarly with activities too: if they   1175a25
differ in kind, we think of what completes them as differing in kind. But the
activities of thought differ in kind from those involving the senses, and they
themselves from each other; so then do the pleasures that complete them.
This will be apparent also from the closeness with which each of the pleasures
is bound up with the activity it completes. For the activity's own pleasure   1175a30
contributes to increasing the activity. It is those who are active and take
pleasure in it that are more discriminating and precise in relation to a given
subject, e.g. those who delight in geometry are the ones that become expert in
geometry, and are always more able to see things, and similarly the lover of
music, or of building, or whatever it may be—each gets better at his own task   1175a35
through taking pleasure in it; and the pleasures contribute to the increase; but
what contributes to increasing something belongs to it as its own, and where   1175b1
things are different in kind, what belongs to each is different in kind. But this
will be still more evident from the way activities are impeded by the pleasures
from different ones. Lovers of pipe-music are incapable of paying attention to
a discussion if they happen to hear someone playing the pipes, because they
take more pleasure in the pipe-playing than in their present activity. So the   1175b5
pleasure in pipe-playing destroys the activity of discussion. This happens in a
similar way in other cases too, when someone is simultaneously involved in
two activities; for the more pleasant one pushes the other out of the way, and
the more so if the difference in pleasure is large, to the point where the other
activity ceases altogether. Hence the fact that when we are deriving intense   1175b10
enjoyment from whatever it may be we are hardly inclined to do something
else, and that if we do turn to other things, it is when we are only mildly
engaged, as e.g. those who eat titbits in the theatre do it most when the actors
are no good. And since its own pleasure gives an activity a sharper edge, and
makes it longer-lasting and better, while other activities' pleasures spoil it,   1175b15
clearly pleasures are widely distinct in nature. For a pleasure that belongs to
another activity has much the same effect as an activity's own pain; for activities are destroyed by the pains belonging to them, as e.g. if writing, or doing

calculations, is unpleasant for someone, and even causes them pain, in the first case there is no writing and in the second no calculating, because the activity
1175b20   is painful. The pleasures and pains that belong, then, have contrary effects on activities, the ones that belong being the ones that supervene on the activity itself. Pleasures that belong to other activities, as we have said, have an effect not dissimilar to that caused by pain: they destroy the activity, only not in the
1175b25   same way. But since activities differ in goodness and worthlessness, and some are desirable while others are to be avoided, and others neither, so it is with pleasures too, since for each activity there is its own pleasure. So the pleasure belonging to a worthwhile activity is good, while that related to a worthless one is bad; for appetites, too, are praiseworthy when they are for fine things, and worthy of censure when they are for shameful things. But the
1175b30   pleasures that are in activities belong to them more closely than the desires for them. For the latter are divided off from the activities both by the time that intervenes and by their nature as desires, whereas the former are close together with them and are so indistinguishable that there is room for dispute whether activity isn't the same thing as pleasure. It certainly does not seem
1175b35   likely that pleasure *is* thinking, or perceiving (for that is a strange idea); but because of their not being separated they appear to some people to be the same thing. Just as activities are distinct, then, so too are their pleasures. But
1176a1   sight differs from touch in purity, as do hearing and smell from taste. So the pleasures, too, differ in a similar way: the pleasures of thinking from these pleasures of sense, and each of the two kinds among themselves. But each kind of creature seems to have its own kind of pleasure, just as it has its own
1176a5   function; for the pleasure corresponding to its activity will be its own. But this will also be evident in each case, if one goes through them: a horse's pleasure, a dog's, and a man's are different, and as Heraclitus says, donkeys will choose sweepings to gold; something to eat is more pleasant than gold, for donkeys. If creatures are distinct in kind, then, their pleasures will be different in kind; and if they are of the same kind, one might reasonably expect their pleasures
1176a10   not to differ. But they diverge to no small degree at least in the case of human beings, since the same things delight some while giving pain to others, and are painful and objects of loathing for the one group while being pleasant and things to love for the other. This happens with sweet things too; the same things don't seem sweet to the person with a fever and the one in good health,
1176a15   nor warm to those who are frail and those who are physically fit. This happens with other things too in the same way. However, in all such cases it is thought to be what appears so to the good person that *is* so. And if this is the right thing to say, as it seems to be, and it is excellence and the good person, in so far as he is such, that is the measure for each sort of thing, then so too with pleasures: the ones that appear so to *him* will be pleasures, and the things *he*
1176a20   delights in will be pleasant. If the things that disgust him appear pleasant to a given person, there is nothing surprising in that, since there are many forms

of corruption and damage to which human beings are subject; pleasant the things in question are not, though they are for these types, and for people in this condition. It is clear, then, that the ones by common consent shameful should be declared not to be pleasures, except for people whose nature is corrupted; but among those thought to be good, what sort of pleasure, or which pleasure, should we declare to belong to a human being? Or is the answer clear, from looking at the different types of activity? For pleasures go in tandem with these. Whether, then, the activities of the complete and blessed man are one or more than one, it is the pleasures that complete these that will be said to be human pleasures in the primary sense; and the rest will be so called in a sense that is secondary or many times removed, just as the activities will be. 1176a25

(X. 6) Now that we have discussed the subjects relating to the different kinds of excellence, of friendship, and of pleasure, it remains to treat, in outline, of happiness, since we suppose it to be the end of things human. Now our account will be more concise if we begin by picking up again what was said earlier. What we said, then, was that happiness is not a disposition; for if it were, even a person asleep his whole life might have it, living a plant's life, or someone who was suffering the greatest misfortunes. If, then, these are not satisfying notions, and happiness is rather to be put down as a kind of activity, as has been said in our earlier discussions, and if some activities are necessary, i.e. desirable because of other things, while others desirable in themselves, it is clear that happiness is to be put down as one of those desirable in themselves, not as one of those desirable because of something else; for happiness is not lacking in anything, but self-sufficient. But the ones desirable in themselves are those from which nothing is sought over and above the activity. Actions in accordance with excellence are thought to be of this kind, on the basis that doing what is fine and worthwhile is one of the things desirable because of themselves. Also thought to be of this kind are the pleasant forms of amusement, since people do not choose them because of other things; after all, they get harm rather than benefit from them, by not taking care of their bodies and their property. But such diversions are the refuge of most of those called 'happy', which is why people who have the supple wit for such diversions are in good standing with tyrants; they make themselves pleasant in ways that fit what the tyrant seeks, and he needs people like that. It is thought, then, that these things make for happiness because those with political power spend their leisure-time on them, but presumably people like that are no indication of anything, since excellence does not lie in wielding power, and neither does intelligence, from which the worthwhile activities flow; nor if these people who have had no taste of refined and civilized pleasure resort to bodily ones should one think because of this that the latter are more desirable, since children too think best what is most honoured among their own group. It is to 1176a30

1176a35
1176b1

1176b5

1176b10

1176b15

1176b20

1176b25   be expected, then, that just as different things appear honourable to children and grown men, so too with bad characters and good ones. So as has often been said, both what is honourable and what is pleasant is what is so for the good person; but for each type, the most desirable activity is the one that accords with his own proper disposition; for the good person as well, therefore, the most desirable is the one that accords with excellence. In that case, happiness does not lie in amusement; for it is indeed a strange thought that the end should be amusement, and that the busy-ness and suffering through-
1176b30   out one's life should be for the sake of amusing oneself. For we value almost everything, except happiness, for the sake of something else; for happiness is an end. To apply oneself to serious things, and to labour, for the sake of amusement appears silly and excessively childish. 'Play to be serious', as Anacharsis has it, seems the correct way; for amusement is like relaxation, and
1176b35   it is because people are incapable of labouring continuously that they need to
1177a1   relax. Relaxation, then, is not an end; for it occurs for the sake of activity. The happy life seems to be in accordance with excellence; and this life is one accompanied by seriousness, not one that depends on amusement. Again, we say that serious things are better than those that occasion laughter and involve
1177a5   amusement, and that the activity of what is better, whether part of a human being or the whole of one, is more serious; but the activity of what is better is superior, which already implies that it is more productive of happiness. Again, just anyone can enjoy bodily pleasures, and a slave no less than the best kind of person; but no one thinks of a slave as having a share in happiness, unless
1177a10   he also has a share in life. For happiness does not lie in diversions of this sort, but in the kinds of activity that accord with excellence, as has been said before.

(X. 7) But if happiness is activity in accordance with excellence, it is reasonable that it should be activity in accordance with the highest kind; and this will be the excellence of what is best. Whether, then, this is intelligence or some-
1177a15   thing else, this element that is thought naturally to rule and guide, and to possess awareness of fine things and divine ones—whether being, itself too, something divine, or the divinest of the things in us, it is the activity of this, in accordance with its own proper excellence, that will be complete happiness. That it is *reflective* activity has been said; and this would seem to be in agree-
1177a20   ment both with what was said before and with the truth. For this is the highest kind of activity, since intelligence too is highest of the things in us, and the objects of intelligence are the highest knowables; further, it is the most continuous, since we can engage in reflection continuously more than we can in getting things done, whatever they may be. Again, we think that pleasure must be an ingredient in happiness, and of activities in accordance with excellence it is the one in accordance with intellectual accomplishment that is
1177a25   agreed to be pleasantest; at any rate the love of it [*philosophia*] is thought to

bring with it pleasures amazing in purity and stability, and it is reasonable that those who have attained knowledge should pass their time more pleasantly than those who are looking for it. Again, the talked-about self-sufficiency will be a feature of the reflective life most of all; for both the intellectually accomplished and the just person, and everyone else, will require the things necessary for living, but given that they are adequately supplied with such things, the just person will need people to be objects of, and partners in, his just actions, and similarly with the moderate, the courageous, and each of the other types, whereas the intellectually accomplished will be able to engage in reflection even when by himself, and the more so, the more accomplished he is—he will do it better, presumably, if he has others to work with him, but all the same he will be most self-sufficient. Again, reflective activity would seem to be the only kind loved because of itself; for nothing accrues from it besides the act of reflecting, whereas from practical projects we get something, whether more or less, besides the doing of them. Again, happiness is thought to reside in leisure from business; for we busy ourselves in order to have leisure, and go to war in order to live at peace. Now the context of the practical activity of the excellences is either the city or war, but actions in these spheres seem to lack the element of leisure, and warlike ones, in fact, lack it utterly (for no one chooses to make war for the sake of making war, or deliberately contrives it: if someone made his friends into enemies in order to create battles and killings, he would seem an utterly bloodthirsty type). But the politician's activity, too, lacks the element of leisure, and aims beyond the business of politics itself—at getting power, or honours, or indeed happiness for himself and his fellow citizens, this being distinct from the exercise of political expertise, and something we clearly do seek as something distinct. If, then, among actions in accordance with the excellences the political and warlike stand out in fineness and greatness, and these actions are lacking in leisure and aim at some end rather than being desirable because of themselves, while the activity of intelligence seems both to possess a greater seriousness, being reflective, and to aim at no end beside itself, and to have its own proper pleasure (and this contributes to increasing the activity); and if, finally, the elements of self-sufficiency, and of leisure, and of freedom from weariness, in so far as these are possible for human beings, and all the other attributes assigned to the blessed, are patently characteristics of this kind of activity: then *this* activity will be the complete happiness of man, if it is given a complete length of life, since nothing about happiness is incomplete. But such a life will be higher than the human plane; for it is not in so far as he is human that he will live like this, but in so far as there is something divine in him, and to the degree that this is superior to the compound, to that degree will its activity too be superior to that in accordance with the rest of excellence. If, then, intelligence is something divine as compared to a human being, so too a life lived in accordance with this will be divine as compared to a human life.

1177a30

1177b1

1177b5

1177b10

1177b15

1177b20

1177b25

1177b30

One should not follow the advice of those who say 'Human you are, think human thoughts', and 'Mortals you are, think mortal' ones, but instead, so far as is possible, assimilate to the immortals and do everything with the aim of living in accordance with what is highest of the things in us; for even if it is small in bulk, the degree to which it surpasses everything in power and dignity is far greater. And each of us would seem actually to *be* this, given that each is his authoritative and better element; it would be a strange thing, then, if one chose, not one's own life, but that of something else. Again, what was said before will fit with the present case too: what belongs to each kind of creature by nature is best and most pleasant for each; for man, then, the life in accordance with intelligence is so too, given that man is this most of all. This life, then, will also be happiest.

(X. 8) But second happiest is the life in accordance with the rest of excellence; for activities in accordance with this are human. For just things, and courageous things, and the other kinds of things we do that accord with the excellences, we do in relation to one another, keeping what befits each person in view, in transactions and dealings and all the various types of actions, and in our affective states; and all of these things appear to be human. Some of them seem also to be consequential on the body, and in many respects excellence of character seems to be bound up closely with the affective states; and wisdom too is yoked together with excellence of character, and this with wisdom, given that the starting points of wisdom are in accordance with the character-excellences, and the correctness of the character-excellences is in accordance with wisdom. Connected as these are with the affective states too, they will have to do with the compound. But the excellences of the compound are human ones; so too, then, is the life in accordance with these, and the happiness. The excellence belonging to intelligence, by contrast, is separate; let that much be said about it (for to go into precise detail is a larger task than the one before us). But it would also seem to have little need for external resources, or less need than excellence of character does. For let the requirement both types have for the necessary things be taken as actually equal, even if the political type exerts himself more in relation to the body and everything of that sort, since the difference might be a small one; but with regard to the respective activities there will be a large difference. For the open-handed type will need money to do open-handed things, and the just type, too, in order to make returns for benefits received (for wishes are invisible, and even those who are *not* just pretend to wish to do the just thing); and the courageous type will need not to be powerless, if he is to achieve anything in accordance with his excellence, while the moderate type will need the opportunity of indulging himself—how else will it be clear that this type, or any of the others, is the type he is? Again, there is dispute about whether excellence is primarily a matter of decision or of doings, on the assumption that it depends on both:

well, in the complete case it clearly will involve both, and one needs many things in order to carry an action through, and more of them, the greater and finer the action is. The person engaged in reflection needs none of these sorts of things, at least for his activity; instead, one might almost say that they are even impediments to him, at least in relation to reflecting; but in so far as he is a human being, and shares his life with others, he chooses to do the deeds that accord with excellence, and so he will need such things for the purposes of living a human life.

1178b5

But that complete happiness is a reflective kind of activity will be evident from the following too. Our belief is that the gods are blessed and happy to the highest degree; but what sorts of practical doings ought we to assign to them? Just ones? Won't they appear comic, carrying on transactions, returning deposits, and everything like that? Courageous ones? Should we think of them as standing up to frightening things, and facing danger because it is a fine thing to do? Open-handed ones? But to whom will they give? A strange notion, too, that they'll have currency or anything like that. And their moderate actions— what would they be? Or would praising them in that way be vulgar rubbish, since they don't have bad appetites? Everything about practical doings, if one looks through all the kinds, will obviously turn out to be petty and unworthy of gods. And yet everyone supposes them to be alive, and if alive, then in activity; for they surely do not think of them as sleeping like Endymion. If, then, living has practical doing taken away from it, and (still more) producing, what is left except reflection? So then the activity of a god, superior as it is in blessedness, will be one of reflection; and so too the human activity that has the greatest affinity to this one will be most productive of happiness. Another indication of this is that the other animals do not share in happiness, being completely deprived of this sort of activity. For the life of gods is blessedly happy throughout, while that of human beings is so to the extent that there belongs to it some kind of semblance of this sort of activity; but of the other animals none is happy, since there is no respect in which they share in reflection. So happiness too extends as far as reflection does, and to those who have more of reflection more happiness belongs too, not incidentally, but in virtue of the reflection; for this is in itself to be honoured. So then happiness will be a kind of reflection.

1178b10

1178b15

1178b20

1178b25

1178b30

But the one who is happy will also need external prosperity, in so far as he is human; for human nature is not self-sufficient for the purposes of reflection, but needs bodily health too, and the availability of nourishment and other kinds of servicing. And yet, if it is not possible to be blessedly happy without external things, still it should not be thought that the happy person will need many of them, and on a large scale, in order to be so; for self-sufficiency does not depend on excess, and neither does action, and even someone who does not rule over land and sea is capable of doing fine things; for it will be possible to act in accordance with excellence even on the basis of moderate resources

1178b35
1179a1

1179a5

(and this one can observe plainly enough, since private individuals seem to perform decent actions no less, or even more, than those with political power), and it is enough to have external things to this amount, since a person's life will be happy if he is active in accordance with excellence. And Solon, too, gave what is perhaps a good depiction of the happy when he said they had been moderately well equipped with external things, had done the finest things, as he saw it, and had lived a sensible life; for it is possible to do what one should if one has moderate possessions. Anaxagoras too seems to have taken the happy man not to be a rich one, or a politically powerful one, when he said he wouldn't be surprised if the happy were to appear to most people a strange sort—because they judge by external things, having eyes only for these. The views of the wise, then, seem to be in agreement with the arguments.

These sorts of considerations too, then, do carry a certain conviction; but in the practical sphere the truth is determined on the basis of the way life is actually lived; for this is decisive. So when one looks at everything that has been said up to this point, one should be bringing it to bear on one's life as actually lived, and if it is in harmony with what one actually does, it should be accepted, while if there is discord, it should be supposed mere words.

And the person whose intelligence is active, and who devotes himself to intelligence, and is in the best condition, seems also to be most loved by the gods. For if the gods have any sort of care for things human, as they are thought to do, it would also be reasonable to suppose both that they delight in what is best and has the greatest affinity to themselves (and this would be intelligence) and that those who cherish this most, and honour it, are the ones they benefit in return, for taking care of what they themselves love, and acting correctly and finely. And quite clearly, all these attributes belong most of all to the intellectually accomplished person. He, therefore, is most loved by the gods. But it is reasonable that the same person should also be happiest; so that in this way too it is the intellectually accomplished person who will be happy to the highest degree.

(X. 9) Well then, if we have accorded adequate discussion, in outline, both to these subjects and to the excellences, and again to friendship and pleasure, should we suppose our programme completely carried out? Or as one says, when it is a question of practical projects is the goal not to reflect on each set of things and to know about them, but rather to get on and do them—so that in the case of excellence too, it is not sufficient to *know* about it, but rather one must try actually to have and to use it, or whatever way it is that we become good? Now if words were sufficient in themselves for making people decent, 'Many and fat the fees they'd earn' (to quote Theognis), and justly, and words would be what had to be provided; but as it is they appear to have the power to turn and motivate those of the young who are civilized, and to be capable of bringing about possession by excellence in a character that is noble

and truly loves the fine, but to lack the power to turn the majority of people   1179b10
towards refinement of excellence. For most people are not of the sort to be
guided by a sense of shame but by fear, and not to refrain from bad things on
the grounds of their shamefulness but because of the punishments; living by
emotion as they do, they pursue their own kinds of pleasures and the means
to these, and shun the opposing pains, while not even having a conception of   1179b15
the fine and the truly pleasant, since they have had no taste of it. What kind of
talking, then, would change the rhythm of their life? For it is not possible,
or not easy, for words to dislodge what has long since been absorbed into
one's character-traits. But perhaps we should be satisfied if, with all the factors
in place through which it is thought that we become decent people, we were
to acquire a portion of excellence. Now some people think we become good   1179b20
by nature, while others think it is by habituation, and others again by teaching. Well, the natural element clearly does not depend on us, but[46] belongs by
divine causes of some kind to the truly fortunate; while talk and teaching may
well not have force under all circumstances, and the soul of the hearer has to
have been prepared beforehand through its habits in order to delight in and   1179b25
loathe the right things, just as one has to prepare soil if it is going to nourish the
seed. For the person who lives according to emotion will not listen to talk that
tries to turn him away from it, nor again will he comprehend such talk; how
will it be possible to persuade someone like this to change? And in general it is
not talk that makes emotion yield but force. Before he acquires excellence,
then, a person must in a way already possess a character akin to it, one that is   1179b30
attracted by the fine and repulsed by the shameful. But it is hard for someone
to get the correct guidance towards excellence, from childhood on, if he has
not been brought up under laws that aim at that effect; for a moderate and
resistant way of life is not pleasant for most people, especially when they are
young. So their upbringing and patterns of behaviour must be ordered by the   1179b35
laws; for these ways will not be painful to them if they have become used to
them. But presumably it is not enough that people should be brought up and   1180a1
supervised correctly when they are young; on the contrary: since they must
observe those patterns of behaviour, and be habituated to them, when they
are grown men too, there will need to be laws covering these aspects too, and
indeed covering the whole of life; for most people are more governed by   1180a5
compulsion than talk, and by penalties than by what is fine. This is why some
think that lawgivers, in the course of laying down laws, should exhort and try
to turn people towards excellence for the sake of what is fine, on the assumption that those whose habits have been decently developed will listen; but that
they should impose forcible constraints in the form of punishments on those
that fail to obey, and are rather poor material; and finally that they should cast
out the incurable for good; the view is that the decent character, his life being   1180a10

---

[46] Reading οὐκ ἐφ' ἡμῖ ν, ἀλλὰ (1179b22).

directed as it is towards the fine, will allow words to govern him, whereas the inferior character whose desire is for pleasure needs forcible constraint by pain like a yoked animal. This is why they also say that the pains meted out should be of the sort most opposed to the attracting pleasures.

1180a15   However this may be: if, as has been said, a person needs to be brought up and habituated in the right way in order to be good, and then live accordingly under a regime of decent behaviour, neither counter-voluntarily nor voluntarily doing what is bad; and if this will come about when people live in accordance with a kind of intelligence or correct principle of order, with the force to make itself felt: well, a father's prescriptions do not have the requisite force, or

1180a20   the element of compulsion; nor indeed do the orders of any single man, unless he is a king or similar person; but law does have the power to compel, being a form of words deriving from a kind of wisdom and intelligence. And people hate any human beings that oppose their impulses, even if the opposition is correct; whereas the law is not felt as burdensome when it orders

1180a25   decent behaviour. But only in Sparta, or in a few places, does the lawgiver seem to have given sufficiently careful attention to upbringing and patterns of behaviour; in most cities there is neglect of such matters, and each man lives as he wishes, 'wielding his law over children and wife' like a Cyclops. The best

1180a30   thing, then, is that there should be communal supervision, of the correct sort; but if things are neglected on the communal level, then it would seem appropriate for each to contribute towards his own children's and friends' acquisition of excellence, and for him to have the capacity to do so, or at any rate to decide to do it. But from what has been said he would seem to be likely to have a greater capacity for doing it if he first acquired the expertise of the lawgiver. For clearly, where supervision is on a communal basis, it is achieved

1180a35   through laws, and where it is of a decent kind, through good laws; whether
1180b1   these are written or unwritten, or whether they are to govern the education of one person or many, it would appear to make no difference, any more than it does in the case of music, or athletic training, or other kinds of discipline. For the things a father says, and the habits he imposes, have the same force in a

1180b5   household as legal provisions and customs in a city; or even more force, because of the bonds of kinship and beneficence; for offspring are naturally predisposed to feel affection for and to be obedient to fathers. Furthermore: education on an individual basis is in fact also superior to its communal counterpart, just as individual medical treatment is superior: rest and fasting

1180b10   are generally advantageous for patients with a fever, while for a given one perhaps not, any more than the boxing trainer will prescribe the same style of fighting for all his pupils. The particular case, then, would seem to be more exactly worked out once there is private supervision, since each person gets to a greater extent what applies to him. But the best supervision in each individual case will be provided by the doctor, or athletic trainer (or whoever it

1180b15   may be), when he has universal knowledge, knowing what applies to all cases or to cases of such-and-such a type (since the different kinds of expert know-ledge are said to be, and actually are, of common features). Granted that there is no reason, despite this, why a given individual should not be well supervised even by someone who, although no expert, on the basis of experience has made precise observations of how things turn out in each situation—just as in fact some people seem to be their own best doctors, even though they would be of no assistance to someone else; still, this presumably does not mean that 1180b20 at any rate if someone does wish to acquire technical knowledge, and the capacity to think reflectively about a subject, he should not proceed to the level of the universal, and familiarize himself with that so far as is possible, for as we have said, this is the sphere of expert knowledge. And perhaps if someone wishes to make people better—whether in large numbers or in small—by exercising supervision over them, he too should attempt to become an expert in legislation, if it's through laws that we'd become good. For the 1180b25 production of a good disposition in any given person, whoever he may be, is not a task for just anybody, but if anyone *can* do it, it is the person with knowledge, as in the case of medicine or any sphere where there is room for wise supervision.

So should we next inquire from what source, or how, one might become an expert in legislation? Or is it (if we follow the model of other kinds of 1180b30 expertise) from the experts in politics? After all, legislation seems, as we saw, to be a part of political expertise. Or is it evidently not the same for political as it is for other kinds of expertise or capacity? For in the others, those who pass on the relevant capacities and those who practise them are plainly the same individuals, as with doctors or painters; but when it comes to things political 1180b35 it's the sophists who profess to teach, but no sophist is a practitioner—rather, 1181a1 the practitioners are rather the politicians, who would seem to do what they do by means of some sort of natural ability and experience, rather than by means of thought, since they are not well known for writing or lecturing on this sort of thing (though it would presumably have been a finer thing than making speeches for the lawcourts or the assembly), or again for having made 1181a5 political experts of their own sons or others close to them. But it would have been reasonable for them to have done so, if they were capable of it; for not only is there no better legacy they could have left to their cities, but there is nothing they would rather choose than this ability to have for themselves, and so for those dearest to them. And yet experience seems to make no small 1181a10 contribution, since otherwise people would not in fact have turned into polit-ical experts through familiarity with the political sphere; hence those who aim for expert knowledge in the sphere of politics seem to need experience as well. But the sophists who profess such knowledge appear to be nowhere near teaching it. For they don't have any knowledge at all even of what sort of thing it is or what sorts of things it is about; if they did, they wouldn't put it 1181a15 down as the same as, or inferior to, rhetorical expertise, nor would they think legislating an easy thing for anyone who has collected together those laws that are well thought of, on the basis that one can then pick out the best—as if the selection were not itself a matter for acumen, and correct discrimination not the greatest task, as in questions of music. For it is those experienced in each

1181a20 sphere that discriminate between the relevant products correctly, and understand by what means and in what way they are brought to completion, and what sorts of things harmonize with what; whereas for the inexperienced it is an achievement if they simply avoid failing to observe that the product has been well or badly produced, as in the case of painting. But laws are like the

1181b1   products of political expertise; how then could someone become a legislative expert, or discern which are the best of them, *from* them? For it doesn't appear that people become medical experts, either, from written texts. It is certainly true that these texts *try* to say not only what the forms of treatment are, but

1181b5   even how patients might be cured, and how one should treat each type of patient, distinguishing the various conditions; and these texts are thought to be beneficial to those with experience, but useless to those without expert knowledge. Perhaps, then, collections of laws and constitutions too might be put to good use by those able to reflect on and to discern what is well done or the contrary, and what sorts of things fit what; but in those who go through

1181b10 such things without any skill there won't be good discrimination, unless of course by accident—and they might perhaps then get to understand more about these things. Well then, since previous thinkers left the subject of legislation unexamined, it is better, perhaps, if we ourselves start a further investigation of it, and of the constitutions in general, so that as far as possible

1181b15 that part of philosophy that deals with things human may be brought to completion.

First, then, if there is anything that has been well said on any particular point by our predecessors, let us attempt to discuss that, and then, on the basis of our collected constitutions, try to observe what sorts of things preserve and destroy cities, and what sorts have these effects on each type of constitution,

1181b20 and what the causes are whereby some cities are finely governed and others the opposite. For when we have made these observations, perhaps we shall have a better view, too, on what sort of constitution is best, and how each type is arranged, and what laws and customs it will have. Let us then make a start on the discussion.

PART III

Commentary, Word List, Select Bibliography, Indexes

Commentary

BOOK I

Ar. begins by arguing that there is a chief good for human beings (chapters 1–2, 1094a1–b11). After some methodological remarks (3–4, 1094b11–1095b13), he turns to the problem of identifying that good which everyone calls 'happiness' (4, 1095a14–18). Having examined some existing views, popular and philosophical (5–6, 1095b14–1097a14), he constructs his own account (7, 1097a15–1098b8) and shows how it diverges from and coincides with received opinions (8–9, 1098b9–1100a9). Some questions about happiness: the main one arises from the fact that human happiness is that of a mortal, subject to chance (10–11, 1100a11–1101b9). Another question: is happiness to be praised or honoured? (12, 1101b10–1102a4). Since he has defined the good for man in terms of *excellent activity of the soul* (7, 1098a16–17), the next task is to examine *excellence*, beginning with an anatomy of the soul (13, 1102a5–1103a10).

I 1, 1094a1–18

Different things aim at different goods; *the* good as that at which everything aims (1094a1–3); some ends are activities, others are products, but either way some are subordinate to others (1094a3–18).

every action [*praxis*] '*Praxis*', often a weightier word than our 'action', indicates a doing in light of which a person's life is seen as going well or not. Only rational animals are capable of it (VI. 2, 1139a20). (But there is not much reason for following those interpreters who claim to find here a special and even weightier sense of '*praxis*' that applies only to actions that are backed by the rationality of a 'decision' (on which see next note). The basis of the claim is that although non-rational or downright irrational action can be said to aim at some good (for it aims at, for example, pleasure, which is a good or anyway good 'for' the agent (see Introduction, pp. 66 and 72–3), it is hard to see how such action belongs among the 'all things' that aim at the *chief* good (1094a3). Probably, however, Ar. is speaking broadly here and simply not thinking of deviant or imperfect cases. The

1094a1

261

present emphasis on universality is more about *kinds* of endeavour that in some sense aim for the chief good, rather than instances.)

1094a2 **undertaking** The term is *prohairesis*: Ar. will give it a stricter meaning ('decision', on which see Introduction, pp. 42 ff.) in the context of his theory of deliberate action; III. 2–3 (1111b4–1113a14), VI. 2 (1139a17–b13).

1094a2 **seems to seek some good** (a) Ar. invokes received views. The 'seems to' does not indicate doubt on his part. (b) To say, for example, that medical expertise 'seeks' the good which is health is not to make a psychological claim about physicians' motives for doing their work. It means, rather, that as physicians they are judged successful or not by their success in promoting the good which is health.

1094a2–3 **Because of that, people are right to affirm that the good is 'that which all things seek** [ephiesthai]**'** (a) The argument turns on a logical contrast between *some* good and *the* good. This is an example of a general distinction, familiar in Ar.'s scholastic circle, between what is F *in a way*, or *with some qualification*, and what is F *without qualification*, or *simpliciter*. *Some* good is the specific good sought by some given kind of project, one among others. Since there are as many kinds of good as there are kinds of project, the good in each case must be marked by a qualifying expression, as in 'the good *of the body*' or 'the good *which is health*'. '*The* good', by contrast, means 'the good *simpliciter*, or without qualification'. The argument is: since specific projects each seek some specific good, the good without qualification must be what is sought by any project whatsoever. The premiss is uncontroversial, but it supports, at most, the hypothetical conclusion: if there is some end such that any project whatsoever seeks it, then this is the good without qualification. *The* good (without qualification) is the topic of practical philosophy or ethics. (b) **people are right to affirm** Ar. may be thinking of Eudoxus (Eudoxus of Cnidus, c.390–340, was a mathematician, astronomer, philosopher, and a member of Plato's Academy). At x. 2, 1172b9–10 Ar. says 'Eudoxus used to think that pleasure was the good because he saw every sort of creature seeking (*ephiesthai*) it'. Note that Eudoxus understands 'seeks' psychologically, as = 'desires'. (Cf. Plato, *Philebus* 20d8–10.)

1094a3 **But there appears to be a certain difference among ends** i.e. among objectives. 'Ends' here is virtually synonymous with 'goods'. The difference between the two kinds of ends is most easily made out in relation to kinds of *expert knowledge* (*technē*): in some, the end is the activity that constitutes exercise of the expertise (so *riding* stands to *horsemanship*); in others, the end is a product which survives the activity (so *bridles* to the *bridle-making* skill). The distinction prepares us for a point made later: *the* good is an activity (see 5, 1095b31–3; 7, 1098a5–6; 8, 1098b31–1099a7).

Where there are ends over and above the activities ... the products are by **their nature better than the activities** e.g. it is better to have harvest without ploughing than the other way round.

the ends of the controlling ones are more desirable than the ends under **them** So far he has spoken only of subordination of expertise etc. to expertise, but this is grounded on the subordination mentioned here, of the end of one expertise to that of another.

It makes no difference ... over and above these One end can be subordinate to another regardless of kind (e.g. bridles (i.e. the product-end of bridle-making) are subordinate to riding (i.e. the activity-end of horsemanship), and riding is in turn subordinate to military victory (i.e. the product-end of generalship)). Ar. is seeking to establish the general point that if expertise E_1 is subordinate to expertise E_2, this is because the former's end is subordinate to the latter's. This will enable him to argue that the existence of an expertise to which all others are subordinate proves that there is a chief end (2, 1094a26–b7).

I 2, 1094a18–b11

If there is an end wished for because of itself and other things because of it, it is the chief good (1094a18–22); knowing about it is of practical importance (1094a22–5); it is the object of the most sovereign type of expertise, i.e. the political kind, since this is in charge of the others (1094a26–b7); the inquiry about the chief good is the same, whether one aims to benefit one individual or a city-state or a nation (1094b7–11).

If then there is some end ... chief good The antecedent of this conditional consists of three clauses together with a parenthetical argument in support of the third:

> (C1) There is an end, *T*, which we wish for (*boulesthai*) because of itself;
> (C2) We wish for everything else for the sake of *T*;
> (C3) We do not choose (*hairesthai*) everything for the sake of something else;
>   (for (P) if we did, the process would go on to infinity etc.).

C1 says much the same as C3; hence like C3 it is grounded in the argument in parentheses. But C2 is controversial and not supported by the parenthetical argument (or by anything else in the context). For the necessity of *some* stopping point for a chain of wishes (or choices: here Ar. seems to use the terms interchangeably; see also 'desire' (*orexis*) at 21) does not entail what C2 implies: that all chains lead to one and the same stopping point. The conditional's consequent is:

> (C4) It is clear that this (sc. the unique ultimate end) is the chief good;

but this cannot be inferred without C2.

On one interpretation (Int₁), the passage is meant to prove C4, and to establish:

(C5) There is a chief good.

Then comes an argument showing *what* the chief good is: it is the end of the political expertise (1094a24–b11). According to Int$_1$, C3 or C1 (backed by P) is meant to support C2. (Some scholars believe that Ar. rests C2 on C3 or C1 through a fallacious inference from 'Every chain of desires ends at some point' to 'There is some point at which every chain of desires ends'.) So, in effect, Ar. affirms all three parts of the antecedent and therefore affirms C4 and C5.

Alternatively (Int$_2$), C2 is unsupported and remains hypothetical, so that C4 is not affirmed. On this interpretation there is no separate argument for C5, which instead is implicitly proved when it is proved what the chief good is (i.e. since it is the objective of political expertise, *which exists*—being in fact practised however imperfectly—the chief good is a real objective).

1094a20–1 **for if *that* is the case . . . empty and vain**   If we choose each thing only for the sake of something else, the chain of wishes which is our chain of reasons for choosing *X* would either come full circle or trail to infinity. (Ar. does not consider the former possibility, but cf. the arguments of *Posterior Analytics* i. 3 against infinite and circular demonstrative chains.) In either case desire would be 'empty' because if I desire *A* only for the sake of *X* and *X* for itself, we say that *X* is what I really desire in desiring *A*, and is what would satisfy me. If I desire *A* for the sake of *B*, *B* for the sake of *C*, etc., and nothing for its own sake, then I desire without its being the case that anything would satisfy me. (In the circular case, I could actually gain all the things I desire, but since I want none of them for its own sake, I gain nothing I really want.)

1094b6 **the end of this expertise will contain** [*periechein*] **those of the rest**   Not: the other goods are in the chief one as parts in a whole; but: (pursuit of) the chief good should limit (pursuit of) the others.

1094b7–11 **For even if the good is the same . . . a political inquiry in a way**   Ar. thinks that the good is the same for a single person and for a city (i.e. city-state, *polis*), not in the sense that the city, like the person, is an individual that can have a good, but in the sense that the question 'What is the chief human good?' concerns anyone organizing human life, whether at the private or communal level (cf. x. 9, 1180b1–2, and 24; see Introduction, pp. 10–11). The reason for the qualifier 'in a way' may be (1) that the usual paradigm of *political expertise* is administrative, rather than reflective about fundamental principles (cf. vi. 8, 1141b24–9); or (2) that the usual paradigm has to do only with public life.

1094b10 **to do it for a nation or for cities is finer and more godlike**   (*a*) Ar.'s usual context in the *Ethics* and *Politics* is the politically autonomous city-state (*polis*). Many such states made up the Greek 'nation' (*ethnos*) on account of shared language and culture and (in many cases) ancestral ties. (*b*) 'godlike' = *theios*, also translated 'divine' (e.g. at vi. 7, 1141b4; x. 7, 1177a15–16 and 28).

I 3, 1094b11–1095a13

The subject matter sets limits to the degree of clarity and precision one should expect, because of its variability (1094b11–1095a2); a suitable student needs experience of life and to be self-disciplined (1095a2–13).

Having established the reality of his topic, Ar. considers what his audience should expect from, and what they should bring to, an inquiry into it.

1. They should not expect mathematical exactness, nor, failing that, conclude that there is no objective truth in ethics. Ethics is full of generalizations, such as 'lying is to be avoided', 'wealth is advantageous', which are not undermined by acknowledged counter-examples (1094b11–1095a2). The audience, therefore, should have had practical experience (since this is what enables one to decide, in a given case, whether an ethical generalization applies to it, and to see why not, if not).

2. They should be self-disciplined, since otherwise the practical lessons of the inquiry will be thrown away (1095a4–11).

Comment: The *Ethics* contains many formal statements which are not rough generalizations: e.g. the proposition that moral virtue is a median disposition, the definition of happiness, the classification of parts of the soul, the conclusion that pleasure is not a process. Why, then, does he characterize ethical truth wholesale as only 'for the most part' (1094b21)? Presumably because by themselves those exact statements have no practical bearing, and ethics is essentially practical. The roughness is an immediate consequence of the practicality.

precision [*to akribes*]   The more self-sufficient an account is, i.e. the less it depends on tacit assumptions, the more precise it is; cf. III 3, 1112b1.   *1094b13*

so that they come to seem fine and just by convention alone, and not by nature   For the view that moral values are man-made rules, see Plato, *Republic* I (Thrasymachus) and *Gorgias* (Callicles). Ar.'s point is that we need not resort to this theory to explain why 'the same' thing is right for one person and wrong for another, since the objective right or wrong of the action varies with circumstances. No one would argue that the value of health is 'only a matter of convention' on the ground that illness sometimes confers advantages.   *1094b16*

I 4, 1095a14–1095b13

The chief good is generally called *happiness*, but there is no agreement on what this is (1095a17–22); a range of views briefly scanned (1095a22–30); we need to be clear about the difference between arguing from first principles (*archai*) and working towards them, and about the difference between what is knowable to us and knowable without qualification (1095a30–b3); since we must start from what is knowable to us, the student of political questions must be a well brought up person (1095b4–13).

1095a17–20   **Pretty well most people . . . the same thing as being happy**   From now on Ar. will often refer to the chief human good as 'happiness' (*eudaimonia*); see Introduction, pp. 12 and 14–15.

1095a25–6   **out of consciousness of their own ignorance they are in awe of those who say something impressive and over their heads.**   Ar. may be implying that these awestruck ones do not understand about inquiry. They are right to realize that popular views are inadequate, but fail to see that this is because the views are only starting points to be modified as inquiry proceeds, not rejected completely. They therefore think that 'the right answer' is something entirely removed from the popular views. (See 1095a30–b1, with comment.)

1095a26–8   **Some people used to think . . . cause for all these too of their being good**   The reference is to the Platonists, whose views will be discussed in 6, 1096a11–1097a14. See Plato, *Republic* VI, 506d–509b, on the Form or 'idea' of the good. On the showing of the present passage, the Platonic theory does not disagree that the 'obvious things that anyone would recognize' (22) are good, but refuses to take their goodness as self-explanatory. Ar., too, thinks of *the* good as cause or ground of the values of other goods (cf. 12, 1102a3–4), although he rejects the Platonic conception of its metaphysical status. For Ar., being cause or ground of value covers a variety of relations; his chief good—or rather, its main ingredient—is excellent rational activity, and wealth is good when it is a means to such activity, pleasure when it is pleasure in such activity, friendship when friendly interaction consists of such activity. Various other desirables are good in so far as they adorn such activity, or their absence casts a shadow on it (8, 1099a33). See also 12, 1102a3–4 with note.

1095a30–b1   **we must keep in mind . . . towards the turn or in the reverse direction**   To claim that so-and-so is *the* good for man in the above value-causal sense is to claim to have identified the theoretical first principle (*archē*) of ethics. (*Archē* also means 'starting point', 'beginning'.) But this would be the result, not the starting point (*archē*), of inquiry seeking to identify the chief good. Since the first principle becomes, in turn, a new starting point for tracing the goodness-'transmitting' relations in which *the* good stands to other goods, we must take care to distinguish these directions of thought. A person who thinks that one or other (or the collectivity) of the plain and obvious goods is the final answer to the question 'What is the chief good?' has shut himself off from inquiring. So has a person who sees that the chief good is not any of the above, but thinks that inquiry must start from identification of it.

1095a32   **Plato too used to raise difficulties . . . he would inquire**   As Burnet points out, the wording suggests personal recollection of Plato's discussions.

1095b2–3   **there is what is knowable *in relation to us*, and what is knowable *without qualification***   See note on 1, 1094a2–3. 'Knowable *in relation to us*' applies to what we can know unsystematically on the basis of ordinary experience; 'know-able *without qualification*' to the first principle(s) of a field of inquiry. In general, '*X* without qualification' signals what Ar. regards as the primary use of '*X*'. The first principles are primarily knowable because knowledge of them makes one a more *perfect* knower of the rest of the field. Cf. *Posterior Analytics* I. 2, 71b9–72a8, on first principles of theoretical science.

Consequently, in order to listen appropriately to discussion about what is fine and just . . . one must have been well brought up   The pre-systematic knowledge relevant to the present inquiry is the decent person's ability to discriminate good and bad, right and wrong. These intuitions are the phenomena or obvious things (cf. 1095b6) from which we start (see Introduction, pp. 11–12, 13–14).   *1095b4–6*

For the starting point [*archē***] is *that* it is so, and if this were sufficiently clear to us . . . there will be no need to know in addition *why***   Although good upbringing provides proper starting points for ethical inquiry, it may not ensure that we always make the best decisions (*prohaireseis*) in life. For this, we may sometimes need to understand the *why*, the principle that explains why the original intuitions were correct. Once philosophy shows the ground of the values of well brought up people, it can also make them aware, by logical extension, of otherwise neglected values (for an example, see Introduction, pp. 76 and 53–4). If these had always been 'sufficiently clear' from the beginning, there would have been no practical need to articulate the principle.   *1095b6–7*

Hesiod   *Works and Days* 293–7.   *1095b9*

I 5, 1095b14–1096a10

Views about the chief good are suggested by three ideal lives commonly proposed: the life of pleasure, the political life, the life of reflection (1095b14–19); the values implied by the first two ideals are criticized, discussion of the third is postponed; the moneymaking life is out of the question (1095b19–1096a10).

This critical discussion of three standard ideals brings out several criteria to be met by a satisfactory candidate for the title of 'happiness'. (Here the life of pleasure replaces that of moneymaking in the traditional trio. The latter is not a candidate, because its focus is not an end in itself; 1096a5–9.)

from which we digressed   i.e. at 4, 1095a30.   *1095b14*

pleasure   Here Ar. goes along with the vulgar assumption that the paradigm pleasures are those of physical indulgence; this is usually behind the view that pleasure tends to conflict with other values. Cf. 8, 1099a24–9, on the Delian inscription.   *1095b16*

the political life   i.e. that of an active citizen, participating in government.   *1095b18*

the life of reflection [*bios theorētikos***]**   often translated 'contemplative life'.   *1095b19*

267

1095b19–20   most . . . decide in favour of a life that belongs to grazing cattle   Ar. cannot realistically mean that most of them live such a life; rather, it is their ideal. Their lives manifest their ideal, according to line 15, but presumably without exemplifying it in most cases.

1095b21–2   in high places . . . Sardanapallus   Ar. may be recalling his experience at the court of Macedon. Sardanapallus (Asshur-bani-pal), the 7th-century BCE ruler of Assyria, was legendary for self-indulgence. Cf. x. 6, 1176b12–18.

1096a3   the books that have circulated   For example, perhaps, his own early work *Protrepticus*, an exhortation to philosophize. Large fragments survive.

1096a4   in what follows   In fact this discussion does not occur until x. 7–8 (1177a12–1179a32).

1096a7–8   one might be more inclined to take as ends the things mentioned before   On some things qualifying as ends (*telē*) more than others, cf. 7, 1097a25–34, where some ends turn out to be more complete (*teleios*; lit. 'final', 'end-like') than others.

1096a9   But it appears that they are not what we are looking for either   This remark does not include the thinker's activity, which has not been discussed.

1096a9–10   and yet there are many established arguments that focus on them   Perhaps his point is that it is surprising that 'the things mentioned before' have been taken so seriously in discussion.

II 6, 1096a11–1097a14

Objections to the notion of the chief good as a Platonic universal: preamble (1096a11–17); seriality among goods (1096a17–23); 'good is said in many ways' (1096a23–9); the plurality of kinds of knowledge (1096a29–34); the 'itself' locution adds nothing, nor does 'eternal' (1096a34–b5); remark about the Pythagoreans and Speusippus (1096b5–8); a problem arising from the distinction between what are goods in themselves and what are goods in relation to the former (1096b8–26); alternative possible explanations of the non-homonymy of 'good' (1096b27–31); anyway, the Platonic Good is not practicable; nor does it help in achieving any practicable good (1096b32–1097a13).

1096a11–17   *Preamble:* Ar. is about to launch a series of technical objections to the Platonic doctrine that the proper referent of the title 'chief good' is a universal Form or 'Idea' (*eidos* or *idea*: Ar. uses these terms interchangeably when speaking of Platonic Forms) which exists apart from all particular good things, being the metaphysical cause of their goodness (see 4, 1095a26–8 with note). But: **such an investigation goes against the grain because it was friends of ours who introduced the forms** (12–13)   Ar. spent the first twenty years of his adult life in

Plato's Academy, leaving only upon Plato's death in 348/347 BCE. Even so, the present expression of compunction is extraordinary. (Elsewhere Ar. argues against Platonist theories, not pulling punches any more than he will here, but without hint of apology.) The explanation may lie in the context. For Plato, the ideal life is that of the thinker. Plato's career and those of some of his associates in the Academy were star examples of such a life. Ar. is not yet ready to produce his own arguments in favour of this ideal (see 5, 1096a4–5), and he is about to argue against the Platonic doctrine of the chief good. Some in the audience might have taken the doctrinal difference to imply rejection of Plato's personal values. (Socrates sometimes argued as if knowing the true theory of the good were necessary and sufficient for living the good life (cf. *EE* I. 5, 1216b2–10): which suggests that fundamental theoretical differences about the nature of the good commit the theorists to fundamentally different lived values.) It was a common-place that friends share values (e.g. VIII. 9, 1159b31; but cf. IX. 6, 1167a22–8 for a careful circumscription of the areas relevant to the like-mindedness of friends). So by declaring his friendship with the Platonists, Aristotle clears the way for his own final position on the ideal life.

to destroy even what is one's own This may indicate that (1) Ar. himself once *1096a15* accepted the Platonic doctrine which he is about to refute; or that (2) because of his intimacy with Plato he understands it as if from the inside. But (3) it may simply be a general remark.

while both friends and the truth are dear, the right thing [*hosion*] **is to honour** *1096a16* **the truth first** For the sentiment, cf. Plato himself, *Phaedo* 91c; *Republic* x, 595b–c and 607c. '*hosion*' implies that the contrary action would be sinful. Ar. may intend this religious overtone, since to him god is pure intellect, and human intellectual activity, conducted purely for the sake of truth, is a kind of worship; see 1096a24–5 and x. 8, 1179a22–32 with notes.

Objection I. (1) Where particular *K*s constitute a series ordered by priority– *1096a17–23* posteriority, there is no Form *K* which explains their common *K*-ness; (2) the categories of being, Substance (or: 'what it is', lines 20 and 24), Quality (20 and 25), Quantity (25), Relative (20–1 and 26), Time (26), Place (27), etc., form a series (or at any rate Relative is posterior to Substance); (3) the term 'good' is said in each of these categories (cf. 23–7); therefore (4) there is no common (i.e. universal) Form of good.

Comments: (*a*) Premiss (1) was a tenet of the Platonists themselves ('those who introduced this view', 17). The argument for it was that if there were a Form of *K* it would be prior to the particulars constituting the series; hence the first item of the series would not be first. (*b*) Although the doctrine of the categories of being in (2) is traditionally ascribed to Aristotle (see his treatise *Categories*), it was fore-shadowed by Platonic distinctions, and seems to have been common ground for many in the Academy. (*c*) A 'relative' is not a relation in the modern sense, but a term whose definition requires reference to a specific other term: thus *slave* is *of-a-master*; *useful* is *for-an-end*. Being a slave, or any other relative, is inessential to the substantial individual to which it applies. (*d*) On the meaning of (3), see comments on objection II. (*e*) The inference to (4) depends on the assumption that since the categories form a series, a corresponding series of goods arises from the fact that 'good' is said in the different categories.

1096a23–9   **Objection II.** (1) 'Good' is said in each of the categories of being; (2) a genuine, unitary, universal would occur in just one category; hence (3) there is no universal corresponding to 'good'.

Comment: The argument is directed against the assumption that the one word 'good' conveys one universal. The exact interpretation of (1) is disputed, but the main point is that information carried by 'good' varies with the category signified. In the domain of how things are qualified, 'good' picks out *excellent* (or *just* or *courageous* etc.); in the domain of how much, it picks out *moderate*, i.e. *neither too much nor too little*; in the domains of time and place respectively it picks out *the right moment* (*kairos*), and *suitable habitation*; in the domain of relatives it picks out *useful*. In the domain of substance, it picks out *god* or *intellect* (since apart from these (if indeed they are different; the connective joining them may indicate alternative expressions) there is no substance such that to be it is *eo ipso* to be good).

1096a29–34   **Objection III.** (1) A single Form defines a single field of knowledge; hence (2) a single Form of good implies a single type of knowledge concerned with all goods. But (3) in reality, there are many kinds of practical knowledge, even for the same category.

Comment: Premiss (1) was accepted by the Platonists. But they could have replied that the different kinds of practical knowledge are all branches of a single science of the good.

1096a34–b5   **Objection IV.** Nothing is gained by talking of an '*X*-itself' (Platonic jargon for 'the Form of *X*'), if (as the Platonists also hold) the definition of *X*-itself is the same as the definition of *X*, which applies to particular *X*s. For in so far as, for example, the good-itself and a particular good fit the definition of good, the former is not more truly called 'good' than the latter. (But in that case it is not the chief good.) That it is eternal does not affect the point.

Comments: (*a*) The assumption that there is a definition of good, as there is of man, is *ad homines*; for according to Ar., a definable term must belong in a single category. (*b*) This may seem a surprising argument if directed against Plato himself, since it is a commonplace of the *Dialogues* that particular *X*s fall short of the Form of *X* in respect of deserving to be called '*X*'. However, (*c*) perhaps objection IV is directed against a possible Platonist response to objection II, as follows: 'Good' as applied to particulars occurs in different categories, but the same is not true of 'good-itself'. This applies only to the Form. And since what is good-itself is obviously good (for it is the chief good), the term 'good' that is applied to the good-itself is not one that belongs to different categories. Thus it is a genuinely unitary term. If this is the position opposed in objection IV, the objection correctly notes its inconsistency with the assumption, attributed here to the Platonists, that *what* we say (i.e. what the definition conveys) of particulars, and *what* we say of the Form, in calling them (respectively) 'good' is the same. It is irrelevant that the particulars live up to the single definition less well than the Form. (*d*) It is debatable that an eternal good is not on that account better than a transient one. It surely would be, if it could be possessed; but see 1096b33–5.

The Pythagoreans ... in the column of goods   The followers of Pythagoras 1096b5–6
(6th-century BCE mathematician, philosopher, and ascetic) based their metaphysics on pairs of contraries forming two columns:

Limit	Unlimited
Odd	Even
One	Many, etc. (*Metaph.* I. 5, 986a22–6)

Ar. refers to the left-hand one as 'the column of goods' even though Good itself appears as an item in it lower down. His comparison with Platonism presumably has to do with the relations in each theory between Good and One. Plato, Ar. tells us, identified them (*Metaph.* XIV. 4, 1091b13–15), whereas the Pythagoreans distinguished them. We can only guess why Ar. prefers the Pythagorean theory to Plato's.

Speusippus   Plato's nephew and successor as head of the Academy.   1096b7

Objection V. Ar. now concedes that the Platonic postulate of the universal Form of 1096b8–26
the good is not meant to explain the goodness of all non-metaphysical goods: the Platonists distinguished things that are good in themselves or per se (8–16) from ones that are good because they promote the former, and the Form was invoked only in connection with the per se ones. Ar. sets up a dilemma: either there are, or there are not, goods per se apart from the Form itself. If there are not, the Form 'has no point' (since it was postulated to account for the goodness of other goods per se). If there are, the explanation of why they are good should be the same for all of them (since the Platonist explanation is that they all participate in the same Form). But this is not so. For example, what wisdom is differs from what pleasure is (the definitions are different), and each is good because of what it is. Hence there is no single universal Form of good (16–26).

Comments: (*a*) It is a sufficient condition for something's being a good per se that it is desirable not merely as a means to or vehicle of something else. Thus pleasure and honour are examples, even though not all pleasure is good, and the value of honour is not self-explanatory (X. 5, 1175b24–8; I. 5, 1095b26–9). (*b*) Objection V brings out the fact that, on the Platonic theory, it is self-contradictory to assert that there are per se goods other than the Form of good. For if each is simply a vehicle for the one universal Form, then whoever has one of them, e.g. wisdom, is put in touch with the same good as if he had another, e.g. honour. But in that case they are not good per se since the distinctive nature of each is irrelevant to its value.

1096b26–9   **But then on what principle *is* it predicated ... other goods, other contexts?** Having emphasized the diversity of kinds of goods in four out of five of the objections so far, Ar. now registers the need for an explanation of their all counting as 'good' even though the word gives different information in each case, yet is not just randomly equivocal. The first two possibilities (if indeed they are different) he suggests offer considerable latitude, since 'derives from' and 'converges on' (alternative expressions) cover a variety of relations. Thus if wisdom were the primary good, honour is good when wisdom is its object, or when it is accorded wisely; and pleasure is good when it is pleasure in the exercise of wisdom, or of some power that contributes to wisdom, etc. In this way, wisdom would be the principle of value, i.e. the cause of the goodness of other goods. See 4, 1095a26–8, and 12, 1102a3–4 with notes.

1096b28–9   **as sight is in the case of the body, intelligence is in the case of the soul**   An analogy familiar to Platonists: see *Republic* VI. 506d ff. According to this, the second suggestion, although 'good' is not said univocally of sight and of intellect, it is applied in accordance with a single principle grounded in the analogy. Another relevant analogy would be: as intellect is to the category of Substance, so excellence is to that of Quality, the useful-for to that of Relative, etc.

1096b30–1   **But perhaps for now we should leave these questions aside ... a different sort of inquiry**   Not only would a discussion of the variety of uses of 'good' be logically technical, but it would have to take account of the non-practicable goodness of god and the universe (on which see *Metaph.* XII. 10, 1075a11–24; XIV. 4, 1091a30 ff.). Perhaps analogy would play an important role in explaining the applicability of 'good' to eternal and also non-eternal things.

1096b31–5   *Objection VI.* Even if it exists, the Platonic Form of good is not the chief good we are seeking, because (being part of the eternal structure of reality) it is not doable or capable of being acquired.

1096b35– 1097a13   *Objection VII.* (*a*) Nor does it function as an ideal model that helps experts such as physicians and carpenters to realize their ends. In fact (*b*), what is sought is never a generality at all: for the physician, it is *this* patient's health in each case.

Comment: both parts of this objection also apply to Ar.'s own account of the chief human good, and perhaps would apply to any account of it. To (*a*) the Platonist can reply that knowledge of the Form of the good should guide the *political* expert; this is the doctrine of the *Republic*. And later on Ar. applies (*b*) to his own results; see x. 9, 1180b7–13.

I 7, 1097a15–1098b8

This chapter contains two quite distinct lines of argument about the chief practicable good, the first (1097a15–b21) showing that it is happiness, the second (1097b22–1098b8) defining it and commenting on the definition.

The various goods are ends (*telē*) of specific activities, so the chief practicable good should be the end (or ends) of all of them (1097a15–24); But some ends are more complete (*teleios*) than others (1097a25–34); happiness more than any other good satisfies the requirements for being complete without qualification (1097a34–b6); it is also (as the chief good should be) self-sufficient (1097b6–16); and most desirable when not counted in with other goods (1097b20).

1097a15–b21

Completeness, self-sufficiency, and being most desirable when not counted in with other goods were recognized features of the chief good that were used in debate not so much to characterize it as to show that certain contenders are *not* the chief good. For the first two, see Plato, *Philebus* 20d–e; for a criterion rather like the third, see *NE* x. 2, 1172b28–34.

this will be the practicable good   i.e. the highest practicable good. The argument echoes I. 1, 1094a1–3.

1097a23

and if there are more than one, it will be these   Some scholars take this to imply that if the chief good is not something unitary, it is a *combination* of different kinds of goods which meet the two criteria jointly, not severally. If so, the happy life is characterized by the combination. However, in x. 6–8 (1176b30–1179a32), a sketch that is reminiscent of Book I (cf. x. 6–7 with I. 5, 1095b14–19; x. 7, 1177a27–b22, with I. 7, 1097a3–b15; x. 7, 1177b25, with I. 7, 1098a18), Ar. recognizes a *disjunction* of kinds of happy life, each characterized by a unitary good that conforms to the two criteria, although one conforms more exactly than the other. The present passage points briefly to the possibility that the chief good is plural, leaving open whether conjunctive or disjunctive. See 1097a30 with notes.

1097a23–4

Thus as the argument turns . . . same point   i.e. where we were at the outset of the *NE*; see I. 2, 1094a18–22.

1097a24

Since, then, the ends [*telē*] are evidently more than one . . . not all are complete   An end is 'complete' (*teleion*) to the extent that attaining it is reaching complete satisfaction. *Teleios* also means 'perfect'.

1097a25–8

and if there are more such things than one, the most complete of these   (a) The possibility of *several* complete things seems to be what Ar. had in mind in speaking of the possibility of the chief good as plural (22–4). But now it is assumed that one of these is *most* complete, and the reference of 'the highest

1097a30

good' ('the best', 28) shifts from the plurality to its most complete member. Cf. 8, 1099a29–31. (b) Note that it was after Ar. had characterized the chief good as 'the end of *all* practical undertakings' that he raised the possibility of its being plural (22). So if it is plural, it is the universal practical end (i.e. the end of political expertise) *as a plurality*. Hence if the chief good is plural, and if one member M of the plurality P now takes on the title 'highest good' as satisfying the criteria more completely than the other(s), we are not entitled to infer that M *alone*, after all, has the status of universal practical end, nor that it is the ultimate end of the other member(s) of P. (c) Since Ar.'s highest good does turn out to be plural, this is as good a place as any to consider whether its structure is conjunctive or disjunctive. The question is complex, since we must consider the highest good both as (1) an ideal for the political expertise, and as (2) realized in an individual life. As to (1): it is clear that Ar. holds that the task of public policy makers is to ensure conditions for the *conjoint* realization in society of the different forms of the highest good. As to (2): no doubt it is possible to live a life in which these forms of the highest good coexist, but on balance (the interpretation is disputed) Book X seems to present them as *exclusive alternatives* for an individual considering the personal question of how to live. Each of the forms is the logical centrepiece of one distinctive kind of life. So from this point of view the highest good is disjunctive. But since (in this interpreter's view) the alternatives have much in common, the path of realization is common too, much of the way (see Introduction, pp. 79–80).

1097a30–1 we say that what is worth pursuing for itself is more complete than what is worth pursuing because of something else   Understand the less complete end here as worth pursuing *only* because of something else.

1097a33–4 what is complete *without qualification* is what is always desirable in itself and never because of something else   (a) 'Complete without qualification' is by contrast with 'complete, but only by comparison with something else less complete'. (b) On this analysis, an end's being complete without qualification is consistent with its not being the end to which everything else is subordinate. Logically, there could be more than one end of unqualified completeness.

1097a34–b5 Happiness seems most of all to be like this . . . supposing that we shall be happy through them   Ar.'s conclusion that happiness above all is complete without qualification is based on ordinary attitudes according to which (1) we should sooner have honour or pleasure etc. than not, even unaccompanied by other things necessary for happiness; and (2) if asked why we want one or another of them, we are as likely to say 'So as to be happy' as 'For itself'; whereas (3) we cannot make sense of wanting happiness because of something other than itself. Since observation of these attitudes precedes Ar.'s philosophical analysis of the chief good and of happiness, the reader is not justified in inferring that Ar. at this point endorses any particular interpretation the ordinary person might give to the words 'I want (say) honour *for the sake of* happiness' (1097b4). For example, it is possible that the ordinary person thinks that happiness is a collection of goods, of which honour is one, and that this is why it makes sense to 'want honour for the sake of happiness'. But there is no reason here to read this into Ar.'s thinking. If one asks 'How is happiness related to the other intrinsic goods?', the gist of the present passage is that 'happiness' constitutes a better answer than any of them to the question 'What is the chief good?' (For the point of establishing this, see Introduction, pp. 14–15.) This leaves open exactly how the highest good is related to other intrinsic goods.

the complete good seems to be self-sufficient   Since the highest good must render one self-sufficient, Ar. calls *it* 'self-sufficient' on the principle that the cause of something's being *F* has first claim to the predicate.   *1097b7–8*

since man is by nature a civic being [*politikon*]   Ar. holds that human nature comes to full development only in the context of the city-state (*polis*); cf. *Politics* I. 2, 1252a24–1253a29.   *1097b11*

an infinite series   Absurd because we are concerned with a *practicable* ideal, and because infinite commitments exclude self-sufficiency.   *1097b13*

on another occasion   Ar. does not return to this question.   *1097b14*

the 'self-sufficient' . . . and lacking in nothing   This suggests a widely inclusive chief good. See 1098a18 with comment.   *1097b14–15*

and moreover [we also think of it as] **most desirable of all things, it not being counted with other goods . . . always more desirable**   This appears to offer a third reason (additional to completeness and self-sufficiency) for accepting that happiness is the highest good. Different construals are possible, yielding opposite meanings: (1) The phrase 'it not being counted with other goods' (*mē sunarith-moumenon*) introduces a necessary condition for thinking happiness the most desirable thing. (2) The phrase introduces a ground for thinking this. On (1), happiness is the most desirable *single* good, but not the most desirable good, since the combination of it plus any of the others would be more desirable. So understood, the passage is inconsistent with the main purpose of the chapter so far, which is to show that the highest (i.e. best, most desirable) human good is rightly identified with *happiness*. On (2), the preferable interpretation, happiness can be seen to be the most desirable thing from the assumed fact that (pre-reflectively) it does not lend itself to being counted along with other goods. Since no other good can be added to it to make a more desirable combination, its status as maximally desirable is assured. Cf. x. 2, 1172b23–34, where a similar principle is used to rule out certain claimants for title of 'highest good'. On this interpretation, lines 17–20, which envisage happiness as being part of a more desirable combination *were* it 'counted in with the least of other goods', invoke a necessarily false hypothesis.   *1097b16–20*

1097b22–1098b8   The chief good is defined by reference to the human function (1097b22–33); the function is practical rational activity of the soul in accordance with excellence or the best excellence (1097b33–1098a18); the human good is this activity in a complete life (1098a18–20); the above is only an outline (1098a20–6); do not expect too much precision (1098a26–33); and do not always seek reasons why, e.g. for starting points (1098a26–1098b3); ways of establishing starting points, and the importance of getting a good one (1098b3–8).

1097b23–4   **a more distinct statement of what it is is still required**   'It' refers to the chief good, not to happiness.

1097b28–33   **So does a carpenter . . . a characteristic function for a human being too**   An inductive argument from these examples to the case of man would be weak, but perhaps the examples are meant rather to illustrate the concept of *characteristic function* (*ergon*). That the being or essential nature of an individual is expressed through a typifying activity is the central doctrine of Ar.'s metaphysics.

1097b33–
1098a3   **For being alive is obviously shared . . . a practical [*praktikos*] sort of life of what possesses reason**   (*a*) The last four words are logically redundant (they are there to introduce the division made in the next sentence), since practicality is essentially rational. Ar. regards thinking as a kind of living (*zoē*) or way of being alive; other ways are sense-perception, growth, and metabolism. (*b*) Some interpreters see a conflict between 'practical' here and the Book x position that the most complete happiness is theoretical reflection. However, at *Politics* VII. 3 Ar. defends the reflective ideal from the charge that it idealizes 'the doing (*prattein*, cognate to *praktikos*, *praxis*) of nothing' (1325a21–3); he maintains that theoretical thinking is properly termed 'a sort of *praxis*' (i.e. doing) (1325b16–21). His argument there (very compressed, and requiring a colon after *telos* in line 21) is that since theoretical activity is one of the fundamental ends of human life, it is a form of *eupraxia* (i.e. doing well: the word is synonymous with *eudaimonia*; cf. *NE* I. 4, 1095a19–20), and therefore is a form of *praxis*. A less verbal consideration, and one that does not depend on passages elsewhere, is that any human activity counts as *praxis* if it is serious and governed by standards of excellence, and if engaging in it is backed by the judgement that this is worth while; see note on 1, 1094a1.

1098a4–5   **of this, one element . . . and itself thinks**   This distinction is explained in ch. 13.

1098a6   **active life**   Active by contrast with quiescent. Even when we fail to engage actively in anything, we continue alive as practical beings (e.g. we can be held responsible for what happens through our inactivity).

1098a6–7   **for this seems to be called a practical life in the more proper sense**   This is a logical or metaphysical point, not one about existing linguistic usage. (If it were, it would be as incorrect for the Greek of Ar.'s time as it is for the English of ours.) In general, the capacity for *F* is *F* in a sense posterior to that in which the activity is *F*, because the capacity is defined as being for that activity.

If the function of a human being is activity of soul in accordance with reason, or not apart from reason . . . the human good turns out to be activity of soul in accordance with excellence   *1098a7–17*   (*a*) At lines 7, 12, and 16, 'if' has the force of 'since'. (*b*) That the function of man is activity of *soul* (*psuchē*) follows from its being a way of being actively alive (1097b33–1098a3), since the *psuchē* is the life-principle of a living thing. (But not all activity manifests life. In Aristotelian physics a stone, which is inanimate, is active in accordance with its nature when it falls.) (*c*) It is not clear what the difference is between 'in accordance with reason' (*kata logon*) and 'not apart from reason' (*mē aneu logou*). If one implies a more intimate relation than the other, it may be that they refer respectively to the activity of the strictly rational part of the soul, and that of the part that merely 'participates in reason' (see 13, 1102b14–1103a3). 'accompanied by reason' (14) presumably covers both relations, if there is a difference. Cf. VI. 13, 1144b26–8 with note. (*d*) **and the function, we say, of a given sort of practitioner and a good [*spoudaios*] practitioner of that sort is generically the same**   The basic meaning of '*spoudaios*' is 'zealous', 'enthusiastic', 'serious', 'committed'. That the word is often synonymous with 'good' shows that, for its users, it was an analytic truth that excellence requires dedication. (*e*) **when a difference in respect of excellence is added to the function**   i.e. a difference from other instances of the same kind of function. (*f*) In Plato's and Aristotle's philosophical usage (1) to say a quality of a given kind of thing is an 'excellence' (*aretē*, often translated 'virtue') is to say that in having it, the thing is *good* (*agathon*) of its kind; and (2) to say it is good of its kind is to say it is in a state or condition to perform its characteristic function *well* (*eu*). Cf. II. 6, 1106a15–24 and Plato, *Republic* I, 352e–353d. The conclusion of the present passage depends on these connections together with the assumptions (3) that the good of a thing of a given kind is 'in its function' (1097b25–8), and (4) that the function-term primarily names an activity as distinct from a capability (1098a5–7). In this conceptual framework the human good is available only to a good human being. But this does not tell us which qualities are the excellences that make a human being good, nor that there is one correct answer to that question.

and if there are more excellences than one, in accordance with the best and the most complete [*teleios*]   *1098a17–18*   (*a*) 'In accordance with' = *kata* (+ accusative). 'In accordance with excellence', ' . . . with justice', ' . . . with badness' are ubiquitous phrases in Ar.'s *Ethics*. Used of activities and actions, they indicate that the activity or action is qualified by the adjective corresponding to the noun 'excellence', 'justice', 'badness', etc. (*b*) On Ar.'s account so far, the human good turns out to be one very general kind of thing, i.e. rational activity in accordance with excellence, as distinct from a combination of diverse goods. But immediately Ar. shows readiness to shift the reference of 'the human good' to the best of the rational activities of excellence, should there turn out to be many (cf. 1097a30). The shift should not surprise those who see this passage as Ar.'s 'definition' of the chief good or happiness (cf. 11, 1101a14–16). For in a definitional context one would expect, if there are different forms of a definiendum O, that the term 'O' would attach in its strictest sense to whichever form (if any) satisfies the definiens most completely. The shift does not cancel the lesser forms' status as genuine forms of O.

1098a18 **in a complete** [*teleios*] **life**   (*a*) The next two lines focus on length of life. This is not just a question of more time rather than less, but of the time required to develop rational maturity (which requires experience; cf. vi. 11, 1143b11–14 and i. 3, 1095a2–8) and exercise it to the full in a variety of situations. Hence a complete life includes abundance of opportunities for such excellent activities, as well as the wherewithal necessary for engaging in them; and elsewhere we learn that it also includes friends and loved ones, the respect of others, and pleasure. (*b*) Presumably, when Ar. put forward the completeness and self-sufficiency criteria for the chief good, he had in mind that an adequate account would include reference to a complete life. However, (*c*) there is a difference here. The ideal whole that is *excellent-rational-activity-in-a-complete-life* meets the self-sufficiency criterion because of the *in-a-complete-life* component; and of course without this component it would be incomplete in the ordinary sense of the word (cf. 11, 1101a14–19). But Ar.'s criterion of unqualified completeness is more technical; it is desirability always and only for its own sake, and the ideal whole meets this condition because of its *excellent-rational-activity* component. (*d*) Given that the happy life must contain some measure of these other goods, as well as excellent rational activity, should we say that happiness is essentially a complex whole to which they and the latter all contribute? A simple affirmative ignores the fact that for Ar. excellent rational activity is evidently the *principal* component of a happy human life: witness the synecdoche in his calling the chief good 'excellent activity' (e.g. 13, 1102a5–6; x. 7, 1177a12), whereas he never calls it after any other component. While fully recognizing that the happiest human life is a plexus of different goods (which is why it is at the mercy of chance), Ar. avoids words that would highlight the complexity, because the paradigm case of a happy life is that of god or the gods, and this consists of nothing but excellent rational activity (x. 8, 1178b18–27; cf. *Metaph.* xii. 7, 1072b14–30). Hence excellent rational activity is *the* happy-making ingredient of a happy human life, which has to include other goods only because, unlike a divine life, it is mortal and dependent on a physical and social environment.

1098a20 **blessed** [*makarios*] **and happy** [*eudaimōn*]   Normally, the Greek words are synonyms except that *makarios* is more elevated.

1098a23–4 **and time seems to be good at discovering such things**   The outline will develop into a richer picture as it is applied and interpreted at different times, whether these are stages of an individual's life or periods in the history of a culture. Ar. may be thinking in particular of the process of putting elements of his *Ethics* into practice through legislation. (This is discussed in the closing pages of the *NE* (x. 9 (1179a33–1181b23)). Plato, *Laws* vi, 769a–770c, uses the simile of filling in an outline in connection with legislation.)

what was said before   i.e. at 3, 1094b11–27.   *1098a26*

One should not demand to know the reason *why* **[***aitia***], either, in the same**   *1098a33–b3*
way in all matters: in some cases it will suffice if *that* **something is so has been well**
shown, as indeed is true of starting points; and that something is so is primary
and a starting point   Having reached his own definition of the chief good, Ar. now treats it as starting point for further inquiry (see next note). He probably does not mean the distinction '*that* it is so'–'*why* it is so' to apply literally to the doctrine (D) that the chief good is excellent rational activity in a complete life. D itself is supposed to provide the *why* of pre-philosophical values (see 4, 1095b4–7 with notes), and it is difficult to see what space there could be for a yet more fundamental explanation of the why of D. Rather, he means an analogy between the inappropriateness of expecting the implications of D to be spelled out with absolute precision, and the inappropriateness of always asking 'Why?'

Of starting points, some are grasped by induction ... others in other ways   *1098b3–4*
Induction (drawing a universal conclusion from a set of specific or particular cases) plays a part in the discovery of scientific first principles (*Posterior Analytics* II. 19, 100b3–4), but it also provides the unsystematized generalizations that are the explananda of an Aristotelian science. These are starting points for a search for first principles. *Perception* gives the starting points of induction (ibid. I. 18, 81a38–b9). *Habituation* is the source of pre-reflective values, which are the starting points of ethical inquiry (cf. 4, 1095b4–6 and II. 1 (1103a14–b26)). In the present passage Ar. particularly has in mind a starting point not grasped by sense-perception or habituation (though induction may play a part; see note on 1097b28–33), namely his own definition of happiness. Although this was reached in the course of inquiry, it launches new inquiries, particularly concerning the excellences.

I 8, 1098b9–1099b8

Our account of the chief good must be considered in the light of received opinions (1098b9–12); it fits in with the opinions that the best goods belong to the soul (1098b12–20), and that the happy person lives well and does well (1098b20–2); the features people expect of happiness belong to the chief good as defined above (1098b22–6); the opinions contain truth even though some are held by ordinary people, others by exceptional ones (1098b27–9); the account fits in with the view that the chief good is excellence or an excellence, but it matters whether one means the disposition or its activity

(1098b30–1099a7); the life of excellent activity is pleasant in itself (1099a7–21); excellent actions are not only pleasant, but also good and fine, to the highest degree, so that one and the same good (contrary to the Delian proverb), namely happiness, is best, finest, and pleasantest (1099a22–31); happiness is held to require external goods too, which accords with our account (1099a31–b8).

1098b9–11   **But we must inquire into it** [*peri autēs*] **not only** [A] **on the basis of our conclusion and the premisses of our argument, but also** [B] **on the basis of the things people say about it** [*peri autēs*]   Grammatically, 'it' should refer to *the starting point*, 1098b7, but this hardly makes sense. In fact, Ar. must mean to refer to *happiness* (last mentioned at 7, 1097b22). Inquiry A will spell out the main implications of the I. 7 definition, and inquiry B, which comes first, will compare it with received views.

1098b12–20   **given the division of goods into three . . . in this way the end turns out to belong among goods of the soul and not among external goods**   (a) The threefold division occurs several times in Plato, and Ar. treats it as a commonplace. (b) 'External' means 'external to the person'. External goods include friends, political power, and honour, as well as material possessions (cf. 1099a31–b2; IV. 3, 1123b20–1). (c) Note that fine practical activities involving the body count squarely as goods of the soul. (d) On the contrast between soul and body, see 13, 1102a32–b12, with note on b2–3.

1098b18   **those who reflect philosophically**   e.g. Heraclitus, Democritus, and Plato *passim*.

1098b18–19   **Our account will be right too in so far as certain actions and activities are being identified as the end**   Ar. takes credit on two scores. (1) The respected opinion that goods of the soul are best confirms his account's explicit reliance on the notion *activity of soul* (16). And (2) it bears out his doctrine that certain practical activities are the supreme end, since a practical activity is a good of the soul, not an external good (18–20; here Ar. argues as if there were only these two divisions of goods). On the meaning of 'practical', see note on 7, 1097b33–1098a4. On the plural 'activities', see note on 7, 1097a23–4 and note (c) on 7, 1097a30.

1098b21–2   **happiness has virtually been defined as a sort of living well and doing well**   It has been defined as a rational sort of living well—in a complete life. Thus the synonymy of 'happiness' with 'living well' is not quite perfect; see note on 10, 1100b8.

1098b23–5   **some people think it is excellence, others that it is wisdom** [*phronēsis*]**, others a kind of intellectual accomplishment** [*sophia*]   (a) Ar. reflects ordinary opinion in writing here as if wisdom and intellectual mastery do not count as excellences in the same way as, for example, courage and justice. Cf. 13, 1103a8–10, with note ad loc. (b) The distinction and contrast between *phronēsis* and *sophia* as the excellences of, respectively, practical and theoretical reason, is Aristotelian (*NE* VI). Thus we should not assume that the original audience was expected to understand the terms in those precise senses here.

for most people the things that are pleasant are in conflict, because they are not such by nature   On one interpretation they conflict with each other, but it is better to understand a conflict between pleasant things and excellence. Ar. is explaining why his result, that pleasure is intrinsic to excellent activity, would surprise a great many people. It is because what is pleasant *for them* is incompatible with excellent activity. But what is pleasant *for them* is not the same as what is pleasant *by nature* or *without qualification* (see note on VII. 12, 1152b29–31, and Introduction, pp. 66 and 72–3), and Ar.'s result holds only for the latter. *1099a11–12*

So happiness is what is best, and finest, and pleasantest, and these qualities are not divided as the inscription at Delos says   (a) 'Best', when contrasted with 'finest' and 'pleasantest', means 'most beneficial'. 'Fine' in Aristotle's *Ethics* is often rendered by 'noble'. (b) 'Divided' means that pursuing any one of the three superlatives entails sacrificing the others. The inscription allows that mediocre levels of the values may be combined. In rejecting it, Ar. commits himself to showing that the pleasures involved in happiness are pleasantest; cf. x. 7, 1177a22–7, and Introduction, pp. 73–4. (c) Delos was a great centre for the worship of Apollo, rivalled in importance by Delphi alone; thus the pessimistic verses must have been credited with the same authority as the Delphic 'Know thyself' and 'Nothing in excess'. Variants occur in the poets Theognis, Simonides, and Sophocles. *1099a24–6*

these, or the one of them that is best   Cf. 7, 1097a30 and 1098a17–18. *1099a30–1*

it clearly also requires external goods in addition, as we have said   Implied at 7, 1098a18. 'clearly', introduces a received opinion that corroborates what 'we have said'. *1099a31–2*

For in the first place many things are done by means of friends . . . and then again, there are some things the lack of which is like a stain on happiness, things like good birth, being blessed in one's children [*euteknia*, lit. 'excellence of children'], **beauty**   (a) The particles *men* and *de* (lit. 'on the one hand . . . on the other hand') at 1099a33 and b2 make clear that there are two reasons why lack of external goods conflicts with happiness: (1) such goods are enabling conditions for excellent activities; and (2) some are such that their absence is a blight even if the excellent activities can be carried on without them. See also the language at 10, 1100b25–9. Friends (*philoi*; the word covers all loved ones, see Introduction p. 57) come under both reasons. (b) It is not entirely clear whether Ar. really means to classify good birth, good children, and physical beauty as external goods. By the triple division at 1098b12–14, beauty is a good of body, and it is a puzzle where good birth should go. (c) It is very surprising that health is not mentioned among the ingredients of a happy life. *1099a33–b3*

1099b3–4   Is the claim here that physical beauty is necessary for happiness, or that ugliness is an impediment?

I 9, 1099b9–1100a9

Consequently, there are conflicting views on how happiness comes about (1099b9–19); it cannot be by chance (*tuchē*) (1099b20–5); our account's emphasis on excellent practical activity fits in with the initial designation of the chief good as the political objective, since the aim of political expertise is to make the citizens excellent in that way (1099b25–32); and with the impossibility of applying 'happy' to brutes (1099b32–1100a1); it is applied to children only in hope (1100a1–5); life is subject to great turns of fortune (*tuchē*), and no one calls happy a figure who, like Priam, flourishes and then suffers a disastrous end (1100a5–9).

1099b9–11   **This is the reason too why people debate whether happiness is something learned ... or even through chance**   Because happiness depends on excellence but also on good fortune (*eutuchia*, 8, 1099b8), people identify it with one or with the other, and disagree correspondingly on how it comes about. (See Plato's *Meno* and *Protagoras* for debate on this.) For Ar., possible ways of its coming about seem at first to divide as follows: (1) we can achieve happiness by our own efforts, whether (1*a*) by habituation or (1*b*) by learning or (1*c*) in some other way; or, alternatively, (2) happiness has a source beyond our control, whether (2*a*) the gods or (2*b*) chance (*tuchē*). At line 15, (2*a*) 'Happiness is heaven-sent' and (1) 'Happiness results from excellence and training on our part' are treated as mutually exclusive. But although Ar. opts for (1), he continues to call happiness 'most divine' (16–18). This insinuates the thought, on which he will build in x. 7–8 (see especially 7, 1177a13–17), that our human nature contains something divine or godlike—how not so, if godlike happiness is in our human power? Thus (1) and (2*a*) are not pointing in opposite directions after all.

1099b19   **It will also be something available to many**   In principle the chief good is achievable by human beings in general; it does not presuppose any special biological endowment. But the necessary education is often lacking; and in so far as the chief good consists in the exercise of intellectual mastery (*sophia*), the necessary attitude is far from common (Introduction, pp. 53–4, 75–6). Ar. writes elsewhere as if most people never attain actual excellence and happiness (e.g. x. 9, 1179b10–18; iii. 11, 1118b23 ff.; ix. 8, 1168b15–25).

1099b16–18   **for the prize and fulfilment [*telos*] of excellence appears to be to the highest degree good, and to be something godlike and blessed [*makarios*]**   The argument is: there is nothing finer than excellence in human life. So since happiness is the *fulfilment* of excellence, there must be something more than human about happiness.

282

if it is better like this than that we should be happy through chance [*tuchē*], **it is reasonable to suppose that it is like this ... in relation to the best** **cause**   The argument is: things of sorts that come about by nature or artifice, but *1099b20–3*
can also come about by chance, are at their best and most themselves when in fact
they come about by these genuine causes, and not by chance. Consequently,
happiness is at its best if it comes about not by chance, but by the best of all
causes, i.e. cultivation of excellence. (And since we are inquiring about happiness
because we are inquiring about the highest human good, we should focus on the
best happiness if some kinds are inferior to others.) (*a*) Having established this
conclusion, Ar. does not in fact envisage an inferior form of happiness that comes
about by chance. It would be of no interest as a practicable goal. (*b*) Strictly
speaking, the conclusion is true only of the *principal component* of Aristotelian
happiness. The components implied by 'a complete life' are not only vulnerable
to chance, but sometimes come about by it.

This will agree, too, with our opening remarks   To the effect that the chief *1099b28–9*
good is the political objective (2, 1094a24–b11). It is an already received opinion
that the function of government is to make excellent citizens who are doers
(*praktikous*) of fine things, and here it provides the middle term that equates the
chief good as explained in I. 2 with the chief good as explained in I. 7.

So it makes sense that we do not call either an ox, or a horse, or any other *1099b32–*
animal 'happy' ... because of their prospects   The inference is from *prakti-* *1100a4*
kous at 31–2. On brutes, Ar. is referring to existing usage. His account of happiness as 'practical' entails that brutes cannot be happy (see note (*a*) on 7, 1097b33–
1098a3); thus existing usage confirms his account. As for children, it is not clear
whether the remark about felicitating them reports a commonly felt nuance, or
tells us what we ought to mean in calling a child '*eudaimōn*'.

Priam   The Homeric king of Troy, who saw his city sacked and burned, his sons *1100a8*
killed, his eldest son Hector's body desecrated, his womenfolk led captive, before
being slaughtered himself at the altar of his palace.

died miserably   See preliminary comments on ch. 10. *1100a9*

I 10, 1100a10–1101a21

Should one then follow Solon, and refuse to call anyone happy who still has
some life ahead of him? (1100a10–11); Solon meant that we should wait
until the person is out of reach of misfortunes (*dustuchēmata*) (1100a11–17);
but this may never be the case, since perhaps the dead are affected by what
happens to their descendants (1100a17–26). (It would be strange if the dead
switched back and forth between happiness and wretchedness because of
how things go with descendants far removed in time, but strange too if
there is no period in which they are affected to some extent (1100a26–30.)
But this problem may be solved by solving the first one (1100a31–2)). The

strange unwillingness to call someone happy *when* he *is* so is because we think that happiness is firm-rooted, whereas people's fortunes go up and down frequently (1100a34–b4); it is right not to think that changes in fortune imply corresponding switches to and fro in a person's happiness-status, because the latter is principally determined by excellent activities, which are firm-rooted and endure through changes of fortune (1100b4–33); misfortune may destroy someone's happiness, but cannot make him miserable, since the true misery is doing hateful things (1100b33–1101a8); it takes major changes of fortune to dislodge someone from happiness or to return him to it (1101a8–13); to count someone happy, must one add to the terms of the existing definition the condition that his present state will continue for the rest of his life? That would be human blessedness (1101a14–21).

Must we agree with Solon, and look to a man's end? Solon was a great political reformer of 6th-century Athens, and one of the legendary Seven Sages. The story surrounding the apophthegm is told by Herodotus, *History* I. 30–3. In the *EE* Ar. indicates agreement with Solon's dictum, without discussion (II. 1, 1219b6). Here he takes issue with it. But first he interprets it charitably. Solon cannot mean 'A person (i.e. one who has lived and died well) *is* a happy being only when dead' (1100a13–17). Solon must mean that only when such a person is dead can we safely ascribe happiness to him, implying that he *was* happy when alive. In that case, Solon assumes (Solonic assumption 1) that happiness is irreversible: if you lose it, you never really had it. (Perhaps his idea is that a good passage of life does not count as happy if it will be succeeded by a disaster.) So, since we cannot foresee the future, 'happy' can be applied reasonably (rather than by guess) only once the person has died, when, Solon assumes (Solonic assumption 2), nothing more can happen to him or her.

Ar. holds: (A) Yes, no one calls 'happy' someone known to have met an end like Priam's (termed 'miserable' at 9, 1100a9; cf. 10, 1100a29, b5); but (B) it is absurd to refuse to call living persons 'happy' who fit the criteria, on the grounds (1) that we cannot foresee reversals of their fortune (*tuchē*) and (2) that happiness is understood to be something lasting and hard to change (1100a33–b3). So (C) grave misfortune can dislodge the happy from their happiness; however (D), just as happiness principally consists in activity of excellence, so its opposite, misery, principally consists in activity of badness. Since these are activities of firmly based dispositions (cf. II. 4, 1105a33), the happy person will not become miserable, no matter what happens to him or her.

Comparing A and D, we see that Ar. begins by going along with the ordinary meaning of 'miserable' (*athlios*), but then replaces this with an ethically defined meaning corresponding to his ethical definition of the contrary term, 'happy'. It is in the ordinary, not the ethical, sense that Priam's end was miserable (9, 1100a9), since in the story he was a good or certainly not a bad man.

B implies that it was reasonable to call someone happy when he or she fitted the criteria, even if (as we now know) unforeseen misfortune struck later. (B taken with ground (1) suggests—what seems reasonable—that it would not be correct to call someone happy now if the misfortune is foreseeable now.) B, therefore, implies that the person *was* happy then, even if not later. But does this not contradict A? No, not if one considers what Ar. and his audience would have meant by 'calling someone happy' (or ' . . . blessed'). It was not simply a matter of applying the predicate 'happy' to a given subject. It was also to demonstrate what happiness is. It was to take the celebrated notion 'happy person' and to say of X or Y 'He/she is an example'. Priam, whose tragic end was legendary, *is* not an example anyone now would choose, even though it was equally legendary that he *was* happy (hence *was* a suitable example) earlier. His earlier happiness does not now exemplify the concept to those who cannot help seeing it as followed by irreversible disaster.

Ar. begins by challenging Solonic assumption 2. Surely the dead are affected well and adversely by the good and bad fortunes (*tuchai*) of their descendants (which, by the same token, will include the good and bad fortunes of *their* descendants) (1100a16–21)? (If so, and if the dead can be so badly affected as to warrant withholding the accolade 'happy' *no matter how well they lived and ended their own lives*, then by Solonic assumption 1, no one, alive or dead, can ever properly be called 'happy'.) On the other hand, it is rather absurd to think of someone who lived and died happy, as then, when dead, switching to and fro between happiness and misery (21–9). (But does this absurdity indicate the general absurdity of switching from happiness to misery? If so, it supports Solonic assumption 1. Or is it, rather, absurd only as applied to the *dead*? If so, is it because they are not after all affected, or not significantly affected, by how things go for their descendants?)

Ar. then (1100a31) sets aside for a while (until 11, 1101a22–b9) the question of descendants' fortunes getting through to the dead, and turns back to 'Call no man happy until he is dead'. He deals with it in two stages, rejection (32–5) and diagnosis (1100b2–16). The rejection takes off from Solon's willingness to call 'happy' or 'blessed' some of the deceased retrospectively (on this, see the story in Herodotus, reference above). Solon, then, is committed to 'They *were* happy'. But if they were happy, this, Ar. assumes, was because of how their lives were then. So it would have been reasonable for someone who knew them then to call them 'happy'. But if so, the same would have been reasonable, once, in the case of one whose life was like that (once) but then took an unforeseeable turn for the worse.

As it stands, this argument is ineffective against Solon, who insists that no part of a life, however good, counts as happy if the end is unforeseen disaster. But why insist this and deny oneself the possibility of pointing out live examples of happiness? (Perhaps because it seems that a good example of something should be timelessly so; thus to posit mutable X as a true example of 'happy' we must wait until X is in the past and out of reach of change. Perhaps Solon as one of the Seven Sages is expected to restrict his statements to timeless truths!) Ar. diagnoses truth beneath the insistence. The truth lies with the respected views (1) that happiness is something stable, and (2) that chance (fortune, luck) is volatile. Unqualified, these jointly imply that chance in the form of misfortune cannot take happiness away (suggesting that happiness can be ascribed only to those out of reach of chance). But Ar. explains that the truth of (1) holds, more precisely, of excellent activity, the principal component of happiness, though not of the other components (1100b4–1101a13). Since the activity depends on oneself, it is not vulnerable to chance. Moreover, true misery implies hateful and vile activity, which is alien to the excellent person. So again (1) is true if interpreted to mean: 'The happy person is safe from becoming truly miserable'.

1100a19 **as much as someone who is alive but not perceiving what is happening to him** The comparison leaves it unclear whether the belief is that (i) the dead exist as human presences, but are insensate; or (ii) they have dim awareness of what happens to their descendants; or (iii) they do not exist but are nonetheless affected by such events. We, too, feel that the departed can be wronged or betrayed without necessarily believing that they actually exist somewhere. Ar.'s psychological and logical theories imply difficulties for all these interpretations. Against (i): there can be no animal, including the human kind, that is not capable of sensation; against (ii): even dim awareness presupposes a living organism, since sense and thought so far as it involves imagination are physiologically based; against (iii): an affection (or being affected) presupposes an existing substance. So why does Ar. accept the belief for discussion at all? Presumably because it will not give way under merely conceptual probing, being an outgrowth of the believers' bond with the departed (11, 1101a22–4; however, at III. 6, 1115a26–7 he says that for the dead, death is the end). So he must take it seriously because, in conjunction with Solon's principle that a person cannot safely be called happy as long as new things can happen to him or her, it threatens to imply that human happiness is never recognizably instantiated. For vulnerability through one's descendants will last as long as their generations (1100a26–7).

1100b7–8 **Or is it completely wrong to track a person's fortunes like this?** i.e. wrong to let changing fortunes determine the pattern of our applying 'happy' and its opposite ('miserable'), so that (a) minor misfortune automatically renders a person less happy, and (b) serious misfortune automatically renders him or her miserable. The ethical implication of 'miserable' is not yet revealed, but is about to become so through the connection with activities (10–11, and see next note).

1100b8 **For they** [*sc. a person's fortunes*] **are not where living well or badly is located** Quality, good or bad, of distinctively human life is quality of rational activity, since the activity *is* the life at highest intensity. Thus living well is not quite the same as happiness (cf. 8, 1098b21).

1100b11–12 **The present difficulty itself bears witness to our account** i.e. the problem of the relation of happiness (supposedly stable) to chance (volatile). The problem would not bother us if its components did not each contain truth. Thus it confirms that Ar. was right to define happiness as principally consisting of something constant, i.e. activity of excellence, although goods subject to chance are also needed.

they seem to be more firm-rooted even than the various kinds of knowledge *1100b14*
we possess   Systematic knowledge is meant. Strictly, the comparison should be between such knowledge and the *disposition* for excellent activity (i.e. excellence). But whoever has *this* disposition will exercise it whenever possible, whereas exercise of mathematical knowledge is sometimes possible but not called for. Thus the activity of excellence is a firm feature of the excellent life. And the excellent person might for some good reason let his mathematics get rusty ('forgetfulness', 17) by ceasing to exercise the skill, but there cannot be a reason he would recognize as good for ceasing to exercise excellence.

'the man who is truly good and four-square beyond reproach'   Words of the *1100b21–2* 5th-century poet Simonides.

for they bring on pains, and obstruct many sorts of activities   This means *1100b29–30* that many activities natural to him become difficult or frustrating, not that he is rendered inactive. A person must be actively admirable for it to 'shine through' (1100b30–1; see also 1101a2–3: 'he *does* what is most admirable given his resources').

as we have said   At 1100b10. *1100b33–4*

though neither will he be blessed if he meets with fortunes like Priam's   So *1101a7–8* far, 'blessed' (*makarios*) has been used as an alternative for 'happy' (*eudaimōn*), e.g. at 1100a33–5; b16–18; 11, 1101b4–5. (Cf. 1100a10, 16, 33, b1, 12; 1101b24, where *eudaimonizein* ('call happy') and *makarizein* ('call blessed') are used interchangeably.) If this is the meaning here, then Ar. is saying what is obvious, that the happy fall from happiness if their lives end in catastrophe. Or he may be using 'blessed' in the different sense explained below in the note on 1101a16–21.

Or must we add that he will also continue to live like that . . . but blessed as *1101a16–21* **human beings**   (*a*) This shows that 'in a complete life' of the original definition does not mean 'to the end of one's life'. (*b*) Usually in Ar. this form of question is tantamount to an affirmation. But given the context, this can hardly be the sense here. He has just said that someone can achieve happiness but then be 'dislodged' from it by great misfortunes (1101a9–11), and he does not in fact add this further condition to his own account of happiness (see x. 7, 1177a25). But now he acknowledges the pull towards denying that *X* was ever happy if *X*'s life ends badly, however good it was before. (One might say that the good part, given what followed, was only incomplete happiness; but happiness, it would seem, cannot be in any way incomplete.) Ar. compromises by declaring that the term we withhold in such a case is 'blessed'. This, unlike the previously synonymous 'happy', is now reserved for those who *will live out their days and die* in happiness. The point is not merely that Priam is not *now* an example of blessedness. (He is also not now an example of happiness, although no doubt he was one in his middle age.) It is that we cannot properly say of Priam that he *was* blessed during the good part of his life, given what we know lay ahead for him. So, reworded to 'Call no human being blessed while alive', Solon's adage is sound (unless, of course, the vicissitudes of their descendants can render the dead unhappy). Since 'blessed' is commonly used of the gods (they are invulnerable to fortune, as Solon thought the dead to be), Ar. points out that the blessedness of a life lived happily to the end is still only human. (Thus it is not so perfect that it would be senseless for humans to hope for it; and, being only humanly blessed, it may not be devoid of small misfortunes.)

I 11, 1101a22–b9

We do not deny that the fortunes of descendants and loved ones make some difference to the dead (1101a22–4); but to get a sense of whether this could dislodge a dead person from happiness (or the reverse), one has to consider that even the living are not much affected by everything that happens to their loved ones, and that a living person's being affected belongs to a different order of magnitude than a dead person's so being (1101a24–34), and that it is controversial whether the dead are affected at all (1101a34–b1); all of which suggests that if anything does get through to them, it is not of a nature to convert happiness to unhappiness or vice versa (1101b1–9).

At 10, 1100a31–2 Ar. said that whether the dead are affected by the actions and fortunes of their surviving relatives might be solved through his first addressing Solon's adage. He now returns to the former question, generalizing it to cover surviving loved ones, whether relatives or not (1101a22). The two issues are connected in the following ways: (1) Via the *centrality to happiness of excellent activity*, which was the basis of the response to Solon. While the excellent person is alive, the fates of his loved ones unfold for him as humanly active: it is only as a humanly active self that he can be made happy or unhappy by what they do or what happens to them (even though these vicissitudes do not weaken his own activity or its excellence). (2) In replying to Solon, Ar. was led to make it clear that the fact that human happiness is not independent of fortune is not to be interpreted as the fact that human happiness is fortune-sensitive. That is: the inference '*F*, a stroke of fortune, happens to *X*; *F* is bad/good; therefore *X*'s happiness is decreased/increased' is to be rejected. Such reasoning could only apply to the excellent, since only they can be happy; but it belongs to the excellent not to be moved by minor changes of fortune (10, 1101a9–13; cf. 11, 1101a28–30). There, Ar. was thinking of vicissitudes directly one's own; now he considers those suffered indirectly (by the living) because loved ones fare badly or well. We are now logically prepared for the thought that even if it is true to say, once *X* is dead, that a good or bad turn in the life of a loved one is a good or bad thing for *X*, still nothing follows about *X*'s happiness.

whether it involves the living or the dead makes much more difference than whether in tragedies lawless, terrible deeds have happened beforehand or are presently being enacted   The dead are necessarily background, and don't (now) have a foreground; but anything significant enough to reverse happiness/unhappiness must occur in someone's foreground.   *1101a31–3*

we must bring in the difficulty, in relation to the dead, whether they share in any good   This does not logically support the conclusion that they cannot be made happy or unhappy, but it makes it sensible for us to judge them happy—or not—entirely on the basis of their own lives.   *1101a35–1101b1*

I 12, 1101b10–1102a4

Happiness—an object of praise or of honour? (1101b10–12); marks of things that are praised (1101b12–21); it follows that the highest goods, such as the gods, the most godlike men, and happiness, are not objects of praise (1101b21–31); praise contrasted with encomia (1101b31–5); clearly, happiness is an honourable and godlike thing, being the principle (*archē*) and cause of the other goods (1101b35–1102a4).

In I. 10–11 Ar. has argued for a conception of human happiness according to which it is just that: thoroughly human. It is supposed to be achievable by human beings; it can coexist with minor misfortunes; it can be destroyed by grave ones; and at its best it is rounded off by death. The object of I. 12, it seems, is to emphasize that human happiness is nevertheless a godlike thing (see note on 7, 1097b20). Ar. does this by arguing that it satisfies a further criterion for being the highest good, one suggested by an argument of Eudoxus. This concludes the examination of happiness in Book I; Ar. will return to the subject in the final pages of the *NE*.

Eudoxus had built an argument for hedonism on the doctrine that the chief good is a per se good *beyond praise*. According to Eudoxus, the chief good, and god, have this status, because it is to them that other goods (including the objects of praise, *ta epaineta*) 'are referred' (1101b27–31). Eudoxus must have gone on to claim that pleasure is a per se good, and to point out that we do not praise people for experiencing pleasure. Ar. accepts the Eudoxan rule, adds one further ingredient, and shows that the resulting criterion is satisfied by happiness as defined by himself. The further ingredient is the assumption that the category of things 'superior to the praiseworthy' is the category of the *honourable*. Ar.'s question, then, is whether happiness is an object of honour, rather than merely an object of praise. In proving the former, Ar. proves that human happiness is godlike, since (it is taken for granted) honouring is the appropriate attitude towards gods and godlike things. (He thereby corroborates the mystique that leads some people to stand in awe of those who speak of happiness as something 'impressive and over their heads' (4, 1095a25–6). And he also secures an advantage against Eudoxus' candidate for highest good, since it might be hard to show that pleasure as such is honourable. For more arguments against Eudoxan hedonism, see x. 2, 1172b9–35).

1101b11–12 **whether happiness comes under the heading of what is to be praised or rather of what is to be honoured; for obviously it is not found among the potentialities** For a fuller treatment of this division of goods (which includes a fourth, that of means for obtaining and preserving goods), see *Magna Moralia* I. 2, 1183b19–37. The author (if not Ar., then one of his students) says:

> By what is to be honoured I mean this sort of thing: the divine, what is better (e.g. soul, intellect), what is more ancient, first principles—these sorts of things . . . The category of goods to be praised includes things like excellences; for praise comes about from actions done in accordance with these. Other goods are potentialities, such as power, wealth, strength, beauty; for these are things that can both be put to good use by the excellent person and be put to bad use by the bad—which is why such things are called potentially good. Goods, then, they are, for they are assessed by reference to the use the excellent person makes of them, not by the use the bad man makes of them . . . The fourth and last category of goods is that of what tends to preserve and produce what is good, in the way that training preserves and produces health, and anything else like this.

(For a similar division see also Fragment 113, Rose[3].)

1101b12 **Everything praised appears to be praised for being of a certain quality and being disposed in a certain way towards something** The excellences predicated by adjectives such as 'just', 'courageous', and 'good' are in the category of Quality because they are defined as dispositions *for* activity of various kinds (see II. 5 (1105b19–1106a13)), and dispositions (*hexeis*) are a type of quality (*Categories* 8, 8b26–9a9). In applying a dispositional term we make reference (cf. 21) to something else, i.e. the activity; and in applying a quality-adjective we presuppose reference to something else, i.e. a substance. Thus when we apply, for example, 'good' as a term of praise, we make reference to something other than the feature in virtue of which we apply it.

1101b14–15 **for we praise the just man . . . and excellence** i.e. these are all *terms* of praise.

1101b18–21 **This is also clear if we consider praises offered to the gods; for they appear laughable if they are offered by reference to our case, and this actually occurs, because of the fact that we have mentioned, that praise is always with reference to something** (*a*) The last point was made by implication at 1101b12–18. (*b*) The Greek wording suggests that it is the praises, not the gods, that appear laughable. In any case, the exact meaning is unclear. Perhaps it is this: in god there is no distinction between disposition and activity, as the divine is pure activity (*Metaph.* XII. 7); and god is a substance such that to be it is *eo ipso* to be good (see 6,

1096a24 with note). So if god is correctly said to be good, 'good' applies to the divine activity and the divine substance. But if the term is used so as to *praise*, the application must refer to something else. In this case, what could that be but *ourselves*, perhaps imagined as connected with divine activity as its beneficiaries? (Thus in praising the gods, we cannot be celebrating them just as they are in virtue of their own nature.) Alternatively, and more simply, the thought may be that praise implies that the object *satisfies our standards*. But if so, the distinction between disposition and activity does not work in this argument.

for we call both gods and the most godlike men 'blessed' and 'happy'   (*a*)   *1101b23–5*
Here Ar. takes it as obvious that the speech-act of *calling* someone *blessed* or *happy* (i.e. felicitation) is not a speech-act of praise. (*b*) The one godlike human activity encountered so far is that of the large-scale (successful) political expert (2, 1094b10). In x. 7–8 Ar. will argue that this is not the highest.

but ranks it blessed [*makarizein*], as being something more godlike and superior   A moment ago (23–5) the happy, rather than happiness, were the targets of   *1101b26–7*
felicitation. As with praise (14–15), Ar. does not distinguish object from ground of felicitation. But in the case of god, this is a distinction without a difference, since god is nothing but god's activity of happiness.

the competition of goods   See Introduction, p. 76.   *1101b28*

it is to these that the other things are referred   See note on 1102a3–4.   *1101b30–1*

praise is appropriate to excellence   Not just excellence of soul; see the   *1101b31–2*
examples at line 16 above.

encomia   (*a*) An encomium was a celebration of a particular deed; see *Rhetoric* I.   *1101b33*
9, 1367b26–35; *EE* II. 1, 1219b8–16. (*b*) The implication is that of *praise, encomium*, and *felicitation*, the latter alone is restricted to things of the soul.

This also seems to be so because of the fact that it is a principle   See the   *1102a2*
Magna Moralia passage quoted in note on 1101b11–12.

for it is for the sake of happiness that we all do everything else we do   This   *1102a2–3*
is not an observation about human motivation, but a normative declaration that everything else be subordinated to happiness. This is the rule that should guide 'political' thinking and acting in the sense of 'political' introduced at the beginning (I. 2, 1094a24–b11, and Introduction, pp. 10–11).

the principle and cause of goods   (*a*) Here Ar. says that *happiness* is the principle   *1102a3–4*
ciple and cause of the value of the other goods. However, happiness does not give value to *excellent rational activity*, for this owes its worth to nothing but itself, and is that in whose absence the other ingredients of the would-be happy life are valueless. It seems to follow that excellent rational activity is the true 'principle and cause of good things', and is therefore the chief practicable good, given that

the chief is principle of value for the others. Then what about happiness? Excellent rational activity may be termed 'happiness' by synecdoche (see note (*d*) on 7, 1098a18), but it is not happiness in the sense of being sufficient to render human beings happy, as Ar. makes clear at 7, 1098a18–20; 8, 1099a31–b8; and 10, 1100b19–1101a11. And surely the chief good which is the goal of 'political' thought and action is not merely *excellent rational activity*, even if this is by far the most important part of the goal, but *excellent rational activity in a complete life*? Perhaps the solution is that someone's excellent rational activity cannot actually exercise its role as cause of the goodness of the other goods unless the latter are present in the person's life as the empirical entities they are—health, friends, social position, children, etc.—to *be* rendered good by their various relations to excellent rational activity. We must understand 'a complete life' as containing these elements *for* excellent rational activity to make worth while. 'Adding' any one of these other things, the *O*s, to excellent rational activity (or it to one of them) is sufficient and necessary for that *O* to count as good. When all *O*s are 'added', we have a combination in which all *O*s are rendered good, and this combination is the one otherwise known as 'excellent rational activity in a complete life'. (It is awkward for clarity that the empirical entities listed are commonly called 'goods' regardless of whether they occur in the context of excellent rational activity. It is also awkward that the 'adding' means different relations for different *O*s. Adding excellent rational activity to wealth would be using wealth in it or to support it. Adding the former to pleasure or to friendship would be, respectively, taking pleasure in it and having a friendship based on it. These last examples show that *pleasure* and *friendship* figure here in a logical and generic way. The 'intersection' of pleasure and excellent rational activity is a different kind of pleasure with a different concrete nature from the 'intersection' of pleasure with some kind of low-level activity, and similarly for friendship. It is not as if literally the same pleasure could now be away from, now be with, excellent rational activity in the way in which this is possible for the identical material resources if they pass from one sort of agent to another.) (*b*) In Platonism, the cause of the *F*-ness of other *F* things is also supposed to be the '*F*-itself', i.e. the purest example of *F* (cf. *EE* I. 8, 1217b1–15). In Ar., by contrast, the purest case of happiness is that of the gods, and it is identical with their excellent rational activity *tout court*. On the divine level there is nothing but perfect activity and no space for anything else there that might be made good by association with it. On the human level it is *our* excellent rational activity, in a life necessarily involving more than just that, that gives other human goods their value. (On the relation of human happiness to divine activity, see Introduction pp. 14–15.)

I 13, 1102a5–1103a10

From inquiring about happiness we pass to inquiring about human excellence of soul, which is anyway a topic for political expertise (1102a5–18); therefore the political expert should know something about the soul

(1102a18–27); for instance, that one part is non-rational, the other rational (1102a27–32); the nutritive part of the non-rational part is common to all living things, and is incapable of human excellence (1102a32–b12); another non-rational part participates in a way in reason: it can and should obey reason, but sometimes fights against it, as happens with self-control and the lack of it (1102b13–1103a3); the distinction between this non-rational part and the rational one implies a corresponding distinction between kinds of excellence: the intellectual excellences versus the excellences of character (1103a3–10).

This chapter marks the transition to the topic of human excellence, the main subject of the *Ethics*. Excellence must be studied (1) because it is part of the I. 7 definition of the chief good, i.e. happiness, and (2) it is the main objective of political expertise (cf. 9, 1099b28–32 with comment). The excellence in question is of soul, not body. Some account of the soul is therefore a necessary preliminary.

the Cretans and the Spartans   The city-states of Crete and Sparta were   *1102a10–11*
famous for their communal methods of moral training. At *NE* x. 9, 1180a24–9, Ar.
laments the rarity of this sort of institution.

in accordance with our original purpose   i.e. to delineate the political expert's   *1102a13*
objective (2, 1094a18–b11).

By 'human excellence' we mean excellence of soul, not of body; happiness,   *1102a16–18*
too, we say, is activity of soul   Here are two reasons for studying excellence of
soul. The second relies on Ar.'s analysis of happiness (7, 1098a7–17), and 'we' in it
refers to himself. The first is based on (1) the fact that we, i.e. ordinary speakers
call someone a good human being in light of qualities of mind and character
rather than health and strength of body, together with (2) the principle that the
excellence of an *F* as such is the quality that makes it a good *F* (II. 6, 1106a15–24).
Here, as at 8, 1098b12–20, Ar. echoes the popular contrast between soul and body,
but see below, 1102a32–b12, with note on b2–3.

If all this is so . . . the political expert should know, in a way, about soul, just   *1102a18–20*
as the person who is going to treat people's eyes should know about the
entire body, too   According to one ancient school of medicine, knowledgeable
treatment of a given organ presupposes an understanding of the whole system.
Ethics is concerned primarily with excellent rational activity, since this is the
core of the chief good; but reason in man is only one part of the soul, and its
nature and the challenges to its development depend on its place in the wider
psychic context, including even the 'nutritive' part of the soul—which has no
share in distinctively human excellence (1102b12), but is the basis of the physical
appetites with which excellence (specifically, moderation) has to be concerned.
The political expert should know about all this 'in a way', i.e. not as a natural
scientist.

1102a26–7   **in our published works**   The reference is uncertain.

1102a28–30   **whether these are delimited like the parts of the body . . . or whether they are two things by definition but by nature inseparable**   (*a*) The first possibility considered here is the association of the rational and non-rational powers of the soul (*psuchē*) with different parts of the body, as in the psychology of Plato's *Timaeus* (69b–70e). This theory included the doctrine that the rational element is immortal (ibid. 41a–43e); thus Ar. may be indicating that the truth or falsity of this, too, is irrelevant to the present inquiry. (*b*) In what follows Ar. seems to lean towards the second of the above possibilities, since he relates the strictly rational and non-rational parts of the distinctively human soul as *director* to *directed* (1102b13–1103a3), which are correlatives like *convex* and *concave*. However, the strictly rational part is more than a mere director of the non-rational, since the theoretic excellence of intellectual accomplishment is also ascribed to it (see 1103a5–9, with note on 8–10). Hence it is not the rational part as such that is related to the non-rational part as convex and concave, or vice versa, but the rational part in its directive role. This is a strictly human role, since reason in its theoretic mode is all there is to the soul of a god.

1102a33   **what is responsible for the taking in of food and for increase in size**   This is the 'nutritive' soul, responsible for metabolism, growth, and also reproduction (*On the Soul* II. 4).

1102b1–2   **and this same one too as being in them when they are full-grown, for it is more reasonable to suppose the presence of this one than of any other**   Since the power of growth is also the power of nutrition, it is the same in immature and mature organisms, although only the former express it through growth.

1102b2–3   **Excellence in the exercise of this capacity . . . appears to be something shared and not distinctively human**   Good growth and metabolism show physical health, a non-rational excellence. Elsewhere in the *Ethics* Ar. falls in with the dualist classification of health as an excellence of body as distinct from soul (e.g. I. 8, 1098b13–16; 13, 1102a16–17; cf. VIII. 11, 1161a35).

1102b13–14   **although participating** [*metechousa*] **in a way in reason**   Cf. 25–6; 30–1. 'Participate' is Platonic; so also 'share in' (*koinōnei*) at 29–30. In Platonism, Socrates' relation to the Form of Man makes it not incorrect to call Socrates a 'man' even though the Form is more properly called 'man' than any human individual. So for Ar. the potentially obedient part of the soul may be called 'reason' and 'rational' because of its relation to the directive part, even though the terms primarily apply to the latter. See 1103a1–3. Note that whereas Plato's 'participate' and 'share' are meant to bring out the fact that a given participant is one of many (the Form is 'one over many'), Ar.'s indicate no more than a dependence that allows transfer of terms.

294

those with and without self-control   Self-control (a good quality but not an   *1102b14*
excellence) is the disposition to refuse to act on desires not approved by reason;
the lack of it (a defect, but not a vice) is the disposition to give way to them. The
topic is studied in VII. 1–10 (1145a15–1152a36).

How it is different is of no importance   Cf.1102a28–32.   *1102b25*

the appetitive and generally desiring part   On the different kinds of   *1102b30*
desire (*orexis*), see III. 2, 1111b10–11 with note. Here Ar. may be omitting the kind
called 'wish', since he usually associates it with the rational part; cf. *Topics* IV. 5,
126a6–13.

it is the way one is reasonable when one *takes* account of advice from one's   *1102b32–3*
father or loved ones, not when one *has* an account of things, as for example in
mathematics   Having an account is being able to demonstrate a result oneself.

we call some of them intellectual excellences, others excellences of charac-   *1103a4–5*
ter   (*a*) **we call**   Ar. refers to his own school. (*b*) **character**   The word is
ēthos, whence 'ethics', 'ethical'. The plural *ēthē*, is rendered by the Latin '*mores*',
whence 'moral', 'morality'. Thus the excellences of the 'listening' part of the soul
are often labelled the 'ethical' or 'moral' virtues.

but we do also praise someone accomplished in something for his disposition,   *1103a8–10*
and the dispositions we praise are the ones we call 'excellences'   This is a
proof that intellectual accomplishment (*sophia*) counts as a human excellence.
Proof is necessary because this quality is not on a par with the others: unlike
them, it is godlike even in human beings (see X. 7–8), and it would not have been
obvious to everyone in Ar.'s audience, or everyone in the communities in which
they would serve, that intellectual accomplishment (especially on Ar.'s interpretation of it) is necessary for complete human excellence (1102a1), and that one of
the duties of political expertise is therefore to encourage its cultivation in everyone. (In calling something a 'human excellence', Ar. implies that it is not a
technique that can be left to a few specialists.)

BOOK II

The topic is excellence of character: its development through practice (1–2,
1103a14–1104b3); its relation to pleasure and pain (3, 1104b3–1105a16); why
developing it does not presuppose already having it (4, 1105a17–b18); its
definition as a *disposition* (5, 1105b19–1106a13) for achieving the *intermediate*

in actions and feelings (6, 1106a14–1107a27); its status as mean between dispositions of excess and deficiency as shown in specific cases (7, 1107a28–1108b10); how it can be confused with either extreme (8, 1108b11–1109a19); how achieving it is hard, and judgements about it sometimes necessarily indefinite (9, 1109a20–b26).

II 1, 1103a14–b25

Intellectual excellence is developed by teaching, excellence of character by habituation, rather than arising by nature (1103a14–26); we acquire the character-excellences by first engaging in the activities (1103a26–1103b6); it is the same as with technical expertise—from engaging in the activity well or badly we become good agents or bad ones (1103b6–21); the dispositions come from the activities and correspond to them (1103b21–3); it makes all the difference how one is habituated from a young age (1103b23–5).

1103a14   **Excellence being of two sorts**   See I. 13, 1103a1–10 with notes.

1103a15   **teaching** [*didaskalia*]   Ar. means a process of getting someone to learn by being shown *why* some moves or responses are correct, others not, as distinct from simply being shown or told what to do.

1103a16–17   **which is why it requires experience and time**   Since the process of habituation (17) also takes time, Ar. must mean that time and experience are necessary before *didaskalia* can begin, whereas habituation begins in earliest youth. Experience precedes analysis and systematic knowledge; it is a familiarity built up from 'many memories of the same thing' (*Metaph.* I. 1, 980b29). Although minimally necessary for abstract theoretical disciplines, experience is the stuff of wisdom (*phronēsis*) (cf. VI. 8, 1142a9–19; 11, 1143b11–14), and prerequisite for getting the most out of Ar.'s discourse on ethics (see I. 3, 1095a2–3 with note). Wisdom is possible only when the lower part of the soul is thoroughly trained to obey reason (VI. 12–13 (1143b18–1145a11)), so it needs time for this training as well as for the accumulation of experience.

1103a17–18   **which is in fact the source of the name it has acquired** [*ēthikē*]**, the word for 'character-trait'** [*ēthos*] **being a slight variation of that for 'habituation'** [*ethos*, short 'e']   '*ethos*' originally meant 'usage' or 'wont', and carried no implication of cultural as distinct from genetic origin. But Ar. takes the supposed etymology as evidence of the former.

1103a18–20   **This makes it quite clear ... no natural way of being is changed through habituation** [*ethistheiē*]   (*a*) In Aristotelian physics the tendencies of earth (the material of stones) to fall and of fire to rise are intrinsic properties of these fundamentally different substances. (*b*) The present argument assumes that if one of a pair of alternative tendencies is impossible to acquire through habituation, the other could not have been acquired in that way either. (*c*) Excellences or defects of character, once acquired, are 'second nature' (cf. VII. 10, 1152a30–3, and *EE* II. 2, 1220a36–b5), i.e. virtually indelible propensities to behave in certain ways.

the excellences develop in us neither by nature nor contrary to nature   This   *1103a23–4*
is true of the intellectual ones too, but Ar. is not thinking of them here (cf. line 26).

What happens in cities testifies to this . . . a good one from a bad one   For an   *1103b2–6*
extended discussion, see x. 9 (1179a33–1181b23). The deliberate use of legislation to make the citizens good is an ideal seldom instantiated, as Ar. admits at 1180a24–8.

every excellence is both produced and destroyed   Given remarks elsewhere   *1103b7–8*
about the durability of excellence (4, 1105a32–3; III. 5, 1114a16–21; cf. I. 10, 1100b11–17), he presumably means that habituation destroys the *possibility* of excellence (unless the statement is a logical slip from ' . . . every excellence and corresponding defect is produced'). Cf. 2, 1104a11–14 and 25–7; 3, 1105a13–15.

II 2, 1103b26–1104b3

Since this inquiry is for the sake of becoming good, not of knowing what excellence is, we must consider how one should act, since acting generates the dispositions (1103b26–31); 'in accordance with the correct prescription' is of course a condition, which will be considered later (1103b31–4); one can only speak in outline and imprecisely about practical things (1103b34–1104a10); yet we should try to help by pointing out that deficiency and excess are what destroy good qualities, whether they are physical ones or excellences (1104a10–27); the conduct through which excellence is generated is the conduct in which it is exercised, once we have it (1104a27–1104b3).

for we are not inquiring into what excellence is for the sake of knowing it, but   *1103b27–9*
for the sake of becoming good, since otherwise there would be no benefit in it
at all   Cf. 4, 1105b11–18 and I. 3, 1095a4–6.

as we have said   i.e. in the previous chapter, 1103a31 ff.   *1103b31*

that one should act in accordance with the correct prescription is a shared   *1103b31–2*
view   'Correct prescription' renders *orthos logos*, sometimes translated as 'right rule', sometimes as 'right reason'. 'Rule' is inappropriate, since the *orthos logos* operates in particular situations, and Ar. does not think that knowing just what to do in a particular situation is given to us by rules. 'Right reason' is misleading if it invites the interpretation 'right reason*ing*', since '*logos*' here means, as often, a *product* of reasoning such as a formula or articulate declaration. What is said to be shared here is the use of the *phrase* 'according to the correct prescription'. It was used both inside and outside the Academy.

1103b32–4　**there will be a discussion about it later, both about what 'the correct pre-scription' is, and about how it is related to the other kinds of excellence**　The reference is to Book VI, or to a projected treatment for which that common book was substituted (see Introduction, p. 4). At times Ar. uses 'the correct prescription' as a label for the excellence (wisdom, *phronēsis*) whose possessors can be relied on to formulate correct prescriptions; see e.g. VI. 1 (1138b18–1139a7).

1104a2–3　**as we also said at the beginning**　See I. 3, 1094b11–27.

1104a10–11　**even though the present discussion is like this, we must try to give some help**　The question is: 'What sort of actions must one practise in order to develop excellence of character?' The preceding answer, 'Actions that accord with the correct prescription', gives no practical guidance, whereas what follows does give some.

1104a24–5　**as boors do, is insensate, as it were**　Boorishness (*agroikia*) later becomes the name of the defect humourlessness; II. 7, 1108a26; IV. 8, 1128a9 and b2. On 'insensate, as it were' see note on 7, 1107b8.

II 3, 1104b3–1105a16

Pleasure or pain in doing good actions is a sign that we have the dispositions (1104b3–11); excellence of character, and the opposite qualities, have to do with pleasures and pains (1104b8–9); arguments for this point (1104b9–28); pleasure is fundamental to us, we are guided by it, therefore every effort must be made to ensure that we feel pleasure and pain as we should (1104b28–1105a16).

1104b3–5　**The pleasure [*hēdonē*] or pain [*lupē*; also sometimes translated 'distress'] that supervenes on what people do should be treated as a sign of their disposi-tions**　(*a*) The educator must be able to tell when a disposition has become established. Relevant *actions* are not always good evidence, since they are possible without the disposition. (*b*) Finding certain actions welcome or unwelcome is not circumstantial evidence for a disposition of character, but a direct expression of it.

1104b7–8　**cheerfully, or anyway without distress**　This is an oversimplification. The cour-ageous person cheerfully, gladly, willingly, and even (as we colloquially say in answer to requests) 'with pleasure', undergoes trials which may in fact be extremely unpleasant. Since as persons we are complex, and we are biological organisms as well as persons, there are different levels of inclination and disinclin-ation. (Ar. tries to do justice to this complexity in the case of courage at III. 9, 1117a32–b16.)

1104b8–9　**For excellence of character has to do with pleasures and pains**　Does he mean the special pleasures and pains that arise from an acquired ethical dis-position, or ones that everyone feels, and which the ethical dispositions deal with well or badly (cf. 5, 1105b25–8)? The next sentence may refer to the latter, but then the connection with the previous sentence is obscure.

as Plato says   *Republic* 401e–402a; *Laws* 653a ff.   1104b12

if the excellences have to do with actions and affections [*pathē*]   (*a*) This   1104b13–14
antecedent is assumed true. (*b*) In a psychological context, *pathē* can often be
rendered 'emotions' (the term also covers impulses and any psychic disturbance),
but in the Academy it also acquired the technical abstract meaning 'affective
quality' (*Categories* 8, 9a28–10a10).

A further proof   i.e. of the proposition that 'Excellence of character has to do   1104b16
with pleasures and pains' (8–9). The argument is: (1) We use forceful correction
(*kolasis*) to inculcate good conduct; (2) forceful correction is essentially painful; (3)
as in medicine, excess of one opposite (e.g. giving in to pleasures) is corrected by
applying the other; (4) pleasure is the opposite of pain; therefore (5) excellence of
character consists in a state that is corrected and healthy in the matter of giving in
to pleasures. A similar argument with 'forceful correction' replaced by 'correction
by blandishment' ('sugaring the pill') in (1) and (2), and 'painful' by 'pleasant' in
(2), gives the additional conclusion that excellence of character consists in a state
that is healthy in the matter of shrinking from pains.

as in fact we said just now   See 2, 1104a27–9.   1104b18–19

people define the excellences as kinds of impassivity and immobility   He   1104b24–5
may be referring to Speusippus (on whom, see comment on I. 6, 1096b7), who
held that the best state is absence of both pleasure and pain; this was linked to the
theory (which Ar. rejects) that pleasure is a kind of movement or coming to be;
cf. VII. 12, 1152b33–1153a17; X. 3, 1173a29–b7, and 4, 1174a14–b9. For Ar., impassivity and immobility cannot as such be excellence, because, as 1104b25–6
implies, they sometimes go wrong.

what is fine, what is advantageous, and what is pleasant   Cf. I. 8, 1099a15–29,   1104b31
where happiness is said to fall into all three categories.

Again, it is harder to fight against pleasure . . . technical expertise and excel-   1105a7–9
lence   This is another proof that excellence of character is particularly shown in
our dealings with pleasure: to do what is more difficult, one needs, in general,
excellence (e.g. in some spheres technical excellence).

Heraclitus   The 6th-century philosopher.   1105a8

II 4, 1105a17–b18
A problem: how can one become just by doing just things if one is not
just already (1105a17–21)? The same problem could be raised about skill or
technical expertise, and the general answer is the same: it is one thing to get
something right, another to do so in the way the skilful or excellent person

does (1105a21–6); a difference between the two cases (1105a26–30); the conditions for acting from excellence (1105a30–b9); reaffirmation that the only way to become just etc. is by doing just etc. things (1105b9–18).

1105a17   **But someone may raise a problem about how we can say**   The problem is reminiscent of Meno's paradox (Plato, *Meno* 80d–e): How can we say we inquire? For we cannot inquire unless already furnished with the knowledge we are looking for. Socrates was afraid that, unsolved, this problem would make some people give up inquiring (81d); perhaps Ar. has a similar concern.

1105a27–31   **the things that come about through the agency of skills [*technai*] contain in themselves the mark of their being done well [i.e. done with skill] . . . whereas the things that come about in accordance with the excellences count as done justly or moderately not merely because they themselves are of a certain kind, but also because of facts about the agent doing them**   Once chance and direction by another have been eliminated (22–3), *X* counts as a work of skill or technical expertise if it is seen to have the qualities typical of products of the expertise in question. But for *Y* to count as a work of justice etc. (under the same conditions) it is not enough that *Y* be seen to be the kind of thing the just person would do: certain conditions must also be seen to hold of the *agent* of *Y*.

1105a31   **first, if he does them knowingly**   (*a*) The 'if' of this and the two subsequent conditions amounts to 'only if'. (*b*) To refuse an excessively rich dish is the sort of thing the moderate person would do, but your refusal does not indicate moderation if you did not know that that was what you were refusing. The parallel point can be made about expertise, as Ar. notes (1105b1–2), but is more likely to be of academic interest there, since in very many cases there is no possibility of producing a highly finished artefact ('such as the expert would produce') without knowing that this is what one is doing.

1105a31–2   **secondly if he decides [*prohairoumenos*] to do them**   (*a*) On 'if' see (*a*) of previous note. (*b*) A 'decision' to do *X* is an undertaking informed by the agent's considered judgement that his or her doing *X* would be good conduct (*praxis*). The determinations of an expertise are not 'decisions' in this Aristotelian sense, because they reflect conceptions of, for example, good music, correct spelling, etc., not of good practice as such. See Introduction, p. 41.

1105a32   **and decides to do them for themselves**   If, as a result of decision, you do what can be described as *D*, where '*D*' (e.g. 'refusing excessively rich food') answers the question (for example) 'In this situation, what would the moderate person do?', this is not evidence that you are moderate unless your decision is indeed *to do D*, as distinct from a decision to (for example) annoy your hostess by refusing her signature dish. (The point is not, as some interpreters think, that the person of excellence decides on the action for its own sake. For it is consistent with moderation to do *D* for the sake of one's health, and to value health just for the sake of happiness.)

and thirdly if he does them from a firm and unchanging disposition [sc. to act in that way]   (*a*) On 'if' see note (*a*) on 1105a31. (*b*) On 'firm and unchanging', see Introduction, p. 19. (*c*) The first condition does not entail the others. The second entails the first, but not the third, since the incontinent person sometimes acts on his decision but sometimes wavers from it. The third entails the first and probably also the second.

but when it comes to having the excellences, knowledge makes no difference, or a small one, whereas the force of the other conditions is not small but counts for everything, and it is these that result from the repeated perform-ance of just and moderate actions   The agent's knowledge is only a sine qua non for his action's counting as done from possessed excellence; normally it adds no positive ground for viewing it thus. But the other two conditions each add positive ground, because they tend to be constitutive of excellence. Because of this they, like excellence itself, and unlike the sheer ability to know what one is doing, develop only through frequent practice.

whereas from not doing these things no one will have excellence in the future either   From the claim, which Ar. has just defended, that we become just by doing just things etc., it follows that those to whom it applies are not just yet but will be so if they (consistently) do just things. He now adds that those who fail to do just things neither are just now nor will be later.

by taking refuge in talk they think that they are philosophizing, and that they will become excellent this way   They make two mistakes: they assume that the difference between would-be excellent and excellent is bridged by talk, not action; and they assume that they philosophize, when a wholly misdirected intellectual activity does not count as 'philosophizing'.

II 5, 1105b19–1106a13

Ar. begins the positive account of what character-excellence is. It is either an affection or a capacity or a disposition (1105b19–28); affections are elimin-ated (1105b28–1106a6); so are capacities (1106a6–10); therefore the genus of excellence is *disposition* (1106a10–13).

Now since the things that occur in the soul fall into three kinds . . . excellence will be one of these   (*a*) What justifies the tripartition? Ar. relies on his audience to remember that excellence in general belongs in the category Quality (cf. I. 6, 1096a25). *Dispositions* (or *hexeis*, which many translators render by 'states'), *capaci-ties* (*dunameis*), and *affections* (*pathē*) are three of the four subdivisions of this category (*Categories* 8). (The fourth is shape.) (*b*) Although there are physical affections, capacities, and dispositions, the argument is confined to psychic ones, since the subject is excellence of soul, not body (I. 13, 1102a16–17). Thus *pathē* here is virtually equivalent to 'emotions', 'feelings' (and shape is excluded from consideration). (*c*) Although some psychic affections, capacities, and dispositions are intellectual (the intellectual excellences are called 'hexeis', and so are the different kinds of expertise), and some are sensory, the present argument is confined to those relating to (one's own) emotions and impulses, since the subject is, specifically, character-excellence, which has to do with emotions (3, 1104b13–14) and is said to belong to the appetitive part of the soul (I. 13, 1102b30). (d) Affections are actualizations of capacities and dispositions; e.g. a particular outburst of temper is an actualization both of the agent's general, human, capacity for anger, and of his or her personal disposition to (for example) get angry when kept waiting. (e) As the above example shows, a disposition is activated immediately by the trigger situation, whereas a capacity is activated because the disposition is. (f) An Aristotelian disposition is defined more narrowly than a disposition in the modern philosophical sense, since the former is defined as a property in virtue of which the subject is *well or badly* disposed in some way (*Metaph.* v. 20, 1022b10–12; and lines 25–6 below).

1105b23   **generally, feelings [*pathē*] attended by pleasure or pain**   See Introduction, pp. 19–20.

1105b25–6   **as for dispositions [*hexeis*], it is in terms of these that we are well or badly disposed [*echomen eu ē kakōs*] in relation to the affections**   The phrase 'to be well/badly disposed (i.e. to be in a good/bad state, condition)' was colloquial Greek. Ar. uses it to explain the more technical term 'disposition'.

1106a2–4   **we are angry and afraid without decision, whereas the excellences are kinds of decision, or anyway involve decision [*prohairesis*]**   (a) On 'decision' see 4, 1105a31–2, with note. (b) The point is not that affections like anger do not arise from decision (this is largely also true of excellences; the actions that give rise to them must be voluntary, but need not be decided upon; cf. III. 2, 1111b4–10); it is that the excellences (and their opposites) are manifested in decisions, whereas unqualified affections are manifested only in impulses. (c) 'Prohairesis' , like 'decision' can mean (i) an act of deciding, (ii) the content of what is decided, and (iii) a policy reached through an act of decision. Being furnished with a decision in sense (iii) resembles an excellence in that both are standing conditions; the state of being furnished with a sense-(iii) decision is what modern philosophers call a 'disposition' to act according to a decision in sense (i) and sense (ii).

1106a10   **earlier**   At 1, 1103a18–26.

II 6, 1106a14–1107a27

The general notion of 'excellence' applied to the human case (1106a15–24); the notions of 'too much', 'too little', and 'intermediate' (relative to us) (1106a26–b5); every sort of expertise does its work well by seeking the intermediate (1106b5–14); therefore character-excellence (which is better than expertise) seeks the intermediate in affections and actions (1106b14–27); so excellence is a kind of intermediacy between extremes (which explains why going right takes one form, while going wrong takes many, and why going right is more difficult) (1106b27–35); excellence, then, is a disposition issuing in decisions, depending on intermediacy that is relative to us and determined by the rational prescription—intermediacy between two bad states, one of excess, the other of deficiency (1106b36–1107a6); hence excellence is defined as intermediacy, but on the scale of goodness it is top (1107a6–8); actions and affections whose names imply their badness, such as malice and murder, do not admit of intermediacy; to expect it is like expecting each member of an excess–intermediacy–deficiency trio to admit, in turn, each of the three possibilities (1107a8–27).

we must also say what sort of disposition it is   It has already been informally   *1106a14–15*
differentiated as being right about pleasures and pains (ch. 3), and about affections (i.e. emotions and impulses, 5, 1105b25–6). But Ar. now offers an account which he regards as more informative, in terms of *the intermediate.*

every excellence, whatever it is an excellence of . . . gives that thing the finish   *1106a15–16*
of a good condition   Since excellence is the good condition, not a distinct source of it, excellence 'gives' it to something only in a logical sense ('having only three angles gives this figure triangularity'); similarly for 'the eye's/horse's excellence makes it excellent' (1106a17–20). Cf. vi. 12, 1144a3–4.

the excellence of a human being too will be the disposition whereby he   *1106a22–6*
becomes a good human being . . . In what way this will be, we have already
said, but it will also be clear in this way, too, i.e. if we consider what sort of
nature excellence has   There are two ways of reading this passage. (1) Take (i) 'good human being' at line 23 as meaning 'one who has an excellent disposition'; (ii) 'whereby he becomes' (23) as meaning 'whereby he is' (excellence is the disposition whereby one 'comes to have' an excellent disposition only in the sense in which the eye's excellence 'makes' it good at seeing (see previous note)); (iii) 'this' (24) as referring to his being a good human being (or to excellence of a human being, 22); (iv) 'in what way this will be' as meaning 'the method by which excellence is developed'. In that case, the backward reference is to ii. 1–2, where the acquisition of character-excellence is discussed. The difficulty with this reading is that it is not clear how the ensuing explanation of character-excellence as 'intermediate' adds to our understanding of how it is acquired. One possibility is that defining excellence as *being* something intermediate confirms the declaration at 2, 1104a11–28 that it is *acquired* through a mixed (not all one way or the other), hence intermediate, set of experiences. Alternatively (2), take (ii and i) 'whereby he becomes a good human being' as meaning 'whereby he acts as a good etc.' (in Greek 'is good' can be used in this way; cf. our 'Be good', where what is enjoined is behaviour); and (iii and iv) 'in what way this will be' as picking out the mode of behaviour that distinguishes good performance of the human function. In that case, the backward reference is to ii. 4, 1105a29–b9, on the differences between

303

doing what the excellent do and acting from excellence, and the ensuing discussion adds that excellent behaviour 'hits upon what is intermediate'. Interpretation 2 seems preferable.

1106a27   **a greater and a lesser and an equal amount**   The Greek expressions can also mean 'too much', 'too little', and 'a fair amount'.

1106b1   **ten minae in weight**   The mina, according to the Attic standard, was just under a pound.

1106b3   **Milo**   A legendary wrestler, said to have eaten the flesh of a bull in one day.

1106b4–5   **Similarly with running and wrestling**   Presumably he means amounts of these activities.

1106b7   **the intermediate, that is, not in the object, but relative to us**   (*a*) the intermediate 'in the object' is the arithmetical mean (1106a35–6). (*b*) Ar. labels the ethical mean 'relative to *us*' because of his illustrations, in which the right amount (of food and exercise) is right for the physique of the person concerned. But where it is a question of the 'right amount' of anger or risk-taking, what is right is so *for the particular situation* (which of course includes facts about the agent).

1106b8–9   **If, then, it is in this way that every kind of expert knowledge** [*epistēmē*] **completes its function** [*ergon*] **well, by looking to the intermediate**   i.e. by being guided by the question 'Is this the right amount (intermediate between too much and too little)?' With many types of expertise, the completed function is a separable product; with human excellence, it is excellent activity (cf. I. 7, 1098a7).

1106b14–16   **and if excellence is more precise and better than any expertise, just as nature is, it will be effective at hitting upon what is intermediate**   (*a*) An a fortiori argument: since expertise, which is inferior to excellence, owes its success to its ability to hit the intermediate, how much more is this true of excellence. (*b*) The argument turns not just on the platitude that excellence is better than expertise, but on the claim that it is more 'precise' (*akribestera*); what can this mean? It seems obvious that some expertises require a degree of precision alien to the ethical sphere, if Ar. is right about the roughness of ethics. Perhaps the point is that excellence is more rigorous because unconditionally uncompromising about its aims, whereas any ordinary practical expertise must be prepared to give way to the wider goals of human life; thus excellence is not only superior in the sense of more commanding, but its operations are more self-sufficient (it is answerable only to itself), hence in a way less haphazard, than those of expertise. See VI. 2, 1139a35–6 with comment; for a similar comparison between wisdom and technical expertise, see VI. 5, 1140b22–4; and cf. III. 3, 1112b1, on the connection of precision with self-sufficiency. (*c*) Presumably nature is mentioned as another example of a power superior to any expert knowledge (*epistēmē*, 8; the word means any sort of systematic knowledge, practical or theoretical), in order to block the objection that 'nothing is superior to *epistēmē* (cf. Plato, *Protagoras* 352b–d). To allow the objection would commit one to the Socratic view that human excellence is a kind of *epistēmē*.

I mean excellence of character; for this has to do with affections and actions, and it is in these that there is excess and deficiency, and the intermediate (*a*) Ar. writes as if hitting the mean is distinctive of character-excellence, and in the *NE* he never applies the triadic scheme to intellectual qualities. Yet he was aware of dimensions in which it could have been applied: e.g. some bring to political science exaggerated standards of rigour (I. 3, 1094b11–27), others confuse it with rhetoric (x. 9, 1181a12–15). At *EE* II, 3, 1221a12, wisdom appears in the manuscripts, at the end of a chart of character-triads, as intermediate between simple-mindedness and unscrupulous cunning; but this idea is not taken up in the actual discussion of wisdom (the main discussion being in the common book *NE* VI = *EE* v). (*b*) Actions now reappear in the discussion. Separate attention is given to the intermediate in affections (18–23) and in actions (23–4) because good affective responses are signs of excellence in themselves, not merely because they motivate good action.

1106b16–18

pleasure and distress in general   These are now grouped along with the affections, whereas before (3, 1104b14–15; 5, 1105b21–3) they were said to accompany them.

1106b19–20

but to be affected when one should, at the things one should, in relation to the people one should, for the reasons one should, and in the way one should, is both intermediate and best   Here it becomes clear that quantity (*too much, too little, median amount*) represents the entire range of respects in which one can be right or wrong whether in engaging or in failing to engage.

1106b21–2

Excellence has to do with affections and actions ... intermediacy belongs to excellence   This passage gives two arguments for 'Intermediacy belongs to excellence': (1) Excess and deficiency go astray; 'intermediate' (i.e. 'neither excessive nor deficient') is a term of praise, meaning 'Got it right'; praise and rightness belong to excellence (1106b24–8). (2) There are many ways of going wrong, only one of going right (so excellence, whereby one goes right, is intermediate because intermediate (i.e. centre) is one and extremes are many) (1106b28–34). Throughout the passage, excellence is treated as intermediate for two reasons which Ar. hardly distinguishes: because of the intermediacy of its own responses it is effective at hitting upon what is intermediate, 27–8; cf. 9, 1109a22–3), and because the two contrasting dispositions are independently labelled 'excessive' and 'deficient' (see Introduction, pp. 20–1). The difference between these reasons is passingly registered at 1107a3 ('and also because').

1106b24–34

the Pythagoreans   See note on I. 6, 1096b5–6.

1106b29–30

'single and straight ...'   Source unknown.

1106b35

1106b36–1107a2   **Excellence, then, is a disposition issuing in decisions** [*hexis prohairetikē*]**, depending on intermediacy** [*mesotēs*] **of the kind relative to us, this being determined by rational prescription** [*orthos logos*] **and in the way in which the wise** [*phronimos*] **person would determine it**   (*a*) On 'decisions' see note (*b*) on 4, 1105a31–2. This element of the definition is difficult, given the repeated emphasis on *affective* response as expressing character (5, 1105b25–8; 6, 1106b16–23, 1107a8–11). For elsewhere, it would seem, actions alone are subject to Aristotelian decision. Moreover, at III. 2, 1112a14–16 and 3, 1113a2–12 he says that decision presupposes prior deliberation; yet many character-expressing actions are not led up to by deliberation. But perhaps 'issuing in decisions' here means 'issuing in determinate responses (cf. III. 3, 1113a3) that reflect the respondent's fundamental values'. (*b*) Conversely the *intermediacy* of a moral excellence distinguishes it from the associated bad qualities, which are also 'dispositions issuing in decisions'. (*c*) As at 1106b33, the intermediacy on which character-excellence depends is a property of the agent's particular responses. (*d*) On the rational prescription, cf. 2, 1103b31–4 with notes.

1107a5–6   **whereas excellence both finds and chooses the intermediate**   Strictly speaking, it is wisdom (*phronēsis*) that 'finds' (*heuriskein*, 1107a5) what is intermediate, whereas excellence of character 'chooses' (*haireisthai*) it. But the focus here is not so much on the difference between finding and choosing as on the contrast between excellence and the vices of excess and deficiency.

1107a6–7   **its essence** [*ousia*] **. . . what it is for excellence to be** [*to ti ēn einai*]   These are technical expressions of Aristotle's school.

1107a8–9   **But not every action admits of intermediacy, nor does every affection**   Ar. now makes clear that excellence can be said to attain the intermediate only when the action or emotion is neutrally described. If attaining the intermediate means responding correctly, there can be no attaining it in the ones about to be mentioned, whose names imply condemnation.

1107a10–11   **malice, shamelessness, grudging ill will** [*phthonos*]   These three are discussed again at 7, 1108a30–b6. (*a*) Shamelessness would seem rather to be lack of feeling. (*b*) At 5, 1105b21–3 grudging ill will is one of the neutral feelings.

1107a11–12   **and in the case of actions, fornication, theft, murder**   Actions falling under these descriptions are wrong prima facie, which is enough to distinguish these from neutral descriptions, but here Ar. takes the stronger position that they are always wrong. However, his discussion of hard choices in III. 1 holds out the possibility that he might consider them excusable under certain circumstances.

1107a20–1   **for that way there will be intermediate excess and deficiency, excessive excess, and deficient deficiency**   The model of something continuous and divisible (1106a26) actually suggests this absurdity. If the intermediate is like a point dividing it, the lines on each side (representing excess and deficiency) should themselves be divisible by an intermediate into excess and deficiency of excess, and excess and deficiency of deficiency.

II 7, 1107a28–1108b10
We must see how the theory fits particular cases as set out in the chart.

how it fits the particular cases   Here, as often, Ar. uses 'particular' not to exclude 'universal' in the logical sense, but as meaning specific by contrast with generic.   *1107a29*

from the chart   i.e. of the triads of dispositions. The chart is not in any surviving manuscript of the *NE*, but is reconstructed as follows: *1107a32–3*

Continuum	Disposition		
	Excessive	Intermediate	Deficient
Fear	Cowardice	Courage	[Nameless]
Boldness	Rashness	Courage	Cowardice
Physical pleasures	Self-indulgence	Moderation	[Nameless]
Money: giving	Wastefulness	Open-handedness	Avariciousness
taking	Avariciousness	Open-handedness	Wastefulness
Grand spending	Vulgarity	Munificence	Shabbiness
Great honours	Conceitedness	Greatness of soul	Littleness of soul
Minor honours	Love of honour	[Nameless]	Indifference to honour
Temper	Irascibility	Mildness	Spiritlessness
Self-presentation	Imposture	Truthfulness	Self-deprecation
Humour	Buffoonery	Wittiness	Boorishness
Affability	Obsequiousness Ingratiatingness	'Friendly'-ness	Contentiousness

the one who is excessively fearless ... the one who is excessively confident   The difference between these is explained at III. 7, 1115b25–33, in the extended study of courage.   *1107b1–2*

many cases are nameless   In the lists that follow, Ar. will: coin some new words (e.g. *anorgētos*, 'spiritless', and *mikroprepēs*, 'shabby', and the cognate nouns); use some that were probably unfamiliar except to those who knew Plato's work; and use some familiar terms in newly extended or newly restricted senses.   *1107b2*

With regard to pleasures and pains ... the intermediate state is moderation   In the extended treatment at III. 10–11 (1117b23–1119a20) the continuum for   *1107b4–6* moderation is physical pleasure, and physical pain is dealt with in the discussion of courage.

1107b8   **let us put them down as 'insensate'** [*anaisthētoi*]   In ordinary use, the word meant 'unconscious' or 'unable to perceive by the senses'.

1107b15   **later**   At IV. 1 (1119b22–1122a17).

1107b21   **later**   At IV. 2, 1122a20–b18.

1107b30–1   **The states themselves, too, are nameless, except that the name given to that of the honour-lover is love of honour**   A name for the opposite quality does not exist, and Ar. does not coin one, perhaps because (as the next lines indicate) it would be arbitrary whether he attached it to the intermediate character or the deficient one.

1107b31–2   **Consequently those at the extremes lay claim to the ground between them**   Since there is no name for the intermediate character (29), each extreme assumes that he and the opposite extreme exhaust the possibilities. Since each sees the other as inferior in matters of honour, he concludes that his own disposition is excellence in this sphere.

1107b32– 1108a1   **even we ourselves sometimes call the intermediate person 'honour-loving', sometimes 'indifferent to honour', sometimes using the first as a term of praise, sometimes the second**   It would not be surprising if the excessive extreme called the intermediate 'indifferent', and the deficient extreme called him 'honour-loving'; this would be because of their distorted ethical points of view (see Introduction, pp. 21–2). In itself this would not indicate that the language has too few terms for the number of dispositions in question (cf. 8, 1108b15–26, where the intermediates mischaracterized by the extremes have their own established names). But if 'we ourselves' (well brought up people; cf. I. 4, 1095b4–6) fluctuate in our names for a certain intermediate, using opposite terms to praise it, this can only be because the disposition is nameless.

1108a2   **We shall talk about the reason for our doing this in what follows**   The reason is that the intermediate state is opposed to each of the extremes; thus if it is nameless it easily comes to be named as if it were the extreme opposite of one or other extreme: see 8, 1108b11–19.

1108a20   **in a sense 'truthful'** [*alēthēs*] ... **'truthfulness'**   An unusual usage, as the main meaning of the Greek words had to do with freedom from error rather than sincerity.

1108a25–6   **the deficient person perhaps a boor** [*agroikos*]   The Greek word originally meant 'rustic'.

1108a27–8   **if someone is pleasant in the way one should be, let us call him 'friendly'** [*philos*]**, and the intermediate state correspondingly**   In fact, Ar. here calls the intermediate state '*philia*', which does not mean 'friendliness', but 'friendship'. Apparently he could find no distinctive word for the quality of general friendliness. In the longer treatment at IV. 6, 1126b20–3, he says the intermediate state 'most resembles *philia*' (using the word in its usual sense), but lacks *philia*'s special bond of personal feeling.

There are also intermediates in the affective feelings [*pathēmata*] **and in relation to things that happen to people** [*pathē*]   Here Ar. introduces two *1108a30–1* examples of a new sort of triad, consisting of excessive, deficient, and intermediate responses to things that befall people. One example consists in responses to things involving oneself, the other in responses to the fortunes of others. It is strange that he classes these triads as affective feelings (i.e. affections), as they seem to be dispositions.

a sense of shame is not an excellence   He speaks of it as an excellence at III. 8, *1108a31–2* 1116a27–8. He gives reasons why it is not an excellence at IV. 9 (1128b10–35).

Righteous indignation is intermediate between grudging ill will and malice *1108a35–b1* Cf. the more complex analysis in *Rhetoric* II. 9, where the present trio becomes a foursome with the addition of pity (i.e. pain at unmerited misfortune).

and the malicious person is so deficient when it comes to being distressed *1108b5–6* **that he is even pleased**   Whereas the other two attitudes involve pain at others' good fortunes, malice involves pleasure in their misfortunes. The extremes of this triad are not mutually exclusive, and in fact at *Rhetoric* II. 9, 1387a1, they are said necessarily to coincide.

But there will be an opportunity to discuss these questions later   For justice, *1108b6–7* see *NE* V; for the other excellences of character, III, 6–IV. 8 (1115a4–1128b9). Ar. returns to proper shame (IV. 9) but not to righteous indignation in the *NE*; see note on IV, 9, 1128b33–4.

how justice in each of the two senses is an intermediate   Some commenta- *1108b8–9* tors think these words spurious, since justice in one of the two senses of Book V (general justice) is not defined as intermediate.

And likewise with the excellences of reason [*hai logikai aretai*] **too**   Presumably *1108b9–10* the reference is to *NE* VI. But this sentence too is suspect. Its mode of designating the intellectual excellences occurs nowhere else in Aristotle. And any implication that these, too, are intermediates seems un-Aristotelian (see note (*a*) on 6, 1106b16–17).

II 8, 1108b11–1109a19
Each member of a triad is opposed in a way to each of the others, with the intermediate being excessive in relation to the deficiency and deficient in relation to the excess (1108b11–19); e.g. the courageous type appears rash to

the coward and cowardly to the rash (1108b19–26); but the extremes are more contrary, and more dissimilar, to each other than either is to the intermediate, since in some cases one extreme resembles the intermediate more than the other does, e.g. rashness and courage (1108b26–35); of the two extremes, sometimes the deficiency is more opposed to the intermediate, e.g. cowardice to courage, and sometimes the excess is, e.g. self-indulgence to moderation (1108b35–1109a5); this is because (1) in some cases one extreme really is closer to the intermediate, so the latter is more opposed to the other extreme (1109a5–12); and because (2) in some cases we ourselves naturally have a greater bent towards one of the two extremes, which therefore seems to us more contrary to the intermediate (1109a12–19).

This chapter supports the theory of triads by explaining why it is easy to make the mistake of thinking that an excellence has just one opposite. (*a*) From the perspective of an extreme (which takes itself to be the excellence), the intermediate can be confused with the other extreme (as a lesser version of it), so that there appear to be two, not three, mutually exclusive dispositions (1108b19–30). (*b*) In some triads there is greater objective resemblance between the intermediate and one extreme than between the intermediate and the other extreme; hence the excellence seems to have just one contrary; e.g. courage versus cowardice because rashness is more like courage (1108b30–1109a12). (*c*) In some cases, three appear two because we are naturally more prone to one extreme than the other, so it seems to us our sole adversary as we battle towards the intermediate (1109a11–19). It is interesting that he does not treat our natural proneness in one bad direction (when it is practically universal, as with self-indulgence versus moderation) as a sign that the other extreme is objectively more similar to the intermediate.

II 9, 1109a20–b26

Summary of main points about character-excellence (1109a20–4); why it is hard to be excellent (1109a30); one should at least achieve the second best of avoiding the extreme that is more opposed to the intermediate (1109a30–b7); we must be always on guard against pleasure (1109b7–13); even so, it is hard to identify the intermediate in particular cases (1109b14–16); we ourselves sometimes praise as excellent persons who deviate from it a little; nor can one give a rule for what will count as a significant deviation in a particular case (1109b16–23); the only safe generalization is that the intermediate disposition is best, and that to approach it one must sometimes incline towards one or other extreme (1109b23–6).

1109a29–30 **getting things right is ... a proper object of praise, and something fine** Getting things right is praiseworthy not just because it hits the mark, but (also) because it is a good thing that is difficult to achieve.

following Calypso's advice In fact the words are spoken by Circe: *Odyssey* XII. *1109a31–2*
219–20.

as the elders of the people felt towards Helen Iliad III. 156–60. In the same *1109b10*
breath the Trojan senators marvelled at her charismatic beauty and wished her far
away from Troy, 'lest grief be the legacy for us and our children after us'.

But to do this is difficult, perhaps So far he has been dealing with the difficulty *1109b14*
of disciplining the non-rational part of the rational soul (cf. I. 13, 1102b11 ff.); now
he refers to the intellectual difficulty of discerning the right response.

we ourselves sometimes praise those deficient in anger ... call them *1109b16–18*
'manly' The pair of examples is chosen to bring out a difference between this
type of error, which is due to the nature of the subject matter, and the kind
that results from occupying an ethically corrupt perspective (8, 1108b23–6). The
coward regularly confuses courage with rashness and never with cowardice,
whereas 'we ourselves' (i.e. well brought up people; cf. 7, 1107b32) sometimes
take one extreme, sometimes the other, to be intermediate.

BOOK III

III 1–5, 1109b30–1115a5
Voluntary action and its conditions (1, 1109b30–1111b3); decision (2,
1111b4–1112a17); deliberation and decision (3, 1112a18–1113a14); wish (4,
1113a15–b2); whether we become ethically good or bad depends on us (5,
1113b3–1114b25); summary, and transition to next subject (1114b26–
1115a5).

III 1, 1109b30–1111b3
Preamble on the voluntary and the counter-voluntary (1109b30–1110a1);
force (1110a1–3); duress ('constraint') and hard choices (1110a4–b9); we are
not 'forced' by pleasant things or fine things (1110b9–17); ignorance, with
and without regret (1110b18–24); acting *because of* ignorance versus acting *in*
ignorance (1110b24–1111a2); different cases of acting because of ignorance
(1111a3–21); summary on voluntary and counter-voluntary action
(1111a22–4); actions done from appetite and temper are no less voluntary
than actions based on reason (1111a24–b3).

sympathy [*sungnōmē*] i.e. readiness to see the case from the agent's point of *1109b33*
view. Appeals to this attitude can be of two types, which Ar. does not distinguish:

(*a*) when the agent defends an apparently wrong-headed or disgraceful action by trying to show that under the circumstances it was right, reasonable, acceptable, etc.; and (*b*) when he or she admits wrongdoing but asks for leniency because of mitigating circumstances, such as provocation, duress, etc.

1110a11   **mixed**   i.e. there is ground for calling them 'counter-voluntary' and ground for calling them 'voluntary'.

1110a16   **the instrumental** [*organika*] **parts**   i.e. the parts of the body that we move at will in carrying out actions. Ar. conceives of voluntary movement as the natural mode of functioning for animals, and parts like legs and wings as natural instruments for the purpose.

1110a17–18   **if the origin** [*archē*] **of something is in himself, it depends on himself whether he does that thing or not**   (*a*) Some commentators object that natural physical processes which we cannot control have their origin in the organism. But by 'in him' Ar. may mean 'in him as a rational or potentially rational individual'. Cf. 3, 1112a32–3, where man and nature (which includes human biological nature) are contrasted as distinct types of cause. (*b*) Ar. does not allow here for the fact that I may be in charge of what I do under one description, not under another. It may be that, under threat, I cannot control whether I give the tyrant the information he wants, even though it is by my own controlled movements that I do things (arriving at a meeting, speaking) that constitute passing the information. Here, Ar. assumes that because these movements are voluntary, my *giving the tyrant the information* is voluntary too; but see *EE* II. 8, 1225a12–13, for a more nuanced view.

1110a26   **But perhaps in some cases there is no such thing as 'being constrained'**   i.e. one cannot get off the hook by pleading that one was under extraordinary pressure. Ar. does not distinguish citing extraordinary pressure as (1) justification where the subject admits responsibility, from citing it as (2) a mitigating circumstance where the subject admits responsibility for wrongdoing. And here he does not recognize extraordinary pressure as (3) grounds for judging what happened counter-voluntary. Apparently Alcmaeon murdered his mother in order to avoid his father's curse. Ar. will not accept that the paternal threat made matricide (1) right, or (2) excusable, or (3) counter-voluntary. Against (3): Alcmaeon himself was the source of his action; against (2): since killing the mother and accepting the father's curse are *each*, taken by itself, humanly unbearable (so that considering either of them against a background of normal alternatives, one is certain that one would not do it unless literally forced or because of ignorance), it does not make sense to do one of them voluntarily and then claim that one was constrained to do it because the other was unbearable.

1110b13–14   **It is ludicrous . . . to put the responsibility on external objects, rather than on oneself for falling an easy victim to such things**   See 5, 1113b3–1114b25, where he will argue that character is a voluntary acquisition.

312

regret [*metameleia*]   Not 'remorse' or 'repentance', since the agent is innocent   *1110b19*
of wrongdoing. However, his or her regret is not a bystander's sadness *that* the
accident happened; it is regret at having caused it. ('*Metameleia*' does sometimes
mean remorse or repentance; it never means a bystander's sadness.)

but he has not acted counter-voluntarily [*akōn*] **either, in so far as he is not**   *1110b21–2*
distressed at it   Here *akōn* applies retrospectively, in view of the subject's
regret. Logically, Ar. ought in the same sense to say that an agent who acts
through ignorance but is later pleased at what he has effected is 'voluntary'
(*hekōn*) in relation to it; but this would have been too paradoxical.

let him be 'non-voluntary'; for since he is different, it is better that he should   *1110b23–4*
have a name to himself   This appears to contradict line 18, where everything
done because of ignorance is said to be not voluntary. But what 18 denies is the
relation to the action (namely, responsibility for it) that would have obtained
(absent force) *at the time of* acting had the person not acted through ignorance;
whereas lines 23–4 mark the *retrospective* contrast between those who regret and
those who do not, both having acted because of ignorance.

Acting *because of* ignorance also appears to be distinct from acting *in* igno-   *1110b24–5*
rance   These are labels for acting from inadequate information versus acting
from a perspective distorted by intoxication, rage, or badness of character. The
fact that Ar. treats these three together may, but need not, suggest that he sees bad
people as acting in a daze or a haze. In any case, even the drunken and the angry
may have a clear grasp of the aspects of the situation that matter to them; but the
wrong aspects matter or they matter in the wrong way.

but because of one of the things just mentioned   i.e. drunkenness or anger.   *1110b27*
The argument is: to say that someone acted because of ignorance sounds like an
excuse; but if the ignorance is due to drunkenness or rage, then it is more
accurate to go to the prior cause and say they acted because of *it* — which no
longer sounds like an excuse.

ignorance in decision-making [*prohairesis*] **. . . ignorance at the level of the**   *1110b31–2*
universal   Both ways of characterizing the state of one who has wrong values,
wrong priorities. On the meaning of 'decision' in Ar., see Introduction, pp. 42–3.
Since this sort of ignorance does not normally give rise to distress about the
action, one might have expected Ar. to deny that it makes an action *non*-voluntary,
not counter-voluntary. But he must be thinking of Plato, who held that 'no one
acts unjustly except counter-voluntarily' (*akōn*) (*Laws* IX, 860d).

no one, unless he were mad   It is remarkable that Ar. mentions insanity but   *1111a6–7*
does not stop to discuss its implications for the ascription of voluntary agency (cf.
3, 1112a20). (However, at V. 8, 1136a6–9 he says that actions done from pathological feelings are counter-voluntary. At VII. 5, 1148b15–1149a20 he considers
pathological pleasures; and at VII. 6, 1149b34 he says summarily that the insane
lack reasoning and decision.)

1111a10 **as Aeschylus said about the Mysteries** i.e. the Eleusinian Mysteries.

1111a13 **pumice stone** Porous and lightweight.

1111a25 **temper or appetite** i.e. non-rational impulses.

1111a26 **none of the other animals will act [*praxei*] voluntarily, nor will children** It is crucial that voluntary action is open to children, who do not count as rational. Children develop good character through being encouraged to do and refrain from certain things, and encouragement implies that they are aware of what they do so far as they see it as what is encouraged, and that the movements are their own response, not forced. In implying that they act only from non-rational impulse, Ar. does not mean that children cannot reason at all, only that they cannot yet conduct their lives by reason.

III 2, 1111b4–1112a17

Decision (*prohairesis*)—what it is not (1111b4–1112a13); decision is reached through deliberation (1112a13–17). The discussion of decision in this and the next chapter fills out Ar.'s formula for character-traits as 'dispositions issuing in decisions' (II. 6, 1106b36; 4, 1105a31–3; 5, 1106a3–4).

1111b6 **and to indicate the differences between people's characters more than actions do** This is because an Aristotelian decision is not a detached conclusion of deliberation, but encapsulates all the reasons and priorities informing the conclusion.

1111b7–8 **Decision, then, is clearly something voluntary, but is not the same thing as the voluntary, for the voluntary is a wider type** (*a*) By 'decision is voluntary' he means 'what is decided-for is voluntary'. (*b*) Although deciding agents are a sub-division of voluntary agents, Ar.'s discussions of the voluntary and of decision take opposite perspectives. As voluntary, actions were considered as deeds done (III. 1); as subjects of decision they will be considered prospectively.

1111b10–11 **Those who say that it is appetite, temper, or wish, or a sort of judgement . . .** (*a*) Appetite (*epithumia*), temper (*thumos*), and wish (*boulēsis*) are the three types of desire (*orexis*). An appetite is an impulse towards the pleasant or away from the painful. Temper, which often takes the form of anger (*orgē*) in response to aggression or insult, is a pre-rational concern for one's worth and for its being recognized and respected. (This includes concern for other things and other people in so far as one's sense of one's own worth is bound up with them.) Both these types of desire tend to be aroused by present objects and to issue in immediate action. Wish has for its object something judged good, and not immediately attainable (so that reason is necessary to form the initial judgement and to reason out means to the end) or not attainable at all. (*b*) The thinkers referred to here would not have used '*prohairesis*', which becomes a philosophically significant term only with Ar. He means that they proposed one of the four items as *immediate source of rational action*.

314

the person without self-control acts from appetite, but not from decision   On lack of self-control, see VII. 1–10 (1145a15–1152a36).   *1111b13–14*

appetite goes contrary to decision, whereas appetite does not go contrary to appetite   Having an appetite for *X* is compatible with deciding for not-*X*, but not with having an appetite for not-*X* (cf. *Metaph.* IV. 3, 1005b29–30, on the contrariety of believing *p* and believing not-*p*).   *1111b16*

appetite for what is pleasant and what brings pain   i.e. these are its foci.   *1111b16–17*

And yet neither, for that matter, is it wish, although it appears quite closely related to it   When the wish is attainable, effective deliberation converts it into a decision.   *1111b19–20*

immortality   i.e. immunity from biological death.   *1111b22–3*

that a particular actor or athlete should win   Dramas were staged in competition with each other at festivals.   *1111b24*

wish is more for the end [*telos*] **whereas decision is about what forwards the end** [*ta pros to telos*]   The object of wish only becomes an end when one sets oneself to attain it, e.g. by deliberating. Thus when it is an end there is already consideration of means. But the original wish for that which then becomes an end is innocent of any thought of means, which are therefore the concern of something different, namely decision. But since nothing can be a means in the abstract, decision must always be about means-for-a-given-end.   *1111b26–7*

neither should it be identified with a certain kind of judgement [*doxa*]   i.e. judgements or opinions about good or bad things as such.   *1112a1*

decision is praised more by reference to its being for what it should be, or to its being correctly made, whereas judgement is praised by reference to how true it is   Elsewhere, however, he speaks of a good decision as 'truth' VI. 2, 1139a17–b5; cf. 5, 1140b5 and 20–1).   *1112a5–7*

So is it, at any rate, what has been reached by prior deliberation?   Not a real question but the expression of Ar.'s view.   *1112a15*

even the name [*prohairesis*] **indicates that what we decide to do is chosen** [*haireton*] **before** [*pro*] **other things**   This may mean 'in preference to alternative actions', or 'chosen in advance of action', or 'chosen (not as the end, but) as preceding realization of the end'. In any case deliberation is presupposed.   *1112a16–17*

III 3, 1112a18–1113a14

The subject matter of deliberation (1112a18–b15); the process of deliberation (1112b15–1113a2); its termination in decision (1113a2–9); summary definition of decision (1113a9–14).

1112a26   **sometimes one way, sometimes another**   i.e. sometimes it happens, some-times not, in accordance with no rule.

1112b2   **as e.g. with writing (for we are not in two minds about how to write)**   Apparently this refers to correct spelling, not formation of letters. A poor speller may of course be in two minds about what the correct spelling is of a certain word; but Ar.'s point is that we do not think that different spellings might each be good, and wonder which is right for the present occasion.

1112b13   **a doctor does not deliberate about whether he'll make his patients healthy** ...   (*a*) According to one interpretation, the point is that one cannot deliberate on whether to *succeed* in curing etc., since success does not depend entirely on the agent. But this does not give a contrast between end and steps towards it, since it is equally true that one cannot deliberate on whether to succeed in actually *taking* the steps, but only on whether one should try taking them. Alternatively and preferably, the point is that every process of deliberation presupposes, hence cannot itself establish, an end which sets the problem of means. (*b*) The examples suggest that just as the doctor as such necessarily aims to cure (though he may have to give up on curing a particular patient), so there is some one kind of end at which the human being as such necessarily aims. Presumably this is happiness. We should bear in mind that happiness, on Ar.'s own account of it, is not *just* an objective aimed at. For in so far as it consists in the activity of human excellence, including wisdom (*phronēsis*), the quality by which we deliberate well (VI. 5 and 9), the good person, even while deliberating, already instantiates happiness. At the same time, such an agent deliberates with the unattained purpose of discovering and then *doing* what is right for someone in his situation; so in so far as right action is central to excellent activity, he necessarily aims for the latter, and therefore for happiness (even if he does not know its Aristotelian definition). However, elsewhere Ar. seems to recognize that human deliberation generally focuses on some end more specific and contingent than happiness, one of many that we aim for at different times. (*EE* II. 10, 1227a14–18, a passage reminiscent of *NE* III. 3, 1113a6, says 'e.g. wealth, pleasure or anything else of the sort that happens to be our object'. See also the plural 'ends' at 1112b34.) The agent who deliberates so as to do what is right in this situation must also have some more specific end in view, or the starting point of his deliberation will be without content.

1112b19   **the first cause**   A loaded phrase, signalling that, despite the inexactness of its subject matter, practical thinking is as much an exercise of reason as scientific thinking. *The* function of reason is to track down first causes (e.g. the basic constituents of a geometrical figure, as in the comparison which follows). It is not clear whether the reference here is to the action finally decided upon, or the final decision itself. Either can be considered the first cause (starting point) of the external process of realizing the end, and it would be quite Aristotelian not to make the distinction.

similarly in the other cases too   Presumably the reference is to the practical   *1112b30*
expertises used as illustrations at 1112b14. In so far as they each take account of
considerations relevant to just one specific objective (this is true even of political
expertise, mentioned at 14), their conclusions are not decisions strictly speaking.
See Introduction, pp. 42–3.

as has been said   At 1112a33.   *1112b31*

actions are for the sake of other things   'Actions' here means what, through   *1112b33*
deliberation, you find out you should do, as distinct from the end which your
deliberation has presupposed. Thus the end or its coming about appears here as
other than the action. However, Ar. often speaks as if the entire project of
attaining-end-*Y*-by-means-*X* is the action.

So there will not be deliberation about particulars either   i.e. the particular   *1112b34*
facts, which, like the end, are given. By comparison, even the most detailed plan
of action is a universal in the sense of indeterminate, i.e. capable of alternative
physical realizations until carried out. In *NE* vi. 7 Ar. links deliberation to particulars (1141b8–16), but there the contrast is with scientific reasoning about universal
truths. The properly baked bread example suggests deliberation ending in a
decision to eat something healthful; cf. the examples at vii. 3, 1147a25–33.

What we deliberate about and what we decide on are the same   Just as it is   *1113a2–3*
the same diagram unanalysed and analysed: 1112b20–1.

the kings would announce to the people what they had decided   i.e. the   *1113a8–9*
kings decided on their own. This is to establish that the part of us that decides is
the part that rules, i.e. reason. This blocks any suggestion that practical reason is
responsible only for framing universal ideals, and that day-to-day decisions spring
from a humbler part of the soul.

decision too will be deliberational desire [*bouleutikē orexis*]   Not clear whether   *1113a10–11*
he means that it is wish (one of the three familiar kinds of desire; (2, 1111b11)
that has been subjected to deliberation, or a new kind of desire that is formed
through deliberation.

III 4, 1113a15–b2

Is wish for (*a*) the good or (*b*) the apparent good? (On the former position,
cf. Plato, *Gorgias* 468d–e.) In the argument that ensues Ar. assumes (1) that if
X is wished for, then *X* is an object of wish (*boulēton*), and (2) that being an
object of wish entails being an object *to be* wished for. The Greek '*-ēton*'
ending sanctions such a combination of, or ambiguity between, 'is φ-ed' and
'is to be φ-ed'. (*a*) Those who say that the good is the object of wish (which
follows from saying that wish is for the good) face the problem that someone who chooses badly wishes for what is not an object of wish. (*b*) Those
who say that the apparent good is the object of wish (which follows from

saying that wish is for the apparent good) face the problem that there is no 'natural' object of wish, i.e. there is nothing such that to wish for something other than it is to wish wrongly. A modern philosopher would probably reply to (a) by pointing out that from the first-person perspective, wish is for the good, but that if we are describing someone else we may well say 'He or she wishes for what (only) appears good to him or her, but it isn't really good'. (Note that in such a case the modern philosopher would have to abandon one or other of Ar.'s two assumptions.) And the modern philosopher would probably reply to (b) by saying: 'To say that each person wishes for what appears good to him or her is not to imply that there is no real good. What appears good to some, *is* good, i.e. is the "natural" object of wish. Thus in this case, what is wished for is both what appears good, and what is good.' The modern replies show that each side of the original question has some truth in it. Predictably, Ar.'s treatment shows this too. But his treatment is different from the modern one. He says: 'The good is the object of wish (hence to be wished for) *without qualification* or *tout court*; what appears to So-and-So to be good is the object of wish (hence to be wished for) *in relation to So-and-So*' (1113a23–4). And it is characteristic of Ar. that instead of going on to explain the difference between the two parts of this claim in terms of the difference between first- and third-personal points of view, he goes on to explain it in terms of the difference between a subject in good, and another in bad, ethical condition. The good person's object of wish is the good, and the good is, without qualification, an object of wish; whereas the bad one's object of wish is the apparent good, and this is an object of wish in a qualified way, i.e. in relation to himself. Now, given that the bad person wishes for his object of wish, assumptions (1) and (2) above entail that Ar. cannot logically interpret 'it is an object of wish in relation to S' as meaning 'it appears to S to be an object of wish' (where this is consistent with: 'but really it isn't'). And it seems that Ar. does not interpret what we express as 'in relation to' (conveyed in Greek by the dative case) in this way. He draws a parallel with physically healthy and sick subjects in a way that suggests that what the bad person wishes for is indeed *to be* wished for, i.e. *is desirable*, for a being like him. Looked at in this way, what is wrong with him is not that things that are not desirable at all seem to him desirable; it is that the things that are desirable for him—things by which someone like him can thrive—are desirable only for the rotten thriving of someone in a rotten condition. In so far as his error is cognitive, it is the mistake of holding that these things are to be wished for *tout court* as distinct from wished for only by someone like him. This mistake arises out of the universal and natural tendency to assume that what oneself wishes for is to be wished for *tout court*. But only the good person is justified in giving in to this tendency. Cf. vii. 12, 1152b26–33, 1153a2–7; and Introduction, pp. 72–3 (on pleasure).

the things that are truly healthful These are not (as we might think) things that both appear to be healthful and are so, versus things that appear to be so but are not, but rather: things that really are healthful without qualification, versus things that to diseased people seem healthful without qualification but really are healthful only for them.

III 5, 1113b3–1114b25

The main aim is to show that persons of poor character are not just passive recipients of their dispositions. Ethical dispositions are 'voluntary' because they 'depend on us', which means, minimally, that we do not just acquire or find ourselves with one regardless of what we voluntarily do. Ar. begins by arguing (1) that good actions depend on us (1113b3–6). Then (2) if the good ones depend on us, so must the bad (1113b6–14); therefore (3) it depends on us whether we are good or bad. Further, (4) if we deny badness to be voluntary we imply the absurdity that 'man is not the source and begetter of his actions' (1113b16–21). (5) That this is absurd is shown by the practices of punishment and reward (1113b21–30). (6) Similarly, we are punished not only for certain actions, but also for certain kinds of ignorance that result in bad actions; this shows that it depended on us not to be ignorant. So also for carelessness (1113b30–1114a3). But (7) what if one is *the kind of person to be careless*? Well, that is because one voluntarily grew to be of this nature even if it is now hopelessly ingrained. Similarly for unjust and self-indulgent persons: they originally had it in their power not to become like that (1114a3–21). (8) We are blamed for physical (as well as ethical) defects, but only when it was in our hands to prevent them; this shows that it was in our power to avoid ethical defects, since we are blamed for them (1114a21–31). (9) Someone may say: (A) everyone aims at what appears to him (*phainomenon*) good (cf. ch. 4), but we cannot control our *phantasia*, i.e. the susceptibility by which things appear to us one way or another, for this is a function of the sort of person one is; so (B) either each of us is somehow responsible (*pōs aitios*) for our own ethical condition (the sort of person one is), and therefore somehow responsible (indirectly) for how the good appears to us; or we are *not* somehow responsible for our ethical condition, because it is part of our genetic endowment (1114a31–b12). (10) Ar. accepts the above disjunction, and argues against the second disjunct that if it is true, excellence is no more voluntary than vice, since they are on a par (1114b12–b16). By now it is taken for granted that excellence is voluntary. So (11) something from the human agent himself goes into forming his ethical disposition. This can be so in either of two ways: (i) the end is not a biological given, or (ii) even if it is, the actions constituting the means are not biologically given but are taken voluntarily. So the resulting dispositions are voluntary, bad ones as well as good (1114b16–21).

The passage from (1) and (2) to (3) needs an extra assumption. This may be provided at 1113b13–14, where Ar. actually equates doing fine or shameful actions with being a good or bad person. He may allow himself this assimilation of activity to disposition, even though earlier in the *NE* he took pains to distinguish them, because he is now about to argue against the well-known philosophical view that 'no one is bad voluntarily' (1113b14–15), and the philosophers (Socrates, Plato) did not properly distinguish disposition and activity when putting it forward. The same assimilation would also account for the curious assertion of (4). Possibly, however, Ar. is already relying on the principle, not stated clearly until 1114a4–10, that ethical dispositions naturally and foreseeably result from voluntary actions. Given that principle, and the absurdity of denying that we are voluntary agents of good and bad actions, it follows that the human voluntary agent is (as such) the source of his ethical dispositions. For if they did not arise from him, it could only be because the actions did not. It is no objection to say that once a bad disposition is fixed, the person cannot act so as to undo it: it is still voluntary, because of its origin.

The hypothetical interlocutor at (9) states that if each individual is not somehow responsible for his own ethical condition, then 'no one is responsible for its being the case that he himself does bad things' (1114b3–4). The interlocutor seems to base this on the thought that if we are not somehow responsible for our own ethical condition, it is because that condition is entirely genetically determined, together with the thought that acting from genetically determined badness would be acting from a kind of ignorance (1114b4). It is unclear whether Ar. is simply describing someone's theory, or whether he endorses this part of the interlocutor's argument. Perhaps we should assume that he does not reject it, since he lets it go by without objection. Now the kind of ignorance the interlocutor has just invoked is the kind—'ignorance on the level of the universal'—that Ar. earlier said does *not* exculpate or render an action counter-voluntary (1, 1110b30–4). And surely according to the earlier twofold criterion for voluntary action (not done because of force, not done because of factual ignorance), actions can be voluntary whether the corresponding disposition is acquired or genetically determined. However, even if Ar. endorses this part of what the interlocutor says, he would not be about to revise the twofold criterion so as to allow that ignorance on the level of the universal counts against the voluntary status of actions expressing such ignorance. (If he were to do this, the revised criterion would, like the original one, apply regardless of whether the 'ignorance' in question is acquired or genetically determined, whereas the present argument is directed specifically against the second possibility.) Rather, Ar. would be focusing here on a condition that gives meaning to the entire practice of establishing whether an action is voluntary or not. This condition is the link between the voluntary, and praise and censure (1, 1109b31). These attitudes make sense only on the assumption that they will encourage one kind of conduct and discourage another. If we were genetically endowed not with a mere general propensity to be guided by praise and censure from others (cf. II. 1, 1103a 23–6), but with specific ethical dispositions, then we should act in accordance with them regardless of praise and censure (cf. 1113b26–30), which would therefore be rendered meaningless. Since Ar. does not question the value, and effectiveness in principle, of these existing practices, he rejects the genetic endowment theory, i.e. the theory that specific ethical dispositions are entirely a matter of genetic endowment. Since no other alternative is considered, this rejection entails that the dispositions are voluntarily acquired, i.e. that voluntary agency makes *some* contribution to their development.

and this [sc. doing fine things and shameful things]**, it is agreed, is what it is to be, respectively, a good person and a bad one**   Here he speaks as if one's being a good person or a bad one consists in the very doing of (presumably, a multitude of) the corresponding actions.   *1113b12*

no one is vicious voluntarily   The saying is attributed to Epicharmus, an early 5th-century comic writer. We see from *Protagoras* 345d–e that the idea was a commonplace. For Plato's own endorsement see *Laws* v. 731c, 734b; and especially IX. 860d–e, where Plato shifts between speaking of actions and of dispositions.   *1113b14–15*

what has just been said   (a) This refers either to 'It depends on us whether we are good or bad' just above, or to 'Man is a source of actions' at 3, 1112b31–2. (b) The absurdity of 'Man is not an origin' (18–19) is perhaps not so much that, if man is not the origin of his actions, then some other sort of being is (i.e. of the actions we ordinarily ascribe to human beings), as that if man is not an origin of actions, then man as such is not an origin of any changes in the world. For it is only by producing actions that man as such produces changes. Ar. nowhere draws on the distinction between actions and movements (or changes). However (c), what he rejects at 19–20, sc. that we can 'trace actions back to origins beyond their origins in us', does not quite fit what goes before, for now (unless the writing is careless) he momentarily envisages origins in us *and* different origins that can be traced back past us. This kind of scenario is familiar from Homer, where human agents both act voluntarily and are being manipulated by the gods.   *1113b17*

as when penalties are doubled   Pittacus of Mytilene, one of the Seven Sages, made a law to this effect.   *1113b31–2*

it runs counter to reason to suppose that the person engaged in unjust action does not wish to be unjust . .   He may not think of himself as 'unjust' (cf. II. 8, 1108b23–6), and may wish the term not to be true of him, but he is willingly doing what he is doing, and therefore willingly becoming the sort of person who does that.   *1114a11*

1114a15 **he is ill voluntarily** [*hekōn*]   To the ordinary ear this would have sounded as the paradox 'he is gladly ill'.

1114a22–3 **with some people those of the body are so too, and these people too we blame**   i.e. as well as those with defects of the soul. The analogy between moral and physical defects was commonplace, and Plato used it to argue that vice is not voluntary. However, Protagoras in Plato's dialogue makes the point Ar. makes here (*Protagoras* 323d–e).

1114b11–12 **to have been born well and beautifully endowed in this respect will be to be naturally well endowed in the full and true sense**   A person is usually said to be naturally well endowed (*euphuēs*) because of his physique, but if the word were to apply in light of his conduct, that would be the true sense (since soul is prior to body). Ar. may be taking the existing usage as a mild piece of evidence that native good qualities do *not* include ethical dispositions.

1114b18 **whether the end is natural** [*phusikon*]   i.e. having it is a function of our biological nature alone.

1114b22 **as people say**   The reference is perhaps to 1113b14–15, using his own definition of blessedness (happiness), in which excellence is central.

1114b23 **for we ourselves are partly responsible, in a way, for our dispositions**   Ar. now shows that the conclusion he has been pursuing throughout the chapter is that we as voluntary agents play *some* part in the formation of our characters. The other cause, with which we share influence, is nature. Elsewhere Ar. is explicit that people are naturally predisposed to various ethical traits (vi. 13, 1144b3–9).

III 5, 1115a4–5
Transition to the discussion of the specific character-excellences, beginning with courage.

1115a4 **how many they are**   See Introduction, pp. 22–3.

III 6–9, 1115a6–1117b22, on courage
Courage the intermediate in the continua of fear and boldness (6 and 7, 1115a6–1116a15); genuinely courageous action distinguished from kinds that resemble it (8, 1116a16–1117a28); pain and pleasure in courageous action (9, 1117a29–b22).

III 6–7, 1115a6–1116a15
Not everything we fear is an occasion for courage and not all fearlessness is courageous (1115a7–24); courage has to do with danger of death—not in all cases, but in the finest, e.g. in war (1115a25–1115b6); courage does not imply superhuman fearlessness (1115b7–11); with respect to fear and

boldness, the courageous person 'gets it right' in all the many ways, and acts for the sake of the fine (1115b11–24); excessive fearlessness (1115b24–8); excessive boldness, i.e. rashness (1115b28–33); excessive fear, i.e. cowardice (1115b34–1116a2); further contrasts between the dispositions (1116a2–12); dying in order to escape pain is not courageous (1116a12–15).

people define fear itself as expectation of what is bad   See Plato, *Laches* 198b, *Protagoras* 358d.   *1115a9*

or in general the sorts of things not due to badness, or to one's own agency   Not that one should not be moved to ward off poverty and illness, but a good person need not hold them in dread. Strictly, given the present point, a good character need not dread undeserved loss of reputation (see 13) either.   *1115a17–18*

Nor, then, is a person cowardly if he fears assault on his children and wife, or fears grudging ill will   If this is consistent with 1115a17–18, and the assault and ill will target him from outside, these are fears he should not have. The point then is that they do not make him a *coward* (even though he is less than admirable). But in the parallel passage of the *EE* the worry about grudging ill will is lest one become a source of it towards others (III. 1, 1229a36). If this is the meaning here, it is conceivable that the first fear is lest he himself abuse wife or children.   *1115a22–3*

nor is he courageous if he is bold when facing a whipping   Perhaps because a whipping is not something of supreme importance (cf. next line), perhaps because he is assumed to deserve it, in which case the accolade does not fit.   *1115a23–4*

the most fearsome thing is death; for it is an end, and there seems to be nothing any longer for the dead person that is either good or bad   Just the reason why, if it is true, death is not to be feared at all, according to Socrates and Epicurus. Cf. Ar.'s 'being alive is something that is good and pleasant in itself, since it is determinate, and the determinate is of the nature of the good' (IX. 9, 1170a19–21). 'Nothing any longer, either good or bad' is the ultimate indeterminacy.   *1115a26*

optimistic because of their experience   This is not a kind of courage at all; cf. 8, 1116b3–13 and 1117a9–14.   *1115b3–4*

in every case, an activity's end is the one that accords with the corresponding disposition. This, then, holds for the courageous person too. Now, courage is something fine [*kalon*]. So the end [of courage], too, is such [i.e. it is the fine], since each thing is distinguished by its end. So it is for the sake of achieving the fine that the courageous person stands firm and acts in those ways that accord with courage   The aim of this passage is clear, although the detail is obscure and the text at line 21 uncertain. Ar. is emphasizing that an action is correctly said to be done from courage only if it is, and is done as, an instance of the *fine*, rather than, say, because it is useful, or because one will be punished otherwise. This will   *1115b20–4* be the main criterion that distinguishes actions of real courage from ones belonging to the five false types (see below). In four of these the *fine* is absent, and in one (the first) it is present imperfectly.

1115b25   **earlier**   At II. 7, 1107b1–2.

III 8, 1116a15–1117a28
The five false forms of courage: (1) the 'civic' kind, where the motive is fear of dishonour (1116a17–29) or (2) fear of punishment (1116a29–b3); (3) where the crucial factor is experience (1116b3–23); (4) where it is temper or spirit (1116b23–1117a9); (5) where it is optimism (1117a9–27).

1116a23   *Iliad* XXII. 100.

1116a25–6   *Iliad* VIII. 148–9. Diomedes was the son of Tydeus.

1116a28   **for it comes about through shame**   i.e. from fear of what others will think, not the moral person's autonomous sense of what would be shameful. Shame is not an excellence, but is a major factor in the formation of good character (II. 7, 1108a31–2; IV. 9, 1128b15–21).

1116a34–5   *Iliad* II. 391. The speaker is not Hector but Agamemnon.

1116b4   **Socrates**   That courage is expert knowledge (*epistēmē*) is Socrates' position at *Laches* 194 d ff. and *Protagoras* 360b–361b.

1116b6   **soldiers**   i.e. paid professionals as distinct from citizens taking up arms.

1116b19   **at the temple of Hermes**   In Boeotia. The battle was fought in 354–353 BCE.

1116b27–8   **Homer**   Iliad XI. 11, XIV. 151, XVI. 529, V. 470, XV. 232–3; *Odyssey* XXIV. 318. ('His blood boiled' does not occur in our text of Homer.)

1117a4   **the most natural form**   i.e. it owes less to culture or special experience (or lack of it) than the other types. Cf. VI. 13, 1144b1–9 on natural excellences.

1117a5   **the end for the sake of which**   i.e. the fine; cf. 7, 1115b20–2.

1117a23   **those who act in ignorance** [*agnoountes*]   This is not the technical use of 'in ignorance' of III. 1, 1110b24 ff., reserved for those who act from drunkenness etc., or a bad disposition. The ignorant ones here are said to be 'inferior' to the optimistic because their factual error is the only reason they place themselves in danger at all.

1117a26–7   **what happened to the Argives ...**   The Spartans, by contrast with the Sicyonians, were famous for their toughness in battle. The incident occurred at Corinth, 392 BCE.

III 9, 1117a29–b22

This portion, which emphasizes the painfulness, both physical and mental, of courageous action, is surely placed last to point up the contrast with moderation, to be discussed next. The ideally moderate person feels nothing when he or she refrains from taking too much.

as has been said   The reference may be to 7, 1116a1–2.   *1117a33*

So not all the excellences give rise to pleasant activity, except to the extent   *1117b15–16*
that pleasant activity touches on the end itself   This is an important qualification on the doctrine somewhat glibly laid down at i. 8, 1099a7–21 and then, with the present difficulty in mind, reformulated with regard to courage at ii. 3, 1104b8 ('or anyway without distress'). The reformulation was inadequate, since the courageous man in action does suffer distress. The present passage distinguishes aspects of the activity, implying that it pleases (even the agent) just in so far as it achieves the fine, and blocking the implication that the courageous take pleasure in getting wounded and the like.

III 10–12, 1117b23–1119b18, on moderation

Moderation to do with certain pleasures of touching (10, 1117b23–1118b8); common versus idiosyncratic appetites and pleasures, etc. (11, 1118b8–1119a20); self-indulgence is more voluntary than courage, etc. (12, 1119a21–b18).

III 10, 1117b23–1118b8

The sphere of moderation is among bodily versus mental pleasures (1117b27–1118a1); but not all pleasures involving sense-organs are relevant, but really only certain pleasures of touching (1118a2–b1), involving certain parts of the body (1118b4–8); touch is the sense faculty common to all animals (1118b1–4).

these seem to be the excellences of the non-rational parts   sc. of the soul.   *1117b24*
Usually Ar. speaks, without distinction, of one non-rational part (relevant to ethics); e.g. i. 13, 1102b13 ff. If the point of the present remark is to assign courage and moderation to different non-rational parts, this reinforces Ar.'s pluralism about the character-excellences, as opposed to the reductionism that says that they are all species of moderation or wisdom (see Introduction, pp. 22–3). For reduction fails if one belongs to one part, another to another. The present language recalls the *Republic*'s division into reason and two non-rational elements, temper or the spirited (*thumoeides*) part, and the appetitive (*epithumētikon*) part (cf. also 8, 1116b31 on temper (*thumos*) 'collaborating with' the courageous man). But the psychology of the *Ethics* is different. In the *Republic* appetite is only for the physical pleasures by which Ar. defines moderation, and temper is typified by,

among other things, the love of honour. But for Ar., any liking for something can issue in an appetite for it; the love of honour would be one example (cf. 1117b29), and elsewhere he mentions appetitive desire for health and for learning (1, 1111a31).

1117b24–5 **we have said** II. 7, 1107b4–6.

1117b26 **it relates less, and not in the same way, to pains** i.e. its primary concern is with certain pleasures; the relevant type of pain is the pain of lacking those pleasures, hence it is not an independent primary object (cf. 11, 1119a3–5).

1118a10 **incidentally** i.e. by association as explained at line 13.

1118a12 **perfumes or tasty dishes** [*opsa*] The ancient commentator Aspasius suggests a mental association between perfumes and courtesans. The word *opsa* implies appetizers designed to add interest to a staple such as bread. Xenophon, *Memorabilia* III. 14, portrays the gourmandizer (*opsophagos*; see 1118a32) as one who makes a full meal of *opsa* without bread, thus giving a nutritional luxury the rank of a necessity.

1118a22–3 **'a stag . . .'** Homer, *Iliad* III. 24.

1118a25 **slavish** cf. 11, 1118b21; I. 5, 1095b19–20; x. 6, 1177a6–8; and 1118b4 on pleasures appropriate to free men. On slaves as less than human *qua* slaves, see VIII. 11, 1161b2–8 with comment.

1118a31–2 **or so-called 'venery'** The Greek euphemism is '*ta aphrodisia*', 'Aphrodite's doings'. 'Venery' is from 'Venus', the Roman name for the goddess of sex.

III 11, 1118b8–1119a20

Appetites common to the human species versus ones that are peculiar and acquired (1118b8–15); excess in each kind (1118b15–27); the kind of pain that is relevant to moderation and self-indulgence (1118b27–1119a5); deficient interest in the relevant pleasures hardly ever occurs (1119a5–11); intermediacy of the moderate person (1119a11–20).

1118b10 **nourishment . . . dry or liquid** For Ar., *dry* and *moist* are two of the four fundamental chemical properties, hence are immediately relevant to the organism's ability to be nourished by food.

1118b11 **Homer** *Iliad* XXIV. 130.

III 12, 1119a21–b18

Self-indulgence is more voluntary than cowardice because of their respective relations to pleasure and pain (1119a21–5); and because we have many safe opportunities to learn moderation (1119a25–7); dispositions and particular actions compared in respect of being voluntary or not (1119a27–33); unchecked appetite is like an unchecked child (1119a33–b18).

looks more like a voluntary thing [*hekousion*] According to the theory of III. *1119a21*
5, excellences and defects of character are all equally voluntary, in the sense of
being proper grounds for praise and reproach, because all are predictable results
of voluntary behaviour. Here, however, Ar. reverts to the older meaning of
'*hekousion*', meaning what one welcomes, or does gladly (see Introduction, p.
38). In this sense self-indulgence is more voluntary (one might say, more *wilful*)
than cowardice (and therefore more reprehensible) because it develops from acts
that are pleasant whereas cowardice develops from ones that are unpleasant.
Presumably the point is partly that the incipient glutton etc. is glad, the incipient
coward distressed, to be in the situation where he goes wrong. But there are also
the facts that the latter's distress is more disorientating than the former's pleasure,
and that opportunities to practise moderation, by contrast with courage, are
many and safe (1119a25–7).

But the disposition of cowardice would seem to be voluntary in a way in *1119a27–33*
which the particular acts of cowardice are not . . . for no one has an appetite
to be self-indulgent Having just argued from the more and less voluntary
character of the particular acts to the more and less voluntary character of the
corresponding dispositions, Ar. now compares (*a*) each class of particulars with its
corresponding disposition, and (*b*) the resulting 'voluntariness differences' with
each other. Cowardice is more voluntary than cowardly acts because as a mere
disposition it is free of the distress attendant on the acts; by contrast, self-
indulgence is less voluntary than self-indulgent acts because, unlike them, it is not
in itself pleasant and an object of appetite. This is parenthetical to the main thrust
of the argument, which is that self-indulgence is worse than cowardice.

The term 'indulgence' is one we also apply to the ways children go *1119a33–4*
wrong The word translated 'self-indulgence' (*akolasia*) literally means the
condition of not having been forcibly corrected (*kolazesthai*), childhood being
the stage when this ought to happen.

the fine is goal for both Untrained, the appetitive element is fixed on the *1119b16*
pleasant without discrimination; properly trained, it takes pleasure only in what
reason allows and what is fine; cf. 11, 1119a12–13.

BOOK IV

IV 1, 1119b22–1122a17, on open-handedness
It is an intermediate to do with the use of money (1119b22–1120a9); to do with giving rather than taking (1120a9–23); the open-handed type gives as one should, for the sake of the fine, and with pleasure (1120a23–31); he takes as one should, gives according to his wealth, does not set great store on money (1120a31–1121a7); the wasteful type is excessive in giving, deficient in taking (and the avaricious one is the opposite), impoverishes himself and may be cured (1121a7–30); but most of the wasteful take as they should not, which vitiates their giving, although in any case they tend to spend on self-indulgence (1121a30–b12); but avariciousness is incurable and more innate (1121b12–16); it has two forms, deficiency in giving and excess in taking, which usually do not go together (1121b16–21); misers who are respectable about taking (1121b21–31); scavengers for gain (1121b31–1122a13); avariciousness a worse evil than wastefulness, and people go to greater lengths in it (1122a13–16).

1119b27–8   **Both wastefulness and avariciousness consist in behaving excessively and deficiently in relation to money**   In certain extreme forms each of the defects involves both excess and deficiency.

1119b33–4   **The name 'wasteful', then, is not properly theirs**   This shows that Ar. is writing about abstract types, not concrete persons, since of course the word is 'proper to' all concrete persons who are wasteful, whether or not other characteristics also obtrude.

1119b34– 1120a3   **for by 'wasteful' is meant . . . life depends on these things**   The argument is meant to explain why, or prove that, 'wasteful' (*asōtos*) is the proper term for the type that spends excessively. It depends on the literal meaning of '*asōtos*', i.e. 'lost', 'ruined', and on the ambiguity of 'substance' (*ousia* (1120a1–2), lit. 'being' or 'that by which one subsists', but in ordinary parlance a holding or estate). Since '*asōtos*' is a term of reproach, it must imply that the ruined person is to blame for his own ruin, i.e. is *self*-destructive. But destroying one's own substance, both in the philosophical and in the more relaxed sense of the word, is self-destruction, since one's living depends on that by which one subsists. Hence the *asōtos* destroys or loses what he lives off, i.e. his wealth.

1120a9–11   **giving to the people one should is more the mark of the open-handed person than [a] taking from sources one should take from, and than [b] not taking from sources one shouldn't**   See 1120a11–15 for (*a*); 15–20 for (*b*).

1120a30   **for he would choose money over acting finely**   i.e. although he does give, he would have preferred to be in a situation where it was not called for, instead of welcoming the opportunity as the open-handed person does.

328

everyone is more attached to what they have themselves made   Cf. VIII. 12,   *1120b13*
1161b18–24; IX. 7, 1167b33–1168a8.

as we have said   At 1120b7–9 and e.g. 1120b3.   *1120b23*

This is why we do not call tyrants wasteful   He may be thinking of Philip of   *1120b25*
Macedon, who was notorious for extravagance. 'Wasteful' implies spending not
only indiscriminately, but more than one can afford.

If it turns out that he does not spend as one should, or in accordance with   *1121a1–2*
what is fine   Presumably this could happen to the open-handed person through
misinformation or as the lesser of two evils.

Simonides   The great 5th-century poet, said to have become a miser in old age.   *1121a7*

We have said   At 1119b27–8.   *1121a10*

but only on a small scale   Cf. 1122a3–7.   *1121a15*

'wasteful', in fact, seems to apply to private individuals   Cf. 1120b23–7.   *1121a18*

as we have said   It was roughly implied at 1121a16–17.   *1121a 30–1*

it is reasonable that avariciousness [*aneleutheria*] **should be said to be contrary**   *1122a13–14*
to open-handedness [*eleutheria*]   The Greek affix '*a-*'or '*an-*' negates, so language
even makes it seem as if what we call avariciousness is *the* contrary of open-
handedness. On the 'reasonableness' of this, see II. 8, 1108b35–1109a19.

IV 2, 1122a18–1123a33, on munificence

This too has to do with money, but only with spending, and spending on a
large scale (1122a18–1122b3); the result is grand and beautiful, and the
munificent type is concerned only about that (1122b3–18); relevant kinds of
events and projects (1122b19–1123a9); munificent spending is also judged by
the person's resources (1122b23–9) and the type of occasion (1123a10–19);
the excessive type (1123a19–27); the deficient one (1123a27–31).

fitting out a trireme   i.e. one of the fleet of warships.   *1122a24*

Homer, *Odyssey* XVII. 420.   *1122a27*

we shall discuss these subjects later   At 1123a19–33.   *1122a33–4*

as we said at the outset   At II. 1, 1103b21–3.   *1122b1*

with the same expenditure it can create a greater and more suitable effect   *1122b13–14*
The munificent person also has an eye for the special touch at no more cost.

as has been said   At 1122a25–6.   *1122b24*

as has been said   At 1122a31–3.   *1123a20*

1123a23   **purple**   Since purple dye was rare and expensive, the colour would be unsuitable for the down-to-earth ambience of contemporary comedy. It is not certain whether the reference is to the costumes of the chorus or to hangings over the place where they entered the stage.

IV 3, 1123a34–1125a35, on greatness of soul

Greatness of soul, which is being, and thinking oneself, worthy of great things, and its opposites (1123a34–b15); it therefore has to do with honour, which is the greatest external good (1123b15–26); 'great-souled' implies being great in every excellence (1123b26–1124a4); the great-souled attitude to honours and dishonours, and to good and bad fortune in general (1124a4–20); how high birth and power breed a false kind of greatness of soul (1124a20–1124b6); characteristics of the great-souled with regard to danger, giving and receiving benefits, going in for honours, openness, being impressed, conversation, complaining, possessions, gait, manner of speaking (1124b6–1125a16); of the two opposites (misguided states, rather than bad ones), littleness of soul is more common and worse (1125a17–34).

1123b5   **moderate** [*sōphrōn*]   The word is used here in the general sense; see Introduction, p. 25.

1123b12–13   **for what would he do if he were not worthy of so much?**   One who underrates himself despite being worthy of great things is perverse and despicable in a way in which inferior self-underraters are not. The former's great worth may mask this difference, but when one imagines his particular brand of self-distrust operating from a lower point on the scale of worth, one sees how annihilating it is.

1123b18–20   **greatest of these we would suppose to be the one we mete out to the gods . . . such is honour**   (*a*) But cf. IX. 9, 1169b8–10, where *friends* are the greatest of external goods. (*b*) The connection with the gods not only establishes honour as the greatest external good, but underpins the thought that the proper object of honour *in us* is what is highest in us, i.e. excellence (1123b35–6). The divine connection also narrows the meaning of 'honouring' so that essentially it consists in an attitude expressed in ritual and symbolic gestures rather than material rewards.

1123b21–2   **So the great-souled type has to do with honours and dishonours, in the way one should**   If Ar. had had inverted commas he might have put this in the formal mode. The meaning is not that the great-souled type is preoccupied in the right way with honours etc., but that it is on account of a certain attitude to *these* things that we apply 'great-souled'.

1123b32   **when nothing impresses him**   This is spelled out more fully at 1124a12–19.

1123b35   **honour is a prize of excellence**   This is technically contradicted by I. 12, esp. 1101b31–2, according to which excellence is the object of praise, whereas honour is accorded to happiness. There, however, the comparison is between excellence and its exercise, here between excellence and other goods (or possession of them). But at 1124a25–6 he says that only the good are to be honoured, although the good who also have great external possessions are 'thought to be' worthier of honour than the mere good. This seems a shift from the distinctions made in I. 12, since the combination of goodness and great other possessions more or less amounts to happiness.

it augments them, and does not occur without them   See Introduction, p. 30.   *1124a2–3*

which is actually why Thetis doesn't mention to Zeus the things she did for   *1124b15–17*
him; similarly the Spartans to the Athenians, but they did mention what the
Athenians had done for them   At *Iliad* I. 395–407 Achilles tells Thetis, when she pleads on his behalf to Zeus, to remind the god of how she rescued him when he had been trussed up by the other gods. Thetis is tactful enough not to follow her son's advice when she actually addresses Zeus (ibid. 503 ff.). The second reference is to a request by the Spartans to the Athenians for help against Thebes, 370–369 BCE.

except when being self-deprecating with ordinary people   Since the great-   *1124b30*
souled type has 'refinement of excellence' (*kalokagathia*, 1124a4) we learn from this that self-deprecation only manifests a defective disposition (as it does in ch. 7) when practised towards social equals (and superiors).

day-labourers   i.e. hirelings.   *1125a2*

a deep voice   Indicating maturity versus youth and male versus female. For a   *1125a13–14*
general discussion, see *On Generation of Animals* v. 7, esp. 786b35–787a2.

littleness of soul is more opposed to greatness of soul than conceitedness is . . .   *1125a32–4*
occurs more often and is worse   On the reasoning, see II. 8, 1108b35–1109a19.

IV 4, 1125b1–25, on an unnamed excellence to do with honour
There is an excellence that stands to greatness of soul as munificence to open-handedness (1125b1–8); 'honour-loving' and 'indifferent to honour' are sometimes terms of praise, sometimes of censure, i.e. are sometimes applied to the nameless intermediate state, sometimes to one of the extremes (1125b8–25).

as was said in our first discussions   At II. 7, 1107b24–7.   *1125b1–2*

moderate, just as we said in our first discussions   At II. 7, 1107b33–1108a1,   *1125b13–14*
although the earlier passage does not use 'moderate', which appears here in its broad sense.

so this disposition is praised   i.e. is praiseworthy. Ar. has just been arguing that   *1125b20–1* the intermediate state exists; in now emphasizing that it is praiseworthy, he shows that it is an excellence; cf. I. 13, 1103a9–10; IV. 5, 1125b31–3.

1125b23–4 **This seems to be the case with the other excellences too** See II 8.

IV 5, 1125b26–1126b10, on mildness

The intermediate and extremes in the sphere of anger (1125b26–1126a13); different kinds of excessive disposition (1126a13–29); the excess more common than the deficiency (1126a29–31); general remarks about the impossibility of drawing hard and fast lines between what does and does not count as 'getting it right', and of saying how big an error must be to be significant (1126a31–b4); the only general advice available is that the intermediate is to be praised, the extreme states to be censured (1126b4–10).

1125b26–7 **Because the intermediate lacks a name (as do the extremes, almost)** i.e. no word exactly conveys the intermediate. Thus Ar. finds it necessary to *argue* (at 31–3) that 'mild' is the right label for one who is angry as and when he should be. (The argument is: 'mild' is a term of praise in this area; one who is angry as he should be is praised; therefore . . .) 'Mildness' normally implies *not* being moved to anger, as Ar. acknowledges when he says that it inclines towards deficiency (1125b28, 1126a29, 36–b1).

1126a29 **It is the excessive state that we tend more to regard as opposed to mildness** See II. 8, 1108b35–1109a19.

1126a31–2 **what we said in our previous discussions** i.e. at II. 9, 1109b14–26.

IV 6, 1126b11–1127a12, on a nameless excellence to do with causing pleasure and pain in conversation

The extremes and the intermediate state described, the latter said to resemble friendship (1126b11–22); but it lacks the special bond of friendship (1126b22–6); even so, it observes proper distinctions between people (1126b26–1127a2); it prefers to cause pleasure and is careful not to cause pain unless something important is at stake; the extremes are described and the one that exceeds in pleasing is divided into a kind that does it for its own sake and one that does it for profit (1127a3–11).

IV 7, 1127a13–b32, on a nameless excellence to do with self-presentation

By identifying these nameless qualities we learn about character, and confirm the theory of excellence as intermediate (1127a14–17); the impostor, the self-deprecator, the truthful person (1127a17–32); the truthful one speaks the truth for its own sake, even when there is no question of perjury or fraud if one does not (1127a32–1127b7); the impostor who exaggerates for its own sake versus the one who does it for the sake of something else, and the one who does it for glory versus the one who does it for material gain

(1127b9–22); self-deprecation described; when very ostentatious it smacks of imposture, but in moderate doses is quite endearing (1127b22–32).

which makes him characteristically truthful The word used here is *1127a24* 'alētheutikos', and it seems to have been coined by Aristotle. (It is also used of the great-souled type at 1124b30.)

each type, if he is not acting for some further end, speaks and acts in the way *1127a27–8* **corresponding to his nature, and lives his life in that way** The truthful/ untruthful behaviour, provided that it is an end in itself, implies a truthful/ untruthful agent. (The proviso sets aside exceptional situations, as when a truthful person lies to save someone, or an exaggerator tells the truth under oath. For according to 1127b11–20, one who *habitually* exaggerates for the sake of glory or profit counts as an impostor.)

he leans more towards telling less than the truth about himself Cf. the *1127b7–8* great-souled person, who is self-deprecating with inferiors (3, 1124b30–1).

but it is decision, not capacity … that sort of person This may belong at *1127b14–15* 1127b22, after 'have the features described'.

as indeed Socrates used to do Socrates was famous for his self-deprecation *1127b25–6* (often called 'irony') in discussions.

Spartan dress The Spartans dressed with studied simplicity, advertising the *1127b28* purity of their manners.

The impostor, since he is worse, appears to be more opposed to the truthful *1127b31–2* **person** See II. 8, 1108b35–1109a19.

IV 8, 1127b33–1128b9, on wittiness

The relevant area is relaxation and amusement, which is a necessary part of life (1127b33–1128a1; 1128b3–4); the extremes and the intermediate described and named (1128a2–16); the intermediate state is marked by refinement in humour (*epidexiotēs*), although there is no exact definition of this (1128a16–28); one's standard for deciding what jokes to listen to (or to accept being the butt of) should determine what jokes one makes (1128a28–9); there are laws against certain kinds of verbal abuse, but when it comes to avoiding abusive humour, the person of taste is a law to himself (1128a29–33); the two extremes described (1128a34–b3); summary concerning these three conversational excellences (1128b4–9).

IV 9, 1128b10–35, on the sense of shame, and shamelessness

Shame is not an excellence, because (1) it is an affection (1128b11–15); (2) we only praise it in those who are not supposed to be ethically mature

(1128b15–20); (3) it presupposes the consciousness of wrongdoing, hence the decent person does not feel it (1128b20–9). The fact that shamelessness about wrongdoing is bad does not make shame decent; it is only hypothetically decent (1128b29–33).

1128b11   **it resembles an affection rather than a disposition**   This is not a good reason why there is no excellence under the heading of shame, since there are dispositions to be ashamed, and to be ashamed at different kinds of things. However, a sense of shame should not be, like an excellence, a 'firm and unchanging disposition' (II. 4, 1105a33), for the good person outgrows it.

1128b33–4   **Self-control is not an excellence either, but a sort of excellence that's mixed with something else**   It is a good disposition by comparison with certain others, but not a real excellence, because it entails having an inappropriate desire. By 'mixed' he may mean that, like shame, it is hypothetically decent, self-control being the best condition *if* one has inappropriate desires.

There are discrepancies between these remarks about shame and the preview at II. 7, 1108a30–5. In the preview a sense of shame was said to be praiseworthy (though not an excellence), whereas here it ranks as only hypothetically praiseworthy. More significant: the only opposite mentioned here is shamelessness, whereas in the preview proper shame was intermediate between two opposites. And in the preview the shame triad is followed by righteous indignation and its opposites, but this topic is missing here. Possibly the end of *NE* IV. 9 is lost, in which case the last sentence ('Now let us talk about justice') is an editorial addition. The *EE* and *Magna Moralia* parallel passages have the triads of shame and righteous indignation.

It is also possible, however, that Ar. wrote this chapter as part of a different treatment from the one to which the preview belongs, and that it is complete as it stands. One can speculate that he decided to drop righteous indignation from the list of excellences because he saw that it does not fit well with greatness of soul. To the extent that the great-souled person sets no store on anything but excellence, he is conceptually not in a position to be distressed when the wicked flourish as the green bay tree, since he cannot regard their good fortune as genuine flourishing.

BOOK V

V 1–2, 1129a3–1130b29

This stretch establishes that justice is two different things: general justice, which is coextensive with all the other excellences, and particular justice with its own sphere; and that particular justice and injustice have to do, respectively, with the equal and the unequal.

The starting point is that justice and injustice are dispositions issuing in just and unjust actions (1129a3–11); principles of inference: from acts of contrary kinds to contrary dispositions; from a contrary disposition to its contrary; and from the things and persons that are *F* to the disposition *F*-ness; thus homonymy on the one hand implies it on the other (1129a11–31). The unjust person is a lawbreaker, grasping, and unequal-minded, so the just one is each of the contraries; and correspondingly for what is unjust and what is just (1129a31–1129b1). The grasping person is concerned with a certain subdivision of goods and lesser evils, and is unequal-minded (1129b1–11). As the unjust person is a lawbreaker and the just one law-abiding, everything lawful is just (1129b11–14); but the laws pronounce about every area of life, enjoining us to act in each given area as the excellent person acts (1129b14–25); so in one sense justice is complete excellence defined as 'in relation to another'—this justice is the same as the whole of excellence, but is differently defined, and a corresponding result holds for injustice (1129b25–1130a13). As for particular justice and injustice, the special mark of the latter is graspingness, which is different from all the bad qualities contrasted with the other particular excellences—this shows that there is particular injustice and, correspondingly, particular justice (1130a14–b8). Moreover, the unjust that is the unlawful and the unjust that is the unequal are different, since the unequal stands to the unlawful as proper part to whole; hence there are correspondingly a type of injustice that is the whole and a type that is a part of it; and correspondingly for justice (1130b8–18). (Some of the same points are repeated; 1130b18–26.) An aside on the possible difference between a good man and a good citizen (1130b26–9).

everyone   The *Republic*, however, while taking for granted that justice gives rise to just conduct in society, mainly presents it as an inner relation between parts of the soul.   *1129a7*

with a capacity or expertise [*epistēmē*], the same one seems to relate to both members of a pair of contraries   Capacities and types of expertise do not incorporate the wish to use them for just one sort of end (medical expertise can be used to cure and to kill). But since ethical dispositions 'issue in decisions' (II. 6,   *1129a13–14*

1106b36; cf. 'wish' at 9–10 above), a single one cannot be manifested in contrary kinds of behaviour, any more than health can give rise to sickly symptoms. Cf. the demonstration in Plato, *Republic* I. 333e–334b, that if justice is a species of technical expertise (*technē*), it renders men apt to cheat as well as deal honestly. The present distinction between dispositions and types of expertise was forged in the debate over Socrates' vision of personal excellence as a species of systematic knowledge or intellectual understanding; cf. VI. 13, 1144b17–21; *EE* I. 5, 1216b4–9; and below, 5, 1134a1–2 with comment. See also VI. 12, 1143b24–8 and 1144a3–5, on the assimilation of excellence (in this case, wisdom) to health rather than the science of health.

1129a18 **the dispositions are revealed by the subjects possessing them** e.g. we clarify impiety by considering whom we call 'impious'. More generally we clarify the disposition *F*-ness by considering what we call '*F*', what we call 'tending-to-make-someone-*F*', what we call someone's behaving '*F*-ly', and so forth. For this, and for clarification of contrary by contrary, see *Topics* VI. 9, 147a13–15; I. 15, 106a9–21.

1129a26–8 **Justice and injustice, in fact, *do* seem to be said in more than one way, but we fail to notice the homonymy in their case because the things referred to are close together** Ar. is talking here simultaneously about the words 'justice' and 'injustice' and about the qualities they stand for: this reflects his unquestioned assumption that what we can gather from the meaning of a word immediately reveals the nature of what it stands for. Strictly speaking, it is the words that are said in many ways, whereas for Ar. homonymy is a property of things as distinct from words. In this case, the homonyms are the qualities general justice and particular justice, general injustice and particular injustice. 'Homonym of *X*' means: not a sense other than some given sense of the word '*X*'(where *X* is a thing), but: another kind of thing that has the same name as *X*. Particular and general justice are 'close together' because they both fall under the general heading of 'excellences of the soul', both are defined with reference to other persons (cf. 2, 1130a32–b5), and in so far as general justice is the same as 'the whole of excellence' (1130a8–10) both have to do with the intermediate.

1129a29–31 **the key that locks a door and the one below the neck of an animal are called 'key'** [*kleis*] **homonymously** The one below the neck is the collar-bone.

1129a32–3 **the grasping, i.e. unequal-minded, one** 'Equal-minded' and 'unequal-minded' translate '*isos*' and '*anisos*', of which the basic meanings are 'equal' and 'unequal', but which can also mean 'fair' and 'unfair' whether of states of affairs, actions, or persons. The quantity that is equal (sc. to some *X*) stands between the more-than (*to pleon*) and the less-than (*to elatton*) *X*. These Greek phrases, and equivalents, are also often used to mean (and then are so translated) 'more/less than is equal = fair', i.e. 'too much/little'. Ar.'s arguments about the just and unjust depend heavily on these semantic connections.

In that case, the just is what is lawful and what is equal, while the unjust is what is unlawful and what is unequal 'The just' and 'the unjust' here must refer to the dispositions. *1129a34–b1*

grasping [*pleonektēs*, lit. 'one who goes in for having more'] (*a*) 'Grasping' is always pejorative in Ar. as in Plato, hence cannot be used of the laudable character who seeks more and more of the goods that depend on personal effort alone and are always good for one, namely excellence and excellent activity. (*b*) At *EE* vii. 15 (= viii. 3), 1248b25–33, excellence is said to be the condition under which the things that are 'generally good' (there called 'natural goods') are good *for* the individual. Thus the prayer at line 5 should be for excellence. *1129b1–2*

is a common feature of both i.e. of taking too much of the good and taking too little of the bad. *1129b11*

the laws pronounce 'The laws' (*nomoi*) covers not only written statutes but customs and social norms in general. *1129b14*

and its parts i.e. the excellences and their activities. *1129b18*

not without qualification but in relation to another person In so far as law regulates conduct *in society*, 'in relation to others' was implicit in the equation of just with lawful behaviour (11–14). *1129b26–7*

'neither Evening Star nor Morning equals its wonder' Apparently from the *Melanippe* of Euripides, a lost tragedy. *1129b28–9*

the proverb goes Theognis, 147. *1129b29*

because it is the *activation* of complete excellence (*a*) 'Complete excellence' means the gamut of excellences considered so far. (*b*) Ar.'s reason for endorsing common sense's special regard for justice (in the broad sense) is that it looks to interests beyond one's own. But his rationale is not the utilitarian one that more people thereby benefit. It is, rather, that justice (i.e. respect for law and the rights of others) provides the other excellences with unique opportunities for *activity*. (As well as being the essence of happiness, their activity is their own metaphysical completion, in the sense of end for which they exist.) A sense of justice exposes one not merely to more challenges but to ones of a different order of difficulty, involving as they do persons with whom one does not naturally identify (1130a8). (*c*) The contrast 'in relation to another person . . . by himself' (31–3) is between oneself and family or friends on the one hand, and outsiders on the other. *1129b31*

Bias One of the Seven Sages. *1130a1*

someone else's good Cf. *Republic* i. 343c. *1130a3*

while it is the same disposition, what it is to be the first is not the same as what it is to be the second They are the same disposition in that to cultivate (or undermine) the one is *ipso facto* to cultivate (or undermine) the other. *1130a12*

1130a18 **has thrown away his shield** So as to flee unimpeded; this was the classic cowardly action.

1130a30 **to cowardice if he has deserted his comrade in battle** Since the coward seeks security, which (in so far as it is a good thing) is a kind of advantage or profit, what is the difference between him and the person who behaves in similar fashion because of particular injustice? The former, presumably, seeks security as such, not because he sees it as an instance of the more abstract kind, *profit* or *advantage*, whereas the latter would run risks where necessary for gaining an advantage; and the former shows the wrong attitude to certain kinds of fearsome things (cf. iii. 6), whereas the latter shows the wrong attitude to profit or advantage considered as a finite good that ought to be shared fairly with others. The coward might behave fair-mindedly in non-fearsome situations.

1130a33–b1 **sharing the same name** [*sunōnumos*] **because its definition is in the same genus** This is not Ar.'s technical sense of '*sunōnumos*' in which it applies to two items just in case they have the identical definition. On 'in the same genus', see comment on 2, 1129a27.

1130b2 **the one has to do with honour, or money, or security** These are examples of the kind of good with which graspingness and particular justice are concerned, called 'the things that are generally good' at 1, 1129b2–4.

1130b14–16 **this injustice is a part of injustice as a whole, and similarly too the justice corresponding to it is a part of justice as a whole** This is not a coherent conception, given that he still wants to say that justice as a whole is coextensive with excellence as a whole, but differs by being the activation of the latter in relation to other people (18–20). For it follows either that particular justice is *coextensive with* a part of excellence as a whole, or that particular justice *is* a part of excellence as a whole (cf. 1130a14). The latter is the natural thing to say, since a species is part of its genus, and it is natural to think of justice as a species of excellence coordinate with courage, moderation, and the rest. But this alternative implies that particular justice, which is already defined as relating to others (1130b1–2) is a disposition that can, but may not be, activated in relation to others. If, instead, particular justice is coextensive with a part of excellence as a whole, then presumably the latter is a special excellence that has to do with profit and so on, but is not defined as relating to others—but what is this special excellence? It nowhere appears.

1130b28 **must be determined later** Cf. the discussion in x. 9 (1179a33–1181b23).

1130b28–9 **it is not the case that being a good man and being a good citizen are the same, for every type of citizen** The difference between a good man and a good citizen is discussed at *Politics* iii. 4. In the best type of city-state they would coincide, so that ideally the political expertise (which creates and interprets the law that defines good citizens) works to produce good men, as at i. 9, 1099b29–32. Ar. distinguishes types of citizen according to the type of city-state.

338

V 2, 1130b30–1131a9

Introducing two forms of the just that corresponds to particular justice: distributive and rectificatory. The latter is then subdivided into two kinds: one for wrongs done in counter-voluntary interactions, one for those done in voluntary ones.

Of the justice that is a part, and of what is just in this sense   The discussion of distribution and rectification will focus on certain arrangements. In this context 'justice' does not name a disposition of character; it is the abstract noun corresponding to 'just' as predicated of arrangements and procedures leading to them. 1130b30

one sort is the one found in distributions . . . while another is rectificatory [*diorthōtikos*] **. . . Of the latter, there are two parts, since some interactions are voluntary, some counter-voluntary**   Rectification presupposes a wrong calling for redress or reparation. It follows that there must be wrongdoing in each of the two kinds of interactions where rectificatory justice operates. Thus the ones called 'voluntary' must be dealings where (i) both parties willingly engage, but (ii) one fails to keep its side of the bargain. This is by contrast with 'counter-voluntary' ones, where a perpetrator attacks a victim by stealth or force (both conditions that render the victim a counter-voluntary participant) from the start. (The labels are obviously relative, because the injured 'voluntary' party is not voluntarily injured, while the perpetrator in the counter-voluntary kind is a voluntary agent.) The dual classification hints at the later distinction between torts and crimes. However, according to another interpretation (endorsed by Aquinas), rectificatory justice (1) corrects wrongs committed in the 'counter-voluntary' interactions, and (2) regulates the 'voluntary' ones so that wrongs are *not* committed in them and they conform to a supposed additional type of particular justice, the 'commutative', which has to do with commercial exchange (the main topic of 5, 1132b21–1133b28). Some interpreters take rectificatory justice to divide into two types, corrective strictly speaking, and commutative. Others see the commutative as a third species coordinate with distributive and rectificatory. Making commutative a subdivision of rectificatory (*diorthōtikos*) justice has the following difficulties: '*diorthōtikos*' means 'corrective' rather than 'corrective or regulatory'; Ar.'s discussion of the just in rectification (4, 1131b25–1132b20) deals only with correction of inequalities that have actually been perpetrated; rectification requires an outside arbitrator—not a normal feature of commercial exchange, so he would surely have remarked on this difference if he saw fairness in exchange as a species of rectification. The view that commutative justice is a third coordinate kind receives some support from 5, 1132b32: 'a form of the just that is like this'. 1130b31–1131a3

V 3, 1131a10–b24

The discussion of the just in distribution begins with very general remarks about the more, the less, the equal, and the intermediate (1131a10–24). This passage could serve to introduce a discussion of either sub-type of the particular just, although it seems more likely to have been written with only the distributive one in mind. The fact that distribution first shows up by name quite casually (24) suggests that Ar. wrote 1131a10–b24 at a stage when he thought of the topic of the particular just as more or less identical with that of fair distribution.

1131a18–19   **Necessarily, then, the just involves at least four terms**   This is usually taken to apply only to distribution, but it could apply to correction too. See the diagram on 3, 1132b6–9: EA (reading from left to right) is the victim, CCD is the perpetrator, AE is the loss, CD is the gain.

1131a24–9   Equal distribution is in accordance with merit, which is judged differently under different types of political system; therefore the just is a kind of proportionality, hence requires at least four terms (1131a29–b5); an example is worked out (1131b5–12); this is geometrical proportion, not arithmetical, and discrete, not continuous (1131b12–17); general remarks about more and less, good and bad (1131b17–24).

1131a24   **'according to merit'**   The question of adjudicating between competing criteria of merit (*axia*) is outside the present topic of distributive justice, since just and unjust distribution presuppose one or another merit principle. Ideally, excellence is the criterion of merit (it is so used at VIII. 10, 1160b12–13, and 36–1161a1, but see also *Politics* III. 10–13, which examines the practical difficulties of this option). This choice of criterion, however, is a deliverance of general, not particular, justice.

1131a29   **aristocrats**   'Aristocracy' means 'rule by the best'.

1131a29   **The just, then, represents a kind of proportion**   The reasoning is: the just is the equal; the equal that it is is not that of absolute equality, because merit plays a part; therefore it is proportional equality.

1131a31   **number in general**   i.e. any countable plurality. Justice is not proportionality between the abstract numbers that happen to be instantiated by the amounts of merit possessed by, and the amounts of good assigned to, a set of individuals, since in that case justice would be a purely mathematical property exemplified in every medium in which the proportionality obtained.

1131a33   **so too does continuous proportion**   Having established that distributive justice requires minimally four terms (1131a18–20), Ar. now combats the appearance that continuous proportion requires no more than three, so as to strengthen the conclusion that distributive justice is a sort of proportion (29). (Here, 1131b1–3, he treats proportion as holding between lengths as distinct from numbers.) His argument against the appearance (i.e. that in continuous proportion the intermediate term functions twice, which with the extremes makes four) is also the reason why continuous proportion cannot represent distributive justice: the numerically same entity cannot function both as *recipient* and as *portion* (1130b15–16; this does not rule out the possibility that one recipient's portion might not be measured by the same number as another's merit-ranking, as when five years' service wins ten acres and ten wins twenty).

as A is to B . .   (*a*) A and B are individuals *qua* bearers of amounts of merit; C and D are portions of some distributable good. The just distribution is one that achieves a just 'pairing' between amount of merit and portion of good for each individual, as follows:

1131b5–23

(1)   A : B : : C : D; hence

(2)   A : C : : B : D (from (1) *alternando*, 6–7); hence

(3)   (A + C) : (B + D) : : A : B (from (2) by composition, 7–8).

(*b*) In representing the pairings as sums or wholes, Ar. does not mean that merit and the good to be distributed are addible packets of the same kind of value. (This is ruled out by the remark at 1131b15–16 about why it is impossible to represent a just distribution by a continuous proportion.) The point of the summing is that pairings are just when and only when the ratio between the degree by which the A-individual gains through the accrual of C, and that by which the B-individual gains through the accrual of D, is identical to the ratio of merit A to merit B. (*c*) Where what is distributed is a disadvantage, the differences made to the individuals should be in inverse ratio to their merits. But Ar. accommodates this to his 'summing' model by treating the lesser disadvantage as functionally equivalent to the greater advantage and vice versa (1131b19–23; cf. 1, 1129b6–11).

and the just in this sense is intermediate   i.e. between possibilities in which someone receives more, or less, than he merits.

1131b10

the person who behaves unjustly has too much   Ar. overlooks the case where the unjust distributor is not a recipient; see Introduction, p. 35. In assuming, in effect, that the distributor is necessarily a recipient, Ar. may be following a democratic model in which it is up to potential recipients themselves to work out a distribution. When he does speak of an external arbiter (only in connection with corrective justice, 4, 1132a7, 20–5, 30–2), he merely considers the ideal case where the arbiter is 'the just in living form' (1132a22).

1131b19

V 4, 1131b25–1132b20

The just in rectification differs from the above, in that the former has to do with communal goods, and the latter depends on arithmetical proportion and restoration to absolute equality (1131b25–1132a10). The original interaction, and the restoration to equality, involve gain and loss (1132a10–19). The just and equal as the intermediate; intermediacy and the judge; the intermediate, and the more and less of gain and loss (1132a19–b20).

1131b25   **The remaining form is the rectificatory** [*to diorthōtikon* (at 1132a18, *epanor-thōtikon*)]   The two Greek words are sometimes translated 'corrective'. This makes it easier to think that in dealing with rectification, Ar. is dealing with correctional punishment as much as with reparation, but there is little evidence that this is so. See 5, 1132b31–3, with comment. His word for correctional punishment (usually translated 'forcible correction' in this volume) is '*kolasis*'.

1132a1–2   **arithmetical proportion**   M, N, and O are in arithmetical proportion when M exceeds N by the same absolute amount as N exceeds O. Rather than *effecting* a proportion as distributive justice does, justice in rectification *is guided by* arithmetical proportion in subtracting from M (the wrongdoer's condition) and adding to O (the injured party's) in order to restore the mid-condition (absolute equality), N, for both sides.

1132a8–9   **the effect of the action and the doing of it constitute unequal parts of a division**   The action divides, as it were, a line into two unequal lengths, the larger corresponding to the agent, the shorter to the patient.

1132a9–10   **the aim of imposing a loss on the doer is to equalize things, taking away from the gain realized**   As Ar. says at 1132b12, the words 'loss' (*zēmia*) and 'gain' (*kerdos*) come from voluntary exchange. '*Zēmia*' also means 'fine', 'penalty'.

1132a24   **The just, then, is something intermediate, if in fact the judge is**   The just as embodied in the judge or arbitrator is not the just of a given fair apportionment, but is the very institution of arbitration and going to arbitration. Ar. could have made more of its intermediacy; as an individual, the judge is in some sense intermediate between disputants; but as an institution, arbitration is intermediate between, on the one side, the evil of unresolved conflict between the parties, and, on the other, that in which one of them ends the dispute by superior force.

1132b6–9   **Let there be three lines . . .**

Additional assumptions: DCC and CD are the same lines as CCD and DC respectively; CD = AE (because AE is subtracted from AA and added to CC, whereby it 'becomes' CD); F on CC is the point corresponding to E on AA. Hence CF = AE = CD, and DCC exceeds EA by twice the amount it exceeds BB (= AA, as was).

V 5, 1132b21–1133b28
The reciprocal (*to antipeponthos*): some hold that this defines the just, but it does not fit either of the kinds that have been considered; criticism of the *lex talionis* (1132b21–31). Still, proportional reciprocity in exchange does bind

people together (1132b31–1133a5); an example (1133a5–10); the parties must be of different types, and must be equalized; currency does this by functioning as a common measure for exchangeables, hence it is a sort of intermediate (1133a10–25). But really the common measure is need, since currency exists only by convention (1133a25–31). (Repetition of previous points; 1133a31–b10.) Currency makes transactions possible where one party does not want any commodity the other is able to offer; so the value of currency fluctuates less than values of commodities (1133b10–14). (Repetition of previous points; 1133b14–26.) But exchange of goods can occur without using currency (1133b26–8).

Rhadamanthys   A divine judge who sentences souls in the underworld. The form his justice takes might be thought paradigmatic. The quotation is from Hesiod.   1132b25

there is a great difference between what was done voluntarily and what was done counter-voluntarily   The fact that this point is made here and not also in the discussion of rectification indicates that Ar. sees rectification as primarily compensation of the party that has suffered damage, rather than punishment of the doer (cf. III. 1, 1109b30–5), for it is plausible that the doer should compensate, whether the damage was inflicted voluntarily or not.   1132b30–1

In commercial associations, however, the parties are bound together by a form of the just that is like this, i.e. what is reciprocal in proportional terms, not in terms of numerical equality   (a) This may refer to a new form of particular justice, the 'commutative': see note on 2, 1130b31–1131a3. For a different understanding of the connection of commercial exchange with justice, see Introduction, p. 37. (b) Commercial exchange is different from retaliation (tit for tat) and from rectification, in that in commerce what the parties respectively receive is different in kind from what they give. This allows for the possibility that a unit on one side is worth more or less than a unit on the other, so that the equality achieved must be proportional. Another difference is that in retaliation and rectification the purpose of the 'exchange' (i.e. the 'giving back') is to equalize the parties in accordance with some prior conception of equality, whereas in commerce the parties themselves 'equalize' the commodities (settle on how many of one unit is worth how many of the other) in order to receive what each lacks. Further: while the just in distribution and in rectification is necessary for political society, the achieving of it in a particular instance does not automatically 'hold men together': on the contrary, on equalization, the parties walk away (this is also true in retaliation); but in commerce, once a particular equalization is reached, they come still closer together in actual exchange of goods. It is because he sees this as an important difference that Ar. labours the fact that commercial equalization must precede the actual exchange (1133b1–3; cf. 1133a10–12).   1132b31–3

1133a6–7 **the coupling of diametrical opposites** i.e:

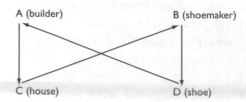

1133a10–12 **If, then, there is first of all equality in proportional terms, and reciprocal exchange occurs after that** i.e. they must agree on the proportion between a unit of one product and a unit of the other *before* exchanging, in order to achieve the just 'coupling of diametrical opposites', in which for agreed upon m and n, the whole consisting of builder-in-receipt-of-m-pairs-of-shoes is 'equal to' that consisting of shoemaker-in-receipt-of-n-buildings. The same point is made at 1133b1–3, on which see comment.

1133a14–17 **This feature is found in the various forms of productive expertise too . . . For it is not two doctors that become partners to an exchange** The point that exchange implies equalization of unlikes is set in a metaphysical perspective. On the one hand, there could *be* no production, nor therefore productive expertise and products to exchange, unless patient undergoes an effect identical in kind and quantity to what agent brings about. On the other hand, production entails that patient initially lacks (and is not about to acquire for itself) exactly what agent provides (cf. *On Generation and Corruption* i. 7).

1133a18 **in general people who are of different sorts and not in a relation of equality to each other** The doctor and the farmer illustrate 'different sorts'. The parties are 'unequal' when they bring to the transaction commodity-units of different value. They are equalized when the proportionate value of these is established. Ar. sees this as establishing a proportion between the parties themselves, each person being represented by the product he brings; cf. 22 and 32–3.

1133a26 **as was said before** At line 19.

1133a26–7 **In truth this one thing is need, which holds everything together** Presumably this is meant to correct the statement that currency is the common measure (20–1), as if it might be thought that currency could encourage exchange in the absence of need for the articles bought and sold. (Such a thought might seem more plausible when the currency consists of pieces of precious metal.) In the background of this association of *that which measures everything* with *that which holds everything together* stands the early philosopher Heraclitus, who made exchanging goods by means of currency ('goods for gold and gold for goods', fr. 90, Diels) a model for the cosmic justice (the *logos*) that structures the cyclic transformation of kinds of matter, and thereby holds the physical world together.

1133a27–8 **for if people did not need things, or if they do not need them to the same extent, then either there will be no exchange, or the exchange will be a**

different one   'The same extent' presumably means ' . . . as each other'. The 'different kind' may mean monetary payment by contrast with barter, or it may mean a relation like friendship between unequals, where the party that needs less is given love or honour, instead of an equal material good (cf. VIII. 7, 1158b20–8).

But one should not introduce them as terms in a figure of proportion when   *1133b1 ff.*
they are already making the exchange . . .   Obscure, but the point seems to be this: in stating, for example, that one *builder's unit* is worth a hundred *shoemaker's units*, we must make it clear that we refer to units possessed before the transaction, i.e. to the builder's and shoemaker's respective products; for if the words refer to what each acquires as result of exchange, then the larger number of units will belong on the same side as the units of greater value: we shall be implying, for example, that one pair of shoes is worth a hundred houses. This is not advice for buyers and sellers, but for the analyst explaining the logic of exchange in terms of proportionality.

they want to give a corn export licence in return   i.e. something not needed   *1133b9–10*
by someone who only has wine to sell.

V 5, 1133b29–1134a16

Doing what is just (dikaiopragia) is intermediate between doing what is unjust (*adikein*) and being subjected to what is unjust (*adikeisthai*; 1133b29–32). And *justice (dikaiosunē)* is an intermediate disposition, though not in the same way as the other excellences, but because it gives rise to the intermediate and the proportionately equal; injustice gives rise to the contrary, i.e. proportional excess and deficiency of good and harm, hence is itself excess and deficiency (1133b32–1134a12).

It is on the basis of the account of (*a*) *the just* as the equal and the intermediate that Ar. now shows how 'intermediate and equal' apply to (*b*) *doing* what is just and to (*c*) *the disposition* justice. (And he similarly shows how the contrary terms apply to doing what is unjust and to the disposition injustice.) The exclusive attention to geometrical proportion shows that this was written before he considered the just in rectification (see comment on 3, 1131a10–b24). The main points here apply to exchange as well as distribution, but he mentions distribution alone (1134a3), and the contrast 'between himself and another' versus 'between different others' (1134a3–6, 9–12) does not apply to exchange. This completes the inquiry, undertaken at 2, 1130b7–8, into 'what, and what sort of thing' particular justice is.

not in the same way as the other excellences   Particular justice resembles the   *1133b32–3*
other character-excellences in achieving the intermediate (II. 6, 1106b28), but differs in that the extremes are achieved not by distinct contrary defects of excess and deficiency, but simply by injustice, which is simultaneously excessive and deficient to different participants in a single apportionment. Another difference:

the intermediate achieved and extremes avoided by justice are (in Ar.'s presentation) necessarily quantitative, whereas the other dispositions are also about non-quantitative ways of getting things right and wrong.

1134a1–2   **justice is the disposition in accordance with which the just person is said to be the sort to do [*praktikos*] what is just, as a result of decision**   This may be an emphasis on the practicality of justice, invoked in case the mathematical approach suggests that the main achievement is identifying the proportions.

1134a12   **there can be disproportion either way**   He means *unjust* disproportion. Whether I give X too much of some good and Y too little, or the reverse, it is unjust to someone either way if neither is myself. But between myself and another, I cannot do what is unjust by giving him too much and myself too little, because one cannot wrong oneself: see 11, 1138a4–28.

1134a12–13   **Of unjust action [*to adikēma*], the 'too small' is a matter of being subjected to what is unjust, the 'too large' of doing what is unjust**   The pair consisting of doing what is unjust and being subjected to what is unjust (1133b31) are now considered as aspects of one thing, unjust action.

V 6, 1134a17–23

This short discussion of the difference between doing what is unjust and being an unjust person is germane to what precedes it, but is probably out of place, since it seems unrelated to the reference to reciprocity at line 24 and to the ensuing discussion of what is just in the 'political' sense (although lines 32–3 hark back to the present passage).

1134a19   **Or will this turn out not to be the way they differ?**   i.e. the difference between the person of unjust disposition and one who merely behaves unjustly does not lie in any special kind of unjust act committed by the former, but in his acting from decision. For a fuller treatment of the difference, see 8, 1135b8 ff.

V 6, 1134a23–b18

What is just/unjust in the primary or unqualified sense is *political*; i.e. it occurs only in the relations of full members of a political community, enfranchised, equal, and living together under the rule of law (1134a26–b1). (Digression on magistrates as guardians of the law, and how they should be rewarded; 1134b1–8.) In relations between masters and slaves, fathers and dependent children, husbands and wives, there are qualified types of the just and the unjust, resembling the unqualified (1134a28–30, b8–18).

For example, parental assignment of chores or rewards to young children is not just/unjust, but just/unjust-in-accordance-with-paternal-justice. This is not to say that a husband's or father's obligations regarding his wife or children are weaker than those to his fellow citizens, but simply that they are not strict examples of particular justice. So far as distribution is

E18 RESOURCE BASE

concerned, this is because the merit of non-adult children, of wives, and (if any) of slaves, cannot be compared with that of the man of the house so as to be brought into proportional equality with his. For Ar.'s theory of natural inequalities (slave to master, female to male), see *Politics* I. 1–8, 13–14. These natural inequalities differ among themselves, for the wife and children are free, unlike the slave, but are not fellow citizens (have no part in political activity).

has been said earlier   See 5, 1132b21–33.   *1134a24*

what we are looking for is both what is just without qualification and what is   *1134a25–6*
just in the context of the political community   (*a*) What follows shows that these are the same. (*b*) 'without qualification' is contrasted with 'what is just in a way and in virtue of a certain resemblance' at lines 29–30.

For there is justice . . . if there can be injustice   The English nouns refer not to   *1134a30–1*
dispositions of character but to types of action and arrangement.

where there is unjust action there is not always injustice   'Injustice' now   *1134a32–3*
refers to the disposition; cf. 8, 1135b22–5.

what is generally good   See 1, 1129b3–4.   *1134a34*

as we stated before, too   At 1, 1130a3.   *1134b6*

chattel   i.e. slave.   *1134b10*

oneself—no one decides [*prohaireitai*] to harm *that*; hence there will be no   *1134b11–13*
injustice in relation to oneself   (*a*) 'Decides' occurs here in its Aristotelian sense; at 9, 1136a32–3, the uncontrolled person (who by definition acts contrary to decision) is said to harm himself voluntarily. (*b*) If, as seems likely, 'injustice' here means acting unjustly, rather than the character-trait, the above is a poor argument, since in general *voluntary harming* is sufficient for *unjustly treating* (8, 1135b22–4). Possibly Ar. assumes that if an action, e.g. harming oneself, is such that one cannot do it from decision, then (even though doable voluntarily) it cannot be said to be done unjustly (or justly) (i.e. the question whether something is an instance of acting unjustly arises only if it is conceivably the manifestation of an unjust disposition, in which case it would have to be a possible object of decision for the agent). But it is anyway plausible that relations towards oneself or parts or extensions of oneself cannot exhibit the unqualified just or unjust. (However, at 11, 1138b5–8, Ar. states that the just does not obtain even in a qualified sense between an individual and himself, taken as a whole.)

nor, therefore, will there be what is unjust in the political sense, or what is   *1134b13*
just [sc. between fathers and dependent children]   The inference assumes that the politically just is just without qualification.

and these were people sharing equally in ruling and being ruled. Hence 'the   *1134b14–16*

just' exists more in relation to one's wife than in relation to one's children and chattels (*a*) Equality in ruling and being ruled is implemented if citizens take turns to rule or different functions of rulership and subjecthood are equally distributed according to some criterion of equal distribution, or if all are ruled by a monarch who does not count as one of them. (*b*) The wife is closer to being an equal than child or slave is, because she rules in important areas of domestic life.

V 7, 1134b18–1135a8

'Natural' versus 'legal' forms of the politically just (1134b24–1135a8); argument against those who hold that it is all a matter of legality alone (1134b24–35).

Whether human justice is grounded on nature or is a legal creation had been a matter of intense debate in the 5th century; see the positions of Plato's characters Callicles (*Gorgias*) and Thrasymachus (*Republic* I). Respect for law, which is the basis of political justice and of justice in the wide sense, depends on the assumption that laws in general are neither arbitrary nor mere reflections of the will of some particular interest group. Ar. rejects the argument that if there were laws reflecting natural justice they would be the same everywhere and immutable. Even if natural justice is in some sense divine (cf. *Politics* III. 16, 1287a29), our human interpretations of it are, of course, different under different circumstances. He does not attempt to give a principle for deciding which laws express natural justice and which are ad hoc or purely conventional, presumably because he assumes that in practice it is easy to tell.

1134b18–19   **What is politically just divides into the natural and the** [merely] **legal**   In ch. 6 'the politically just' was understood as particular justice (see the reference to goods in general at 1134a34), but here the two divisions of it seem to include more than questions of distribution and rectification.

1134b23   **Brasidas**   The Spartan general, killed at Amphipolis in 422 BCE. The Amphipolitans gave him a hero's burial and instituted games in his honour (Thucydides, v. 6. 11).

1134b24   **decrees**   i.e. ad hoc edicts of the assembly. At *Politics* IV. 4, 1292a15–25, Ar. warns against replacing the rule of law with rule by decree, which he likens to rule by a tyrant.

1134b33–5   **for the right hand is superior by nature, and yet it is possible that everyone should become ambidextrous**   Even though all societies have acquired conventional rules in addition to the rules of natural justice (like acquiring left-handed 'dexterity' through special training), this does not alter the fact that the latter are natural, nor does it erase the difference between natural and conventional.

larger where people buy, smaller where they sell It is not clear whether this is an observation about wholesale and retail markets in the same city-state, or about states which import, versus those which export, a given commodity.

1135a2–3

even political constitutions are not the same everywhere, although only one is everywhere the best by nature (a) This seems to be the premiss of an a fortiori argument: institutions, such as the constitutions of states, that are properly assessed in terms of natural justice are not the same everywhere, so certainly conventional arrangements are not. (b) The ideal constitution is rule by the excellent.

1135a4–5

Each of the things that are just in the legal sense ... because it is a universal This balances what precedes. Despite the variation in the legally just, every law is a single constant universal by comparison with the many particular actions that comply with it.

1135a5–8

V 7–8, 1135a8–1136a9

The difference and connection between what is just/unjust (*to dikaion/ adikon*) and a just/unjust act (*dikaiōma/adikēma*) (1135a8–15); a just/ unjust act, i.e. acting justly/unjustly (*dikaiopragein/adikein*), is voluntary (1135a15–23); 'voluntary' and 'counter-voluntary' explained (1135a23–b8); the difference between the merely voluntary and what has been decided for (1135b8–11); three kinds of harming: misfortunes (*atuchēmata*), mistakes (*hamartēmata*), and unjust acts (1135b11–22); the difference between doing an unjust (or a just) act and being an unjust (or just) person (*adikos/dikaios*) (1135b22–5, 1136a1–5); digression on temper and premeditation (1135b25–1136a1); distinctions within the counter-voluntary (1136a5–9).

for what is unjust is so by nature or by prescription, while this same thing, when done, is an unjust act The argument seems to be: that something is unjust is due to one of two causes, nature or prescription, whereas that something is an unjust *act* is only ever due to one type of cause, i.e. that something unjust is *done*; therefore being unjust differs from being an unjust act. (We are using 'act' to refer to the done deed or performance, 'action' to refer indifferently to this and to action considered as *what* is performed.) At lines 19–23 he further specifies that an unjust etc. act is voluntarily done.

1135a9–11

We must consider later Perhaps in the *Politics*.

1135a15

except in an incidental sense i.e. what he does fits the description of an unjust action, but his doing of it, being counter-voluntary, is not unjust.

1135a18

for when something unjust is done voluntarily, it is an object of censure, and at the same time it is, then, an unjust act This is a significant divergence from the doctrine of III.1, which allows that one can voluntarily do something bad yet

1135a20–1

349

not be censured for it, e.g. if it is done as the lesser evil (1110a15 ff.), or under duress in certain cases.

1135a23   **as has also been said before**   *EE* II. 9, 1225b1–10; *NE* III. 1, 1111a22–4.

1135a31–b2   **What is done in ignorance, then, or not in ignorance but without its depending on oneself, or rather, under force, is counter-voluntary. For there are also many of the things … such as ageing or dying**   (*a*) 'in ignorance' here is tantamount to 'because of ignorance' at III. 1, 1110b22–30. (*b*) In III. 1 Ar. did not distinguish what is due to force and what does not depend on us (although he did not equate them either), and he did not recognize a distinct class of inevitable natural processes that are neither voluntary nor due to external force or ignorance (although something like this enters the discussion at III. 5, 1113b26–30). This is probably because III. 1 was not looking for a classification of all phenomena, but for guidelines to safeguard against misidentifying the non-voluntary as voluntary, or vice versa. The question of its being voluntary cannot arise for a universal natural process like ageing.

1135b4–5   **counter-voluntarily [*akōn*], and because of fear**   Two interpretations are possible: (1) 'counter-voluntarily' has its official, Aristotelian, meaning in which it excludes 'voluntarily'. In that case, actions done from fear and the like (the next line speaks of 'constraint', *anankazomenos*) either constitute a new category of the counter-voluntary over and above those due to external force and to ignorance, or there are still two categories based on force and ignorance, but fear etc. now count as kinds of force. (This does not seem very likely from the one example he chooses to illustrate force: 1135a27.) On this interpretation, there is a conflict with 1135b20–3, which implies that actions done from fear are voluntary. (2) 'Counter-voluntarily' is used colloquially to mean 'reluctantly', and the point is that although the agent (voluntarily) does what is just, this is not an example of acting justly (*dikaiopragein*), which requires a positive attitude (so also for 'unjust' and 'acting unjustly' (*adikein*) at 1135b6–8). This interpretation would be more attractive if one could take 'voluntary / counter-voluntary' at 1135a17–20 as meaning 'unreluctant / reluctant', but lines 20–33 rule this out; and in any case there is a conflict with 1135a15–17, which equates voluntary doing of an unjust thing with acting unjustly. (At III. 1, 1110a4–26 actions done under constraint of fear etc. are finally classed as voluntary, while at *EE* II. 8, 1225a19 they are counter-voluntary.)

1135b12   **mistakes**   This term first covers every harm done because of ignorance, but is then restricted to cases of culpable ignorance (17–18).

1135b19   **a misfortune when it is outside him**   e.g. where *A* harms *B* because of *B*'s negligence, the origin is in *B*. This is a wider conception of *external origin* than was used in III. 1, where it was equivalent to *force*.

1135b19–20   **when a person inflicts harm knowingly but without prior deliberation, it is an unjust act**   Ar. draws no distinction between harm that is intended and harm

350

that is a foreseeable consequence of what is intended. (Thus he lacks, or over-looks, the concept of 'intention' in so far as the above distinction sustains it.)

temper and other affections that are inevitable or natural for human beings   *1135b21–2*
Actions done from these impulses are here said to be voluntary (cf. III. 1, 1111a24–b3), but when the feeling is pathological the action is counter-voluntary (1136a5–9). See also 1135b4–5 with comment.

and when the harm *is* inflicted as a result of decision, then the doer is unjust   *1135b25*
and a bad character [*mochthēros*]   (a) 'As a result of decision' presumably covers not only what the agent positively decides to do, but also what he or she finds, on deliberation, to be an acceptable consequence of the former. See comment on 1135b19–20. (b) This differs from the doctrine of Book II according to which a good or bad action based on decision is a necessary but not sufficient condition for having the corresponding quality of character (II. 4, 1105a28–33).

from premeditation   The condition for heaviest culpability under Athenian law.   *1135b26*
Here Ar. sees this legal distinction as confirming his own distinction between the merely voluntary and what is based on decision. However, 'premeditation' does not imply, as Ar.'s 'decision' does, that the agent acts in accordance with his character and values. VII. 6, 1149b13–17 recognizes an agent who is uncontrolled, hence has abandoned his decision, but who acts with premeditation.

Again, the dispute is not even about whether the event occurred, but about   *1135b27*
what is just   This is another reason why it is right to hold that what is done from temper is not premeditated: the two types of motive suggest different courtroom strategies. One who has harmed another from temper is likely, if charged, to plead provocation, in which case he admits the deed but claims some right on his side. He can also present himself as having acted impulsively. By contrast, one who inflicted wrongful harm in the premeditated belief that he would get away with it is more likely to insist that he did not do anything.

anyone who has plotted   i.e. who acted from premeditation. The point may be   *1135b33*
that he knows what he did was unjust, whereas the person who lashed out under provocation mistakenly believes he was justified.

so that one party thinks he is being treated unjustly   Present tense because he   *1135b33–*
continues to be the victim of injustice until the wrong is rectified.   *1136a1*

whenever the action runs contrary to what is proportionate or contrary to   *1136a2–3*
equality of distribution   This restriction makes it clear that particular injustice is the topic.

Of things done counter-voluntarily some are such as to call for sympathy   *1136a5–6*
[*sungnōmē*]**, others not**   'Sungnōmē' covers pity, pardon, compassion, sympathy based on a sense that we ourselves might well have done the same bad deed in the same circumstances. We cannot feel this towards those who do evil from what we

regard as unnatural or inhuman feelings, even though (according to Ar. here), we should count such actions as counter-voluntary. The reason cannot be that they are done 'in ignorance' since this is true of actions done from normal feelings, which count as voluntary (1135b20–2); the thought must be that unnatural feelings represent a force external to the individual's human nature.

1136a6–8 **not only in ignorance but also because of ignorance ... not because of ignorance but** [sc. merely] **in ignorance** The 'because of ... ' locution refers to ignorance of a particular fact, as at III. 1, 1110b24–7. But there, it and 'in ignorance' were mutually exclusive, whereas here 'because of ... ' is a subdivision of 'in ... '.

V 9, 1136a10–1137a4

Questions about passive parties: can one voluntarily receive unjust treatment? (1136a10–23, 31–b14); does undergoing what is unjust imply being unjustly treated? (1136a23–31); if X receives more than his share in a distribution, is it X who acts unjustly, or Y, the distributor? (1136b15–1137a4). The first question leads to: can one wrong oneself? (1136a33–b13). This is taken up again in ch. 11 (1138a4 ff.).

1136a11–12 **the paradoxical lines of Euripides** The quotation is from the lost play *Alcmaeon*.

1136a15 **Is it possible, in truth, to receive unjust treatment voluntarily** (*a*) A conceptual question with practical implications. If the answer is no, then *caveat emptor*: a person who voluntarily accepts a bad bargain cannot claim redress on grounds of having been wronged. (*b*) Having raised the above question, Ar. asks whether the answer is the same for all cases. First he argues that it is: since the opposite of the passive is the active, then (by the symmetry of opposites) being unjustly treated is always whichever it is, voluntary or counter-voluntary, because unjustly treating is always what it is, i.e. voluntary (16–21). He then shows that such an argument cannot be sound because it would establish that being justly treated (which it is assumed is at least sometimes voluntary) is always voluntary; but this is not always the case (as is shown by the fact that most people try to escape just punishment) (21–3).

1136a23–4 **whether every person who has had something unjust done to him is being treated unjustly** On the present tense see comment on 1135b33–1136a1.

1136a32 **the person who lacks self-control** Citing lack of self-control blocks the glib move: if one voluntarily accepts what would otherwise count as harmful treatment, it is not harmful, hence a fortiori not a case of being unjustly treated. It is agreed that the un-self-controlled, in yielding to temptation, voluntarily harm themselves or accept harm from another (1136b1–3), so this is a test case for deciding whether *voluntarily* can coexist with *being unjustly treated*.

Or is our definition incorrect? Should we add ... 'against the subject's   *1136b3–5*
wish'?   Ar. is referring to the definition of unjustly treating at 8, 1135b19–24, and
the questions are his characteristic way of saying the addition *is* necessary. Cf.
1136b23–9, where 'being against one's wish' seems to imply that the action is
initiated by someone else. Thus he concludes at lines 5–6 that one cannot voluntarily be the victim of unjust treatment (although one can voluntarily have done
to one things that are incidentally unjust, according to the distinction explained at
1136a24–9). Now the text becomes very obscure ('for no one wishes it, not even
the person lacking in self-control, who acts, rather, contrary to his wish ...
doesn't do what he thinks he should', 6–9). Perhaps something is missing or
different discussions have been patched together. The difficulty is that if the
un-self-controlled person acts contrary to his own wish (so that 'contrary to one's
wish' does not here imply an external initiator, but has its usual meaning in which
wish is for the good as distinct from the pleasant; cf. *NE* III. 4, 1113a15 ff.; *EE* II. 7,
1223b6–9, 29–35), the augmented definition does not rule out the possibility of
voluntarily undergoing unjust treatment: the uncontrolled agent voluntarily,
through appetite, overrides his own wish and acts so as to harm himself; hence he
is voluntarily treated unjustly (by himself). Ar. could rebut this by appealing to a
principle like the one possibly at work at 6, 1134b11–13 (on which, see comment),
i.e. that if an outcome *O*, say harm to oneself, is such that one cannot *wish* it
(even though one can voluntarily bring *O* about because of appetite), then one
cannot act justly or unjustly by bringing *O* about. But it would be far-fetched to
read this into this passage.

Homer   Iliad VI., 236.   *1136b9*

the problems we decided to discuss   The only relevant reference to problems   *1136b15*
was at 1136a10.

if there exists the possibility we raised before   This refers to the possibility of   *1136b17–18*
treating oneself unjustly; cf. 1136a34–b1. At b12–13 he asserted that this is not
possible, but the argument there was unsatisfactory, and he returns to the question at 11, 1138a4 ff.

by reference to our definition   i.e. as emended at lines 3–5.   *1136b23*

but merely 'does' what is unjust   This is true to the extent that receiving a   *1136b31*
distribution that one did not initiate counts as 'doing something'.

if someone gave an unjust judgement in ignorance, he is not acting unjustly in   *1136b32–4*
terms of the legally just, nor is his judgement unjust, although it is unjust in a
way (since what is just in a legal sense is different from what is just in the
primary sense)   (*a*) What is just in the primary sense is so by nature, in contrast
with what is just only because stipulated by law; cf. 7, 1134b18 ff. The point of
saying that the agent does not act unjustly in purely legal terms seems to be
simply to set up a contrast with the naturally just. A judgement that conflicts with

a naturally just arrangement is, as we might put it, objectively wrong, even if it was made in ignorance; if so, it is 'unjust in a way', although ethically unexceptionable. (*b*) The judge here operates not merely 'in ignorance' but 'because of ignorance', according to the usage of 8, 1136a6–7.

1137a1   **favour or revenge**   Motives for assigning another too much or too little when one does not take an unfair share oneself.

V 9, 1137a4–30
The difference between doing things that are just/unjust, and being a just/unjust person (1137a4–26); the sphere of particular justice (1137a26–30).

1137a4–5   **People think that acting unjustly depends on them**   This thought matches the one rejected at 1136b12: that it can depend on oneself whether one is treated unjustly. In what follows there seems to be no clear distinction between acting unjustly etc., and being an unjust etc. person. At lines 6–9 Ar. argues: because (1) it is easy to commit adultery etc., and doing so depends on us, people confusedly think that (2) doing so unjustly is easy and depends on us. The point is less strange if couched in terms of just action and acting justly. The focus then seems to shift to the difference between knowing which actions of others are just (easy) and being able to tell when they are instances of just agency (difficult) (9–26). The general target may be Protagoras' view that virtually everyone brought up in society is an expert on justice (Plato, *Protagoras* 324d–328a).

1137a11–12   **it is not hard to understand the matters on which the laws utter (although it is not these that constitute what is just** [*dikaia*; see also line 13]**, except in an incidental sense)**   Elsewhere (8, 1135a15–19, b2–6) he made much the same point using 'just act' and 'acting justly' instead of 'what is just'.

1137a17   **And precisely because of this**   i.e. because of the similarity to the case of medicine. This encourages us to misconceive of justice as a two-edged skill; cf. 1, 1129a11–15. On the just person as good at thieving etc., see e.g. *Republic* I, 334a–b.

1137a22–3   **except incidentally**   i.e. the practice of cowardice etc. immediately consists in abandoning-one's-shield-etc.-in-a-certain-frame-of-mind, and only consequentially consists in abandoning one's shield. Cf. VI. 12, 1144a13–20; II. 4, 1105a17–b9.

1137a27   **and who have too much or too little of these**   They are goods in the abstract but not necessarily for a particular person (cf. 1, 1129b1–6) precisely because some individuals have too much of them for their own good, others too little to benefit effectively. If we were gods, no amount would corrupt us, if we were irredeemably wicked no lack of those goods would leave us worse off than we would be anyway. So particular justice is for intermediate beings.

V 10, 1137a31–1138ba3

On reasonableness (*epieikeia*; often translated 'equity'): how is it related to justice? It seems neither the same nor different (1137a31–b5); solution (1137b5–13). The puzzle arises because a quality is needed to rectify law when law fails to fit a given situation, and this quality is reasonableness (1137b13–1138a2).

(The adjective *epieikēs* commonly meant 'ethically good', 'decent', and Ar. frequently uses it in this way: see e.g. IV. 9, 1128b21 ff.) Use of the noun for the specific quality of humane discretion in applying law so as to achieve natural justice suggests that concern for natural justice in all areas is *the* hallmark of the good person (cf. 1, 1129b27–30).

At 9, 1136b20–1 the reasonable person was one who does not press his own claims of particular justice to the full. Note that to act reasonably in that way would necessarily be to act unjustly to someone if it were possible to act unjustly to oneself; this may explain why a discussion of this latter possibility follows the discussion of reasonableness. Now, however, the reasonable person is one who interprets law or goes beyond it when it is too general to determine a fair ruling in a particular case (although see note on 1138a1). In so far as reasonableness is an aspect of the just disposition, it is an excellence of character (cf. 11, 1138b13–14); but its responsiveness to particulars makes it also an aspect of the intellectual excellence, wisdom: cf. VI. 11, 1143a19–24. There is a fuller account of reasonableness at *Rhetoric* I. 13, 1374a20–b23.

either what is just is not a good thing, or if it is, what is reasonable is not just   i.e. we think of a reasonable action as just, and therefore as good, only when the just action would *not* be good. This is paradoxical until we see that sometimes the reasonable is needed to make the difference between a state of affairs that conforms to the legally just, and one that is genuinely fair.   *1137b4–5*

so that decrees [*psēphismata*] **are needed instead**   See comment on 7, 1134b34.   *1137b29*

like the leaden rule used in building Lesbian-style   i.e. a flexible measuring rod. The reference is to the island of Lesbos; presumably the special style involved a variety of curves that had to be made the same or proportionate lengths.   *1137b30–1*

but rather tends to take a less strict view of things   At 9, 1136b20–1 this phrase referred to taking a smaller share of some divisible good than one is entitled to; but it fits better into the present context if here it means a reluctance, in general, not to exact all that the law permits.   *1138a1*

V 11, 1138a4–b28

Is it possible to treat oneself unjustly? Argument for (1138a4–11); arguments and conclusion against (1138a11–28). Digression on its being worse to treat than be treated unjustly (1138a28–b5). In an extended sense there can be just and unjust relations between different parts of the soul (1138b5–13).

1138a4–5   **from what has been said**   Presumably the reference is to 9, 1136b3–5.

1138a5–11   **For part of what is just . . . in that case he is acting unjustly**   Several details are obscure, and some scholars doubt whether Ar. could have written lines 6–7 as given in the manuscripts. But the main point is that one can treat oneself, voluntarily (and moreover not by way of retaliation), in a way forbidden by law; thus in this broad sense of 'unjust' one can (it is argued) treat oneself unjustly. Lines 6–7 may allude to a law that enjoins suicide in certain circumstances (this is envisaged in Plato, *Laws* 873c), the point then being that the law forbids it otherwise. Ar. invokes the particular sense of 'unjust' at 14–20, where he argues the other side of the question.

1138a15–16   **for this is a distinct case from the other one**   'The other one' refers to the unjust in the broad sense, corresponding to 'badness as a whole' (17–18); cf. 1, 1130a10.

1138a20–1   **acting unjustly is something which is both voluntary and based on decision, and involves doing something to someone first**   Ar.'s usual doctrine is that decision is not a necessary condition for acting unjustly, but here he takes the paradigm case.

1138a23–4   **it will be possible to receive unjust treatment voluntarily**   Argued to be impossible at 9, 1136b1–14.

1138a25–6   **no one . . . breaks and enters through his own wall**   'Wall', not (as we might expect) 'window', because the windows of a typical ancient Greek house faced the inner courtyard.

1138a27–8   **the definition introduced in connection with one's being the voluntary recipient of injustice**   See 9, 1136a31–b5, 23–5.

1138a30–1   **what makes for health . . . what makes for fitness**   Presumably these illustrate 'intermediate'.

1138a31–2   **doing injustice is worse**   What some of Socrates' interlocutors found deeply paradoxical (e.g. *Gorgias* 469b–c) now appears uncontroversial.

1138a33–4   **the badness is either complete and possessed without qualification, or nearly so (for not every voluntary unjust act goes with an unjust disposition)**   Here, 'complete badness' seems to refer to the disposition, what is 'nearly so' to a voluntary unjust act. The difference between them, though important elsewhere (cf. 8, 1135b23–5), is minimal in the context of the contrast (in terms of deserving/not deserving reproach) with being unjustly treated.

1138b1   **there is no reason why it should not incidentally be a greater evil**   For Ar. this would have to be a case in which suffering a wrong *A* rather than committing one *B* leads to committing an act worse than *B*.

it is in these sorts of relationships of disparity that the part of the soul   *1138b8–9*
possessing reason stands to the non-rational part   In the *Republic* Plato argues that individual justice is essentially a state of the soul in which reason, the natural ruler, rules. For Ar., this is justice only by resemblance to relations (master–slaves, father–children) that themselves are just only by resemblance to the primary case (cf. 6, 1134b8–17).

BOOK VI

NE VI has been described as 'piecemeal' in character, an inevitable impression if one expects linear progress. It is mainly about wisdom (*phronēsis*), but since Ar. explains the nature of wisdom by showing what it is not, the Book is about other intellectual qualities too. The discussion of wisdom itself moves between three foci: (i) the good *results* that wisdom delivers, i.e. decisions (*prohaireseis*) each embodying a prescription (*orthos logos*) correct for the occasion (1 and 2, 1138b18–1139b13); (ii) the rational *process* leading to such results, i.e. good deliberation (chs. 1, 2, 5 (1140a24–b30), and 9 (1142a31–b33)); and (iii) the *disposition* exercised in the process, which turns out to consist in an alliance of cleverness (*deinotēs*) with excellence of character (12 and 13, 1143b18–1145a11). This duality of wisdom reflects the duality of its result, the good decision, which Ar. analyses as a complex of 'true thought and right desire' (2, 1139a21–4). Differentiating wisdom from technical expertise (*technē*) and from intellectual accomplishment (*sophia*, 'theoretical excellence') requires an excursus into each of these (4, 1140a1–23); 7, 1141a9–b23), and extended comparisons (chs. 4, 7, and 8 (1141b23–1142a30)). And because intellectual accomplishment turns out to combine *systematic knowledge* (*epistēmē*) with *intelligence* (*nous*), these too have to be explained (3, 1139b14–36; 6, 1140b31–1141a8). Ar. also has something to say about different levels of wisdom, about wisdom in politics (8, 1141b23 ff.), about the cognate rational qualities of excellence in comprehension (*eusunesia*) and sympathy (*sungnōmē*) (10 and 11, 1142b34–1143a24), and about the status of wisdom *vis-à-vis* intellectual mastery (12 and 13, 1143b33–5 and 1145a6–11).

In fact *NE* VI is quite well organized. And it seems more obscure than it is if we look in it for solutions to the wrong questions (see Introduction, pp. 51–2, and note on 1, 1138b18–34). That said, it remains true that Ar.'s writing in this Book is often extremely terse and for that reason difficult.

(III. 2–3 (1111b4–1113a14) ranges over some of the same material, but with significant differences. Decision and deliberation (like the preceding topic of the voluntary) are examined neutrally, i.e. without special emphasis on rightness or goodness. Excellence of character is the only disposition considered; wisdom and cleverness are not mentioned. Ar. happily illustrates ethical deliberation by examples of technical and theoretical (geometrical) reasoning (3, 1112b11–24), and is unconcerned to show how it differs from them. There is no emphasis, as there is in VI (7, 1141b15 ff.), on the particularity of the objects of deliberation. In III the discussion of decision is integrated with one of wish (*boulēsis*; III. 4), about which VI is silent.)

VI 1, 1138b18–34

It is a truism that the successful practitioners operate by the correct prescription, adjusting their activity so as to achieve intermediacy, but this is 'not at all illuminating' (1138b26), because it applies not only to matters of conduct but also to 'all other spheres of concern involving specialized knowledge [*epistēmē*]'(26–9). The medical patient is helped by being told *what* sort of treatments he should undergo, not by being told to undergo 'those that medical expertise [i.e. the expertise that generates medically right prescriptions or instructions] dictates' (29–32). Similarly, the student of ethics needs an explanation, which Ar. now undertakes to provide, that marks off the ethical correct prescription and states what is distinctive about it (33–4).

This passage has sometimes been understood as promising to state a rule for correct decision-making, or to identify some single goal that would function as a standard for deciding what to do. But there is nothing in the subsequent chapters to satisfy such an expectation. This is consistent with II. 2, 1104a1–10, according to which there are no exceptionless rules of conduct, and with III. 1, 1110a13–14, which says that 'the end for which actions are done varies with the occasion'. It is true that at 7, 1141b13, Ar. speaks of the good deliberator as aiming at 'what is best for a human being among practicable goods', a phrase reminiscent of references in NE I to the chief good or happiness (e.g. 4, 1095a16; 7, 1097b22; 2, 1094b7). This and similar passages (cf. VI. 5, 1140a28, b5–6, 18–19, 21; also 2, 1139b3–4 and 9, 1142b31–3) suggest that the good deliberator's objective according to Book VI is happiness as Ar. defines it. However, this does not in general constitute a standard for decision-making. In so far as Aristotelian happiness consists in the activity of excellence, of course the good deliberator in a sense aims at happiness (and is already instantiating it; see note (*b*) on III. 3, 1112b13), since he is deliberating in order to find out what it would be good to do; and as he is wise and has the other excellences, his doing what it would be good to do will no doubt be an activity of excellence. But having happiness as one's objective in this way does not help one to decide what, specifically, it would be good to do. And in so far as Aristotelian happiness consists of the elements that make up 'a complete life', a good deliberator who aims to realize one or another of these (whether or not in the name of happiness) does not on that account get definite guidance on what to do, for there are different ways of realizing that sort of goal, and he will want to choose one that is ethically acceptable. Finally, one might be operating in 'political' mode, i.e. aiming to set up conditions of what one represents to oneself as 'a good human life', or 'the way to live' for oneself or one's family or community. One might be pondering a life-shaping decision. In that case, it is probably helpful, as Aristotle thinks it is, to have before one's mind a true general picture of the human good, a picture that reminds one of such things as that wealth is not an end in itself, for the picture might indeed guide one towards one definite decision rather than another. But not all decisions are of this 'political' kind, whereas all good ones involve the 'correct prescription'. It follows that if Aristotle's promise to clarify 'the correct prescription' is a promise to identify a standard for decision-making, statements such as 'The good deliberator aims at the best for a human being among practicable goods' cannot in general fulfil that promise.

In fact, there is little or no evidence in Book VI for the view that what distinguishes Ar.'s wise individual is adherence to a rule commanding promotion of some single goal (whether this be Aristotelian happiness or something else). For the passages such as 7, 1141b13 can be understood as saying simply that the wise person's decisions are good answers to the question 'What would it be good (or best) for me as a human being (as distinct from a doctor, a housebuilder, etc.) to do?' Setting one's sights on the good in this sense is not appealing to a rule or model that provides substantial guidance one way rather than another. Rather, it is setting oneself to evaluate options from a point of view that is open to any sort of humanly relevant consideration.

This interpretation fits with an otherwise recalcitrant passage. At vi. 12, 1144a31–5 Ar. says of the starting point, i.e. the objective, that controls good deliberation: 'for the sake of argument let it be anything one happens to choose'; and then he speaks of objectives in the plural (*archai*) (see also 5, 1140b16; iii. 3, 1112b34 (plural 'ends'); and *EE* ii. 10, 1227a14–15, where he speaks of the end of deliberation as 'wealth or pleasure or anything else of the sort that happens to be our object').

So when at the start of Book VI Ar. offers to say something informative about 'the correct prescription', he is not expressing the intention (one that is never carried out) to state the rule that good agents follow in every decision. Instead, he uses 'the correct prescription' generically, to refer to correct prescriptions of any sort, and he undertakes to explain how the *ethical* sort differs from other types such as we find operative in non-ethical kinds of thinking like the thinking of a technical expert or the theorizing of a natural scientist or philosopher. He does carry out this task in Book VI, or rather he carries out the task of explaining how the disposition and activity that generates ethically correct prescriptions differs from the dispositions and activities that generate the other types. This gives some content to the reference to the correct prescription that occurs in the definition of character-excellence, although the content is still very general and abstract. In medical advice-giving the parallel would be: describing in a general way the kinds of things a well-trained doctor knows and does. This is less useful, for particular problems, than telling a sick person what specific medicine to take, but it gives an idea of the sort of person one would have to become in order to be useful in that way, and also of the sort of person the sick person should turn to for advice.

1138b18   **earlier**   Cf. *EE* ii. 5, 1222a6–12; *NE* ii. 6.

1138b20   **'as the correct prescription prescribes'**   The Greek, like the English, is ambiguous between 'prescription' meaning 'act of prescribing' and meaning 'what is prescribed'.

1138b21–2   **just as with everything else**   This certainly refers to skills or technical expertises, to which excellence of character is so often compared. It may also refer to theoretical accomplishments. One can think of continua where theoretical thinking can err through excess or deficiency (e.g. too abstract versus burdened with irrelevant detail; over-precise versus slipshod).

1138b23   **as he tenses and relaxes**   The reference is probably to tuning a stringed instrument.

1138b32   **dispositions of the soul**   The reference is to character-dispositions, although they are only a subclass of dispositions of the soul.

VI 1, 1138b34–1139a17

Ar. distinguishes two main kinds of reason proper, and sets out to specify the excellence ('best disposition') of each.

1138b35–1139a1   **we said that some of them were excellences of character, others intellectual excellences**   At *EE* ii. 1, 1220a5; *NE* i. 13, 1103a3–5; ii. 1, 1103a14–15.

1139a3   **Previously we said**   For this division of the soul, see *EE* ii. 1, 1220a8–11; 4, 1221b28–31; *NE* i. 13, 1102a18 ff.

1139a6   **Let us assume the parts possessing reason to be two**   Although deliberative reason is not the highest part of the soul (x. 7, 1177a13–18; cf. vi. 12, 1143b34; 13, 1145a6–7), Ar. treats it as a genuine form of reason in its own right. Whereas the non-rational part is derivatively rational because of its ability to obey, the deliberative part does not in turn depend for its rational status on some relation to the highest part.

things whose principles cannot be otherwise   Things whose principles are *1139a7–8* necessary are themselves necessary, while contingent things (8) have contingent principles (see *EE* II. 6). This distinction corresponds to that between *theoretical* and *deliberative* activity (12). Not only mathematics, but physics and, strictly speaking, history, fall under theoretical: physics because it studies general patterns which in individual cases are necessary-unless-something-interferes, and history because it studies things that were once contingent but are now necessary, being past (*De Interpretatione* 9; cf. *NE* VI. 2, 1139b8–11). However, Ar. ignores history and equates the theoretical with mathematics and the sciences.

they have cognition in accordance with a certain likeness and affinity to their *1139a10–11* **objects**   This standard view was interpreted differently by different thinkers, as saying, for example, that cognitive faculties must resemble their objects in order to cognize them, or that in cognition faculties become like their objects in some way. For the present argument Ar. needs only the point that differences in types of objects imply differences in types of cognitive power. It would be pressing the passage too hard to extract the doctrine that theoretic reason is imperishable because its objects are.

let the first be called 'scientific' [*epistēmonikon*]**, the second 'calculative'** *1139a11–12* [*logistikon*]   (*a*) Although '*epistēmē*' was used of any sort of systematic knowledge (cf. Ar.'s own usage at 1, 1138b26–7), its referent par excellence for Ar. is the scientific grasp of a body of necessary and universal truths. What distinguishes scientific grasp of a fact *p*, according to Ar., is the ability to 'demonstrate' it. A demonstration is an argument that exhibits the cause or explanation of *p* by showing how *p* follows syllogistically from premisses representing the fundamental principles of the science in question. However, Ar. does not make this clear until 3, 1139b18–36. (*b*) Ar. may be following Plato in using 'calculative' for the deliberative part (cf. *Republic* IV, 439d), even though (i) Plato never distinguished the theoretical from the deliberative (see Introduction, pp. 46–7), and (ii) literal calculation has to do with necessary truths of arithmetic. To (ii) one can reply that calculation, unlike science in Ar.'s sense, is not concerned to give explanations, and is used for practical purposes.

VI 2, 1139a17–b13

The argument is: in order to understand the excellence of *X*, one must understand *X*'s characteristic function or work (1, 1139a16–17; cf. *EE* II. 1, 1218b37–1219a23; *NE* II. 6, 1106a15–18). The work (or objective) of any sort of rational thinking is truth (1139a29, b12). Hence practical thinking has its own kind of truth (1139a26–7 and 18 with comment). Practical truth turns out to be nothing other than right decision (*prohairesis*) (since it is the function of practical thinking, or deliberation, to arrive at this). Decision is a combination of thought (*dianoia*) or intelligence (*nous*), and desire (*orexis*) concerning the same thing; hence in good or right decision the thought and the desire are each as they should be: i.e., respectively, true and right (pointing in the right direction). This combination is practical truth (1139a22–b5; see especially 26–7).

General comments:

(*a*) 'Truth', 'true', etc. in this chapter connote, not a semantic property of propositions, but a property which the mind has when it is in the best relation to the objects in the domain it is addressing.

(*b*) This strange notion of practical truth is central for Aristotelian ethics. If Ar. cannot make it plausible, he should abandon either the principle that truth is the proper work of rational thought or the doctrine that practical wisdom is an excellence of reason.

1139a17–18 **the things determining action and truth are three: perception, intelligence [*nous*], and desire** (*a*) 'action and truth' is a hendiadys for 'practical truth' (cf. 26–7). (*b*) '*nous*' means the faculty of intellect in some Aristotelian contexts, but generally in *NE* VI it means intelligence — the excellence whereby that faculty attains truth.

1139a19 **perception [sc. sensory] is not an originator [*archē*] of any sort of action [*praxis*]** Having just used '*praxis*' in a wide sense that would include the purposeful movements of animals (18), Ar. now restricts it to mean 'conduct', i.e. action as viewed from the ethical perspective. He does not imply that sense-perception plays no part in action in this narrow sense. The point is that the goodness of good conduct does not depend on the well-functioning of sense-perception as such, whereas it does depend on the well-functioning of rational thought and desire as such.

1139a21–2 **What affirmation and denial are in the case of thought, pursuit and avoidance are with desire** Because decision involves desire, it is not simply a state of truth, for desire as such cannot be *true* but at best is *right*. So in case the presence of desire should seem to undermine the claim of good decision to count as a kind of truth, Ar. draws an analogy between thought's true-or-false affirmation/denial and desire's right-or-wrong pursuit/avoidance. The analogy shows that the desire-element in decision, which differentiates it from a conclusion that is true-or-false *tout court*, has a similar bivalent nature, and is subject to rational assessment.

1139a23 **decision is a desire informed by deliberation** Cf. 1139b4–5. This echoes or is echoed by the language at III. 3, 1113a10–11.

1139a24–6 **both what issues from reason must be true and the desire must be correct for the decision to be a good one, and reason must assert and desire pursue**

the same things   (*a*) Since desire presumably makes reference to the end and reason to the means (for this, cf. 9, 1142b32–3; 12, 1144a8–9, 20–6; 13, 1145a5–6), they can converge only if each refers to both means and end. Reason says: 'M is the means to O' (cf. 'rational reference to an end' at 1139a32–3), and the desire for O becomes a desire for O via M. (*b*) Why does Ar. write as if this convergence, which is necessary for any decision at all, is not to be taken for granted any more than the goodness of a good decision? Presumably because an excellent decision (which is the case that interests him here) forms precisely when character-excellence screens out or rejects some of the means that reason presents, i.e. the unacceptable ones. Thus, in the good case, it is not automatic that the desire for O becomes a desire to pursue it by the means actually chosen (see Introduction, pp. 49–50). (*c*) Given that the good decision itself is practical truth, what sort of truth does Ar. here attribute to reason's distinct contribution to the decision? It is not the truth sought by scientific reason (see next note). Is it then truth in the semantic sense (i.e. the facts accord with the proposition)? What reason says must be true in at least this sense (recognized at *Metaph.* IX. 10, 1051b1 ff.), but Ar. may mean something more here. He might withhold the accolade 'true' from information that was factually correct but (to the good person) ethically irrelevant.

in the case of thought that is theoretical [*theorētikē*]**, and not practical nor**   *1139a27–8*
productive, 'well' and 'badly' consist in the true and the false   (*a*) These words may suggest that theoretical truth is just truth *tout court*, and that practical truth is this combined with the additional factor of right desire that accords with it. However, practical truth cannot be a synthesis of *theoretical* truth and right desire, because theoretical truth is about the eternal and necessary. (*b*) 'productive': i.e. technical as distinct from practical in Ar.'s ethical sense. When he distinguished the two kinds of reason in ch. 2, Ar. may have meant the calculative (deliberative) to include both practical and productive abilities, since both have to do with things that can be otherwise. Or he may not have been thinking of production at that point.

in terms of the source of the movement, not its end   One of Ar.'s stock   *1139a31–2*
distinctions between modes of explanation, the efficient as distinct from the final cause.

Hence intelligence and thought, on the one hand, and character-disposition   *1139a33–4*
on the other are necessary for decision   Since the excellences of character and their opposed defects were defined as 'dispositions' (II. 5), these words may seem to imply that decisions spring only from excellences or defects, i.e. more or less unchangeable conditions of character (II. 4, 1105a33). But this was not implied by the discussion of decision in III. 4, and of character-dispositions in relation to it at II. 4, 1105a28–b4 (cf. 5, 1106a3–4 and 6, 1106b36). Moreover, in Book VII self-control and the lack of it are standardly described as tendencies to resist or give way to desires that conflict with one's decision (e.g. 8, 1150b30; 9, 1151a29–34):

but agents characterized by these tendencies are neither excellent nor defective according to the classification in Book II (cf. VII. 1, 1145a15–b2). In the present passage Ar. is probably using 'disposition' to cover any condition of the non-rational part of the soul, the contrast here being between that and the deliverances of the rational part. At VII. 1, 1145a25 he uses 'disposition' of a condition that falls outside the Book II classification; and cf. 1145a36–b2.

1139a35–b1   **Thought by itself sets nothing in motion; thought that sets in motion is for the sake of something and practical. For this also controls productive thought**   Purely reflective (theoretical) thought is not oriented towards bringing about change in the world; productive (technical) thought is so oriented, but not autonomously: the builders build because of someone's practical decision to expand his house or extend the city wall.

1139b4–5   **decision is either intelligence qualified by desire or desire qualified by thought**   Cf. 1139a23–4.

1139b5   **human beings are originators of this sort**   There may be an implicit contrast not only with brutes, but with god. If god is an efficient cause, then god's effects are necessary (cf. *EE* II. 6, 1222b20–3), and they are unmediated by discursive thought.

1139b5–9   **Nothing that happened in the past is subject to decision ... not to have happened**   These lines seem out of place, but it is not clear where else they should go. If 1139b5 does invoke a contrast between divine and human agency (see previous comment), the present passage may be a side glance at the one constraint they share: the inescapability of the past. Agathon (9) was a distinguished 5th-century tragedian. The feast in Plato's *Symposium* was a celebration of his victory at one of the dramatic festivals.

VI 3, 1139b14–36

Having established that reason takes two fundamental, autonomous, forms, each of which seeks its own kind of truth, Ar. continues to investigate the corresponding excellences, which have so far remained nameless. But instead of focusing just on them, he approaches 'from a more general standpoint' (1139b14). It being now clear that the excellences in question put reason in possession of truth (2, 1139b12–13), he proceeds by examining a wider set (it is presumably complete) of named and acclaimed attributes which are known to be 'states by which the soul has truth through affirmation and denial' (1139b15; cf. 6, 1141a3–5). There are five of them: technical expertise (*technē*), systematic knowledge (*epistēmē*), wisdom (*phronēsis*), intellectual accomplishment (*sophia*), and intelligence (*nous*). Ar.'s question is 'Which of these is identical with excellence of practical reason, which with excellence of theoretical reason?', and he answers it by presenting definitions of each. Later the five reduce to three, because intellectual accomplishment turns out to be a combination of intelligence and systematic knowledge (6, 1140b31–1141a8).

Ar. starts with systematic knowledge (1139b18–34). The doctrine here is that, strictly speaking, the only kind of cognitivity to deserve the title 'systematic knowledge' is Aristotelian syllogistic explanation ('demonstration') of necessary and universal truths. Anything else counts as systematic knowledge only because of resemblance to the former. 'Systematic knowledge' (like the names of the other four qualities at 1139b16–17) is an accolade; so whatever truly deserves it is in this respect superior to what receives it by resemblance. If either of the rational excellences is to be identified with systematic knowledge, it would be with systematic knowledge of the most excellent kind.

We all believe that it is not even possible for what we know in this sense to be otherwise   This alone shows that the excellence of *practical* reason is not to be identified with systematic knowledge. 'We' refers to the Academy. He says 'not *even* possible' perhaps to bring out this modal improvement on Plato's doctrine that systematic knowledge is of what *is*. |1139b19–21|

everything that is by necessity, without qualification, is eternal   This is by contrast with what is hypothetically necessary for some end that is contingent; e.g. if there is going to be a house, it is necessary that there are going to be foundations. |1139b23–4|

in the *Analytics*, since some of it takes place through induction [*epagōgē*], **some by means of deduction** [*sullogismos*]   The reference is to *Posterior Analytics* I. 1. Induction extracts a universal truth from a set of particular or special cases. By 'deduction' he means the syllogistic kind using subject–predicate propositions in which both terms are logical universals. (Syllogistic premisses need not be universal in the modern sense of universally quantified.) |1139b27–8|

Systematic knowledge, then, is a disposition that is active in demonstration, and so on (we list the further defining features in the *Analytics*)   (*a*) We have systematic knowledge of *p* (which it is assumed we already believe to be so) just in case we can demonstrate it from (i.e. explain it as following from) underlying principles (starting points, *archai*). For 'further defining features', see especially *Posterior Analytics*. I 2. (*b*) Compare the formulae defining technical expertise and wisdom as dispositions that are 'rational and 'truthful', differentiae which can be taken for granted in the case of systematic knowledge; see 4, 1140a10 and 5,1140b5; also 11, 1143a24 on sympathy. |1139b31–3|

the starting points are known to him—since if they are not clearer than the conclusion, he will have the knowledge only in an incidental sense   'Clearer' means 'standing in less need of explanation'. Unless we grasp the demonstrandum *as needing*, and the starting points *as not needing*, explanation, then even if we are in possession of the propositions that represent the starting points and of the conclusion, and see the logical connection, we cannot see the former as explaining the latter, and we only have a simulacrum of systematic knowledge. |1139b34–5|

VI 4, 1140a1–23

Is the excellence of practical reason a kind of *technical expertise*? No, because (1) technical expertise is productive (1140a6 ff.); and (2) the practical and the productive are different, and neither is a species of the other (1140a2–6).

1140a3–5 **so that rational disposition in the sphere of action** [*hexis meta logou praktikē*] **will also be different from rational productive disposition** [*hexis meta logou poētikē*] The inference is from difference between the activities themselves to difference between dispositions, since the latter are defined by the former.

1140a5 **By the same token, nor is either of them a species of the other** i.e. the dispositions do not stand in this relation because the activities do not (lines 5–6, where the statement that action is not production nor production action means '. . . is not . . . essentially'). No argument is given here for the latter claim, but it is easy to generate one from the principle that if *A* is a species of *B*, then a good/bad *A* is a good/bad *B*. An instance of fine production is not necessarily one of good conduct, as when excellent clothes are produced fast and cheaply through the use of child labour, and vice versa, as when Penelope repeatedly wove and unravelled the tapestry so as to stay faithful to her husband.

1140a6–10 **But since building is one sort of technical expertise . . . technical expertise will be the same as productive disposition accompanied by true rational prescription** (*a*) The proposition at lines 8–9, 'there is [no] technical expertise that is not a productive disposition accompanied by rational prescription', is reached by generalization from building, which is clearly a technical expertise and whose name points to a product. A sort of argument for the converse proposition (9) may be implied by the comparison with 'things that are or come to be by nature' (15). For if it is typical of productive dispositions to be, like building, defined by reference to their products, then a given productive disposition will always be directed towards an end of the same empirical type. But Ar. recognizes just two such kinds of regular cause in the sphere of contingent things: the nature (*phusis*) of a natural substance, and technical expertise (cf. *Physics* ii. 8). A natural substance *S* considered as origin of change is essentially identical with *S* considered as undergoing change (*Physics* ii. 1, 192b9–34), whereas in a rational productive disposition such as building, the source is evidently other than the material worked upon. Such a disposition, then, is technical expertise. (*b*) 'True' applies because 'rational' does; cf. 2–3, 1139b12–16. (*c*) Ar. is pinning the term 'technical expertise' down to a narrower than ordinary use, since normally it would cover certain theoretical skills too. He is also using 'productive' in a wider than the ordinary sense (in which a product is a thing or a condition that continues to exist after it has been produced), so that it covers all activities that aim to bring about a standard effect; cf. 5, 1140b6–7 with comment.

1140a18–19 **chance** [*tuchē*] **and technical expertise occupy the same field, just as Agathon says** Chance is mentioned as one 'kind of cause' along with necessity, nature, and technical expertise; cf. the list at III. 3, 1112a31–3. The present point, tailored to the quotation from Agathon (on whom, see comment on 2, 1139b9), is surely not meant to imply that chance impinges more on the operations of technical expertise than on those of action proper (*praxis*).

VI 5, 1140a24–b30

The chapter divides into three parts: (1) 1140a24–b11; (2) b11–20; (3) b21–30. (Lines b20–1 repeat the conclusion of part (1); cf. b4–6.)

(1) To see what wisdom is, Ar. asks what sort of people we call 'wise'. The answer: those who can deliberate well about their own good from the point of view of life in general. Deliberation (which is about contingent things) distinguishes wisdom from any sort of systematic knowledge; the point of view of life in general distinguishes it from any sort of productive disposition or technical expertise. Being neither purely reflective nor productive, wisdom must be a true disposition accompanied by rational prescription relating to *action* (*praxis*); i.e. it is a quality of the rational practical part of the soul.

(2) Ar. sketches the argument, given more fully in chs. 12–13, that wisdom presupposes excellence of character.

(3) Whereas (1) shows (*inter alia*) simply that wisdom is not a technical expertise, the third section shows that wisdom is not a productive technique, but an *excellence* (cf. 12, 1143b18–28 and 1144a1–2).

it is thought characteristic of a wise person to be able to deliberate well   Ar. both appeals to ordinary usage ('it is thought') and improves on it. It would generally be agreed that excellence in deliberation etc. is a reason for calling someone 'wise', but he now proceeds as if nothing else is a reason. This was not supported by contemporary usage; it simply expresses his determination that from now on 'wisdom' is to designate a single determinate quality.   *1140a25–6*

about the things that are good and advantageous to himself   Ar. is not preaching egoism, but pointing out a difference between wisdom and good production. The wise person considers how to further his own projects, which of course will include things done for other people; whereas the producer considers how to make what customers or clients expect from him. Cf. 7, 1141a25; 8, 1141b30; 1141b33–1142a11.   *1140a26–7*

An indication of this is that we also call those in a specific field wise if they succeed in calculating well towards some specific worthy end on matters where no exact technique [*technē*] applies   Ar. is speaking here about productive expertise, which requires deliberative calculation only when there is no pre-established technique in the sense of a set of rules; cf. III. 3, 1112a34–b8, and *Physics* II. 8, 199b28: 'Technique [sc. like nature] does not deliberate'. But for deliberative ingenuity to count as 'wisdom', the end must be a weighty one. Thus we say 'a wise doctor', 'a wise financial consultant', but not 'a wise cook'. The fact that we say 'wise doctor' etc. of those who meet the above conditions shows that   *1140a28* unqualified 'wise' is the proper epithet for those who reason well to achieve the unqualified end, i.e. the best *all* things considered.

1140a35   **since all these things can in fact be otherwise**   The reference is to things whose starting points can be otherwise. A starting point that can be and not be must have effects that are neither impossible nor necessary (since in the latter case they would exist independently of the starting point).

1140b3–4   **because action and production belong to different kinds**   This argument assumes the conclusion announced in the next sentence, that wisdom relates to action (*praxis*). A substantial reason why wisdom is not a technical expertise is that the technical expertises serve departments of life (implied at 1140a27–8 above). Two more reasons are given at 1140b21–4.

1140b6–7   **For the end of production is something distinct from the productive process, whereas that of action will not be; here, doing well [*eupraxia*] itself serves as end**   The question governing production is 'What is the best I can do *to achieve special end* T?' whereas the question governing good action is 'What is the best I can *do*?' This does not mean (as is sometimes thought) that the wise agent does not seek means to ends, or does not act for the sake of ulterior objectives, or that he is concerned only with his action as opposed to its consequences ('action for its own sake'). Doing *M*-for-the-sake-of-*O*, and doing *A*-with-foreseeable-consequences-*C*, *D*, *E* are familiar kinds of doing (*praxis*), and he asks whether doing something like that is the best he can do. The present distinction also allows that the 'product' of an expertise be something that cannot exist independently of its producer's activity, e.g. a dance or a musical performance in the days before audio and video recording.

1140b8   **Pericles**   The statesman who led Athens to the height of her glory in the 5th century.

1140b9–10   **what is good for themselves and what is good for human beings in general**   (*a*) See comment on 1140a26–7. (*b*) The reference to human beings is not to mankind at large, as if the aim were to do the greatest good to the greatest number, but to the agents themselves *as* human beings, as distinct from doctors, builders, etc.

1140b10–11   **we think that this description applies** [sc 'capable of forming a clear view of what is good for themselves and for human beings'] **to those who are good at managing property and at politics**   Ar. will say a little more about the relation of wisdom to economic management and statesmanship in ch. 8.

1140b11–12   **That is why we give *sōphrosunē* ['moderation'] its name, as something that *sōzei tēn phronēsin* ['preserves wisdom']**   'Moderation' is meant in a broad sense here. That it preserves wisdom is supposed to distinguish wisdom from intellectual mastery and technical expertise. Ar. overlooks the fact that immoderate desire for fame or money might induce wishful thinking, even on the professional level, in a theoretical scientist or a technical expert.

once someone is corrupted through pleasure or pain, he fails to see the 1140b17–18
starting point [*archē*]   The starting point or principle is whatever matters most,
what should be controlling one's response to the situation. The reference here
may be to the general principle 'Do what's best' or to some specific commitment
which wise deliberation would put first. Although 'Do what's best' issues in no
specific instruction, taken seriously it makes a practical difference: the deliberator
will be more vigilant and open to all considerations.

there is such a thing as excellence in technical expertise, not in wisdom   i.e. 1140b21–2
one can say 'a good doctor' etc., but not 'a good wise person' (as if there could be
bad ones).

with technical expertise it is more desirable if someone voluntarily gets 1140b22–4
something wrong, whereas with wisdom, as with the excellences, it is less
so   The excellences are those of character. It was a standard point that one
cannot both be courageous (for example) and voluntarily act in a cowardly way,
whereas one can be a technical expert and deliberately misuse the expertise.

the part with which we form opinion   The wording invokes the Platonic con- 1140b26
trast between systematic knowledge and opinion (*doxa*, often translated 'belief').
In the *Republic* (v, 477a–478b) these are assigned different sets of objects, but in
the *Theaetetus* (201c ff.) opinion about *X* is considered as possibly becoming systematic knowledge of *X* (through addition of an 'account'). However, this promotion is possible only if *X* is a necessary thing or truth (cf. 3, 1139b19–21). The
present passage signals (*a*) rejection of the Platonic epistemology according to
which practical wisdom belongs to the scientific (*epistēmonikon*) part, and (*b*)
acceptance of the point that practical wisdom (because it deals with the contingent) deals with items which, in Platonic terms, can never be more than objects
of opinion.

neither is wisdom a disposition accompanied by rational prescription, merely, 1140b28–30
as is indicated by the fact that this sort of disposition can be forgotten,
whereas wisdom cannot   One can let go of an expertise (which is a rational
disposition) through forgetfulness, but the wise person logically cannot under-
value his wisdom so as to let it 'get rusty'. Cf. i. 10, 1100b12–17.

VI 6, 1140b31–1141a8
Intelligence has for its objects the starting points of systematic knowledge.

for what is systematically known is demonstrable   This follows from the 1140b35
definition of systematic knowledge as a 'disposition that is active in demonstrations' (3, 1139b31–2). Since we cannot demonstrate starting points of demonstration, they are not objects of systematic knowledge. Therefore what grasps
them is something else, which by further elimination is identified as intelligence
(cf. *Posterior Analytics* ii. 19).

1141a1–2 **Neither, then, are the starting points objects of intellectual accomplishment, as it is part of intellectual accomplishment to be able to demonstrate certain things** (*a*) the reasoning assumes that just as systematic knowledge is *of* demonstrables and nothing else, so there must be another kind of truth-achieving disposition that is *of* demonstrative starting points and nothing else. (*b*) 'Certain things', because intellectual accomplishment is concerned only with the highest things (7, 1141a20), whereas systematic knowledge is wider (cf. Introduction, p. 53).

General comments:

(*a*) Even if the starting points are not *what* scientific knowledge demonstrates, they must be invoked in demonstrating *from* them. Therefore the person who can demonstrate from them has some kind of cognition of them. Is this what Ar. means by 'intelligence' of them, or is intelligence something more? If the former, then anyone with any sort of systematic knowledge automatically has intelligence of the relevant starting points. And since Ar. is going to define intellectual accomplishment as the combination of systematic knowledge and intelligence concerning the highest things, it would follow that whoever has systematic knowledge about such things automatically has intellectual accomplishment. However, at 7, 1141a16–17 Ar. states that intellectual accomplishment is 'the most precise of the kinds of systematic knowledge'. This rather suggests that the former goes beyond ordinary systematic knowledge in a way that amounts to more than the triviality that whoever can demonstrate has to grasp something more than *what* he demonstrates, namely the starting points *from which*. In that case, what Ar. must mean by 'intelligence' (*nous*, which is an honorific title) is the ability to discover or help discover explanatory starting points, as opposed to simply explaining non-fundamental truths by means of starting points one has received from others. The highest level of intelligence would be the ability to discover them for oneself, but Ar. surely recognizes less exalted levels such as the ability to appreciate such discoveries, and to criticize and improve on them.

(*b*) How does the doctrine that intelligence is grasp of explanatory starting points fit in with the earlier point that those starting points are established by induction (*epagōgē*; 3, 1139b27–31)? These claims are not incompatible. Take one of Ar.'s examples in the *Posterior Analytics*: we go by induction from particular cases to the universal: 'Non-transparent objects can block the passage of light.' This truth is obvious to everyone because the particular cases are so many and so familiar; but it takes (in addition) unusual *intelligence* to see in it the explanation of eclipses.

(*c*) In assigning the honorific 'intelligence' as he does, Ar. may be declaring that a talent for theoretical explanation is intelligence par excellence (cf. note on 3, 1139b18–34 on 'systematic knowledge'). Elsewhere, however, he also speaks of intelligence in the practical sphere: 2, 1139a18–19, 33, b4; 11, 1143a35–b5; 13, 1144b8–13.

VI 7, 1141a9–b22

Ar. begins by arguing that since we say that someone is accomplished (*sophos*) in some restricted expertise because of the precision of his work, intellectual accomplishment *sans phrase* must be the most precise among the kinds of systematic knowledge (1141a9–16). The argument parallels the one for wisdom at 5, 1140a25–31, with 'precision' (*akribeia*) playing the role played there by 'good deliberation'. From this, Ar. argues that intellectual accomplishment not only (1) has cognition of what follows from the starting points, but also (2) has a true grasp of the starting points (17–18). (1) follows from the premiss that intellectual accomplishment is a kind of systematic knowledge. (2) follows from the consummate precision (*akribeia*) of intellectual accomplishment. For this implies a completely thorough and penetrating grasp of the subject matter, which will therefore include intelligent grasp of its starting points. Next: the objects of intellectual accomplishment are sublime (20). In this it differs from political expertise and wisdom, which are about human affairs—since man is not the best thing in the universe (1141a20–b8). The parenthetical passage 1141a22–33 points out another difference between intellectual accomplishment on the one hand, and wisdom and political expertise on the other (1141a28–33). More on what distinguishes wisdom from intellectual accomplishment (1141b8–14; very similar remarks at 5, 1140a25 ff. distinguished it from systematic knowledge). We then have the new point that wisdom is concerned with particulars (1141b14–22).

As for accomplishment, this we ascribe, in the case of the various kinds of technical expertise [*technai*], to those experts in them who are most precise   Ar. appeals to a commonplace.   *1141a9–10*

Pheidias . . . Polycleitus   The great 5th-century sculptors.   *1141a10–11*

as Homer says in the *Margites*   A mock-heroic poem attributed in antiquity to Homer. The quotation is not meant to prove that we think that there are accomplished persons, but to illustrate the phrase 'accomplished *in* something'. Ar. is employing the contrast between 'accomplishment without qualification' and 'accomplishment qualified by something else [i.e. by reference to a specific domain]'.   *1141a14*

For it is a strange thing to think . . . that political expertise, or wisdom, is what is to be taken most seriously; unless, that is, man is the best thing there is in the universe   (*a*) What Ar. says is strange was presumably the actual assumption of many in his audience. Nor does he disagree that politics is a high calling: see I. 2, 1094b7–10. (*b*) The reasoning assumes (i) that to identify *X* as (true) intellectual accomplishment is to identify *X* as the best excellence (this too must have been a commonplace), and (ii) that the excellence of a branch of intellectual activity depends on the worth of its subject matter.   *1141a20–1*

1141a22–6 **Now if healthy and good are different for human beings and for fish, while white and straight are always the same, everyone will agree that what is intellectually accomplished, too, is always the same thing, whereas what is wise differs; for each kind of creature asserts that what is wise is what successfully considers the things relating to itself, and will hand over decisions to that** (a) The antecedent is assumed true. (b) 'itself' (25) probably refers to the kind of creature in question. Cf. 5, 1140b5–6; 9. See also 1140a26–7 with note.

1141a30–1 **there will be many kinds of accomplishment** [sc. concerning the same type of question] (Ar.'s rejection of this seems to rule out the possibility of different and equally brilliant theories of the same phenomena. But the essential contrast with the practical–political still holds: the value of each theory does not depend on the specific nature of its adherent.)

1141a33–4 **Even if man is the best thing possible out of all animals** As was said by, for example, Isocrates, *Panegyricus* 48.

1141b3–4 **Anaxagoras and Thales** Thales of Miletus (6th century) is traditionally regarded as the earliest Greek philosopher. He was said to have fallen into a well while stargazing. Anaxagoras of Clazomenae (5th century) was a philosopher and cosmologist who (like Aristotle himself) lived much of his adult life at Athens, where he was not a citizen, and so could play no part in political life. It was said that when asked why one should choose to have been born rather than not, he replied: 'To study the heavens and the whole order of the universe' (*EE* I. 5, 1216a11–14). See also *NE* x. 8, 1179a14–15.

1141b16–17 **the sphere of action is constituted by particulars. That is why sometimes people who lack universal knowledge are more effective in action than others who have it** (a) A universal, for Ar., is a shared property, and particulars are what share it. *Meat from birds* is a particular in relation to *light* and *healthy*, since white fish too has those properties. (b) Each party in the example has partial knowledge. But by theoretical standards, one who knows (only) that light meats are easily digestible and healthy is more knowledgeable than one who knows only that meat from birds is light and healthy; this is because the former commands two levels of explanation (healthy because digestible, digestible because light), the latter not even one. The latter, however, is more practical only if he can also recognize chicken etc. (cf. 8, 1142a20–30).

1141b18 **experienced people** This is spelled out more fully at 8, 1142a14–19.

1141b21–2 **so we need to have both sorts of excellence—no, we need wisdom more** i.e. if we can have only one of them. Wisdom is more necessary to us, even though it is inferior (cf. 1141a20–2).

VI 7–8, 1141b22–1142a30

The last sentence of ch. 7 (according to the chapter divisions we are using) clearly goes with what immediately follows in ch. 8.

Ground-level wisdom by which one carries out one's own affairs *versus* architectonic wisdom; the ground-level form is wisdom more properly speaking (1141b22–31; this passage continues to emphasize that wisdom is above all about particulars. The contrast now is not with theoretical universals, but between a type of wisdom that is more, and one that is less, remote from particulars). But what count as *one's own* affairs? (1141b33–1142a11). Wisdom depends on experience (1142a11–16), and is concerned with the terminus of deliberation (1142a23–30).

And here too there will be a kind that is architectonic [*architektonikē*]   i.e. in the sphere of the practical, just as there is in the sphere of production. The *architektōn* is the master-builder; he effects change by instructing the manual workers (29). By 'architectonic wisdom' Ar. presumably means the ability to frame good policies for people in general. (This includes, but is not restricted to, philosophical ethics and political theory.)   *1141b22–3*

Political expertise and wisdom are the same disposition, but their being is not the same   i.e. they differ in definition, but are developed by the identical training. The difference here seems to be that political expertise operates through civic institutions, i.e. by constitutional methods, whereas wisdom operates less formally. Thus architectonic wisdom would be the excellence of the wise despot (cf. *Politics* i. 13, 1260a16–17). (*a*) In what follows (24–30) Ar. seems to be answering the question 'Since wisdom takes an architectonic form as well as a ground-level one (in which the agent is the immediate source of the changes), why is our discussion of wisdom all about the latter (as it has been so far)?' The answer is: 'Look at political expertise, which is the same disposition. It too has architectonic and ground-level forms, of which the former is called "legislative expertise", whereas the latter gets called "political expertise" although this is really the name of both. Since ground-level political expertise issues the day-to-day decrees (*psēphismata*) by which the state is managed, the fact that it gets the common name shows that we think the name belongs more to this more immediately practical type of political expertise. So (by analogy, or because wisdom is the same disposition as political expertise), although the ability to make good decisions about our personal situation, and the ability to make good general proposals, are both called "wisdom", the former counts as "wisdom" more than the latter.' (*b*) The analogy with manual workers versus master-builder is in respect of practical immediacy; it does not imply that the business of ground-level wisdom is essentially to implement plans laid down by architectonic wisdom. (*c*) It seems clear that someone can have ground-level wisdom without having architectonic wisdom (and likewise administrative political expertise without legislative expertise). Hence in saying that political expertise and wisdom are the same disposition, Ar. may be identifying the architectonic forms with each other, and the ground-level forms with each other (cf. x. 9, 1180b28–1181b15, where legislation is said to be the business of those who do philosophical ethics; see especially   *1141b23–4*

1181b12–14). If he identifies all four forms, it is presumably because he sees the ground-level forms as natural bases for developing the architectonic kinds or kind. (In the digression or later addition at 1141b31–3, he seems to classify the two forms of political expertise as forms of wisdom; cf. lines 24–5. He also adds another form of wisdom, the ability to manage one's household and property, and he subdivides the ground-level political form into 'deliberative' and 'judicial'.)

1141b28　**what comes last**　i.e. the conclusion of deliberation. The decree (*psēphisma*) was the civic equivalent of decision.

1141b34　**knowing things for one's own benefit**　This standard way of conceiving of wisdom (cf. e.g. 5, 1140a26) is now interpreted as minding one's own business, and is contrasted with political involvement in general.

1142a2　**Euripides**　The lines are from his lost play *Philoctetes*. They go on to say that the busybodies are the ones who get civic honours, presumably to compensate for their trouble.

1142a9–10　**and yet presumably one's own well-being is inseparable from managing a household, and from political organization**　Ar. now balances the contrast between 'political' (busybody) and 'wise' (minding one's own business) by pointing out that 'one's own' includes household and city. Cf. 5, 1140b6.

1142a11　**An indication of what we have said**　The reference is probably to 7, 1141b14–16, on the particularity of wisdom's knowledge.

1142a20　**the definitions**　These are the a priori starting points of mathematical demonstration; the contrast is with starting points that derive from experience.

1142a24　**wisdom . . . has for its object what comes last [*eschaton*] in the process of deliberation, as has been said**　(*a*) Something like this was said at 1141b26–8, in reference to the conclusion of deliberation. (*b*) Wisdom is exercised throughout deliberation, but it is now particularly associated with the conclusion because it is only at this point that wisdom becomes fully practical. (*c*) There are two ways of interpreting the above reason why wisdom is not systematic knowledge: (1) 'what comes last' means starting points of demonstration (they are reached last by analysis of the proposition to be demonstrated), but the objects of systematic knowledge are demonstrated *from* such starting points; (2) (suggested by *Metaph.* xi. 1, 1059b26) 'what comes last' means particulars (reached last in a taxonomic descent from the widest genera), but the objects of systematic knowledge are universals. This whole difficult passage 1142a23–30 should be compared with 11, 1143a32–b5.

1142a25–7　**So wisdom is antithetical to [*antikeitai*] intelligence; for [*gar*] intelligence has as its objects the definitions for which there is no account [*logos*], whereas wisdom has as its object what comes last [sc. in deliberation], and this is not an object of systematic knowledge [*epistēmē*], but of perception**　(*a*) Theoretical intelligence and wisdom are antithetical in several respects — the objects of one are universal, eternal, and necessary; of the other, particular, transient, and contingent. (*b*) These contrasts are due to (*gar* in 26) the fundamental difference between theoretical and practical reason, which is that the former does well ('intelligently') when it hits upon basic definitions ('accounts') which make other things intelligible, while the latter does well ('wisely') by reaching good decisions through which other good things become practicable. (*c*) That there are 'no accounts' for the basic definitions means that nothing in the body of systematic knowledge stands to them as they stand to what is demonstrable from them. It does not mean that basic definitions are not framed through thinking.

not perception of the sensibles special to each sense, but like that by which   *1142a27–30*
we grasp that the last element in mathematical analysis is the triangle …
(However, this is more a case of perception than of wisdom, but a different
kind of perception from the one of the special sensibles)   Wise perception is
first contrasted with hearing, taste, etc. by being likened to the perception of a
geometer who sees, for example, a hexagon as consisting, finally, of triangles.
(The contrast is: we can immediately taste simple qualities such as bitter and
sweet, and so on for the other sense-modalities; whereas we cannot see the
triangles *as* the last two-dimensional elements of the hexagon, or see such-and-
such a particular action *as* the right decision, without first considering the
*un*analysed hexagon or the *un*analysed project.) Ar. then ('However, this is more a
case of perception than of wisdom') worries lest this shared contrast with sense-
perception make the geometric case seem too much like wisdom; and finally ('but
a different kind of perception from the one of the special sensibles') worries lest
his correction for the last worry make the geometric kind look too much like
sense-perception. He is working against a Platonic background in which theoretical and practical reason were not properly distinguished, and in which a crude
contrast between reason and sense-perception was commonly treated as exhaust-
ive. For more on the perception of what comes last, see 11, 1143a36–b1 with
comment.

VI 9, 1142a31–b33
An examination of deliberative excellence (*euboulia*).

a kind of correctness, but neither of knowledge nor of judgement   (*a*) There   *1142b8–9*
is no correctness of knowledge, any more than incorrectness of it; cf. 5, 1140b22,
'there is no excellence of wisdom'. (*b*) Deliberative excellence is not truth (i.e.
correctness of opinion, 1142b11), because truth (understood as a condition of the
soul; see general comment (*a*) on *NE* vi. 2) is what is sought by inquiry; once it is
attained the inquiry (deliberation being a kind of inquiry) is over. The difference
between truth in this sense and deliberative excellence corresponds to the difference at 1142b13–15 between an assertion (which is what a judgement is) and an
inquiring.

1142b11–12 everything that is the subject of a judgement is also already determinate   To judge that *p* is to judge that there is already a determinate fact of the matter. Deliberating whether *p* assumes that it is not yet determinate that *p* or that not-*p*. For Ar. this indeterminacy is ontological (as distinct from epistemic indeterminacy, where one is merely open-minded whether *p* or not-*p*); see *De Interpretatione* 9.

1142b12–13 It remains, then, for it to be correctness of thinking [*dianoia*]   This is not thinking *that* something is so (i.e. judging), but pondering or considering. Its correctness consists in its being on the right track.

1142b16–17 so it is deliberation — what it is, and what its object is — that needs to be inquired into first   Surprisingly, there follows neither a discussion of this, nor a reference to a previous one such as that in III. 3.

1142b18–20 the person without self-control, or the one with a bad character, will achieve what his project requires, thereby having 'deliberated correctly', although he will have got himself a great evil   The text may well be corrupt here, but the main point seems clear. On the calculating or plotting of a person without self-control, see VII. 6, 1149b14.

1142b24 the intermediate premiss being false   i.e. the premiss about means. It is not clear whether what is false is a judgement about the means' effectiveness (in which case the agent attains the end by sheer accident), or about their ethical suitability.

1142b27 The former case, then, still won't count as deliberative excellence   Since deliberative excellence is not the ability to hit on what one is looking for irrespective of how it is carried out (24–6), it is not the ability to do this quickly either.

1142b31–3 So if it is characteristic of the wise to deliberate well, deliberative excellence will be that sort of correctness that corresponds to what conduces to the end, of which wisdom is the true grasp   This passage is often taken to mean that good deliberation presupposes wisdom's true grasp of the end, the assumption being that good deliberation *begins from* this. But 'true grasp' is reminiscent of the 'practical truth' of ch. 2, which refers to the *upshot* of good deliberation, i.e. good decision. See 9, 1142a25–7 and comment (*b*) ad loc. One has theoretical truth (in the richer than merely semantic sense) about a fact-to-be-explained when one sees how it follows from fundamentals, and one has practical truth (i.e. wisdom, cf. 5, 1140b4–6, 20–1) about the end-to-be-attained when one is ready to actualize it in full knowledge (the result of deliberation) of how this is best done in the circumstances. The difference between deliberative excellence and wisdom in this chapter corresponds to that between seeking for (cf. 1142a31–2, b15) and being in possession of truth.

VI 10–11, 1142b34–1143a24

Ar. introduces two more ethical-rational excellences, which are 'critical' rather than practical: excellence in comprehension (*eusunesia*; 'comprehension' is *sunesis*) and sympathy (*sungnōmē*). As before, assigning names is his way of bringing out latent distinctions. Excellence in comprehension is the ability to judge well the wisdom of someone else's proposal. Sympathy takes account of the agent's situation, and is the mark of a 'reasonable' (*epieikēs*) person.

Comprehension is neither having wisdom nor acquiring it; but just as seeing the point is called 'comprehending' when one is exercising systematic knowledge, so ... when someone else is speaking   (*a*) 'Acquiring wisdom' here probably means reaching a wise decision, not acquiring a wise disposition. (*b*) Comprehension is not either of these, because they are, respectively, having and exercising a *practical* disposition, and comprehension is not practical (14–15). (*c*) 'To see the point' (*manthanein*, from which 'mathematics') was particularly used in the context of *theoretical* learning; here Ar. explains ethical comprehension, too, in terms of 'seeing the point' (which in its original, theoretical, context is also called 'comprehending'; line 3). (*d*) But his explanation is complicated by the fact that 'He sees the point' is said in two senses: of the pupil learning (acquiring) something for the first time, and of someone who has command of the subject matter and is exercising his knowledge of it. This ambiguity was an old chestnut in the Academy; cf. Plato, *Euthydemus* 275d–278b. Ar. therefore emphasizes that ethical comprehension is an exercise, not an acquisition, of good judgement (13–14). This passage is a good example (there are many) of how much Academic knowledge on the part of the reader Ar. takes for granted in *NE* vi. (*e*) **when someone else is speaking**   i.e., in the ethical context, when someone else is deliberating aloud or explaining how they reached a certain deliberative conclusion. At x. 9, 1181a17–19 there is a nice example of the exercise of *sunesis* (there translated 'acumen') as applied to judging the qualities of existing laws. *1143a11–15*

The quality called 'sense' [*gnōmē*] ... is making correct discrimination of what is reasonable   Here Ar. defines 'sense' in terms of the 'correct'. However, '*gnōmē*' can also mean any judgement, true or false, and presumably it has this meaning at line 23, where it is qualified by 'correct'. On the quality of reasonableness, see v. 10. *1143a19–20*

VI 11, 1143a25–b17

A summing-up section which concludes the enterprise of defining wisdom and intellectual accomplishment.

The critical excellences and wisdom go together. The former resemble wisdom in being concerned with practicable things, things that come last, and particulars. And they all, including wisdom, have it in common that they show reasonableness (*epieikeia*) in dealings with others. These qualities involve intelligence (*nous*) too (1143a25–35). This ethical kind of intelligence is compared and contrasted with the kind that is part of intellectual accomplishment (1143a35–b9). It depends on experience (b11–14).

1143a26–7   **we attribute sense, comprehension, wisdom, and intelligence** [*nous*] **to the same people**   Note the difference from ch. 6, where 'intelligence' was restricted to the theoretical kind (see also 8, 1142a25). Here, with the support of ordinary usage ('we attribute'), Ar. fully recognizes a practical-critical (or ethical) kind of intelligence. He might have said, but does not, that the theoretical kind is intelligence strictly speaking, the practical only by 'resemblance'; contrast the treatment of 'systematic knowledge' at 3, 1139b18–19.

1143a35–6   **And intelligence has as its objects what is last in both directions**   It is as if theoretical and practical intelligence work at opposite ends of the universe of thought. Cf. 8, 1142a25: 'wisdom is antithetical to [theoretical] intelligence'.

1143a36–b1   **for both the primary definitions** [sc. of a body of systematic knowledge] **and what is last in practical reasoning are to be grasped by intelligence, not with an account** [*logos*].   In both theoretical and practical reasoning there are two classes of objects: those that are adequately known when and only when they have been resolved into elements or starting points which cannot be resolved further; and these elements themselves. 'Accounts' are *of* objects of the first class, and are articulated in terms of objects of the second. 'Intelligence' is *of* the elements (i.e. as elements, as constituting the solution to the initial problem). On the theoretical level, to see an object of the first kind (it may be a fact) as made up of its elements is to have the explanation (systematic knowledge) of why it is as it is. The practical analogue is: seeing the general aim of pursuing some desired objective in terms of a decision that reflects an analysis of the particular circumstances, thereby making the general aim into something that a good person in those circumstances can bring to realization. See 9, 1142b31–3 with note. On this interpretation, 'what is last' in the practical sense refers equally to the decision and to the situational particulars as they appear under final analysis. That these ultimates are not grasped 'with an account' (cf. 8, 1142a26–7) is of course consistent with their coming to light through reasoning: deliberation in the practical case, scientific working back to first principles in the theoretical. But does their coming to light through reasoning fit with the thought that in each case they are objects of a sort of *perception* (1143b5; cf. 8, 1142a27–30)? Yes, because rational probing into something unclear would be ineffectual if we could not also, applying whatever the criteria of adequacy, *see* when we have reached an adequate answer. Also, once we have the answer there is no room for further thinking of the sort that led to it, just as when we are actually in literal perceptual contact with something, there is no room for trying to reckon what it would look or feel like if one could perceive it.

1143b2–5   **while the object of the sort** [of intelligence] **that operates with practical dispositions is what is last and contingent, and belongs to the second premiss. For these are the starting points** [*archai*] **of that for the sake of which, since things that are universal consist of particulars. So one must have perception of these, and this is intelligence**   (*a*) Schematically, the first premiss of deliberation refers to an end aimed at, the second one to the particular situation.

Practical intelligence is associated with the latter, because it is easy to know in a general way what one is aiming at (this is the beginning of deliberation), whereas it is difficult (requires good deliberation) to see all the relevant particulars. (*b*) That-for-the-sake-of-which is the end, and, on the interpretation proposed here, its 'starting points' are the perceived particulars of the situation: they give rise to the end (i.e. to its realization) by filling out the general aim so as to convert it into a decision. 'things that are universal consist of particulars':   i.e. generalities come into being only as particularized. (However, some interpreters think this passage says that intelligence sets up the end from which the process of deliberation begins; see comment on 9, 1142b31–3. Some translate 'universals come from particulars', and see a reference to induction from particular cases of good conduct to a 'universal' (i.e. general) conception of the good, which then becomes available for deliberation to begin from. The role of intelligence is to 'perceive' those particular cases, and possibly to see the universal in them. One difficulty with this view is that, according to it, intelligence has done its work in advance of deliberation, whereas the present passage as a whole seems to be about its contribution *in* deliberation, i.e. to the formation of the final decision.)

This is why the things in question are thought to be natural growths   He is *1143b6* referring to the qualities cited at 1143a26. Because of the relation to particulars, having them depends on experience and their findings are not fully articulable in concepts. Consequently there is no formal training for acquiring them, so they seem, when they occur, to have developed as a natural part of the ageing process.

[Because of this, intelligence is both starting point and end. For demonstra- *1143b9–11* **tions** [*apodeixeis*] **are based on these and about these.]**   The order of the text is uncertain. With these sentences in their present position, the referent of 'these' is very obscure. If they belong at all in this general context, the meaning must be: since the objects of intelligence are grasped by a sort of perception, intelligence (here equated with its objects) is both a starting point (of 'demonstrations') and an end (because analysis stops at the starting points). This adds little except the conceit 'is both starting point and end'. If the passage belongs hereabouts, its referent must at least include practical or ethical intelligence. In that case 'demonstrations' must include explanations of actions given by the wise, the sympathetic etc. and 'these' includes (at least) particulars. The ethical explanations are of ('about') particular decisions or actions done with certain ends in view, and they are in terms of ('based on') situational particulars. Although Ar. usually restricts '*apodeixis*' to theoretical explanation, he uses it again at lines 12 and 13 to refer to the ethical kind. Giving and assessing this type of explanation are characteristic activities of the critical excellences. However, wise people may also come up with wise remarks and opinions that are not explained (11–13).

because they have an eye, formed from experience, they see correctly   It is an *1143b13–14* eye for the relevant particulars; cf. 8, 1142a11–19; 12, 1144a29–30; 13, 1144b10–12.

VI 12–13, 1143b18–1145a11

The account of the intellectual excellences is followed by an epilogue addressing two questions: (1) Of what use to their possessors are wisdom and intellectual accomplishment? (12, 1143b18–33); and (2) Wisdom is supposed to be inferior to intellectual accomplishment, but how can this be if wisdom is what 'prescribe[s] on everything'? (12, 1143b33–5; cf. 7, 1141a21–2). No doubt these were standard questions, telling us something of the dialectical environment in which Ar. composed *NE* VI.

The response to (1) occupies most of the epilogue. It mainly focuses on wisdom, which the question initially portrays as an expertise whose products we can enjoy without being that sort of expert ourselves (1143b20–33). But most of the response is aimed at a different target: the view that wisdom adds nothing to good conduct that is not already taken care of by excellence of character (12–13, 1144a11–1145a6). (The value of character-excellence is never in question.) In effect, (1) (so far as it concerns wisdom) represents a dilemma: either wisdom is an expertise that can benefit us without our having it ourselves, or there is no such thing as wisdom over and above excellence of character. Ar. accepts the second disjunct to the extent that it implies that wisdom and excellence of character are inseparable. But he rejects any implication that wisdom belongs to a part of the soul that has nothing in common with theoretical reason. He is treading a fine line here, for as far as character-excellence is concerned, Ar. holds that it grows up in a part of the soul that does have nothing in common with theoretical reason. (It is derivatively rational entirely on account of its relation to *practical* reason; cf. I. 13, 1102b13–31 and x. 8, 1178a16–22 on 'the composite'.

The response to (2) fills just over five lines (13, 1145a6–11).

Response to (1): (i) Since there are parts of the soul of which intellectual accomplishment and wisdom are the excellences, these qualities are desirable in themselves even if they produce nothing further (12, 1144a1–3). But (ii) in a sense they do produce something good, namely happiness, when they are exercised (1144a3–6). (iii) Wisdom is necessary for good conduct, and is not the same as excellence of character (1144a11–29). ((iv) But there is no wisdom without excellence of character; 1144a29–b1.) In fact, (v) excellence of character is not fully itself without wisdom (13, 1144b1–17, 20–7). Thus (vi) the different character-excellences are essentially connected via wisdom to reason, although Socrates' intellectualization of them was exaggerated (1144b17–30). (This common connection with reason means that they cannot occur apart from each other; 1144b32–1145a2.)

For the response to (2), see text and comment ad loc.

1143b24–6 **knowledge of them does not make us any more doers of them, given that the excellences are dispositions** [*hexeis*]**; just as with things relating to health, or**

things relating to physical fitness (i.e. the ones to which the terms apply not because they produce but because they flow from the disposition) The term 'relating to health' applies to every item whose concept makes reference to health. Some items fall under it because they flow from the disposition (*hexis*, lit. 'having') of health, others because they produce that disposition. An item of the latter kind, such as expertise for healing, can be realized only in one who has knowledge of the field, but this knowledge is not necessary for the *having* of health or for doing the healthy actions that flow from having it. The present objection assumes that whereas the excellences are 'havings', wisdom is an expertise for *producing* such qualities. Given that the ability to produce X is not, as such, a having of X, the objection implies that wisdom is not an excellence. And, given the identification of wisdom's knowledge of just, fine, and good things with the supposed expertise for making people just, fine, and good, the analogy with health implies that one can be just etc. without oneself being wise.

if excellences they are, each of one of the two soul-parts in question The reference is to the two rational parts distinguished at 1, 1139a5–15. If each of these has its own excellence (cf. 1, 1139a15–16), these intellectual excellences are necessary parts of 'excellence as a whole' (1144a5; cf. *EE* ii. 1,1219a35–9, 'happiness is activity in accordance with complete excellence'), i.e. of a whole of several parts none of which is lacking. (NB, this is not the same thought as *NE* i. 7, 1098a17–18, 'happiness is activity in accordance with the best and most complete' (excellence, sc. 'if there are more excellences than one'), which singles out one part of the *EE*'s complete whole of excellence). However, given the objection explained in the previous comment, Ar. cannot take it for granted that wisdom *is* an excellence rather than a sort of productive expertise. But the above objection does not apply to intellectual accomplishment, the good disposition of theoretical reason (mentioned on its own at 1144a5). No doubt he hopes that *its* status as an excellence will go unchallenged, and that this will facilitate acceptance that practical reason has its own excellence too — and what can this be if not wisdom? *1144a2*

they are in fact productive: not in the way medical expertise produces health, but in the way health does In a logical sense the condition of health 'makes' one healthy. Analogously, the excellence of intellectual accomplishment helps (through being possessed) to make one completely excellent, and through being exercised it makes one happy. *1144a3–4*

Again, the 'product' [ergon] is brought to completion by virtue of a person's having wisdom and excellence of character i.e. the happiness is produced through wisdom etc. This is an additional point, since the previous one focused on intellectual accomplishment. *1144a6–7*

excellence makes the goal correct, while wisdom makes what leads to it correct (*a*) Here and frequently in the epilogue 'excellence' is used as synonymous with 'character-excellence' and contrasted with wisdom (cf. ii. 6, *1144a7–9*

1106b36–1107a6). This is the usage of those who question whether wisdom is an excellence (unless it is the same as undisputed character-excellence). (*b*) For the interpretation, see Introduction, pp. 49–50.

1144a13–19   **Just as we say that in some cases people do what is just without being just themselves . . . because of decision, and for the sake of the things being done themselves**   This passage recalls earlier ones where the difference between merely doing just things and doing them as the just person would was understood as the difference between not yet having and having justice considered as excellence of character (cf. II. 4, 1105a21–b9; v. 8, 1135b22–5). Ar. now begins to focus on it as the difference between having and not having the intellectual excellence of wisdom.

1144a20–2   **The decision, then, is made correct by excellence, but the doing of whatever by the nature of things has to be done to realize that decision is not the business of excellence but of another ability**   Cf. 1144a7–9 with comments. A decision is a decision to act *for* some goal *by* such-and-such determinate means. Here Ar. speaks as if it were just 'for some goal', whereas elsewhere he often speaks as if it were just concerned with means.

1144a25   **able to carry these out**   Cleverness appears here as executive rather than deliberative, perhaps because the epithet (translated 'unscrupulous') applied to clever wrongdoers is *panourgoi* (27–8), which means: 'they stop at nothing'.

1144a29–30   **This eye of the soul does not come to be in its proper condition [*hexis*] without excellence**   The proper condition is the one in which a thing functions as it should. The purpose of cleverness is not to see clearly and distinctly all the facts in the situation (whatever that could mean), but to focus on what is relevant for a good decision. Hence it should be the cleverness of a just, courageous, mild, etc. person.

1144a30–1   **as has been said**   At 5, 1140b16–19; cf. III. 4.

1144a31–6   **for chains of practical reasoning have a starting point—'since the end, i.e. what is best, is such-and-such' (whatever it may be: for the sake of argument let it be anything one happens to choose), and this is not evident except to the person who possesses excellence, since badness distorts a person and causes him to be deceived about the starting points of action**   Here, the starting point is a statement describing the end, and it is a starting point of practical arguments or reasonings. (Compare 11, 1143b4, where the starting points were the particulars, and they were starting points of the end considered as a project for realization.) The present passage repeats the first half of the point made at 12, 1144a7–9 (cf. 12, 1144a20–1; 13, 1145a5–6), i.e. that character-excellence makes the aim right, whereas the intellectual side of wisdom takes care of the steps towards it. According to the interpretation proposed in the Introduction (pp. 49–50), this means that excellence of character is responsible for its remaining true throughout the deliberation (or until deliberation about that objective is abandoned) that the thing originally aimed at as 'best' is indeed best to aim at, given the circumstances.

VI 13, 1144b1–1145a11

as wisdom stands to cleverness (not the same thing, but similar), so 'natural' *1144b2–4* [*phusikē*] **excellence too stands to excellence in the primary sense** (*a*) Ar. means: as wisdom is to cleverness, so excellence in the strict sense is to 'natural' excellence. (*b*)'Natural' excellence may be a place-holder for any good character-state unfinished by wisdom, in which case it includes tendencies acquired through upbringing. (These are put on a par with natural (i.e. innate) excellence at VII. 8, 1151a18–19.) For bare 'natural' courage in action, see III. 8, 1117a4–5; cf. 1116b35.

but if a person acquires intelligence Since intelligence is an excellence with- *1144b12* out qualification (and the activity of excellence is good), what he acquires would not strictly speaking count as 'intelligence' if he were not already of decent character.

This is why some say that all the excellences are kinds of wisdom i.e. *1144b17–18* because they are drawn to the truth though they fail to grasp it accurately.

he was wrong in so far as he thought that all the excellences are kinds of *1144b19–20* **wisdom** For Socrates, this was the same as the view that all the excellences are forms of systematic knowledge; see 1144b28–9. Cf. Plato, *Protagoras* 357a–d and *Phaedo* 69b–c; Xenophon, *Memorabilia* IV. vi. 2–6, 10–12.

it is not just the disposition [to act] **according to the correct prescription** [*kata* *1144b26–7* *ton orthon logon*]**, but the disposition** [to act] **accompanied by the correct pre-scription** [*meta tou orthou logou*] **that constitutes excellence** The standard for-mula fits a condition of simple readiness to obey the right prescription; Ar.'s improvement implies this plus *self*-directedness. Cf. '*meta logou*' in the definitions of wisdom and technical expertise, 4, 1140a10; 5, 1140b4–5, 20. The substantial point, that the excellent person is autonomous, has been perfectly clear for a long time; Ar. is only correcting the *language* that is used.

if wisdom, which is one, is present, they will all be present along with it (*a*) *1145a1–2* Wisdom could not always decide what is best all things considered if there were departmental wisdoms, one for each excellence of character, etc. There may be concrete situations calling for the exercise of several excellences of character, but it is *one* decision that has to be made. (*b*) If wisdom, like the character-excellences, is a 'firm and unchanging disposition' (II. 4, 1105a33), i.e. a readiness to operate in every type of situation that could call for it, then wisdom needs all the character-excellences, since the lack of one would disable it for the corresponding field. (*c*) If wisdom is unchanging in this way, then none of the character-excellences strictly speaking can be found without all the others, given that each requires wisdom. But surely some people are moderate or good tempered in peaceful contexts, but would lose their heads and act in a rash or cowardly way in battle? Ar. himself allows a less than ideally strict use of excellence-terms when he says that some people are both open-handed about wealth and cowardly (III. 6, 1115a20–1).

1145a2–4 **even if it did not lead to action** [*ei mē praktikē ēn*] **. . . there would be a need for it because of its being an excellence of its soul-part** This is part 1 of a two-part summary. It harks back to VI. 1, 1138b35–1139a17 (cf. 12, 1144a1–3).

1145a4–6 **a decision will not be correct in the absence of wisdom, or in the absence of excellence; for the one causes us to act** [sc. well] **in relation to the end, the other in relation to what forwards the end** Part 2 of the summary, harking back to VI. 2, 1139a22 ff., on good decision; and also, since the good decision is the same as the correct prescription, to VI. 1, where Ar. undertook to explain the latter; cf. 13, 1144b21–8.

1145a6–7 **But neither is wisdom sovereign over intellectual accomplishment, or over the better of the two rational parts** That theoretical reason is superior to practical follows from the superiority of its excellence, which reflects the superiority of its subject matter (7, 1141a20–b9).

1145a9 **it prescribes on its behalf, not to it. It is as if one said that political expertise rules over the gods, because it issues prescriptions about everything in the city** (*a*) For wisdom to give orders to intellectual accomplishment would be for it to dictate research programmes and the like. Ar.'s remark encapsulates the idea of academic freedom, but not in a form in which it could do much of the protective work it does today, since political and social topics lie outside the province of Aristotelian intellectual accomplishment (7, 1141a20–2; a33–b8). (*b*) Some interpreters suppose that, for Ar., all wise decisions, either on the personal or on the political level or both, are directed towards promoting intellectually accomplished activity. But (since Greek city-states were not theocracies) the simile here suggests that this is or should be just one of several important responsibilities for the wise person.

BOOK VII

Chapters 1–10 of this Book (1145a15–1152a36) are on self-control and the lack of it; chapters 11–14 (1152b1–1154b34) are on pleasure.

VII 1–2, 1145a15–1146b8

Introduction and methodological remarks (1145a15–b7); existing views (1145b8–20); questions, puzzles, and preliminary arguments (1145b21–1146b8).

The discussion of lack of self-control proceeds by accepting (or assuming) what is obvious and laying out existing views (*tithenai ta phainomena*, 1145b3), then raising problems and solving them in ways that accommodate or explain the data as far as possible. This is Ar.'s characteristic method, but here for once he describes it (1145b2–7).

Homer's   See *Iliad* xxiv. 258–9.   *1145a20–2*

later   See 5, 1148b15–1149a20.   *1145a34*

we have discussed badness earlier   i.e. while discussing the character-   *1145a34–5*
excellences in Books ii, iii (5–12, 1115a4–1119b18), iv, and v.

As in other cases   Other places where Ar. begins a topic by laying out the   *1145b3*
various views and raising puzzles and questions include *Metaph.* i–ii, *On the Soul* i,
Physics i.

about these ways of being affected   In fact, they are *dispositions* to be affected   *1145b5*
(or not) in morally significant ways.

in regard to temper, honour, and profit as well   i.e. as well as bodily pleasures.   *1145b19–20*

But one might raise the problem: in what sense does a person have a correct   *1145b21–2*
grasp when he behaves uncontrolledly?   This is often mistranslated as follows:
'how, if someone grasps the situation correctly [e.g. that it is a situation in which
he should do D], can he act uncontrolledly [so as to fail to do D]?' On this reading,
Ar. is sceptical about the very possibility of acting against one's better judgement.
But in fact, he is about to declare (1145b28) that Socrates, in denying this possibility, is contradicting what patently appears to be the case (*ta phainomena enargōs*; cf.
1145b3). Elsewhere Ar. takes it for granted that un-self-controlled behaviour
occurs (e.g. *EE* ii. 7, *passim*; *NE* v. 9, 1136a32–3; most of vii; i. 13, 1102b14–28,
where it grounds the division of the ethical soul; iii. 2, 1111b13–14). The mistrans-
lation has led many interpreters to view Ar. as a philosopher who is reluctant to
accept the ordinary belief that 'the un-self-controlled person acts because of his
affective state, *knowing* that what he is doing is a bad thing' (1145b12, emphasis

added). They then read his response to the puzzle (ch. 3) as a series of attempts to show that the un-self-controlled are *not really aware* of what they do. This represents Ar. as virtually denying that lack of self-control is possible, since the un-self-controlled are essentially voluntary (free and knowing) doers of what they take to be wrong. The assumption behind this interpretation ('interpretation A') is that Ar. finds it metaphysically baffling that people knowingly act against their better judgement. (That Socrates found it so is understandable, because he lacked the developed psychology which allows for a part (or in Plato's case, parts) of the soul which 'listens to reason' not automatically, but as a result of training.)

In fact, according to the interpretation preferred in this commentary ('interpretation B' below), Ar. does think that voluntarily acting against one's better judgement is a phenomenon to be explained; but for him as for common sense the explanation is ready to hand: the phenomenon occurs because one is affected by appetite or emotion (3, 1147a24 ff.); and if some people are more prone to temptation by appetite etc. than others, or more prone to give in, this is because of their lack of discipline in the past (cf. III. 1, 1110b9–14). But according to interpretation A, Ar. holds that the immediate cause or explanation of uncontrolled behaviour consists, in every case, in a failure to be fully aware of the situation one is in or of what one is about to do. It is only because passion causes a breakdown of awareness that it can cause one to act against one's better judgement. Consequently, on this view, Ar. ought to deny the possibility of giving in to temptation while in a state of psychologically perfect awareness that this is what one is doing. It is true that not all uncontrolled behaviour follows this pattern, but common sense recognizes it as one familiar possibility, and Ar. seems to do so too when he distinguishes *impulsive* and *weak* lack of self-control (7, 1150b19–28; see also *Magna Moralia* II. 6, 1203a32–3, and *NE* VII. 6, 1149b13–14, on 'plotting'). The classic example, Euripides' Medea, is clear-headed enough to soliloquize: 'Yes, I know how evil a thing it is that I am about to do, but rage is stronger than my reasonings' (*Medea* 1078–9). (However, Medea, for Ar., might be a logically peripheral case because of her unnatural savagery; see VII. 5.)

On interpretation B, Ar. accepts as unproblematic in itself the thought that the un-self-controlled know what they are doing and that it is wrong. (Cf. V. 9, 1136a31–b6, where he does not hesitate to speak of them as harming themselves voluntarily and therefore knowingly.) But Ar. sees a logical need to distinguish the sense in which one says that they know (cf. 3, 1146b9; 2, 1145b29). They *know* in so far as the relevant facts are available to them; they do not need to check again to see if they have made a good decision, they are not unconscious, hypnotized, etc. On the other hand, their knowledge (or understanding of the situation) is not making the kind of difference that it should. It is not on active duty when it ought to be, or not fully so (for it might be making them ashamed even as they act). Any entity E is 'there' in full actuality (in *energeia*, a central distinction in Ar.'s metaphysics) when and only when (absent external impediment) E is making its own distinctive or typical difference to the world. 'Typical' has a teleological connotation here. The point of being aware of what one should be doing in a situation is to *do* it, not to *contrast it with what one is actually doing so as to feel ashamed* (or *feel ashamed later*). (This is so even if shame itself is typical of the un-self-controlled.) A Cartesian dualist might say that the awareness or occurrent belief has made all the difference it can—namely, to the state of the uncontrolled person's *mind*, simply by being there. But on this way of thinking it becomes incomprehensible why beliefs about practical matters (or, for that matter, desires) guide observable behaviour at all. On interpretation B, the un-self-controlled's non-performance of the right action (or performance of the wrong one) is the ground for saying that he or she *does not know* or *is ignorant*. But this is not because the failure of knowledge to be 'there' explains the non-performance, in the way in which feeling sleepy or dizzy, or being distracted—which are special psychological conditions—might explain a stumble. Saying that someone exhibits this failure of knowledge is not ascribing a special psychological condition that then explains something else: instead, it is placing the non-performance itself in a certain ethical category, i.e. saying that it is behaviour uncontrolled by the agent's knowledge of what he should do. This knowledge both is and is not knowledge; for on the one hand it was (we can suppose) acquired in the way in which such knowledge is acquired, i.e. by intelligent, well-informed, right-minded deliberation; but on the other hand it is now causally nullified by the contrary appetite or emotion. (Similarly, a dead man both is and is not a man; the corpse cannot be classified as any other species than human, yet it is man in name only, since it cannot function as human being: see *Parts of Animals* I. 1, 640b35–641a5.) It is immaterial whether the onset of appetite etc. temporarily alters the agent's state of mind, making him or her empirically unconscious of or inattentive to the good decision or the present facts, or whether it coexists with a clear and steady awareness. Either way, knowledge has been disabled and nullified. The problem raised at 1145b21–2, then, is simply that of finding ways to say, without self-contradiction, that the uncontrolled both knows and does not know what he should do.

On the whole interpretation B is preferable, although see 1145b29 with comment.

it would be an astonishing thing if, when knowledge [epistēmē] is in us ... something else overpowers it and drags it about like a slave This recalls Socrates' words at *Protagoras* 352c. *1145b23–4*

the agent's affective state [*pathos*]   Presumably this refers to the uncontrolled surrender to appetite. **if it is because of ignorance**   Here Ar. speaks of ignorance as the *explanation*, which fits interpretation A. However, this is only hypothetical; he has not yet developed his own position; and the wording may just echo his summary of Socrates' account (27; cf. *Protagoras* 357d). *1145b29*

that nothing is superior to knowledge   Ambiguous between 'better' and 'stronger'. The conflation implies that mere opinion or belief, being less valuable than knowledge, has weaker effects. *1145b32*

1146a3–4   **there is no sympathy for badness, nor for any other object of censure**   It is assumed that lack of self-control is an object of censure; therefore it cannot consist in a weak or hesitant grip on the belief that ought to resist appetite, since we sympathize when a belief caves in from this sort of cause.

1146a8–9   **we have shown before that the wise person is of a sort to act [*praktikos*] (being of a sort concerned with 'what comes last'), and is someone who possesses the other excellences**   See VI. 11–13, 1143a25–1145a5. However, implementing decisions was never discussed in Book VI. Ar. may now be optimistically taking it for granted that the excellence necessary for being a good decision-maker excludes lack of self-control in implementing decisions. More likely he is (i) reaffirming that 'wise' implies 'of a sort to *act*' and 'excellent', even though in Book VI this was established without reference to implementation, and (ii) now asserting that the latter two terms fail to apply to the un-self-controlled person.

1146a19–20   **as e.g. in the case of Sophocles' Neoptolemus, in *Philoctetes***   Neoptolemus, the son of the hero Achilles, agreed to take part with Odysseus in a disgraceful plot against the disabled hero Philoctetes, but then could not bring himself to do so.

1146a35   **'when water is choking you, what will wash it down?'**   i.e. the best cure doesn't work. If persuading someone that he should do *D* fails to result in his doing it, there is nothing more one can do for him.

VII 3, 1146b8–1147b19

Ar. begins his resolution of the problems. The introductory passage, 1146b8–24, seems to consist of two versions of the agenda, the second beginning at line 14. The rest of the section, 1146b24–1147b19, is about lack of self-control and knowledge. It falls into three parts.

(1) At 1146b24–31 he argues, contra the theorists at 2, 1145b32–5, that it makes no difference whether the unself-controlled is said to have systematic or reasoned knowledge (*epistēmē*) or only a true judgement or belief (*doxa alēthēs*). (In the argument which follows, as in many modern discussions of acting against one's judgement, it also makes no difference whether the judgement is even correct. But this is part of a treatise for educators, whose task is to train characters that will make and carry out (what the educators take to be) *right* ethical judgements.)

(2) At 1146b31–1147a24 he returns to the question raised at 2, 1145b21–2 (on which see comment) and introduces three refinements which make it logically possible to say that the un-self-controlled both knows and not-knows: (*a*) He or she knows, i.e. *has* knowledge, but also not-knows, i.e. is not at this moment *using* it (1146b31–5). Here the knowledge may be understood as a simple particular gerundive, e.g. 'I should eat this', where 'this' refers to something required by health. (*b*) The above gerundive is viewed as the resultant of a combination of *universal* and *particular* premises, and the agent is said both to have and to use the universal one, but only to have the particular (1146b35–1147a10). (*c*) 'Having

knowledge' is said to be ambiguous, so that under the mode of having knowledge one can both know and not know (1147a10–24).

(3) At 1147a24–b17 Ar. gives a psychological explanation of how appetite puts people of un-self-controlled disposition into the predicament of both knowing and not knowing, according to the above distinctions.

whether what distinguishes the self-controlled person and the unself-controlled is type of object or manner   Cf. III. 5, 1115a5.   *1146b15–16*

Heraclitus   The 6th-century philosopher, whose extant fragments show him pronouncing with oracular assurance.   *1146b30–1*

using   According to interpretation B, this implies using the practical knowledge properly, i.e. for the purpose for which one acquired it in the first place. Cf. Ar.'s *Exhortation to Philosophy* (*Protrepticus*):   *1146b32*

> The use of anything, then, is this: if the capacity is for a single thing, then it is doing just that thing; if it is for several things, then it is doing whichever is the best of these. E.g. a flute: a man uses a flute only or especially when he plays it. Thus we must say that he who uses a thing aright is most truly said to 'use' it; for he who uses something well and accurately uses it for the natural end and in the natural way (B 84, Düring; translation based on the Revised Oxford Translation).

According to interpretation A, a piece of knowledge is 'used' if it merely comes to mind.

having regard to [*theōrōn*] **it**   Theoretical knowledge was a standard example   *1146b33–4*
for the Academic distinction between having and using: thus using came to be equated with *theōrein*, i.e. reflecting on or operating intellectually with something one has learned. In the present context, *theōrein* may simply be a stand-in for the practical analogue, in which case it is tantamount to 'act upon'. But adherents of interpretation A understand it here as 'be aware of' or 'think about' (cf. VI. 7, 1141a25), and take the point to be that we have to postulate psychological unawareness of the situation or what it calls for in order to explain the failure to act. However, another standard example for the distinction was exercise versus mere possession of the builder's skill. Here, actual building (not mere thinking about it) is said to be the exercise (cf. *On the Soul* II. 5, 417b8–10; *Metaph.* IX. 6, 1048b1; 8, 1050a11–12). By analogy, again, 'to have regard to' or use knowledge of what one ought not to do is to act upon it. In that case, not to act upon it is not to know it (in the use mode), regardless of whether one is conscious of it or not.

this is what is thought astonishing [*deinon*]   This responds to what Socrates   *1146b35*
thought astonishing (2, 1145b23–4). 'Astonishing' may seem too weak for interpretation B, given that according to the latter 'While having regard to/using the knowledge he is not acting upon it' is not merely astonishing, but logically inconsistent. However, in the light of the *Exhortation* passage quoted *ad* 1146b32, 'using and not acting on it' is inconsistent *provided acting upon practical knowledge is the proper way to use it*. Thus any suggestion that 'using and not acting on it' might be

true amounts to a suggestion that proper use might consist in something other than acting according to the knowledge; this may not be self-contradictory, but it is certainly 'astonishing'.

1146b35–1147a1   **there are two types of premiss**   These premisses are not starting points of a deliberative process, but factors in a gerundive such as 'I should eat this', whether it expresses the result of deliberation or a sheer impulse. Ar. analyses such a gerundive G as the synthesis of a universal premiss such as: 'Dry food is good for humans', and particular ones such as 'I am human', 'This food is dry'. (On premisses as materials of the conclusion, see 1147a26–7 and *Metaph.* v. 2, 1013b20; on the practical 'syllogism' so called, see references in comment (c) on 1147a24 below. Un-self-controlled failure to act on G (in which 'this' refers to some dry food) is now (1147a2–3) more precisely identified as failure to use a particular (*kata meros*) premiss. This is meant to underline the impracticality of lack of self-control (3–4; cf. vi. 7, 1141b16–22). Difficulties: (*a*) It seems arbitrary to pick on the particular premisses. For it is equally true that the agent (by eating something greasy and fattening instead) behaves as if (so far as he or she is concerned) the universal one were not the case. (*b*) Ar. implies that the un-self-controlled does use the universal one. But what can this mean if not that he or she applies it to the relevant particular premisses, and does this not imply using them as well? Alternatively, what can non-use of one or more particular premiss mean if not that the universal fails to be brought to bear, and surely this implies failing to use it too? (*c*) If using the universal is applying it to the relevant particulars, and this involves using them, too, as premisses, then all the components of G are in active use. How, then, is G itself not in use? But if it is, the un-self-controlled failure to act on it is not a case of having but not using it, which contradicts what was said at 1146b31–5. Response: although the universal cannot be used (in a practical way) except in the context of relevant particulars, which in turn cannot be used except in the context of it, the respective uses and non-uses do not stand and fall together. The universal is fully used when, given the particulars, it tells you what to do; but the particulars count as fully used only if, in addition to their subserving the universal's role in forming the instruction, the instruction is obeyed. The rationale for this asymmetry is that the sense-faculty, which delivers particulars inviting action here and now, and the physiological apparatus which, in an obedient subject, is set in motion accordingly, are organically related in a teleological system; thus voluntary failure to engage in the right movements is first and foremost failure to use information gathered by this system. Cf. 1147b13–17.

1147a3–4   **not the particular** [*kata meros*] **one; for it is particulars** [*ta kath' hekasta*] **that are acted on**   The connection here is not quite as close as it looks in English, where the word 'particular' translates different expressions.

1147a12–13   **such that a person both has knowledge in a way and does not have it**   This possibility surfaced at 1147a7, where it applied to the particular premiss. In one sense, *having* (*echein*) knowledge is being in a state of readiness to use it whenever called for. The point of the comparison with sleep, intoxication, and madness is that, in these, one has knowledge in that one has acquired it, but not in such a way as to be ready to act on it if the occasion arises.

Empedoclean verses Empedocles was a Sicilian scientist and sage, 5th century. *1147a20*
He wrote epic verse entitled *On Nature* and *On Purifications*.

actors on the stage The point of the comparison is not that the un-self- *1147a23*
controlled do not mean their better judgement, or feel that they are playing a part when they utter it, but that it does not make the difference in the real world that it should, any more than events on the stage have the effects they would if real.

Furthermore, one can also, in the following way, look scientifically at the *1147a24–5*
cause (*a*) According to interpretation B, this is where Ar. begins to consider the cause of un-self-controlled behaviour (since the preceding discussion of knowing and not-knowing was meant only to find a logically coherent way of speaking about un-self-controlled knowledge and ignorance, and not to explain the behaviour as due to the ignorance). According to interpretation A, the cause now begins to be considered from a scientific point of view, but has already in VII. 3 been under consideration from one or more other points of view. (*b*) Ar. some-times contrasts a natural science perspective with one that is logical, dialectical, or very abstract (cf. *On the Heavens* I. 10, 280a32; *On Generation and Corruption* I. 2, 316a11–14; II. 9, 335b24–5; *NE* VIII. 1, 1155b2). (*c*) So far, he has considered the universal and particular premisses of the action which the un-self-controlled per-son ought to perform, but fails to. Ar. holds, however, that action in general, including the behaviour of non-human animals and of un-self-controlled human beings, is structured by a combination of such premisses (cf. *On the Movement of Animals* 7, esp. 701a29–36). Action occurs when premisses 'about making some-thing happen' are brought together to form 'a single proposition', given that the agent is capable of acting and not prevented (1147a25–31). Un-self-controlled behaviour gives an example of 'prevention' of one action by another in the same agent. There are two pairs of premisses, e.g.:

Pair 1: {U_1: (Do not taste anything of kind K) and P_1: (This is of kind K)}
     versus
Pair 2: {U_2: (Everything sweet is pleasant) and P_2: (This is sweet)}

('This' has the same referent in both pairs.)

Pair 1 generates the conclusion 'avoid this', and by itself it would thereby generate the action of turning away from the object. In a moderate agent, even if pair 2 were also present, it would generate nothing more than the conclusion 'This is pleasant' (an observation; in itself, pair 2 is not 'about making something happen'), and the action expressing pair 1 would go forward unobstructed. But in a subject of un-self-controlled disposition, when pair 1 and pair 2 are present *along with appetite* (i.e. unreflective desire for the pleasant), P_2 in pair 2 becomes active:

i.e. (in line with Interpretation B, see above) the agent acts on it. Note that P_2 is active (acted upon) *as a member of its pair*, i.e. as placing its referent under the term 'pleasant', supplied by U_2; and that the presence of appetite converts U_2 (for the time being) into an imperative to sample whatever is sweet. There is conflict because (i) P_1 and P_2 refer to the same object; and (ii) activity of P_1 (as a member of pair 1) means action in the opposite direction to that dictated by pair 2, given appetite.

It is permissible to substitute 'sweet' for 'of kind K' in the above. If we do, P_1 and P_2 are logically identical, but they are not so from the point of view of natural science: each is dynamic, if at all, only in context of the pair of which it is a member. Thus according to this interpretation, the logically same particular premiss can be both unused (in the pair 1 context) and active (in the pair 2 context). (If, as this interpretation holds, 'used' means 'used as it should be', and 'active' means 'acted upon', then 'used' and 'active' are not interchangeable, as interpreters often assume.)

1147a27–8 **the soul necessarily assents, in one type of case, to what has been concluded** This is the type of case where the premisses have no practical import. For the parallel between assent and action, cf. VI. 2, 1139a21–2.

1147a29–30 **if everything sweet should be tasted, and *this* ... is sweet** This pair of premisses, with the implied conclusion that 'this' *should* be tasted, implicitly followed by the action itself if possible, is an illustration of the practical syllogism in general. It is confusing that Ar. then (31–4) chooses similar subject matter (sweet, tasting) to illustrate the special case of two potentially conflicting premiss pairs, especially as the practical directive in one of them is to *refrain from* tasting.

1147a34 **then the first one** [*hē men*] **says 'avoid this'** The reference is to the proposition that is the conclusion from pair 1.

1147a35–b3 **So it turns out that uncontrolled behaviour is due to reason, in a way ... to the correct prescription** It would have been a natural question for philosophers whether the un-self-controlled's good judgement is overcome by appetite or by a contrary rational judgement. (Some, like Hume, might have argued that there can be conflict only between a judgement and its logical contrary, not between a judgement and a 'passion'.) Ar.'s answer: the un-self-controlled agent does act for a reason, for he can explain why he acts on P_2 by citing the universal U_2 (animals cannot do this; cf. 1147b3–5); but the practical tension between these premiss-pairs is due to the presence (incidental, cf. 1147a33–4) of appetite for pleasure, not to the conceptual content of the premiss-pairs themselves.

1147b9–17 **But since the final premiss is both a judgement about something perceived, and what determines actions, either he does not have this ... but the perceptual kind** This passage brings to bear a general point from Ar.'s theory of action: action at a given moment is triggered by perceptual information (called 'the final premiss') received at that moment. Ar. goes on to claim that it is information of this kind (P_1), rather than a universal premiss, that the un-self-controlled agent does not have, or not in a way that counts as knowing it. But since the conclusion of pair 1, which because of appetite fails to be enacted, is generated from U_1 as well as P_1, one might think that each of these premisses represents knowledge that fails to be operative. Why then does Ar. single out P_1 as the location of the failure? Perhaps it is because P_1 is thought of as pertaining to just this one occasion (so that in effect it says 'This here now is of kind K'); thus its unreadiness to be used as it should have been used, i.e. to generate action in accordance with the prohibition in U_1, is a complete and absolute failure on its part, whereas U_1 applies to other occasions, perhaps ones where appetite is not present, and so lives to fight another day. (See also comments on 1146b35–1147a1.) At any rate, by locating the trouble in P_1 Ar. can hand a sop to Socrates: the last premiss (*ho eschatos horos*, 1147b14), not being universal, seems less like an object of systematic knowledge (*epistēmē* at 15; cf. 13) than the unvanquished U_1 does. This in a way confirms Socrates' theory that appetite cannot knock knowledge off its throne. (Further: in the case where P_1 and P_2 are the same proposition, one can think of appetite as wrenching a single piece of *perceptual information*, PI, out of the environment of U_1 (which itself is untouched) where PI should do practical service, and into the environment of U_2. Like a slave (2, 1145b24), PI dictates no practical direction by itself; it becomes practical only when working under something like U_1 or under something like U_2 allied with appetite; and only one of these is its rightful master. Where P_1 and P_2 are different propositions paired with U_1 and U_2 respectively, one can think of appetite as pulling *perceptual attention*, PA, away from P_1 where PA belongs (given P_1 is with U_1), and over to P_2.)

for it is not what seems to be knowledge in the primary sense that the affective state [*to pathos*] in question overcomes (nor is it this kind of knowledge that is 'dragged about' because of the state), but the perceptual kind We read *dokousēs periginetai* at line 16 (Stewart's conjecture), since the received text gives an unacceptable sense. (Translated it runs: 'for the affective state in question does not occur in the presence of what seems to be knowledge in the primary sense—nor is it this kind of knowledge that is dragged about— but in the presence of the perceptual kind'. The difficulty is that nothing in the account so far suggests that the affective state does not occur *in the presence of* the universal.) *1147b15–17*

In the scientific passage Ar. has explained what makes the un-self-controlled do wrong: it is appetite. He does not try to explain why appetite has this effect on some and not others. The same elements are present in self-controlled behaviour. Since Ar. says that 'self-controlled' describes those who resist where the average person succumbs, and 'un-self-controlled' those who succumb where the average resists, and that the self-controlled's appetite is strong (7, 1150a11–14; 2,

1146a15–16), he is unlikely to think that the un-self-controlled yield simply because of stronger appetites. Rather: some people simply have the disposition to yield, others to stand firm. Ar. has given a coherent analysis of yielding against one's better judgement, and this (together with obvious facts) is all that is needed to prove contra Socrates (2, 1145b25–6) that such a disposition exists.

VII 4, 1147b20–1148b14

VII. 4–6, 1147b20–1150a8 is devoted to clarifying the unqualified form of lack of self-control by comparisons with different qualified types. The question 'Which form is unqualified?' was raised at 2, 1146b2–5. In VII. 4 the unqualified emerges as relating to the same objects as self-indulgence, by contrast with qualified forms relating to other kinds of normal pleasures. The distinction rests on a division of pleasure-giving things into 'desirable in themselves' and 'necessary' (1147b23–31), and then on what appears to be a more elaborate division (1148a22–8).

1147b24   **some of the things that produce pleasure are necessary**   See Introduction, p. 26 (on moderation).

1147b28   **we stated to be the sphere of self-indulgence and moderation**   See III. 10, 1117b26 ff.

1147b30   **winning, honour, wealth**   On wealth as something desirable in itself, see Introduction, p. 56.

1147b35   **as with the man who used to win Olympic victories, called Man**   Anthrōpos was the given name of a boxer who won in 456 BCE. 'Lack of self-control' said without qualification can function as a generic term covering the various sorts of lack of self-control, but its meaning is different when it is used as the 'proper name' of lack of self-control proper.

1148a12   **people are also called soft in relation to these sorts of pains**   i.e. bodily ones. Ar. assumes that lack of self-control and softness operate at opposite ends of the same range.

1148a25   **the distinction we made before**   The reference may be to the division into pleasant things that are necessary and ones that are desirable in themselves at 1147b23–31, but the classification is now significantly different. Three groups are now distinguished: 'by nature desirable', 'by nature undesirable' (the contrary), and 'neither of the above' (in between); and the term 'necessary' does not appear.

1148a27   **i.e. for desiring and 'loving' [philein] them**   Greek standardly forms compounds with 'philo-' such as 'philotimia' (love of honour'), 'philosophia' ('love of wisdom'). Satyrus' nickname at 1148a34–b1 is 'philopatōr'. Cf. I. 8, 1099a8–11.

1148a33   **Niobe**   ('all tears', Shakespeare) boasted (with tragic consequences) that her children made her the rival of Leto, mother of the divine Apollo and Artemis.

1148b1   **Satyrus**   May have been a king's son who deified his father.

VII 5, 1148b15–1149a24

Unqualified lack of self-control is now contrasted with dispositions that are brutish, or pathological, or perverted by abuse. Self-control and lack of it occur with abnormal desires too, but we do not view failure here as 'lack of self-control', but as *brutish or pathological* lack of self-control'. The qualification places those dispositions beyond ethical assessment. In this comparison the *normal* qualified forms discussed in ch. 4 (lack of self-control in relation to honour, wealth, etc.) make no appearance. The examples of brutish or pathological pleasures all have to do with eating or sex. However, the generalization at 1149a4–9 presumably allows for such kinds as pathological pleasure in revenge.

Phalaris   A 6th century Sicilian tyrant.   *1148b24*

any more than one would call women un-self-controlled because they have   *1148b32–3*
the passive rather than the active role in copulation   This is by contrast with the case of two males: the role of catamite (let alone enjoying taking it) was considered disgraceful.

So on the one hand *having* each of these sorts of dispositions is something   *1148b34–*
outside the limits of badness of character, just as brutishness in general is; on   *1149a3*
the other, having them and exercising control, or failing to exercise control, is
not the unqualified lack of self-control but the one by resemblance   (*a*) If merely having one of the above inclinations counts as brutishness, then brutishness here is compatible with a kind of self-control and lack of it: this was not envisaged in the taxonomy at 1, 1145a16 ff. (*b*) The point of 'on the one hand . . . on the other' may be that although the inclinations are beyond ethical assessment, this is not true of controlling them or not. 'Lack of self-control' and its contrary always refer to ethical qualities even when used with qualification, as here.

house-weasel   Presumably it would have been used for mousing.   *1149a8*

VII 6, 1149a24–1150a8

Unqualified lack of self-control is now compared with the counterpart that relates to temper (1149a24–b27); brutishness is compared with human badness (1149b27–1150a8). Presumably temper and brutishness are considered in the same discussion (see the reference at 1149b27) because both have a biological basis.

reason, or sensory appearances, indicate . . . rush off to enjoy it   See Introduc-   *1149a32–6*
tion, pp. 56–7, on the relative rationality of human temper.

temper or irascibility is more natural than appetites for excess and appetites   *1149b6–8*
for unnecessary things   i.e. excessive temper is more likely to be hereditary. In so far as appetites are congenital, they have a natural limit and are for necessary

objects. The congenital is more forgivable because it is more difficult to over-come. Cf. 10, 1152a27–30.

1149b14–15   **does not plot ... but is open**   However, at IV. 5, 1126a19–25, Ar. recognizes a type of anger that simmers covertly.

1149b17   **Homer's**   See *Iliad* XIV. 214–17 (where in fact sexual desire, stimulated by Aphrodite's girdle, is about to deceive Zeus, not turn him into a deceiver).

1149b21–3   **If, then, the things that most justify anger are the more unjust, so too is the lack of self-control that comes about because of appetite**   A paradigmatic case of anger (and therefore of un-self-controlled anger) would be in response to (the perception of) prior aggression issuing from un-self-controlled lust.

1149b27   **As we said at the beginning of this discussion**   i.e. at 5, 1148b15 ff.

1149b34–   **for they do not have decision, or reasoning, but are a falling away from nature,**
1150a1   **like madmen among human beings**   Since Ar. is talking about entire animal species that run amok, they have not fallen away from their species-nature (as have human lunatics) but from some general set of natural limits prevalent in most species. They are called 'self-indulgent' (and the limit-observing species are called 'moderate') by analogy: falling away from the general natural limits is like a human individual's falling away from his decision (cf. 1, 1145b11–12; 2, 1146a18; 8, 1151a1; 9, 1151b4).

1150a6–7   **The comparison is similar ... to that between injustice and an unjust human being**   The one is worse because injustice is its essence; the other, because it can *do* wrong.

VII 7, 1150a9–b28
Lack of self-control and self-control are different from softness (*malakia*) and resistance, (*karteria*) (1150a12–b19). Impulsiveness is one kind of lack of self-control, weakness another (1150b19–28).

1150a17–18   **neither is deficiency**   This has to do with pain. Beyond a certain point, the failure to tolerate it is necessary; up to that point the tendency to fail is a deficiency.

1150a21   **since he necessarily has no regrets**   '*Akolastos*' literally means 'uncorrected' or 'incorrigible'. The unregretful cannot be corrected (*kolazesthai*). However, at IX. 4, 1166b5–25, Ar. depicts particularly wicked people as hating themselves and 'full of regret'(24–5). Something like this is also implied at III. 5, 1114a13–15.

1150a27–32   **[But everyone would think a person worse ... worse than the un-self-controlled one.] of the types in question, then, one is more softness—of a sort, whereas the other is self-indulgence**   Omitting the passage in square

396

brackets, which seems clearly out of place, the argument is: the non-deciding types (25) are divided into the weak about pleasure and the weak about bearing pain; hence there is a corresponding difference among bad types that act from decision ('the types in question', 31). Of these, the one that exceeds in avoiding pain is now called 'a *sort of* softness', i.e. not softness proper, since that is the name of the non-deciding disposition (1150a14).

resisting is a matter of withstanding, whereas self-control [*enkrateia*] **is a**   *1150a33–5*
matter of overcoming [*kratein*].   It is not clear whether this presupposes the distinction at 1150a13–14, where self-control and the lack of it were in face of pleasure, resistance and softness in face of pain; or whether the main difference now is between overcoming (or failing to) and withstanding (or failing to) as applied to both pleasures and pains. Presumably 'overcoming' in this contrast means getting to the point where the pleasure or pain no longer bothers one, whereas when 'withstood' they remain as intense as at the beginning.

weakness for comfort is a kind of softness   Here (cf. 1150a31–2) he means a   *1150b3*
subspecies of softness proper.

Theodectes . . . Carcinus . . . Xenophantus   Theodectes studied with Ar. His   *1150b9–12*
plays, like those of Carcinus, are lost. The reference to Xenophantus is obscure.

As for lack of self-control, part of it is impulsiveness, part weakness   These   *1150b19*
are then distinguished as failure to deliberate versus failure to stand by the results of deliberation (19–22). However, both kinds must involve an abandoned decision, and therefore (by Ar.'s usual doctrine) a prior deliberation. Lines 22–5 show that what distinguishes the impulsive type is being caught off guard by temptation; i.e. the failure to 'deliberate' is a failure to prepare oneself imaginatively for the reality of being offered a tasty but unhealthy dish and the like.

if one has tickled the other person first   Cf. *Problems* xxxv. 6, 965a11–18, 'Why   *1150b22*
can one not tickle oneself?' Answer: being tickled depends on being taken by surprise.

the bilious sorts of people   A modern equivalent might be 'highly strung'. Bile   *1150b25–6*
was one of the 'four humours' of ancient medical theory.

VII 8, 1150b29–1151a28
Comparison of lack of self-control with self-indulgence, focusing on the paradoxical appearance raised at the beginning, that the latter is better because easier to cure (2, 1146a31–b2).

as has been said   At 1150a21.   *1150b29*

when we listed the problems   At 2, 1146a31–b2.   *1150b31*

1151a8   **Demodocus**   A native of Leros, near Miletus.

1151a15–19   **For excellence and badness respectively keep healthy, and corrupt, the fundamental starting point [*archē*], and in action this is that for the sake of
which [*to hou heneka*], just as in mathematical arguments the initial posits
[*hupotheseis*] are starting points. Neither in that case, then, does reasoning
[*logos*] teach us the starting points, nor does it in the present one; instead, it is excellence, innate or resulting from habit-training, that gives
us correct judgement about the starting point**   Compare VI. 11, 1143a35–b5,
where it was particulars grasped by intelligence that were said to be the starting
points (for the realization) of that for the sake of which, and to be beyond *logos*
(i.e. rational analysis) like the first principles of demonstration. Here, Ar. does not
consider the intellectual side of action, because of the context. He is explaining
why, although the self-indulgent are in a way more rational than the uncontrolled,
since their actions cohere with their convictions, they are less open to reform
through criticism of their behaviour. It is because they act from conviction; conviction is grounded in character rather than the reverse (1151a13–14); and discussion cannot help change an unrepentant character. Cf. VI. 5, 1140b13–20; 12,
1144a31–6; x. 9, 1179b4–18.

VII 9–10, 1151a29–1152a36

Discussion of problems raised at the beginning: are the self-controlled and
uncontrolled to be defined as sticking/failing to stick to any decision, or only
a good one? (1151a29–b22; cf. 2, 1146a16–18); is the wise man self-controlled?
(1151b32–1152a3; cf. 1, 1145b14–15); can someone be both wise and
uncontrolled? (1152a6–14; cf. 1, 1145b17–19, and 2, 1146a4–7). There is some
repetition of points covered earlier, indicating different versions. A new
question: are self-control and uncontrol two of a triad? (1151b23–32).

1151a33   **(the problem we raised before)**   At 2, 1146a17 ff.

1151a33–4   **incidental . . . in themselves**   Academic jargon whose literal meaning contributes nothing here. A clumsy illustration follows at 1151a35–b2. The contrast is
between the logically primary case and others.

1151b5–6   **who are called stubborn, the ones who are hard to persuade, i.e. not easily
persuaded to change their minds**   Lines 10–16 below show that rational persuasion is meant, and that not being open to it (rather than refusing to change
one's mind at all) is the essence of stubbornness.

1151b16–17   **so they are more like the un-self-controlled type than they are like the self-
controlled**   Either because the uncontrolled, too, regret that what they decided
was not carried out; see 8, 1150b31–2, for 'decrees' cf. 10, 1152a20; or because
both kinds are governed by pleasure and pain, not reason.

Neoptolemus in Sophocles' *Philoctetes*　Cf. 2, 1146a19–20.　　*1151b18–19*

one of these two is in evidence only rarely, in a few people　Cf. ii. 7, 1107b6–7;　*1151b30–2*
iii. 11, 1119a5–7.

in our original discussion　The reference is to vi. 12, 1144a23 ff.　*1152a12–13*

but like someone asleep or drunk　Cf. 3, 1147a11–15.　　*1152a15*

He is not unjust either, since he is not a plotter　The general claim that the　*1152a17–18*
un-self-controlled is not a plotter is surprising, given that we have just been told
that lack of self-control can occur along with cleverness (1152a10). The claim also
appears inconsistent with 6, 1149b13 ff.—although that said that (sexual) appetite
is a plotter, not that the person struck by it is. Presumably 'plotter' here means a
constitutional plotter such as the unjust person, rather than someone in the grip of
an uncontrolled plotting appetite.

the bilious type　See comment on 7, 1150b25–6.　　*1152a19*

Anaxandrides　Of Rhodes, a comic poet.　　*1152a22*

Evenus　Of Paros, an acquaintance of Socrates.　　*1152a31*

VII 11, 1152b1–24
Reasons for discussing pleasure (1152b1–7); existing views and arguments
about pleasure, mostly disparaging it (1152b6–24).

for he is the 'architectonic' craftsman of the end, to which we refer when　*1152b2–3*
calling each sort of thing without qualification good or bad　For 'architectonic' cf. I 2, 1094a6–8; for happiness as cause and reference point of the other
goods, cf. i. 12, 1102a2–4; for an example of the latter, see vii. 13, 1153b21–5.

we laid down　*EE* ii. 1, 1220a34–6; 5, 1222a11–16; *NE* ii. 3 (1104b3–1105a16).　*1152b5*

some think that no pleasure is a good, either in itself or incidentally, their　*1152b8–10*
reason being that the good and pleasure are not the same thing　We are not
told why these thinkers hold that pleasure is not *the* [sc. chief] good, but presumably it is because they reject the implication that everything pleasant is good in
itself, on the ground that there are disgraceful pleasures. To deny that pleasure is
the good is to imply that, for all x, if x is good in itself, the explanation of this is
not that x is a pleasure or pleasant; and if x is good incidentally, i.e. good because
related in some way to something good in itself, the explanation of this is not that
x is related in that way to a pleasure or something pleasant. It seems to follow that
no pleasure (or pleasant thing) is, as such, good in itself. (It is not clear how it
seems to follow that no pleasure or pleasant thing is, as such, an incidental good.)
In fact, the above inference is invalid, because it may be that a certain kind of
pleasure or pleasant thing is good not merely because it is a pleasure or pleasant,
but because it is the kind of pleasure or pleasant thing that it is, and if this is so it

would not misrepresent the fact to say that this kind of pleasure or pleasant thing is, as such, good. For example, if pleasure in excellent activity is not merely something that is both good and a pleasure, but is a kind of pleasure (rather as green is a kind of colour), then this is a kind of pleasure that is, as such, good. (In fact, there is no reason why a certain kind of pleasure might not be the chief good; cf. 13, 1153b7–9.)

1152b11–15 **Further, there is a third one of these positions: even if all count as a good . . . belongs to the same kind as a house** (*a*) This completes a trio of anti-hedonic positions of which the other two were 'No pleasure is good' (1152b8), and 'Some pleasures are good, some (most) are not' (10–11). (*b*) See Plato, *Philebus* 53c–54d for the theory of the 'subtle thinkers' that pleasure is a process of coming to be in the natural state (or escape from a painful unnatural condition), and the inference that it is not good as an end in itself; cf. also 31b–32b. For 'perceived' process of coming to be, see 33d–34a. Ar. himself once defined pleasure as a 'movement [i.e. a kind of coming to be] by which the soul as a whole is consciously brought into its normal state of being' (*Rhetoric* I. 11, 1369b33–1370a1). (*c*) 'Good' at lines 11–12 means 'good in itself'.

1152b15–16 **the wise person pursues what is painless, not what is pleasant** Cf. *Philebus* 32e–33b.

1152b18–19 **that pleasure is not the object of any expertise, and yet everything good is the product of some expertise** This turns on its head the reasoning in Plato, *Gorgias* 462b–465e, where it is argued that since oratory aims to produce a kind of pleasure (one that is only a seeming good), it is not an expertise (but a 'knack'), since a true expertise aims at a real good.

1152b23–4 **These, then, are the views expressed, more or less** One may be surprised that almost all the views collected are negative about pleasure. However, it is easy to read off various positive views they are intended to counter, so this chapter may be said to introduce several sides of the Academic debate about the value of pleasure.

VII 12, 1152b25–1153a35

The above objections to pleasure are answered.

Against those pointing out that there are bad pleasures (11, 1152b10–11, 20–2), Ar. argues that just as (1) some things are good without qualification, while others are not, but are good only *for someone in an abnormal state*, so with pleasures: (2) some are pleasures without qualification, others are pleasures only for someone in an abnormal state (1152b26–33, 1153a2–6). (The norm is an adult, healthy, excellent human being.) Those against whom he is arguing presumably accept (1) and the general distinction 'without qualification'/'for someone in an abnormal condition'; hence it would be reasonable of them to accept (2). If they do, (*a*) it is not clear that they can point to any pleasures that are both pleasures without qualification and bad without qualification (i.e. both pleasant for and bad for a physically and ethically healthy subject); and (b) the analogous logical behaviour of 'good' and 'pleasure' should lead them to suspect a close connection between the two. (See Introduction, pp. 72–3; and cf. x. 5, 1176a10–22, and III. 4 (1113a15–b2) with comments.)

those that are accompanied by pain and are for the sake of healing   There   1152b32
may be something diseased or disturbed about pleasures that depend in some way on pain to make their point as pleasures (cf. *Philebus* 44e–51a), but instead of concluding, as some did, that pleasure as such is diseased or disturbed, Ar. says that the pleasures in question are those of a diseased or disturbed subject, and, in effect, that involving pain is not typical of pleasure. Moreover, here he connects the painful pleasure with healing rather than with the trouble needing to be healed.

This leads towards a reply to the objection that pleasure is only a perceived coming to be of the healthy state (11, 1152b12–15, 22–3).

Further, given that the good is part activity and part disposition ... where   1152b33–
there is no depletion of the natural state   The process of restoration to a   1153a2
completely natural or healthy state is not, as such, pleasant; rather, what is pleasant is something in which the restoration consists, i.e. the activity of the residual good state that survived depletion. (One needs residual health to get one back to full health.) Thus even in such cases, the pleasure is a function of what is good, not of its absence or of what is bad. If the restoration were pleasant *qua* restoration (and if perceived restoration is what pleasure essentially is) there should be no pleasures not preceded by painful depletion. Cf. 14, 1154b15–20. But see also 14, 1154a29–31, where pain or lack is said to be responsible (through contrast) for the *intensity* of restorative pleasures (though not for the pleasures themselves).

An indication is that ... so too are the pleasures deriving from them   This   1153a2–7
passage matches the two distinctions 'without qualification' / 'for someone in an abnormal condition' and 'restored state' / 'process of repletion'. What the other side identify as pleasures without qualification are only pleasures for the abnormal, though, according to the previous point, they are a function not of their abnormality so much as of their partial normality. It is not easy to see how this applies on the ethical as distinct from physiological level. Is taking pleasure in bullying or cheating people necessarily to be analysed as pleasure in the activity of some partly decent ethical disposition?

Ar. now (1153a7–17) turns directly to the claim that pleasure is only the coming to be of a further end, and is therefore always inferior to the end. He states that pleasures are not comings to be, but 'activities and an end' (9–10). He then states that not all activities are for the sake of a further end, seeming to imply that some activities are comings to be after all (11–12). However, from what we have seen already, this means only that there are activities (of the underlying good state) in which restorations to complete health consist. (It is now clear that not only are the metaphysical categories 'end-state' and 'coming to be [in the end-state]' mutually exclusive, as the opponents saw, but so are the categories 'coming to be' and 'activity'. Cf. *Metaph.* IX. 6, 1148b18–34, and *NE* x. 4, 1174a14–b10. Now it is common ground between Ar. and the other side that merely having or being in a good condition is less good than exercising or using it (cf. 1152b33). But the restorative pleasure that is really the activity of the organism's partial health is of the same metaphysical kind as the activity of complete health once health is restored. It follows that even the restorative pleasure belongs to the category of what, in general, is metaphysically superior to the end-state of a coming to be.) It is a mistake to define pleasure as a 'perceived coming to be' because it is an activity, and (new point) because 'unimpeded' should be substituted for 'perceived' (1153a12–15). 'Unimpeded' suggests, contra the objection at 11, 1152b11–18, that pleasures interfere with thinking, that the activity interfered with would itself be a pleasure absent the hindrance, and the point is made at 12, 1153a20–3. 'Perceived' is eliminated presumably because, given 'activity', or 'unimpeded activity', it is redundant—although the reason for this becomes clear only from IX. 9, 1170a13–1170b10, and x. 4–5 (especially 5, 1175b33–5): activities that are pleasures (according to the doctrine of *NE* VII) are cognitive ones—perception, sensation, and intellection—and they are necessarily self-aware.

1153a15–17 **Some people think it is a coming to be on the basis that it is good in the primary sense; for they suppose that activity is coming to be, whereas it is something different**   (*a*) 'good in the primary sense' means both: 'good in itself' as opposed to 'good incidentally', and 'good without qualification' as opposed to 'good for someone in a certain condition'. (*b*) 'on the basis that it is good in the primary sense' must be part of the view of the thinkers referred to; hence theirs is a different theory from the one at 11, 1152b12–15. See Plato, *Theaetetus* 152d–153d, for the thought that to be in a good condition is to be perpetually coming to be.

1153a17–18 **To argue that pleasures are bad because some pleasant things bring disease**   The original objection, 11, 1152b21–2, was not as illogical as this, but Ar. attacks its assumption that healthy things are automatically good and disease-causing things bad.

1153a20–2 **Neither wisdom nor any disposition at all is impeded** [sc. in its exercise] **by the specific pleasure deriving from it, but only by alien ones**   Cf. 11, 1152b16–18. The point is more fully developed in x. 5.

1153a23–4 **That no pleasure is the product of expertise is what one would reasonably expect**   Cf. 11, 1152b18–19. The reason, namely that products are only 'capacities', i.e. resources which may or may not be activated by use, confirms the definition of pleasure as *activity*. Dispositions such as health, and objects such as perfumes and delicacies, are 'capacities' here.

That the moderate person avoids pleasures, and that the wise man pursues
the painless life, and that small children and animals pursue pleasure—these
points are all resolved by the same means   Cf. 11, 1152b15–16 and 19–20. The
resolution consists in applying the 'pleasant without qualification/pleasant for
someone' distinction drawn at 1152b26–31, to show that the pleasures that attract
the immoderate, the immature, etc. are not pleasures without qualification (even
though they seem to be so to many, for whom they have 'taken over the title to
the name "pleasure"'; 13, 1153b33).

VII 13, 1153b1–1154a7

Since pleasure is the opposite of pain, and pain is bad, pleasure is good
(1153b1–7). Happiness might be identical with a certain kind of pleasure; in
fact, it must be, given the definition of pleasure as unimpeded activity. This
explains why human happiness requires some external goods, and is con-
firmed by the universal behaviour of animals (1153b7–25). For human
beings, equating pleasure with physical pleasure is a mistake, but a natural
one (1153b33–1154a1). That pleasure is an element of happiness shows that
it is good (1154a1–7).

Speusippus' attempted rebuttal of this argument does not succeed   (*a*) On
Speusippus, see comment on i. 6, 1096b7. (*b*) The rebuttal consisted in pointing
out that just as being larger than *x* has two contraries: being equal to, and being
smaller than, *x*, so pain has two contraries: pleasure and freedom from both
pleasure and pain; consequently, the badness of pain (which Sp. does not question) does not prove the goodness of either contrary in particular. On independent grounds Sp. held that the neutral state is the good one of the three; this,
presumably, is why Ar. objects 'he would not say that pleasure was essentially
something bad', as if this is what Sp. logically ought to say, the thought being that
if the good corresponds to the neutral equal, any departure from it in either
direction is bad.

that some pleasures are bad is not a reason why the chief good is not a
certain kind of pleasure, any more than the fact that some kinds of know-
ledge are bad is a reason for its not being a certain kind of knowledge   (*a*)
For the argument, see 11, 1152b8–10, with comment. (*b*) The parallel with knowledge recalls the *Philebus* contest of pleasure and knowledge for title of 'the
Good': in several *Philebus* passages the same arguments are used for or against
both candidates.

whether happiness is the activity of all of them or of one of them   By 'dispositions' he means 'excellences'. Cf. i. 8, 1099a30–1, and 7, 1098a17. The argument is: since unimpeded activity is better than impeded, and happiness is activity,
and nothing is better than happiness, happiness is an unimpeded activity, which,
by 12, 1153a14–15, means that it is a pleasure.

1153b13–14   **even if most pleasures turned out to be bad, even without qualification**   This seems to be directed against 11, 1152b10–11: 'most [pleasures] are bad'.

1153b23–5   **for even good fortune is an impediment when it is excessive—and perhaps then one should no longer call it good fortune, since its limit is determined by reference to happiness**   Not only does the definition of pleasure as unimpeded activity explain why happiness needs the external goods of fortune, but it also explains why they are not happiness, and thereby sets the limit beyond which they do not count as good: there can be excess of them; there cannot be excess of happiness; they are excessive when they impede the essential activity of happiness.

1153b25–32   **that all animals, and indeed human beings, pursue pleasure indicates that it is in a way the chief good ... for everything by nature contains something godlike**   (a) As a biologist who holds that nature's arrangements for each kind of living thing are for the good of members of the kind, Ar. cannot accept that the universal tendency towards pleasure is typically a tendency towards something bad. Here he suggests that the tendency springs from something divine in each animal, and that the obvious differences between the pleasures of the different species mask a deeper sameness of the pleasure that is sought. He may be thinking that this fundamental pleasure is in sheer being alive (cf. x. 4, 1175a10–21), or that it is in approximation to the divine. Activity unimpeded by external obstacles or weariness certainly accords with traditional notions of the immortal gods. At *On the Soul* II. 4, 415a26–b7 Ar. says that plants and non-rational animals participate in the divine through biological replication of their types. Human beings who equate their supreme good with, for example, the pleasure of sexual activity are seeking the divine, but do not realize that human approximation consists in activity of rational excellence (since, according to *Metaph.* XII. 6–7, god is eternal activity of thought). (b) The quotation is from Hesiod, *Works and Days* (763–4). The pleasure-seeking behaviour of all animal species is treated as the expression of a universally held value-judgement.

1153b33–4   **It is the bodily pleasures ... that have taken over the title to the name 'pleasure'**   This fact, which he is about to explain, is what has given pleasure a bad name and made it seem the opposite of anything godlike.

1154a1–7   **if pleasure, and the activity that is pleasure, is not a good, it will not be the case that the happy person lives pleasantly ... Neither, then, is the life of excellence more pleasant, unless the activities that belong to it are so too**   Ar. argues that pleasure is a good on the basis of the received view 'The happy person lives pleasantly' (I. 8, 1099a7–16; cf. 11, 1152b6–8). Since this proposition is meant to hit off something essential about happiness, it fails to 'be the case' if a pleasureless happy life is even possible—which would be so if pleasure-activity were not a good, since a life without such activity would not therefore lack anything valuable, hence could be a happy life. At this rate, even a painful life can be happy, since if pleasure does not improve a life, pain does not mar it. (As at 1153b5–7, against Speusippus, he insists that if pleasure and pain are not opposed as good and bad, they must have the same status: both bad, or both neither good nor bad, as here.) But then why do the would-be happy avoid pain? The last sentence, with its shift of focus to 'the life of excellence' (*ho bios ho tou spoudaiou*), is obscure. The point may be that if in general pleasure is not a good, then an excellent person's pleasure in his typical activities is not a good; which implies, absurdly, that such pleasure is superfluous to and not characteristic of the excellent person (the sole candidate for 'happy one'), and that such a character may take no more pleasure in good activities, hence have no pleasanter a life, than one who (other things equal) is not yet excellent and for whom good activities go against the grain of his nature.

VII 14, 1154a8–b34

On the bodily pleasures: Ar. defends them against those who reject them as altogether undesirable (1154a8–13); division of activities and pleasures into those where excess is possible and those where it is not; the bodily pleasures are of the first kind, and are bad only when excessive (1154a13–21); the necessity of explaining why bodily pleasures in general give the illusion of being much more desirable than in fact they are (1154a22–6); a variety of explanations, some ethical, some physiological (1154a26–b15); pleasures in respect of which there is no excess—they pall because of our mortal nature (1154b15–31).

with those dispositions and movements for which 'exceeding the better amount' is not possible, there cannot be excess of pleasure either   The possibility of excess is intrinsic: i.e. the processes of fulfilling bodily needs have a natural terminus. An activity and pleasure of the contrasted type, where there is no natural terminus, can be engaged in 'excessively' in an extrinsic sense, e.g. under the wrong circumstances, or detrimentally to some other interest.   *1154a13–15*

for pain is not contrary to excess except for the person pursuing excess   This qualifies the previous statement in case it should be taken to sanction pursuit of excess as contrary to (hence as escape from) the pain of not indulging in the excess. In effect the latter is set aside as being not painful without qualification, but only *for* a malfunctioning person.   *1154a20–1*

having is better than coming to be   i.e. having the healthy condition is better than being restored to it.   *1154a34–b1*

to many what is neither pleasant nor painful is painful, because of their nature   The neither pleasant nor painful condition, i.e. the natural, undepleted, state, was held to be best by Speusippus (cf. 13, 1153b5). But it is painful *for* or *to* most people, because in that state one continues to exercise the sense-faculties, and according to science even this involves physical wear and tear. One way out is   *1154b6* to stop using those faculties, but for most people this would mean lapsing into unconsciousness, hence ceasing to be fully alive, so they contrive physical needs (1154b3–4) so as to distract themselves with the pleasures of restoration. The Aristotelian answer to the wear and tear of ordinary sensory activity is twofold: (1) engage as far as possible in intellection instead (for this, according to his theory, is not the activity of a faculty based on some organ of the body: see *On the Soul* III. 4–5); (2) compensate not by gross bodily activities that add to the problem of ordinary wear, but by using the senses on or for objects that are fine and determinate and least bogged down in physiological materiality (cf. x. 5, 1175b36–1176a3). (Interestingly, the misguided flight to gross pleasures is viewed here as a sort of reaction against physical embodiment.)

1154b11   **bilious people**   See note on 7, 1150b25–6.

1154b15–16   **the pleasures that are not accompanied by pains cannot be taken to excess**
These are the ones that do not involve satisfaction of a lack (assumed to be painful); cf. 12, 1152b34–1153a2. Without a lack to be satisfied, there is no natural cut-off point beyond which the pleasure is excessive.

1154b16–17   **these are the pleasures relating to things that are pleasant by nature and not incidentally**   i.e. pleasant because of what they are, not because they are associated with something else that is pleasant. But in the next lines, Ar. says that the process of being cured seems (not even: is incidentally) pleasant because it is incidental to (which here means 'results from') the activity of the underlying health.

1154b20–2   **But in no case is one and the same thing always pleasant, because our nature is not simple, but also has in it an element of a different sort, in so far as** [*kath' ho*] **we are mortal**   (*a*) Ar. has to explain why even well-constituted people get tired, on particular occasions, of one or another of the finer pleasures. That this happens might suggest that even these pleasure-activities have a natural terminus, and can be pursued to excess. Alternatively, it might suggest that the supposed natural terminus of a physical pleasure is not a stopping point dictated by the nature of that pleasure, but just a weariness in the subject who would do better just to keep going if he could. Ar. preserves his distinction between kinds where excess is possible and ones where it is not by arguing that the latter pall, not because of what they are in themselves, but because we who enjoy them are mortal, and therefore are composed of different elements (cf. *Metaph.* IX. 8, 1050b24–8). These elements have to operate unevenly if we are to experience either pleasure or pain at all; hence with every pleasure a moment comes when the underlying unevenness becomes physiologically intolerable, and the organism has to turn to something else. (*b*) The phrase translated 'in so far as we are mortal' could also be translated 'whereby we are mortal'. This, with the application to god at line 26, suggests that 'element of a different sort' means 'different from the divine element in us'.

there is activity not only of movement [kinēsis] **but also of immobility** [akinēsia]   *1154b26–7*
For god is both absolutely immobile and perfectly active; cf. *Metaph.* xii. 7.

as the poet says   Euripides, *Orestes* 234.   *1154b29*

BOOK VIII

VIII 1, 1155a3–b16
Common observations about 'friendship' (*philia*) (1155a3–31); theoretical questions about it (1155a32–b16).
   On the range of bonds comprised under '*philia*', see Introduction, p. 57.

very necessary   By contrast with *fine* (*kalon*), which applies to friendship   *1155a4*
because friendship in the primary sense is linked with excellence. See below, 1155a28–9, and ix. 11, 1171a24–6.

'When two go forth together'   *Iliad* x. 224. The passage continues: 'one or the   *1155a15*
other notices first how to get the advantage. A man on his own might notice it, but his wits do not reach so far, and his plotting and planning is weak.'

which is why we praise those who love mankind [philanthrōpoí]   This is not   *1155a20–1*
about philanthropy as it is now understood, i.e. as large-scale generosity in the public interest. The general point is that members of a given species are good members of it to the extent that they love their fellow members as such; this is why 'we', being members of the human race, praise (i.e. predicate 'good' of) human beings who love human beings as such.

it is also a fine thing. For we praise those who cherish their friends   i.e.   *1155a29–30*
'cherisher of friends' (*philophilos*) is a term of praise, and praise is reserved for the fine. Cf. 8, 1159a34.

having many friends   The possibility and desirability of this are discussed at viii.   *1155a30*
6, 1158a10–18, and ix. 10 (1170b20–1171a20).

the proverbial potters   'Potter contends against potter'; Hesiod, *Works and*   *1155a34–5*
Days 25.

Euripides   Fragment 898 (Nauck).   *1155b2*

Heraclitus   The 6th-century philosopher; the fragment is DK 8.   *1155b4*

Empedocles   The 5th-century natural philosopher.   *1155b7*

1155b11–13 **whether it is impossible for those who are bad characters to be friends, and whether there is one kind of friendship or more than one**   The first question is discussed in VIII. 4, 1157a16–20 (where it is closely linked with the answer to the second); see also IX. 4, 1166b25–9. The second is discussed in VIII. 2–3 (1155b17–1156b32); cf. 6, 1158b5–11.

1155b13–15 **For those who think that there is one kind on the ground that friendship admits of more and less have based themselves on an insufficient indication, since things different in kind too can be compared as more or less**   Ar. rejects the dogma that only members of the same kind *K* can be compared as more or less *K* than each other. He will argue that, of the three kinds of friendship, the one based on excellence is such that the partners are *most* 'friends', i.e. they are friends *more than* partners in the other kinds; see 3, 1156b7–10; cf. 9, 1159b34–5. 'Most' and 'more' here are formal, not material: the meaning is that excellence-friendship is the kind that most strictly deserves the title of friendship.

1155b16 **earlier**   The reference is uncertain. However, Ar.'s own habit (see I, *passim*) of referring to the human good as 'the best' (i.e. what from the point of view of practical philosophy is most entitled to be called 'good'), given his arguments against the Platonists that 'good' does not pick out a single nature (I. 6 (1096a11–1097a14)), has already made it abundantly clear that philosophical comparisons of more and less need not presuppose a single kind.

VIII 2, 1155b17–1156a5
Analysis of the friendship relation in terms of (i) the three types of 'lovable' (*philēton*, also translated 'object of love') and (ii) the common structure of mutually recognized reciprocal good will. This is provisional, for the all-important element (iii) *living together*, i.e. *sharing lives* (see VIII. 5–6 (1157b5–1158b11)) is not yet included, and it will affect the threefold division. For it is held to be typical of the elderly to make friends solely on the basis of usefulness (3, 1156a24–6), and the elderly are supposed not to enjoy company (5, 1157b13–19; 6, 1158a1–5); consequently, element (iii) undermines the claim of usefulness to be a basis of genuine friendship (cf. 3, 1156b19–20; 6, 1158a18–21).

1155b18–19 **the lovable is good, or pleasant, or useful**   The trio recalls I. 8, 1099a24–9, and II. 3, 1104b31, with 'useful' instead of 'beneficial' and 'good' instead of 'fine' (*kalon*). Possibly Ar. avoids using '*kalon*' here because in a discussion of love and friendship the term might be misunderstood as meaning physical beauty.

1155b19–21 **that would seem to be useful through which some good or pleasure comes about, so that it will be the good and the pleasant that are lovable as ends**   When the friendship is based on utility, the basis is not an end in itself, as in the other two types; but it does not follow that the utility-friend is regarded purely instrumentally. See Introduction, p. 58, and the comment on 1155b28–9.

408

there is a similar difference in the case of the pleasant too   On the difference   *1155b23*
between *pleasant* and *pleasant for someone*, see comments on VII. 12 and Introduction, pp. 72–3.

But that will make no difference   i.e. *good* still lines up with *lovable* whether we   *1155b26*
mean what is really good and lovable, or what is only seemingly good and
therefore only seemingly lovable.

nor wishing for the other's good   *Wishing the other's good for his own sake*   *1155b28–9*
(*ekeinou heneka*; cf. 31) is central to the traditional notion of friendship. Hence Ar.
will argue that one type of friendship is 'complete' (*teleios*), i.e. more fully and
truly friendship than the others, on the ground that it involves this feature in a
way in which the others do not (3, 1156b7–11). However, he gives *wishing the
other's good for his own sake* a wide and a narrow interpretation. In the wide one,
operative in the present passage, the contrast is with wishing that something or
someone be safe and sound simply in order that the thing or person serve some
purpose of one's own (1155b29–31). The wide sense is a condition of each of the
three types of friendship. On the narrow sense, see 3, 1156b7–11, with comments
(*a*) and (*b*).

VIII 3, 1156a6–b32
The three principal kinds of friendship (11156a6–19); comparison in respect
of stability (1156a19–b6); excellence-based friendship is the complete (*teleia*)
kind, as it also implies the advantages of the other two kinds (1156b7 ff.)

these things differ in kind; so, then, does the loving, and so do the friendships   *1156a6–7*
This is a familiar Aristotelian set of definitional dependencies: the type of the
object determines that of the activity directed towards it, and the type of activity
determines that of the corresponding capacity or disposition. For example, vision
is defined in terms of seeing, and seeing in terms of the proper visibilia.

those who love each other wish good things for each other in the way in   *1156a9–10*
which they love   i.e. the general type of wishing goods to each other that
characterizes all friendship has three subdivisions corresponding to the three
lovable qualities.

do not love them for themselves [*kath' hautous*]   If *M* is friends with *N* because   *1156a10–11*
he finds *N* useful or fun to be with, the friendship depends on an extrinsic
relation, not on *N*'s own nature. See 1156b7–11 with comment.

incidentally   i.e. based on inessential features.   *1156a16–17*

Such friendships . . . are easily dissolved   By comparison with those founded   *1156a19–20*
on excellence, which is proverbially stable (I. 10, 1100b12–17).

guest-friendships   A guest-friendship (*philia xenikē*) was a hospitality-arrange-   *1156a30*
ment, often going back many generations, between families belonging to

different city-states. Note that the word '*xenos*' applies to both host and guest, just as '*philos*' does to all parties in a friendship.

1156b7–11   (*a*) Above, the traditional assumption that a friend wishes goods for his friend *for the latter's own sake* was interpreted through a contrast with wishing something or someone to be safe and sound just because one finds it or him useful or pleasant to oneself (2, 1155b29–31). In that sense, the phrase picked out a feature of all three kinds of friendship. Now it is interpreted through a contrast with wishing goods for someone because of incidental facts about him. Since being pleasant or useful to some particular person are incidental, the only type of friendship that exhibits the new sense of 'wishing goods for him for his own sake' is the one based on goodness (excellence). Ar. concludes that (given the traditional assumption) friendship based on excellence is friendship in the fullest sense (since it fits the traditional assumption twice over, as against the others' once). (*b*) For another example of Ar.'s taking a traditionally recognized feature and interpreting it first in one, then in another, sense to characterize first Y in general and then the primary form of Y, see i. 7, 1097b6 ff. with x. 7, 1177a27–b1, where Y is happiness and the feature is self-sufficiency. (*c*) At 1156b10 'wishing good things for their friends, for their friends' sake' is immediately inferred from 'wishing goods for them *because of* themselves' (*di' hautous*); there seems to be no difference between the latter and 'loving them *for themselves*' (*kath' hautous*) at 1156a11. Cf. also 'he is good in himself' (*kath' hautous*) at 1156b9, and *di' hautous* at 4, 1157a18 and b3. (*d*) The emphasis on friend N in himself as distinct from his role in certain relations to friend M needs to be corrected in case it should be sophistically taken as implying that friends in the truest friendship stand in no relation to each other. Ar. makes the correction at 13: 'and good for his friend'.

1156b15   **for the good are both pleasant without qualification and pleasant for one another**   Usually, 'pleasant without qualification' and 'pleasant for someone' are mutually exclusive, the latter meaning 'pleasant merely for someone', but see comment (*d*) on 1156b7–11.

1156b18–19   **all the attributes that friends should have**   The 'should' has logical force.

1156b19–20   **every kind of friendship is because of some good or because of pleasure**   'Some good' presumably includes both excellence and usefulness.

1156b23   **these most of all are objects of love**   The focus now seems to be restricted to the good, i.e. excellent, and the pleasant. They are 'most lovable' because they are 'ends'; see 2, 1155b20–1.

VIII 4, 1156b33–1157b5

Mostly repetition of points made in ch. 3, the most important advance being that friendships based on pleasure and on usefulness are now relegated to the status of 'friendships by virtue of resemblance' (1157a1–3, 25–32). There is a brief discussion of friendships where one side gets the useful, the other the pleasant (1157a6–10).

lover and beloved   This refers to the traditional relation between older man and youth, in which the former was the latter's lover (or at least erotic admirer) and mentor. The main point to note is that in the stereotypical case, the roles of lover and beloved were mutually exclusive; hence this is a friendship of unlikes, and therefore, for Ar., one of the many (logically) marginal forms of friendship. One would suppose he would have more to say about it if he considered this type of liaison to be in general particularly valuable for the young person's cultivation— or if he considered it pernicious. *1157a6*

for the bad [*kakoi*] **get no gratification** [*chairein*] **from each other, unless they might get some benefit**   He assumes that they recognize each other's quality and dislike it. But at 8, 1159b7–10 he says that the *mochthēroi* (a more specifically ethical word, usually translated 'bad') enjoy (*chairein*) each other's badness (*mochthēria*). *1157a19–20*

VIII 5–6, 1157b5–1158b11

New points: (i) There is a distinction between the disposition of friendship and its active exercise in living together (*suzēn*; 1157b5–24). (In general, for Ar., the nature and value of a disposition is determined by that of its activity, and activity generates and maintains the disposition (cf. technical skills and moral qualities in II. 1–2, 1103a3–b23, 1104a11–b3); hence living together is what is most characteristic of friendship; 1157b19.) (ii) The notion of active living together is brought to bear on the usefulness/pleasantness/excellence division, and on the question of friendships in youth and old age (1157b14–17, 1158a1–10); and it shows that pleasure-based friendship is closer than utility-friendship to the complete type (1158a18–26). (iii) In complete friendship, reciprocal loving involves decision (1157b28–32). (iv) The requirements of active living together and stability entail that complete friendship is possible only with a few (1158a10–17). (v) Combining the advantages of pleasure-friendship and those of usefulness-friendship is a problem normally to be solved either by cultivating the friendship of excellence or by a lifestyle of power and subservient friends (1158a27–33); which brings us to the question of equality and inequality between friends or loved ones (1158a33–b1).

because asleep or separated by geographical distance   'Asleep' is a metaphor here for the suspension of activity due to geographic separation. For its literal use to make the same abstract point, cf. I. 5, 1095b32–3; I. 8, 1099a1–2. *1157b8–9*

'Cut off . . .'   Author unknown. *1157b13*

which seems to be characteristic of comradely [*hetairikē*] **friendship**   'Comrades' (*hetairoi*) are close and lasting friends one *makes*, as distinct from the loved *1157b23–4* ones with whom one is connected by birth. There may also be a reference here to the *hetaireiai*, political clubs.

1157b28–9   **And loving … a disposition**   Ar. invokes the standard trichotomy: *capacity, affection, disposition* (cf. II. 5 with comment on 1105b19–21). Obviously neither loving nor friendship is a mere capacity.

1157b30–1   **reciprocal loving [*antiphilēsis*] involves decision, and decisions flow from dispositions**   (The context shows that this is a point about excellence-based friendship.) To the extent that one-sided loving (*philēsis*) is to be classified as an *affection* of the soul, it does not involve decision; hence we now learn that reciprocal loving (anyway in the paradigm case of friendship) is more than *M*'s loving *N* plus *N*'s loving *M*, plus their both knowing about it (2, 1155b33–4). What 'decision' adds is that intrinsic to *M*'s love for *N* is a sense of the value of *N*'s love for him, and vice versa; and presumably, therefore, a settled commitment on each side to maintaining the other side's valuation, and to making it true by living up to it.

1158a22   **while the blessedly happy have no need of useful friends, they do need pleasant ones**   (*a*) They of course will need the services of others, but presumably they count as blessedly happy (*makarioi* as distinct from *eudaimones*) partly because they are prosperous enough not to need useful *favours* from anyone. (*b*) He implies that living with those who are not pleasant is painful. (*c*) The present observation seems to be a further reason for regarding pleasure-based friendship as closer than profit-based friendship to the complete type. The principle is: for any two sub-types, F_1 and F_2, of a type of good F, the one more closely linked with the supreme good is closer to being exemplary of the type.

1158a24–5   **no one would put up even with the good itself [*auto to agathon*], if it were painful to him**   An allusion to Plato's *Philebus*, where it is argued that if the chief good consisted in wisdom without a grain of pleasure, it would be a good no human being would want (21d–e).

1158a27–34   **People in powerful positions … appear to keep their friends distinct … But simultaneously pleasant and useful is what the good person has been said to be**   (*a*) The back-reference is to 3, 1156b17–19, and 4, 1156b33–1157a3. Cf. 4, 1157a33–6, where the combination of useful and pleasant is said to be a rare coincidence except in the context of friendship based on excellence. (*b*) Since the powerful tend to be looked up to (IV. 3, 1124a21–4), the present passage suggests caution about admiring their lifestyle of multiple compartmentalized friendships; the fact that those who 'can have whatever they like' choose this pattern, which is out of reach for most, gives it no weight as a standard. For an explicit such warning about certain pleasures, cf. X. 6, 1176b12–21. In fact, it is better to be forced by modesty of resources to look for a few friends who essentially combine the useful and the pleasant, for then one will not be satisfied by anything less than

412

friendship based on excellence. See Introduction, pp. 61–2, on the Delian inscription. (*c*) On 'witty friends' (31): although wittiness is an excellence of character, here and at x. 6, 1176b14 Ar. is fairly dismissive of the witty.

this sort does not become friends with someone his superior in power unless he is exceeded by him in excellence too; otherwise he is exceeded, but cannot effect a proportional equalization   Excellence cannot honour the powerful in return for favours in the way that the powerful expect—unless the powerful are more excellent still (Ar. may have been thinking of his own friendship with Hermias, the ruler of the state of Atarneus in Asia Minor. After Hermias was treacherously murdered, Ar. commemorated him with a poem likening his excellence to that of demi-gods and legendary heroes.   *1158a34–6*

though as we have said, these are at the same time friendships to a lesser degree, and less long-lasting   Here he means friendships where the basis is different for each party; the reference is to 4, 1157a5–10. But the following lines seem also to cover the unmixed friendships of utility and pleasure.   *1158b4–5*

VIII 7, 1158b11–1159a 12
Friendship relations between unequals.

there is a different excellence of each of these, and their function is different   Cf. *Politics* I. 13.   *1158b17–18*

what is equal does not seem to take the same form in just interactions and in friendship   On equality in the former, see v. 3–5 (1131a10–1134a16).   *1158b29–30*

primary ... secondary ... a great disparity   In justice (equated here with distributive), quantitative equality is posterior to equality in proportion to merit, because it is a special case of it; in friendship, quantitative equality is prior because the proportionate kinds are called 'friendships' on account of likeness to it. That is why the greater the disparity, the further one is from *friendship* (whereas justice applies regardless of the degree of disparity of merit).   *1158b31–3*

This is most evident in the case of the gods   Ar. is discussing relationships between unequals where equalization is possible through mutual cultivation in proportion to worth. In this sense there cannot be love between men and gods; cf. 14, 1163b15–18, and 12, 1162a4–5.   *1158b35*

the problem ... as to whether friends might sometimes not wish the greatest goods for their friends, e.g. being a god   The question is whether the well-meant banality 'Friends wish friends the greatest goods' is literally true. The point seems to be that it cannot be characteristic of *friendship* to wish (even in fantasy) for a situation in which, though both parties exist, their friendship (not merely the activity of it; cf. 5, 1157b5–13) is impossible, and where N is so placed that M's existence as a friend could have no value to N. (It may, however, be characteristic of one-sided *loving* for M to wish N a good that N cannot have in the context of a   *1159a6–7* reciprocal bond between them; cf. 8, 1159a28–33 on mothers who give up their infants for adoption.)

1159a12 **for each person wishes good things for himself most of all**   The meaning is not that one prefers, or ought to prefer, one's own interests to those of one's friend, but that not to wish any goods for *x* when *x* is *oneself* is the extreme of paradox. The well-meant 'I wish you all that's good' (11) is absurd if it implies that the well-wisher wants none of the good things in the world for himself.

VIII 8, 1159a12–b24
The desire to be loved, and how it differs from the desire for honourable recognition; being loved is a good in itself, but the ethical value of friendship lies in loving rather than being loved; more on equality/inequality, likeness/unlikeness, between friends.

1159a22–3 **are seeking to confirm their own** [sc. good] **opinion of themselves**   Hence they do not value being honoured in itself. Cf. i. 5, 1095b26–8.

1159a27–8 **But it seems to lie in loving more than in being loved**   Here Ar. equates friendship (the subject of this sentence) with what is fine about friendship. He then proves (28) this point by considering a case which is not *philia* because not reciprocal (cf. 2, 1155b28). The proof is not in the mothers' attitude but in ours: the fact that we admire them for loving even when not loved in return (whereas we do not admire the children for being loved) shows that what we admire about the friendship of actual friends is the loving on each side, not the being loved. Since loving is an activity of the soul, whereas being loved is not, the former is closer to happiness; cf. i. 7, 1098a6–7; 8, 1098b12–19, b31–1099a7.

1159a35–b1 **so that it will be those between whom this occurs according to worth that will be lasting friends**   i.e. each *loves* the other in proportion to the latter's worth. A contrast is implied with the situation in which each *is loved by* the other in proportion to the latter's worth. As stability is a feature of perfect friendship, the instability of a relation between unequals *M* and *N*, where *M* is loved more by *N* than *N* is by *M* in proportion as *N* is superior to *M*, proves that loving is more fundamental to friendship than being loved, although both are necessary.

1159b15–16 **lover and beloved**   See comment on 4, 1157a6.

1159b24 **hardly germane** [sc. to ethics]   Cf. 1, 1155b8–9.

VIII 9, 1159b25–1160a30
Friendship, justice, and community are closely connected topics. Just as there are many kinds of just obligation, so there are many kinds of friendly bond. In the context of a friendship, unjust acts are worse, and more is expected under the heading of justice. Every kind of association that exists for some purpose common to its members is the basis for a distinct sort of friendship.

as we said at the beginning   i.e. at 1, 1155a22–8.   *1159b25*

Between brothers and between comrades   The word for brothers, '*adelphoi*',   *1159b32*
can be translated 'siblings' but Ar. probably takes it for granted that our attention
will be on male *adelphoi*. On comrades, see comment on 5, 1157b23–4.

fellow members of a tribe or a deme   The tribes (*phulai*) and demes (*dēmoi*)   *1160a18*
were subdivisions of the citizenry. Membership in each was hereditary.

the whole of life ** making   The asterisks mark a lacuna in the text.   *1160a23*

VIII 10–11, 1160a31–1161b10
Ar. develops the idea (originating with Plato, *Statesman* 291d–292a) that
there are three types of good political constitution (also three corresponding
deviations), and draws parallels between these and the three basic familial
relationships.

There are three kinds of political constitution, and an equal number of devia-   *1160a31–2*
tions   What is common to the healthy and the deviant kinds, respectively, is that
government in the former seeks the common good, in the latter the good of
those in power.

thirdly one based on property assessments, the proper name for which   *1160a33–5*
appears to be 'timocracy', though most people are in the habit of calling it
'constitutional government'   (*a*) Whereas Plato, *Republic* VIII, 545b, used 'timocracy' for the rule of those to whom honour (*timē*) is the highest value, Ar. takes
the meaning to follow the cognate *timēma*, 'property qualification'. (*b*) The word
translated 'constitutional government' (*politeia*) is the same as that for 'constitution'. In the *Politics* (IV. 7–8; cf. III. 7, 1279a37–9) Ar. himself uses it of a form of
majority rule where the majority is somehow exclusive (e.g. through a property
qualification); this type of constitution is usually labelled 'Aristotelian polity'. The
usage may reflect the belief that the corresponding deviant form, i.e. democracy
(non-exclusive majority rule) tends towards tyranny or despotism, where there is
no 'constitutional' framework.

king by lot   i.e. as if chosen at random.   *1160b6–7*

From timocracy the change is to democracy   Democracy is a 'deviation'   *1160b16–17*
because in giving equal say to all citizens, it gives equal say to uneducated and
educated. Ar. probably takes it for granted that the former will always be by far
the majority. He of course envisages the ancient, direct, form of democracy, in
which policy and legislation were decided by citizens' votes.

Homer, too, calls Zeus 'father'   Since Zeus is king of gods and men, Homer's   *1160b26*
practice confirms that *father* parallels *king*.

this type of rule . . . is clearly correct   Ar. sanctions slavery, but his considered   *1160b30–1*
views on the institution are quite complex. See *Politics* I. 3–7, 13.

415

1161a32–4   **For where there is nothing in common between ruler and ruled, there is no friendship either**   This is an unfinished dab at explanation, because there is at least a definitional element in common between craftsman and tool (*organon*); e.g. *he* is a builder—*it* is for some building operation. So also between soul-functions and organs and limbs of the body, according to Ar.'s theory in *On the Soul*.

1161a35–b2   **for these are all benefited by their users, but there is no friendship towards inanimate things, nor justice either**   The tools etc. have no value except in the context of use by another.

1161b6–7   **for there seems to be a kind of justice that obtains for any human being in relation to anyone capable of sharing in law and taking part in agreements**   Since this applies to slaves, Ar. implies both that slaves have rights, and that the right not to be enslaved is not one of them. Here he thinks of the enslaved as *both* a slave, which is a less than human thing to be since the slave is someone else's instrument or tool, *and* as a human being. It is shaking to us that he sees no inference from 'is a human being' to 'has the right not to be a slave'. This is different from the doctrine of 'natural slaves' (*Politics* I. 3–7), which seems designed in response to the objection that a full human being should not be a slave; cf. *Politics*. I. 13, 1259b21–7.

VIII 12, 1161b11–1162a33

Ar. now sets aside the more formal kinds of relationship to focus on those of personal intimacy, family ones in particular.

1161b11–12   **as has been said**   At 9, 1159b29–30.

1161b31   **for the self-sameness [*hē ... tautotēs*] of their relation to *those* produces the same with each other**   The Greek words for 'the same' (*ho autos*) and for 'self' are almost identical. That siblings are the same in their relation to their parents makes them each other's selves to each other.

1162a5   **and human beings' for gods**   The analogy of children and parents suggests that the gods have provided the greatest benefits (6) to us as extensions of themselves, and that we love them in return as having in some way sprung from them (1161b17 ff., 27–31).

1162a17–18   **man is naturally a coupler more than he is naturally a civic being**   But in a different sense of 'natural', having to do with a thing's fulfilment, man is by nature a civic being more than a familial one. Cf. *Politics* I. 2 (where the priority stated here is reversed, in accordance with final causality; 1253a19 ff.); and *Physics* II. 1, 193a9–b18, on senses of 'nature'.

VIII 13, 1162a34–1163a23

Here and in the next two chapters (VIII. 14 and IX. 1 (1163a24–1164b21)) Ar. re-examines the three principal types of friendship, this time from the point of view of conflict between friends and ways of avoiding it. Ch. 13 is about cases where the friends see themselves as equals.

as was said at the beginning   At 3, 1156a6–7.   *1162a34*

it is a fine thing to do good to someone without meaning to be repaid, but it   *1162b36–*
is to one's benefit to have good done to one   Thus a benefactor easily bestows   *1163a1*
favours as if not expecting repayment, and becomes angry later that the other
took this at face value.

and the measure looks as if it is the decision [*prohairesis*] of the doer   i.e. M   *1163a22*
determines ('measures') how to respond to a friendly initiative from N not by
reference to the advantage it actually brought him (since this is not a relation
based on usefulness) but by interpreting N's intention, which is what matters
most in questions of excellence and character (cf. IX. 1, 1164b1–2).

VIII 14, 1163a24–b28
Conflict (and how to avoid it) in friendships between acknowledged
unequals.

one cannot at the same time receive money from communal sources and be   *1163b8–9*
accorded honour   The reason comes in the next sentence: the public would
then be 'getting the smaller share' in every respect.

as has been said   The reference could be to the entire discussion 13, 1162a34 ff.   *1163b12*

But if the son is a bad character, then for him assisting his father is something   *1163b25–6*
to be avoided, or something not to take trouble about   So the father may not
lose much support by repudiating him.

Let this, then, be our account of these subjects   Since the discussion of friend-   *1163b27–8*
ship continues in Book IX, this formula, which signals the end of a topic, must
have been inserted by an early editor who misidentified the end of a Book (i.e. a
scroll of a certain standard size) with the close of a discussion.

BOOK IX

IX 1, 1163b32–1164b21
Conflict and avoidance of it in heterogeneous friendships (i.e. where the
basis is different in kind on each side).

as has been said   Presumably the reference is to VIII. 14, 1163b11–12, although   *1163b33*
the emphasis there was not on heterogeneity but on inequality.

1163b34–5   **the return . . . is measured by their worth**   This is discussed in v. 5, 1133a5–b 28.

1164a12–13   **as has been said**   In VIII. 3–4.

1164a24   **Protagoras**   The 5th century sophist. The sophists to whom Ar. refers as such at 1164a31 were probably his own 4th century contemporaries; see also x. 9, 1180b35–1181a1 and 1181a12 ff.

1164a27   **'to each man his fee'**   From Hesiod, *Works and Days* 370, where the advice is 'Fix the fee in advance'.

1164a35   **as has been said**   At VIII. 13, 1162b6–13; cf. 31–2.

1164b3   **those who have imparted philosophy** [*koinōnēsasin*, lit. 'having given a share'] **to him**   'Philosophy' means the finest intellectual culture, whatever it may be. See Introduction, pp. 52–4.

1164b4   **since its worth is not measured in relation to money**   So sophists who charge a fee, or (like Protagoras) leave it to the student to determine one, either misunderstand the value of philosophy (see previous note) or are professing to teach something else.

IX 2, 1164b22–1165a35
Questions about priority as between different kinds of friendly connection.

1164b23–5   **should one trust a doctor when sick, and elect an expert in warfare to a generalship**   i.e. rather than one's father.

1164b33–4   **But perhaps even this is not a universal rule**   i.e. giving priority to repayment of loans (a stranger's ransom money being considered as lent to the person redeemed). Ransoming one's father takes priority.

1165a1–2   **For it would seem that one should ransom one's father even before oneself**   This implies that one should ransom one's father rather than one's own ransomer (and a fortiori rather than repaying a creditor who has not been taken captive), on the assumption that ransoming one's own ransomer does not have higher priority than ransoming oneself.

IX 3, 1165a36–b36
Ending a friendship when the other is no longer the same.

1165b6   **as we said at the beginning**   The reference is probably to VIII. 13, 1162b23–5, which is near the beginning of the discussion of the breakdown of friendships.

1165b16–17   **it has been said that like is friend to like**   At VIII. 1, 1155a32–4, this was mentioned as one view among others.

1165b31   **we have discussed these things**   At VIII. 5–6 (1157b5–1158b11).

IX 4, 1166a1–b29

Ar. argues that the marks of friendship for another characterize the decent person's attitude towards himself (see Introduction, pp. 60–1). One purpose is reconciliation of existing views. Each 'mark' stands for a view about the nature of friendship; hence a plurality of marks stands for a plurality of competing views. Ar. reconciles them by showing that each is a special case of 'How I am towards my friend is how I am towards myself'.

so it is with mothers towards their children, and with friends who are angry with each other   Cf. VIII. 8, 1159a28–33, where the natural mother continues to love her adopted child even though the child is ignorant of the relationship. A quarrel creates a similar situation in both directions: each continues to care about the other although the other's back is turned to him.   *1166a5–6*

as has been said   At III. 4, 1113a25–33.   *1166a12*

since even as things are god has the good   I am no better off now on account of the fact that another being, god, is in possession of the absolute good now; so how can I be better off in future if another (whom I turn into) has all goods in the future?   *1166a21–2*

And he most of all shares his grief and pleasure with himself   For Ar. this only makes sense in so far as the self is viewed as many in some way; here, it is my self today and my past and future selves.   *1166a27*

Let us set aside for the present whether there is or is not friendship for oneself   The closest Ar. comes to returning to this in the *NE* is in IX. 8 (1168a28–b2) where the question is whether one should love (*philein*, also 'befriend') oneself most of all. Perhaps Ar. holds back from asserting that the 'friendly' features of a person's attitude to himself ground a literal notion of reflexive friendship because he sees it as harbouring paradox, given that a friend is another (good) self; for in that case, if a good self is literally a friend to himself, then the good self is another good self than himself. According to *EE* VII. 6, friendship with oneself is only by analogy, the literal relation requiring separate individuals.   *1166a33–4*

in so far as a person is countable as two or more   He may be thinking of functional 'parts of the soul', like the two ethically relevant parts in *NE* I. 13, or the three of Plato's *Republic*; or he may be thinking of the temporal plurality of 24–9, which could be threefold (the past, the present, and the future self).   *1166a35*

Certainly no one who is really bad and does unspeakable things has these attitudes, or even appears to have them. And this is more or less true of inferior people too   The connection between badness and self-conflict is reminiscent of Plato. It is not at all obvious that the wicked are necessarily at odds with themselves, still less that ordinary bad persons are so too. Without argument, Ar. treats them as making self-destructive choices instead of going for the good,   *1166b5–7* *which they themselves take to be good*, although elsewhere he equates badness with ignorance of the good (III. 1, 1110b28–30). However, this need not be a contradiction: he can say, as of the uncontrolled with whom he compares them (1166b7–10), that in a way they know what is good, in another way are ignorant of it (cf. VII. 3, 1146b31 ff.). But this leaves it unexplained why we should think that the wicked and bad are necessarily self-conflicted. Some scholars see this discussion as belonging to a different stage of Ar.'s development from the study of lack of self-control in Book VII, where the uncontrolled person's conflict is contrasted with the self-indulgent one's unanimity of decision and appetite (VII. 4, 1148a6–20, and ch. 8). But again, there may not be an outright contradiction, since here the bad person's conflict is said to be between *wish* and appetite (1166b7–8), not between *decision* and appetite, which is the mark of the uncontrolled in Book VII. Thus in the present passage the bad man's wishes for the good never turn into decisions. The result, given that he has an appetite for harmful pleasures (1166b9–10), is not exactly a *practical* conflict, since the wish lacks practical force (recall that we can wish for what we take to be impossible; III. 2, 1111b22–3), but it is still a rift in the soul. Reflectively, one may find one's personality hateful, even if in practical situations one always falls into enacting its characteristic purposes. But we are given no reason for holding that it is always like this with bad or even extremely bad people.

IX 5, 1166b30–1167a21
Good will.

1166b32 **this is something we have said before, too**   At VIII. 2, 1155b32–1156a3.

1167a12–14 **though not the kind that exists because of the useful, or the one that exists because of the pleasant, since neither does good will arise on the basis of these**   Some understand the last clause as saying that, in general, there is no good will in relationships based on utility or pleasure. This would contradict the account covering all three types of friendship given at VIII. 2, 1155b27–1156a5 (where 'good will' is said to be a name for wishing the other's good for his own sake; cf., however, VIII. 4, 1157a14–16). It is better to take the clause as saying that just as the useful and the pleasant do not give rise to the friendship based on excellence (referred to indirectly at line 12), so they do not give rise to the inactive mutual good will that can develop into friendship (10–12). If I bear someone good will because he is or has been useful or pleasant to me, this is fair enough (14–15 below), but it is not a case of mutual inactivity. If I wish someone well who has not yet interacted with me, and do so not on account of his excellence, this can only be because I hope to get something out of him, and this is not genuine wishing *him* well (15–18). The difference between this situation and a usefulness-*friendship* is that in the latter one does wish the other well for his own sake, even though in this case interactive usefulness constitutes the context for good will (see Introduction, p. 58). Hence good will that is both inactive and genuine must be directed towards the other's excellence. Given the assumption that a pre-friendly interest in someone's usefulness, pleasantness, or excellence develops (if it does) into the corresponding type of friendship, it follows that inactive good will can only develop into excellence-friendship. Here, as at 9, 1169b33–1170a4, someone's excellence can touch us simply through contemplation of it.

For a person who has been benefited . . . because of some use [chrēsis] **he**   *1167a14–18*
wants to get out of it   This should be taken to apply to the pleasant as well as the useful; thus *chrēsis* includes 'enjoyment'.

IX 6, 1167a22–b16
Like-mindedness.

Pittacus   6th-century ruler of Mytilene. Unanimously elected to the office, he   *1167a32*
eventually stepped down because he wanted to.

Phoenician Women   Euripides' play; the subject is the rivalry of Oedipus' sons   *1167a33*
for the throne of Thebes.

like the Euripus   i.e. the strait between Boeotia and Euboea, full of strong,   *1167b7*
changing currents.

IX 7, 1167b17–1168a27
Why do benefactors seem to love their beneficiaries more than the latter them?

Epicharmus   5th-century comic writer.   *1167b25*

But it would seem that the explanation lies, rather, in natural philosophy   *1167b28–9*
[*phusikōteron*]   The comparison is with his usual method in the *Ethics* of tapping received views. The explanation from natural philosophy, which runs from 1168a5 to 15, is preceded by an argument bringing the benefactor case under the common-sense generalization 'The maker loves what he has wrought' (i.e. his *ergon*; 1167b31–1168a5; cf. 1168a21–6). (The benefactor's *ergon* is the difference he makes to beneficiary.) It is this that is to be explained. Typical of this natural philosophy approach is that it applies to all animals as such, it makes sophisticated use of the concepts of *agent*, *patient*, and *actuality* (*energeia*, also translated 'activity'), and it invokes the metaphysical connection between pleasure and *energeia* which will be clarified in x. 4–5 (1174a13–1176a29). Cf. 9, 1170a13ff.

in a way, the work is the maker in actuality   This is explained at lines 8–9, 'for   *1168a7*
what he is in potentiality, the work shows in actuality'. The poem is not evidence from which we infer to the author's skill, but is a determinate instance of that skill 'out in the world'.

he delights in the one in whom it occurs   This alludes to the doctrine that a   *1168a10–11*
process of change (*kinēsis*) is an actuality occurring *in* its subject, the patient, and *by* (*hupo*) the agent: see *Physics* III. 3; *Metaph.* IX. 8, 1050a30–4. Ar. here treats an action (*praxis*) as a sort of *kinēsis*. The benefactor contemplates, in the recipient,

something of himself that is fine, hence gets pleasure from the recipient as such. This prepares the way for one argument for the major thesis that friendship is essential to happiness, i.e. 9, 1169b30–1170a4, where again one person's activity is in a way located in another. One may wonder whether, on this view, benefactors can properly be said to *love* their beneficiaries, willing them good for *their* sake, any more than creditors love their debtors (1167b20–31). The answer perhaps is that normally one confers a benefit in the first place because one independently wishes the other's good, and the special feeling which Ar. is trying at this point to explain is consequential on the good deed. To confer a benefit solely or largely in order to enjoy contemplating one's fine deed 'in' the recipient would be to some extent self-defeating, because the action, although beneficent, would be less fine than one motivated by good will for the other.

1168a11–12   **whereas for the recipient there is nothing fine in the one who gave the benefit, but at most something advantageous, and this is less pleasant and less lovable**   (*a*) i.e. the recipient finds nothing fine about *himself* in the benefactor. This ignores the possibility that the recipient sees the benefactor's action as something fine about the benefactor, and takes pleasure in it accordingly; for in that case the recipient operates like any appreciative bystander, not specifically as recipient. (*b*) On the association of pleasantness with the fine (by contrast with the useful), cf. *Rhetoric* I. 9, 1366a33–5: 'the fine is what is both good and pleasant because good', whereas the useful is not as such pleasant (cf. VIII. 3, 1156b19–23).

1168a16   **the fine survives the passage of time**   If the deed was fine at the time, then it still is, though past; substitute 'useful', and the point does not hold.

1168a18–19   **expectation seems to be the other way round**   i.e. more pleasant when the object is something useful to oneself, less so when it is something fine that one will do.

1168a19–21   **loving is like doing something to something, whereas being loved is like having something done to one; and it is to those who exceed in respect of being an agent that 'loves' and the features of friendship apply**   This is still part of the explanation why benefactors love beneficiaries rather than the reverse. The argument is: 'to benefit', like 'to love', is active by contrast with passive, a resemblance that implies that, for two parties X and Y, 'loves' is predicated of benefactor X rather than beneficiary Y. The point, a logical one, is not that the benefactor necessarily loves the beneficiary, but that if the question 'Which of the two of them loves?' arises in such a case, the answer is 'The benefactor'. This belabouring of the obvious reflects an anxiety to be clear that true application of a predicate such as ' . . . loves . . . ', for which there must be two logical subjects, depends not merely on picking a pair to which it applies, but also on putting them in the right order (the anxiety itself arising from the metaphysical desirability of treating a relation and its converse as in a way identical: see *Physics* III. 3). The phrase 'those who exceed in respect of being an agent' is a schematic way of distinguishing agents whose action is not reciprocated; with reciprocity, there is equality (cf. v. 4, 1132a13 ff., for the same idea in the context of reparation), and the order in which the subjects are plugged in to '... loves ...' makes no difference to the truth-value of the resulting sentence.

IX 8, 1168a28–1169b2
Self-love.

The phenomenon discussed in the last chapter, that benefactors love bene-ficiaries more than the reverse, is paradoxical only on the assumption that getting a material benefit is more precious than doing a fine action (although without this assumption the curious may still want to understand the phenomenon). The same assumption sets up the problem of ch. 8, which is a conflict between common opinions about self-love: (O_1) that a bad person loves himself most of all, and acting from self-love precludes acting because of the fine (1168a29–35); (O_2) that one ought to love oneself most of all (on the ground that one is one's own best friend, and one ought to love one's best friend most) (1168a35–b10). Ar. first argues as if the solution depends on distinguishing senses of 'self-love' corresponding to the different types of goods which the self-lover vulgarly so called, and the agent who acts for the sake of the fine, wish for themselves respectively (1168b12–28). He then argues that the latter is the true self-lover, (*a*) because he wishes for himself better goods than the other does for *himself*, and (*b*) because reason, the element within him which he favours by seeking these goods, is more truly himself than any other element (1168b28–1169a6). So (O_1) is false for self-love in the true sense. Ar. now (1169a11) turns to (O_2), and finds it true for the good man, false for the bad (1169a11–18). He ends by showing that the better goods which the true self-lover seeks for himself include just the kinds of actions that are vulgarly deemed unselfish and self-sacrificing (1169a18–b1).

The topic of this discussion is not egoism and altruism, but true and false self-love.

But people's behaviour is out of tune with these statements, and not without   *1168a35–b1*
reason. For they say that ...   Much of the time they indulge their natural self-love, and are justified by the views that follow.

what each side means by 'self-love'   Ar. presents the proponents of (O_2) as a   *1168b14*
different group from those of (O_1), and as if they intend 'self-love' in the enlight-ened sense. But in fact it is unenlightened common sense going to and fro between (O_1) and (O_2) that sets up the opening question.

So people who are grasping about these things indulge their appetites, and in   *1168b19–21*
general the affective elements and the non-rational part of the soul   The reference is probably to those who pursue such things from decision or regular policy, not to the uncontrolled person. Thus the difference here between reason

and the appetites is not one of function or activity (reason *decides*, appetite *urges*) but lies in the types of objects. The proper objects of reason are fine actions, which there can be no need to fight over (18), since one person's having more of these goods does not entail another's having less.

1168b25–8   if anyone were always eager that *he* most of all should do what was just . . . no one will . . . censure him   Homeric nobles are urged by their fathers: 'Always be best and superior to the others'. Ar. may be sketching someone who acts always with an eye on his own ethical performance, in which case we should find fault, since in much right action one's attention should be on others. But the passage also fits someone who is not thus self-absorbed in the course of particular actions, but on reflection is pained more by his own ethical failings than by anyone else's, or/and more pained by his ethical than his other failings.

1168b29–30   he assigns the finest things, the ones that are most good, to himself   (*a*) This (likewise 18–27) may be the language of eulogy, not of psychological description from the agent's point of view. (*b*) The point is not that he assigns the finest goods to himself rather than to others, but that the goods *he* chooses, as distinct from those chosen by the self-lover in the pejorative and false sense, are finest.

1168b35–1169a1   it is actions accompanied by reason that people most think they have done themselves, and voluntarily   Elsewhere Ar. is definite that voluntary actions include those done from impulse or out of negligence; see III. 1–2, 1111a24–b14, 1110b9–17; 5, 1113b33–1114a3.

1169a8–9   if everyone vied for what is fine   At 1168b19–20 and 1169a20–1, the fine is contrasted with 'fought-over' goods. If this epithet means that they are goods such that if one person has more, another necessarily has less (although in fact this is more the reason why they are fought over), the rivals for the fine cannot each be bent on being ahead of everyone else in excellence, since only one can fill that position. In that case, what Ar. describes as 'vying' is not a competition, but is presumably a process in which each party's performance, through mutual comparison, is seen as articulating a standard which others (and he) can now aim to pass, in order to raise the quality (not in order to be one, or the one, who raises it). Alternatively: that the fine is not a fought-over good means: it is not such that *men can snatch it from each other by force*. Thus genuine rivalry for the position of first in excellence does not count as *fighting over* this good, given that fighting over something is essentially the alternative to accepting a fair assignment. For whoever does come first in excellence necessarily deserves the good of being first. (The point holds, of course, for excellence in any field.)

1169a11–14   Thus the good person should be a self-lover . . . but the bad one should not; for he will harm both himself and . . .   By favouring their appetites, the bad identify themselves with these, erroneously. It is only 'themselves' according to this false view of what they are that the bad ought not to love, not merely because the object is not lovable, but also because in loving it they harm their real selves.

he will choose intense pleasure for a short duration over mild pleasure for a *1169a22–3*
long one   (*a*) The reference is to the man who lays down life for country or
friends, but we need not suppose that 'intense short pleasure' aims to describe his
actual feelings in battle or at the moment of being cut down (cf. the more realistic
description at III. 9, 1117a29 ff.). Given Ar.'s metaphysical connection of pleasure
and life (x. 4, 1174a13 ff., prefigured in IX. 7–9, 1167b17–1170b19), preferring an
intense short pleasure is tantamount to preferring an intense short vital activity.
(*b*) Ar. does not say here that the alternative to choosing the intense short pleasure
would be a disgraceful choice, only that it would be humdrum. Why then should
reason necessarily choose the former? Presumably because complete excellence
includes greatness of soul, which holds itself ready to do few but illustrious deeds
(IV. 3, 1124b24–6).

IX 9, 1169b3–1170b19

A traditional puzzle: to be happy, does one need friends? (See Introduction,
pp. 62–5.)

   On grounds of material prosperity it seems that not (1169b4–8). On the
contrary, friends are needed for the best *use* of prosperity (1169b8–16); and it
is absurd to make the blessed person solitary, since it is human nature to live
together (*suzēn*; 1169b16–22). Why the negative answer seems plausible
(1169b22–8). Three arguments showing why the affirmative is correct:
according to the first two, full pleasure in one's own excellent activity is
impossible without friends (1169b28–1170a4) and (1170a4–13); while the
third shows that the friend's existence holds, for the good person, a good
and a pleasure as central, almost, as the good and pleasure of his own
existence (1170a13–b19).

   In fact, the arguments apply to all sets of friends who regard themselves
and each other as excellent. It is not clear that Ar. faces the possibility that
they could be systematically mistaken. But this is irrelevant in the context of
an argument about happiness, where genuine excellence is presupposed.

'To those . . .'   Euripides' *Orestes*, line 667. *1169b7–8*

friends, something that seems greatest of the external goods   Cf. the div- *1169b9–10*
ision of goods at I. 8, 1098b12–14. At IV. 3, 1123b20–1 honour was said to be the
greatest external good.

if it is finer to do good to friends than to strangers   Not clear why this should *1169b12*
be so.

whether one needs friends more in good fortune or in bad   This is the subject *1169b14*
of IX. 11, 1171a21 ff.

the blessedly happy [*makarios*] **will have no need of friends of this kind**   Cf. VIII. *1169b24*
6, 1158a22.

425

1169b26–7   **adventitious pleasure**   Cf. I. 8, 1099a7–21.

1169b28   **it was said at the beginning**   At I. 7, 1098a6; 8, 1098b31–1099a7.

1169b32   **and pleasant in itself, as was said at the beginning**   At I. 8, 1099a7–21.

1170a1   **for those actions have both of the attributes that are naturally pleasant**   They are (i) good and (ii) (in a way) our own (*oikeios*).

1170a2–3   **given that he decides to observe** [*prohaireitai theōrein*] **decent actions that bear the stamp of his own** [*oikeios*]   (*a*) Ar. does take this as given, presumably not as something we know from experience, but as a theoretical assumption justified by its role in the explanation being offered. (*b*) The emphasis is not on self-knowledge with a view to criticism and improvement, but on self-appreciation. (*c*) It is not clear why N, in whose excellent action M sees his own, must be a *friend*. Perhaps because, to be enjoyed while going on, N's activity must be immediately comprehensible, which for activities of any depth or complexity requires a background of familiarity. (*d*) At 1170a1 Ar. follows ordinary usage in saying that N's activity is pleasant to M who observes it. But according to the doctrine of x. 4–5 (1174a13 ff.), the subject's pleasure, strictly, is in his *own* activity, in this case that of observing the other's. (*e*) Since M here *observes* N's activity, the latter, in the paradigm case, would be one in which M is not engaged as participant.

1170a5–6   **for being continuously active is not easy by oneself**   Cf. x. 4, 1175a 3–6, on tiring of an activity, and VII. 14, 1154b20–31, on the need for variety.

1170a7   **being pleasant in itself**   i.e. not because it is, for example, the remembering or expecting of some other pleasure.

1170a12–13   **as Theognis says**   Perhaps the line quoted at 12, 1172a13–14.

1170a13–14   **if we examine the matter more from the point of view of natural philosophy, it seems that the good friend is naturally desirable for the good person**   (*a*) See 7, 1167b28–9 with comment. Almost all the elements of the ensuing argument are from technical philosophy, except for the proverbial 'the friend is another self' (1170b6–7). (*b*) 'naturally desirable' entails 'is desired, and rightly so'. (*c*) In outline, the argument from natural philosophy goes:

(1) (Premiss) The good person's own vital activity (i.e. his active existence) is a good for him and is necessarily felt as pleasant by him (argued for in 1170a14–b5);

(2) (Premiss) The friend is another self (b5);

(3) The good man's existence is desirable for the good person (from (1));

(4) The friend's existence is a good for the good person and is felt as pleasant by him (provided that they engage in joint living) (from (1) and (2));

(5) The friend's existence is naturally desirable for the good person (1170b14–17; from (4)); QED (see 1170a13–14).

Most of the work here goes into the argument for premiss (1). Yet at 1169b31–2 Ar. takes almost the identical proposition for granted, and few would dispute it. However, the argument for (1) brings out two important points: (*a*) M's pleasure in, and awareness of the value of, his own self-aware being (when it is not divided against itself) are intrinsic and central to his being; thus the good and the pleasantness to M of friend N's existence is similarly intrinsic and central for M. (*b*) We (and indeed all sentient beings, according to *On the Soul* III. 2, 425b11 ff.) are essentially aware of our perceiving (and in the human case, of our thinking); thus far from being in the first place monolithically alone, we are essentially always (when awake) monitored by or in the presence of someone; thus it is our nature to be-with or live-with even when we are by ourselves.

it has been said   e.g. at III. 4, 1113a21–33. Usually the point is that the good person's judgement on what is good is authoritative; here it is that what is good in itself is a benefit to him.   *1170a14*

people define being alive in the case of animals by capacity for perceiving, and in the case of human beings by capacity for perceiving or thinking   Cf. *On the Soul*, III. 12, 434a31; II. 3, 414b3–4, 18–19.   *1170a16*

perceiving (*aisthēsis*)   It could also be translated 'awareness'.   *1170a16*

since it is determinate, and the determinate is of the nature of the good   (*a*) Being alive is determinate because a dead human being or a dead mouse is man or mouse in name alone; it has no definite nature, because the nature of a substance is defined by reference to its typical activity (cf. I. 7, 1097b24 ff.), and death is cessation of activity. Moreover, life at its fullest is activity, which is determinate by comparison with the corresponding capacity or disposition. For example, the activity of seeing is realized only in particular episodes each with its own particular object or set of objects that makes that episode the determinate one that it is, whereas the capacity is only for seeing visible things in general. (*b*) The association of goodness and determinacy was a Pythagorean and late Platonic doctrine; see *Philebus* 25d ff., and note on *NE* I. 6, 1096b5–6 where the column of goods is headed by Limit, the principle of determinacy. Here the point seems to be that the determinate as such is good; for the converse, see x. 3, 1173a15–16.   *1170a20–1*

such a life is indeterminate   Because pain blurs its distinctive activities; see x. 5, 1175b17–20, the probable reference of 1170a25. He does not say that the bad life is indeterminate, but the proposition follows from lines 20–1.   *1170a24*

the subject of pain, however, will be given clear treatment in the sequel   See IX. 11, 1171a27–b11.   *1170a24–5*

if being alive is itself good and pleasant   The truth of this was proved from determinacy at lines 19–21; now it is proved from the love of life, strongest in the good (and those who believe themselves good); cf. III. 9, 1117b7–13, on the courageous man.   *1170a25–6*

1170a29   **the one who sees perceives that he sees**   Cf. *On the Soul* III. 2, 425b11–25.

1170a32–3   **if perceiving that we perceive or think is perceiving that we exist**   Compare Descartes, who (in one formulation) infers 'I exist' from 'I think'. By contrast, Ar. is as directly aware of the fact of his existence as of the fact of his thinking (for example) since these facts are identical. Since not everyone is a philosopher, Ar. would surely allow that one could be aware of one's own thinking and perceiving without using or even having the theoretical knowledge that for human beings, life and therefore existence *is* perceiving and thinking. Even so, he holds that *what* such a person is aware of when aware of his perceiving or thinking is the fact of his existence (or perhaps his existence itself), and not merely some aspect of that fact (or of the existence itself). For it is awareness of life or existence as such that is pleasurable for the good person (1170b1–5).

1170b10–11   **In that case, he needs to be concurrently perceiving** [*sunaisthanesthai*] **the friend —that he exists, too**   M needs to be aware of his friend N's active existence along with being aware of his own. It may be implied that M is aware of N not as an object, but as subject of his (N's) own thoughts and perceptions. Given reciprocity, this would presumably be equivalent to M's being aware of N as co-constituent of a joint point of view. The corresponding passage in the *EE* (VII. 12, 1245b21–2) links '*suzēn*' and '*sunaithanesthai*' in a way that directly suggests that 'living-with' implies sharing the other's perceptions (and presumably awareness of them).

IX 10, 1170b20–1171a20

Many friends or few? Many are either unnecessary or impossible in friend-ships based on utility and pleasure (1170b20–9). For those based on excel-lence, the number of friends is limited by what is involved in friends' sharing their lives (1170b29–1171a15). Those who are friends 'with everybody' seem not to be friends of anyone (1171a14–17); but these must be distinguished from civic friends (1171a17–19).

1170b21–2   **'Host not many . . .'**   Hesiod, *Works and Days* 715.

1171a2   **as we said**   E.g. at VIII. 5, 1157b19.

1171a14–15   **there are not numerous parties to the comradely type of friendship**   See on VIII. 5, 1157b23–4. The legendary examples are duos, such as Achilles and Patro-clus, Theseus and Peirithous.

1171a17   **people call them obsequious**   Cf. IV. 6, 1126b11 ff.

IX 11, 1171a21–b28

We need friends in good times and in bad, for different kinds of reasons (1171a21–30). The presence of friends when one is in distress (1171a22–b12) . . . and when one is prospering (1171b12–14). When one should invite them eagerly, when hesitantly; when one should go to them eagerly, when hesitantly (1171b15–27).

if he doesn't make excessive efforts to avoid distressing them [*alupiai*]**, he won't abide the pain being caused them**   (*a*) 'if' here may have the logical force of 'even if'. (*b*) On the wording, cf. iv. 6, 1126b14, where *alupos* occurs in the sense of not causing distress to others. (*c*) Ar. seems to imply a triad: the extremes are putting up a wall between friends and one's own trouble, and being in a hurry to draw them into it.   *1171b7–9*

'One's suffering is enough'   Author uncertain.   *1171b18*

IX 12, 1171b29–1172a15
Shared living (*suzēn*) is the most desirable thing about friendship (1171b29–32), because shared living is the activation of a desirable awareness—that of the friend's existence (1171b32–1172a1). Whatever activity most counts as 'living' to M, this he wants to do with his friend (1172a1–8). The friendship of the bad is a bad friendship, and makes them worse, while that of the good makes them better (1172a8–14).

'For from good men . . .'   Theognis, 35.   *1172a13–14*

BOOK X

Chapters 1–5 (1172a19–1176a29) are on pleasure; chapters 6–8 (1176a30–1179a32) are on happiness; 9 (1179a33–1181b23) is on the implementation of excellence.

Why pleasure is an important topic (1, 1172a19–b8); existing views, positive and negative, with replies (2–3, 1172b9–1174a12); Ar.'s own account of pleasure (4, 1174a13–1175a21); consequences concerning pleasure and activity, and the variety of pleasures (5, 1175a21–1176a29).

X 1, 1172a19–b8, introduction
Pleasure is a subject for ethics because (1) the hedonic propensity is fundamental to our nature (1172a20), and affects our actions throughout life (20–3). And (2) the topic is very controversial (27). The two main views are that pleasure is the supreme good (1172a27–8), and that pleasure is bad (27). Proponents of the latter are divided into those who believe it and those

who preach it on pragmatic grounds (29–33). Ar. deals with the latter group (33–b7) before turning to the views themselves.

1172a33   **that way they will arrive at the intermediate**   At II. 9, 1109a30 ff. Ar. recommended an exaggerated hostility to pleasure as corrective to our natural partiality. Now he points out the danger of preaching more austerity than one could reasonably practise. If the preacher sometimes pursues pleasure, belying his words, his audience will think they are justified in ignoring the preaching completely.

X 2, 1172b9–1173a13, on Eudoxus' hedonism

On Eudoxus, see note on I. 12, 1101b27–31. Here Ar. ascribes to him four arguments for the view (E) that pleasure is the supreme good. Eudoxus' first argument (1172b9–15): E follows from (1) All beings seek pleasure, together with (2) What all things seek is the supreme good. Ar. does not reject (1), and he endorsed (2) at I. 1, 1094a2–3. So should he not accept E? No, because the supreme good is something of singular nature. Thus E follows from (2), given (1), only if 'pleasure' in (1) refers to just one thing. Eudoxus probably assumed that pleasure is a single reality occurring in different causal contexts. But in x. 5 (1175a21–1176b29) Ar. will stress the essential diversity of pleasures. What is common to all pleasures is an abstraction, which no being pursues.

Eudoxus' second argument (1172b18–20): (1) Pain and pleasure are contraries; (2) Pain in itself is to be avoided; therefore pleasure in itself is to be pursued. (It is assumed that what is to be pursued is good.) The conclusion falls short of E, since it claims only that pleasure in its own right is *a* good, not that it is the supreme good.

Eudoxus' third argument (1172b20–3): E follows from (1): What is most desirable is what we choose only for its own sake, together with (2): No one asks: 'For the sake of what are you enjoying yourself (taking pleasure in so-and-so)?' As before, Ar. would accept the premises, but the argument proves E only on the assumptions (i) that we choose only one thing for its own sake, and (ii) that pleasure is unitary. If (ii) is false, the argument proves the absurdity that there are as many supreme goods as there are distinct pleasures. For Ar.'s own elaboration and use of premiss (1), see I. 7, 1097a18–b6, and x. 7, 1177b19–20. Premiss (2) does not rule out the possibility of justifying doing something for pleasure by reference to some further end, as when we engage in enjoyable recreation on doctor's orders (cf. x. 6,1176b33–1177a1). The point is that taking pleasure in the activity is not itself something we decide to do for the sake of something else. Ar. will elaborate *in propria persona* on the end-like nature of pleasure in x. 5.

Eudoxus' fourth argument (1172b23–5): E follows from (1) Adding pleasure to any other kind of good G (such as just action or moderate behaviour) makes G better (more good), because (2) 'the good is increased by itself' (25). Premiss (2) is mysterious, and it is not clear how E even seems to follow. However, we know that Eudoxus held a doctrine of immanent Forms (Ar., *Metaph.* I. 9, 991a13–17), so perhaps the thought is this: goods of different kinds are all good because of the presence in them of the Good. Hence they (or perhaps even: the Good in them) can only be made better by adding more of the Good. Hence by (1) pleasure is the Good. (This metaphysical idea of the F (for any predicate 'F') as the principle of F-ness for all (other) F things goes back to Plato. Although Ar. rejects Plato's identification of the Good with a separately existing universal common to all good things (I. 6; cf. I. 4, 1095a26–8), he does not reject the metaphysical notion itself, but applies it to human happiness at I. 12, 1102a2–4.) The fourth argument, too, is flawed because it presupposes the unity of pleasure. Moreover, even if one grants that by adding pleasure you add more of the Good, this could be true not because pleasure itself is the Good, but because of the presence in it of the Good: i.e. because pleasure is *a* good, as is just action. According to Ar., (1) and (2) support only this weaker conclusion (1172b26–7).

Why, it is by this sort of argument that Plato See *Philebus*, esp. 20e–22b, 60a– 61a. Since the Good is the source of the goodness of all other goods, no other good can make *it* good or better; consequently, if pleasure with wisdom is better than pleasure alone, pleasure is not the Good. Cf. I. 7, 1097b14–20. 1172b28

What, then, is there of this nature, which we have a share in [koinōnoumen] **too?** This can be interpreted in two ways. (A) The question concerns the Good as something practicable by human beings, as distinct from the Platonic Form, or something accessible only to eternal beings (cf. Plato, *Parmenides* 133c–134d). The question arises because Ar. has just adduced Plato's argument against Eudoxus, namely that if pleasure were the Good, nothing could be added to pleasure that would make it more desirable: a criterion by which not only human pleasure falls short, but so, perhaps, does any comparable candidate such as human wisdom or excellence (1172b24, 30, 31–2). This seems to open the way for Platonists to infer that the Good is none of these perishable (and realizable) things, but something beyond the realm of change. Ar. wants to retain the Platonic criterion while rejecting the Platonist inference: his own candidate, happiness, both fits the criterion and is practicable by us (cf. I. 6, 1096b32–5, and I. 7, 1097b16–20 with comment). (B) 'we' refers to himself and those who are going along with *his* inquiry into the good, by contrast with others whose formal criterion (see above) Ar. shares, though he uses it to draw a different conclusion. 1172b34–5

Those, on the other hand, who contend that what all creatures seek is not good may well be talking nonsense ... has as its object their own proper good Although premiss (1) of Eudoxus' first argument cannot sustain the conclusion, it is a truth of great significance for ethics. For it signals that pleasure is a fundamental good: a result which any adequate ethical theory must recognize and explain. Intelligent animals would not seek pleasure if the pleasure they seek were not to their good, and in unintelligent ones the impulse towards pleasure is a natural mechanism directing them towards what is good for them. 1172b35–1173a5

But the point about the contrary ... this, then, is the way they are 1173a5–13

opposed This rebuts an objection to Eudoxus' second argument, according to which pleasure's contrariety to pain, which is bad, may be due to its being a contrary kind of bad thing (as, for example, wastefulness is contrary to avarice), or due to its being of indifferent value (as tepid, which is neither hot nor cold, is contrary to cold). Ar. cannot accept any objection to thesis E that entails the universal conclusion that pleasure is not good. At VII. 13, 1153b1–7 Ar. attributes a similar objection to Speusippus, who held that pleasure is neither good nor evil. Ar.'s rebuttal, that we pursue pleasure as if it is a good and shun pain as if it is an evil, is made on the assumption that these practical attitudes constitute evaluations which the ethical theorist ought to take seriously. The fundamental contrariety of pleasure and pain consists in their being, respectively, attractive and repulsive; hence if we respect our practical evaluations, we must conclude that the contrariety of pain to pleasure is a contrariety of evil to good.

X 3, 1173a13–1174a12

Ar. now rebuts three Academic arguments. The first two purport to show that pleasure is not a good; the third that it is not the Good.

(1) Pleasure does not fall into the category of Quality (1173a13–14). The argument may have been that if pleasure were a good, it would be a good quality; but it is not any sort of quality. Ar. responds (14–15) that happiness, the highest good, is not a quality either, since it is the *activity* of excellence (i.e. good quality; cf. I. 6, 1096a25).

(2) The good is determinate, but pleasure is indeterminate, because it admits of more and less (16–18). Ar agrees that what is good is, as such, determinate (IX. 9, 1170a20–1). His present response shows him rejecting the assumption that what admits of more and less is indeterminate (cf. *Philebus* 23c–27e). His response is: if the argument is based on 'being pleased', i.e. on taking pleasure in a given thing X—so that the point is that, for any X, one can take pleasure in X more and also less—then the argument proves too much, since excellences and excellent activities also admit of more and less (17–22; see also 23–8 on health). But if the argument is based on comparing different kinds of pleasures, the point being, for example, that the pleasure of listening to music is more of a pleasure than that of winning a hard-fought boxing match, then the argument fails to give the right explanation, which is not that pleasure as such is susceptible of less and more, but that some pleasures are, and some are not, mixed with pain, the contrary of pleasure (22–3; cf. *Philebus* 46a ff.). In any case, some things which the opponents define as 'determinate', such as health (cf. *Philebus* 25d–26a) admit of more and less (24–8).

(3) The Good is complete (or final, *teleion*), but pleasure is a movement (*kinēsis*) or a coming to be (*genesis*), and therefore is incomplete (29–31). ('Movement' covers not only locomotion, but also qualitative and quantitative change, and sometimes even coming to be and passing away.) For the argument, cf. *Philebus*

53d–54d. Ar., too, holds the Good to be complete or final (cf. I. 7, 1097a28–b6), and defines movement as 'incomplete activity' (*Physics* III. 1). But he shows (i) that pleasure in the sense of being pleased is not a movement, and (ii) that it is not a coming to be. The argument for (i) is that *quick* and *slow*, which qualify movements (cf. *Physics* VI. 2, 233b20–1), have no application to pleasure in the sense in question (1173a34–b4). The argument for (ii) rests on the assumptions (*a*) that any coming to be has the triadic structure laid out in *Physics* I. 7: it is *of Y* (the new state or thing), *from X* (the old one), and *in* a subject; and (*b*) that if pleasure is the coming to be of *Y* from *X*, pain is the opposite process, i.e. the passing away of *Y* into *X*. The theorists whom Ar. is opposing held that pleasure is the coming to be of a state of natural satiety from a state of lack, which is pain (b7–8). Thus they identified pain with *X*, which infringes (*b*). (They should care about this mistake, since they draw a fundamental distinction between a process and its *terminus ad quem*: this is the basis of their claim that pleasure is incomplete.) And since the states they had in mind were states of the body, they must regard the body as subject of the coming to be that is pleasure. But this implies that pleasure is an attribute of the *body*, which does not seem right (8–11). Moreover, pleasures of the mind and of sensory cognition do not presuppose any painful lack which they proceed to fill (15–20).

Ar. considers two further arguments aiming to show that in general pleasure is not a good.

(4) There are reprehensible pleasures (1173b20–1). Ar. offers a variety of responses. (i) Reprehensible pleasures are not pleasures properly speaking; they are merely pleasures *for* their ill-conditioned subjects (21–5; see note on 5, 1176a12–24). (ii) By the same token wealth and health are not goods, since one can come by them, too, in disgraceful ways (25–8). (iii) Pleasures from fine things and from inferior ones differ in kind, and are available respectively only to persons of the corresponding character (28–1174a4). (Thus if there are bad pleasures, this is not because of the nature of pleasure as such, but because there are persons of inferior character.) Reply (iii) does not sit well with (ii), where pleasure is assimilated to an external good whose specific kind does not depend on the character of whoever has it. At this stage, however, Ar. is pointing out flaws in existing opinions, rather than constructing his own.

(5) There are many things we should value even if they brought no pleasure (1174a4–8). This is undeniable, but all it shows is that there are goods other than pleasure.

it seems to be characteristic of every movement to be quick or slow, and if   *1173a32–3*
not in itself, as e.g. the movement of the cosmos, then in relation to something else   In general, one stage of a thing's movement between two termini may be faster than another: this is the movement's being quick or slow 'in itself'. However, the movement of the cosmos (the revolution of the circle of fixed stars) cannot speed up or slow down; but it can still be said to be quick or slow by comparison with some other movement.

X 4–5, 1174a13–1176a29

Ar.'s positive account of pleasure. It has three main tenets: (I) pleasure is something complete or perfect (*teleios*; 1174a14–b14); (II) pleasure completes or perfects (*teleioi*) good activity; (1174b14–1175a21); (III) pleasures are as diverse as activities in kind and in ethical quality (1175a21–1176a29).

I. Pleasure is something complete or perfect (1174a14–b14)

Ar. proposes the *completeness* of pleasure as the reason why pleasure is not a movement towards, or a coming to be of, something beyond itself. He compares pleasure with the activity of seeing, of which the form or nature (*eidos*; also translated 'kind') is complete at every moment of the time the seeing lasts (1174a14–19). (What I saw may have been incomplete, e.g. a show interrupted by bad weather, but my seeing of what I did see was not therefore lacking in anything required for it to count, fully, as seeing.) By contrast, a process ('movement') such as a temple's getting built is essentially incomplete as long as its object remains unfinished. (The completeness of pleasure in this sense does not entail that pleasure is necessarily always at a maximum; cf. 3, 1173a15–28. The point is that taking pleasure in something is not the gradual accomplishing of some end beyond the pleasure. On the completeness of seeing, and the contrast with movement, see also *Metaph.* IX. 6.)

1174a21 **So that will be either in the whole time, or in this** [sc. the moment of completion] It is not clear whether the temporal location of a complete movement is the whole time (*chronos*) it takes or the final moment, but either way the movement is incomplete while still going on. This is because the form or nature (*eidos*) of a movement (by contrast with that of an activity) is given by a pair of termini ('the where from/where to'), 1174b5. These define an interval within which the movement is as yet incomplete.

1174a21–b5 **But if it is divided up into temporal parts, ... determines the form** This passage seems intended to forestall the objection that as a movement goes on, its successive stages (except for the last, however one identifies that) are completed; hence the movement is made up of complete constituents, and the contrast with pleasure is no longer compelling. In response, Ar. emphasizes (*a*) the incompleteness of the individual stages (1174a22, 26, b4), and (*b*) their difference in character from each other and from the whole (1174a22–b2). The meaning of (*a*) may be either (*a*1) that each stage, like the whole movement, is incomplete while it is going on; or/and (*a*2) that each stage (except for the last) is incomplete *even when completed* in a way in which the whole is not, since the real goal of each earlier stage is not its own completion but that of the whole movement. Both (*a*1) and (*a*2) refute the attempt to reduce an ongoing movement to completed elements. The point of emphasizing (*b*) is perhaps that since the stages are not merely small-scale versions of the entire process (since each is characterized by its own pair of termini) completeness on the level of stages, even if it were admitted, would not justify calling the ongoing whole complete.

the triglyph   A decorative element in the frieze of a Doric temple.   *1174a26*

flying, walking, leaping, and so on   A biologist's classification of locomotion.   *1174a31*

nor is crossing this line the same thing as crossing that one   The lines marked   *1174a34*
stages on the race-track. Since the lines are differently located (b1–2), every pair of lines constitutes a distinct 'where from / where to'.

a precise account of movement has been given elsewhere   In *Physics* III. 1–3;   *1174b2–3*
V; VI.

And this would also seem to follow from the fact that it is not possible to   *1174b7–9*
move, while it is possible to be pleased, without taking time [*mē en chronōi*];
for what occurs in the now [*to nun*] **is a whole of some kind**   Here we
have what purports to be a new reason for holding that pleasure is not a movement, and is something whole and complete (6–7). It turns on the Aristotelian
contrast between *now*, which is a durationless instant, and *a time*, which is a
divisible length bounded by successive 'nows' (*Physics* IV. 10–14). Presumably the
argument is: experience shows that (1) pleasure can hit all at once in an instant
(e.g. joy in the instantaneous event of seeing one's favourite athlete finish first);
it follows that (2) getting pleased does not require a length of time; but (3)
movement in a now is impossible (see *Physics* VI. 3); therefore . . .

For one does not talk of a movement or coming to be of everything . . .   *1174b10–14*
because it is a kind of whole   One reason why pleasure is not a movement or a
coming to be, namely that it occurs completely all at once, is also a reason for
holding that there is no coming to be *of* pleasure (13). Aristotle understands
coming to be as a gradual development whose temporal stages correspond to
different stages of completeness in the product. The 'of' is logically different in
'there is no movement of pleasure', which means that there is no movement of
which pleasure is subject in the way Socrates is subject of walking from gym-
nasium to lawcourts. This is because for Ar. only objects with spatial magnitude
can be subjects of movement ('in movement')' strictly speaking; see *Physics* VI. 4.

II. Pleasure completes or perfects good activity (1174b14–1175a21)

(*a*) Ar. has used the activity of *seeing* as an obvious example of something
which neither is a movement towards, or a coming to be of, something else
(1174a14–17) nor is built up through one (1174b12). The comparison may
suggest that pleasure, too, is an activity. Ar. now corrects this impression,
arguing that pleasure is what *perfects* an activity such as seeing. (*b*) The
activities he considers are essentially conscious ones; cf. *On the Soul* III. 2; *NE*
IX. 9, 1170a14–b10; and VII. 12, 1153a12–15 with note ad loc. (*c*) When such
an activity gives us pleasure, it is because it is good of its kind (1174b14–
1175a3). (*d*) It does not seem that he is committed to the view that, when

435

asked *what* we are enjoying, we should strictly speaking always mention our own activity. The statements that pleasure is *in* the activity, and that the activity is pleasant (e.g. 4, 1174b20, 1175a1), can be understood as assigning the pleasure a metaphysical location; in which case they are consistent with our not even being aware of the underlying activity, but aware only of what we are seeing, hearing, etc.

1174b23–6 **pleasure does not complete it in the same way . . . causes in the same way of being healthy**   Pleasure does not render the activity complete or perfect in the way the excellent object and excellent sense-faculty do, i.e. as preconditions of perfect functioning. And whereas each of them helps perfect the activity because it is good of its kind, this is not so of pleasure, since if a pleasure is good this is because the associated activity is (see 5, 1175b24–1176a29). Thus 'completes/ perfects' covers different kinds of relations, as does 'because of' in 'X is healthy because of <the previous healing action of> the doctor' (efficient causality) and 'X is healthy because of <the presence in him of> health' (formal causality). (Scholars have struggled with the gratuitous question 'In which of the various causal modes does pleasure stand to the activity, according to this passage?' But the passage simply illustrates the ambiguity of 'completes/perfects' by pointing to the presumably more familiar ambiguity of 'cause'.) However, it is not yet clear whether, given an activity guaranteed by the excellences of its subject and object to be a complete/perfect example of its type, the pleasure in it is (*a*) just that completeness of the activity as such, or (*b*) a completion/perfection additional to the latter although inseparable from it. (This is a matter of metaphysical detail that makes little difference for ethics, which is perhaps why Ar. touches on it only briefly and in passing, at 5, 1175b32–5.)

1174b31–3 **Pleasure completes . . . as a sort of supervenient end, like the bloom of manhood on those in their prime**   This seems to tell in favour of (*b*) above. However, the point of 'a sort of supervenient end' (*epiginomenon ti telos*; see also 1175b21–2) may be not that pleasure is distinct from the activity, even if this is assumed to be so, but that although end-like (cf. 2, 1172b20–3), it is not a goal in its own right; it can be attained only by aiming to make the activity as good of its kind as possible.

1175a3–10 Why is pleasure not continuous? This is easily explained if pleasure is the replenishment of a lack, or is essentially dependent on such a process. But on Ar.'s theory, the paradigmatically pleasurable activities have no built-in terminus marking the completion of what was previously incomplete. They can go on and on unless interrupted from outside, so why do we cease to enjoy them after a while? The answer is 'fatigue'. (For a different answer, see VII. 4, 1154b20–6 with note.)

1175a10–20 Why is pleasure universally desired? Since Ar. rejects the explanation that Eudoxus might give (Eudoxus might think that the universal desire for it not only proves pleasure's status as the supreme good (2, 1172b9–15) but is somehow explained thereby), he must offer an alternative: activity is life; the living desire to be as alive as possible; therefore it makes sense (*eulogōs*, 16) that they should also desire pleasure as the perfection of activity and life. (On cognitive activities as modes of being alive, cf. *On the Soul* II. 2–3.) Ar. sets aside the question of the exact relation between desiring vital activity and desiring pleasure (18–19). From a scientific standpoint he may think that pleasure and the desire for it are nature's mechanisms for ensuring that a living being does engage in its proper vital activities (cf. 2, 1173a4–5). But this makes pleasure subserve activity, which might seem to conflict with the doctrine that pleasure is end-like.

III. The diversity of pleasures (1175a21–1176a29)
Since activities differ in kind (*eidos*), so do the associated pleasures. For (1) what completes one kind of thing is as different from what completes another as the things from each other (1175a21–8). And (2) what belongs to (*oikeios*; sometimes translated as '[something]'s own') one kind of thing is as different from what belongs to another (*allotrios*) as they are from each other. That pleasures belong to activities is shown by the fact that a given activity is strengthened by taking pleasure in it, since what strengthens X belongs to X (29–b1). (But Ar. should explain how, if pleasure supervenes on activity (4, 1174b31), it also strengthens it.) That pleasures differ in kind is also shown by the fact (3) that the pleasure that belongs to an activity is inimical to an activity of another kind (hence the pleasure that belongs to the latter differs correspondingly; 1175b1–24).

the lover of music, or of building   Getting a particular edifice built is one of Ar.'s   *1175a34*
favourite examples of 'movement' (cf. *Physics* III. 1), the structure of which is antithetical to that of pleasure (see ch. 4); but there is no inconsistency in his allowing that one can get pleasure from exercising one's skill in an activity of that sort.

For a pleasure that belongs to another activity has much the same effect as   *1175b16–17*
an activity's own [*oikeios*] **pain**   The pain belonging to an activity is one's specific dislike of it.

But since activities differ in goodness and worthlessness . . .   A desire derives its   *1175b24ff.*
worth from the worth of the activity desired. A fortiori, a pleasure derives its worth from that of the activity, since the relation of pleasure to activity that pleases is more intimate (28–33). Some people (e.g. Ar. himself in VII. 11–14) actually identify them, even though it is absurd to say that pleasure in thinking or seeing etc. *is* thinking or seeing etc. (Presumably the absurdity is of the same general kind as proves that pleasure is not process. Just as one cannot apply 'quick' and 'slow' to pleasure, so one cannot apply to it the typical characteristics of thinking and seeing, e.g. 'true/false', 'clear/dim'. In Book VII Ar. does not use the quickly/slowly argument against the doctrine of pleasure as process.)

At 1175b36–1176a3 Ar. ranks pleasures by ranking cognitive activities in order of 'purity'. Sight and hearing are superior to touch and taste, intellectual activities to sensory, one kind of thinking (purely reflective) to another (practical). The degrees of purity are degrees of independence from physical involvement with the object of cognition; such independence is assumed to carry greater cognitive refinement. Purity is also a property of the corresponding pleasures; cf. x. 7, 1177a25–6 on the superior purity of philosophical pleasures.

The connections between life, activity and pleasure entail that each kind of living being has its own kind of pleasure (1176a2–8). But why then are the same things pleasurable to some human beings and distressing to others (1176a10–12)? If there is no one kind of pleasure characteristic of human beings, we may have to question the link just forged between pleasure and activity, or else question Ar.'s fundamental doctrine that there is an activity distinctive of man (i. 7, 1097b24–1098a8). Ar. tries to settle this by distinguishing pleasures in an unqualified sense, and relative pleasures. Honey may taste bitter to a sick person, but the healthy man's judgement is the authoritative one. Similarly with the pleasure-judgements of the morally stunted or corrupt versus those of the virtuous. Ignoble pleasures are not *pleasant* (i.e. pleasant without qualification), but only *pleasant-for* those who enjoy them (12–24; see vii. 12, 1152b25 ff. with comment, and Introduction, pp. 72–3). In this way Ar. reduces the apparent diversity of human *pleasures*.

The theory explains why many human beings are unmoved by the higher pleasures even though these are proper to our species (1176a28): they can only be experienced by those who engage in the corresponding activities (cf. 6, 1176b19–21; 9, 1179b15–16), and engage in them well. But to engage well in activities of reason presupposes intellectual qualities which have to be cultivated. The theory also goes some way, though not far enough, towards explaining why people are captivated by baser pleasures. It is because they have not developed the bent for higher activities, but must find pleasure somehow, since the desire for it is inseparable from the will to live.

1176a6–7 **as Heraclitus says** DK fragment 9.

X 6–8, 1176a30–1179a32

Ar. returns to the question of happiness (6, 1176a30–1), defined in i. 7 as 'rational activity of excellence in a complete life' (1098a16–17). That was only an outline (1098a20 ff.) which has now largely been filled in with detailed discussions of the character-excellences wisdom, friendship, and pleasure. So far it seems clear that the happy human being is one who lives a good and active *practical* life, blessed with friends and sufficient property. But nothing has yet been said about the non-practical excellence of intellectual accomplishment (*sophia*). By classifying this as a human excellence (i. 13, 1103a4–10; cf. vi. 12, 1144a5), Ar. has already hinted at its vital connection with happiness. That connection is the topic of x. 7–8, with ch. 6 providing a preparatory argument.

But it is a problematic connection. This much is obvious from Book VI, where intellectual accomplishment is shown to be fundamentally different from practical wisdom. Whereas wisdom is inseparable from the excellences of character (VI. 12, 1144a7–b1), it can hardly have escaped Ar. that someone might be intellectually accomplished without being wise (and vice versa). By ordinary intuitions, then as now, someone who is intellectually accomplished, but cowardly or unjust or atrociously bad-tempered, may be admirable in a way, but is not a good human being. So how is Ar. justified in classifying intellectual accomplishment as a human excellence at all, given that human excellence is what makes good human beings (II. 6, 1106a15–23)? Yet in x. 7–8 he seems to imply that the intellectually accomplished individual stands, as such, higher than the unintellectual wise one. For intellectual accomplishment is the excellence of the best element in us (7, 1177a11–20). And he argues that the activity of intellectual accomplishment, carried on in a full span of life, is 'the complete happiness of a human being' (7, 1177b24–5). Hence a full span characterized by that sort of activity is the happiest human life, whereas one characterized by excellent practical activity is only 'second happiest' (7–8, 1178a7–9).

Since x. 6–8 relies on positions developed in Book I, we cannot suppose that Ar. simply changed his mind about the nature of happiness. In fact, references in Book I to 'the best and most complete excellence' (7, 1098a16–18) and 'the one best activity' (8, 1099a29–31) seem with hindsight to prefigure the conclusions of x. 7–8. So why is it not already stated in Book I that happiness has two forms, higher and lower? Or that the supreme human good lies in purely reflective activity? Why is the reflective life mentioned there only to be put aside (I. 5, 1096a4–5)? And why, if the supreme good is essentially a matter of reflection disengaged from practice, is the *NE* in general so preoccupied with practical excellence?

On the first three questions, which go together: we can only guess at Ar.'s reasons for his indirectness in Book I, while noting the rhetorical effect of saving the dichotomy of happiness to the end. A slow climb brings us to the previously hidden view of a greater mountain beyond our mountain. The fourth question is not a puzzle unless we assume that the general fact (which seems clear) that intellectual accomplishment can coexist with undesirable practical and ethical qualities is a reason for supposing that Ar. (unless he shuts his eyes to that fact) thinks that this is true *of the intellectual accomplishment of his Book X paragon*. On this, see the Introduction, pp. 79–80.

x. 6–8 harks back to the three lives each proclaimed best by its supporters: that of 'pleasure' vulgarly understood; of political involvement; and of reflection (I. 5 (1095b14–1096a10)). The happiest *life* will be the one whose characteristic *activity* best deserves the title 'complete happiness'. But what is it for an activity to characterize a life? We need not assume a relationship in which the activity fills every waking moment of the corresponding life, or (slightly less unrealistically) functions as the sole ultimate end of actions.

439

For a life or a person to be stamped 'reflective', 'political', etc., it is enough that the relevant activity be a conspicuous life-shaping concern. In fact, we are probably to think of the special lifestyles as options for those whose ordinary responsibilities allow for considerable leisure (cf. 6, 1176b28–33; 7, 1177b4–6). Vulgar pleasures are said to be the leisure-occupations of tyrants (6, 1176b16–17), and the political person is portrayed as busy when he might have been at leisure (7, 1177b12–18). Leisure is the opportunity for 'honourable' as distinct from 'necessary' activities (*Politics* VII. 14, 1333a15 ff.; cf. *NE* I. 12 on happiness as honourable). Thus our choice of leisure-activity, whether we realize it or not, expresses our sense of what is honourable. At VIII. 9 leisure is associated with religious celebration. Our choice of leisure-activity also expresses our idea of 'heaven', since at leisure we are free of mortal toil. So our use of leisure attests to our highest value, in a sense of 'highest' that does not entail that everything else we do should be subordinate to the activity.

Arguing from non-controversial criteria, several of which have appeared in I. 7–8 and 12 (happiness must be an activity that is desirable only for itself, pleasant, an end worth striving for, serious (or worth while), fine, honourable, continuous, self-sufficient, and leisurely), Ar. dismisses vulgar pleasures (ch. 6), and ranks reflective thought above political activity (ch. 7). In ch. 8 he compares these two in respect of dependence on external goods (1178a23–b7); theologizes to show that the reflective thinker's 'idea of heaven' is the most plausible (1178b7–27); and invokes the support of respected opinions and 'lived facts' (1179a8–22). The *NE*'s discussion of happiness then ends with a proof that the intellectually accomplished exemplar is 'most loved by the gods'—another reason for counting him happiest (1179a22–32).

X 6, 1176a30–1177a11

1176a31 **in outline** Cf. 9, 1179a34. (1) Ar. skirts topics where close discussion goes beyond ethics; e.g. 8, 1178a22–3, on the separateness of intellect. And (2) his account of complete happiness may be meant to allow for new applications. See note on 8, 1178b28, and Introduction, pp. 80–1.

1176a32–3 **what was said earlier** In Book I. See 5, 1095b31–1096a1; 8, 1098b31–1099a2 (activity, 1176a33–b2); 7, 1097a30–b21 (desirable for its own sake, self-sufficient, lacking in nothing, 1176b2–7, and again at x. 7, 1177a27–b1, and 8, 1178a23–b3); 8, 1099a7–16 (pleasant, 1176b9; x. 7, 1177a22–7).

1176b8–9 **doing what is fine and worth while** [*spoudaios*; also means 'serious'] **is one of the things desirable because of themselves. Also thought to be of this kind are the pleasant forms of amusement** [*paidia*, from *pais*, 'child'].

1176b24–5 **as has often been said** e.g. at 5, 1176a15–19.

For we value almost everything, except happiness, for the sake of something   *1176b30–1*
else   '*almost* everything, except happiness', because we value excellent activity
for its own sake, even when not in a complete life; cf. I. 10, 1100b19–1101a6.

Anacharsis   A legendary sage. The adage brings out the difference, easily   *1176b33*
missed, between relaxation and leisure. Relaxation is *from* toilsome work; leisure
should be *for* a kind of work that is not toilsome. Relaxation is the sphere of
wittiness, the excellence whose sphere is fun; see IV. 8 (1127b33–1128b9). On right
and wrong uses of leisure, see *Politics* VII. 14, 1333a16 ff., and ch. 15.

just anyone . . . unless he also has a share in life   On bodily pleasures as slavish,   *1177a6–9*
cf. I. 5, 1095b19–20. The slave *qua* slave lacks a human life (VIII. 11, 1161b2–6), and
humans alone (apart from the gods) are capable of happiness (8, 1178b24; I. 9,
1099b32–1100a1).

X 7, 1177a12–1178a8
Whether, then, this is intelligence [*nous*] or something else, this element that   *1177a13–16*
is thought naturally to rule and guide, and to possess awareness of fine things
and divine ones   whether being, itself too, something divine, or the divinest
of the things in us   (*a*) The intelligence that is the subject of this sentence is
both practical (ruling and guiding) and theoretical (its objects are eternal entities).
(This is different from the doctrine of VI. 1, 1139a3 ff., which postulates two parts
of the rational soul, corresponding to the two types of object / concern.) Having
identified the highest element in us as that which naturally rules and guides etc.,
Ar. goes on to argue that its '*own proper* [*oikeios*] excellence' is of a non-practical
nature. The phrase means the excellence that the highest element would still be
able to exercise even if (*per impossibile* for the human case) it were separated from
the non-rational part of the soul (hence had nothing beneath it to rule and guide).
This excellence does not include the practical one of wisdom (*phronēsis*), which is
bound up with the excellences of the non-rational part (cf. 8, 1178a14–21). Behind
all this is the following thought: in the practical sphere, intelligence (or whatever
one calls it) is the natural ruler not because ruling is simply what this element is
for, as the stomach is for digesting food, but because it is 'better and more
honourable' than anything non-rational; i.e. its entitlement to rule rests on something about it beyond the fact that ruling is a task it does well. This yields
the notion of the highest element in us as being also the potential subject of
some activity other than ruling. (*b*) Ar. leaves it open whether our highest element
is in fact intelligence or 'something else'; also whether it actually *is* divine (*theios*)
or an approximation. Cf. *EE* VII. 14 (= VIII. 2), 1248a20–9, which identifies
god as the source of human rational inspiration; also Simplicius' observation
(= Aristotle, F 49 R³) that in Ar.'s work *On Prayer* (lost to us) god is said to be
either intelligence or something even beyond intelligence.

That it is *reflective* (*theōretikē*) activity has been said   (*a*) The closest Ar. has   *1177a17–18*
come to saying this in the *Ethics* is VI. 7, 1141b2–8. The reference might be to the

441

Protrepticus (one of his early works, surviving only in part) B43 and B66–70 (Düring). (*b*) We should not assume that at this point in the *NE*, before the comparison of the best lives is fully under way, Ar.'s audience understood '*theōrētikos*' quite as we understand 'theoretical', i.e. as sharply contrasted with any kind of practical thinking. The fact that the common books (see Introduction, pp. 4–5) may not belong with the original *NE* is relevant here, since it means that the audience for whom Ar. wrote *NE* x may not have had the benefit of the division of thinking into (mutually exclusive) practical, productive, and 'reflective' (*theōrētikos*) that we find in the second common book = *NE* vi (2, 1139a27–b1). And even in the common books Ar. freely uses the verb '*theōrein*' for active reflection in general (e.g. *NE* vi. 4, 1140a11 (technical–productive); 7, 1141a25 (practical); vii. 3, 1146b33–5 (theoretic–scientific; also practical, of the particular premiss)). x. 7–8 is a place where the notion of purely theoretical thinking gets carved out (see also *Metaph.* i. 1–2).

1177a20   **the objects of intelligence are the highest knowables**   For example, the 'constituents of the universe' (vi. 7, 1141a34–b7). For a systematic discussion of true intellectual acccomplishment and its subject matter, see *Metaph.* i. 1–2.

1177a21   **the most continuous**   Because least fatiguing, since the body is minimally involved.

1177a25–7   **the love of it** [*philosophia*].   According to its root meaning, 'philosophy' is prizing of intellectual accomplishment (*sophia*). The former, an attitude one must have in order to become intellectually accomplished, is here exhibited as a learner's attitude. Ar.'s argument is a fortiori: if the activities of *philosophia* are extraordinarily pleasant, those of achieved accomplishment must be superlatively so. (The activities of *philosophia*, like those of other 'loves', such as love of art, love of football, love of wine, will include eager discussion of criteria for excellence in the field, and indeed for what counts as belonging to the field. So far as they are activities of learners, they depend to some extent on teachers, hence are less self-sufficient than those of full-blown accomplishment.)

1177a27–b1   **Again, the talked-about self-sufficiency ... he will be most self-sufficient**   Here Ar. distinguishes what is necessary simply to live from what practitioners of the different kinds of excellence require for their respective fine activities. In terms of the first, the intellectually accomplished are on a par with everyone else; in terms of the second they are far more independent.

1177b8   **warlike ones ... lack it** [the element of leisure] **utterly**   The point is not simply that warlike activities leave one with no leisure, but that they are utterly unsuitable occupants of leisure left over from anything else.

1177b12–15   **the politician's activity ... aims beyond the business of politics itself—at getting power, or honours, or indeed happiness for himself and his fellow-citizens, this being distinct from the exercise of political expertise**   On happiness (whether for one or many) as the proper goal of politics, see I. 2, 1094a26–b10. Does the point made here contradict x. 6, 1176b6–11, where fine activities in general, including (presumably) political ones, are characterized by 'nothing is sought from them over and above the activity' (6–7)? No, because even if the best reason for engaging in politics is that the activity in itself is worth while, once you do engage, you are committed to pursuing particular political goals (such as getting certain legislation passed) where a successful result depends on factors besides your own activity.

while the activity of intelligence seems both to possess a greater seriousness, being reflective, and to aim at no end beside itself   (*a*) This does not imply that intelligence is not active in practical thinking too; by '*the* activity of intelligence' he means the activity of its own proper excellence. See 1177a17, with comment on 1177a13–16. (*b*) The comparison in respect of 'seriousness' (*spoudē*) is, presumably, with 'pleasant forms of amusement', considered against 'worth while' or 'serious' (*spoudaios*) activities at 6, 1176b8–10. (The connections between excellence and seriousness are presumably as follows: (i) Achieving excellence at X requires serious application to X; (ii) if X offers no purchase for serious application (e.g. what is important in X is random, or all on the surface), there can be no excellence regarding X; (iii) being good at X, even when effort is needed, counts as an excellence (unqualified) if and only if X is 'worth while', i.e. unconditionally merits serious application.) (*c*) It seems fairly clear that reflecting about something is a way or a part of being serious about it; thus the activity called 'reflective' par excellence is, as such, serious and worth while (since its objects are assumed to be such as reward that sort of attention).

1177b19–20

***this* activity will be the complete happiness of man ... in so far as there is something divine in him**   A paradox. The completely happy *human* life is *higher than human*, because the human being is not just human, since the best element in us is similar to the divine (just as a slave is not only a slave, but human: see VIII. 11, 1161b5–8). However, human beings tend to identify with their best and ruling element (1178a3; cf. IX. 4, 1166a16–17, 22–3; 8, 1168b28–33); so when philosophy explains that this part of *us*, though mainly occupied with practical things, is most truly itself when detached and purely reflective, we may look upon this activity as godlike, but we cannot consistently regard it as not our human business too.

1177b24–8

the compound   Either: of intelligence with an animal body (from which it follows that intelligence is joined to a non-rational level of soul); or: of intelligence with (immediately) a non-rational level of soul.

1177b28–9

in accordance with the rest of excellence   See note on 8, 1178a9.

1177b29

even if it is small in bulk, the degree to which it surpasses everything in power and dignity is far greater   (*a*) 'Small in bulk', i.e. in volume or power of occupancy. The point is probably that in the uncultivated soul, activity of the

1177b34– 1178a2

443

non-rational side is much more likely to block activity of intelligence than vice versa. 'Far greater' suggests that far more injustice is done to intelligence if its operation is not allowed to prevail than is done to the non-rational side by silencing its *naturally* louder voice. (*b*) The 'power' of intelligence is perhaps the capacity by which Ar. defines it in *On the Soul* III. 4: that of 'thinking all things'. (*c*) The phrase 'surpasses . . . in power and dignity' (*dunamei kai timiotēti . . . huperechei*) recalls *Republic* VI, 509b9–10, '*presbeiai kai dunamei huperechontos*', referring to the Form of the Good).

X 8, 1178a9–1179a33

1178a9 **But second happiest is the life [*bios*] in accordance with the rest of excellence** That there is a plurality of *happiest* lives suggests that the class of happy lives can be divided between merely happy and outstandingly so. The outstanding kinds are the two whose claims to exemplify 'complete happiness' can be taken seriously (although only one of the claims is true).

Between chs. 7 and 8 Ar. seems to waver about the activity characteristic of the second-happiest life. At 8, 1178a27 the person who lives this life is said to be 'political', but whereas the political activity considered in ch. 7 was outstanding 'in fineness and greatness' (1177b17), in ch. 8 the second-happiest life is described in humdrum fashion as 'in accordance with the rest of excellence' (i.e. the practical excellences). This description (given the natural assumption that the second-happiest life is an *alternative* to the one that outranks it) has helped create the impression that, for Ar., ordinary practical excellent activity is not part of the ideal life of intellectual accomplishment. (To avoid this conclusion some scholars have held that the life 'in accordance with the rest of excellence' is not an alternative to the life of the ideal intellectual master, but is the practical aspect of that same person's existence. (In this sense we speak today of someone's having a family life and also a professional life etc.) Thus the same paragon lives both the happiest lives. But there is no linguistic warrant for taking '*bios*' to mean one aspect of a many-sided existence.) However, characterizing the second-happiest life by reference to 'the rest of excellence' does not imply that practical excellent activity is missing from the supremely happy human life. Its presence there is not emphasized because it is not what distinguishes this life. By contrast, activity in accordance with 'the rest of excellence' *only* (i.e. the whole of excellence except intellectual accomplishment) does distinguish the life called second happiest.

But why, having previously characterized the latter (the political life) as one of outstanding public achievements, does Ar. now describe it in low-key terms that would apply to a life of ordinary practical happiness? It is because his argument in x. 7–8 proceeds in two stages. (1) At 7, 1177b26 he reaches the conclusion that purely reflective activity is superior to its only serious rival to the title 'complete happiness'. Then (2) at 7–8, 1177b26–1178b32 he expounds the nature of this superiority: it is that of the divine to the merely human (or secular). (There is an interlude at 7, 1177b31–1178a7 defending the human relevance of the theoretical ideal.) In stage (1) purely reflective activity is compared with that of the great leader—a much more familiar ideal; cf. Anaxagoras' saying at 8, 1179a15—and is proved superior by a set of criteria which it satisfies more fully, although the other satisfies them, too, up to a point. Here, the more familiar ideal in all its brilliance sets the base line for appreciating its rival's greater perfection. In stage (2) the focus is on the mundane or metaphysically 'compound' nature of *all* practical activity, which is why it is inferior *in kind* to the theoretical. From the point of view of this contrast, differences of degree within each kind are not important.

for activities in accordance with this are human   It is not clear whether this is   *1178a9–10*
meant as a justification of 'second' or of 'happiest' in 'second happiest' from the previous line. If the former, the point is that these activities are *merely* human, as opposed to godlike. If the latter, it is that they *are* human, even though not godlike; i.e. the doctrine that purely reflective activity is both godlike and characteristically human is not to be understood as entailing that any lower activity is subhuman and therefore cannot count as 'happiness' (cf. I. 9, 1099b32–1100a1; x. 8, 1178b27–8). It is, presumably, the undividedly human quality of the practical excellences that supports the intuition that an intellectually accomplished human being who lacks wisdom and the virtues of character is a worse *human being* than the wise person who lacks intellectual accomplishment. (But a wise person who promotes intellectual accomplishment when possible is a better human being than one who neglects such opportunities, since the preference itself is *practical*, showing wisdom (VI. 13, 1145a6–9) and perhaps also greatness of soul (IV. 3, 1123a34–1125a35).)

separate   This means, minimally, that intelligence can be defined without refer-   *1178a22*
ence to the body or to the non-rational part of the soul. See *On the Soul* III. 4–5.

For let the requirement . . . living a human life   This repeats the argument at 7,   *1178a25–b7*
1177a27–34, adding the points that responsibilities of wealth impede theoretical activity (1178b4–5); and that since the intellectually accomplished paragon chooses to exercise the practical excellences, he needs the external wherewithal (1178b3–7). 'chooses' (*haireitai*) at 1178b6 does not imply that the choice lacks warmth or might easily have gone otherwise; the cognate *hairetos* is regularly translated 'desirable'.

like Endymion   A beautiful youth loved by the Moon. He was given immortal-   *1178b19–20*
ity but on condition of suspended animation, since he is in eternal sleep.

Another indication of this is . . . share in reflection [*theōria*]   The argument is: *1178b24–8*
(1) human beings are the only mortal animals capable of happiness, and the only ones capable of reflection for its own sake; hence (2) the capacities are the same (or the first is based on the second); hence (3) purely reflective activity (which is closest in nature to the divine life; cf. 23) is man's greatest happiness. The argument assumes that practical intelligence is not exclusively human. In Ar.'s biological works a sort of non-rational practical cunning is ascribed to various subhuman species; see also *NE* VI. 7, 1141a25–8, and *Metaph.* I. 1, 980a27–b25. According to the present argument, human happiness can take a practical form

too only because the activity of practical reason is 'some kind of semblance' of purely reflective activity (26–7). It is like it in respect of the criteria for happiness, which it fulfils to a lesser degree.

1178b28–9   **So happiness too extends as far as reflection does**   This may refer to (1) the proportion of time someone spends on reflection (this by contrast with the gods, whose happiness is coextensive with their life, 25–6). But the context equally suggests reference to (2) a range of kinds of activity which the term 'reflection' can cover. In that case, the point is that grounds for calling an activity 'reflection' are grounds for calling it 'happiness'. Thus Ar. can concede that divine reflection may be immeasurably different from that of the human philosopher or scientist, and that human reflection, hence also happiness, might take forms not considered in the *Ethics*.

1178b29–30   **and to those who have more of reflection more happiness belongs too**   If 'have more of reflection' means 'reflect for more time', the clause repeats line 28 on interpretation (1) of the latter (see previous note). But it may mean 'reflect in a way worthier of the name of reflecting' (i.e. closer to the divine paradigm; see 1178b24–8 with note).

1178b33–   Here Ar. shows how the reflective ideal reconciles the accepted views that happi-
1179a16   ness is (1) fine activity, and (2) best suited by moderate prosperity. The conclusion will be drawn by those who understand that perfect human happiness is godlike, and that it makes no sense to imagine the gods as holding high office or enjoying magnificent material possessions.

1179a9ff.   **And Solon too ... when he said**   The pluperfects reporting Solon's words reflect his refusal to call anyone happy before death. 'as he saw it' may distance Ar. either from this part of Solon's view or from his conception of 'the finest' things. Solon's examples in the story are all, of course, practical. (See I. 10 (1100a10–1101a21), and the note on 1100a11.)

1179a13–14   **Anaxagoras too seems to have taken the happy man not to be a rich one, or a politically powerful one**   See note on VI. 7, 1141b3–4, for Anaxagoras, and below *ad* 1179a22–32.

1179a17   **of the wise**   The Greek is '*sophoi*', here used colloquially.

1179a17–22   **These sorts of considerations too, then, do carry a certain conviction; but in the practical sphere the truth is determined on the basis of the way life is actually lived; for this is decisive**   'These sorts of considerations' are such facts as that the views of Solon and Anaxagoras chime in with Ar.'s own conclusions. This kind of confirmation is then contrasted with a different kind, where the touchstone is not reputable beliefs but the way people live their lives. Who are the people concerned? They cannot just be Solon and Anaxagoras (if these are still in the discussion at all); certainly these figures chose lives that fitted their words, but what we have here is quite general. Given his pessimism about 'the many' (see e.g. 9, 1179b10–16), Ar. cannot mean that his conclusions must be judged against the way people around us live. The meaning must be that those for whom he is writing are to check his conclusions against their own lives. That is, he exploits the fact that the question whether these conclusions are true is pragmatically equivalent to the question whether one should accept them. Since the 'well brought up' (cf. I. 4, 1095b4–6) will not tolerate serious divergence between what they think they should accept and what they do accept, especially concerning the human good, the question then becomes, for each, 'Do I accept these conclusions?' Given that, at this stage, the soundness of Ar.'s arguments is not an issue, the question can only be answered by considering what sort of life one is in fact committed to. If it is definitely of a sort that does not, in some way, honour the reflective ideal, then one has arrived at the answer that the conclusions are not true. In effect, then, one rejects the arguments as 'mere words' (1179a2), i.e. as not saying anything that *should* make a difference to 'real life'. This, of course, makes it true that, as far as oneself is concerned, they will turn out to have been 'mere words' in the sense of *actually* making no difference. Again: if one does not question the soundness of the arguments, yet shrugs off any practical implications, then it turns out that all along one has been someone who, in Ar.'s much earlier words, 'will not be an appropriate listener to discussion about what is fine and just, i.e. about the objects of political expertise in general', a deficiency which Ar. immediately connected with not being well brought up (I. 4, 1095b4–6). Presumably, then, he relies on his audience's self-respect to make it harder for them not to take his present conclusions with practical seriousness. (There is no need to assume that taking them seriously in this way means, for each listener, that he or she is personally headed for a career of reflection; it is enough if each is willing to support such activity in the city-state.)

And the person whose intelligence is active, and who devotes himself to intelligence . . . in this way too it is the intellectually accomplished person who will be happy to the highest degree   The preceding passage, 1179a17–22, *1179a22–32* is a coda to the discussion of 'complete' happiness that began at 6, 1176a30, and that constitutes the last stage of the *NE*'s entire inquiry into the nature of the human good. 1179a17–22 is also a natural point of transition to the discussion in ch. 9 (1179a33ff.), which is about ways to make this goal a reality. But in between, Ar. offers this proof that the intellectually accomplished paragon is 'most loved by the gods' (24, 30), and for this reason too is 'happy to the highest degree' (32). The position of this argument suggests that its object is not simply to strengthen the main conclusion of x. 6–8 by showing that it harmonizes with the traditional belief that happiness is the mark of divine favour (cf. I. 9, 1099b11–14). Had this been the sole point, the argument would surely have been placed before the coda. Instead, it is reasonable to suppose that the argument's main purpose is to identify intellectually accomplished reflection as that which (in human beings) *the gods love most*. This is, in effect, a reinterpretation of piety (*to hosion*), a standardly recognized excellence which is not discussed elsewhere in the *Ethics*. For it was a commonplace that piety is what makes men loved by the gods (cf. Plato, *Euthyphro* 7a ff.).

As well as seeing that connection, Ar.'s original audience will also have related the present argument to the preceding reference to Anaxagoras (1179a13), who fled Athens as a result of an indictment for engaging in and publishing impious *cosmological reflections*. (He held that the sun and moon were fiery rocks.) According to anecdote, on being asked to describe the happy individual Anaxagoras described himself (*EE* I. 5, 1216a10–16; see VI. 7, 1141b3–8 with comment ad loc.). Given traditional connections between happiness and divine favour, and the latter and piety, it is necessary to clarify the nature of piety (even if for no other reason) so as to remove suspicion that the character of Anaxagoras' life undermines his claim about happiness.

The argument has baffled interpreters. It is true that Ar. says only: *if, as they are thought to do*, (1) the gods care about men, then it *would* be reasonable to hold that (2) they return good for good, treating as friends those human beings who honour the divine element in themselves (1179a24–9). But he must assent to (1) and therefore to (2), since he concludes unconditionally to (3): the intellectually accomplished is most loved by the gods (a30). Yet scholars have thought it impossible to reconcile (1) and (2) with what they regard as Ar.'s official conception of divinity. The astral deities of *Metaph.* XII. 7–9 are not cognizant of things on earth; and purely reflective activity, which is the essence of god, is not about contingent particulars such as human choices (cf. VI. 3). Consequently, it has been claimed that the argument is served up *ad homines* to vulgar adherents of (1) and (2). But its conclusion depends on the assumption that god is pure intellect, and this was not part of the vulgar conception.

It is not as if Ar. needs this argument to establish the superiority of the life of intellectual accomplishment, since he has already built a powerful case for that. And why would he wish to add an argument based on assumptions which he himself found absurd? (This would be a discouraging example of 'devoting oneself to intelligence' (23)—trying to sell a view by pretending to beliefs one does not share, especially when he has just declared that the people should test ethical positions by checking them against their own lives and conduct!)

It is more reasonable to suppose that Ar. states (1) and (2) *in propria persona*, and that he bases them not on traditional views about gods rewarding sacrifices with recovery of health, or rain for the crops, or electoral victory, but on the fact, familiar from experience, that working one's mind often brings increased understanding—sometimes seemingly out of nowhere. This can be interpreted as showing that those who accord intelligence the ultimate honour of exercising it solely for its own sake receive, in the act, the divine reward of understanding. (In the human case, understanding would be as much a reward for the *practical* choice of devoting oneself to reflection, as for excellence in the activity itself.) Here, crossing (i) the intellectualized conception of divinity which has already been established at 1178b7–22, with (ii) a fact of every thinker's experience, produces simultaneous definitions of human piety and divine repayment. (Cf. *EE* VII. 14 (= VIII. 1), 1248a16–29, which argues that god gives rise to the movements of human intellect.) As for how this fits in with the cosmological deities of *Metaph.* XII, Ar. would be within his rights in regarding that as a question for a different type of inquiry (cf. 1178a22–3).

As a rule Ar. states what he means, but in this instance, given the example of Anaxagoras (not to mention Socrates), there are reasons of political—and per-haps also religious—caution for leaving the simultaneous definitions implicit. Faced with Ar.'s challenge to check views against lives (see 1179a17–22 with comment), the audience can hardly have failed to note that their teacher's view on complete happiness stands up splendidly to the test of his own lifestyle; having, then, tacitly drawn attention to his own mainly reflective life, Ar. might understandably prefer to leave suggested rather than stated his new interpretation of 'pious' and 'loved by the gods', since anything more would amount to a declaration of his own piety.

This interpretation of 1179a22–32 should also take in the fact that in the next section of the *NE* (which there is no reason to suppose is not part of the same continuous composition) Ar. alludes disparagingly to claims made by Isocrates in the *Antidosis* (1181a12–19; on Isocrates, see Introduction, pp. 53–4). Ar.'s subject at this point is not the gods or piety. But, as his audience would very well know, the *Antidosis* was Isocrates' *apologia pro vita sua*, occasioned by the fact that he lost a legal battle about financial responsibility for equipping a warship (see Introduc-tion, p. 28). In this work, by an absurd fiction, Isocrates chose to present himself as answering charges such as those brought against Socrates: capital charges of corrupting the young, and *impiety*. The speech, which contains numerous echoes of Plato's *Apology of Socrates*, winds up as follows:

> I know myself to have spoken so piously [*hosiōs*] and justly about the city, about our ancestors, and most of all about the gods, that if they care at all about human affairs [cf. *NE* x. 8, 1179a24–5], nothing, I believe, of what is happening to me is escaping their attention. Therefore I do not dread the outcome that you [the fictional jury] will deliver on me; on the contrary, I am bold and optimistic that the end of my life will come when it is good for me that it should. The sign on which I base this hopefulness is that I have lived my past years, up to this day, in the way that befits those who are reverent [*eusebeis*] and are loved by the gods [*theophileis*]. (*Antidosis*, 321–2)

Looking back at *NE* x. 8, 1179a22–32, we now see that the question of who is 'most loved by the gods' was also the question of who is the true heir to Socrates.

for taking care of what they themselves [sc. the gods] **love** [*hōs tōn philōn autois*   *1179a28* *epimeloumenous*].   The Greek can also mean 'for caring for their [the gods'] friends'.

X 9, 1179a33–1181b23

Ar. has completed his account of the political thinker's end (on the meaning of 'political' in this context, see Introduction, pp. 10–11); but the inquiry is not yet over (1179a34–5). All along, the purpose has been practical (1179a35–b4;

cf. I. 2, 1094a22–5; 3, 1095a5–6; II. 2, 1103b26–9). But a philosophical under-standing of the human good can make no practical difference to lives that are not pre-reflectively disposed towards excellence (1179b4–31). Thus the next question is how best to foster such a disposition.

'By means of law' is Ar.'s answer. (*a*) Ideally, the upbringing of children should be controlled by civic legislation (1179b34–5, 1180a24–30). (*b*) Civil laws in general have great influence on character, since they set standards of practice for well brought up adults (1180a1–24). (*c*) The rule of law is prefer-able to rule by a paternalistic individual, since its enforcement is impersonal (1180a18–24). (*d*) Even where upbringing is left entirely to individual fam-ilies, as in most city-states, a head of household can do more for his charges if he has acquired some 'legislative expertise', i.e. understanding of the principles of legislation, since the father's rule in the home is analogous to rule by law in the community (and law in the community should be made by those who have some understanding of what they are trying to do) (1180a24–b12). (*e*) It is true that tailoring upbringing to the needs of the individual young person gives better results than applying general rules wholesale, but even going case by case one does a better job if one 'knows the universal' (1180b7–16). (*f*) It is true that, without this level of knowledge, one might carry out the task successfully in some single case with which one is intimately acquainted, but anyone who wants, more generally, to 'make people better' should try to acquire some legislative expertise (1180b16–28).

So how does one acquire it (1180b28–9)? Not from the practical politi-cians, for although they have the right experience they cannot articulate the principles of statecraft. Still less from the 'sophists', who claim to teach political expertise but have no political experience and do not know what they are talking about (1180b29–1181b2). No, it is the business of the phil-osopher of ethics to think about the fundamentals of legislation and politics in general. Without these studies, to which we now turn, ethical philosophy will be incomplete (1181b12–23).

1179b6   **to quote Theognis**   *Elegies* 432–4, appropriated by Plato at *Meno* 95e. (The theme of the *Meno* is: how do we become excellent?)

1179b9   **possession** [*katokōchimos*] **by excellence**   The word is used of divine possession and of military occupation.

1179b10   **refinement of excellence** [*kalokagathia*]   This quality last appeared in connec-tion with greatness of soul (IV. 3, 1124a4). It involves not only all-round excellence, but the deliberate prizing of excellence (cf. Introduction, pp. 30–1).

1179b18–20   **But perhaps we should be satisfied . . . a portion of excellence**   We should be glad of the excellence we can achieve when the right conditions are present, rather than lament the impotence of words to produce it when those conditions are absent.

while talk and teaching . . . repulsed by the shameful   The same theme as at *1179b23–31*
1179b4–18.

some think that lawgivers . . .   The reference is to Plato, *Laws* iv. 718b ff., where   *1180a6 ff.*
it is argued that laws should address decent people via explanatory exhortations,
as well as announcing punishments for lawbreakers. If the laws are felt to appeal
only to our desire to avoid the evil of sanctions, they will not be respected for
their own sake and will lose their power to transmit values.

neither counter-voluntarily nor voluntarily doing what is bad   Good upbringing   *1180a16–17*
cannot protect against doing something bad counter-voluntarily in the sense
explained at iii. 1 (1109b30–1110b17)—a sense in which the action is no indication
of a defective character. Here, then, Ar. must be using the words in colloquial
senses of 'reluctantly' and 'willingly'. Colloquially, un-self-controlled action is
'counter-voluntary' (since the agent does it against his own wish) and shows a
faulty character.

unless he is a king or similar person   i.e. a 'natural' king or person of extra-   *1180a20–1*
ordinary excellence. See *Politics* iii. 15–17.

people hate any human beings that oppose their impulses   The contrast is   *1180a22–3*
with law not merely as impersonal, but as expression of divine reason; cf. *Politics*
iii. 16, 1287a29–32.

like a Cyclops   See Homer, *Odyssey* ix. 114.   *1180a28*

proceed to the level of the universal   Cf. *Metaph.* i. 1 on this transition.   *1180b21*

as we have said, this is the sphere of expert knowledge [*hai epistēmai*]   He   *1180b22–3*
means the kinds of productive expertise; the reference is to 1180b15–16.

the sophists   i.e. the teachers of rhetoric, in particular Isocrates (see comment   *1180b35*
ad 1181a14–17, and Introduction, p. 54).

making speeches for the lawcourts or the assembly   These are the domains   *1181a4–5*
of rhetoric. If politicians never express ideas except in speeches of these types, it is
not surprising that political science should come to be confused with rhetoric; see
1181a15. On the politicians' failure to pass on their skill, cf. Plato, *Protagoras*
319e ff. and *Meno* 92b ff.

if they did, they wouldn't put it down as the same as, or inferior to, rhetorical   *1181a14–17*
expertise, nor would they think legislating an easy thing for anyone who has
collected together those laws that are well thought of   Ar. is referring—with
a verbal echo—to the views of Isocrates. In his *Antidosis* (composed in 354–353),
Isocrates maintains that one becomes a good legislator by picking out, from
round the Greek world, laws 'that are well thought of'; and argues that since
doing this is very easy by comparison with mastering rhetoric, the rhetorician
ranks higher than the lawmaker (*Antidosis* 79–83). For Ar.'s contrary ranking
(given that legislative expertise is an aspect of political), see i. 2, 1094b2–7.

1181a21 **for the inexperienced** The sophists' lack of experience was implied at 1180b35–1181a1. The charge may not be fair to Isocrates, who did take part in public life. But his forte (on which he prided himself) was the design and promulgation of large-scale policy rather than the daily conduct of affairs.

1181a23–b2 **But laws are like the products of political expertise; how then could someone become a legislative expert, or discern which are the best of them, *from them*?** To make a well-founded judgement of the quality of a product one needs something of the expert understanding that produced it; good laws are or should be products of political expertise; but the sophists claim, in effect, that we can tell at a glance which existing laws are good, and thereby have all the knowledge we need to legislate well (whether they think we do this by copying existing laws, or by reproducing what they seem to have in common). This insistence on going back to first principles is very much in the spirit of the Socrates of Plato's dialogues.

1181b3–5 **For it doesn't appear that people become medical experts, either, from written texts ... distinguishing the various conditions** An a fortiori argument. If studying medical texts, which go into detail about the application of remedies in different kinds of case, is no substitute for experience, this is all the more true of studying existing laws, given their greater generality.

1181b7 **collections** Such as Ar.'s own collection of 158 constitutions, of which one survives, *The Constitution of Athens*.

1181b8 **those able to reflect on and to discern** Ar.'s criticisms of the politicians and the sophists (1180b35–1181a12) implied that legislative expertise requires (*a*) experience and (*b*) articulate thought. Having focused on (*a*) at 1181a19–b5, he now turns to (*b*).

1181b12–13 **since previous thinkers left the subject of legislation unexamined** This can hardly be meant to include the author of the *Laws*, referred to at 1180a6. Focusing as it does on the fundamental problem of ethical education, this chapter is squarely in the Platonic tradition. The reference is probably to 5th- and early 4th-century theorists of rhetoric.

1181b16 **our predecessors** Including Plato, this time.

Word list

This is not a complete list of key words. It is a list of translations used in the present work for key words that tend to be rendered differently by different translators and interpreters of Aristotle's *Ethics*.

adikēma	unjust act (i.e. deed done)
aisthēsis	perception, sense (i.e. sensory capacity)
akolastos	self-indulgent
akousios, akōn	counter-voluntary
akratēs	lacking self-control, uncontrolled, un-self-controlled
akribēs	precise
alazōn	impostor
anankazein	constrain (in the context of voluntary agency)
aneleutherios	avaricious
archē	beginning, origin, principle, source, starting point
areskos	obsequious
aretē	excellence
asōtos	wasteful
athlios	miserable
bia	force
boulēsis	wish
dianoia	thought
dianoētikos	intellectual, having to do with thought
dikaiōma	just act (i.e. deed done)
doxa	judgement, opinion
dunamis	capacity
eirōn	self-deprecating
eleos	pity
eleutherios	open-handed, civilized, worthy of a free man
endoxa	received opinions, existing views

energeia	activity, actuality
enkratēs	self-controlled
eph' hēmin	dependent on us
epichairekakia	malice
epieikēs	decent; reasonable (in v. 10)
epistēmē	knowledge, scientific knowledge, systematic knowledge
epithumia	appetite
ergon	function, work, product
ēthikos	to do with character
ēthos	character-trait
eudaimonia	happiness
gnōmē	sense (as in 'good sense')
haireisthai	to choose
hairetos	desirable
haplōs	without qualification
hekousios, hekōn	voluntary
hexis	disposition
kakia	badness, bad state
kalokagathia	refined excellence, nobility
kalos	fine
kata sumbebēkos	incidentally
kath' hauto	in itself
kinēsis	movement, process
kolasis	forcible correction
kolax	ingratiating
krinein	to discriminate, discern, judge
lupē	distress, pain
megaloprepēs	munificent
megalopsuchos	great-souled
mesos	intermediate
metameleia	regret
mikoprepēs	shabby
mikropsuchos	little-souled
mochthēros	bad, of bad character, depraved
nous	intelligence
ōphelimos	beneficial

orexis	desire
orthos logos	correct prescription
pathos	affection, affective state, emotion
phaulos	bad, inferior
phronēsis	wisdom
phthonos	grudging ill will
pleonektēs	grasping
ponēros	bad
praos	mild
prohairesis	decision
psogos	censure
skopos	target, goal
sophia	intellectual accomplishment
sōphrōn	moderate
spoudaios	excellent, serious
sumpherein	to be advantageous
sunaisthanesthai	to perceive concurrently
sunesis	comprehension, acumen
sungnōmē	sympathy
suzēn	to live with, share life with
ta pros to telos	what forwards the end, what leads to the end
technē	technical expertise, skill
teleios	complete
tharros	boldness
theios	godlike, divine
theōrein	reflect on, observe; have regard to (VII. 3)
theōrētikos	reflective, purely reflective, theoretical
thrasus	rash
thumos	temper
tuchē	chance, fortune

Luton Sixth Form College
Learning Resources Centre

Select Bibliography

Aristotle's philosophy

Ackrill, J. L., *Aristotle the Philosopher* (Oxford: Oxford University Press, 1981).
Barnes, J. (ed.), *The Cambridge Companion to Aristotle* (Cambridge: Cambridge University Press, 1995).
Barnes, J., *Aristotle: A Very Short Introduction* (Oxford: Oxford University Press, 2000).
Lear, J., *Aristotle, the Desire to Understand* (Cambridge: Cambridge University Press, 1988).
Ross, W. D., *Aristotle* (London: Methuen, 1949).

Aristotle's ethics in general

Anton, J. P. and Preus, A. (eds.), *Aristotle's Ethics*, Essays in Ancient Greek Philosophy, vol. iv (Albany, NY: State University of New York Press, 1991).
Aristotle, *Eudemian Ethics Books I, II, and VIII*, trans. with comm. M. Woods, 2nd edn. (Oxford: Oxford University Press, 1992).
Barnes, J., Schofield, M., and Sorabji, R. (eds.), *Articles on Aristotle*, ii: Ethics and Politics (London: Duckworth, 1977).
Bostock, D., *Aristotle's Ethics* (Oxford: Oxford University Press, 2000).
Broadie, S., *Ethics with Aristotle* (New York: Oxford University Press, 1991).
Cooper, J. M., *Reason and the Human Good* (Indianapolis: Hackett, 1986).
—— *Reason and Emotion: Essays in Ancient Moral Psychology and Ethical Theory*, pt. ii (Princeton: Princeton University Press, 1999).
Hardie, W. F. R., *Aristotle's Ethical Theory*, 2nd edn. (Oxford: Oxford University Press, 1980).
Hughes, G. J., *Aristotle on Ethics* (London: Routledge, 2001).
Kraut, R., *Aristotle on the Human Good* (Princeton: Princeton University Press, 1989).
Reeve, C. *Practices of Reason: Aristotle's Nicomachean Ethics* (Oxford: Clarendon Press, 1995).
Rorty, A. O. (ed.), *Essays on Aristotle's Ethics* (Berkeley: University of California Press, 1980).
Urmson, J. O., *Aristotle's Ethics* (Oxford: Blackwell, 1988).

Method in ethics

Barnes, J., 'Aristotle and the Methods of Ethics', *Revue Internationale de Philosophie*, 34 (1980), 490–511.
Bolton, R., 'Aristotle on the Objectivity of Ethics', in J. P. Anton and A. Preus (eds.), *Aristotle's Ethics*, Essays in Ancient Greek Philosophy, vol. iv (Albany, NY: State University of New York Press, 1991), 7–28.

457

The chief good, the human function, happiness

Achtenberg, D., 'The Role of the *Ergon* Argument in Aristotle's *Nicomachean Ethics*', in J. P. Anton and A. Preus (eds.), *Aristotle's Ethics, Essays in Ancient Greek Philosophy*, vol. iv (Albany, NY: State University of New York Press, 1991), 59–72.

Ackrill, J. L., 'Aristotle on "Good" and the Categories', in S. M. Stern, Albert Hourani, and Vivian Brown (eds.), *Islamic Philosophy and the Classical Tradition* (Oxford: Oxford University Press, 1972), 17–25; repr. in J. Barnes, M. Schofield, and R. Sorabji (eds.), *Articles on Aristotle*, ii: *Ethics and Politics* (London: Duckworth, 1977), 17–24.

Broadie, S., 'Aristotle's Elusive *Summum Bonum*', *Social Philosophy and Policy*, 16 (1999), 233–51.

Charles, D., 'Aristotle on Well-Being and Intellectual Contemplation', *Aristotelian Society Proceedings*, suppl. vol. 73 (1999), 225–42.

Cooper, J. M., 'Aristotle on the Goods of Fortune', *Philosophical Review*, 94 (1985), 187–216; repr. with postscript in Cooper, *Reason and Emotion: Essays In Ancient Moral Psychology and Ethical Theory*, pt. ii (Princeton: Princeton University Press, 1999), 292–311.

—— 'Contemplation and Happiness: A Reconsideration', *Synthese*, 72 (1987), 187–216; repr. in Cooper, *Reason and Emotion: Essays in Ancient Moral Psychology and Ethical Theory*, pt. ii (Princeton: Princeton University Press, 1999), 212–36.

Defourny, P., 'Contemplation in Aristotle's Ethics', in J. Barnes, M. Schofield and R. Sorabji (eds.), *Articles on Aristotle*, ii: *Ethics and Politics* (London: Duckworth, 1977), 104–12.

Depew, D. J., 'Politics, Music and Contemplation in Aristotle's Ideal State', in D. Keyt and F. Miller (eds.), *A Companion to Aristotle's* Politics (Oxford: Blackwell, 1990), 346–80.

Farwell, P., 'Aristotle and the Complete Life', *History of Philosophy Quarterly*, 12 (1995), 247–63.

Gómez-Lobo, A., 'The Ergon Inference', in J. P. Anton and A. Preus (eds.), *Aristotle's Ethics*, Essays in Ancient Greek Philosophy, vol. iv (Albany, NY: State University of New York Press, 1991), 43–57.

Kraut, R., 'The Peculiar Function of Human Beings', *Canadian Journal of Philosophy*, 9 (1979), 467–78.

—— 'Two Conceptions of Happiness', *Philosophical Review*, 88 (1979), 167–97.

Irwin, T. H., 'Permanent Happiness: Aristotle and Solon', *Oxford Studies in Ancient Philosophy*, 3 (1985), 89–124.

Kenny, A., *Aristotle on the Perfect Life* (Oxford: Clarendon Press, 1992).

Lawrence, G., 'Aristotle and the Ideal Life', *Philosophical Review*, 102 (1993), 1–34.

Richardson, G., Appendix on 'Self-Sufficiency' in *Happy Lives and the Highest Good*, Princeton University Ph.D. dissertation, 2001.

Roche, T., '*Ergon* and *Eudaimonia* in *Nicomachean Ethics*, I: Reconsidering the Intellectualist Interpretation', *Journal of the History of Philosophy*, 26 (1988), 175–94.

Santas, G., 'Aristotle's Criticism of Plato's Form of the Good', *Philosophical Papers*, 18 (1989), 137–60.

Scott, D., 'Aristotle on Well-Being and Intellectual Contemplation', *Aristotelian Society Proceedings*, suppl. vol. 73 (1999), 225–42.

White, N. P., 'Good as Goal', *Southern Journal of Philosophy*, 27, suppl. (1988), 169–93.

White, S. M., *Sovereign Virtue: Aristotle on the Relationship between Happiness and Prosperity* (Stanford, Calif.: Stanford University Press, 1992).

Character-excellence (general)

Burnyeat, M. F., 'Aristotle on Learning to be Good', in A. O. Rorty (ed.), *Essays on Aristotle's Ethics* (Berkeley: University of California Press, 1980), 69–92.

Gómez-Lobo, A., 'Aristotle's Right Reason', *Apeiron*, 28 4 (1995), 15–34.

Hursthouse, R., 'A False Doctrine of the Mean', *Aristotelian Society Proceedings*, NS 81 (1980–1), 57–72.

Hutchinson, D. S., *The Virtues of Aristotle* (London: Routledge & Kegan Paul, 1986).

Irwin, T. H., 'Aristotle's Conception of Morality', *Proceedings of the Boston Area Colloquium in Ancient Philosophy*, 1 (1985), 115–43.

Owens, J., 'The *KALON* in the Aristotelian *Ethics*', in D. J. O'Meara (ed.), *Studies in Aristotle* (Washington, DC: Catholic University of American Press, 1981).

Urmson, J. O., 'Aristotle's Doctrine of the Mean', *American Philosophical Quarterly*, 10 (1973), 223–30; repr. in A. O. Rorty (ed.), *Essays on Aristotle's Ethics* (Berkeley: University of California Press, 1980), 157–69.

Specific character-excellences

Aubenque, P., 'The Twofold Natural Foundation of Justice according to Aristotle', in R. Heinaman (ed.), *Aristotle and Moral Realism* (London: UCL Press, 1995), 35–47).

Burger, R., 'Ethical Reflection and Righteous Indignation: *Nemesis* in the *Nicomachean Ethics*', in J. P Anton and A. Preus (eds.), *Aristotle's Ethics*, Ethics in Ancient Greek Philosophy, vol. iv (Albany, NY: State University of New York Press, 1991), 127–40.

Cooper, N., 'Aristotle's Crowning Virtue', *Apeiron*, 22 (1989), 191–205.

Curzer, H., 'Aristotle's Much Maligned *Megalopsychos*', *Australasian Journal of Philosophy*, 69 (1991), 131–51.

—— 'Aristotle's Account of Justice', *Apeiron*, 28, 3 (1995), 201–38.

Engberg-Pedersen, T., 'Justice at a Distance — Less Foundational, More Naturalistic: a Reply to Pierre Aubenque' in R. Heinaman (ed.), *Aristotle and Moral Realism* (London: UCL Press, 1995), 48–60.

Hardie, W. F. R., '"Magnanimity" in Aristotle's Ethics', *Phronesis*, 23 (1978), 63–79.

Leighton, S. R., 'Aristotle's Courageous Passions', *Phronesis*, 33 (1988), 76–99.

Pears, D., 'Courage as a Mean', in A. O. Rorty (ed.), *Essays on Aristotle's Ethics* (Berkeley: University of California Press, 1980), 171–87.

Shiner, R., 'Aristotle's Theory of Equity', in S. Panigiotou (ed.), *Justice, Law and Method in Plato and Aristotle* (Edmonton, Al.: Academic Printing and Publishing, 1987), 173–90).

Williams, B. A. O., 'Justice as a Virtue', in A. O. Rorty (ed.), *Essays on Aristotle's Ethics* (Berkeley: University of California Press, 1980), 189–99.

Young, C., 'Aristotle on Justice', *Southern Journal of Philosophy*, 27 (suppl.) (1988), 233–49.

—— 'Aristotle on Temperance', in J. P. Anton and A. Preus (eds.), *Aristotle's Ethics*, Essays in Ancient Greek Philosophy, vol. iv (Albany, NY: State University of New York Press, 1991), 107–25.

—— 'Aristotle on Liberality', *Proceedings of the Boston Area Colloquium in Ancient Philosophy*, 10 (1994), 313–34.

Zembaty, J. S., 'Aristotle on Lying', *Journal of the History of Philosophy*, 31 (1993), 7–30.

Action and the voluntary

Ackrill, J. L. 'Aristotle on Action', *Mind*, 87 (1978), 595–601; repr. in J. P. Anton and
A. Preus (eds.), *Aristotle's Ethics*, Essays in Ancient Greek Philosophy, vol. iv (Albany,
NY: State University of New York Press, 1991), 93–101.

Anscombe, G. E. M., 'Thought and Action in Aristotle', in R. Bambrough, *New Essays on
Plato and Aristotle* (London: Routledge & Kegan Paul, 1965), 143–58; repr. in J. Barnes,
M. Schofield, and R. Sorabji (eds.), *Articles on Aristotle*, ii: *Ethics and Politics* (London:
Duckworth, 1977), 61–71.

Charles, D., *Aristotle's Philosophy of Action* (New York: Oxford University Press, 1984).

Curren, R., 'The Contribution of *Nicomachean Ethics* iii 5 to Aristotle's Theory of
Responsibility', *History of Philosophy Quarterly*, 6 (1989), 261–78.

Furley, D. J., 'Aristotle on the Voluntary', in J. Barnes, M. Schofield, and R. Sorabji (eds.),
Articles on Aristotle, ii: *Ethics and Politics* (London: Duckworth, 1977), 47–60.

Hursthouse, R., 'Acting and Feeling in Character: Nicomachean Ethics 3.i', *Phronesis*, 29
(1984), 252–66.

Kenny, A. *Aristotle's Theory of the Will* (London: Duckworth, 1979).

Meyer, S. S., *Aristotle on Moral Responsibility* (Oxford: Oxford University Press, 1993).

Sorabji, R., *Necessity, Cause and Blame: Perspectives on Aristotle's Theory* (London:
Duckworth, 1980).

Deliberation, decision, wisdom

Bolton, R., '*Phronesis*: Aristotle's Conception of Moral Knowledge', in M. Gifford (ed.),
Intellectual Virtue: Essays on Aristotle, Nicomachean Ethics Book VI (Kelowna, BC:
Academic Printing and Publishing (forthcoming 2002).

Fortenbaugh, W. W., 'Aristotle's Distinction between Moral Virtue and Practical
Wisdom', in J. P. Anton and A. Preus (eds.), *Aristotle's Ethics*, Essays in Ancient Greek
Philosophy, vol. iv (Albany, NY: State University of New York Press, 1991), 97–106.

Gottlieb, P., 'Aristotle on Dividing the Soul and Uniting the Virtues', *Phronesis*, 39 (1994),
275–90.

Irwin, T. H., 'Disunity in the Aristotelian Virtues', *Oxford Studies in Ancient Philosophy*,
suppl. vol (1988), 61–78.

Louden, R. B., 'Aristotle's Practical Particularism', in J. P. Anton and A. Preus (eds.),
Aristotle's Ethics, Essays in Ancient Greek Philosophy, vol. iv (Albany, NY: State
University of New York Press, 1991), 159–78.

Mele, A. R., 'The Practical Syllogism and Deliberation in Aristotle's Causal Theory of
Action', *New Scholasticism*, 55 (1981), 281–316.

Sorabji, R., 'Aristotle on the Role of Intellect in Virtue', *Aristotelian Society Proceedings*, NS
74 (1973–4), 107–29; repr. in J. P. Anton and A. Preus (eds.), *Aristotle's Ethics*, Essays in
Ancient Greek Philosophy, vol. iv (Albany, NY: State University of New York Press,
1991), 201–19, and A. O. Rorty (ed.), *Essays on Aristotle's Ethics* (Berkeley: University of
California Press, 1980), 201–19.

Telfer, E., 'The Unity of Moral Virtues in Aristotle's *Nicomachean Ethics*', *Proceedings of the
Aristotelian Society*, NS 90 (1989–90), 35–48.

Tuozzo, T. M., 'Aristotelian Deliberation is not of Ends', in J. P. Anton and A. Preus (eds.),
Aristotle's Ethics, Essays in Ancient Greek Philosophy, vol. iv (Albany, NY: State
University of New York Press, 1991), 193–212.

Walsh, M. M., 'The Role of Universal Knowledge in Aristotelian Moral Virtue', *Ancient Philosophy*, 19 (1999), 73–88.

Woods, M., 'Intuition and Perception in Aristotle's Ethics', *Oxford Studies in Ancient Philosophy* 4 (1986), 145–66.

Lack of self-control

Broadie, S., 'Another Problem of *Akrasia*', *International Journal of Philosophical Studies*, 2 (1994), 229–42.

Cooper, J. M., 'Some Remarks on Aristotle's Moral Psychology', *Southern Journal of Philosophy*, 27, suppl. (1988), 25–42; repr. in Cooper, *Reason and Emotion: Essays in Ancient Moral Psychology and Ethical Theory*, pt. II (Princeton: Princeton University Press, 1999), 237–52.

Dahl, N. O., *Practical Reason, Aristotle, and Weakness of the Will* (Minneapolis: University of Minnesota Press, 1984).

Gosling, J., 'Mad, Drunk or Asleep? Aristotle's Akratic', *Phronesis*, 38 (1993), 98–104.

Mele, A., 'Aristotle on *Akrasia* and Knowledge', *Modern Schoolman*, 58 (1981), 137–59.

Rorty, A. O., '*Akrasia* and Pleasure: *Nicomachean Ethics* Book 7', in A. O. Rorty (ed.), *Essays on Aristotle's Ethics* (Berkeley: University of California Press, 1980), 267–84.

Love and friendship

Cooper, J. M., 'Aristotle on Friendship', in A. O. Rorty (ed.), *Essays on Aristotle's Ethics* (Berkeley: University of California Press, 1980), 301–40.

—— 'Political Animals and Civic Friendship', in G. Patzig (ed.), *Aristoteles' Politik* (Göttingen: Vandenhoeck & Ruprecht, 1990), 221–41; repr. in Cooper, *Reason and Emotion: Essays in Ancient Moral Psychology and Ethical Theory*, pt. II (Princeton: Princeton University Press, 1999), 356–77.

Pakaluk, M., *Aristotle*, Nicomachean Ethics *Books VIII and IX*, translation and commentary (Oxford: Oxford University Press, 1998).

Price, A. W., *Love and Friendship in Plato and Aristotle*, rev. edn. (Oxford: Oxford University Press, 1997).

Stern-Gillet, S., *Aristotle's Philosophy of Friendship* (Albany, NY: State University of New York Press, 1995).

Pleasure

Annas, J., 'Aristotle on Pleasure and Goodness', in J. P. Anton and A. Preus (eds.), *Aristotle's Ethics*, Essays in Ancient Greek Philosophy, vol. iv (Albany, NY: State University of New York Press, 1991), 285–99.

Gonzalez, F. J., 'Aristotle on Pleasure and Perfection', *Phronesis*, 35 (1991), 141–59.

Gosling, J., and Taylor, C., *The Greeks on Pleasure* (Oxford: Oxford University Press, 1982).

Gottlieb, P., 'Aristotle's Measure Doctrine and Pleasure', *Archiv für Geschichte der Philosophie*, 75 (1993), 31–46.

Urmson, J. O., 'Aristotle on Pleasure', in J. Moravcsik (ed.) *Aristotle* (London: Macmillan, 1968), 323–33.

Relation of Ethics to Politics

Bodéüs, R., *The Political Dimensions of Aristotle's Ethics*, trans. J. E. Garrett (Albany, NY: State University of New York Press, 1993).

Cashdollar, S., 'Aristotle's Politics of Morals', *Journal of the History of Philosophy*, 11 (1973), 145–60.

Some cultural background

Dover, K. J., *Greek Popular Morality in the Time of Plato and Aristotle* (Oxford: Blackwell, 1974).

Jaeger, W., *Paideia: The Ideals of Greek Culture*, trans. Gilbert Highet (Oxford: Oxford University Press, 1986), vol. iii, chs. 2 and 6.

Natali, C., '*Adoleschia*, *Leptologia* and the Philosophers in Athens', *Phronesis*, 32 (1987), 232–41.

Index of Names

Index of Subjects

E18 RESOURCE BASE